The Cambridge Dictionary of
Linguistics

The Cambridge Dictionary of Linguistics provides concise and clear definitions of all the terms any undergraduate or graduate student is likely to encounter in the study of linguistics and English language or in other degrees involving linguistics, such as modern languages, media studies and translation. It covers the key areas of syntax, morphology, phonology, phonetics, semantics and pragmatics but also contains terms from discourse analysis, stylistics, historical linguistics, sociolinguistics, psycholinguistics, computational linguistics and corpus linguistics. It provides entries for 246 languages, including 'major' languages and languages regularly mentioned in research papers and textbooks. Features include cross-referencing between entries and extended entries on some terms. Where appropriate, entries contain illustrative examples from English and other languages, and many provide etymologies bringing out the metaphors lying behind the technical terms. Also available is an electronic version of the dictionary which includes 'clickable' cross-referencing.

KEITH BROWN is an affiliated lecturer in the Department of Modern and Medieval Languages at the University of Cambridge. He taught linguistics at the University of Edinburgh from 1965 to 1983 and then at the University of Essex, where he was Research Professor in Linguistics. He is a former Chair of the LAGB and President of the Philological Society. His major research interest is in English grammar. His previous publications include *Syntax: A Linguistic Introduction to Sentence Structure Second Edition* (with Jim Miller, 1991) and he is Editor-in-Chief of the *Encyclopedia of Language and Linguistics Second Edition* (2006).

JIM MILLER is Professor Emeritus at the University of Edinburgh. He taught linguistics at the University of Edinburgh from 1967 to 2003 and the University of Auckland from 2003 to 2007. His major research interests are the grammar and discourse organization of spontaneous spoken language and how they differ from written language, and grammatical categories, especially case, tense and aspect. He is the author of *A Critical Introduction to Syntax* (2011) and *Spontaneous Spoken Language: Syntax and Discourse* (with Regina Weinert, 2009).

The Cambridge Dictionary of
Linguistics

KEITH BROWN and **JIM MILLER**

CAMBRIDGE
UNIVERSITY PRESS

CAMBRIDGE
UNIVERSITY PRESS

University Printing House, Cambridge CB2 8BS, United Kingdom

Published in the United States of America by Cambridge University Press, New York

Cambridge University Press is part of the University of Cambridge.

It furthers the University's mission by disseminating knowledge in the pursuit of education, learning and research at the highest international levels of excellence.

www.cambridge.org
Information on this title: www.cambridge.org/9780521766753

© Edward Keith Brown and James Edward Miller 2013

This publication is in copyright. Subject to statutory exception and to the provisions of relevant collective licensing agreements, no reproduction of any part may take place without the written permission of Cambridge University Press.

First published 2013

Printed and bound in the United Kingdom by CPI Group Ltd, Croydon CR0 4YY

A catalogue record for this publication is available from the British Library

Library of Congress Cataloging-in-Publication Data
Brown, E. K.
The Cambridge dictionary of linguistics / Keith Brown and Jim Miller.
   p. cm.
ISBN 978-0-521-76675-3 (Hardback)
1. Linguistics–Dictionaries. I. Miller, J. E. (James Edward), 1942– II. Title.
III. Title: Dictionary of linguistics.
P29.B76 2013
410'.3–dc23   2012029086

ISBN 978-0-521-76675-3 Hardback

Cambridge University Press has no responsibility for the persistence or accuracy of URLs for external or third-party internet websites referred to in this publication, and does not guarantee that any content on such websites is, or will remain, accurate or appropriate.

CONTENTS

List of abbreviations vii
Phonetic symbols for English ix
Introduction 1

The Dictionary 3

ABBREVIATIONS

ABBESS	abessive
ABL	ablative case
ABS	absolute
ADJ	adjective
ACC	accusative
ADV	adverb
ADVP	adverbial phrase
AGR	agreement
ALL	allative case
AOR	aorist
AP	adjective phrase
APPL	applicative
CAUS	causative
CGEL	Cambridge Grammar of the English Language
CGE	Comprehensive Grammar of English
CLF	classifier
COMP	complementizer
CONJ	conjunction
DAT	dative case
DO	direct object
ELAT	elative
ERG	ergative
ESS	essive
FOC	focus
GEN	genitive
GER	gerund
GB	Government and Binding
IMP	imperative
IND	indicative
INSTR	instrumental
IPFV	imperfective aspect
LFG	Lexical-Functional Grammar
LOG	logophoric
MP	Minimalist Program
NOM	nominative case
NP	noun phrase

OBLQ	oblique
OO	oblique object
OPT	optative
PART	participle
PFV	perfective aspect
PL	plural
POSS	possessive
PRS	present
PRT	participle
PRTV	partitive
PP	prepositional phrase
P&P	Principles and Parameters
PROG	progressive
PROP	proprietive
PST	past
RRG	Role and Reference Grammar
S	subject
SG	singular
SG	Systemic grammar
SPE	Sound Pattern of English
SUB	subjunctive
SUP	supine
TRANSL	translative
VOC	vocative
VP	verb phrase
1	first person
2	second person
3	third person
2PL	second-person plural, etc.
1SG	first-person singular, etc.

PHONETIC SYMBOLS FOR ENGLISH VOWELS

i	as in *see*	/si/
ɪ	as in *pit*	/pɪt/
e	as in *pet*	/pet/
a	as in *pat*	/pat/
ɑ	as in *part*	/pɑt/
ɔ	as in *paw*	/pɔː/
ɒ	as in *pot*	/pɒt/
ʊ	as in *put*	/pʊt/
ʌ	as in *cup*	/kʌp/
u	as in *too*	/tu/
ɜ	as in *bird*	/bɜd/
ə	as in *about*	/əbaʊt/
eɪ	as in *pay*	/peɪ/
əʊ	as in *home*	/həʊm/
ai	as in *high*	/hai/
aʊ	as in *how*	/haʊ/
ɔɪ	as in *boy*	/bɔɪ/
ɪə	as in *here*	/hɪə/
eə	as in *hair*	/heə/
ʊə	as in *pure*	/pjʊə/

INTRODUCTION

This Dictionary has been written primarily for undergraduate students and MA students whose curriculum includes a linguistics module, but we hope that undergraduate honours and postgraduate students in general will find it useful. Judging that our intended readers would not find concise and possibly dense definitions of technical terminology particularly helpful, we have gone for more extended explanations. We have included examples wherever possible, adapting the aphorism that one picture is worth many pages. Many of the examples are English, and many of these are real examples from informal English, others are from languages we know or from languages that we know well enough to be able to consult grammars. Some examples come from articles published in journals such as *Language*.

What ground should be covered in a dictionary of linguistics that is limited to 3,000 entries or so? We were guided in our choice by the topics that in our experience are covered in linguistics programmes and courses at British universities, focusing on items typically addressed in introductory textbooks, though not restricted to these. We have kept in mind that in addition to degrees in linguistics, linguistics is also taught as part of a variety of other degrees, and therefore in addition to terms from the central areas of linguistics – syntax, morphology, phonology, phonetics, semantics, pragmatics and discourse analysis – we have included terms from stylistics, historical linguistics, sociolinguistics, psycholinguistics, computational linguistics and corpus linguistics. In making our choice of terms. in addition to our own experience we have drawn on the work of our predecessors, especially, Crystal, Trask and Matthews.

Some entries provide etymologies. JM discovered during a four-year stint at Auckland University that the large numbers of Chinese students taking one of his courses were baffled by much of the technical vocabulary. The main problem seemed to be that the terms were not in everyday use in speech or writing and were quite opaque. Etymologies removed the opacity and, for some terms, exposed the metaphor underlying the original use and helped the students to handle the terminology. It turned out that many of the native speakers of English in the class also appreciated the etymologies. We suspect and hope that many of the users of this dictionary will appreciate them too.

We have included a selection of language names, including languages regularly mentioned in linguistics textbooks and 'major' languages. As linguists, we recognize that all languages are equal with respect to phonology, morphology and syntax. (And the vocabulary of any language can be expanded as required with the creation of native words or the borrowing of words from other languages. To take one area of the vocabulary of English, technical terms in the sciences are all built on roots borrowed from classical Greek and Latin.) In contrast, as members of a particular society and culture in a particular geographical location, we know well that with respect to numbers of speakers, economic power, quantity and quality of written literature and so on, some languages come to the attention of our intended audience more often than others, and we have included them. For many of the languages, we thought it useful to indicate the number of speakers, using data from *Ethnologue* and updating the figures on the basis of information in the *CIA World Factbook*. Such numbers are always approximate, but our goal is to give readers a better idea of the relatively large numbers of speakers that many languages have – and also of the dismayingly few speakers that other languages have.

The choice of technical terms to be defined, of languages to be listed and of appropriate examples requires judgement. The text of the definitions reflects the intended audience. Half of the entries in this dictionary were written by KB and the other half by JM: KB was responsible for entries in phonetics, phonology, historical linguistics, sociolinguistics, computational linguistics, half the psycholinguistics entries, and 'general'; JM was responsible for entries in syntax and morphology, semantics and pragmatics, discourse and stylistics, and the other half of the psycholinguistics entries.

We are grateful to generations of students and colleagues, to Helen Barton, our editor at Cambridge University Press, and to a number of specialist reviewers for comments which have materially improved the dictionary and, occasionally, saved us from error – any errors that remain are, of course, ours.

Layout of general entries

The heading is in bold capitals. The body of the entries is in plain font, apart from terms which have their own entry. They are in bold lowercase. Many entries conclude with a list of related entries in bold capitals. These lists will allow users to follow up a particular topic.

Layout of language entries

The entries are mainly in note form. Their structure is

[**Language family**: Number of speakers: Countries where spoken: Additional comments.]

Numbers are abbreviated as in the following examples: 10M = ten million, 500K = five hundred thousand. Where the total of speakers is less than a thousand, the number is expressed in full, e.g. 250, 680.

AAC
See **AUGMENTED AND ASSISTED COMMUNICATION**.

AAVE
African American Vernacular English, also known as **Black English Vernacular (BEV)** and **Black English**. A variety used by many African Americans, characterized by being non-**rhotic** and the frequent deletion of the verb 'to be'.

A-BAR-BINDING
In **Government and Binding Theory**, **Principles and Parameters** and the **Minimalist Program**, the **binding** between a **pronoun** and an **NP** in a non-**argument** position. In *That guy$_i$, I'm sure I saw him$_i$ in your office yesterday*, the NP *that guy* is not an argument of *saw*, but *I* and *him* are. There is binding between the pronoun *him* and the non-argument *that guy*, as signalled by the subscript *i*; *him* picks out the same person as *that guy*. See **ANAPHORA**, **BINDING THEORY**, **BOUND** .

ABBREVIATION
A conventional short way of writing a word or phrase: *mgs* 'milligrams', *cm* 'centimetre'. Abbreviations are often used in grammatical labels, e.g. *adj(ective)*, *prog(ressive)*. See **ACRONYM**, **CLIPPING**, **INITIALISM**.

ABDUCTION
A process of reasoning which does not follow the rules of logic but is widely used, e.g. by children acquiring their native language, and can lead to changes in a given language. The first step is for learners to guess at a rule for some pattern. The rule may be wrong but may yield some correct results. 'Wrong' results may become established as a new stable pattern. To take a real example: a young learner of English apparently devised the rule: verb forms with a change of vowel in the stem are past tense forms. When producing a past tense form, he argued to himself: 'I want to produce a past tense form, and therefore it will have a change of vowel.' This led to the temporary production of verb forms such as *slope* for *slept*. See **DEDUCTION**, **INDUCTION**.

ABDUCTIVE
Being produced by abduction, such as certain examples of language change.

ABESSIVE
Case marking signalling absence of a thing or an action. E.g. Finnish *sanaakaan sanoma-tta* 'word-ACC saying-ABESS', 'without/not saying a word'.

A-BINDING
In **Government and Binding Theory, Principles and Parameters** and the **Minimalist Program**, an element in an A (**argument**) position binds an element B if A **c-commands** B and A and B are co-indexed: in *The dog_i injured herself_i*, *The dog* is an argument of *injured* and c-commands *herself*, that is, it A-binds *herself*. See **ANAPHORA, ANTECEDENT**.

ABKHAZ
Caucasian. 100K speakers, mainly in the Abkhaz Republic in Georgia.

ABLATIVE
Case marking signalling movement from a place. E.g. Turkish *Ankara* 'Ankara', *Ankara-dan* 'from Ankara'. It may also signal cause – *on-dan* that-from, 'for that reason' – and partitive relations – *kitap-lar-dan biri* book-pl-ABL one 'one of the books'. See **CASE**.

ABLATIVE ABSOLUTE
An **absolute construction** in Latin typically consisting of a **noun** and a **participle**, both in the **ablative** case. The **construction** is subordinate to the rest of the sentence and the two chunks have different **subjects**: e.g., *Caesare interfecto* (Caesar-ABL-sg killed-ABL-sg), *Marcus Antonius ita locutus est* (Mark Antony thus spoken is) 'Caesar having been killed, Mark Antony spoke thus'.

ABLAUT
An alternation in the **vowel** of a **root** or **stem**, e.g. the **inflectional** variation in English 'strong verbs' to mark **past tense**, *sing–sang–sung*, and past participle, *think–thought*, or the derivational variation in English deverbal nouns *sing–song*; *think–thought*. Most frequently used of such variation in older **Indo-European** languages.

ABRUPT RELEASE
In **plosive** consonants, when the oral **closure** is released it is usually accompanied by **aspiration**, as in [tʰɪk], *tick*. In some environments, as in consonant clusters such as *st-*, the closure is released abruptly, i.e. suddenly, with no aspiration, as in [stɪk], *stick*.

ABSOLUTE
A word or phrase from which an expected **modifier** is missing: *This program runs quicker* (than the others), *She talks more sensibly* (than her brothers).

ABSOLUTE ADJECTIVE
An **adjective** denoting a constant property. Colour is a constant property but size is not. Thus, a grey squirrel is a grey animal but a small elephant is not a small animal because different scales of size apply to the set of elephants and the set

of all animals. *Grey* is an absolute adjective and *small* is a relative adjective. See **HYPONYMY, OPPOSITENESS**.

ABSOLUTE AUDITORY THRESHOLD
In acoustic phonetics the point at which a listener is able distinguish sound.

ABSOLUTE CONSTRUCTION
A phrase subordinate to the rest of a sentence without the relationship being overtly marked: e.g. *The rain having stopped, the children ran outside.* Compare *When/since the rain had stopped, the children ran outside.*

ABSOLUTE FORM
A form of a word with no affixes; e.g. Turkish *ev* 'house' vs *ev-e* 'house-DAT to the house' and *ev-i* 'house-3POSS his/her house'.

ABSOLUTE TENSE
See **RELATIVE TENSE**.

ABSOLUTE-RELATIVE TENSE
See **RELATIVE TENSE**.

ABSOLUTE UNIVERSAL
A property found in every human language; e.g. having **vowels** and **consonants**, marking **reference** and **predication**. See **PREDICATE (2), REFERENCE**.

ABSOLUTIVE
In **ergative** languages, the case form for the **subject** of an **intransitive verb** and the **object** of a transitive verb. See **CASE, TRANSITIVITY**.

ABSORPTION
In phonology, the process whereby one element is incorporated into another. Particularly in **tone languages** where, for example, if a high-low contour precedes a low tone giving the sequence, HL+L, one low might be absorbed into the other to yield H L. See **CONTOUR, SPREADING**.

ABSTRACT NOUN
A noun denoting a state or property which cannot be seen, touched, etc; *truth, courage, guilt*. See **CONCRETE NOUN**.

ABSTRACT SEGMENT
Some theories of phonology propose an abstract underlying segment which does not correlate directly with any single surface representation to account for some particular phonological feature; for example the feature [**syllabic**] may be used to identify segments that can serve as syllable nucleus, i.e. vowels, nasals, etc.

ABSTRACT STRUCTURE
A representation differing from **surface structure** but showing, for example, grammatical relations and other relations that are not immediately apparent in the surface. For instance, a **discontinuous construction** like the 'past progressive'

was jumping might be given an abstract representation as {past}+ {BE+-ing} + {JUMP}, where the discontinuous constituents are brought together – {BE+ing} represents the progressive. This corresponds to a less abstract reordered representation as {BE+past} {JUMP+-ing.}. See **SURFACE STRUCTURE**.

ACCENT

1. A speech variety differing in its pronunciation from other varieties. The variation may be due to regional factors, (a London, Geordie, Somerset, etc. accent), social factors (an RP accent), whether a speaker is a native speaker or not (a French, Chinese, etc. accent). Varieties differing grammatically are usually referred to as **dialects**. Accent and dialect typically go together, but need not do so. 2. In variation studies. Those features of a person's pronunciation that identify regional or social origin. Dialect studies are also concerned with grammatical and lexical features. Regional accents can be characteristic of urban (e.g. Liverpool) or rural (e.g. Norfolk) communities. The term is also often applied to the pronunciation of speakers of 'foreign' languages (e.g. a Russian accent). Social accents relate to the social, cultural or educational circumstances of a speaker. In Britain received pronunciation, RP, is the name of an accent with no regional affiliation traditionally associated with the 'Queen's English', a public school education, the professions, the court, BBC newsreaders, etc. 3. Auditory prominence within a word or syllable, also referred to as stress. Thus in *com'puter* the second, stressed, syllable, *-pu-* is perceived as more prominent than its neighbours. Differences in accent may mark different word meanings, e.g. *'protest: pro'test*. The auditory weight may derive from a variety of factors, raised pitch, additional volume, additional length. etc. 4. In metrics. Accent, or stress, is partially responsibility for the rhythm of metrical verse as in *To'be or'not to 'be, 'that is the 'question*. 5. Diacritic marks that indicate pronunciation, etc,, e.g. the acute accent: á; the grave accent à.

ACCEPTABILITY

A property of words, phrases, clauses and sentences. A given example may be judged by native speakers to be more or less acceptable; that is, to correspond more or less to normal usage. In linguistics, examples are graded according to whether they are judged to be marginally possible (?), marginally impossible (*), totally impossible (**) and so on. (Judgements are indicated by question marks and asterisks as in the preceding sentence.) Speakers make their judgements on various grounds, and different speakers may judge examples differently. A distinction is generally drawn between acceptable and grammatical. An example may be constructed according to the rules of a given language but be unacceptable, say because it is too long or too complex, like *I know that she knows that the manager is aware that the teller suspected that something was wrong*. Examples may be grammatical but unacceptable because they are impolite or scatological. In contrast, an example such as *We drank wine expensive* is unacceptable because the grammar of English requires adjectives to precede nouns in such constructions: *We drank expensive wine*. An example such as *She likes* is ungrammatical and hence unacceptable because it is incomplete. *Likes* requires a direct object, as in *She likes cats*. In contrast, ungrammatical sentences may be acceptable as catchphrases such as, from a television programme, *Nice to see you – to see you nice*.

ACCESSIBILITY
See **ACCESSIBILITY HIERARCHY**.

ACCESSIBILITY HIERARCHY
1. A scale of grammatical functions or relations in which **subject** (NP) is the most accessible to **modification** by **relative clauses**, followed by **direct object**, **indirect object** and **oblique** object in declining order of accessibility. For a given language, if less accessible **NPs** can be modified by a relative clause (or relativized), all the more accessible NPs can be relativized. All languages relativize subject NPs: in *The boy was playing with the hammer*, *The boy* is the subject and can be replaced by *who* to give the relative clause *who was playing with the hammer*. There are languages that do not allow oblique object NPs to be relativized: *the hammer with which the boy was playing* is possible in English but not in many **Bantu** languages. **2.** A scale of NP types graded according to how easily the listener (in the speaker's judgement) can pick up their **referents**. Highly accessible referents may require no overt NP or just a pronoun: *(I) hope you will manage to visit us* (in a letter or e-mail); inaccessible referents require a full NP: *I have contacted a firm in Sheffield that makes the equipment*. In declining order of accessibility a hierarchy proposed for English is zero anaphora, agreement, stressed independent pronoun, right dislocated definite NP, neutral ordered definite NP, left dislocated definite NP, cleft, indefinite NP. See **ANAPHORA, CLEFT CONSTRUCTION, DEIXIS, LEFT DISLOCATION, NOUN PHRASE, RIGHT DISLOCATION**.

ACCIDENCE
An older term for **inflectional morphology**.

ACCIDENTAL GAP
A phonologically well-formed sequence that happens not to represent a real word, e.g. *blick, brillig*. See **SYSTEMATIC GAP**.

ACCOMMODATION
Adjustments in **accent**, etc. made by a speaker to resemble their interlocutor more closely, thus reducing social distance.

ACCOMPLISHMENT
Accomplishments are situations consisting of an **activity** phase and an **achievement**. Writing an e-mail involves the activity of writing, and the event is brought to completion (reaches its final bound or boundary) with the writing of the last word. Driving to a destination involves the activity phase of driving along a road and the achievement phase of arriving at the destination.
See **AKTIONSART**.

ACCUSATIVE

In **nominative-accusative languages** a case marking for **direct object** or **patient** nouns See **CASE**.

ACCUSATIVE AND INFINITIVE

A **construction** borrowed from **Latin**. Verbs of judging, such as *consider, judge, believe, think*, can be followed by a complement clause, as in *They believed that she had won* or *I judge that he is the most competent*, or by a direct object and infinitive, as in *They believed her to have won* and *I judge him to be the most competent*. In Latin direct object nouns are in the accusative case and the English pronouns have different subject and object forms, e.g. *she* vs *her*, *he* vs *him*.

ACHIEVEMENT

Achievements are situations conceived as happening instantaneously. Achievement verbs in English are *recognize, reach, see* (in the sense 'catch sight of'), *catch*. They are the verbs that typically occur in achievement clauses, combining with time phrases such as *in five seconds*, but not *for five seconds*, but rarely occurring in the Progressive – ?*I was recognizing my old teacher*. See **ACTIVITY, ACCOMPLISHMENT, AKTIONSART**.

ACOUSTIC

Related to the physical properties of sound. See **ACOUSTIC CUE, ACOUSTIC DISTINCTIVE FEATURE, ACOUSTIC PHONETICS**.

ACOUSTIC CUE

An **acoustic** characteristic of a speech sound used in its recognition.

ACOUSTIC DISTINCTIVE FEATURE

A property of a speech sound when analysed by acoustic phonetic techniques, as opposed to an auditory or articulatory feature. For example, **fundamental frequency**. In some versions of distinctive feature theory, acoustic features define the binary oppositions that characterize a phonological system. See **DISTINCTIVE FEATURES, ACOUSTIC; J&H DISTINCTIVE FEATURE THEORY, SPE DISTINCTIVE FEATURE THEORY**.

ACOUSTIC PHONETICS

The branch of phonetics that deals with the physical properties of speech sounds. It relies on electronic instrumentation and, increasingly, on computational analysis. Acoustic analysis can be used to support articulatory or auditory analysis. Sometimes, particularly in the analysis of intonation, acoustic, instrumental and auditory analyses can appear to be in conflict.

ACROLECT

In a **dialect continuum**, the variety (or **lect**) that is most prestigious. In the Jamaican **post creole continuum**, the acrolect is standard English and the **basilect** is Jamaican creole. See **MESOLECT**.

ACRONYM

A word formed from the initial letters of two or more words, e.g. *PIN* 'personal identification number'. Like *PIN*, many acronyms can be pronounced as a word. Others, such as *EU* 'European Union', have to be spelled out. See **INITIALISM**.

'ACROSS-THE-BOARD'

Of a process that applies to all the members of a linguistic system; e.g. a sound change affecting all intervocalic voiceless **stops** or affecting all the members of some coordinate structure: *the books I bought and actually read and enjoyed* can be thought of as derived from *the books [I bought the books and I actually read the books and I enjoyed the books]*. A process called object deletion applies across the board to delete all the instances of the direct object *the books* inside the square brackets. See **INTERVOCALIC, VOICELESS**.

ACROSTIC

A text, usually a poem, in which particular letters, such as the first letter in each line, make up a word.

ACTANT

French term for the phrases in a clause referring to the **participants** in the process denoted by the clause. See **ROLE**.

ACTION

A dynamic situation involving change, expenditure of energy and an agent: e.g. *The children are playing cricket, John is building a terrace*. See **AKTIONSART, PROCESS, STATE**.

ACTION NOUN

Noun formed from a verb and denoting an action or process: *dig – digging, transmit (a broadcast) – transmission of a broadcast*.

ACTION VERB

See **AKTIONSART, DYNAMIC**.

ACTIVE

1. See **VOICE**. 2. Vocabulary which a speaker uses as opposed to passive vocabulary which a speaker recognizes but does not use.

ACTIVE ARTICULATOR

The description of the place of articulation of a consonant identifies the place of contact or constriction between a moveable articulator, the active articulator, usually the tongue, and an immobile articulator, the passive articulator, usually the roof of the mouth.

ACTIVITY

Activities are situations presented as having duration and lacking an end-point. Verbs in activity clauses combine with time phrases such as *for hours, for two weeks* and allow the Progressive. *The children were running round the pond* is an Activity;

The children were running to the pond is an **Accomplishment**, since the event concludes when the children reach the end point, the pond. See ACHIEVEMENT, AKTIONSART.

ACTOR

Especially in **Role and Reference Grammar**, a macro-role covering different microroles. E.g. on one analysis, in *The water flowed out of the dam*, *water* is a **theme** and in *The engineers drained the dam*, *engineers* is an **agent**; but both *water* and *engineers* are actors. See LOGICAL SUBJECT, ROLE, UNDERGOER.

ACTOR-ACTION-GOAL

The basic construction type in declarative clauses. More common labels nowadays are **agent** for 'actor' and **patient** for 'goal'. See CONSTRUCTION.

ACTUAL WORD

A word that has been attested in the use of some community of speakers or writers. *Supercalifragilisticexpialidocious* is not an actual word, although many people have heard it in the film *Mary Poppins*. *Tifting* is not known to many users of this dictionary, but it is an actual word used by the community of architects specializing in Scottish architecture.

ACTUALIZATION

1. In syntax and morphology. See REALIZATION. 2. Especially in literary texts, the creation by an author of a text establishing a believable world of characters, settings and events and the activity of readers in interpreting the text using the author's clues.

ACUTE

1. An acoustic distinctive feature involving a concentration of energy in the upper frequencies of the spectrum, associated with a front or medial articulation, i.e. front vowels and consonants with a non-peripheral articulation, dental, alveolar, palatal. Opposite **grave**. See J&H DISTINCTIVE FEATURE THEORY.
2. In J&H Distinctive Feature Theory, an acoustic **distinctive feature** involving a concentration of energy in the upper frequencies of the spectrum, associated with front vowels and consonants with a non-peripheral articulation, e.g. dental, alveolar, palatal. Opposite grave. See DISTINCTIVE FEATURES, ACOUSTIC. 3. The accent mark ´ as in *café*.

ADDRESSEE

One of the roles played in turn by the participants in a **dialogue**, that of the person being spoken to. See SPEAKER.

ADEQUACY

1. In *Aspects of the theory of syntax*, Chomsky proposed a set of levels of adequacy for evaluating grammars. A grammar was said to be observationally adequate if it generated all the sentences of a language, that is, all the sequences of words. A grammar was descriptively adequate if it assigned correct (**constituent**) **structure** to the sentences. A theory of grammar (or a grammar of a language)

was said to be explanatorily adequate if it explained how speakers arrive at a descriptively adequate grammar of their language. 2. A grammar is weakly adequate if it generates the desired set of sequences of symbols. It is strongly adequate if it also assigns satisfactory structures to the sequences.

ADESSIVE

Especially in the analysis of **Finno-Ugric** languages, **case** suffixes indicating position adjacent to or in the interior of (literal and metaphorical); *talve* 'winter' – *talvella* 'in winter'; *pöydä* 'table' – *pöydällä* 'on the table', *auto* 'car' – *autolla* – 'by car'.

ADJACENCY PAIRS

In an **exchange**, pairs of utterances by different interlocutors, the second being a conventional and predictable response to the first; e.g. question and answer. Another example from English is the check followed by backchannel exchange: *You turn right and then take the second on the left, OK? Uh-huh/right*. With *OK*, the speaker checks that the addressee has understood and with *uh-huh* or *right* the addressee-turned-speaker signals that they have understood. See BACKCHANNEL, CHECKING, CONVERSATION ANALYSIS TURN.

ADJECTIVAL CLAUSE

See RELATIVE CLAUSE.

ADJECTIVAL PHRASE

See ADJECTIVE PHRASE.

ADJECTIVALIZATION

Conversion into an **adjective**, e.g. *drink* → *drinkable*, etc. In early transformational grammars, the term was also used for the transformation of a predicative adjective into an attributive adjective: e.g. *the argument is convoluted* → *the convoluted argument*. This usage is now obsolete.

ADJECTIVE

A member of a class of words that either **modify** a noun in a noun phrase or function as the **complement** of a copula verb. In *my new house, new* is an attributive adjective or an attribute modifying *house*. In *Our house is new, new* is a predicative adjective. It denotes a property that the speakers predicate of or assign to their house. Syntactically it is a complement of the **copula** *is*. See PREDICATE (2), PREDICATIVE.

ADJECTIVE PHRASE

A **phrase** with an **adjective** as its **head**: *unbelievably rich* has *rich* as its head, *less obnoxious than them* has *obnoxious* as its head, *poor as a church mouse* has *poor* as its head.

ADJOIN

1. See ADJUNCTION. 2. In the **Minimalist Program**, an operation expanding a phrase by adding an adjunct at its edge; e.g. *at the zoo* is added to *We saw penguins* to yield *We saw penguins at the zoo*.

ADJUNCT

1. Especially in a **clause**, a typical adjunct is a completely optional modifier of the main verb, not required or excluded by any verb: e.g. *yesterday* in *We booked our tickets (yesterday)*. 2. In **X-Bar syntax**, items that are neither **Complement** nor **Specifier** but optional, e.g. adverbial phrases (AdvP) such as *very slowly* in *The snow thawed very slowly*, prepositional phrases (PP) such as *in the garden* in *We looked for you in the garden*, and clauses such as *When autumn comes* in *When autumn comes the swallows fly south*. 3. See **ADVERBIAL**.

ADJUNCTION

Any operation of adding structure to a **tree**. In **transformational grammar** three types of adjunction were available. Sister-adjunction inserted a constituent as a sister of a constituent already in a tree, while daughter-adjunction inserted a constituent as a daughter. **Chomsky-adjunction** created a copy of a **constituent** in a tree and attached as daughters the original constituent and the constituent being added, as in the figure below. The **Minimalist Program** allows an operation called simply 'Adjoin'. It is Chomsky adjunction but is confined to the insertion of an **adjunct**. E.g. when applied to $_{VP}$ [left for Paris] it gives $_{VP}$ [$_{VP}$ [left for Paris] yesterday] as shown in the figure below.

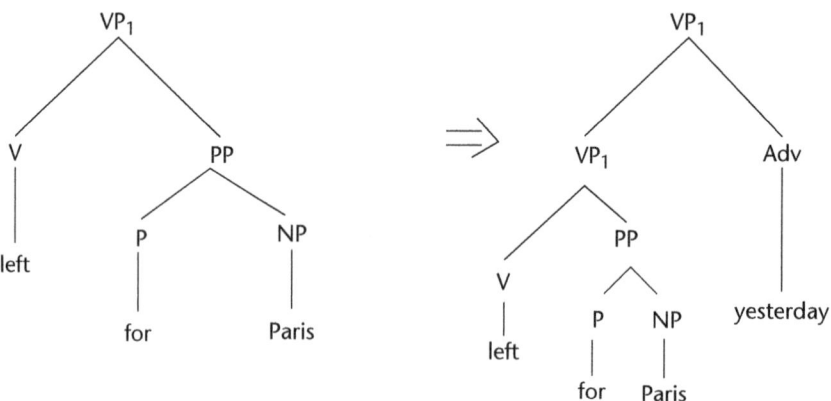

ADNOMINAL

Any constituents in a noun phrase modifying the head noun: *singing* in *The Singing Detective*, *under the chair* in *the crumbs under the chair*, *Emperor's* in *the Emperor's new clothes*. They are next to a noun. *Singing* is sometimes labelled an adnominal form of the verb, in contrast with *The detective is singing*; the adnominal use of *under the chair* contrasts with the **adverbial** use in *The crumbs were lying under the chair*. *The Emperor's new clothes* is an example of the construction called either the adnominal possessive or the Saxon genitive. (Latin *ad* 'to', *nominalis* 'pertaining to a *nomen* "noun"'.)

ADNOMINAL POSSESSION

See **ADNOMINAL**.

ADPOSITION

A general term for prepositions and postpositions. Prepositions come before nouns, postpositions follow them; both are next to nouns (Latin *ad* 'to', *positus* 'placed'.) See **POSTPOSITION, PREPOSITION**.

ADSTRATE

In **language contact** situations, a language that influences a neighbouring language through donating loan words, or **borrowing**. The language that has the higher prestige is the **superstrate** and the language with less prestige is the **substrate**.

ADVANCED TONGUE ROOT, ALSO ATR

A distinctive feature used in the description of vowel harmony systems in some African languages. [+ATR] segments are articulated with the root of the tongue drawn forward in the mouth. e.g. In Akan the oral vowels /i ɪ e ɛ u ʊ o ɔ/ can grouped into two sets: [+ATR]: /i e u o/ and [−ATR]: /ɪ ɛ ʊ ɔ/. Any of the vowels can be a stem vowel, e.g. di 'eat'; kɔ 'go', but the vowels in prefixes fall into one or other set, e.g. 3sg prefix: o ~ ɔ future marker: be ~ bɛ– and they must have a vowel from the same set as the stem: o-be-di *'he/she will eat'*; ɔ-bɛ-kɔ *'he/she will go'*. In some recent work [+/−ATR] replaces the earlier feature [+/− tense]. See **VOWEL HARMONY**.

ADVENTITIOUS

A disorder that is not innate but that occurs as a result of some event.

ADVERB

A large **word class** containing items that are the heads of adverb phrases, e.g. *clearly* is the head of *very clearly* in *Philippa speaks very clearly*. They have adverbial function, modifying adjectives (*very clear, amazingly fast*), verbs (*acted decisively*), prepositional phrases (*immediately in front of you, directly opposite the entrance*) and other adverbs (in *wrote extremely unclearly* – *extremely* modifies *unclearly* and *unclearly* modifies *wrote*). The classic adverbs are those derived from adjectives by means of the suffix *-ly*. They modify verbs and denote manner: e.g., *swiftly* in *They responded swiftly to the threat* and *loudly* in *The children laughed and shouted loudly*. Another large class of adverbs in *-ly* are sentence adverbs, which modify entire clauses and sentences; for instance, *regrettably* in *Regrettably we can't afford it* modifies the clause *we can't afford it*, and *fortunately* in *Fortunately we found Juliet at home* modifies the clause *we found Juliet at home*.

Unfortunately, outside linguistics the term is applied indiscriminately. *On Monday* in *They arrived on Monday* is traditionally labelled 'adverb of time'. In **form** it is a prepositional phrase (denoting a time) with an **adverbial** function. Even further removed from the classic adverbs are items such as *even* in *We even invited our cousins* and *only* in *I only took one suitcase*. Some words prove difficult to classify. In *Is Mike in?* the word *in* is variously analysed as an adverb, a prepositional adverb, a particle or a plain preposition – cf. *Is John in ?* and *Is John in the* *house/his room?*, *She came across the room and spoke to us* and *She came across and spoke to us*. See **PARTICLE, PREPOSITION, PREPOSITIONAL ADVERB**.

ADVERB PHRASE
A phrase with an **adverb** as its head.

ADVERBIAL
In a construction, a function fulfilled by constituents such as adverb phrases, prepositional phrases and adverbial clauses. CGEL distinguishes four types of adverbial. The adjunct function is closest to those of **subject**, **predicate** and **complement** and is played by items denoting manner – *They attacked courageously*, place – *He relaxed in the garden*, time – *The building collapsed next day*, direction/goal – *The children ran to the gate*. ('Adjunct' in this sense encompasses both **adjunct 1** and complement 1.) Adjunct items are relatively integrated with the structure of clauses. CGEL recognizes a class of subjunct items, which are more subordinate and less integrated with clause structure; many of them express viewpoints and other modalities and stand at the front of the clause (in English). In written English they may be separated from the body of a clause or sentence by a comma: *Morally, these proposals are vile*; *Kindly, she offered us a meal*.

The other two types of adverbial function recognized in CGEL are **conjunct** and **disjunct**. They both modify entire clauses and sentences. Disjuncts correspond to what are also called 'sentence adverbs' and express speakers' attitudes: *Obviously they will reject the offer*; *Frankly, the proposal is idiotic*. Conjuncts link clauses and sentences to what precedes them; they may also express speakers' attitudes: *The food is terrible; nonetheless you have to attend the conference*; *You must read this book, otherwise you won't pass the exam*. In contemporary work 'conjunct' and 'disjunct' are rarely used, analysts preferring 'discourse marker' or 'discourse particle'. See **ADVERB, CLAUSE, DISCOURSE MARKERS, SENTENCE**.

ADVERBIAL CLAUSE
See **CLAUSE**.

ADVERBIAL CLAUSE OF CONCESSION
A subordinate adverbial clause which speakers use to concede a point while asserting another point by means of a **main clause**. The classic construction is introduced by *although* or *though*, as in *Although they play elegant football, they do not win games*; *Though he's slow, he's thorough*. Another construction is introduced by *while*, as in *While Lucie doesn't know much Spanish, she's an expert speaker of German*. See **ADVERBIAL, CLAUSE, CONDITIONAL-CONCESSIVE CLAUSE, CONJUNCTION**.

ADVERBIAL CLAUSE OF CONDITION
A subordinate adverbial clause expressing conditions or circumstances which must obtain in order for some event to occur. The latter event is expressed by a **main clause**. E.g. *If they arrive on time, I'll be astonished*; *If they had arrived on time, I would have been astonished*; *Unless you go away, I'll call the police* (= *If you don't go*

away,…); <u>Provided you are properly equipped</u>, *you can climb the mountain safely* (= *If you are properly equipped, …*). See **ADVERBIAL, CLAUSE, CONDITIONAL CLAUSE, CONJUNCTION**.

ADVERBIAL CLAUSE OF PURPOSE
A subordinate adverbial clause expressing purpose or intention. E.g. *He checked in early <u>so that he wouldn't have to wait in a queue</u>*. See **ADVERBIAL, CLAUSE, CONJUNCTION**.

ADVERBIAL CLAUSE OF REASON
A subordinate adverbial clause expressing reason or cause: e.g. *The bank collapsed <u>because it had no capital</u>, They're not pleased, <u>as their flight has been cancelled</u>, <u>Since she's accepted the post</u>, I will have to leave.* Note the subordinating conjunctions of reason or cause: *because, as, since.* See **ADVERBIAL, CLAUSE, CONJUNCTION**.

ADVERBIAL CLAUSE OF RESULT
An **adverbial clause** expressing a result or consequence: e.g. *I was so angry <u>that I resigned immediately</u>.* See **ADVERBIAL, CLAUSE, CONJUNCTION**.

ADVERBIAL CLAUSE OF TIME
A subordinate adverbial clause setting the time of some other event: e.g. *<u>When we reached the house</u>, it was already ablaze; <u>While we were sitting in the garden</u>, it started to rain; <u>After he left</u>, I found his wallet.* See **ADVERBIAL, CLAUSE, CONJUNCTION**.

ADVERBIAL PHRASE
See **ADVERB PHRASE**.

ADVERB PHRASE
A phrase with an **adverbial** function and an **adverb** as its head.

ADVERSATIVE
A form or construction indicating a contrast or **antithesis**. E.g. *but* in *I've brought glasses <u>but forgotten the corkscrew</u>* and *however* in *Go ahead and marry him. <u>However, you'll regret it</u>.*

AEROMETRY
The measurement of airflow during speech.

AFFECTED OBJECT
A **direct object** NP referring to an entity already in existence and affected, but not created, by the **action** denoted by a given verb; e.g. *I pruned <u>the currant bush</u>.* See **EFFECTED OBJECT**.

AFFECTIVE MEANING
Part of the **non-descriptive meaning** of an utterance that has to do with the speaker's emotions or attitude. In *Shut the bloreforming door! There's a helluva strong draught, blooming* and *helluva,* instead of *very,* signal the speaker's attitude or emotional state. See **DESCRIPTIVE MEANING**.

AFFIRMATIVE
Any form that is not **negative**, especially a clause used to assert or affirm that something is the case.

AFFIX
A **morpheme** which is part of a word. Affixes cannot stand on their own but are **bound** and must be added to a **root** or **stem**. *Computerization* consists of the root *compute* plus the affixes *-er*, *-ize* and *-ation*. *Unyielding* consists of the root *yield* plus the affixes *un-* and *-ing*. Affixes that precede the root are called prefixes; affixes that follow the root are called suffixes. Adding an affix is called affixation, adding a suffix is suffixation, and adding a prefix is prefixation. See **CIRCUMFIX, INFIX, INTERFIX, SUPERFIX**.

AFFIX HOPPING
In **transformational grammar**: an analysis of the English verb phrase in which **auxiliary** verbs were broken up into a stem and an **affix** and the affix hopped round, and attached itself to, the next verb on the right. Tense was thought of as the first item in any sequence. Thus, Past HAVE + *en* BE + *ing* DREAM yielded HAVE+Past BE+*en* DREAM+*ing*. This sequence was then realized as *had been dreaming*.

AFFIXING LANGUAGE
A language in which words typically consist of a stem plus affixes. E.g. Turkish *adamlar* 'men' consists of the **stem** *adam* 'man' and the **affix** *-lar* 'plural'. See **ROOT**.

AFFRICATE
A term in the description of the manner of articulation of oral consonant sounds, as in [tʃ] chin, [dʒ] judge. A plosive stop, e.g. [t] is released into a fricative, [ʃ], at the same, or nearly the same, place of articulation. In English, affricates are typically analysed as a single phoneme. Generally the duration of the friction is not as long as it would be in the corresponding independent fricative – compare *chin* [tʃɪn] and *shin* [ʃɪn]. The duration of the friction can sometimes be very brief indeed, as in Cockney [tˢi] *tea*. Such cases are often regarded as affricated stops.

AFFRICATION
See **AFFRICATE**.

AFRIKAANS
Germanic, Indo-European. 6M speakers, South Africa. Descended from Dutch spoken by the seventeenth-century colonists.

AFROASIATIC
A language family including the **Berber, Chadic, Cushitic, Egyptian, Omotic** and **Semitic** families. More than 250M speakers, Northern, Central and Eastern Africa. The oldest documented languages in the world belong to the Egyptian and Semitic families.

AGE GRADING
The organization of individuals in a particular community on the basis of their age.

AGENT
See ROLE.

AGENTIVE
1. Signalling the role of Agent; *runner* is an Agentive noun with the Agentive suffix *-er*. See ROLE. 2. Designating any process by which an Agent noun is formed.

AGENTIVE ROLE
One of the **qualia roles**; it relates to entities viewed from the perspective of how they came about, what agent or agency was involved. The agentive role encompasses the builder's view of a house and the process of putting the individual parts together to form the whole vs the view of its inhabitants. See CONSTITUTIVE ROLE, FORMAL ROLE, TELIC ROLE.

AGENTLESS PASSIVE
See VOICE.

AGGLUTINATING LANGUAGE
A language in which words are formed by **agglutination**. See AGGLUTINATIVE.

AGGLUTINATION
Process by which **agglutinative** words are formed.

AGGLUTINATIVE
Word structure in which, ideally, each abstract morpheme is realized by an independent morph. Turkish comes close to the ideal, as in, e.g., the word *okundular* 'they were read', which divides into *oku* 'read' – *n* 'Passive' – *du* 'Past' – *lar* '3pl'.

AGNOSIA
In **clinical linguistics**, lack of ability to correctly interpret sensory information.

AGRAMMATISM
In **clinical linguistics**, a speech disorder in which a **function word** or an **inflection** marker is omitted.

AGRAPHIA
In **clinical linguistics**, lack of ability to write.

AGREEMENT
A device for signalling the syntactic linkage between words. Typically the words that are linked all change their shape, in Indo-European languages by changes in inflectional suffix. One pattern of agreement is found in noun phrases, where nouns and adjectives agree in certain properties. E.g. in the following Italian noun phrases, the demonsrative *questo* and the noun *ragazzo* or *ragazza* agree in number

and **gender**: *quest-o ragazz-o* 'this boy', *quest-a ragazz-a* 'this girl', *quest-i ragazz-i* 'these boys', *quest-e ragazz-e* 'these girls'. Note also the **copula** constructions: *Il ragazz-o è piccol-o* 'The boy is small', *La ragazz-a è piccol-a* 'The girl is small'; *Il ragazz-o è arrivat-o* 'The boy is/has arrived', *La ragazz-a è arrivat-a* 'The girl is/has arrived'. Agreement is said to be masculine, as for *ragazzo*, or feminine, as for *ragazza*; these terms are applied to nouns denoting animate beings and inanimate objects: *tavola* 'table' imposes feminine agreement, *telefono* 'telephone' imposes masculine agreement. Some Indo-European languages have a third pattern of agreement, called neuter, and other language families possess even more complex agreement patterns.

Another pattern of agreement applies in clauses, to subject nouns and finite verbs, which in many languages agree in person and number. E.g. Russian *Ja idu domoj* 'I am-going home', *Petr idet domoj* 'Peter is-going home', *My idem domoj* 'We are-going home'. Agreement plays an important role in **reference tracking**. See **DEIXIS, GOVERNMENT, PERSON**.

AGREEMENT MAXIM

One of the maxims associated with Leech's **Politeness Principle**. In an ideal dialogue the speaker should maximize agreement with the hearer, by emphasizing points of agreement and minimizing (reducing or playing down) points of disagreement.

AI

See **ARTIFICIAL INTELLIGENCE**.

AINU

Language isolate. Nearly extinct but once spoken widely in the northern part of the main Japanese island of Honshu as well as Hokkaido island and in the Kurile Islands. The current Ainu population is estimated to be around 24K.

AIRSTREAM

The flow of air used in the production of speech.

AIRSTREAM MECHANISM

The process which initiates an **airstream**. The main initiator is the lungs, the **pulmonic airstream**. Air can be drawn into the lungs on an **ingressive** airstream, or expelled on an **egressive** airstream. The **glottalic airstream** is produced by closing the glottis and drawing it sharply downwards for a glottalic ingressive airstream. **Consonants** produced on a glottalic ingressive airstream are **implosives**. The glottalic egressive airstream is created by closing the glottis and drawing it sharply upwards. Consonants produced on a glottalic egressive airstream are **ejective**. The **velaric airstream** is created by two oral closures: one towards the front of the mouth and the other by the back of the tongue moving backwards against the velum. When the front closure is released, an egressive velaric airstream is produced. Consonants produced on a velaric egressive airstream are **clicks**. See **VOWEL**.

AKAN

Niger-Congo. Approx. 8.5M speakers, Ghana. Group of closely related dialects including Asante, Fante and Twi.

AKKADIAN

Semitic. Now extinct. Spoken in the later second millennium BCE in Mesopotamia (roughly = today's Iraq) by the Babylonians and Assyrians. It was written on clay tablets in the cuneiform script.

AKTIONSART

German for 'action type'. Traditionally conceived as the lexical class of a given verb, hence the alternative term 'lexical aspect': *know* denotes a **state** and is a **stative verb**; *recognize* typically denotes an instantaneous event and denotes an **achievement**; *walk* denotes an **activity**; *read the whole book* denotes an **accomplishment**. It is now recognized that Aktionsart applies to clauses: *We were walking* denotes an activity, without any end point mentioned but *We were walking to the park* denotes an accomplishment. When the walkers reach the park, the event is completed and another event begins. The difference may reside in the direct object: *Joe was eating a pie* denotes an accomplishment in that when the pie is finished, the event is finished. *Joe was eating pies* does not mention any possible end point and is an activity. On this interpretation, states, activities and so on are seen as different types of situation and some recent work on aspect uses the term situation aspect.

ALBANIAN

Indo-European. 3.6M speakers Albania, 1.6M Kosovo, 500K Macedonia, 33K Montenegro.

ALETHIC MODALITY

In logic, a **modality** in which propositions must logically be true, such as *All men are mortal*. No natural language has a special grammatical expression for this modality.

ALEXIA

In **clinical linguistics**, loss of ability to read. Cf. **DYSLEXIA**.

ALGONQUIAN

Language family including Cree, Ojibwa, Potawatomi and Shawnee. Formerly spoken along the east coast of North America, around the Great Lakes, and in the foothills of the Rocky Mountains. They were the first North American languages to be encountered by French and English explorers.

ALGORITHM

The specification of an effective process, a sequence of operations that automatically and correctly convert some object into another object. Examples are the operations that convert 25×82 into 2050 and the operations (in transformational grammar) that convert an active, declarative clause, say *The rain stopped play*, into a passive, interrogative clause, *Was play stopped by the rain?*

ALIENABLE POSSESSION

Many natural languages have one construction for alienable possession, that is, the possession of items, such as a car, that are not considered to belong inherently to someone, and another construction for inalienable possession, that is the possession of items that are considered to belong inherently to someone, such as body parts. Cf. French *J'ai cassé son verre* 'I broke his glass', which has the possessive pronoun *son* 'his', and *Je lui ai cassé le bras* 'I broke his arm', which has the dative pronoun *lui* and definite article *le*

ALIGNMENT

1. In Optimality Theory models of morphology, the positioning of prefixes, roots and suffixes relative to each other. Alignment constraints accept correct sequences and reject incorrect sequences. For instance, any morph that is to count as a prefix must have its left edge aligned with the left edge of a word; any morph that is to count as a suffix must have its left edge aligned with the right edge of a root. **2.** In Optimality Theory, the positioning of syntactic and phonological phrases relative to each other. One constraint might be that the left edge of a syntactic phrase be aligned with the left edge of a phonological phrase. That is, the beginning of the syntactic phrase and the beginning of the phonological phrase coincide. **3.** In parallel corpora it is normally a prerequisite for analysis that a text segment and its translation equivalent are aligned, i.e. placed side by side. See **PARALLEL TEXT**. **4.** In typology, the assignment of **roles** and **case** marking to the arguments in the **predicate-argument structure** for a given verb. Thus, a transitive verb such as *crush*, as in *He crushed the piece of paper* or *The hail crushed the flowers*, has two arguments, one of which is agent, or more agent-like, and the other of which is patient, or more patient-like. In nominative-accusative languages the agent argument is assigned nominative case and the patient argument is assigned accusative case. In a language with prototypical ergative morphology, the agent argument is assigned **ergative** case and the patient argument is assigned absolutive case. See **ERGATIVITY**.

ALIGNMENT TYPOLOGY

The study of the different combinations of predicate-argument structure, roles and case marking found in the languages of the world. See **ALIGNMENT 3**.

ALLATIVE

A **case** expressing movement to a place or person. Finnish *koulu* 'school', *menen koulle* 'I-am-going to-the-school'.

ALLEGORICAL

Applied to a text depicting events and characters which can be read simply as a story but can be given a deeper interpretation. E.g. Orwell's *Animal Farm* is on the surface a story (a fantasy) of animals taking over a farm but on a deeper level is a political critique. See **PARABLE**.

ALLEGRO
Rapid and fluent, typical of rapid colloquial speech.

ALLEGRO FORM
Phonologically reduced forms typical of rapid colloquial speech, e.g. *wazzat* for *what's that?*

ALLITERATION
The repetition of a consonantal sound, often the first sound in a sequence of words: e.g. *with beaded bubbles winking at the brim*. See **ASSONANCE**.

ALLO-
A nominal prefix designating a variant form. See **ALLOGRAPH, ALLOMORPH, ALLOPHONE, ALTERNANT**.

ALLOCUTOR
See **ADDRESSEE**.

ALLOGRAPH
1. Alternate form of a **grapheme**, the minimal contrastive unit in a writing system. For instance, *E, ɛ, e* are allographs of *e* in different environments in English. Upper- case *E* is found sentence initially and initially in proper names (and elsewhere), while the use of the allographs *ɛ* and *e* varies from individual to individual. 2. One of a set of alternative spellings, e.g. the variant realizations of the phoneme [eə] in *hair, there, care*, etc. See **ALLO-**.

ALLOMORPH
See **MORPH**.

ALLOPHONE
A particular realization of a phoneme, usually a positional variant. Thus in British English /l/ may be velarized as [ɫ], the 'dark l' of *ball*, or palatalized as [lʲ], the 'light l' of *leave*.

ALPHABET
A writing system in which linguistic units are represented by letters. The Roman alphabet distinguishes between consonants and vowels. Semitic alphabets often distinguish only consonants.

ALTAIC
Language family including **Turkic, Mongolian** and **Tungusic**. Spoken in central and north-eastern Asia, in Siberia and also in northern China. Perhaps related to **Korean** and **Japanese**.

ALTERNANT
One of the varying forms in an **alternation**.

ALTERNATION

The relation between different variant forms or alternative realisations of a linguistic form. For example the forms -/s/~/z/~/Iz/ are alternants of the plural morpheme in English (*cats, dogs, horses*). The symbol ~ represents the alternation. *Men* is the plural alternant of *man*; *go ~ went* are non-past and past alternants of *go*. See **MORPH**.

ALVEOLAR

A term in the description of the **place of articulation** of consonant sounds. The **tip** or **blade** of the tongue comes against the alveolar ridge, the teeth ridge, as in the voiceless alveolar stop [t] as in *tin*; or the voiced alveolar stop [d] as in *din*. English has a wide range of alveolar articulations, the stops [t] and [d], the fricatives [s] and [z] the lateral [l] and the nasal [n]. Articulations towards the back of the teeth ridge can be described as post alveolar.

ALVEO-PALATAL

A term in the description of the place of articulation of consonant sounds. The front of the tongue comes against the front of the hard palate e.g. [tʃ] *church*.

ALZHEIMER'S DISEASE

A form of dementia. See **DEMENTIA**.

AMBIENT CLAUSE

See **IMPERSONAL CLAUSE**.

AMBIENT IT

See **DUMMY SUBJECT**.

AMBIGUITY

Ambiguity occurs when a word, phrase or sentence, said to be ambiguous, has two or more interpretations. Two main types are recognized. **Lexical ambiguity** results from a lexical item having two or more meanings. For example, *She hates the chair* can be interpreted as 'She hates this piece of furniture' or 'She hates the person who is chairing the meeting'. **Grammatical ambiguity** results from a sequence of words being the **realization** of two different constructions. E.g. *I tripped up the thief with the golf club* can be interpreted as *the thief with the golf club* being tripped up, in which case *with the golf club* modifies *thief*, or as the speaker using the golf club to trip up the thief, in which case *with the golf club* modifies *tripped up (the thief)*. *I didn't drive straight after taking the medication* describes either a dangerous situation, if *straight* modifies *drive*, or a sensible one, if it modifies *after*. Because the differences are not always reflected in pronunciation, the term constructional homonymy is sometimes used. Ambiguity should be distinguished from **vagueness**, as in *He is a good candidate*, where the sense of *good* is unclear and could mean 'morally good', 'most suitable' and so on. See **CONTEXT, HOMONYMY, LEXICAL AMBIGUITY**.

AMBIGUOUS
The property of a word, phrase or clause that can be understood in more than one way. See **AMBIGUITY**.

AMBISYLLABIC
A consonant simultaneously forming part of two syllables. In *petrol* the /t/ may be analysed as syllable final in *pet-* and as syllable initial in *-trol*. Phonetically the /t/ may be glottalized, [pɛt^ʔ], a syllable final feature, and the /r/ may be devoiced and possibly affricated as part of a syllable-initial consonant cluster tr-.

AMELIORATION
A change that makes the meaning of a lexical item more positive and impressive. E.g. the Scots word *quine* has kept its original meaning of 'woman', whereas the related English word *queen* has come to mean 'the wife of a king'. See **PEJORATION**.

AMHARIC
Semitic, Afroasiatic. More than 20M speakers. The official language of Ethiopia and widely spoken in the Horn of Africa. Its written history dates back to the fourteenth century.

A-MORPHOUS MORPHOLOGY
A theory of **morphology** which makes no use of **morphs** and morphemes but focuses on relations between whole **words** and on general principles governing the relations. See **MORPHOLOGY**.

AMPERSAND
&, the character standing for *and*.

AMPLIFIER
See **INTENSIFIER**.

AMPLITUDE
The property of a sound wave associated with perceived loudness.

ANACHRONISM
The use of a word or expression not appropriate to the time in which a text is, or purports to be, produced. For example, dialogue in a novel may contain a word that is outdated, such as *wireless* for *radio* in a dialogue set in 2011, or a word or phrase that had not yet come into use, for instance *dead clever* or *dead brilliant* in a novel set in 1800.

ANACOLUTHON
A sentence which begins with one construction but finishes with another, the writer or speaker failing to 'follow on'. A (real) written example is *His letter is a conglomeration of wild and senseless accusations and ends his letter with a nom-de-plume*. A spoken example is *I was going to – Oh do whatever you like*.

ANACUSIS
In **clinical linguistics**, Loss of ability to hear.

ANALOGICAL LEVELLING

The process whereby the number of forms in a **paradigm** is reduced by analogy with another, usually more frequent, paradigm thus making the paradigm more regular: e.g. the paradigm for English 'strong verbs' distinguishes between the simple past and the past participle (*sing, sang, sung*). but this distinction is levelled to the paradigm for 'weak verbs' which do not distinguish between the simple past and the past participle (*walk, walked, walked*). So *dive dove dived* is levelled to *dive dived dived*.

ANALOGY

The process whereby a form is altered so as to make it more like another form. Most usually irregular forms are adjusted to make them more like regular forms. Thus the irregular older English *brethren* gives way to *brothers* by analogy with other regular plurals.

ANALYSIS BY SYNTHESIS

A theory of speech perception that proposes that a listener processes an incoming acoustic signal by synthesizing a replica. The synthesis is, in effect, an analysis of the input.

ANALYTIC

An analytic construction is one in which some grammatical category is expressed by a sequence of words, i.e. as a piece of syntax. E.g. the English **Perfect** *has left* vs **Progressive** *is leaving* are analytic but the Simple Past *left*, being a single word, is not analytic but synthetic. A synthetic construction is one in which some grammatical category is expressed by changes to a stem, i.e. morphologically: e.g. Latin *laboravit* 'has worked' vs *laborabat* 'was working' vs *laborabit* 'will work'. See **MORPHOLOGY, TENSE AND ASPECT**.

ANALYTIC COMPOUND

See **ROOT COMPOUND**.

ANALYTIC MOOD

See **MOOD**.

ANALYTIC PROPOSITION

See **PROPOSITION**.

ANAPHOR

See **ANAPHORA**.

ANAPHOR RESOLUTION

See **ANAPHORA**.

ANAPHORA

The use of anaphors to pick up the **referent** of a full **noun phrase** occurring earlier in a text. Anaphors are **pronouns** that pick up the referent of full noun phrases occurring earlier in some text. Thus, in *My sister liked the house but <u>she</u> didn't buy <u>it</u>*, *she* picks up the referent of *My sister* and *it* picks up the referent of *the house*. Traditionally, *she* and *it* are said to refer back to *My sister* and *the house*, but it is more accurate to say that they refer to whatever these noun phrases refer to. *She* is an anaphor of, alternatively, is anaphoric to, *my sister*; *it* is anaphoric to *the house*. *My sister* and *the house* are the **antecedents** of *she* and *it*. Other anaphors are reflexive pronouns, such as *herself* in *The doctor has removed herself from the list of candidates*, and *so*, in *I approved Philippa's proposal and so did the Chairman*, where *so* refers to the act of approving Philippa's proposal. Determining the antecedents of anaphors in texts is known as **anaphor resolution**. See BOUND, CATAPHORA, PRO-FORM.

ANAPHORIC

See ANAPHORA.

ANAPTYXIS

The insertion of an extra vowel in a word thus producing an additional syllable, as in *filum* /filəm/, *athaletic* /aθəlɛtɪk/. See EPENTHESIS.

ANARTHRIA

In **clinical linguistics**. Loss of ability to articulate speech sounds. See DYSARTHRIA.

ANATOLIAN

Indo-European. Languages spoken in the second millennium BCE in what is now Turkey and preserved in cuneiform script. The principal languages were **Hittite** and Luvian.

ANCHOR

In discourse, a set of elements that the speaker assumes the hearer can infer from their knowledge of the world. For instance, in *We went to see my parents at Christmas. We managed to get the presents and the tree into our car*, the set of elements {things that are central to Christmas festivities} is the anchor that enables the hearer to interpret the phrases *the presents* and *the tree*. See ANCHORING, FRAME SEMANTICS, SCRIPT.

ANCHORAGE MARKER

See ANCHORING.

ANCHORING

The tying of sentences to particular contexts, without which they cannot be interpreted. The interpretation of texts is aided by anchorage markers, words and phrases that help the listener or reader to interpret events as sequential or overlapping and to assign them to specific points or periods of time. E.g. *On Thursday the Chairman resigned. By Friday, having reflected, he regretted his action*. *On Thursday* and *By Friday* anchor the events of resigning and regretting to particular times and signal change of time. See ANCHOR.

ANDATIVE
A term applied to constructions containing an **auxiliary** verb or verb **affix** derived from the lexical verb corresponding to 'go'. Venitive constructions contain an auxiliary or affix derived from 'come'. E.g. in the Polynesian language Tokelau a venitive **particle** *mai* signals that an action is continuing while the andative particle *atu* signals that an action is about to begin.

ANGLO FRISIAN BRIGHTENING
A sound change in Old English and Old Frisian in which the back vowel /a/ was fronted to /æ/ in some environments. See **FRONTING**.

ANIMACY
The property of being **animate**.

ANIMACY HIERARCHY
See **GRAMMATICAL HIERARCHY**.

ANIMAL COMMUNICATION
The study of the communicative systems of animals – e.g. danger calls in monkeys, the bee dance, etc. These are not usually thought to be linguistic systems.

ANIMATE
1. An animate noun denotes a set of humans or animals: *woman, dog, cheetah, president, teacher*. What counts as animate is to some extent culture-dependent. In Cree, trees, pipes and snowshoes are classified as animate. In Russian, *Moskvich* 'Muscovite' also denotes a type of car and in colloquial Russian is treated as animate when referring to the car. 2. In grammar, a class of nouns (or gender class) denoting animate beings and involved in patterns of **agreement** and **government**. E.g. Russian has a special **accusative** case suffix for certain animate nouns: *kot* 'tom-cat', *stakan* 'drinking glass', *videl kota* 'saw the-cat' vs *videl stakan* 'saw the glass'.

ANNOTATION
See **TAGGING**.

ANOMALY
A linguistic unit that is abnormal with respect to some pattern is said to present an anomaly or to be anomalous. An anomaly can be grammatical, semantic or pragmatic. The clause *Dogs growls* is anomalous with respect to number agreement in standard English. *The snow thawed into ice* is anomalous because of the clash in meaning between *thaw* and *ice*. A French speaker addressing a person senior in age and status by the intimate pronoun *tu* is committing a pragmatic anomaly, social rules requiring the polite form *vous*. See **PRAGMALINGUISTIC NORMS, SOCIOPRAGMATIC NORMS, ZEUGMA**.

ANOMIA
In **clinical linguistics**, loss of ability to name things. See **DYSNOMIA**.

ANTAGONISM

A property of ambiguous lexical items, which have various interpretations that are antagonistic, i.e. cannot be held simultaneously. E.g. *We're enjoying his good spirits* could be interpreted 'We are happy that he is in a good mood' or 'We find his whisky and brandy enjoyable'. However, the interpretations are mutually exclusive. See **FACETS, HOMONYMY, MONOSEMY, POLYSEMY, SENSE (2)**.

ANTAGONIST

In Talmy's theory of force dynamics, entities participating in a situation exert forces. Agents, Agonists in Talmy's account, exert a force, which may be countered by a force exerted by an Antagonist. In the situation described by *The car kept moving despite the flat tyre*, *the car* is the Agonist and *the tyre* is the Antagonist. See **ROLE**.

ANTECEDENT

In a **sentence** or a larger piece of text, a noun phrase specifying the **referent** of an anaphor occurring later in the text. In *Sam arrived late. He had lost his way*, *Sam* is the antecedent of *He*, *He* is bound to *Sam*, and *He* and *Sam* are in a relation of **anaphora**.

ANTECEDENT-GOVERNMENT

A antecedent-governs B if A governs B and is co-indexed with it.
See **C-COMMAND, EMPTY CATEGORY PRINCIPLE, GOVERNMENT, PROPER GOVERNMENT, THETA-GOVERNMENT**.

ANTERIOR

In distinctive feature theory anterior segments that have a stricture in front of the palato-alveolar region. **Labial, dental** and **alveolar** consonants are [+ant] while **palatal, velar** and **uvular** consonants etc. are [−ant]. All **vowels** are analysed as [−ant]. This is not an entirely satisfactory feature since neither [+ant] nor [−ant] segments form a natural class.

ANTICIPATORY ANAPHORA

See **CATAPHORA**.

ANTICIPATORY ASSIMILATION

Also **regressive assimilation**. See **ASSIMILATION**.

ANTICIPATORY CO-ARTICULATION

The tendency of a segment to share some aspect of the articulation of a following segment. Thus, in *too*, the /t/ may acquire lip-rounding in anticipation of the lip rounding on /u/ and in *tea* the /t/ may acquire lip-spreading in anticipation of the lip-spreading on /i/.

ANTICIPATORY SUBJECT

See **DUMMY SUBJECT**.

ANTICLIMAX
See **BATHOS**.

ANTILANGUAGE
The private or secret language of various typically socially disadvantaged groups, including criminals and vagrants. The language is often phonologically distorted, as with **pig latin**, **back slang**, etc., and uses private slang extensively. It is usually spoken rather than written. For example, 'thieves cant', **polari**.

ANTINOVEL
A work of fiction that deliberately flouts the traditional conventions of novel writing.

ANTIPASSIVE
A construction found in many languages with an **ergative** system of **case** marking and seen as the opposite of the passive constructions in English, French, Latin and so on. Across languages antipassive constructions have various functions. One common property of antipassives is that the direct object does not denote a given, topical entity but a new entity or one that is non-specific. Inuktitut, an Inuit language spoken in Greenland, has ergative and antipassive constructions. The ergative clause *inu-up qimmiq-Ø takuvaa* 'person-ERG dog-ABS saw, The/a person saw the dog' treats the dog as given, that is as able to be identified by the listener. The antipassive clause *innu-k qimmir-mik takuvuq-Ø* 'person-ABS dog-OBLQ saw, The/a person saw a dog' treats the dog as new, that is as not previously mentioned, not obvious from the context and therefore not easily identifiable by the listener. In Yucatan Maya the antipassive construction combines with incorporation to yield a construction in which the patient noun is non-specific. Examples are the ergative clause *t-in- čak-Ø-ah čeʔ* 'Comp-1sg.ERG-chop-3sg.ABS-PFV tree, I chopped down a tree' vs the antipassive clause (consisting of a single word) *čak- čeʔ-n-ah-en* 'chop-tree-antipassive-PFV-1sg.ABS, I chopped wood'. The independent patient noun in the ergative construction, *čeʔ*, is in the antipassive incorporated into the verb and the agent noun loses its ergative marking. In some languages, such as Tzutujil (a Mayan language spoken in Guatemala), the antipassive allows the patient noun to be omitted altogether, much as in English one can say *He's outside chopping*. Work on **transitivity** has demonstrated that the transitivity of a clause is strongest when the patient noun denotes a single, specific and given entity, but is reduced by patient nouns denoting more than one entity, or a non-specific entity. And where there is no overt patient, transitivity is very low. What is common to the above examples is that the antipassive reduces transitivity. English has transitive verbs that do not require a direct object, as in *Keith is cooking, Barnabas is drawing, Susan buys for a large department store*. Either the missing objects denote a very limited range of things – cooking food, drawing pictures – or the clause denotes a habitual and institutionalized activity. Whether the term 'antipassive' should be extended to such examples is not clear.

In Native Australian languages antipassive constructions have other functions. In Diyari (a language spoken in South Australia) the antipassive lowers the transitivity of a clause. The verb *danka* 'find' denotes finding after a deliberate search; in its antipassive form it denotes accidental finding and is equivalent to 'run into (somebody)' or 'come across (something)'. In Dyirbal (a language spoken in north Queensland) the **pivot** noun phrase, i.e. the one that is deleted, in relative clauses and conjoined clauses has to be in the **absolutive** case, i.e. the case for the subjects of intransitive verbs and the objects of transitive verbs. In the Dyirbal equivalent of *The man saw the woman*, ergative case is assigned to *man* and absolutive case to *woman*. In the Dyirbal equivalent of *The woman came*, absolutive case is assigned to woman. The two clauses (in Dyirbal) can be conjoined to yield *The woman came and the man saw*. In the second clause the patient noun, in the absolutive case, is deleted. To combine the clauses *The man came* and *The man saw the woman*, the antipassive is required. Without it, *man* in the second clause is in the ergative case and marked as an agent, but nouns in the ergative case cannot be deleted. The antipassive construction changes the case marking: *man* is absolutive and *woman* is dative. The clauses can be conjoined to give *The man came and saw the woman*. See **ERGATIVITY, GIVEN AND NEW, INCORPORATION, INFORMATION STRUCTURE, NARRATIVE, PROGRESSIVE, ROLE, VOICE**.

ANTIPHONY

See **APOPHONY**.

ANTIPODAL OPPOSITES

A subtype of **directional opposites**, namely pairs of lexical items denoting the opposite points on some axis. Examples are NORTH and SOUTH, EAST and WEST, which are diametrically opposed in diagrams. Other examples are RIGHT and LEFT, ABOVE and BELOW, BEHIND and IN FRONT OF. Like converses, they allow a clause containing one member of a pair to be converted into a clause containing the other member, while keeping the other lexical items in the clause constant. (Converses differ in not being diametrically opposed.) Thus *X is north of Y* converts to (and entails) *Y is south of X*, and *X is to the right of Y* converts to and entails *Y is to the left of X*. See **OPPOSITENESS**.

ANTITHESIS

The contrasting of ideas by means of contrasting phrases and clauses: e.g. contrastive focus structures such as *not good but evil, They chose not Gordon but Tony*.

ANTONYM

See **ANTONYMY**.

ANTONYMY

Antonymy is the relation between pairs of lexical items whose meanings are related by being opposed to each other in some domain. Such pairs are called antonyms; because they denote properties that can be graded, they are also known as gradable opposites. Unlike complementaries, a given pair of antonyms does not divide up some domain completely but leaves a middle ground. For example, the antonyms BIG and SMALL leave a middle ground; humans are regularly described as neither big nor small, or as being of average height. Antonyms combine with words such as *very* and have comparative and superlative forms: *This dog is bigger than that dog, This is the biggest dog*. In a pair of antonyms, one may be unmarked or neutral and the other marked. The question *How big is the dog?* makes no assumptions about the size of the dog but *How small is the dog?* assumes that the dog is small. BIG is unmarked or neutral, SMALL is marked.

Comparative forms such as *longer* and *shorter* do not entail the positive forms *long* and *short*: *This book is longer than that one* does not entail that 'this book' is long; it might have sixty pages but the other one might only have forty pages. Similarly for *short*. One book might have 1,000 pages and the other 900 pages. The comparatives are said to be impartial, though uncommitted might be a better term. With other antonyms, such as HAPPY and SAD, the comparative forms both entail the positive: *Fiona is happier than Sheena* entails *Fiona is happy* and *Fiona is sadder than Sheena* entails *Fiona is sad*. Antonyms such as HAPPY and SAD (also BITTER and SWEET, PROUD OF and ASHAMED OF) are called equipollent antonyms and their comparatives are said to be committed.

With antonyms such as GOOD and BAD, the question *how good?* is neutral: *How good was the exhibition?* can receive the responses *Terrible* or *Excellent*. The question *How bad was the exhibition* is not neutral. The speaker presupposes that it was bad but wants to know just how bad it was. *Absolutely terrible* and *A total flop* are possible replies but not *Excellent*. The question *how bad?* is said to be committed, and GOOD and BAD are examples of **overlapping** antonyms. See **OPPOSITENESS**.

AORIST

In grammars of Homeric, classical and New Testament Greek, an **aspect** of the verb that was used to present a situation as having occurred in the past. The term comes from the Greek *aoristos*, which meant either 'without boundaries'/ 'unlimited' or 'indefinite'. A situation was presented with no limitations or boundaries relating to completion, or action in progress or repetition. In classical Greek the aorist *eluse*, e.g., as in *eluse ton doulon* 'he-freed the slave' contrasted with the imperfective *elue* as in *elue ton doulon* 'he-was-freeing the slave'. Completion was not an essential component of its meaning but a property that could be inferred from context. The term 'aorist' is used in grammars of Turkish for an aspect that presents a situation as timeless. Thus, the aorist *yazarim* means 'I am a writer' (but am not necessarily writing something at the present moment), in contrast with (*mektup*) *yaziyorum* 'letter I-am-writing, I am writing a letter' (the action is taking place now). The Turkish aorist is used in proverbs and stage directions and to present situations that are in the future, *mektup yazarim* 'I'll write a letter (one of these days)'. See **IMPERFECTIVE, PERFECTIVE, TENSE AND ASPECT**.

A-OVER-A
A principle relating to structures with a constituent A containing a smaller A. Rules applying to A must apply to the higher A. E.g. in *Sue photographed her friend's house*, *her friend's house* is an NP containing the NP *her friend's* and the NP *the house*. Only *her friend's house* moves: *Her friend's house was photographed*, **Her friend's was photographed house*.

AP
See **ARTICULATORY-PERCEPTUAL STRUCTURE, INTERFACE, MINIMALIST PROGRAM**.

APERTURE
The size of the opening in the mouth during articulation, especially of vowels.

APHAERESIS
The omission of segments at the beginning of a word, as in *opossum → possum, nadder → adder*.

APHASIA
In **clinical linguistics**, loss of ability to produce or understand language. **Broca's aphasia** is associated with syntactic problems and **Wernicke's aphasia** with lexical and comprehension problems.

APHEMIA
In **clinical linguistics**, loss of ability to speak. See **mutism**. Other linguistic abilities, e.g. reading, writing, comprehension, are not usually impaired.

APHONIA
In **clinical linguistics**, loss of voice, thus limiting speech production to whisper.

APHORISM
A phrase or clause, concise and possibly memorable, expressing some piece of everyday wisdom: e.g. *Handsome is as handsome does*. See **MAXIM, PROVERB**.

APICO-
Sounds formed with the tip (apex) of the tongue. Apico-dental, apico-alveolar, apico-palatal, etc.

APOCOPE
The omission of segments at the end of a word, as in *Diana → Di; margarine → marge*.

APODOSIS
See **CONDITIONAL CLAUSE**.

APOLLONIUS DYSCOLUS
A Greek linguist working in Alexandria in the mid second century CE. He produced an innovative theory of **word class** which he applied in his analysis of Greek.

APOPHONY
The vowel alternation in inflectionally related words as in English *run – ran*, or in reduplicative words as in *shilly shally*. See also **ABLAUT**.

APOSIOPESIS
Falling silent before a sentence is completed: e.g. *We could* might meet the response *We could what?*, inviting the speaker to complete the sentence. (Greek *apo* 'from', *siope* 'silence'.)

APOSTROPHE
An interruption in a speech or written text to address some person, usually not present, or some inanimate object. (Greek *apo* 'from', *strophe* 'turning', the metaphor being that speakers turned away from the main content of their text.)

APPARENT TIME STUDIES
Comparing usage by different age groups at a single sampling time intended to replicate linguistic change over real time.

APPLICATIVE
Especially in **Bantu** languages, a **construction**, and the form of the **verb** occurring in the construction, that converts an **oblique** object into a **direct object**. E.g. Rwanda *y-a-anditse ibaruwa n-ikaramu* 3sg-S-PST-write letter with-pen 'He wrote the letter with a pen' is converted to *y-a-andik-ish-ije ikaramu ibaruwa* 3sg-S-PST-write-APPL-aspect pen letter 'He wrote the pen the letter'. This is equivalent in sense to 'He used the pen to write the letter'. The direct object of the applicative construction, but not oblique objects, can be made the **subject** of the passive. See **GRAMMATICAL FUNCTION, OBLIQUE**.

APPLIED LINGUISTICS
The application of linguistics to language-related social issues. Often used particularly for the application of linguistics to language teaching.

APPLIED PRAGMATICS
The study of language use in particular contexts where difficulties of communication arise from the use of technical language, formal written language, the need for translation and so on. Examples are exchanges in court, medical consultations, immigration procedures, etc.

APPOSITION
A relation between two phrases, especially noun phrases, in which the two phrases are simply juxtaposed. The second noun phrase refers to the same entity as the first one and merely adds extra information. In *This is Jacob, the soccer player in the family*, *Jacob* and *the soccer player in the family* refer to the same person, the second phrase conveying extra information. In *Do you know our Mandarin speaker, Alan?* the extra information is provided by the noun phrase *Alan*. The phrases *the soccer player in the family* and *Alan* are said to be appositional, or in apposition, to *Jacob* and *our Mandarin speaker*.

APPROXIMANT

A term in the description of the manner of articulation of oral consonant sounds, as in [w] *win*, [j] *year*, [l] *leaf*. The articulators approach each other and there is a non-turbulent airflow without **closure** or **friction**. Sometimes called frictionless continuants.

APRAXIA

In **clinical linguistics**, loss of ability to make muscular movements required for speech

ARABIC

Semitic, Afroasiatic. Approx 280M speakers throughout the Middle East. The liturgical language of Islam. Official language of most countries of the Middle East and Northern Africa. Classical Arabic, the language of the Koran, was first described between the eighth and tenth centuries. Modern Standard Arabic is a descendant of Classical Arabic.

ARAMAIC

Semitic, Afroasiatic. Group of languages spoken throughout the Middle East from tenth century BCE. The spoken language of Palestine in biblical times. Gradually replaced by Arabic from approx. 700 CE but still not extinct. Includes Syriac, the language of the Syrian Church from the fourth century CE. Still in use as a liturgical language.

ARAWAKAN

Arawakan languages are spoken in South and Central America.

ARBITRARINESS

See **ARBITRARY SIGN**.

ARBITRARY SIGN

A sign whose shape does not in any way reflect its meaning. English *dog*, French *chien* and Russian *sobaka* all denote the class of dogs; there is no connection between the phonetic form of the words and their meanings. All arbitrary signs are conventional; the convention governing their use has to be learned. A few items bear some **iconic** relation to entities in the world, especially onomatopoeic lexical items like *splash, whisper*. Arbitrariness is held to be a defining characteristic of language. See **DESIGN FEATURES, EMBLEM, ICONIC SIGN, ONOMATOPOEIA, SOUND SYMBOLISM**.

ARC PAIR GRAMMAR

A formal model developed from **Relational Grammar** and published in 1980 by David Johnson and Paul Postal. The structure of sentences is represented by graphs in which the constituents are connected by arcs representing grammatical relations such as **subject** and **object**.

ARCHAISM

A word or construction retained from an older form of the language, e.g. *thou art* for *you are*. Archaisms are typically found in religious (*with this ring I thee wed*) and legal (*heretofore, the party of the first part*) language and also in nursery rhymes (*whither wilt thou wander*).

ARCHIPHONEME

In **Prague School** phonology, a segment representing the neutralization of two or more phonemes in some particular environment. For example, the English plural **affix** can be realized as /-s/, /-z/ or /ɪz/ depending on the environment (orthographically *cat-s*, *dog-s*, *hors-es*). There is no opposition of voice in the final segment. The segment can be represented as the archiphoneme /Z/ realized as voiceless following a voiceless segment and voiced following a voiced segment, with the insertion of /ɪ/ following a sibilant. An analysis permitting archiphonemes is strongly at odds with a classical phonemic account. The notion can be captured in distinctive features: two segments share all features except the one feature that distinguished the two segments. See **BIUNIQUE, INVARIANCE, PHONEME**.

AREAL LINGUISTICS

That branch of linguistics that is concerned with the way linguistic characteristics (particularly phonological, morphological and syntactic properties) are shared through borrowing, language contact, etc. among languages in a particular geographical area. For example, the Balkans, the Baltic, South-East Asia.

ARGOT

Special vocabulary used by close-knit groups of people, typically of low social class, such as beggars and thieves.

ARGUMENT

1. In a **clause**, any **constituent** required by a **verb**. The term is borrowed from logic, where predicates such as *yawn* or *kick* are said to be 1-place, 2-place and so on in accordance with how many arguments they take: *place* is a 3-place predicate, as in *She placed the letters on the desk*; *yawn* is a 1-place predicate, as in *The students yawned*. In syntax the term is extended to adjectives: in *The headmaster is domineering*, *headmaster* is an argument of *domineering* and in *Taipans are dangerous*, *taipans* is an argument of *dangerous*. Alternatively, *headmaster* and *taipans* are arguments of *is domineering* and *are dangerous*, and in *Fiona is the professor*, *Fiona* is an argument of *is the professor*. See **COMPLEMENT 1, VALENCY**. 2. A set of statements of **propositions**, some of which are **premises**, taken for granted, the others following from the premises. See **CALCULUS**.

ARGUMENT FOCUS

A proposition consists of a predicate and arguments. When a proposition is expressed by means of a clause in an utterance the **focus** may be on one of the arguments. E.g. in *Are you buying a flat? – No, we need a whole house*, the focus in the reply falls on *a whole house* and *house* carries the focal accent. See **END FOCUS, PREDICATE FOCUS, SENTENCE FOCUS**.

ARGUMENT SLOT

In some representations of the structure of a clause, the **arguments** are presented as occupying particular slots. Different constructions have different sequences of slots. E.g. subject-verb-direct object as in *The children watched the players* or goal-verb-subject in *Out of the hole came a badger*.

ARGUMENT STRUCTURE

1. For a given verb (but also noun or adjective), the number and type of **arguments** it takes. 2. The theory of how argument structures are represented and linked with syntactic structures consisting of verbs, noun phrases, prepositional phrases, adjective phrases and adverbial phrases. See **LEXICAL-CONCEPTUAL STRUCTURE, LEXICAL-FUNCTIONAL GRAMMAR**.

ARISTOTLE (384–322 BCE)

One of the most important Greek philosophers, famous for his theories of **meaning** and **word class**.

ARRERNTE

Pama-Nyungan. Two closely related languages spoken in Central Australia. One is virtually extinct; the other has only a few thousand speakers.

ARTICLE

A **determiner** which signals whether a speaker is treating the **referent** of a noun phrase as definite or indefinite. Noun phrases too are said to be definite or indefinite. A definite noun phrase such as *(I left) the book (on the floor)* signals that the book has been mentioned already and/or is salient in the context. The speaker expects the listener to pick out the book with ease. An **indefinite noun phrase** such as *(I left) a book (on the floor)* signals that the book has not been mentioned before. The speaker does not expect the listener to pick out the book and may provide further information. Not all languages have articles, and usage differs among those that do. See **DEFINITE ARTICLE**.

ARTICULATION

A term covering the movements of the various parts of the mouth, etc. that modify the **airstream** moving in or out of the mouth and produce the various types of speech sounds (see figure below). Sounds are classified in terms of the **airstream mechanism** involved, the commonest being the pulmonic egressive airstream; the action of the vocal cords, whether the sound is **voiced** or not; the position of the **velum**, whether the sound is oral or nasal; and activity by other organs in the mouth, especially the tongue and lips, which modify the **place of articulation** (the position where there is a major obstruction or constriction to the airflow), the **manner of articulation** (the nature of the obstruction or constriction; the configuration of the lips is characterized in terms of their spreading and rounding, the way they are stretched away from a neutral position. Most sounds are produced with a single place and manner or articulation. A few also have a secondary place or manner of articulation – labiovelars like [gb] have both a labial and a velar place of articulation; **affricates** like [tʃ] combine a stop and a fricative articulation, and nasal vowels have both an oral articulation and nasalization. See **VOICE**.

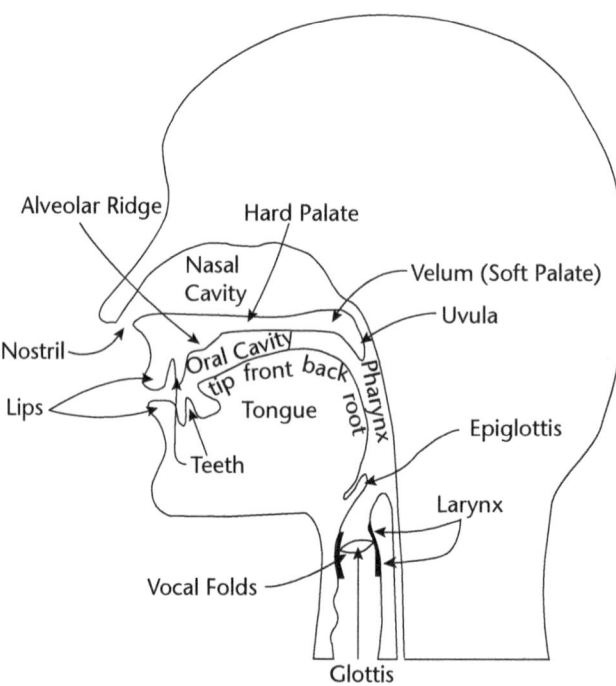

ARTICULATOR
Any part of the vocal apparatus involved in the production of a sound.

ARTICULATORY ANALOG
A representation of the vocal tract in **speech synthesis**.

ARTICULATORY DISTINCTIVE FEATURE
See DISTINCTIVE FEATURES, ARTICULATION, SPE DISTINCTIVE FEATURE THEORY.

ARTICULATORY FEATURE
A distinctive feature related to the shape of the articulatory organs. See **SPE DISTINCTIVE FEATURE THEORY**.

ARTICULATORY GESTURE
In **SPE Distinctive Feature Theory**. A gesture that relates to the **place of articulation** of a segment; other gestures include the phonatory gesture, relating

to **phonation**, especially voicing, and the oro-nasal gesture, relating to nasality. See **FEATURE GEOMETRY, VOICE**.

ARTICULATORY OVERLAP
Where some feature of the articulation of a segment is influenced by that of a preceding segment. See **ASSIMILATION**.

ARTICULATORY-PERCEPTUAL STRUCTURE
See **MINIMALIST PROGRAM, INTERFACE**.

ARTICULATORY PHONETICS
That branch of phonetics concerned with the articulation of speech sounds. The descriptive terminology is derived from anatomy and physiology and from observation and listening. It is the basis of the classification of sounds used in the **International Phonetic Alphabet** and hence in transcription. It has traditionally been the basis of the training of teachers of phonetics and subjects involving phonetics like speech therapy etc. It is usually supplemented by some instrumental techniques, **palatography**, **aerometry**, etc. Sometimes opposed to **acoustic phonetics**, the study of the physical properties of sound. In recent times articulatory phonetics has been overshadowed by **instrumental** phonetics, the study of the physical properties of sound waves etc using electronic instruments and computational techniques deriving from computer science and artificial intelligence. See **INSTRUMENTAL PHONETICS, IPA**.

ARTICULATORY SETTING
The overall configuration of the articulators providing a general impression of a particular individual, accent or dialect. These settings may be relatively permanent, as when an individual has a 'husky' or a 'nasal' voice. The velarized quality of the Liverpool accent is often said to be the result of a particular articulatory setting. See **VELARIZATION**.

ARTIFICIAL INTELLIGENCE
The ability of computers to perform tasks that resemble human capacities such as reasoning, learning and using natural language and the development and elaboration of software that supplies computers with these abilities.

ARTIFICIAL LANGUAGE
An invented language. Some invented languages, such as Esperanto, were intended to be used as a neutral **lingua franca** by speakers of different languages. Others were devised for use in logic or computer programming.

ARTIFICIAL LARYNX
A device available to a speaker whose larynx has been surgically removed. It simulates the vibration of the vocal folds. See **LARYNX**.

ARTIFICIAL SPEECH
Synthesized speech.

ASCENSION
See RAISING.

ASCRIPTIVE
See COPULA.

ASH
The name of the symbol æ used in Old English orthography and in some phonetic and phonemic transcriptions to represent an unrounded front vowel as in *cat* /kat/.

ASIDE
1. A remark that is outside the main topic and flow of a conversation. 2. In drama, a remark made to the audience by one of the characters in a play.

ASPECT
See TENSE AND ASPECT.

ASPECTUAL
To do with ASPECT.

ASPECTUALIZER
In English grammar, a verb such as *begin*, *stop* and *finish*, which denotes various stages of a **situation** that is an **activity** or **accomplishment**. See AKTIONSART.

ASPIRATION
The puff of breath that can follow the release of a **plosive** consonant, usually a **stop**, symbolized by a following raised [ʰ], as in [pʰɪn].

ASR
See AUTOMATIC SPEECH RECOGNITION.

ASSERTIVE
A **speech act**, and any grammatical device, by which speakers commit themselves to what they are saying. **Declarative** clauses are typically assertive, **interrogative clauses** are typically non-assertive. Verbs and phrases such as *assure* and *know for a fact* are assertive, increasing the level of commitment: *I assure you that the work has been completed, I know for a fact that he has emigrated*. **Particles** and phrases such as *apparently* and *as far as I know* reduce the commitment: *Apparently she likes the proposal, As far as I know there are no plans to close ten universities*. The use of modal verbs reduces commitment by signalling that the speaker is making a guess: *A red pick-up truck? That would be Steve, They'll be in the library*. Other modal verbs, sometimes combined with negation, increase commitment: *She must have accepted the job (judging by the evidence), They can't not accept the offer*. There is a view that the strongest commitment is expressed by straightforward declarative clauses. See VERB (2). In Searle's classification, a speech act, such as asserting or concluding, that commits speakers and writers to the truth

of whatever proposition is conveyed by their utterance. See **COMMISSIVE**, **DIRECTIVE**, **EXPRESSIVE**.

ASSIMILATION

The phonetic or phonological processes whereby a segment becomes more similar to an adjacent segment. In **regressive assimilation** (also known as **anticipatory assimilation**) we have assimilation to a preceding segment, as in the pronunciation of *one man,* [wVn man], as [wVm man] – the final /n/ of /wVn/ has assimilated in place of articulation to the preceding segment, the bilabial /m/. This is particularly common in English with word final alveolar consonants: [ɪʃʃi] for *is she* (assimilation of voice and place of articulation [zʃ] → [ʃʃ]); [haf tə] for *have to* (assimilation of voice [vt] → [ft]). In **progressive assimilation** (also known as perseverative assimilation) we have assimilation to a following segment as in [beikŋ] for *bacon*, where the velarity of /k/ is copied onto the following /n/ yielding /ŋ/. In the pronunciation of *has she* as /haʃʃi/, the /z/ of *has* has fricated under the influence of the following segment. In mutual assimilation (also known as **coalescent assimilation**) there is mutual influence, that is, adjacent segments merge. Thus in *don't you* [dəʊnt ju] pronounced as [dəʊntʃu], /t/ and /j/ coalesce to /tʃ/. Vowel harmony has been analysed as distant assimilation (i.e. assimilation between non-adjacent segments). Assimilation is a particularly important process in historical phonology. *Orchard* derives from Old English *ortgeard*: *ort* derives from Latin *hortus* 'garden', *geard* survives as Modern English *yard*; *t+g* by mutual assimilation becomes *ch*.

ASSOCIATION

In **autosegmental phonology** a line drawn to represent the relation between elements of tiers of phonological representation.

ASSOCIATIVE FIELD

See **LEXICAL FIELD**.

ASSOCIATIVE MEANING

See **DESCRIPTIVE MEANING**.

ASSOCIATIVE RESPONSE

The typical response to a word stimulus. A distinction is sometimes made between **paradigmatic** responses, responses in the same word class, e.g. *cat* stimulates *dog*, *mouse*, etc., and **syntagmatic** responses, responses of syntactically associated words, e.g. *cat* stimulates *black* etc.

ASSONANCE

The repetition of a vowel sound. See **ALLITERATION**.

ASTERISK

Used to mark forms judged to be unacceptable: e.g. **I read quickly the letter*, **explicitivity*.

ASYNDETON

The joining of syntactic units without a **conjunction**: *Books, papers, disks – all were lost in the fire; I'm exhausted, I've had a terrible day, I don't want any complaints*. Such structures are called asyndetic. (From the Greek *a-sun-detos* 'not-together-bound'.) See **HYPOTAXIS, PARATAXIS**.

ATELIC

In **aspect** theory, a **situation** represented in language as having no built-in end-point. and a verb or verb phrase that denote such situations. Thus, *I carried the parcel inside* and *I was carrying the parcel inside (when I tripped and fell)* both denote a situation that comes to an end once the parcel is inside. This situation is telic or bounded, and the phrases *was carrying the parcel inside* and *carried the parcel inside* are said to be telic. *The dog carried the bone around* and *The dog was carrying the bone around* denote a situation with no built-in end-point. Carrying something around can go on for as long as the carrier has the strength and inclination. The situation is labelled atelic or non-bounded and *carried the bone around* and *was carrying the bone around* are said to be atelic. **Achievements** and **accomplishments** are telic, states are atelic and an **activity** may be telic or atelic. (Greek *a-* negative prefix, *telos* 'goal'.) See **AKTIONSART, TENSE AND ASPECT**.

ATN

See **AUGMENTED TRANSITION NETWORK**.

ATOMISTIC THEORIES OF WORD MEANING

See **LEXICAL DECOMPOSITION**.

ATR

See **ADVANCED TONGUE ROOT, VOWEL HARMONY**.

ATTITUDINAL MEANING

See **AFFECTIVE MEANING**.

ATTRIBUTE

See **ADJECTIVE**.

ATTRIBUTE-VALUE MATRIX

See **UNIFICATION**.

ATTRIBUTIVE

Applied to a **definite referring expression** that is used to refer, not to a specific person or thing, but to anyone or anything that fits the description. Suppose a speaker declares, in connection with an upcoming social event, *The person sitting in the corner tomorrow will get a surprise*. The definite referring expression *The person sitting in the corner* is used attributively to refer to whoever will be sitting in the corner. The speaker who announces *The person sitting in the corner is my dentist* uses the same definite referring expression referentially, to refer to a particular person. The attributive use is more commonly called *de dicto* (Latin 'about the-said, about what is said'), the referential use is more commonly called *de re* (Latin 'about the-thing'). See REFERENCE.

ATTRIBUTIVE ADJECTIVE
See ADJECTIVE.

AUDIENCE DESIGN
Stylistic variation made in response to those gathered to watch, listen, etc. to an event, etc. See ACCOMMODATION.

AUDIOGRAM
In **clinical linguistics**, a graph representing an individual's ability to hear **pitch**.

AUDIOLOGY
In **clinical linguistics**, the study of hearing and hearing disorders.

AUDIOMETRY
The measurement of hearing and hearing loss.

AUDITORY DISCRIMINATION
The ability to distinguish between speech sounds.

AUDITORY PHONETICS
The branch of phonetics concerned with ways in which the ear and brain hear speech sounds, as opposed to acoustic phonetics, the study of the physical properties of sound waves.

AUGMENT
A segment or syllable added to a **stem** when **suffixes** are added to it, for example the suffix *-al*, as in *margin-al*, often requires a stem augment, often, *-i-*, as in the *professor* → *professor-i-al*. The phenomenon is common in Indo-European (e.g. Greek) and Indo-Iranian (e.g. Sanskrit) and also in Bantu.

AUGMENTATIVE
An **affix** indicating that something or someone is perceived as large: e.g. Russian *dom* 'house', *domishche* 'huge house'. See DIMINUTIVE.

AUGMENTED AND ASSISTED COMMUNICATION
Methods of supplementing language, especially speech, for people with impaired linguistic abilities.

AUGMENTED TRANSITION NETWORK
A method of parsing used in **Artificial Intelligence**.

AURAL MEDIUM
The spoken medium of communication as perceived by the ear, distinguished from the oral medium, communication transacted by word of mouth. Both are distinguished from the written medium.

AUREATE
Of an exceedingly ornate style with many Greco-Latinate words.

AUSTIN, John Langshaw (1911–1960)
A British philosopher and Oxford professor who worked on the philosophy of ordinary language and laid the foundations of **speech act** theory.

AUSTRALIAN LANGUAGES
Before Australia was colonized there were approximately 250 indigenous Aboriginal languages. Today only a handful are learned by children, the others are either extinct or endangered. The largest language family is **Pama-Nyungan**, covering most of the continent and including **Arrernte**, **Guugu Yimidhirr**, **Jiwarli**, Kalkutungu, **Kayardild**, **Kaytetj**, **Pitjantjatjara**, **Wambaya** and **Warlpiri**. There are also many English-based pidgins and creoles.

AUSTROASIATIC
Over 150 languages spoken in South-East Asia, central India and Vietnam. The principal language families are **Mon-Khmer**, including Vietnamese and Munda.

AUSTRONESIAN
Perhaps the largest language family in the world with more than 1,000 languages covering an enormous area stretching from Taiwan and Hawai'i in the north to New Zealand in the south, from Easter Island in the east to Madagascar in the west. Includes **Balinese, Bikol, Cebuano, Fijian, Flores Languages, Formosan Languages, Hawaiian, Ilocano, Indonesian, Javanese, Kapampangan, Madang, Madurese, Malagasy, Malay, Malukan, Maori, Motu, Niuean, Riau Indonesian, Samoan, Sunda, Tagalog, Tahitian, Tamambo, Tongan**.

AUTHORIAL VOICE
The voice of an implied author. In *David Copperfield* the authorial voice is that of David Copperfield, but the real author is Charles Dickens.

AUTHORSHIP ATTRIBUTION
The process of establishing the author of a given text. The process may lead to a specific person being named as the author, or to the author of a given text being the same as the unnamed author of another text, or to no decision. See **STYLOMETRY**.

AUTOBIOGRAPHY
A person's account of his or her own life.

AUTOHYPONYMY
A relationship between two senses of a lexical item, when one sense is general and unmarked and the other sense is more specific and marked. *Dog* is typically used to refer to any dog, male or female, but, in contrast with *bitch* meaning 'female dog', it also has the more specific meaning 'male dog'. *Bitch* and *dog* with these meanings are more likely to be used by dog breeders. (Greek *autos* 'self' +

hyponymy. A lexical item with two such interpretations is thought of as a hyponym of itself.) See **HYPONYMY, MARKED 4**.

AUTOLEXICAL SYNTAX

A model of grammar created by Jerry Sadock in the early 1980s. The model has independent levels of morphology, syntax and semantics, each with its own independent organization and representation. The lexicon plays a central role in the interface between the independent representations.

AUTOMATIC ALTERNATION

Phonological variation that is predictable, has no exceptions and is determined by a context-sensitive phonological rule. E.g. the past-tense marker *-ed* is realized as /ɪd/ after alveolar segments (eg /patɪd/ *patted*); /-d/ after voiced segments (eg /bang-d/ *banged*) and as /-t/ after voiceless segments (e.g. /wɒkt/ *walked*). See **MORPH, SUFFIX**.

AUTOMATIC SPEECH RECOGNITION

The computational transformation of spoken language to machine readable text.

AUTONOMOUS

Autonomous linguistics is linguistics studied as a discipline in its own right, i.e. not as dependent on logic, literary criticism, etc.

AUTONOMOUS PHONEME

A **phoneme** defined without consideration of its relationships to other linguistic levels, e.g. morphology or syntax, in contrast to **morphophoneme, systematic phoneme** where the definition involves matters other than the purely phonetic.

AUTONOMY OF SYNTAX

The idea that syntax can be studied independently of other components of the language system, especially semantics. It plays a central role in Chomskyan models of **generative grammar**. See **CHOMSKY**.

AUTOSEGMENT

In **autosegmental phonology** an element that occurs on one of the parallel tiers proposed.

AUTOSEGMENTAL PHONOLOGY

A classical phonemic phonological representation proposes a single linear sequence of segments, phonemes, which are not themselves resolvable into smaller units, distinctive features or the like. Early **generative phonology** proposes a single linear sequence of segments, this time represented as matrices of distinctive features together with boundary symbols indicating word, phrase and sentence boundaries and tone and stress markers. Autosegmental phonology proposes a representation consisting of more than one simultaneous linear sequence, called tiers, with phonological information distributed between the different tiers. Each tier is composed of autosegments, and relations between autosegments on different tiers are represented by **association** lines. Segments in traditional phonology are represented as bundles of distinctive features on a segmental tier. An early insight of autosegmental phonology was the recognition that **tonal** features are independent of segmental features and cannot readily be represented with distinctive features like segments. A separate level of representation is therefore proposed, a tonal tier. This led to the proposal that stress and intonation in English can be analysed in a comparable fashion, thus a timing tier. These various tiers, with different features appearing on different tiers, enabled investigation of the internal structure of segments and the possible ways in which they may interact in phonological operations such as deletion or spreading, as in **vowel harmony** and **nasal harmony**. It also enabled investigation of the **feature geometry** of phonological systems. See **SPE DISTINCTIVE FEATURE THEORY, TIER, AUTOSEGMENT, TIMING TIER.**

AUXILIARY

In English and many other languages, a verb which requires a lexical or full verb with it in a **clause**. It is auxiliary in that it 'helps' the **lexical verb** by supplying information about **mood, tense and aspect**. In English, *may* and *must*, e.g., express possibility or necessity: *may complete (the course)*; *have* expresses **Perfect** tense: *hasn't completed the course*; *do* expresses tense in negative and **interrogative** clauses: *does not like cheese*; *be* expresses **aspect**: *was learning German* vs *learned German*. Some languages, such as **Turkish**, express possibility and necessity, not by auxiliary **words**, but by **affixes** attached to main verbs. Auxiliaries may have their own grammatical properties, such as the **nice properties** of English auxiliaries. E.g. *not* or *n't* are added direct to auxiliaries whereas ordinary verbs require *do*: *can't help* vs *does not help*, *has not phoned* vs *did not phone*. Auxiliary verbs occur at the front of interrogative clauses, ordinary verbs do not: thus, *Can she help?* but *Did she help*, not **Helped she?* See, **MODAL VERB, NEGATIVE, TENSE AND ASPECT, VERB PHRASE.**

A-VALENT

A **verb** that has no **arguments**; e.g. Latin *pluit* 'rain-3sgPRS It is raining'. See **ARGUMENT STRUCTURE, VALENCY.**

A-VERSE

The first half of a line of verse.

AVERSIVE

In some Native Australian languages, a case affix signalling an NP as referring to something that is feared or avoided. E.g. Yidiny *mujam yarngga-ng gudaga-yiida* 'mother fear-PRS dog-aversive, mother fears the dog'.

AVESTAN

Old **Iranian**, **Indo-Iranian**, **Indo-European**. The language of the sacred texts of Zoroastrianism.

AXIS

In Bloomfield, the **constituent** governed by a **verb** or **preposition**; e.g. *them* in *avoided them* or *(bought a house) for them*.

AYMARA

A language family with approximately 2M speakers in Bolivia, Chile and Peru. Aymara-speaking people have been in close contact with their **Quechua**-speaking neighbours for many centuries.

AZERBAIJANI, NORTH

Turkic, **Altaic**. Approx. 7.4M, Azerbaijan, south Dagestan. Smaller numbers in Armenia and Central Asia.

AZERBAIJANI, SOUTH

Turkic, **Altaic**. Approx. 15.9M, Iran. Smaller numbers in Afghanistan, Iraq, Jordan, Syria, Turkey.

B

BABBLING
Sounds produced by infants in the prelinguistic stage. It often resembles reduplicated adult CV syllables, *bababa*, etc.

BABYLONIAN
See **AKKADIAN**.

BABY TALK
1. Speech used by young children. See **BABBLING**. 2. See **CARETAKER SPEECH**.

BACK
1. The part of the tongue opposite the soft palate. See the figure at **articulation**. 2. Vowels articulated with the back part of the tongue such as [A] in *bar* or [ɔ] in *got*, or consonants articulated in the back part of the mouth, such as the velar consonants /g/ and /k/. 3. In **SPE Distinctive Feature Theory**, segments, especially vowel segments, that are articulated with the tongue bunched and retracted, for example [u], [Q]. See **FRONT**.

BACK SLANG
A form of **antilanguage**, where words are pronounced backwards, e.g. *boy > yob*.

BACKCHANNEL
In conversation, a secondary channel of communication by which the listener, without interrupting the speaker's turn, signals whether the speaker's message has been understood (*OK, Right, Uhuh*) or not (*eh?, sorry?*) or caused amazement (*Really?*) and so on. See **CONVERSATION ANALYSIS**.

BACK-FORMATION
A **word** created from another word which is interpreted as having a **stem** and an **affix**, although originally it did not. E.g. *buttle* from *butler*, *pea* from *pease* (which sounds like a **plural**, although the spelling shows that it is not).

BACKGROUNDING
The process of making less prominent certain parts of a text and the information they carry; e.g. by putting them into subordinate clauses, finite or non-finite, by using short passives or middles with the agent missing (or defocused). See **CLAUSE, FOREGROUNDING, VOICE**.

BACKSHIFTING
See **INDIRECT SPEECH**.

BAHUVRIHI
See **COMPOUND WORD**.

BAKHTIN, Mikhail Mikhailovich (1895–1975)
A Russian professor of literature. His work on **dialogue** was unrecognized during his life but has had enormous influence on current philosophy of language.

BALINESE
Austronesian. Approx. 4K speakers, Indonesia (Java, Bali).

BALTIC
Balto-Slavic, Indo-European. A family consisting of two surviving languages, **Latvian** and **Lithuanian**. A third language, Old Prussian, is extinct.

BALTO-SLAVIC
Indo-European. **Baltic** languages include Latvian and Lithuanian, **Slavic** languages include **Russian**, **Ukrainian**, **Czech**, **Polish**, **Slovak**, Croatian, **Macedonian** and **Bulgarian**.

BALUCHI
Indo-Iranian, **Indo-European**. Approx. 7.3M speakers, mainly in Iran, southern Afghanistan and West Pakistan. It has an impressive oral literature.

BANTU
Niger-Congo. With some 1,500 languages, spoken by some 250M people, Bantu is the largest of the families in Niger-Congo. Bantu languages are spoken from Cameroon in Western Africa to Uganda in Eastern Africa and in most of Central and Southern Africa. **Kinyarwanda**, **Luganda**, **Nyanja**, **Shona**, **Tswana**, **Xhosa**, **Zulu** and **Swahili** are major Bantu languages. A well-known characteristic of Bantu languages is their extensive noun class system.

BAR
See **X-BAR SYNTAX**.

BAR NOTATION
See **X-BAR SYNTAX**.

BAR PROJECTION
See **X-BAR SYNTAX**.

BARE ARGUMENT ELLIPSIS
A type of ellipsis that deletes all the material in a clause apart from one argument, as in *By this time tomorrow James will be enjoying the company of his cousins – not his aunt's food though*. The phrase *not his aunt's food though* can be thought of as derived from *By this time tomorrow James will not be enjoying his aunt's food though*.

BARE PASSIVE
A construction consisting of a passive **participle**, without the **auxiliary** verbs *be* or *get*. It is found in **catenatives**, as in *We had the books <u>shipped out to New Zealand</u>*

and *I keep the documents <u>locked in my safe</u>*, and as reduced relative clauses in NPs, as in *an application <u>rejected by the town council</u>*. See **VOICE**.

BARE INFINITIVE

In English grammar, the verb stem without any grammatical marking and not preceded by *to*: e.g. *whine* in *The noise made the dog <u>whine</u>* and *finish* in *You must <u>finish</u> the exercises*. See **NON-FINITE VERB**.

BARE PHRASE STRUCTURE

See **X-BAR SYNTAX**.

BARRIER

In **Government and Binding Theory**, a boundary which prevented **government** from operating. See **GOVERNING CATEGORY, PRINCIPLES AND PARAMETERS**.

BARTHES, Roland (1915–1980)

A French critic who developed a theory of **signs** both linguistic and non-linguistic and proposed that each field of human activity involves a special type of discourse organized by language.

BASE

1. In morphology, any form to which a process applies. In English, *dog* is the base for the plural *dogs*, *snow* is the base for *snowy*, which in turn is the base for *snowier*. An analysis may require an abstract base, a form that does not actually occur. The base for Latin *nik-s* 'snow-NOM' and *niw-is* 'snow-GEN' is *nikw-*. *Nikws* is realized as *niks* and *nikwis* is realized as *niwis*. In some theories such abstract bases are called underlying forms. In classic **generative phonology** different forms of the same **lexeme** are derived from the same underlying abstract form. See **DERIVATION, MORPH, ROOT, STEM**. 2. In **Cognitive Grammar**, part of the representation of conceptual structures. A given concept is profiled in bold against a base. The base corresponds to some domain of conceptual structure. For instance, the concept of 'sibling' is profiled against a set of kinship relations and the concept of 'in' is profiled against an entity and the space contained by the entity. See **COGNITIVE LINGUISTICS**. 3. See **CATEGORIAL COMPONENT**.

BASE AND PROFILE

In the representations used in **Cognitive Grammar**, the base of a predication is the **domain** in which a given **predicate** applies. The profile of the base is that part of the domain highlighted or designated by the predicate. E.g. *blade* applies to the domain of cutting instruments and designates or profiles their cutting part. *Cognac* applies to the domain of alcoholic liquids, designating one type. See **CONSTRUAL**.

BASE COMPONENT

In **transformational grammar** the base component, consisting of a set of context-free **phrase structure rules** and a **lexicon**, generated **deep structure** representations which were mapped into **surface structure** representations by **transformations**. See **CONTEXT-FREE**.

BASHKIR
Turkic, Altaic. 1.7 M speakers, Russia (Urals).

BASIC CONSTRUCTION
In a given language, the **construction** that is most frequent and can be interpreted independently of other constructions. The construction is unmarked, nothing being highlighted or emphasized. The basic construction in English is active, positive and declarative, as in *The workmen demolished the wall*. Other constructions, such as the interrogative *Did the workmen demolish the wall?* and the passive *The wall was demolished by the workmen* have to be interpreted with reference to the active, declarative clause. Concepts such as 'subject' and 'basic word order' are defined in relation to the basic construction. See GRAMMATICAL FUNCTION, WORD ORDER.

BASIC FORM
See BASE.

BASIC LEVEL
See LEVEL.

BASIC WORD ORDER
See WORD ORDER.

BASILECT
In a dialect continuum, the variety (or lect) that is least prestigious. In a Jamaican post-creole continuum, the basilect is Jamaican creole. See ACROLECT, MESOLECT.

BASQUE
Language isolate. Spoken along the Pyrenees in France and Spain. The only pre-Indo-European language still spoken in Europe. Unsuccessful attempts have been made to relate Basque to other languages, especially Finno-Ugric and Caucasian.

BATHOS
A change from elevated language and ideas to the ludicrously banal, typical of Mr Micawber in *David Copperfield*: *The blossom is blighted, the leaf is withered, the God of day goes down upon the dreary scene, and – and in short you are for ever floored.*

BAUDOUIN DE COURTENAY, Jan (1845–1929)
A Polish linguist, who worked in both Poland and Russia. He laid the foundations of modern **phonology**, introducing the term '**phoneme**' and developing the concept.

BEHAVIOURISM
A school of psychology concerned with measurable and observable behaviour, associated with the American psychologist Skinner. In linguistics particularly

associated with the American linguist Leonard Bloomfield and his school in the 1930s. Opposed to **MENTALISM**.

BELL, Alexander Graham (1847–1922)
The son of Alexander Melville Bell, he invented the telephone and methods for teaching the deaf to speak.

BELL, Alexander Melville (1819–1905)
A British phonetician who emigrated to Canada and the USA. He produced a general **phonetic** theory to be applied in **speech therapy**, the education of the deaf and foreign language teaching.

BELORUSSIAN
Slavic, Indo-European. 3.5M speakers, Belarus (small number in Poland).

BENEFACTIVE
See **ROLE**.

BENGALI
Indo-Iranian, Indo-European. 156M speakers, Bangladesh (official language).

BENUE-CONGO
A large branch of the **Niger-Congo** languages including the Bantu languages and Efik.

BENVENISTE, Emile (1902–1976)
A French linguist who carried out major studies of **Indo-European** and general linguistics, including important work on communication which emphasized the centrality of the **speaker** and the fundamental role of **deixis**.

BERBER
Afroasiatic, perhaps the 'Aboriginal' language of Northern Africa. It is spoken in Morocco (Tamazight), Algeria (Kabyle), and Libya, and by the Tuaregs in Niger and Mali

BEV
Black English Vernacular. See **AAVE**.

BICONDITIONAL
A conditional that is interpreted as 'if and only if'. From the (true) **proposition** *If and only if it has rained, does the Gibson desert bloom,* it follows that *It has rained* entails *The Gibson Desert is in bloom* and *The Gibson Desert is in bloom* entails *It has rained.* See **ENTAILMENT**.

BIDIALECTALISM
The use of two or more dialects by an individual or community.

BIGRAM
A group or **n-gram** of two letters, two syllables or two words. Such groups are the starting point for the statistical analysis of text.

BIKOL

Austronesian, a group of three languages spoken in the Philippines. Related to **Tagalog**.

BILABIAL

A term in the description of the place of articulation of consonant sounds. The two lips come together as in the bilabial nasal [m] *mine*, or the bilabial stop [p] *pine*. For the use of the lips in vowel sounds, see **ROUNDED** and **SPREAD**.

BILATERAL

In **Prague School** phonology an **opposition** that involves two segments contrasting in a feature that they alone share. English /t/ and /d/ are the only units in the system that are [+alveolar] and [+plosive]; they differ in voicing – /t/ is [–voice], /d/ is [+voice]. This opposition is bilateral and contrasts with a multilateral opposition.

BILATERAL IMPLICATION

See **BICONDITIONAL**.

BILINGUAL EDUCATION

Education using two or more languages.

BILINGUALISM

The use of two or more languages by an individual or community. See **COMPOUND BILINGUALISM, COORDINATE BILINGUALISM, SUBTRACTIVE BILINGUALISM, MONOLINGUALISM, MULTILINGUALISM**.

BINARY BRANCHING

In **tree diagrams**, configurations in which any given **node** is connected with two and only two lower nodes. Some formal models of syntax allow only binary branching.

BINARY FEATURE

A feature which has two values, positive, represented by [+], i.e. having a given feature, and minus, represented by [–], not having a given feature. Binary features are appropriate for properties such as animacy or voicing, since entities are either animate or inanimate and sounds are voiced or voiceless. Binary features are not suited to properties such as vowel height, where four levels must be recognized. See **ANIMATE, FEATURE, VOWEL**.

BINDING

The relationship between an **antecedent** and an **anaphor**. E.g. in *Meg cut herself on the bread knife*, *Meg* binds *herself*; in *The dogs chased each other*, *the dogs* binds *each other*. See **BINDING THEORY**.

BINDING THEORY

Especially in **generative grammar**, a theory controlling the linking of an **anaphor** and its **antecedents**. It consists of three conditions. Condition A ensures that the antecedent of a **reflexive pronoun** is in the same **clause**: e.g. *Kirsty trusted herself to make the right decision* but not **Kirsty thought that herself could make the right decision*, where *Kirsty* is in the **main clause** and *herself* in the **complement clause**. Condition B prevents a pronoun from having an antecedent in the same clause: e.g. *him* in *John prefers him* cannot refer to John, but it can in *John thinks that Celia prefers him*. Condition C ensures that referring expressions, that is, NPs with full nouns, are not linked to any anaphors: e.g. in *Celia prefers her* and *She prefers Celia,* neither *her* nor *she* can refer to Celia. See **ANAPHORA, BOUND, REFERENCE**.

BINYAN

In Hebrew grammar, a term for **roots** consisting of two, three or four consonants. Words are created by the insertion of different patterns of vowels. This pattern is typical of **Semitic** languages, e.g. Arabic *ktp*, *kitab* 'a book', *maktab* 'office'.

BIOLINGUISTICS

The study of the biological foundations of the language ability.

BIOSEMIOTICS

The study of semiotic systems in living creatures. See **ANIMAL COMMUNICATION**.

BISLAMA

Creole. An English-based creole, one of the three official languages of the Republic of Vanuatu (Pacific).

BISYLLABLE

See **DISYLLABLE**.

BIT

In computing, the basic unit of digital information. It is the information that can be stored in a device that has only two states, hence each bit has the binary value of 1 or 0. See **BYTE**.

BIUNIQUE

A one-to-one correspondence between a phonemic and a phonetic representation and vice versa. A biunique representation would not permit a phone to be assigned to more than one **phoneme**; for example, the glottal stop, [?], could not be analysed as an allophone of both /t/ as in *bat* [ba?] and /k/ as in *back* [ba?].

BLACK ENGLISH

See **AAVE**.

BLACK ENGLISH VERNACULAR (BEV)

See **AAVE**.

BLACK LETTER WRITING

A style of writing, also known as Gothic. It was common in mediaeval times and was the basis of early printers' type in Germany.

BLADE

That part of the tongue lying opposite the alveolar ridge, between the tip and the front. Also known as **laminal**. See **TONGUE**, and see Figure 'Articulators' at **ARTICULATION**.

BLADYLALIA

In **clinical linguistics**, slow speech.

BLEEDING

Applied to a rule that destroys the context in which a subsequent rule might apply. The first rule bleeds the second. See **FEEDING, GENERATIVE PHONOLOGY, RULE ORDERING**.

BLEND

1. In **derivational morphology**, a word formed by blending the first part of one word and the last part of another; e.g. *Chunnel* from *Channel* and *Tunnel*, *motel* from *motor* and *hotel*. 2. In **syntax**, the blending of two **constructions**, phrases or clauses also known as **anacoluthon**. Thus the contemporary idiom *keep an eye out for something* is a blend of *keep a look out for something* and *keep an eye open for something*.

BLENDING

See **CONCEPTUAL BLENDING**.

BLINDNESS

A characteristic affecting language acquisition. Blind children do not have access to visual speech clues and typically acquire language more slowly than sighted children.

BLOCK LANGUAGE

The language of newspaper headlines, notices, road signs, book titles and so on, with its own patterns of syntax, mostly single words or phrases, e.g. *Heavy plant crossing*, *till January 30th* (of exhibition), but occasionally complete clauses, as in the motorway sign *For Glasgow follow Carlisle*.

BLOCKING

1. In phonological systems, a particular segment or boundary acts as a barrier to some process. Thus, in a **vowel harmony** system where the domain of the harmony is the word (i.e. where there is harmony within a word but not across word boundaries), the word boundary blocks the propagation of the harmony. 2. In word formation, a derived form may be blocked by the existence of an independent word. For example *thief* blocks the formation of **stealer*.

BLOOMFIELD, Leonard (1887–1949)

One of the most influential linguists of the twentieth century. He produced outstanding analyses of Algonquian languages but is best known for his theoretical monograph *Language* (1933).

BOAS, Franz (1858–1942)
Born and educated in Germany and went to the USA in 1886. He organized linguistic fieldwork on Native American languages. He emphasized the need to develop new categories for the analysis of languages very different in structure from Latin and Greek.

BODY OF TONGUE
A distinctive feature which accounts for different positions of the body of the tongue during articulation. See **ATR, BACK, HIGH, LOW, TONGUE.**

BOOLEAN
To do with sets of things and set theory. (George Boole, a nineteenth-century mathematician.)

BOOTSTRAP
1. Part of a computer program used to trigger the whole program. 2. See **BOOTSTRAPPING.**

BOOTSTRAPPING
The prelinguistic child has no obvious knowledge of the phonological, syntactic and semantic structure of the language being acquired. 'Bootstrapping' addresses the question of what it is that triggers acquisition. Prosodic bootstrapping hypothesizes that the infant recognizes and exploits rhythmical regularities to identify syllable structure and pauses to identify word and phrase boundaries. Syntactic bootstrapping assumes that the infant can establish word classes by associating items with objects and actions in the real world, perhaps drawing on innate linguistic knowledge.

BOPP, Franz (1791–1867)
A German linguist regarded as the founder of comparative **Indo-European** linguistics. His major work is a comparative grammar of Sanskrit, Armenian, Greek, Latin, Lithuanian, Old Slavic, Gothic and German.

BORROWING
The process whereby one language takes lexical items, syntactic constructions and so on from another. See **LOANWORD**.

BOTTOM-UP
Analysis of the structure of clauses and sentences going from the smallest units to the largest, words to phrases to **clauses** to **sentences**. The opposite approach, used in automatic parsing, is top-down.

BOULOMAIC MODALITY
Modality having to do with hopes, fears, desires and regrets. (Greek *bouleuo* 'I wish'.) Also called 'volitive modality' (Late Latin *volitio* from *volo* 'I wish, desire, intend'.).

BOUND
1. See MORPH. 2. See ANTECEDENT.

BOUND EXPRESSION
See FIXED EXPRESSION.

BOUNDARY
A real or hypothesized demarcation that marks the edge of something separating it from other similar things. E.g. **syllable** boundary (-) as in *bleed-ing*. **morpheme** boundary (+), as in *KICK+past; kick+ed;* **word** boundary (..#..) as in *kicked#the#cat*, phrase **boundary** (..##..) as *in the man ## in the mo*on; phonological phrase **boundary** (..||..) to distinguish separate intonation units, as in *hello || she said*. Boundaries demarcate units within which particular processes apply.

BOUNDARY MARKER
See BOUNDARY.

BOUNDARY SYMBOL
See BOUNDARY.

BOUNDEDNESS
1. See TELICITY. 2. Especially, but not exclusively, in **cognitive linguistics**, the property of space and time on which rests the distinction between count and mass. Humans can conceive of physical substance as individual chunks, each chunk separated by a boundary from other chunks. Examples are *tree, stone* and *book*. They can also conceive of physical substance as unbounded masses, such as *sand, earth* and *water*. Actions can be construed as individuated chunks with boundaries, as in *Jane has written a novel*, or as a mass without boundaries, as in *Jane does a lot of writing*. See AKTIONSART, COUNT NOUN, MASS NOUN.

BOUNDING THEORY
In Government and Binding Theory, the module that sets the bounds or boundaries over which constituents can or cannot be moved.

BOUSTROPHEDON
A style of writing in which the lines of a text go alternately from left to right and right to left. (Greek *bous* 'ox', *strophe* 'turning'. The metaphor is of a field being ploughed.)

BRACHYGRAPHY
See SHORTHAND.

BRACKET
1. In syntax, a graphical device for indicating which items in a sequence 'go together'. Round or square brackets are used for showing the structure of a

word, phrase or clause: [happi [ness]], [[this] [[very new] [idea]]]. Labels can be attached to brackets showing types of word, phrase and clause, as in NP [Det[this] Det AdjP [very new] AdjP N [idea]]NP This representation is called a labelled bracketing or a labelled bracketed string. Strictly speaking, a **phrase structure rule** generates labelled bracketed strings which are converted into tree diagrams. The latter are much easier to interpret, as demonstrated in the figure below.

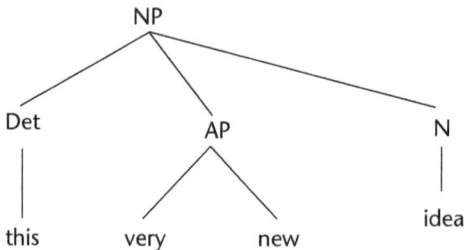

Round brackets are used to indicate that an item is optional. The rule a → (b) c produces the sequences 'c' or 'bc'.

Curly brackets or braces are used to combine two rules into one. The rule b → v/ V___V (b becomes v between vowels) and b → p/ ___# (b becomes p at the end of a word) can be combined thus:

$$b \rightarrow \begin{cases} v/V\_\_\_V \\ p/\_\_\_\# \end{cases}$$

At one time curly brackets were used to represent words as sequences of morphemes: *rejects* – {reject} {prs}{sg}. Curly brackets are used to represent sets of elements: {1, 3, 5} is the set whose members are 1, 3 and 5. See **TREE DIAGRAM**.

BRACKETING PARADOX

Refers to the situation in which a **phrase** or **clause** requires two different bracketings depending on perspective. E.g. In *Daphne arrived yesterday*, *arrived yesterday* is a phrase and the bracketing is [Daphne [arrived yesterday]]. From a semantic point of view *yesterday* modifies the whole clause *Daphne arrived* and the bracketing is [[Daphne arrived] yesterday]]. See **BRACKET**.

BRAHUI

Dravidian. 2.2M speakers, Pakistan.

BRAILLE

A system of writing for blind people to 'read' by touch. The letters take the form of patterns of raised dots.

BRANCH

In a **tree diagram**, a sequence of lines leading from a higher **node** to a lower node, possibly via intermediate nodes.

BRANCHING

In a **tree diagram**, the arrangement wherein a higher **node** A is connected to two or more lower nodes, B, C, etc. A single line comes down to A and then branches, as in the figure below. See **LEFT BRANCHING, RIGHT BRANCHING**.

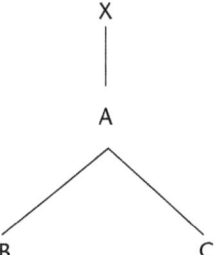

BREAKING

A sound change in Old English involving the diphthongization of short vowels /ɛ/ and /æ/ to /eo/ and /æɒ/ when followed by /h/, /r/ or /l/: (wErpan -> weorpan 'to throw'; (fællAn -> fæAllAn 'to fall').

BRÉAL, Michel (1832–1915)

Professor of Comparative Grammar at the Collège de France. He emphasized the need to study both forms and meaning and laid the foundations for its study in his *Essai de Sémantique* (1897).

BREATH GROUP

Speech produced on a single exhalation of breath.

BREATHY VOICE

A **phonation type** where air escapes through the vocal folds while they are vibrating. Breathy voice is a permanent feature for some speakers and for others it is used for paralinguistic effect. Breathy voice is sometimes characterized as a 'sexy' voice.

BRETON

Celtic, Indo-European. Approx. 500K speakers, Brittany, France. The only Celtic language spoken on the European continent. Related to **Cornish** and **Welsh**.

BRIDGING

A process whereby the referent of a definite referring expression is established via knowledge of the immediate context of utterance, of a particular culture or of the world. In the context of an orchestra rehearsal, *the flute* in *The flute always arrives late for rehearsal* is understood to refer to the flute-player; in *A car stopped and the driver got out*, hearers interpret *the driver* via their knowledge that all cars have a driver. See **CONTEXT (2), COMMON GROUND, DOMAIN 3, EXPLICATURE, METONYMY, NEO-GRICEAN PRAGMATICS**.

BROAD
A **transcription** that represents only major features, contrasting with a **narrow** transcription, which tries to be as exhaustive as possible.

BROCA, Paul (1824–1880)
A French doctor who identified the type of **aphasia** called after him, **Broca's aphasia**, and the area of the brain associated with it, **Broca's area**.

BROCA'S APHASIA
See **APHASIA**.

BROCA'S AREA
The part of the brain that lies in front of and above the left ear and is associated with language. See **APHASIA**.

BRUGMANN, Karl (1849–1919)
A German linguist, a leading member of the **Neogrammarians**. His major work is a four-volume comparative grammar of **Indo-European**.

BUCCAL
In **articulatory phonetics**, sounds made in the oral cavity, especially as relating to the cheeks.

BÜHLER, Karl (1879–1963)
A German psychologist who emigrated to the USA in 1938. His book *Sprachtheorie* (1934) focused on the functions of language and presented the first theory of **deixis**. His work has influenced all the recent functional models of language.

BULGARIAN
Slavic, Indo-European. 6.6M speakers, Bulgaria. Smaller numbers in Greece, Moldova, Romania.

BUNCHING
In **articulatory phonetics**, the body of the tongue held high in the mouth and rather tense, as in close front vowels like [i] or **alveo-palatal** consonants like [ʃ].

BURMESE
Tibeto-Burman language. 32.6M speakers, Burma (Myanmar). Approx. 10M second-language speakers. Written records from tenth century CE.

BURST
The audible explosion that can accompany the forceful release of an oral plosive as in [pʰɒp], *pop*. In acoustic phonetics the sudden burst of energy in these circumstances. See **ASPIRATION**.

BURUSHASKI
Language isolate. Approx. 90K speakers, North Pakistan.

B-VERSE
The second half of a line of verse.

BYTE
In computing, a unit of digital information. The number of **bits**, usually eight, used to encode a text character. Computer memory is measured in bytes.

C

C
Symbol for **complementizer**.

CADDOAN
Caddoan languages are spoken on the central and southern Plains of the United States. The best documented are Arikara and Pawnee. Speakers of these languages have been in contact with Europeans since the sixteenth century. The languages are all either extinct or nearly extinct.

CALCULUS
A formal system with rigorously defined symbols and explicit rules for combining the symbols. In **logic**, calculuses are used to state explicitly the exact conditions in which patterns of argument are valid or invalid. The propositional calculus handles complete propositions. Its symbols include lower-case letters of the Roman alphabet standing for propositions and other symbols representing connectives, such as & 'and', and ¬ 'negation'. The expression $p \& q$ is read as 'The propositions p and q are true'. ¬ p is read as 'The proposition p is false'. Rules of derivation state when a conclusion follows from given premises. The **predicate calculus** has the same aim as the **propositional calculus**, but propositions are assigned a structure consisting of a **predicate**, one or more **arguments** and one or more **quantifiers**.

CALQUE
A word-for-word translation of a **word** or **phrase** borrowed from another language. Thus Italian *fine settimana* is a calque on English *week-end*; English *free verse* is a calque on French *vers libre*.

CANON
1. In Christianity, the set of writings recognized as constituting the Old and New Testaments. 2. In literary theory, the works recognized as written by a particular author or as being good representatives of a particular **genre**, e.g. the classic English novel. (Greek *kanne* 'a reed', Latin *canon* 'a straight rod'.)

CANONICAL
Typical or most general pattern (usually the most basic one) of syllables, clauses and so on and usually also the basic pattern. CVC, as in *sad* or *pad*, is a canonical example of **syllable** structure in English and other languages. In

English, the canonical or basic **clause** is **declarative**, **active** and **positive** (non-**negative**), as in *James climbed the mountain in four hours*. The **syntax** and the semantic interpretation of all other types of clause are based on the syntax and semantics of the canonical clause. Non-canonical clauses can be more or less distant from the canonical pattern. *James didn't climb the mountain in four hours* is quite close, differing only in the presence of the negative **auxiliary** *didn't*; *Wasn't the mountain climbed by James in four hours* is more distant, being **interrogative** and not declarative, passive and not active, and negative not positive. In the UK, *blackbird* is a canonical example of the class BIRD, as opposed to, say, *vulture*. See BASIC CONSTRUCTION, INTERROGATIVE CLAUSE, PROTOTYPE, VOICE.

CANONICAL ENCOUNTER
See CANONICAL ORIENTATION.

CANONICAL ORIENTATION
1. For the analysis of **deixis** and spatial expressions, the normal stance of **speakers**, upright, facing forwards and communicating with **interlocutors** face to face. 2. In the analysis of spatial expressions, certain entities, such as buildings, have canonical backs and fronts. *The cars were parked behind the house* can be used only if the cars were on a space adjacent to the side of the house that counts as its back. In contrast, *The boy was hiding behind the wall* can be used whenever the wall is between the observer and the boy. It does not matter which side of the wall the boy is next to.

CANT
The specialized vocabulary of any social or occupational group, such as lawyers, bankers, snooker fans and so on. Includes **argot**, but the term is now slightly old-fashioned and infrequently used. See JARGON.

CANTONESE
See CHINESE.

CARDINAL NUMERAL
A **numeral** used for counting items, e.g. *one, six, fifteen, fifty-five*. Cardinal numerals generally fall into a word class of their own with their own **morphology** and **syntax**. See ORDINAL NUMERAL.

CARDINAL VOWELS
An arbitrary set of fixed reference points established by the British phonetician Daniel **Jones** to classify **vowel** sounds. The system identifies a set of primary cardinal vowels based on a combination of articulatory and auditory criteria, as shown in the schematic vowel quadrilateral shown in the figure (p. 63).

Cardinal vowel 1, is a **close** vowel represented as [i]. It is made with the tongue as **high** and a far **front** in the mouth as possible without producing audible friction. Cardinal vowel 5, phonetically represented as [ɒ], is made with the tongue as **low** and as far **back** in the mouth as possible. These two vowels define the limits of the **vowel space**. Cardinal vowels 2 [e], 3 [ɛ] and 4 [a] are front vowels auditorily equidistant from each other and on the front edge of the vowel space. Correspondingly, cardinal vowels 6 [ɔ], 7 [o] and 8 [u] are back vowels auditorily equidistant from each other and on the back edge of the vowel space. Conventionally the primary cardinal front vowels are **neutral** or **unrounded** and the back vowels **rounded**. In terms of the categories of vowel classification explained in vowels, they may be described thus: the phonetic symbols are those traditionally allotted by the IPA.

	front (unrounded)		back (rounded)	
close	1	[i]	8	[u]
half-close	2	[e]	7	[o]
half-open	3	[ɛ]	6	[ɔ]
open	4	[a]	5	[ɒ]

Reversing the lip position yields a set of secondary cardinal vowels.

	front (rounded)		back (unrounded)	
close	9	[y]	16	[ɯ]
half-close	10	[ø]	15	[ɤ]
half-open	11	[œ]	14	[ʌ]
open	12	[Œ]	13	[ɑ]

A further set of six **central** vowels completes the set. 17 [ɨ], and 18 [ʉ], respectively rounded and unrounded, represent the highest point the centre of the tongue can reach. The others represent the **half-close** and half-open correlates:

	mid (rounded)		mid (unrounded)	
close	17	[ɨ]	18	[ʉ]
half-close	19	[ɘ]	20	[ɵ]
half-open	21	[ɜ]	22	[ɞ]

The system can be represented in the vowel quadrilateral of the figure below.

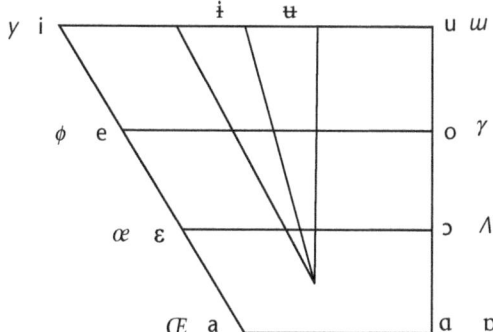

The cardinal vowels are not the vowels of any particular language, but the vowels of a particular language or dialect can be plotted with reference to them. Thus the /i/ vowel of British English *beat* is slightly lower and somewhat retracted from cardinal 1; and the corresponding vowel in Scots is not quite so low as the English vowel and hardly retracted from cardinal 1. See **OPEN**.

CARET

A mark in a written **text** indicating where another piece of text, such as a **punctuation mark**, letter or word, is to be inserted.

CARETAKER SPEECH

Speech used by adults addressing infants. Typically simplified phonologically, syntactically and lexically. See **CHILD-DIRECTED SPEECH, FOREIGNER TALK, MOTHERESE, PIDGIN**.

CARIBAN

A large family from the Amazonian region and Guyana.

CARNAP, Rudolf (1891–1970)

A German mathematician, philosopher and logician who emigrated to the USA in 1935. His work in semantics and formal logic was very influential.

CARTESIAN PRODUCT

Given two or more sets of elements, the Cartesian product is the set of all ordered pairs. Given set A containing {a,b} and set B containing {1,2}, the Cartesian product A x B is {a,1}, {a,2}, {b,1}, {b,2}. The Cartesian product B x A is {1,a}, {1,b}, {2,a}, {2,b}.

CASE

1. The classic concept of case concerns the use of noun-suffixes to signal the relations between verbs in clauses and their dependent nouns. It arose in

the analysis of **Indo-European** languages but applies to other language families, e.g. **Finno-Ugric**, **Turkic** and **Australian languages**.

In the Russian **clause** *Tat'jana priglasila Mariju* 'Tat'jana invited Mary', the **subject** is *Tat'jana*, with the **suffix** -*a*, and the **direct object** is *Mariju*, with the suffix -*ju*. If Mary invited Tat'jana, the clause would be *Marija priglasila Tat'janu*, where *Tat'janu* is now direct object and *Marija* is subject. **Russian** has several case suffixes that are attached to, e.g., subject nouns. Nouns belong to different classes; the class of a given noun determines which suffix is used. The set of subject suffixes is said to mark **nominative** case, while the set of direct object suffixes marks **accusative** case.

Other case suffixes are the **genitive**, which signals possession – *pis'mo Tat'jany* 'the-letter of-Tat'jana', the **dative**, which signals a recipient – *Marja otpravila pis'mo Tat'jane* 'Marija posted a-letter to-Tat'jana'. Case suffixes denote roles such as **patient** – *Tat'janu*, and **recipient** – *Tat'jane*. Grammatical cases mark **grammatical functions**, **semantic cases** mark roles, but the distinction is not always easy to apply. Another controversy is whether roles such as patient are to be seen as particular interpretations of broader meanings such as movement and location.

In Russian the subject of a **transitive verb** and the subject of an **intransitive verb** receive the same case: *Marija priglasila Tat'janu* and *Marija spala* 'Mary was-sleeping'. Russian is said to have a nominative-accusative case system. In other languages the subjects of transitive verbs have different case markers from the subjects of intransitive verbs; the latter have the same marking as the direct objects. An example is Basque. In *Gizonak* 'the man' *ogia* 'bread' *jan du* 'has eaten', *gizonak* has the suffix -*k* and *ogia*, the direct object, has a zero suffix. (See **absolute form**.) In *Gizona* 'the man' *ethorri da* 'has come', *gizona* is the subject of the intransitive verb *ethorri da* and has no suffix, just like *ogia*, the direct object of *jan du*. Basque is said to have an **ergative** case system.

Relations between verbs and nouns in clauses can be signalled by (a) **word order**, as shown by the contrast in meaning between *Tat'jana invited Mary* and *Mary invited Tat'jana*; (b) prepositions, as in *Mary took the money from Tat'jana*, where *from* marks the **source** of the money; (c) **postpositions**, such as *entgegen* in the German *Sie ging dem Baum entgegen* 'She went the tree towards'; (d) by **affixes** on verbs, as in the Swahili example below. A broader concept of case includes noun affixes, prepositions, postpositions, verb affixes and word order. All these devices come under the heading of case marking.

Verbs can be considered the **heads** of clauses; the other phrases are dependent on the verbs. Case systems like the Russian one are **dependent-marking**. In contrast, Swahili, e.g., marks some relations on the head of the clause. In *omukazi enkoko aligigoba* 'the-woman the-chicken will-chase', the initial *a* on the verb signals that *omukazi* is subject and -*gi*- signals that *enkoko* is direct object. Its case system is **head-marking**. 2. English does not have case suffixes like those of Russian but word order is equivalent to nominative and accusative case in signalling subject and direct object. Chomskyans treat English subjects and direct objects as having abstract case, i.e. a case feature that is not realized in the actual forms of nouns (except in the pronouns, e.g. *she* vs *her*). This abstract case is subject to **government** in the Government and Binding model and to **checking** in the **Minimalist Program**. See ABESSIVE, ABLATIVE, ADESSIVE, GRAMMATICAL CASE, INESSIVE, INSTRUCTIVE, INSTRUMENTAL, LOCATIVE, PRINCIPLES AND PARAMETERS, REALIZATION.

CASE FILTER
See CASE THEORY.

CASE FRAME
See CASE GRAMMAR.

CASE GRAMMAR
A **transformational grammar** developed in the late 1960s. In it the **deep structure** showed **dependency** relations between the **verb** and the nouns in a **clause**, the dependencies being labelled with '**case**' labels – really **role** labels – such as agent, patient, instrument. In the lexicon, each verb had a case frame, showing which cases or roles it required.

CASE MARKING
See CASE.

CASE RELATION
The relation between verbs and nouns in **Case Grammar**.

CASE THEORY
The component of **Government and Binding Theory** dealing with abstract cases. Central to case theory is the assignment of case features to nouns. Verbs and prepositions assign the feature [accusative] to object noun phrases, and the feature [nominative] is assigned to the subject **noun phrase** of a **clause** by a constituent labelled 'I' for Inflection. The latter contains, among other things, Tense. A case filter ensures that a case is assigned to all noun phrases containing a full noun, functioning as **subject** or **object** of a verb and expressing **agent** or **patient**. It also ensures that no case is assigned to empty noun phrases. Sentences which do not meet these conditions are rejected by the grammar. As part of **government**, case theory plays a role in controlling the movement of phrases in sentences, in particular the movement of phrases containing wh words such as *who*, *whom*. See CASE, THETA ROLE, THETA THEORY.

CATALAN
Romance, Indo-European. 6.8M speakers Spain, 700K France.

CATAPHOR
See CATAPHORA.

CATAPHORA

The use of certain words and phrases to pick up the referents of noun phrases occurring later in a text: e.g. *These are the items you will need: three planks of wood, superglue, a dozen screws*. *These* functions as a cataphor, pointing ahead to the referents of *three planks of wood, superglue* and *a dozen screws*. In the next example *the following* functions as a cataphor. *The following are essential: sunblock, a broad-brimmed hat, walking boots*. See ANAPHORA, DEIXIS, REFERENCE.

CATEGORIAL COMPONENT

The **base component** of a **transformational grammar**. In it, context-free **phrase structure rules** specified the syntactic structure of clauses/sentences, and a **lexicon** contained lexical items that were inserted into syntactic structures.

CATEGORIAL GRAMMAR

A formal grammar devised by the Polish logician Ajdukiewicz in the 1930s. A set of basic categories is defined. A set of rules specifies how more complex categories can be constructed from the basic ones, and another set of rules specifies how categories are combined into sentences. Suppose that **Sentence** and **Noun** are the basic categories. **Intransitive Verb** is defined as a category that combines with Noun to give Sentence: *multiply* combines with *rabbits* to give *Rabbits multiply*. **Transitive Verb** is a category that combines with Noun to give Intransitive Verb: *eat* combines with *carrots* to give *eats carrots*. *Eat carrots* is like *vanished*; it combines with Noun to yield Sentence, as in *White Rabbits eat carrots*. **Adjective** is defined as a category that combines with Noun to give Nouns: both the single noun *rabbits* and the adjective + noun *white rabbits* combine with an intransitive verb to give a sentence, as in *Rabbits eat carrots* and *White rabbits eat carrots*. A **relative clause** can be treated as an adjective. In its central ideas categorial grammar has affinities with **dependency grammar** and **Word Grammar**. See DEPENDENCY, TRANSITIVITY, VERB.

CATEGORIAL RULE

In **generative grammar**, a rule applying to syntactic categories; e.g. NP → Det N. (Rewrite NP as the sequence Det N.)

CATEGORICAL SENTENCE

A **sentence** in which some entity is presented and then categorized. That is, the speaker predicates a property of the entity and thereby puts it into some category. Categorical sentences have a **topic and comment** and contrast with **thetic sentences**.

CATEGORY

Any set of grammatical or lexical items that share a property or properties. Nouns such as *cement, apple* and *hammer* refer to things that can be seen, handled, etc.; they share certain grammatical properties such as being preceded by **determiners** and functioning as the **subject** and **object** of verbs; they belong to the syntactic category of Nouns. In Latin *-em* in *regem* 'king-ACC' and the *-i* in *regi* 'king-DAT, to the king' signal the relationship between the verb in a clause and these nouns. The relationship is called **case**. *-em* and *-i* belong to the morphosyntactic category of case suffixes, and the meaning they carry is the grammatical category (or morphosyntactic category) of case. *Run, walk, swim, ride,* etc. belong to the lexical category of verbs of movement. Categories typically have good central members, known as **prototypes,** that possess all or most of the properties of the category. Prototypes contrast with peripheral members that possess few of the properties. See DEPENDENCY, GRAMMATICAL CATEGORY, GRAMMATICAL FUNCTION, MORPHOSYNTACTIC CATEGORIES, PROTOTYPE THEORY.

CATEGORY BOUNDARIES

Especially in **prototype theory**, the categories need to be assigned boundaries to distinguish items in the category and items outside it. Category boundaries are fuzzy.

CATEGORY VARIABLE

In **generative grammar**, a symbol, typically one of the last letters in the alphabet such as W, X, Y or Z, which stands for a number of categories, say **Noun** and **Adjective**, or **Preposition** and **Adverb**.

CATENATIVE

In English, full (lexical) verbs that are followed by other verb forms: e.g. bare infinitive *I helped clear up the mess*, to infinitive *The children need to return their library books*, gerund *The saleswoman keeps phoning*. See NON-FINITE VERB

CATENATIVE COMPLEMENT

A non-finite clause functioning as the **complement** of a **verb** in a **catenative** construction; e.g. *to like your cooking* in *My brother seems to like your cooking* and *barking* in *The dog keeps barking*. See CLAUSE, COMPLEMENT CLAUSE, GERUND, NON-FINITE VERB.

CAUCASIAN

A family of some thirty-five languages spoken in Georgia, the Russian Caucasus and parts of Azerbaijan and Turkey. They include **Abkhaz**, Circassian, Lezgian, Nakh, Svan and **Georgian**. Known for having very large consonantal inventories with minimal vowel systems.

CAUSAL CLAUSE

See ADVERBIAL CLAUSE OF REASON.

CAUSATIVE

Applied to **constructions, verbs** or **affixes** expressing causation. E.g. the English syntactic constructions *I had my hair cut very short* and *I had them march through the town* (= *I marched them through the town*) which is causative vs *They* marched through the town – no causer is mentioned or even hinted at) and the Turkish causative suffix *-ir*, as in *sebze pis-iyor* 'the-vegetables cook-PROG, The vegetables are cooking' vs *sebze-yi pis-ir-iyor* 'vegetable-ACC cook=CAUS=PROG, He/she is cooking the vegetables'.

CAUSE

A relationship between two situations whereby the existence of one situation brings about the existence of the other. Cause can be expressed by adverbial clauses of reason, as in *Ken left because he was not promoted*, or by prepositions, as in *Because of the snow the concert was postponed*, or by the simple coordination of two clauses, as in *The boss didn't promote him and Ken left* or *The boss didn't promote him so Ken left*. See **ABLATIVE, CAUSATIVE**.

CAVITY

Any of the chambers within the **vocal tract** – **oral, nasal**, oesophagal. See **DISTINCTIVE FEATURES, PLACE FEATURES, PULMONIC AIRSTREAM**.

CAVITY FEATURES

See **DISTINCTIVE FEATURES**, See **PLACE FEATURES**.

C-COMMAND

In a **tree diagram**, a relationship between two **nodes** which is defined in various ways in the literature. A node X c-commands a node Y if the first branching node dominating X also dominates Y. That is, there is no direct path down the tree from X to Y or from Y to X. but from the first branching node above X there is a path down the tree to Y. In Figure 'C-command (a)', node B c-commands nodes C, D, E and F. Node C c-commands node B and node E c-commands node D. In *The dog injured herself*, *the dog* c-commands *herself* (see Figure 'C-command (b)') and is its antecedent. In *Herself injured the dog*, *herself* c-commands *the dog* (see Figure 'C-command (c)'). Since **reflexive pronouns** cannot c-command their **antecedents**, *herself* cannot be interpreted as the antecedent of *the dog*. See **ANAPHORA, DOMINANCE, X-BAR SYNTAX**.

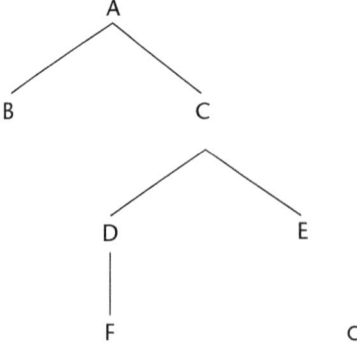

C-command (a)

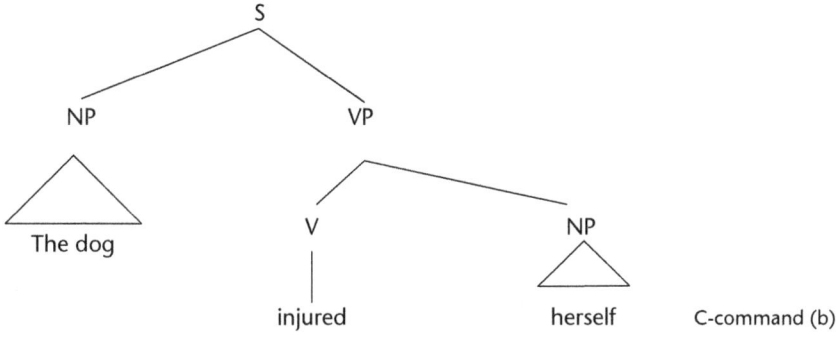

C-command (b)

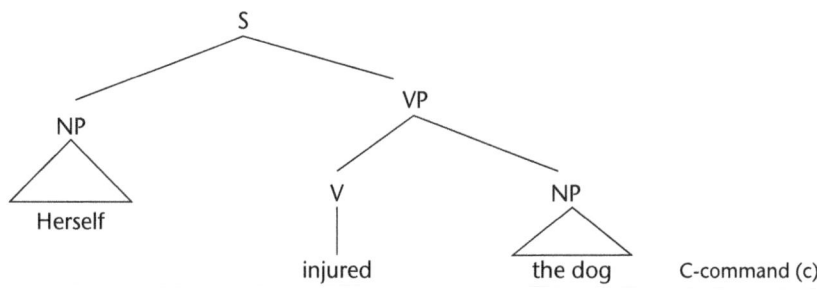

C-command (c)

CD

See **COMMUNICATIVE DYNAMISM**. See **FUNCTIONAL SENTENCE PERSPECTIVE**.

CEBUANO

Austronesian. 12.8M speakers, the Philippines. It is similar to Tagalog.

CELTIC

Indo-European. Only four Celtic languages survive – **Breton**, **Irish Gaelic**, **Scottish Gaelic** and **Welsh**. The 'Continental' Celtic languages, such as Gaulish, are all extinct.

CENTERING THEORY

A theory arising from work in AI and **computational linguistics** which exploits the choice of entity to be the focus of attention in a text and the choice of **referring expression** (personal pronouns, demonstratives, full noun phrases) in order to account for how coherent a text is and whether it is easy or difficult to process. See **ARTIFICIAL INTELLIGENCE**.

CENTRAL

Vowels made in the central part of the vowel space, e.g. [ɜ] in *bird* or [ə] in *a'bout*. Some urban dialects of English are characterized by **centralized** vowels. Those English **diphthongs** which involve a **glide** towards the centre of the **vowel space**, [iə] in *near* or [ɔɪ] in *boy* are referred to as 'centring' diphthongs.

CENTRALIZED

A vowel that is more **central** than the nearest **cardinal vowel**. E.g. [ɪ] in British English *bit* is more central than cardinal vowel 2.

CENTRE

The mid part of the **tongue** between front and back, used in the **articulation** of mid or **central vowels**.

CENTRE-EMBEDDING

The **embedding** of a **clause** in the middle of another clause. Figure 'Centre-embedding (a)' shows the structure of *The leaky house that the firm that you recommended built for us had to be demolished*. The **relative clause** *that you recommended* is embedded in the middle of the relative clause *that the firm ... built for us*. In Turkish **complement clauses** are regularly embedded in the middle of main clauses, between the subject and the verb, as shown in Figure 'Centre-embedding (b)' with the structure of *Orhan, [Aysenin Fransa'da oldugunu] anladi* 'Orhan [of-Ayse in-France her-being] realized, Orhan realized that Ayse was in France'. Centre-embedding can be difficult to process, as in *The rat that the cat that the dog chased killed was eating the malt*. See **CONSTRUCTION, GRAMMATICAL FUNCTION**.

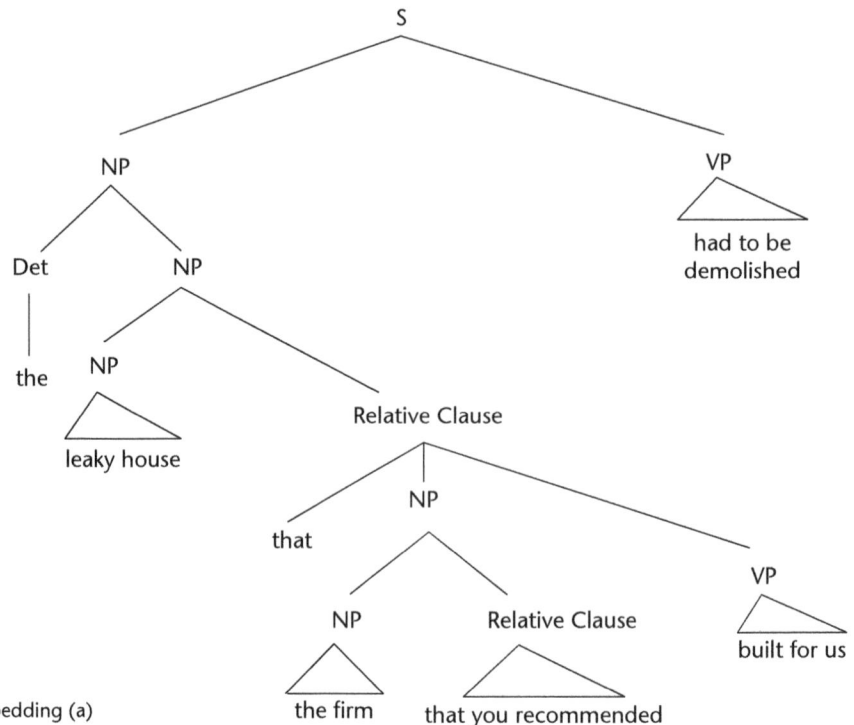

Centre-embedding (a)

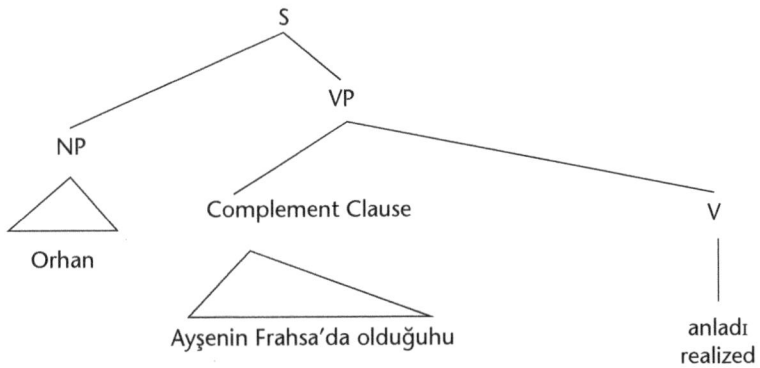

Centre-embedding (b)   Orhan Ayşe-of france-in le-being
'Orhan realized that Ayşe was in France'

CENTUM AND SATEM LANGUAGES

Centum languages are those **Indo-European** languages that retained the proto **Indo-European** velar stops, e.g. /k/, as opposed to the satem languages, where the velars became affricates or fricatives, e.g. /s/ or /ʃ/. The name 'centum' derives from the Latin *centum* 'hundred'. The centum languages include **Celtic** (e.g. **Scottish Gaelic**), **Germanic** (e.g. **English**), Hellenic (e.g. **Greek**) and **Italic** (e.g. **Latin**). The Satem languages include **Balto-Slavic** (e.g. **Russian**) and **Indo-Iranian** (e.g. **Sanskrit**) languages.

CF

See **CONTEXT-FREE**.

CGEL

A Comprehensive Grammar of the English Language. With respect to the quantity of data, the most extensive single **reference grammar** of English. Written by Sir Randolph **Quirk** et al. and published by Longman in 1985.

CHADIC

Afroasiatic. Spoken to the west, south and east of Lake Chad in Western Africa. It contains about 140 languages, the best known of which is **Hausa**.

CHAIN

1. In **Systemic Functional Grammar**, the equivalent of **syntagmatic**. The constituents *Some, dogs, chase, any* and *cat* combine in a chain: *Some dogs chase any cat*. At each point or link in the chain, there is a choice. *All, their* or *no* could be chosen instead of *some*. *Attack, irritate, bite* could be chosen instead of *chase*, and so on. 'Choice' is related to **paradigmatic**. 2. In historical linguistics, see **CHAIN SHIFT**. 3. In Government and Binding Theory, a sequence of constituents containing an NP and its co-indexed trace. See **CO-INDEX, PRINCIPLES AND PARAMETERS**.

CHAIN SHIFT

A sequence of interdependent **sound changes**. A distinction is usually made between a drag chain, where some **segment** changes leaving a hole into which another segment moves, and a push chain, in which some segment begins to move into the space of another, forcing it to move out of the way. The **Great Vowel Shift** in English has been analysed as a drag chain and the first Germanic Consonant Shift as a push chain.

CHAINING STRUCTURE

A sequence of **verbs** in which only the last verb has all the usual **suffixes**. E.g. the **Turkish** sequence *kalk-tı-k git-ti-k* 'GET UP-PST-1pl, GO-PST-1pl, We got up and went' can be replaced by *kalk-ıp git-ti-k*, in which *kalk* has the 'dummy' suffix *-ip*. See **CLAUSE CHAINING, CONVERB**.

CHAMPOLLION, Jean François (1790–1832)

A French scholar, the founder of modern Egyptology and the first to decipher the complex system of the Ancient Egyptian hieroglyphics.

CHANGE FROM ABOVE

Linguistic innovations within a **speech community's** awareness. Change from above does not necessarily involve social class, though it typically does, as in the case of borrowings from a higher prestige speech community.

CHANGE FROM BELOW

Linguistic innovations where speakers are unaware that change is taking place; that is, the change is below the level of awareness. Change from below does not necessarily involve social class and, in contrast with change from above, is typically the result of internal linguistic factors rather than social factors.

CHANGE IN PROGRESS

Linguistic innovations currently in progress.

CHANNEL

In **information theory**, that part of a communication system that connects the transmitter, the source of the message, to the receiver, that is, the route by which information is transmitted: the aural channel, the visual channel, and, for Braille, the haptic channel. More than one **medium** may be transmitted by the same channel: marks on paper and hand gestures are both transmitted by the visual channel. See **HAPTICS**.

CHARACTERIZATION

The properties or character attributed to a person, real or fictional, in a story, newspaper report, etc.

CHART

See **CHART PARSING**.

CHART PARSING

A **parsing** procedure extensively used in **computational linguistics**. It collects alternative analyses in a chart, organizes and evaluates them. It has been particularly successful in the analysis of syntactically ambiguous sentences. See **AMBIGUITY**.

CHAT

See **CHILD LANGUAGE DATA EXCHANGE SYSTEM**.

CHECKED

A **distinctive feature** associated with **ejective** and **implosive** consonants

CHECKING

In the **Minimalist Program**, a process by which **subcategorization** (c-selectional) features are checked and deleted. E.g. *put* has subcategorization features indicating that it combines with an NP and a PP. In a given structure, if *put* does combine with an NP and a PP the subcategorization features are checked and deleted. This process leaves only features with semantic content (interpretable features) which can be interpreted by the semantic component of the grammar. The deleted features have no semantic content and are uninterpretable. See **STRICT SUBCATEGORIZATION, SUBCATEGORIZATION FRAME**.

CHECKING TAG

See **TAG QUESTION 1**.

CHEST PULSE

A contraction of the chest muscles causing air to be exhaled from the lungs. Often connected with emphatic speech. In one account the chest pulse is central to an explanation of **syllables**.

CHIBCHAN

A family of languages in South Central America and the neighbouring South American countries.

CHILD-DIRECTED SPEECH

See **CARETAKER SPEECH**.

CHILD LANGUAGE DATA EXCHANGE SYSTEM (CHILDES)

A computerized database of child language data in a variety of different languages, with a set of **transcription** conventions (CHAT) and analysis tools (CLAN).

CHINESE

Sino-Tibetan. 1,225M speakers. A cluster of languages or dialects many of which are, in the spoken form, mutually unintelligible. They are however all written in the same script and hence available to literate speakers. The largest group of dialects is **Mandarin**, spoken by more than 600M people and including the native language of Beijing. This has become the basis for the standard language, called Putonghua. After the founding of the People's Republic in 1949, this was adopted as the national language. The standard romanized spelling is called Pinyin. Other major non-Mandarin dialects include Cantonese, the native language of Hong Kong, and Guangdong (Canton), Shanghainese, spoken in Shanghai and surrounding provinces and the Fuzhou dialects, including Hokkien, spoken *inter alia*, in Taiwan and Hainan. Cantonese and Hokkien are the languages of a large Chinese diaspora.

CHIROGRAPHY
The study of the various styles of handwriting.

CHOCOAN
A small language family in Colombia and Panama.

CHOICE
See **CHAIN (2)**.

CHÔMEUR
In **Relational Grammar**, a **noun phrase** that has been downgraded from a **complement** in the **core of a clause** to an **adjunct** on the periphery. E.g. the subject noun phrase *a policeman* in *A policeman was directing the traffic* is downgraded to part of an optional prepositional phrase in the passive *The traffic was being directed (by a policeman)*. *Chômeur* in French means 'unemployed person'. See **CLAUSE**, **GRAMMATICAL FUNCTION**.

CHOMSKY, Noam Avram (b 1928)
An American linguist who in the early 1950s developed the theory of **generative grammars**. The first model, **transformational grammar**, reached a wide audience through the book *Syntactic Structures* (1957). After a long series of refinements and reformulations, the latest in a long chain of models is the **Minimalist Program**. More important than any single model has been his theory that much of the grammatical structure of language is innate. He is the most influential theoretical linguist of the second half of the twentieth century, but is known to a larger audience as a proponent of radical political views and severe critic of American policies abroad.

CHOMSKY ADJUNCTION
In generative grammar, a procedure for inserting a constituent into a **tree**. Given, e.g., a structure $_{VP}$[phoned her brother]$_{VP}$ a copy is made of the VP node, the existing VP is adjoined to the new VP node and any adverbs are adjoined to the new VP node too: $_{VP}$ [$_{VP}$ [*phoned her brother*] $_{VP}$ *immediately*]$_{VP}$. This structure shows that *immediately* modifies not just *phoned* but *phoned her brother*. See Figure 'Adjoin/Chomsky adjunction' at **ADJUNCTION**.

CHOMSKY HIERARCHY
A ranking of **finite state grammars**, **context-free** and **context-sensitive** phrase structure grammars and unrestricted rewrite systems in terms of their **weak**

generative capacity. Relates to work by Chomsky in the 1950s. See ADEQUACY, STRONG GENERATIVE CAPACITY, REWRITE RULE.

CHOREA
See HUNTINGTON'S DISEASE.

CHRESTOMATHY
A little-used and now old-fashioned term for an anthology of texts held to be outstanding examples of a particular language or **genre** and collected for the use of learners. (Greek *xrestos* 'useful', *mathein* 'to learn'.)

CHUKOTKO-KAMCHATKAN
A small language family spoken in north-eastern Siberia. All of the languages except Chukchi, are endangered.

CHUNK
1. In **psycholinguistics**, a portion of an **utterance**, **sentence**, etc. 2. In **computational linguistics**, information stored and hence retrievable as a unit, typically the basic phrases of a sentence. Available memory is defined in terms of the number of chunks that can be handled simultaneously.

CHUNKER
A computer program that identifies chunks. See CHUNK.

CHUNKING
The breaking up of an **utterance** into chunks. See CHUNK.

CI
See CONCEPTUAL-INTENTIONAL STRUCTURE, INTERFACE, MINIMALIST PROGRAM

CIRCUMFIX
A combination of **prefix** and **suffix** that is considered to form a complex **affix** attached to a **stem**. In German, the **past participle** of *frag* 'ask' is formed by adding the prefix *ge-* and the suffix *-t*: *gefragt*. *Ge-* requires *-t*, but *-t* can occur without *ge-*, as in *passier-t*, the past participle of *passieren* 'happen'. English forms such as *awooing*, as in *A frog he would awooing go*, can be analysed as consisting of the stem *woo-* and the circumfix *a...ing*. Many analysts reject the concept of circumfix.

CIRCUMFLEX
The **diacritic** ^ placed over a **vowel**, as in *rôle*.

CIRCUMLOCUTION
A round-about way, typically complex, of expressing some idea. (Latin *circum* 'around', *locutio* 'something said'.)

CIRCUMSTANTIAL

An **adverb** indicating the **setting** of a **situation**, especially time and place. Contrasts with the participants in a situation, agent, patient, instrument and so on. From French *circonstant*, as elaborated by **Tesnière**. See **ROLE**.

CITATION FORM

The form of a word spoken in isolation. The form that is conventionally used as a **lemma** in dictionaries. See **LEMMATIZATION**.

CLAN

See **CHILD LANGUAGE DATA EXCHANGE SYSTEM**.

CLASS

Any collection of forms, such as **morphs**, **words** and **constructions**, that have properties in common. E.g. *this*, *that* and *the* belong to the class of **determiners**; they all immediately precede any **adjectives** and the **nouns** in **noun phrases**: *this black dog, the dog*. The properties may be functional: nouns can function as subject or object of a verb. See **CATEGORY, GRAMMATICAL FUNCTION**.

CLASS-CHANGING

Applied to derivational **affixes** that change the **word class** of a **word**. The **suffix** *-al* changes **nouns** to **adjectives**, as in *education* and *educational*. See **DERIVATIONAL MORPHOLOGY**

CLASS DIALECT

A dialect associated with a particular social class.

CLASS-MAINTAINING

Applied to derivational **affixes** that do not change the **word class** of a word. The **suffix** *-hood* derives nouns from **nouns**, as in *parent* and *parenthood*. See **DERIVATIONAL MORPHOLOGY**.

CLASSICAL THEORY OF CONCEPTS

Traditional approach, traceable as far back as Aristotle, which defines categories in terms of necessary and sufficient conditions. E.g. for an animal to count as a ewe, it is necessary for it to be female and to be a sheep. Neither condition is sufficient on its own: a female animal need not be a sheep, and a given sheep might be male.

CLASSIFICATION

See **TAXONOMY**.

CLASSIFIER

Grammatical words or **affixes** indicating the class to which a noun belongs, classifiers relate to properties such as **animacy**, humanness and shape, and typically combine with **numerals** and **demonstratives**. Classifiers are found, e.g., in **Bantu** languages, **Chinese** and languages of Central America. In **Swahili**, for example, plural nouns take *aba-* if they denote humans, *en-* if they denote animals and *emi-* if they denote trees and plants: *aba-kazi aba-satu* 'CLF-woman CLF-three, three women'. See **GENDER**.

CLAUSAL NEGATION

Negation applying to a whole **clause** or **sentence**. A test for whether an instance of negation is clausal is whether a **tag question** can be added, e.g. *has it?* in The *message hasn't arrived (has it?)* and *did we?* in *We didn't know that when we applied (did we?)*. See **CONSTITUENT NEGATION**.

CLAUSE

A unit of syntax containing a **main verb** (with or without an **auxiliary** verb). The main verb can be considered the **head** of the clause; in many languages a **finite verb** alone can constitute a complete clause, for instance Turkish *Okuyorlar* 'They are reading'. The main verb may be modified by a **noun phrase** – *We eat haggis*, an **adjective phrase** – *The tree grew tall*, a **prepositional phrase** – *The dog is digging in the garden* or an **adverbial phrase** – *They responded quickly*, or by a combination – *The firm quickly sent apologies to the customers*.

In analyses of English and many other languages, the **subject** and **direct object** noun phrases are closest to the verb. All English clauses require a subject noun phrase, and even in languages where the subject noun phrase is not obligatory, it is closely connected with the verb by links of **agreement**. In all languages some verbs require direct object noun phrases and other verbs exclude them, and similarly for **directional** or **goal** phrases. These three types of phrase are closely linked to the verb and are called **complements**. **Place phrases** and **Time phrases** are optional, allowed by all verbs and are **adjuncts**. The verb and its complements constitute the **core of a clause**; the adjuncts are on the periphery of the clause. The complements make up the **valency** or **argument structure** of verbs. Some analysts split the core into the **nucleus**, which is the verb, and the core, which is the nucleus plus its complements.

A major distinction is between main and subordinate clauses (sometimes called independent and dependent clauses). Many main clauses can stand on their own as a complete piece of text; subordinate clauses on their own cannot. Main clauses may or may not contain a subordinate clause but are never themselves part of a larger clause. Main clauses allow a very wide range of syntactic constructions and all the distinctions of **aspect**, **tense** and **mood**. In contrast, subordinate clauses allow a smaller range of syntactic constructions. For example, main clauses in English allow **interrogative**, **imperative** and **exclamative constructions**; subordinate clauses do not. Main clauses allow **negative-fronting**, but subordinate ones do not: *Never have I heard such rubbish*, **I am dismayed, because never have I heard such rubbish*. In many languages the verb in subordinate clauses occurs in the **subjunctive** mood, whereas verbs in main clauses typically occur in the **indicative** mood.

In many languages three major types of finite subordinate clause can be recognized. (Particular languages may offer more types.) These are **relative clauses**, **complement clauses** and **adverbial clauses**. Grammars of individual languages provide detailed descriptions of each type of subordinate clause, but the essential distinction has to do with what they apply to. Relative clauses depend on nouns – *the book which I was reading*; complement clauses depend on verbs, either as object – *The bank declared that it was infallible* – or as subject – *That the bank was infallible was news to me*; adverbial clauses depend on whole clauses – in *We left because we didn't like the music*, *We didn't like the music* gives the reason that *we left*; in *We left when they returned*, the adverbial clause *when they returned* applies to *We left*, specifying the time at which that event happened. A further type of complement clause depends on nouns, but in English cannot be introduced by *which*, *who*, etc.: *We accepted the proposal that the land be sold* vs *We accepted the proposal which the land be sold*.

There are finite and non-finite clauses, which contain, respectively, finite verbs and non-finite verbs. (Non-finite clauses are also called **verb phrases**.) In English, **infinitives** or infinitive clauses depend on verbs – in *We all like to make fun of this theory*, *to make fun of this theory* modifies *like*; gerunds or gerund clauses also depend on verbs but have a suffix -*ing* – in *I love swimming in the sea*, *swimming in the sea* depends on and is the direct object of *love* (see **grammatical function**); free participles or participial clauses are also marked by a suffix -*ing* but depend on whole clauses – in *Reading his latest novel, I fell asleep*, *Reading his latest novel* specifies the reason or the time: *I fell asleep because I was reading…* or *I fell asleep while I was reading…* Participial clauses are equivalent to **reduced adverbial clauses**; other non-finite clauses with -*ing* forms are equivalent to **reduced relative clauses**: e.g. *The book lying on your desk (the book that is lying on your desk) is the one I was looking for*. See **CONJUNCTION, COSUBORDINATION, DEPENDENT, EXCLAMATIVE, GERUND, INTERROGATIVE CLAUSE, MOOD, NEXUS, NON-FINITE VERB, TENSE AND ASPECT.**

CLAUSE CHAINING

A **construction** in which two or more **clauses** are combined but in which only one clause has a full verb form, the other clauses having reduced verb forms. E.g. Turkish *bahçede oturup, çay içiyordum* 'Garden-in sit-suffix, tea I was drinking, I was sitting in the garden and drinking tea', only the second verb has the aspect marker -*iyor*, the past tense marker -*du* and the person and number marker -*um*. Negation can also be omitted: e.g. *Beni görüp, selam vermedi* 'Me see-suffix, a-salaam he-did-not-give, He did not see me or greet me'. Only the verb in the second clause has the negative affix -*me*, the past tense marker -*di* and the zero third-person singular marker. Lack of a final suffix signals third **person** and singular **number**. See **CHAINING STRUCTURE, CONVERB, TENSE AND ASPECT.**

CLAUSE COMBINATION

Especially in the analysis of spoken language, a group of clauses that occur one after the other and make up a text, but which analysts avoid organizing into **text sentences** in the absence of reliable criteria for doing so. See **SENTENCE, SYSTEM SENTENCE, TEXT.**

CLAUSE MATES

Constituents in a **sentence** which belong to the same **clause**. In *My brother said [he would let him know]* he and *him* are clause mates in the **complement clause** and must refer to different people. See COMPLEMENT CLAUSE, REFLEXIVE, REFLEXIVE PRONOUN, REFLEXIVIZATION.

CLAUSE OBJECT

See COMPLEMENT CLAUSE.

CLAUSE RELATIONS

See COHESION.

CLEAR

A **lateral** made without **velarization**, as in [lait] 'light', compared with a dark l, as in [bɔtəɫ.].

CLEFT CONSTRUCTION

Many languages use **word order** and **particles**, in combination or separately, to highlight or **focus** on parts of a **clause** or **sentence**. Some languages use special cleft constructions, of which English has a relatively large number in frequent use. The central cleft constructions are the it-cleft (also simply called the cleft) and wh clefts (also called pseudo-clefts). Behind the word *cleft* is the idea that a single clause is cleft into two parts, which are then linked by a **copula**; e.g. *My boss sent the e-mail last week* becomes *It was the e-mail that my boss sent last week*. *The e-mail* becomes the complement of *is* in a copular construction with the dummy subject *it* and *my boss sent [] last week* becomes a **relative clause**. The speaker presupposes that the boss sent something last week and specifies the something as an e-mail as opposed to a parcel, postal letter or form, hence the contrastive effect of many it-clefts. Compare *It was last week that my boss sent the e-mail* – the speaker presupposes the boss sent the e-mail and specifies the time as last week.

Wh-clefts consist of a **free relative clause**, a copula and a **noun phrase** or **verb phrase**: *What my boss sent last week was the e-mail* [noun phrase: *the e-mail*], *What they did was cut off the gas* [verb phrase: *cut off the gas*]. With *What my boss sent last week was an e-mail* the speaker again presupposes that the boss sent something, which is specified as the e-mail. (Compare *When my boss sent the e-mail was last week*.) Wh clefts are used to draw a line under some part of a discussion and to move on to the next part. The latter function is what enables them to be used to open a text: *What I'm going to discuss in this lecture is aspect*.

Th clefts consist of *this* or *that* followed by a copula and a **free relative clause**: e.g. *That's why I hate spinach*, *That's where she hid the letter*. Th clefts are typically used to finish a piece of text by emphasizing some point.

Reverse-wh-clefts have the same constituents as a wh cleft but in the reverse order: a phrase, a copula and a free relative clause: *A new striker is what they need*, *Handling the accounts is what Mary does*. See INFORMATION STRUCTURE.

CLEFT PALATE

A congenital birth defect in which the soft tissues of the **palate** have not fused together properly, thus leaving an opening between the roof of the mouth and the **nasal** cavity. Cleft palates can lead to speech problems with **palatal** sounds and sometimes children with cleft palates cannot close off their nasal cavities during speech.

CLEFT SENTENCE

See **CLEFT CONSTRUCTION**.

CLEFTING

See **CLEFT CONSTRUCTION**.

CLICHÉ

A fixed expression that originally conveyed a new **metaphor** but through overuse has become a hackneyed fixed expression. E.g. *The bottom line is...*, *We will arrange to touch base*.

CLICK

A **stop consonant** produced on the ingressive **velaric airstream**. Clicks can be articulated at a number of **places of articulation**: **bilabial**, [ʘ], **dental** [ǀ], **alveolar** [ǃ] and **lateral** [ǁ]. Clicks are phonemic in some South African languages. In English they are used paralinguistically – a kiss is [ʘ]; '*tut tut*' [ǀ ǀ] and [ǁ] is the sound to encourage horses. See **AIRSTREAM MECHANISM, PARALINGUISTIC**.

CLIMAX

The moment of greatest tension and excitement in a **narrative**. The typical and most successful narrative structure is one in which a series of events leads up to the climax, which takes place near the end of the story. The tension is released via a resolution: the police arrive in the nick of time, the villain is thwarted, the heroine escapes and so on.

CLINE

A series of items in which any one is similar to its neighbour, but the first and last are clearly distinct. Alternatively, a scale going from Ø to 100% on which objects can be placed with respect to some property. **Prototype theory**, for instance, holds that speakers of English in the UK put robins and blackbirds higher on a cline of 'birdiness' than kiwis or penguins. **Adjectives** can be placed on a cline. Near the top are words such as *big*, having all the properties distinguishing adjectives from other word classes; near the bottom are words such as *major*, having few of these properties. See **GRADIENCE, SQUISH**.

CLINICAL LINGUISTICS

The discipline which involves the application of linguistic theories and analytical techniques in the field of speech, language and communication impairment. It concerns itself with the description, explanation and remediation of a range of impairments in children and adults.

CLIPPING

A process of **word formation** in which either a single word is shortened or clipped, as in *plane* for *aeroplane*, or two or more words are clipped and the remaining chunks combined, as in *sci-fi* for *science fiction* and *hi-fi* for *high fidelity*. The latter are also known as clipping compounds. See **COMPOUND WORD, DERIVATIONAL MORPHOLOGY**.

CLIPPING COMPOUND

See **CLIPPING**.

CLITIC

A grammatical form which is neither clearly a **word** nor clearly an **affix**. English examples are *–'ll* in *He'll be here* and *'s* in *Katie's books*. *'s* can be added to phrases, as in *the leader of this party's bizarre policies*, in which *'s* is added to *the leader of this party*. An Italian example is *devo telefonarti* 'I-must phone-you', in which *ti* 'you' is added to the **infinitive** *telefonare*. Clitics such as *'ll* that follow their base are enclitics; clitics that precede their base are proclitics, e.g. Italian *lo scrivo* 'it I-write, I'm writing it'. (Classical Greek *enklitikos* 'leaning on', from *klino* 'to slope', the source of **cline**.)

CLITIC DOUBLING

A clause **construction** in which a **clitic** 'doubles' a full noun phrase functioning as **subject** or **object**. E.g. in the Bulgarian *Momcheto go njama* 'boy-the him not-has, The boy is missing', the clitic *go* doubles the object *momcheto*.

CLOSE

In the four-level classification of tongue heights used in the system of **cardinal vowels**, cardinal vowels 1, [i] and 8, [u] are close vowels made with the tongue as **high** in the mouth as possible without producing audible friction. The other terms in the system are **half-close**, **half-open** and **open**.

CLOSE APPROXIMATION

A term in the description of the **manner of articulation** of oral **consonant** sounds. The **articulators** are brought close together and cause turbulence in the airflow producing a **fricative**, as in [f] *fin*. See **OPEN APPROXIMATION**.

CLOSE TRANSITION

A transition between adjacent sound **segments** such that there is no audible gap. In **homorganic** sequences like [sʌm men], *some men*, there is complete continuity between the segments; in **heterorganic** sequences like [teɪk pleɪs]. *take place*, there may be articulatory overlap.

CLOSED

In **phonology**, a **syllable** that ends in a **consonant**, e.g. [pɪt]. See **OPEN**.

CLOSED CLASS
A **class** of items to which new members are rarely added and which can be set out in a (short) list. E.g. English **personal pronouns**, *I*, *you*, *he*, etc. In contrast, the **noun** class is a very large open class which continually acquires new members.

CLOSED INTERROGATIVE
See **INTERROGATIVE CLAUSE**, See **OPEN INTERROGATIVE**.

CLOSING
The final stage in a conversation; the techniques for bringing a conversation to a close.

CLOSURE
In **phonetics**, contact between the **articulators** such as to obstruct the airstream. There is complete closure with **stops**, and **nasals**, partial closure with **laterals** and **fricatives** and intermittent closure with **trills**, **flaps** and **taps**. See **AIRSTREAM MECHANISM**.

CLUSTER
A sequence of adjacent **consonants** occurring initially, e.g. *still*, *string*, or finally, e.g. *last*, *fifth*. In English up to three consonants can occur initially, e.g. *string* [str-] *splash* and up to four finally *glimpsed* – [-mpst].

CLUSTER ANALYSIS
A type of multivariate analysis for grouping variables or individuals into classes on the basis of particular properties. The members of each class are as like each other as possible and as unlike the members of other classes as possible.

CLOZE TEST
A form of comprehension test in which subjects are asked to supply appropriate words for gaps in a text.

CLUTTERING
In **clinical linguistics**, a speech disorder affecting fluency. Attempting to speak too quickly can lead to distorted articulation and speech rhythm, and to interference in **syntactic structure**.

CNA
See **COGNITIVE NARRATIVE ANALYSIS**.

COALESCENCE
See **MERGER**.

COALESCENT ASSIMILATION
An **assimilation** where two adjacent **segments** mutually influence each other so that a merger occurs, e.g. *must you*: [mʌst ju] → [mʌstʃu]. Also known as mutual assimilation. See **ASSIMILATION**.

CO-ARTICULATION

A term in the description of the **manner of articulation** of **consonant** sounds, simultaneous or overlapping articulation at more than one point in the **vocal tract**. **Labiovelars** like [kp] or [gb] are found in West African languages.

COCHLEA

The spiral cavity of the inner ear.

COCKTAIL PARTY PHENOMENON

Selective listening, which enables interlocutors to focus on a particular conversation in a context where many conversations are taking place.

CO-CONSTRUCTION

See **CO-NARRATION**.

CODA

1. See **NARRATIVE**. 2. In **phonetics** and **phonology** **syllables** are analysed as consisting of an **onset**, a **nucleus** and a **coda**. For instance, in *hat* the vowel is the nucleus; [h] is the onset, and [t] forms the coda.

CODE

A systematic set of rules assigning meanings to symbols. In linguistics this has been used to describe languages (English, Chinese and so on), dialects (Cockney, Tyneside and so on) and especially sociologically determined communication systems. See **CODE MIXING, CODE SWITCHING, ELABORATED CODE, RESTRICTED CODE**.

CODE MIXING

Code switching in situations where it is difficult to determine which language is dominant. Common in, for example, educated interaction in Singapore and Hong Kong (Chinese and English) and in Gibraltar (English and Spanish).

CODE SWITCHING

Switching between two languages or dialects in the same conversation, usually dependent on social or other contextual factors. There are different types of switching. Individual lexical items can be used because there is no direct equivalent in the other language or the precise nuance cannot easily be conveyed (lexical switching): this is sometimes difficult to distinguish from **borrowing**. Switching can occur within a sentence (intrasentential switching), or at a sentence or clause boundary (intersentential code switching). An example from Gibraltar – Spanish, in italics, and English, underlined: *No puedo ir* shopping *porque* I have to work late. Anyway, *te llamo esta noche* OK? *(I can't go shopping because I have to work late. Anyway I'll phone you tonight, OK?).*

COGNATE

Languages or words derived from a common ancestor are said to be cognate. French and Italian, both being descendants of Latin, are cognate languages.

Similarly Italian *notte* and French *nuit* are cognate words both being derived from Latin *nox*

COGNATE OBJECT
A **direct object** which parallels its governing verb in form and meaning: e.g. *He dreamed strange dreams, She slept the sleep of the just*. See **GOVERNMENT**.

COGNITIVE GRAMMAR
A theory of linguistic structure developed from the mid 1970s. It takes language to be an integral part of human cognition, not an independent module as in the Chomskyan approach. The basic units of analysis are semantic and phonological, meaning is handled as dependent on human experience of the world and on human ability to construe the 'same' situation in different ways, all grammatical **morphs** are considered meaningful, **prototypes** and **grammaticalization** are key concepts, and **constructions** are central to the analysis of grammar. See **CONSTRUCTION GRAMMAR, FIGURE, LANDMARK**.

COGNITIVE LINGUISTICS
An approach to language and cognition that established itself in the late 1980s. It grew out of work on metaphor and Cognitive Grammar, which it subsumed. A central tenet is that knowledge of language is part of a set of cognitive capacities, not a separate module as in Chomskyan generative grammar. Research mainly focuses on **metaphor; lexical meaning, concepts** and **prototypes; frames;** modelling the cognitive processes involved in the interpretation of discourse. Many proponents of cognitive linguistics regard it as encompassing **grammaticalization** and Construction Grammar (with particular reference to the meanings of **constructions**). See **CONCEPTUAL BLENDING, FRAME SEMANTICS, MENTAL SPACES, PROTOTYPE THEORY**.

COGNITIVE MEANING
See **DESCRIPTIVE MEANING**.

COGNITIVE NARRATIVE ANALYSIS
A theory (CNA) whose subject matter is the way people understand narrative and narrative as a way of understanding and explaining ideas and concepts. CNA developed out of story grammar theory, which held that all narratives in all cultures have the same basic underlying structure, and work in AI on knowledge representation, how people store knowledge, interpret complex but expected sequences as described in narratives and interpret and remember unusual sequences of events, all with a minimum of textual clues. See **FRAME, NARRATIVE, SCRIPT**.

COGNITIVE SEMANTICS
Any approach to the study of meaning that focuses on the relationship between grammar and mental representations of the outside world and how humans **construe** a given situation in different ways. This approach contrasts with the classic theory of **truth conditions** which related language directly

COHERENCE
The property that makes individual sentences or clauses cohere into a **text** that makes sense, as opposed to a sequence of random sentences. For a text to count as coherent, the writer and reader, or speaker and hearer, must have similar world-views and experience of the world and obey the same cultural conventions when presenting ideas and **propositions** and narrating events.

COHESION
1. The property of texts whereby grammatical and lexical features tie clauses and sentences together so as to parallel an underlying coherence of content. Typical devices are the use of conjunctions (e.g. *however, moreover, besides, then*), pronouns, and non-finite clauses (e.g. *Having finished the book, she returned it to the library*). See **COHERENCE**. 2. See **UNINTERRUPTIBILITY**.

COHESIVENESS
The extent to which a text is cohesive or a word uninterruptible. See **COHESION**.

CO-HYPONYM
Lexical items that are hyponyms of the same superordinate item are co-hyponyms of each other. APPLE, PEACH, PEAR, etc. are co-hyponyms, since they are all hyponyms of FRUIT. See **HYPONYMY**.

CO-INDEX
To assign indices, usually subscript, to show whether phrases have the same or different referents. In *Angus$_i$ doesn't know if he$_i$ will be there*, *Angus$_i$* and *he$_i$* have the same **index** *i* and refer to the same person. They are said to be co-indexed. In *Angus$_i$ doesn't know if he$_j$ will be there*, *Angus$_i$* and *he$_j$* have different indices, *i* and *j*, and refer to different persons. The process of assigning indices is co-indexing. See **TRACE**.

COLLAPSE
In **phrase structure grammars**, to reduce two or more rules to one by means of various notational devices. NP → N and NP → Det N can be collapsed into the single rule NP → (Det) N.

COLLECTIVE NOUN
A noun denoting a number of individual things or animate beings as a group or collection: *congregation* of people in church, *flock* of sheep, *charm* of nightingales. Sometimes the collective noun denoting the type, *aristocracy, clergy*, is similar in form to the noun denoting individuals, e.g. *aristocrat, clergyman*.

COLLIGATION
See **COLLOCATION**.

COLLOCATION

The relation between individual **lexical words** such that they frequently occur together or one requires the other: e.g. *brand* and *new* in *brand new*, *staple* and *diet* in *staple diet*. Colligation is the relation between general units in a **construction**: e.g. between **adjective** and **noun** in a **noun phrase**, as in *slow thinker* and *fast runner*.

COLLOQUIAL

Applied to vocabulary and grammar typical of informal speech and not normally used in formal speech and writing. Colloquial features are used by speakers of standard and **non-standard** varieties alike. *We're stuck with this set-up* is colloquial but not non-standard. See **STANDARD LANGUAGE**.

COLLOSTRUCTIONAL ANALYSIS

A type of collocational analysis that pays particular attention to the syntactic properties of **constructions**. It measures the degree to which particular **slots** in a construction prefer particular sets of lexical items. Constructions may be **stem** plus **affixes**, semi-fixed phrases, or **clauses**, with the focus on **verbs** and their **arguments**. See **ARGUMENT SLOT, ARGUMENT STRUCTURE, COLLOCATION, CONSTRUCTION GRAMMAR, FIXED EXPRESSION**.

COLOURING

The property of having a particular **secondary articulation**, such as a vowel phoneme having 'rhotacization', or 'r-colouring' in some varieties of American English, 'nasal colouring' in some varieties of French, or a particular phonation type – e.g. **'creaky voice'**. See **RHOTIC**.

COMBINATORIAL

Dealing with the way in which grammatical or lexical units combine, or with the rules for combining symbols in a system of logic or mathematics.

COMBINING FORM

Forms of words used only in **compound words** or in longer words: e.g. *tele-* in *television, telepathy* and *anthropo-* in *anthropology, anthropomorphic*. They are obligatorily **bound** morphs. See **MORPH, NEO-CLASSICAL COMPOUND**.

COMITATIVE

A participant or case **role** with the meaning 'together with'. Expressed in, e.g., English by the preposition *with* – *Fiona left with Susan*, and in, e.g., Russian, by a preposition and case suffix – *s Ivanom* 'with Ivan'.

COMMAND

Relationships between constituents in **tree diagrams**. The relationships are based on the positions occupied by constituents relative to each other in different arrangements. See **C-COMMAND, CONSTITUENT STRUCTURE, M-COMMAND**.

COMMENT

See **TOPIC AND COMMENT**.

COMMENT CLAUSE

A **clause**, added at the beginning, the middle or end of another clause and expressing a (**parenthetical**) comment. The prototypical case is a comment on the speaker's attitude, as in *It is, I suspect, going to be difficult to prove; I wonder, will the plane be delayed?; They, I think, regretted his resignation*. It has been extended to clauses commenting on the hearer or on a third person: *As she knows, I will be away; I don't have enough time, you see; You know, this is a waste of time*.
See **PARENTHESIS**.

COMMENTARY AND ANALYSIS

See **PRACTICAL CRITICISM**.

COMMISSIVE

In Searle's classification, a **speech act**, such as promising, vowing, offering, undertaking, that commits the speakers to some future action. See **ASSERTIVE, DECLARATIVE, DIRECTIVE, EXPRESSIVE**.

COMMITMENT

In performing certain speech acts speakers take on a commitment. An assertion commits the speaker to the truth of a **proposition**; promises and offers, e.g., commit the speaker to some action. See **ASSERTIVE, COMMISSIVE, SPEECH ACT**.

COMMON GENDER

1. The gender of nouns which can have either **masculine** or **feminine** agreement. E.g. French *professeur* 'teacher' can take masculine **agreement** – *le professeur, il est beau* 'The teacher-3sg-m is handsome, The teacher (he) is handsome' – or feminine agreement – *Le professeur, elle est belle* 'The teacher-3sg-f is beautiful, The teacher (she) is beautiful'. In the Caucasian language Archi, the word *lo*, e.g., takes three patterns of agreement depending on whether it denotes a boy, a girl or a young animal. 2. The **gender** of nouns which have only one pattern of agreement but can denote male or female humans or animals: e.g. Russian *akula* 'shark-f' and *kit* 'whale-m', and French *chien* 'dog-m'. 3. In, e.g., Dutch and Swedish, the gender assigned to the single class of nouns produced by the merging of the older classes of masculine and feminine nouns.

COMMON GROUND

The background assumptions and knowledge shared by the members of a community or by particular speakers and hearers through their shared experience.

COMMON NOUN

A noun denoting a class of entities (animate beings or inanimate things, whether abstract or concrete); e.g. *gorilla* denotes any animal that can be classed as a gorilla. In contrast, speakers use proper nouns or proper names to refer by name to an individual person, place or thing, or a set of things, that they deem unique in a given context: e.g. *Prince Charles, Diana, Dad, The Barossa Valley* are proper nouns and the names of unique entities in particular contexts.
See **ABSTRACT NOUN, CONCRETE NOUN, COUNT NOUN, MASS NOUN**.

COMMUNICATIVE COMPETENCE

In relation to any given language, a speaker's **grammatical competence** plus knowledge of the rules and conventions governing the accurate, appropriate and effective use of the language in a wide range of social settings. See PRAGMALINGUISTIC NORMS, SOCIOPRAGMATIC NORMS.

COMMUNICATIVE DYNAMISM

See FUNCTIONAL SENTENCE PERSPECTIVE.

COMMUNITY OF PRACTICE

A group participating in communication tasks together, sharing particular aims and assumptions about communication and often using a specialized code, such as the language of medicine, of the law, of marketing. See also ENGLISH FOR ACADEMIC PURPOSES, ENGLISH FOR SPECIFIC PURPOSES, REGISTER.

COMMUTATION

In the work of Hjelmslev, the substitution of one item for a contrastive item in the same context. See CONTRAST.

COMP

See COMPACT, COMPARATIVE, COMPLEMENT, COMPLEMENTIZER.

COMPACT

In **J&H Distinctive Feature Theory**, an acoustic distinctive feature involving a concentration of energy in the central area of the spectrum, associated with **open** vowels and **palatal** and **velar** consonants. Opposite **diffuse**. See DISTINCTIVE FEATURES.

COMPARABLE CORPORA

Corpora of similar texts in more than one language or variety in order to compare different languages or varieties in similar communicative circumstances.

COMPARATIVE

A **construction**, syntactic or morphological, allowing two or more entities to be compared: *noisier than Naples, as noisy as Naples, more beautiful than Taranaki, more eloquently than Cicero*. The **adjective** and **adverb** forms that occur in the construction, whether single words like *noisier* or two words like *more beautiful* and *more slowly*, are said to be comparative or to be in the comparative. See GRADABLE ADJECTIVE, SUPERLATIVE.

COMPARATIVE CLAUSE

A **clause** by means of which a comparison can be made. E.g. *She's kinder than my aunt was*, *We left as soon as we could*.

COMPARATIVE LINGUISTICS

Linguistic approaches that involve language comparison. In historical linguistics this refers to the use of the **comparative method**. In **applied linguistics** this is often referred to as **contrastive linguistics**.

COMPARATIVE METHOD

A way of comparing languages to determine relationships between them and their relation to a possible common ancestor language, the **proto language**. This involves comparing **cognate** forms of two or more languages to establish regular **sound correspondences** from which regular **sound change** can be postulated. If the two languages show a number of regular correspondences and chance similarities can be ruled out, a genetic kinship can be postulated. In this way the protolanguage can be reconstructed from its daughter languages. This account assumes that sound change is regular, and that there is no **borrowing**. The relationships are often represented by a **family tree**. See NEOGRAMMARIAN HYPOTHESIS.

COMPARATIVE PHRASE

A phrase following a **comparative** adjective or adverb. In English, phrases with *than* or *as* – *bigger than Beijing*, *as bright as a button*. In Russian, a noun in the genitive case – *bogache Ivana* 'richer Ivan-GEN, (is) richer than Ivan'. In Turkish a noun in the **ablative** case – *Türkiyeden büyük* 'Turkey-ABL big, bigger than Turkey'.

COMPARATOR

The entity against which a comparison is made: *Croesus* in *(richer) than Croesus*, *(as rich) as Croesus*.

COMPARISON

Changes in the shape of an **adjective** or **adverb**, or the addition of a word, to express degrees of some property: e.g. *fast–faster–fastest, slowly–more slowly–most slowly*.

COMPENSATORY LENGTHENING

A **phonological process** whereby a vowel is lengthened when a following consonant is lost. Examples are West Germanic γ*ans* → Old English *gōs* (Modern English *goose*); West Germanic *finf* → Old English *fīf* (Modern English *five*).

COMPETENCE

An idealization of speakers' knowledge of their language, excluding slips of the tongue, limitations of memory and instances of **anacoluthon** and **aposiopesis**, etc. An account of such knowledge is a competence grammar. See GRAMMATICAL COMPETENCE, COMMUNICATIVE COMPETENCE, LANGUE.

COMPETENCE GRAMMAR

See COMPETENCE.

COMPLEMENT

1. In a **construction**, dependents on the **head** that are obligatory or are in a close relationship with the **verb** in that some verbs require them, while others exclude them. *Vanish* excludes a direct object; *put* requires both a direct object and a directional phrase – *Put the shoes in the cupboard!* but **Put the shoes!* Direct

objects and directional/goal phrases are complements of verbs. **Noun phrases** are complements of **prepositions**: **arrived with* vs *arrived with my brother*. See **MODIFIER 2**. **2**. Short for 'complement clause' – see **CLAUSE, COMPLEMENT CLAUSE**. **3**. In **copula** constructions, the subject complement, i.e. an **adjective phrase** or noun phrase modifying the subject: e.g. *exciting* in *This film is exciting*, *downcast* in *Sue seemed downcast*, *President* in *Roy was elected President*. **4**. In certain constructions, the object complement, i.e. an adjective phrase or noun phrase modifying the direct object: e.g. *ill* in *The pollution made him ill* and *President* in *The voters elected Roy President*. **5**. In **X-Bar syntax**, the item that is the sister of the X-head. See **RESULTATIVE, SMALL CLAUSE**.

COMPLEMENT CLAUSE

The classic complement clause is finite and complements **verbs**, **nouns** or **adjectives**. The ones that modify verbs are sometimes called noun clauses because they function as the **subject** or **object** of verbs, occupying slots in clauses that can be occupied by noun phrases. In *Katarina declared that she was leaving*, *that she was leaving* is a complement clause functioning as the object of *declared*. In *That she didn't leave surprised us*, *that she didn't leave* is a complement clause functioning as the subject of *surprised*. Complement clauses may have no **complementizer**, as in *I know his solution is wrong*; an overt complementizer may be *that* or a **wh form**, as in *We asked whether the car could be repaired*, *We wondered why the dog was barking*. Complement clauses can also modify nouns, typically nouns like *plan, report, theory, hypothesis*, as in *the report that the bank was going bust*, *the theory that the earth is flat*. These complement clauses cannot be introduced by wh words – **the theory which the earth is flat* – and convey the content of the report, theory, etc. Note the difference between *the report which I wrote for the council*, where *which I wrote for the council* is a relative clause, and *the report that the bank was going bust*, where *that the bank was going bust* is a complement clause. Finally, complement clauses can modify adjectives, as in *I'm certain I left the car here* and *We're confident that nothing will go wrong*. See **CLAUSE, COMPLEMENT, CONTACT CLAUSE, FINITE CLAUSE, FINITE VERB**.

COMPLEMENT FEATURE

In the **Minimalist Program**, features on verbs controlling what type of **complement clause** they take.

COMPLEMENTARIES

Pairs of **lexical words** whose meanings are opposed to each other and divide some **domain** of meaning between them leaving no middle ground. The members of such pairs are said to complement each other. One such pair is *dead* and *alive*. Normally a creature that is dead is not alive and a creature that is alive is not dead. In contrast, *big* and *small* leave a middle ground; humans are regularly described as neither big nor small, or as being of average height. The latter type of lexical items are called **antonyms** and the relationship is **antonymy**. See **OPPOSITENESS**.

COMPLEMENTARY DISTRIBUTION
Relationship between two or more items such that one occurs in contexts where the other does not, or the others do not. E.g. *an* occurs before **nouns** and **adjectives** beginning with a **vowel** – *an egg, an azure sky*; *a* occurs before all nouns and adjectives beginning with a **consonant** – *a yacht, a large bull*.

COMPLEMENTIZER
Originally a **subordinating conjunction** introducing a **complement clause**: *that* in (*knew*) *that he was right*, *whether* in *ask whether the train has left*. Now extended by some analysts to all subordinating conjunctions. Often referred to as COMP. See **CONJUNCTION**.

COMPLEMENTIZER PHRASE
Especially in Chomskian theories of syntax, a phrase containing a **complementizer**, which is considered the head of the complementizer phrase or CP. In *asked whether the repairs had been done*, the complementizer phrase *whether the repairs had been done* functions as the **complement** of *asked*. The complementizer phrase contains a complementizer for an **adverbial clause** or a **complement clause** and the wh pronouns of a **relative clause**. The **main clause** in many languages is analysed as having a complementizer phrase containing a **null** complementizer.

COMPLETE FEEDBACK
A proposed characteristic of human language whereby speakers can assess how effectively they have addressed their audience.

COMPLETE SENTENCE
Especially in written language, a **sentence** with no missing obligatory **constituents**. *A book* is an incomplete sentence in answer to *What did she buy?* See **COMPLEMENT, CONSTITUENT STRUCTURE, CORE (OF A CLAUSE), NUCLEUS**.

COMPLETIVE
1. Equivalent to **perfective**. 2. An **Aktionsart** expressing the thorough carrying out of an action: Russian *kusat'* 'sting', *iskusat'* 'sting all over'.

COMPLEX
A unit that involves more than the simplest **construction**, in contrast with a simple or simplex unit. See **COMPLEX SENTENCE, COMPLEX NOUN PHRASE, COMPLEX SYMBOL, COMPLEX WORD, SIMPLE SENTENCE, SIMPLEX**.

COMPLEX CONJUNCTION
A sequence of two or more **words** that can be treated as a single **subordinating conjunction**: e.g. *as long as, in order that*.

COMPLEX INTRANSITIVE
Mainly used in CGEL, the term denotes both a type of **clause** and the type of verbs that occur in it. The **verbs** are intransitive but take a subject complement; e.g. *Brian looks <u>disappointed</u>, He fell <u>ill</u>*. See **COMPLEMENT 3, COMPLEX TRANSITIVE**.

COMPLEX NOUN PHRASE

A **noun phrase** with a **head** noun and a subordinate clause, e.g. *the thought that the world will end tomorrow, my wish to be in bed by midnight*.

COMPLEX NOUN PHRASE CONSTRAINT

In **transformational grammar**, a **constraint** preventing the movement of, e.g., a **wh form** out of a **subordinate clause** inside a **noun phrase**. Thus, in *She heard the news that the bank was buying what*; *what* is in the **complement clause** *that the bank was buying what*. It in turn is part of the noun phrase *the news... What* cannot be moved to the front of the sentence: **What did she hear the news that the bank was buying?*.

COMPLEX PREPOSITION

A sequence of two or more **words** that can be treated as a single **preposition**: *in front of, in spite of*. Some complex prepositions are completely fixed, such as *in lieu of*; others allow some manipulation, such as *with regard to*, which allows the addition of *due*, as in *with due regard to*.

COMPLEX SENTENCE

A **sentence** consisting of a main **clause** and at least one **subordinate clause**. E.g. *When the fire brigade arrived, the houses were ablaze*, with the main clause *the houses were ablaze* and the subordinate clause *When the fire brigade arrived*; *I think that we have met before*, with the main clause *I think that we have met before* and the subordinate clause *that we have met before*.

COMPLEX STOP

A **plosive** with two points of **articulation**: See **CO-ARTICULATION**.

COMPLEX SYMBOL

In mid-1960s **transformational grammar**, a symbol consisting of a bundle of features, some related to properties of **nouns**, such as being common, proper, concrete, abstract, animate and so on; others related to properties of **verbs**, such as taking a **direct object** NP, or a **complement** Adjective Phrase (*seemed anxious*). These sets of features were dominated by category symbols such as N, for Noun, and V, for Verb. They played a central role in generating the correct combinations of a verb and its complements in a clause. See **COMMON NOUN, PHRASE STRUCTURE RULE, SELECTIONAL RESTRICTION, STRICT SUBCATEGORIZATION, SUBCATEGORIZATION FRAME**.

COMPLEX TONE

In **phonetics**, a tonal **contour** involving at least two **pitch** movements, e.g. a fall rise. See **CONTOUR TONE**.

COMPLEX TRANSITIVE

Both a type of **clause** and the type of **verbs** that occur in it. The verbs are transitive, with a direct object, and typically have a complement noun phrase or adjective phrase modifying the object; e.g. *The returning officer declared him Member* *of Parliament for East Cheam* – complement noun phrase, *They sprayed the car bright blue* – complement adjective phrase. See **COMPLEMENT, COMPLEX INTRANSITIVE, TRANSITIVITY**.

COMPLEX WORD

A **word** consisting of a **stem** and at least one derivational affix. An example is *affixation*, with the stem *affix* and the derivational affix *-ation*. See **DERIVATION, DERIVATIONAL MORPHOLOGY**.

COMPONENT

1. See **GENERATIVE GRAMMAR**. 2. A semantic feature. See **COMPONENTIAL ANALYSIS**.

COMPONENTIAL ANALYSIS

The analysis of sets of **lexical words** as bundles of meaning components, represented by **features**. For a given set, the components show whatever meaning the lexical items have in common and what distinguishes them one from the other. To take a familiar example, the lexical items MAN, BULL, STALLION, boy contain the basic meaning component 'male', while the lexical items WOMAN, COW, MARE, GIRL contain 'female'. MAN and BOY, WOMAN and GIRL all contain the component 'human'. MAN and WOMAN contain the component 'adult' and BOY and GIRL contain 'non-adult'. See **LEXICAL DECOMPOSITION, MEANING POSTULATE, NATURAL SEMANTICS**.

COMPOSITIONAL

Relating to **compositionality**.

COMPOSITIONALITY

The principle that the meaning of a **sentence** is obtained by combining or composing the meanings of its constituent **words** and **phrases**. E.g. the meaning of *The cat watched the birds* is obtained by first combining the meanings of *the* and *cat* and *the* and *birds*. The meaning of *the birds* combines with the meaning of *watched*, and the meaning of *watched the birds* combines with the meaning of *the cat*. The meanings of idioms such as *spill the beans* and *do the hard yards* are non-compositional.

COMPOUND BILINGUALISM

A form of **bilingualism** in which a speaker has a single set of concepts related to two different sets of **words** in two different languages. See **COORDINATE BILINGUALISM**.

COMPOUND SENTENCE

A **sentence** consisting of at least two main **clauses**, typically connected by a **conjunction**: *One bank has failed* and *another one is in trouble*.

COMPOUND WORD

A **word** consisting of two or more **stems** which may themselves be words, as in *arm+chair*, or parts of words, as in *retro+spect*. Compounds are formed by the process of compounding or composition. Different types of compounds are recognized. A dvandva or copulative compound consists of two co-ordinated stems, as in *tragicomic* and *hunter-gatherer*. (*Dvandva* is **Sanskrit** for 'couple'.) Tatpurusha (Sanskrit for 'his-man') (also determinative or exocentric) compounds consist of two stems in something like a modifier-head relation. There are two subtypes. Possessive compounds such as *whitethroat* and *paperback* – *white* modifies *throat* and *paper* modifies *back* but the whole compound denotes a bird possessing a white throat (kind of bird) or a book possessing a paper back (kind of book). The second type is attributive: in *blackbird, black* modifies *bird* and the whole compound denotes a kind of bird. The possessive subtype is also known as a bahuvrihi compound, *bahuvrihi* being Sanskrit for '(having) much-rice'. See **NEO-CLASSICAL COMPOUND, ROOT COMPOUND, SYNTHETIC COMPOUND.**

COMPREHENSIBILITY

The property of **sentences** and **clauses** such that the choice of lexical items and the combinations of words, phrases and clauses make it possible for listeners and readers to work out their **literal meaning**. See **INTELLIGIBILITY, INTERPRETABILITY.**

COMPUTATIONAL LINGUISTICS

The use of computers in linguistics and the development of software which can perform linguistic tasks, e.g. parsing, data management. See **PARSE**.

COMPUTATIONAL STYLISTICS

The use of computational techniques for stylistic analysis such as studying authorship, lexical frequencies. See **CONCORDANCE, KEYWORD, KWIC.**

COMPUTER LANGUAGE

See **PROGRAMMING LANGUAGE.**

CO-NARRATION

The telling of a story by two or more speakers. A typical pattern is for one speaker to do the main storyline while other speakers add details. In some societies this is the major method of storytelling and is controlled by strict conventions.

CONATIVE

Especially in the analysis of **Russian** aspect, the use of verbs in the imperfective aspect to refer to actions that are attempted. E.g. *V techenie goda Petr brosal kurit'*. 'In course of-year Petr throw-IPFV to-smoke, During the year Peter was trying to give up smoking'.

CONCATENATION

Originally a mathematical operation for juxtaposing symbols to form a sequence. In **formal grammar** it is applied to the linking of constituents to form a sequence: e.g. **Determiner, Adjective** and **Noun** can be linked to form the **Noun Phrase** sequence Determiner +Adjective+Noun. The operation is denoted by +.

CONCATENATIVE MORPHOLOGY

Any morphological system in which **syntactic linkage** and **grammatical categories** are signalled by the simple addition of **affixes** to **stems**. The morphs are linked by concatenation. See AGREEMENT, CONCATENATION, GOVERNMENT.

CONCEPT

A mental representation constructed from information about the surrounding world received and processed by human beings. It is generally assumed that humans are innately predisposed to perceive the information supplied by their senses in terms of discrete objects with particular properties. A central tenet of theories such as **cognitive linguistics** is that language relates directly to concepts and through them to the outside world. See PROTOTYPE, PROTOTYPE THEORY.

CONCEPTUAL BLENDING

In **cognitive linguistics**, a model of the process by which listeners and readers construct new meaning, putting two **mental spaces** in correspondence. E.g. the sentence *The firm is on the rocks* is interpreted by taking a source space, COMMERCE, and mapping it onto a target space, SAILING. The COMMERCE space contains a packet of information including FIRM, RUNNING A FIRM, FAILURE, while the SAILING space contains a packet including SHIP, SAILING A SHIP, GOING ONTO ROCKS. The source and target spaces, the input spaces, are put in correspondence via a generic space which contains general pieces of information that function as cover terms for the pieces of information in the input spaces; e.g. OPERATIONAL UNIT, CONTROLLING THE UNIT, CHOOSING CORRECT ACTIONS, ADVERSE EFFECTS OF INCORRECT ACTIONS. Via the generic space a blended space is created, e.g. FIRM/SHIP, RUNNING A FIRM/SAILING A SHIP, FAILURE/GOING ONTO ROCKS. The spaces and the interconnections form an integration network. See CONCEPTUAL METAPHOR THEORY, DOMAIN, METAPHOR.

CONCEPTUAL-INTENTIONAL STRUCTURE

See MINIMALIST PROGRAM.

CONCEPTUAL MEANING

See DESCRIPTIVE MEANING.

CONCEPTUAL METAPHOR THEORY

In **cognitive linguistics**, the theory that thought is essentially metaphorical and that conceptual structure involves a complex set of correspondences between different domains. The source **domain** is typically concrete and well structured, and the target domain is abstract. Source domains provide a way of talking about and conceptualizing intangible areas of experience, often the only way of talking about them. Familiar examples are the conceiving of argument as war and of anger as heat and pressure, states as locations and change as movement. See CONSTRUAL, FICTIVE MOTION, METAPHOR.

CONCEPTUALISM

See CONCEPTUAL SEMANTICS.

CONCEPTUAL SEMANTICS

A theory of **semantics** set in a formal generative framework. It has been developed and elaborated since the mid 1970s. Key points are that semantic structures are conceptual, that to analyse meaning is to analyse mental representations and that it is the latter that map onto syntactic structures. The theory has affinities with **localism** and can be seen as a precursor of **cognitive linguistics** and Conceptual Metaphor Theory.

CONCESSIVE

A concessive is an **adverbial clause of concession**, or a **preposition** such as *despite*, or a **discourse particle** such as *though*, signalling that the speaker is conceding some point while maintaining another: *Despite the traffic jams, we reached the airport on time*; *John is clever – he's not very hard-working though*.

CONCESSIVE CLAUSE

See ADVERBIAL CLAUSE OF CONCESSION.

CONCGRAM

An **n-gram** of items co-occurring either in a sequence or in various orders and possibly not immediately next to each other. See CO-OCCURRENCE, CO-OCCURRENCE RESTRICTION, COLLOCATION.

CONCORD

See AGREEMENT.

CONCORDANCE

A list of the words in a text. The words are shown in alphabetical order and accompanied by a given number (say seven) of words that precede them and the same number of words that follow them.

CONCORDANCE LINE

See KWIC.

CONCORDANCER

A computer program that produces concordances.

CONCRETE NOUN

A **noun** denoting a set of concrete objects, such as can be touched, seen, handled and so on: e.g. *dog, pillow, tree, water*. See ABSTRACT NOUN, COMMON NOUN, COUNTABLE NOUN, DENOTATION.

CONDILLAC, Étienne de (1714–1780)

A French philosopher whose theory of knowledge gave a central role to language. His thinking laid the basis for work on linguistic relativism and the idea that each language has its own peculiar genius.

CONDITIONAL CLAUSE

A type of **adverbial clause** stating the condition under which a given event will happen, the given event being stated in a **main clause**. The **canonical** conditional clause is introduced by *if*. In *If Katarina resigns, Freya will be surprised*, the main clause is *Freya will be surprised*, but Freya's surprise will be caused by Katarina's resigning. The two clauses are combined in a conditional **construction**. Conditions can also be expressed by clauses with an **auxiliary** verb in first position and the **subject** noun phrase in second position: *Were Katarina to resign, Freya would be surprised*. An imperative clause can also be used to express a condition: *Resign and the firm will collapse* (= *if you resign ...*). In this construction the traditional name for the conditional clause is protasis, from the classical Greek word for 'proposition', connected with the verb 'stretch something out in front of (someone)'. The traditional name for the main clause is apodosis, a classical Greek noun meaning 'payment' or 'giving back'. See **CLAUSE, COUNTERFACTUAL, REMOTE PAST, SUBJECT-AUX INVERSION**.

CONDITIONAL-CONCESSIVE CLAUSE

An **adverbial clause** that is both like a **conditional clause** in stating some condition and like an **adverbial clause of concession** in being used by speakers to concede a point, specifically that some condition or situation might exist. English conditional-concessive clauses are typically introduced by *even if*: *Even if you don't like the taste, you have to take the medicine.* See **CLAUSE**.

CONDITIONAL CONSTRUCTION

See **CONDITIONAL CLAUSE**.

CONDITIONAL SENTENCE

A **sentence** consisting of a **main clause** and a **conditional clause**.

CONDITIONAL TENSE

A term applied in some grammars of English to the **verb** forms used in **conditional constructions** in which the **conditional clause** expresses a condition as possible but not very likely: E.g. *were* and *would relax* in *If Mary Jane were to eat her pudding, her mother would relax*. The term 'conditional tense' is better thought of as denoting a special use of the **past tense** and the **past perfect** not as a separate tense. See **TENSE AND ASPECT**.

CONDITIONED VARIANT

See **CONDITIONING**.

CONDITIONING

Variation in the form of a **morph** depending on its surroundings. There are different types of conditioning. Phonological conditioning is variation controlled by the phonological context. E.g. in Latin the /k/ in the stem /rek/ 'king' is realized as voiceless [k] before the voiceless fricative /s/ in the nominative *reks*, but as voiced [g] between the voiced vowels in the genitive *regis*. [k] and [g] are said to be conditioned variants. Lexical conditioning is variation controlled by particular lexical items, e.g. the plural **suffix** *-en* in *oxen* and the **past tense** form *ran* for the lexical item RUN. Grammatical conditioning is variation controlled by the grammatical context or **construction**. A French example is the use of **subjunctive** verb forms in the third person **imperative** construction: *Il vient demain* 'He is-coming tomorrow' vs *Qu'il vienne demain* 'That he come tomorrow, Let him come tomorrow'. See **MORPH**.

CONDUCTIVE DEAFNESS

In **clinical linguistics**, hearing loss where sound fails to reach the inner **ear** because it is inadequately conducted through the external or middle ear.

CONFIGURATION

See **CONFIGURATIONAL LANGUAGES**.

CONFIGURATIONAL LANGUAGES

Languages in which syntactic constituents are arranged in configurations, with smaller constituents (e.g. words) combining in fixed orders to build bigger constituents. Thus the **head** and its **modifier** are adjacent. The configurations are easily represented by a **tree diagram**. In non-configurational languages, such as many native **Australian languages**, syntactic constituents, especially of the types that in English would combine to form a **noun phrase**, are separated in the **clause** and do not form a larger unit. The same phenomenon is found in the spoken varieties of other languages. Compare English *an interesting book* in *Find me an interesting book* and the following Russian example, in which the adjective 'interesting' agrees in **gender, number** and **case** with the noun for 'book' but is at the other end of the clause: *knigu najdite mne interesnuju* 'book-ACC find-IMP 1sgDAT interesting-ACC, a-book find me interesting, i.e. Find me an interesting book'. It is possible that non-configurationality is a property of spontaneous spoken language as opposed to formal written language. See **AGREEMENT**.

CONGENITAL

Applied to a condition existing since or before birth.

CONGRUENCE

The property enabling **words** to combine in a **construction**. In Latin, *parva* 'small' is **feminine, singular** and **nominative** case, as is *femina* 'woman'. The two words are congruent and can combine to form a **noun phrase**. *Vidi* 'I saw' requires an **object** noun in the **accusative** case; *feminam* is in the accusative **case**. Being congruent, these two words can combine to form a **verb phrase**. See **AGREEMENT, GOVERNMENT**.

CONJ

See **CONJUNCTION**.

CONJOINING

The process by which constituents are conjoined by a **conjunction**.

CONJUGATION

1. For a given **verb**, all its forms, consisting of a **stem** and an **inflectional affix**: Italian *parlava* 'I was speaking', *parlavi* 'you were speaking', *parlavamo* 'we were speaking', *parlo* 'I am speaking', etc. **2**. A class of verbs that take the same set of inflectional affixes: in Latin, *laboro* 'I work' belongs to the first conjugation and takes the **suffix** *-at* in *laborat* 'he/she works', etc.; *rego* 'I rule' belongs to the third conjugation and the form corresponding to 'he/she rules' is *regit*, with the suffix *-it*.

CONJUNCT

1. Any item linked with another in a **coordinate structure**. 2. In CGEL, a type of **adverbial**.

CONJUNCTION

An item joining two or more syntactic units such as **words**, **phrases** and **clauses**. Coordinating conjunctions join two or more units of the same status: e.g. English words such as *and* and *or* – The dog <u>and</u> the cat are in the kitchen, She likes Bach <u>and</u> he likes Bartok. The most common Turkish coordination conjunction is a particle: *sen, ben, kardesin de* 'You, I, brother-your CONJ, you, I and your brother'. Subordinating conjunctions join two clauses, one of which is subordinated to the other (often, but not always, a **main clause**). Modern usage is for the term to be applied particularly to conjunctions introducing **adverbial clauses** – [We relaxed] <u>when</u> the guests left, [I don't like her], <u>although</u> she is very charming. In traditional usage the term was also applied to the **complementizer** of a complement clause [I announced] <u>that</u> the taxi had arrived, [We asked] <u>if/ whether</u> they would stay.

CONJUNCTION REDUCTION

A rule in **transformational grammar** reflecting the view that all instances of conjoined/coordinated constituents derive from conjoined **clauses**. E.g. *My aunt sent me a book and a cheque* derives from *My aunt sent me a book and my aunt sent me a cheque*. The conjoined clauses are reduced to give one clause with conjoined **noun phrases**.

CONJUNCTIVE

See **SUBJUNCTIVE**.

CONJUNCTIVE ADVERB

See **CONNECTIVE**.

CONJUNCTIVE ORDERING

Property of sets of rules that all apply, in a particular order, to the same arrangement of constituents.

CONNECTED SPEECH

A stretch of spoken language, usually informal everyday speech, used for the analysis of features typical of such speech such as **elision** and **assimilation**. This type of analysis contrasts with the analysis of the articulation of single words in **citation form**, in isolation and out of context.

CONNECTIONISM
A psycholinguistic model of cognition based on associationist psychology and mathematical models of neural processing.

CONNECTIVE
1. An item linking a **clause** or **sentence** to the preceding clause or sentence. E.g. *therefore* in *They couldn't pay their mortgage and therefore lost their house* and *but* in *She phoned but nobody answered*. 2. In logic, an element linking two or more propositions, such as & 'and', V 'or', → 'entails'. See **conjunction**.

CONNECTIVITY
See **COHESION**.

CONNECTOR
See **CONNECTIVE**.

CONNOTATION
See **NON-DESCRIPTIVE MEANING**.

CONSECUTIVE CLAUSE
See **RESULT CLAUSE**.

CONSONANCE
In verse, the repetition of final **consonants** in words or phrases but with different **vowels**, as in *rustle* and *whistle*. In contrast, **alliteration** is the repetition of consonant sounds at the beginning of words, and **assonance** is the repetition of vowel sounds to produce half rhymes.

	/ka θ/	*cath*	'cat'	(root)
[k] → [Nh]	/v ŋhaθ/	*fyn ghath*	'my cat'	(**nasal** mutation)
[k] → [g]	/i gaθ/	*ei gath*	'his cat'	(soft mutation)
[k] → [x]	/i χaθ/	*ei chath*	'her cat'	(**spirant** mutation)

CONSONANT
Consonants can be defined phonologically or phonetically. Phonologically, they are segments that form the **margin** of a **syllable**, i.e. as the **onset**, 't' in *tin*, or **coda**, 'n' in *tin*, of a syllable. Phonetically, they are defined in terms of their properties as speech sounds. In most languages the two definitions largely, but not entirely overlap (see **approximant** below). To distinguish between phonological and phonetic consonants, the latter are sometimes referred to by the general term **contoid**.

Phonetically, consonants are sounds formed by modifying the airstream moving in or out of the mouth at some point in the **larynx**, throat or mouth.

The commonest **airstream mechanism** is the pulmonic egressive airstream, dealt with here: for other airstreams, see **airstream**. Consonants are described in terms of their **place of articulation** (the position where there is a major obstruction or constriction to the airflow), their **manner of articulation** (the nature of the obstruction or constriction) and the **voice** of the segment. This yields a 'three-term label': [f] is a voiceless, labiodental, fricative.

The **place of articulation** (see the figure below) identifies the place of contact or constriction between a moveable articulator, the **active articulator**, usually the **tongue**, and an immobile articulator, the **passive articulator**, usually the roof of the mouth. Thus, from the lips: **bilabial** (the two lips), **labiodental** (the lower lip against the teeth, **dental** (the tip of the tongue against the teeth), **alveolar** (the blade of the tongue against teeth ridge), **retroflex** (the tip of the tongue curled back against the front part of the hard palate); **alveo-palatal** (the front of the tongue against the back of the teeth ridge); **palatal** (the front of the tongue against the hard palate; **velar** (the back of the tongue against the soft palate or velum); **uvular** (the back of the tongue against the uvula); **pharyngeal** (in the pharynx); **glottal** (in the larynx by the closure or constriction of the glottis).

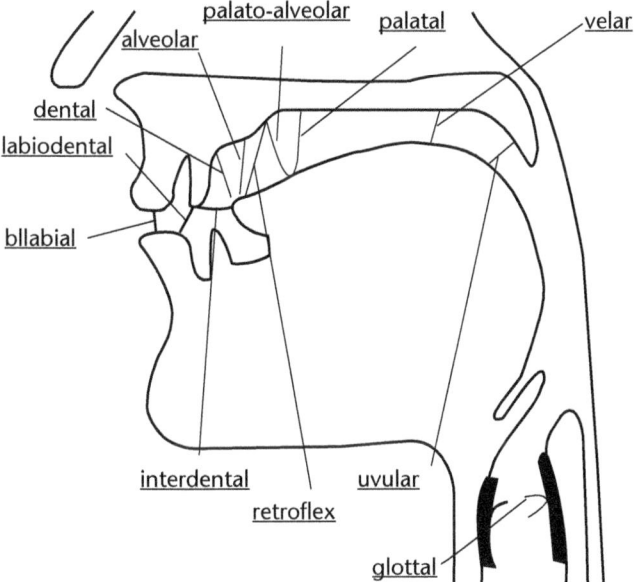

The **manner of articulation** identifies the type of obstruction that occurs in the production of a speech sound. With **nasal** consonants, the **velum** is lowered so that air escapes through the nose and there is complete oral **closure** at some point of articulation. With oral consonants the velum is raised so that no air escapes nasally. The airflow through the mouth is completely blocked in a **stop** consonant. In a fricative the articulators may be brought into **close approximation** sufficient to cause turbulence in the airflow. In an **approximant**

the articulators may be in **open approximation**, that is, brought towards each other but not enough to cause audible friction. If the oral closure is partial and air can escape round the sides of the tongue, the result is a **lateral**; and if the closure is very brief, the result is a **tap** if there is a single contact or a **trill** if the closure is repeated.

Voice is the sound produced by the vibration of the **vocal cords**. Sounds produced while the cords are vibrating are **voiced**: consonants like [b], [z], [m], etc. Sounds produced with no such vibration are **voiceless** consonants like [p], [s], etc.

An **approximant** functions like a consonant, but may have the articulation indistinguishable from the corresponding vowel. Thus, the initial segments in *we* and *you* are phonologically consonants, but phonetically they are produced with the same kind of **stricture** as [u] and [i]. See the figures 'IPA consonants pulmonic' and 'IPA consonants non-pulmonic' at **INTERNATIONAL PHONETIC ALPHABET**.

CONSONANT CLUSTER

A sequence of two or more **consonants** within a single word. English permits clusters of up to three consonants word initially (e.g. spr-ɪŋ (spring), /str-ɪŋ/) and up to four word finally (e.g. /twe-1fθs/ (twelfths), /glɪ-mpst/ (glimpsed). There are severe restrictions of permissible clusters.

CONSONANT HARMONY

A feature of some languages where all the consonants in a word must share some phonological property. This is found in some American Indian languages. It is also attested in language acquisition among English-speaking children where, for example, /dɔg/ becomes /gɔg/. See **VOWEL HARMONY**.

CONSONANT MUTATION

Sound changes that lead to alternations between **consonants**. They are typically triggered by the grammatical environment,. They are found in many language families, e.g. several African languages, some North American languages, and are particularly characteristic of the Celtic languages. For example in Welsh:

CONSONANTAL

1. In **SPE Distinctive Feature Theory**, segments that are produced with an audible constriction in the vocal tract, that is segments that are obstruents, nasals or liquids. See **obstruent, nasal, liquid**. 2. In **J&H Distinctive Feature Theory**, an acoustic **distinctive feature** involving low energy and an obstruction of some kind in the vocal tract, associated with consonants. Opposite **non-consonantal**.

CONSONANTAL ASSONANCE
See **CONSONANCE**.

CONSPIRACY
In 1970s **generative phonology**, a state of affairs in which two or more separate rules, each independently motivated, 'conspire' to produce a general phonological pattern expressed by none of the rules in question. E.g. a rule that deletes a **vowel** may conspire to change a pattern involving open syllables, CVCV, to a closed syllable, CVC. In Slavic, for instance, the verb *sûpatî*, where *û* and *î* represent extra-short vowels, was changed from a phonological structure with three CV syllables to a structure with an initial consonant cluster and a single closed syllable, *spat'*. See **SYLLABLE**.

CONSTANT
A symbol whose value does not change. In algebra, *4* is a constant, whereas *x* is a variable. In **logic**, symbols such as &, 'and', and ¬, 'negation', have a constant value, but letters of the alphabet have a varying value. E.g. in logic 'all alpacas' is rendered 'For all x, such that x is an alpaca'. *x* does not stand for a particular individual alpaca but for any alpaca that might be the topic of conversation.

CONSTATIVE
In early **speech act** theory, constatives were utterances that conveyed statements, questions and commands, that is, utterances that were used for reporting or questioning states of affairs or for requiring a particular state of affairs to be brought about or prevented. In contrast, performatives were utterances whose production was an essential part of some public ceremony.

CONSTITUENT
Any unit which is part of a larger unit. **Morphs** are constituents of **words**, words of **phrases**, phrases of **clauses**, clauses of **sentences**. See **CONSTITUENT STRUCTURE**.

CONSTITUENT NEGATION
Negation applying to a **word** or **phrase** in a **clause** but not to an entire clause or **sentence**; e.g. *You saw her not five minutes ago*, *The report is incomplete*.

CONSTITUENT SENTENCE
See **EMBEDDING**.

CONSTITUENT STRUCTURE
Especially in syntax, the structure of the **phrase**, **clause** and **sentence** are seen as consisting of a set of small units which are combined to form or constitute bigger units, which in turn are combined, and so on. The units making up a bigger unit are constituents. The grouping of smaller units into bigger units

produces structure consisting of different levels, with the smallest or ultimate constituents on the lowest level, bigger constituents on the next level up, and so on, with the biggest constituent on the highest level. This arrangement is known as hierarchical structure. Thus, as shown in Figure 'Constituent structure (a)', *about, the, very, complex* and *ideas* are the smallest constituents of *about the very complex ideas*. *Very* and *complex* are the immediate constituents of *very complex*; *very complex* and *ideas* are the immediate constituents of [*very complex*] *ideas*; *the* and *very complex ideas* are the immediate constituents of *the* [[*very complex*] *ideas*]; and *about* and *the very complex ideas* are the immediate constituents of the whole phrase: [[*about*] [*the very complex ideas*]]. The structure of a main clause is shown in Figure 'Constituent structure (b)'. The general relationship between constituents is called constituency, but this term also refers to the constituents and constituent structure of a given unit. See **DISTRIBUTION, EXPANSION, FRAME, PHRASE**.

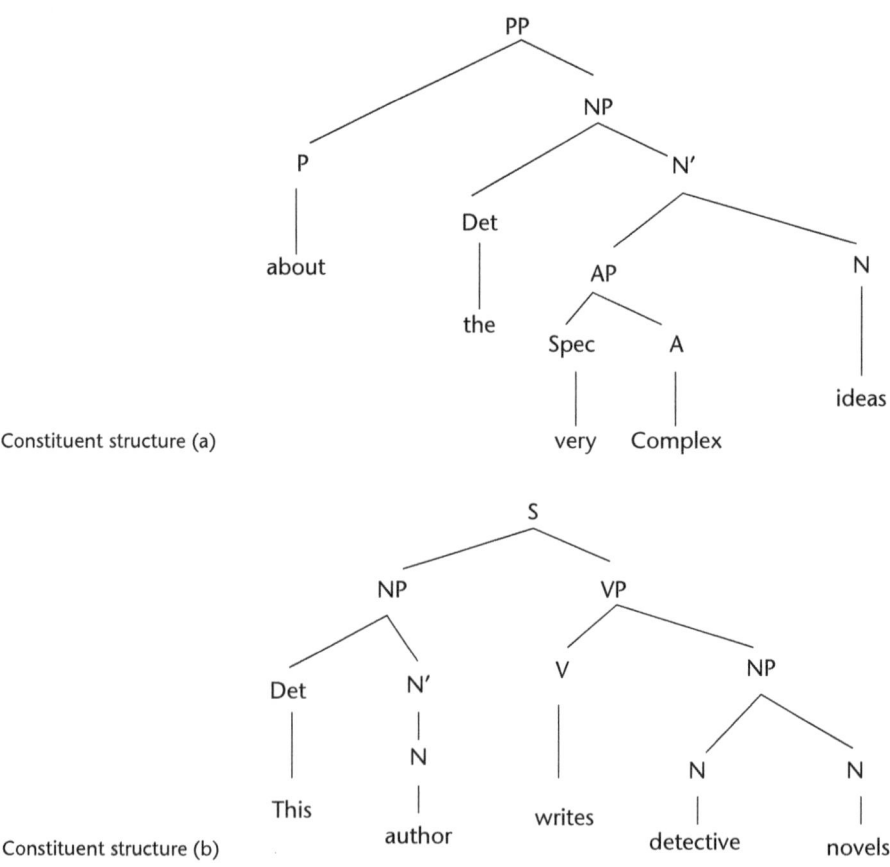

Constituent structure (a)

Constituent structure (b)

CONSTITUENT STRUCTURE GRAMMAR
A grammar that specifies **constituent structure**.

CONSTITUTIVE ROLE
One of the qualia roles in the theory of the dynamic lexicon. It relates to the perspective of how an entity is built up, the various parts it consists of. E.g. one can think of a European house as consisting of stones or bricks, planks of wood, tiles or slates, insulating material, doors and so on in contrast with a place to live in, bring children up in, and so on. See AGENTIVE ROLE, FORMAL ROLE, TELIC ROLE.

CONSTRAINT
1. A restriction, preferably as general as possible, limiting the operation of a rule. See COMPLEX NOUN PHRASE CONSTRAINT, CROSSOVER CONSTRAINT, SUBJACENCY CONDITION. 2. A restriction on, e.g., sequences of phonemes, words or phrases. *Mgl* is excluded as a word-initial sequence of phonemes in English but is allowed in Russian – *mgla* 'mist'. **Which have you read book?*, with modifier *which* separated from its head *book*, is excluded in English but is a possible order of words in Russian. See OPTIMALITY THEORY.

CONSTRICTED GLOTTIS
In SPE Distinctive Feature Theory, segments that are articulated with the the vocal cords held together, so that air cannot pass through, e.g. voiceless consonants, ejectives. See EJECTIVE.

CONSTRICTED
See SPE DISTINCTIVE FEATURE THEORY.

CONSTRICTION
In the description of the **articulation** of sounds, the narrowing of some part of the **vocal tract**. See STRICTURE.

CONSTRUAL
1. The act of construing a construction or a situation. 2. The mental representation of a situation resulting from an act of construing. See CONSTRUE 2, COGNITIVE GRAMMAR, DOMAIN 2, DOMAIN 3, DYNAMIC CONSTRUAL.

CONSTRUCT STATE
In Semitic languages certain **constructions**, such as **possessive** noun phrases and compound nouns, consist of two juxtaposed nouns. Some nouns take on a special form in these constructions. E.g. Arabic *'ilba* 'box' becomes *ilbit* in the construction *ilbit kabriit* 'box matches, a box of matches'. See COMPOUND WORD.

CONSTRUCTION
A pattern of units. Patterns can be described relative to the type of units – **noun, adverb, preposition** and so on, their shape, and their ordering – the

order or **words** in a phrase, **phrases** in a **clause** and, where possible, clauses in a **sentence**. Constructions are held to have meanings, called construction meanings, which are imposed on the combinations of lexical items that realize a particular construction. Some constructions, such as the 'let alone' one, have a highly idiosyncratic meaning, *I can't stand spiders, let alone scorpions*. Other constructions impose an interpretation on particular lexical items or phrases; e.g. *She sneezed the letter right off the table* can be seen as acquiring a caused-movement interpretation from the construction, although *sneeze* is not a verb of caused-movement such as *put* or *shove*. See **BASIC CONSTRUCTION, CONGRUENCE, AGREEMENT, GOVERNMENT, CONSTRAINT, CONSTRUCTION GRAMMAR**.

CONSTRUCTION GRAMMAR

Various models of grammar that take **constructions** as basic units of analysis. Constructional meaning plays an important role, and concepts such as **word classes** are related to particular constructions. An extreme view takes even the classic test of **distribution** to be unreliable because it cuts across many constructions. See **GRAMMATICAL MEANING**.

CONSTRUCTIONAL HOMONYMITY

See **GRAMMATICAL AMBIGUITY**.

CONSTRUE

1. (old-fashioned) To analyse the syntactic relationships in a **clause**, **sentence** or **phrase**. 2. In **cognitive linguistics**, to assign alternative structures to a domain or situation depending on perspective or viewpoint. For example, a picture of a river and a wood connected by a path can be construed 'A path runs down from the wood to the river' or 'A path runs up from the river to the wood'. See **COGNITIVE GRAMMAR, CONSTRUAL**.

CONSULTANT

See **INFORMANT**.

CONTACT CLAUSE

A finite subordinate **clause** that has no **complementizer** but is placed directly next to, in contact with, the word it modifies. E.g. *we watched* in *the programme we watched* and *Sabrina had won* in *They said Sabrina had won*. See **RELATIVE CLAUSE, RELATIVIZER**.

CONTACT LANGUAGE

A language used between speakers whose native languages differ. This often gives rise to a **pidgin**, which may itself become a contact language. See **CREOLE**.

CONTENT

The meaning of a **word**, **phrase** or **clause** as opposed to its form.

CONTENT CLAUSE
In **CGEL**, a very general type of **subordinate clause**.

CONTEXT
1. The linguistic context of a sound, **morph**, **word** and so on. E.g. in *Get over it*, *get* and *it* are the linguistic context of *over*. See **FRAME**. 2. The immediate context of an **utterance**, which consists of the physical surroundings in which a given utterance is produced. *Give that to me tomorrow* can only be understood with reference to this type of context: *that* refers to something known to the **speaker** and hearer, *me* refers to the speaker and *tomorrow* refers to the day after the one on which the dialogue takes place. This type of context is what enables the hearer (and eavesdropper) to interpret *Get over it* as 'Pull yourself together' and not as 'Climb over the wall'. 3. The background context of the general knowledge of the world held by speakers and hearers. See **COMMON GROUND, ADDRESSEE**.

CONTEXT-FREE
1. A type of **phrase structure grammar** in which the phrase structure rules apply regardless of **context**. E.g. the rule NP → Det N' applies whenever the symbol NP occurs and is interpreted as saying that a **noun phrase** consists of a **Determiner** followed by an N'. 2. A context-free language is a language (sequences of symbols) that can be generated by a context-free grammar. See **GENERATIVE RULE**.

CONTEXT OF SITUATION
See **CONTEXT**.

CONTEXT OF UTTERANCE
See **CONTEXT**.

CONTEXT-SENSITIVE
1. A type of **phrase structure grammar** in which an individual **phrase structure rule** applies in a particular context. E.g. the rule $V \rightarrow V_{plural}/NP_{plural}\_\_$ applies to a V only if the latter is preceded by a plural NP. 2. A context-sensitive language is a language (sequences of symbols) that can be generated by a context-sensitive grammar.

CONTEXTUAL ANCHORING
Deictic items need to be anchored to the immediate context of utterance to be correctly understood. A speaker can say *The box is this big and the flap tucks in like so*, but unless the deictic terms *this* and *so* are anchored to some gestures they cannot be interpreted. See **ANCHOR, ANCHORING, CONTEXT, DEIXIS**.

CONTEXTUAL VARIANT
See **CONDITIONED VARIANT**.

CONTIGUOUS
In phonetics, two or more adjacent consonants involving adjacent parts of the same articulator, e.g. [p] and [b], which are both labial. See **HOMORGANIC**.

CONTINUANT
1. A speech sound with no complete closure of the airstream within the vocal tract, e.g. **vowel, fricative**. Opposite **stop, non-continuant**. See **DISTINCTIVE FEATURES**. 2. In **SPE Distinctive Feature Theory**, segments that are produced with no significant obstruction in the vocal tract so that air passes through in a continuous stream. Non-continuous segments have some obstruction to the airflow at some point of articulation. See **ARTICULATION, PLACE OF ARTICULATION**.

CONTINUOUS
See **PROGRESSIVE**.

CONTOID
A **consonant** defined phonetically as a speech sound. To distinguish such sounds from phonological consonants.

CONTOUR
In **intonation**, a tone unit realized with a changing pitch, such as a fall, a rise or a fall-rise, etc. The term 'dynamic tone' is also used. See **CONTOUR TONE**.

CONTOUR TONE
A single tone realized with a changing pitch such as a fall, a rise and a fall-rise. The term 'dynamic tone' is also used. See **TONE GROUP, TONE UNIT**.

CONTOUR TONE LANGUAGE
A **tone language** that uses gliding tones, for instance **Chinese**. See **REGISTER TONE LANGUAGE**.

CONTRACTION
A short way of speaking or writing a sequence of words: *won't* for *will not*, *I'd've* for *I would have*, French *comme d'hab* for *comme d'habitude* 'as usual'.

CONTRADICTORY
1. Two **propositions** are contradictory if they cannot both be true or both be false. That is, each contradicts the other. E.g. of the propositions *The boy broke the window* and *The boy didn't break the window*, one must be true and the other one false. (*The boy* refers to the same person and *the window* to the same window.) Contradictory propositions can contain **complementaries** such as *dead* and *alive* or **reversives** such as *up* and *down*. Of the propositions *The plants are dead* and *The plants are alive* (assuming that in both propositions *the plants* refers to the same plants), one must be true and the other false. The same holds for *The lift is going up* and *The lift is going down*, assuming that the lift is moving. See **CONTRARY, OPPOSITENESS**.

CONTRARY

Two contrary **propositions** cannot both be true, but they can both be false. E.g. *My dog is small* and *My dog is large* cannot both be true, but the dog may be neither small nor large but just average size. Contrary propositions typically contain **gradable** opposites such as *small* and *large*. See **CONTRADICTORY**, **OPPOSITENESS**.

CONTRAST

The **opposition** between two or more phonetic segments in some particular environment and corresponding to different meanings. Each segment will be assigned to different **phonemes**. E.g. [b] in [bɪn] and [p] in [pɪn] are in contrast in the environment [-ɪn] and can be assigned to two different phonemes /b/ and /p/.

CONTRASTIVE DISTRIBUTION

A pattern of **distribution** in which two or more items occur in the same context and contrast in meaning. E.g. in Latin *laboro* 'I am working' and *laborat* 'He/She is working', *-o* and *-at* both occur in the context [*labor__*] and contrast in meaning, one being first **person** and the other third person. See **FRAME**.

CONTRASTIVE LINGUISTICS

See **COMPARATIVE LINGUISTICS**.

CONTRASTIVE STRESS

Stress placed on some element in order to contrast it with another.

CONTROL

The relation by which the **subject** or **object** of a **clause** containing a **non-finite clause** determines or controls the subject of the latter. E.g. in English *Bill agreed to leave*, *Bill* is the subject of *agreed* and the **understood subject** of *to leave*. In *They persuaded Fred to resign*, *Fred* is the object of *persuaded* and the understood subject of *resign*. Verbs such as *persuade* and *agree* are control verbs and *Bill* and *Fred* are controllers. See **MINIMAL DISTANCE PRINCIPLE**.

CONTROL THEORY

That component of the **Government and Binding Theory** model dealing with **control** relations. See **PRO**.

CONTROL VERB

See **CONTROL**.

CONTROLLER

See **CONTROL**.

CONVENTIONAL IMPLICATURE

See **IMPLICATURE**.

CONVENTIONAL SIGN

See **ARBITRARY SIGN**.

CONVENTIONALISM
See NOMINALISM.

CONVERB
A reduced form of verb, lacking tense and often **person** too, associated with **clause chaining**. See CHAINING STRUCTURE, TENSE AND ASPECT.

CONVERSATION ANALYSIS (CA)
1. The theory of how natural conversations are organized and successfully carried out. 2. The analysis of such conversations using audio and/or video recordings. Observation is given priority and general principles are established on the observed patterns. Classic CA focuses on the means by which an **interlocutor** takes turns at speaking, catches their interlocutor's attention, checks that their interlocutor is following, uses **backchannel** signals to indicate that their interlocutor's message has been understood, repairs misunderstandings, and keeps conversation coherent and cohesive. See ADJACENCY PAIRS, COHERENCE, COHESION, ETHNOMETHODOLOGY, EXCHANGE, INSERTION SEQUENCE, POSITION, PRE-SEQUENCE, STANCE, TRANSITION RELEVANCE PLACE, TURN.

CONVERSATIONAL IMPLICATURE
See IMPLICATURE.

CONVERSATIONAL INFERENCE
A prediction of what will follow at a particular stage in a conversation.

CONVERSATIONAL TURN
See TURN.

CONVERSES
Pairs of **lexical words** whose meanings are loosely opposed to each other. Their key property is that a **clause** containing one of the pair can be converted into a clause containing the other, but keeping all the other lexical words constant, with only a change of order. For example, brother and sister are converses: the converse of *Angus is Fiona's brother* is *Fiona is Angus' sister*. Lend and borrow are examples of converse verbs: *Angus lent money to Fiona* converts to *Fiona borrowed money from Angus*. See OPPOSITENESS.

CONVERSION
A process in **derivational morphology** by which a **form** changes its **word class** without the addition of an **affix** or other alteration in the **word** form such as changes in **vowel**, vowel **length** or **tone**. E.g. *John likes to garden, John has a large garden; They've upped the bank rate, Can you run up that hill?, I have my ups and downs but I'm OK*. The process is also known as zero-derivation; there are zero markers of the derivation of **verb** from **noun** or verb from **preposition**, etc. A third term is functional shift.

CO-OCCURRENCE

The relation between two or more items that can be present together in the same unit: e.g. two phonemes may co-occur in a **syllable**, two morphemes in a **word**, two words in a **phrase** and so on.

CO-OCCURRENCE RESTRICTION

Any restriction on which items can co-occur in a unit. Restrictions are usually stated either in terms of **features** on a **head** matching features on its **dependents** or in terms of features on a root node in a **tree diagram** determining features on its **daughter** nodes. See AGREEMENT, CO-OCCURRENCE, GOVERNMENT, SELECTIONAL RESTRICTION, STRICT SUBCATEGORIZATION.

COOPERATIVE PRINCIPLE

A principle proposed by Paul Grice to account for the inferences that **interlocutors** make in the course of conversation. For instance, the question *How much food has he in the house?* and the answer *Even the mice have decamped* will lead the questioner to infer that there is no food at all in the house. Such inferences are not sanctioned by classical **logic**. The principle is stated thus by Grice: Make your conversational contribution such as is required, at the stage at which it occurs, by the accepted purpose or direction of the talk exchange in which you are engaged. The principle is elaborated by four **maxims of conversation**. See CALCULUS, ENTAILMENT, INDUCTION, PREMISE.

COORDINATE BILINGUALISM

A form of **bilingualism** in which a speaker has two different sets of concepts each related to a different set of words in two different languages. See COMPOUND BILINGUALISM.

COORDINATE CLAUSE

See CONJUNCTION.

COORDINATE STRUCTURE

A structure containing two or more **words** or **phrases** joined by a coordinating **conjunction**: e.g. *bought tea and coffee, washed and dried* the dishes.

COORDINATE STRUCTURE CONSTRAINT

In **transformational grammar**, a constraint preventing the movement of, e.g., wh constituents out of a **coordinate structure**. E.g. in *Jennifer has sold her house and her old car*, *her car* cannot be extracted and questioned. *Which car has Jennifer sold her house and?*

COORDINATING CONJUNCTION

See CONJUNCTION.

COORDINATION

A type of linkage between **words**, **phrases** and **clauses**. See CONJUNCTION.

COORDINATOR

See **COORDINATING CONJUNCTION**.

COPTIC

See **EGYPTIAN**.

COPULA

A verb that has no **content** but simply links two words or phrases. The classic copula is *be* in English and its equivalent in other languages. Several copula constructions are recognized: the **equative** one identifies one entity with another – *That elegant woman is my wife*; the ascriptive one assigns (or ascribes) a property to an entity – *My wife is elegant*; the **locative** one expresses location – *My wife is in York*. Some languages have no copula, especially in the present tense, as in Russian *moja zhena shotlandka* 'my wife Scot, My wife is a Scot'. A fourth construction is the **existential**, as in *There is a snake in the garden*. (Latin *copula* 'rope, connection'.)

COPY TAG

See **TAG QUESTION**.

COPYING

1. A general process by which **features** are copied from one constituent to another. E.g. **agreement** can be thought of as the copying of features from the head noun in a **noun phrase** to the **adjectives** that modify it. 2. In the **Minimalist Program** copying is the device for handling **movement**. Given two constituents X and Y that can occur in the order XY or the order YX, a basic order is chosen, say XY, a copy is created of X, giving XYX, and the first X is realized as zero. Copying replaces the use of **traces** in the **Government and Binding Theory** and **Principles and Parameters** models. See **AGREEMENT**, **MINIMALIST PROGRAM**, **REALIZATION**.

CORE (OF A CLAUSE)

The core of a **clause** consists of the **verb** plus any obligatory **arguments**. See **NUCLEUS**.

CORE GRAMMAR

In the Government and Binding and **Principles and Parameters** models, the **constructions** in the grammar that are determined directly by the principles of **universal grammar** and the setting of **parameters**. Any other constructions are said to be on the periphery of the grammar. See **LINGUISTIC UNIVERSALS**.

COREFERENCE

Two **noun phrases** that refer to the same entity are said to be **coreferential** or in a relationship of coreference. In *Folkestone is expanding. The Channel port is busier than ever*, the full noun phrases *Folkestone* and *the Channel port* are coreferential. In *Gordon had had a trying day. He had been rebuffed by Alastair*, the full noun phrase *Gordon* and the pronoun *he* are coreferential.

COREFERENTIAL

Referring to the same referent. Full noun phrases may be coreferential – *the woman Angus married* and *Angus' wife* – and a full noun phrase and a pronoun – *my sister* and *she* in *I invited my sister but she couldn't come.*

CORNISH

Celtic, Indo-European. Approx. 600 speakers. Closely related to **Welsh** and **Breton** and less closely to **Irish Gaelic** and **Scottish Gaelic**. Died out in the late eighteenth century but has recently been revived.

CORONAL

1. In **phonetics**, a **segment** articulated with the **tip** or **blade** of the **tongue** raised, that is, **alveolar, dental** or **alveo-palatal**. 2. In **SPE distinctive feature theory**, a cavity feature, a property of segments that are articulated with the tip or blade of the tongue raised and fronted, for example [t], [n] or [s].

CORPUS

A collection of **texts**, originally stored in writing on paper or card but nowadays stored in digital form. A corpus is not random but a collection of texts representing the same medium, spoken or written, and/or the same types of texts or genres and in the same quantities. For example, the Australian contribution to the International Corpus of English consists of 2,000 word samples, 200 of spoken English and 300 of written English. The spoken samples are of dialogue, private and public, and monologue, scripted and unscripted. News broadcasts are classed as scripted, discussion programmes as unscripted. See **DIMENSION, GENRE, REGISTER.**

CORPUS LINGUISTICS

1. The study of language on the basis of data from corpora. 2. The development and application of techniques for collecting digital corpora, annotating them, and extracting lexical and grammatical patterns and interpreting the patterns statistically.

CORRELATION

In **Prague School** phonology a set of **oppositions** characterized by the same feature. Thus [p], [t], [k] are in opposition to [b], [d], [g] by the correlation of voice.

CORRELATIVE

Any two-part **construction**, the parts being **clauses** or **phrases** and containing parallel, linking **pronouns** or adverbs. E.g. *where* and *there* in *Where the bee sucks, there suck I*; *kto* and *tot* in Russian *kto pozvonit, tot uznaet* 'Who phones, that-one will-find-out'; *as* and *so* in *As you sow, so shall you reap.*

CORRELATIVE CONJUNCTIONS

Conjunctions linking the two parts of a **correlative** construction: *if* and *then* in *If she resigns, then I will stay*; *either* and *or* in *Either the python goes or I go.*

CORRESPONDENCE
See **SOUND CORRESPONDENCE**.

CORRESPONDENCE THEORY
The theory that a **proposition** is true only if it corresponds to some objective state of the world. See **COGNITIVE SEMANTICS, CONSTRUAL, CONSTRUE, DYNAMIC CONSTRUAL, TRUTH CONDITIONS**.

COSUBORDINATION
See **SUBORDINATION**.

CO-TEXT
May be taken as equivalent to **context 1**, but is also understood as the larger textual context of some piece of text. For example, the co-text of a line of poetry can be the whole poem or the particular stanza in which it occurs; the co-text of a **clause** in a novel can be the **sentence** in which it occurs or the entire paragraph or even chapter.

COUNT NOUN
A noun denoting an individual entity that can be counted; e.g. *book – five books, child – two children, car – many cars*. See **MASS NOUN**.

COUNTABLE NOUN
See **COUNT NOUN**.

COUNTER-AGENT
See **ANTAGONIST**.

COUNTERFACTUAL
A conditional construction in which the **conditional clause** expresses a condition that can no longer be met and the main clause expresses an event or state which can no longer come about because it depended on the condition being met. In English the conditional clause contains a past perfect verb, which in main **clauses** locates a situation in remote past time but in the conditional locates it as remote from reality. The main clause contains the **past tense** of *will* or *shall* and the **past perfect**. E.g. *If he had been fit, we would have won (but there's nothing we can do about it now)*.

COVERT
A **grammatical category** not apparent from observable forms but relevant to the grammar of a language. Thus **gender** is covert in French since it is not overtly marked on nouns but is marked in agreement patterns in articles and adjectives etc. In English, **transformational** relationships between sentence types, e.g. active and passive, are covert, since you cannot from a surface inspection determine whether a particular verb will occur in the passive. See **VOICE**.

COVERT PRESTIGE
See **PRESTIGE**.

CP
See **COMPLEMENTIZER PHRASE**.

CRANBERRY MORPH
A bound **morph** such as *cran* in *cranberry* that occurs in only one combination. *Kith* in *kith and kin* and *-ric* in *bishopric* have been cited as possible examples.

CREAK
See **CREAKY VOICE**.

CREAKY VOICE
In the classification of **voice quality**, the auditory effect produced by the slow vibration of the **vocal cords**. It is a permanent feature of the speech of some individuals, but is usually used for **paralinguistic** effect.

CREE
Algonquian. Approx. 20K speakers, Canada (subarctic, northern prairies).

CREEK
Muskogean. Approx. 6K speakers. Once widely spoken in the south-eastern United States, now spoken mainly in Oklahoma.

CREOLE
Historically a **pidgin** language, but one which has over time acquired a community of native speakers, and thus has become a **native language**, or a **first language**. The reduction processes associated with pidginization are usually partially reversed.

CRITICAL APPLIED LINGUISTICS
The use of applied linguistics in projects for the transformation of society.

CRITICAL APPRECIATION
See **PRACTICAL CRITICISM**.

CRITICAL DISCOURSE ANALYSIS
The analysis of texts in relation to social and political structures and power, especially in the light of Marxist theory. See **CRITICAL LANGUAGE AWARENESS**, **CRITICAL LINGUISTICS**.

CRITICAL LANGUAGE AWARENESS
Awareness of the linguistic choices open to speakers and the possible ideological reasons for doing so; e.g. the use of the passive **construction** to avoid mentioning agents, the use of *convener* instead of *chairman*. See **VOICE**.

CRITICAL LINGUISTICS

The application of linguistics in the analysis of texts such as state propaganda, pamphlets supporting political parties and advertisements. See **critical language awareness**, **critical discourse analysis**.

CROSS-CULTURAL COMMUNICATION

The study of how individuals from different cultures communicate with each other.

CROSSOVER CONSTRAINT

A constraint preventing two **noun phrases** referring to the same person from 'crossing over' each other in a **clause** or **sentence**. E.g. in *I hated myself for failing to help them*, *I* and *myself* both refer to the speaker but cannot cross over each other to give **Myself was hated by me for failing to help them*. See **CONSTRAINT**.

CROW

Siouan. Approx. 4K speakers, south-east Montana.

CS

See **CONTEXT-SENSITIVE**.

C-STRUCTURE

In **Lexical-Functional Grammar**, the component that handles **constituent structure**.

CUED SPEECH

A system of communication used with the deaf or hard of hearing to make spoken language more accessible by supplementing it with handshapes representing **consonants** and **vowels**.

CUMULATION

The 'piling up' of two or more morphemes, realized by a single **morph**. In the Russian noun *rabota* 'work', the suffix *-a* realizes the morphemes singular **number**, feminine **gender** and nominative **case**.

CUMULATIVE

A lexical aspect or **Aktionsart** denoting events in which a certain amount of something is accumulated: Russian *kupit'* 'buy', *nakupit'* 'buy a quantity of', e.g. *nakupit' knig* 'buy a-number-of-books'.

CURLY BRACKETS

See **BRACKET**.

CURTIUS, Georg (1820–1885)

A German linguist who taught some of the leading **Neogrammarians** and established a lasting reputation through his research on Greek **etymology**, **comparative linguistics** and **sound change**.

CUSHITIC

A branch of **Afroasiatic** spoken in Eritrea, Ethiopia, Djibouti and Somalia. It contains about thirty languages including **Somali** and **Oromo**.

CV

A notation representing the sequence of **consonant** and **vowel** types in a **syllable**. CV represents a syllable consisting of a single consonant followed by a vowel, e.g. *go*. Compare CVC, a syllable consisting of a single consonant followed by a vowel followed by a single consonant, e.g. *got*, or CCV, a syllable consisting of two consonants followed by a vowel, *stop*, etc.

CV PHONOLOGY

See **autosegmental phonology**.

CV TIER

See AUTOSEGMENTAL PHONOLOGY, SKELETAL TIER.

CVC

See CV.

CYBERNETICS

The study of communication and control systems, especially comparing the capacities of humans in comparison with computers and other electronic devices.

CYCLE

See CYCLIC PRINCIPLE.

CYCLIC NODE

See CYCLIC PRINCIPLE.

CYCLIC PRINCIPLE

Especially in **transformational grammar** of the 1960s, a principle whereby a set of rules applies first to the smallest relevant constituent, then to the next largest and so on. Figure 'Cyclic Principle (a)' (see overleaf) shows the structure of *The mole revealed the report that the bank made big losses*. Various rules apply to the smallest **sentence**, S_2, to create the passive *big losses were made* (as in Figure 'Cyclic Principle (b)') and then apply to the bigger sentence, S_1, to create the passive *The report that big losses were made by the bank was revealed by the mole*. The structure of S_1 is shown in Figure 'Cyclic Principle (c)'. The various rules are said to apply in a cycle, especially to the cyclic nodes S and NP. See CONSTITUENT STRUCTURE, PHASE, TRANSFORMATION.

118 CYCLIC PRINCIPLE

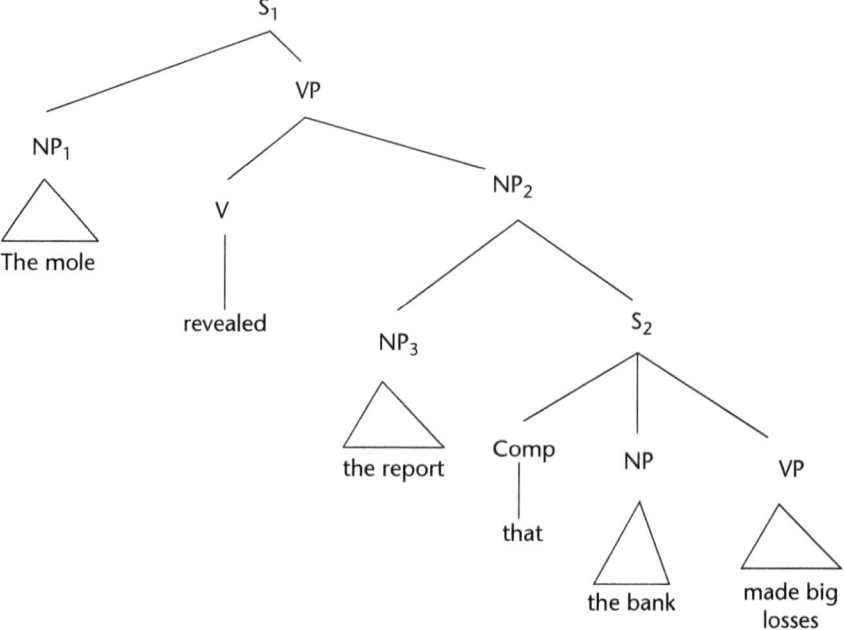

Cyclic Principle (a)

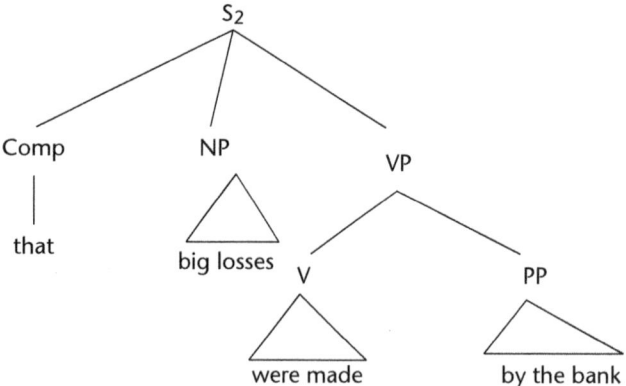

Cyclic Principle (b)

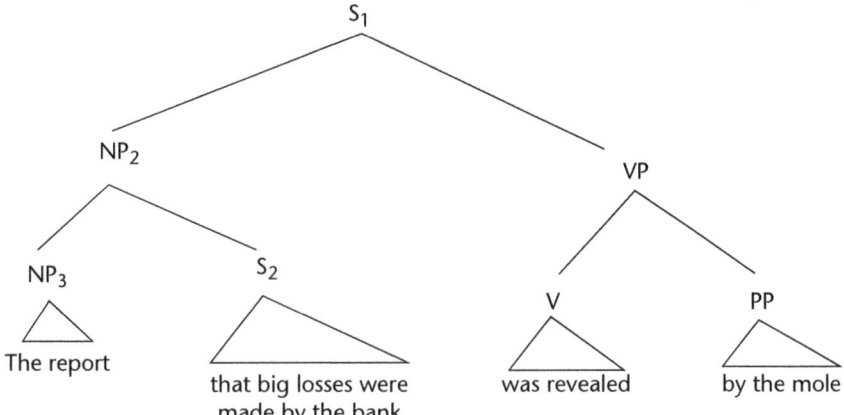

Cyclic Principle (c)

CYCLIC RULES

In **transformational grammar** of the 1960s, transformational rules that apply in a cycle and in the same order within the cycle. See **CYCLIC PRINCIPLE**, **TRANSFORMATION**.

CZECH

Slavic, Indo-European. Approx. 10M speakers, Czech Republic.

D

DA
See DISCOURSE ANALYSIS.

DACTYL
See FOOT.

DAF
See DELAYED AUDITORY FEEDBACK.

DALGARNO, George (c. 1619–1687)
A Scottish philosopher who worked on a philosophical language in which each symbol was to correspond to a universal concept. He had the modern idea of having a small number of basic symbols which could be combined to produce complex symbols.

DANGLING PARTICIPLE
An **absolute construction** in which the **understood subject** of a **participle** does not match the subject of the **clause** it modifies: *Flying over Australia, the turbulence was terrifying* (= *As we were flying…*). *We* does not match *turbulence*. The **construction** is condemned by prescriptivists but is so widely used as to be an unofficial norm. See **DEPENDENCY, MODIFIER**.

DANISH
Germanic, Indo-European. Approx. 5.5M speakers Denmark, approx. 50K North Germany. The second language of people in the Faroe Islands and Greenland.

DARI
Indo-Iranian, Indo-European. Approx. 15M speakers, North-West Pakistan, Kashmir and Afghanistan.

DARK
A velarized **lateral**, [ɫ] as in the pronunciation of *bottle* as [bɔtɫ]. Opposite **clear**. Typical of **Estuary English**. See **VELARIZATION**.

DATABASE
A collection of data, especially for computer analysis.

DATIVE
Case marking signalling a **recipient**: e.g. Latin *miles* soldier-NOM vs *militi* soldier-DAT as in *Marcus militi gladium dedit* Marcus-NOM soldier-DAT sword-ACC

give-PST 'Marcus gave the soldier a sword'. The dative case in classical **Greek** occurs with **prepositions** of place, and the dative in **Turkish** signals both transfer of items to a person and movement to a place, e.g. *adam* 'man' – *adama* 'to the man', *Ankara* – *Ankaraya* 'to Ankara'.

DAUGHTER
In a **phrase structure tree**, a **node** A hanging from a node B is a daughter of B.

DAUGHTER DEPENDENCY GRAMMAR
A type of **dependency grammar** that developed into **Word Grammar**.

DAUGHTER LANGUAGE
A language descended from a parent language. Thus French and Italian are daughters of Latin.

DE DICTO
See **ATTRIBUTIVE**.

DE RE
See **ATTRIBUTIVE**.

DEAD LANGUAGE
A language, such as Latin, that is no longer in everyday spoken use. See **LANGUAGE DEATH**.

DEAD METAPHOR
A metaphor that is no longer perceived as one because of language change or overuse. E.g. *to be a tower of strength, we're scuppered*.

DE-ADJECTIVAL
Formed from an **adjective**. E.g. the **noun** *rapidity* derives from *rapid*; the **verb** *deafen* derives from *deaf*. See **DERIVATIONAL MORPHOLOGY**.

DEAF-BLINDNESS
Concomitant visual and hearing impairments.

DEAFNESS
Hearing loss. Prelinguistic hearing loss generally involves slower **language acquisition** in phonology, lexicon and syntax. Profoundly deaf children often encounter literacy problems.

DE-AUTOMATIZATION
The process, and its result, of making users aware of the form and content of language that has been blunted by frequent and automatic use in everyday communication.

DECIBEL
The unit used in **acoustics** for expressing the **intensity** of a sound relative to a reference point, usually set as the average human threshold of perception.

DECISION PROCEDURE
In **Chomsky's** mathematical work of the 1950s, a procedure that would determine whether a given grammar was the best for a particular language.

DECLARATIVE
1. A **clause** that is used primarily to make **statements**. See **MODALITY**.
2. A type of formal grammar in which rules that generate structures are replaced by declarations of **constraints** on possible structures. The latter determine whether sentences are **well-formed**. See **OPTIMALITY THEORY**. 3. In Searle's classification of speech acts, a speech act that brings about a change in some situation. This is Searle's equivalent of Austin's original ceremonial **performatives**, such as marrying, passing judgement in court, nominating a candidate. See **ASSERTIVE, COMMISSIVE, DIRECTIVE, EXPRESSIVE, SPEECH ACT**.

DECLENSION
For a given **noun, pronoun** or **adjective**, the set of its forms, each consisting of a **stem** and a **suffix**. Also a set of nouns, etc. that take the same affixes. E.g. nouns of the 'second declension' in Latin have the **nominative** suffix -*us*, the **accusative** suffix -*um*, nouns of the first declension have the nominative suffix -*a*, the accusative suffix -*am* and so on.

DECLINE
To take **affixes** or **inflections**. In **Latin, Greek, Russian** and other languages **nouns, pronouns** and **adjectives** are said to decline. (From the Latin verb meaning 'fall away'. The underlying metaphor is of nominative case, the case of subject nouns, as the upright case from which the other cases represent a falling away.)

DECODING
The interpretation of a message.

DECONSTRUCTION
An approach to the analysis of texts that plays down the role of linguistic structure and focuses on whatever assumptions and prejudices and intentions might lie concealed in texts. See **POST-STRUCTURALISM**.

DECONSTRUCTIONIST
A proponent of deconstruction or an analysis informed by the theories and methods of deconstruction.

DECONTEXTUALIZE
To analyse language without taking account of the **context** in which particular examples have been used or might be used. It is a moot point whether sentences can be judged grammatical or not if taken out of context. See **GRAMMATICALITY**.

DECREOLIZATION

The process whereby a **creole** language comes to take on features of the **standard language**. See **POST CREOLE CONTINUUM**.

DEDUCTION

A process of reasoning which begins with a general **proposition**, say *All cars of make X are reliable*. The next proposition is a particular one, about a particular car: *This car is of make X*. The third proposition is deduced from the combination of the first two: *This car is reliable*. Two of the major principles governing deduction are the *modus ponens* and the *modus tollens*. By the first, if proposition q follows from proposition p, and if p is true, then q is true. By the second, if proposition q follows from proposition p, and if q is false, then p is false. Given *Freya has grown* and *Freya is bigger than she was*, if the first is true, the second must also be true. But if the second is false, i.e. Freya is not *bigger* than she was, then the first is not true either. (Latin: *modus* 'mode' *ponendo ponens* 'by-placing placing'; i.e. by placing p, you can also place q. *tollendo tollens* 'by-removing removing'; i.e. by removing q, you can also remove p.) See **ABDUCTION, HYPOTHETICO-DEDUCTIVE, INDUCTION**.

DEEP STRUCTURE

Especially in **Chomsky's transformational grammar** of the 1960s, the most abstract level of structure from which surface structure was derived. E.g. a **clause** in deep structure had constituents in the order for an active **declarative** clause and transformational rules transformed the deep structure into the surface structure of a passive, **interrogative clause** and so on. An example such as *This novel was written by Dickens* was derived from a deep structure 'Dickens wrote this novel'. This showed the logical relationship between *Dickens* and *this novel* (**direct object**). Deep structure was held to determine the semantic interpretation of a **sentence**, but by the mid 1970s it had been renamed D-structure and was thought to play no part in **semantics**. D-structure was abandoned completely in the **Minimalist Program**. See **TRANSFORMATION, VOICE**.

DE-FAMILIARIZATION

See **DE-AUTOMATIZATION**

DEFAULT

When no special conditions apply, the default is the type of constituents that occur, the order in which they occur, the **rule** that applies, the meaning that is understood. Thus in English **plural** formation, if no special rule applies (vowel change as in *man:men*; no alternation as in *sheep:sheep*, etc), the default formation /-s – -z – ɪz/ applies (*cat-s; dog-s; hors-es*). In this case the default is also the regular formation. In written English the past tense of verbs is formed with *-ed* unless the verb is a strong one such as *swim*. The interpretation of a declarative **clause** is that the speaker is making a statement, unless the context makes it clear that the speaker is really giving a command: *It's very draughty in here* (= *Shut the door!*).

DEFAULT MEANING

The interpretation assigned to **lexical words** or to **grammatical categories**, other things being equal. Thus, in, e.g., *Mary baked a cake for her mother* the interpretation of the **Simple Past** tense that comes to mind first is of a single event. Replace *a cake* with *cakes*, and the interpretation as a **habitual** event becomes possible. Add a phrase such as *on Saturdays*, and the habitual interpretation is the only one. Similarly, if asked to draw a picture of the situation denoted by *I saw a cat*, children draw a domestic cat. This is the default meaning of *cat*, although it also denotes lions and tigers. See **DENOTATION**.

DEFECTIVE

A **lexical word** that does not take the full set of **affixes** available to members of its class. E.g. French *falloir* 'be necessary' only has third-person singular forms. See **NUMBER, PERSON**.

DEFINING RELATIVE

See **RELATIVE CLAUSE**.

DEFINITE ARTICLE

A **determiner** attached to a **noun phrase** to indicate that the noun phrase refers to an entity that the hearer can pick out in context: *the dog*. Not all languages have definite articles; many signal definiteness by **case** affixes or by **word order**. Different languages with definite articles have different patterns. In Italian definite articles combine with proper nouns – *il Giorgio* 'the George', i.e. 'George'; in English they do not. See **INDEFINITE NOUN PHRASE, PROPER NOUN, REFERENCE**.

DEFINITE DESCRIPTION

In philosophy, any definite **noun phrase**, that is, any noun phrase containing a **definite article** (*the girl I saw you with yesterday*), a **demonstrative** (*those noisy neighbours upstairs*), a **possessive pronoun** (*your brother*), a **pronoun** or a proper name (*Dave*). Such phrases refer to entities that the speaker thinks can be easily identified by the listener. See **COMMON NOUN, DEIXIS, GIVEN AND NEW**.

DEFINITE NOUN PHRASE

See **NOUN PHRASE**.

DEFINITE REFERENCE

See **REFERENCE**.

DEFINITE REFERRING EXPRESSION

See **REFERENCE**.

DEFOCUSING

See **BACKGROUNDING**.

DE-GRAMMMATICALIZATION

The process by which items such as **affixes** are converted into **clitics** or full **lexical words**. E.g. *ism* in English in such examples as *What a long list of new isms*. The process is far less frequent than **grammaticalization**.

DEGREE

A property of **adjectives** showing the extent or degree to which an entity has some property. The positive degree signals that an entity has some property: *The garden is big/pleasant*. The **comparative** degree signals that an entity possesses a property to a greater degree than another entity (*The garden is bigger than theirs*) or than at another time, past or future (*The garden is bigger than it was*.) The **superlative** degree signals that an entity possesses a property to a greater extent than all the other entities in a set (*The garden is the biggest in the street*) or simply in the highest degree (*The garden is most pleasant*).

DEGREE ADVERB

An **adverb** that specifies the degree to which an entity has some property. See **INTENSIFIER**.

DEICTIC

A word that has a pointing function that is used in deixis.

DEIXIS

The use of certain linguistic items to refer to entities by pointing at them linguistically instead of providing information about their type, size, colour and so on. E.g. in context speakers can say *Could you pass me that?* rather than *Could you pass me the large, red notebook?*. Items that can be used for such linguistic pointing are deictic items or deictic categories. They include **demonstratives** – *this* vs *that*, **personal pronouns** – *I* points to the **speaker**, *you* to the hearer, and *he, she, it* and *they* to persons other than speaker and hearer, the adverbs of place *here* and *there*, tense (indicates time relative to the time at which the speaker is speaking). See **ANAPHORA, CANONICAL ORIENTATION, CATAPHORA, DEFINITE DESCRIPTION, DEMONSTRATIVE, DISCOURSE DEIXIS, EXOPHORA, SOCIAL DEIXIS**.

DELAYED AUDITORY FEEDBACK

An experimental technique where subjects hear their own speech with a short time delay.

DELAYED RELEASE

1. The gradual release of breath in a **fricative consonant** distinguishing an **affricate** [+delayed release] from a **plosive** [−delayed release]. 2. In SPE **Distinctive Feature Theory** this feature differentiates between a **stop** and an **affricate**. See **DISTINCTIVE FEATURES, ARTICULATORY**.

DELAYED VOICE ONSET TIME

In the articulation of a voiceless plosive consonant, the period between the release of the plosive and the start of voicing of a following voiced segment can be delayed. See **VOICE ONSET TIME**.

DELBRÜCK, Berthold (1842–1922)

A German linguist who was a leading **Neogrammarian**. He produced outstanding research in syntax and wrote a classic introduction to Neogrammarian theory.

DELETION

In **syntax**, removing from a piece of syntactic structure a constituent A that is (almost) identical with another constituent B. B usually precedes A. E.g. *She asked me to write the report and I am (writing the report)*. See **EQUI-NP-DELETION**.

DELICACY

In **Systemic Functional Grammar**, the term relating to the amount of detail in an analysis; the more detail, the more delicate the analysis.

DELIMITATIVE

A type of lexical aspect or **Aktionsart** expressing limits on the duration of a situation: Russian *rabotat'* 'to work', *porabotat'* 'to do a bit of work'.

DEMENTIA

Cognitive dysfunction due to the deterioration of the brain, often associated with ageing. Depending on which area of the brain is affected, it may affect language (**grammar**, **lexicon**, etc.) or cognitive function (memory, attention, etc.) or both. See **ALZHEIMER'S DISEASE**.

DEMONSTRATIVE

A **pronoun** or **determiner** that is used to point to entities, locating them as near to or remote from the speaker *this watch* vs *that watch* (and archaically, *yonder castle*), *not this but that*. See **DEIXIS**.

DEMOTE

Especially in **Relational Grammar**, to change the **grammatical function** or **grammatical relation** of a **noun phrase** so that it is lower on the hierarchy of grammatical relations, **subject** being the highest and **oblique** object the lowest. E.g. in the change from the **active** construction, as in *Bill repaired the car*, to the **passive**, *The car was repaired by Bill*, *Bill* is demoted from subject to oblique object and *the car* is promoted from direct object to subject. See **RELATIONAL GRAMMAR, VOICE**.

DEMOTION

See **DEMOTE**.

DENOMINAL

Formed from a **noun**. E.g. the **adjective** *successful* derives from the noun *success*, the verb *beautify* derives from the noun *beauty*. Not all denominal words have an **affix**: *butter (the bread)* derives from the noun *butter*. See **DERIVATIONAL MORPHOLOGY**.

DENOTATION

1. The relation between a **lexical word** and set of entities to which speakers can refer using that lexical word. 2. The set of entities to which speakers can refer using that lexical word. It can be understood as information about the **extension** or **intension** of lexical words. Thus, the lexical word *kiwi* denotes the class of such birds. Denotation differs from reference. In order to carry out the act of referring to a particular kiwi, speakers and writers of English have to combine the lexical word *kiwi* with an **article**, a **demonstrative** or a **possessive pronoun**: *the kiwi, (I've just seen) a kiwi, this kiwi, your kiwi*. Denotation also differs from **sense**, which has to do with the network of relations among lexical items. See **DEFINITE ARTICLE, DENOTATUM, MORPH, REFERENCE**.

DENOTATUM

Equivalent to **denotation**. The denotatum of the lexical item *kiwi* is the set of kiwis, the denotatum of *nocturnal* is the set of nocturnal entities. (Alternatively, a property of certain entities.) *Kiwi* is said to denote a class of birds, *nocturnal* is said to denote either a property or a class of entities.

DENOTE

See **DENOTATUM**.

DÉNOUEMENT

The outcome of a series of events, either in real life or in fiction.

DENTAL

A term in the description of the **place of articulation** of **consonant** sounds. The **tip** of the **tongue** comes against the teeth as in the voiceless **dental fricative** [θ], as in *thigh*; or the voiced dental fricative [ð] as in *thy*. Where there is no special IPA symbol the subscript [̪] is used; as in the representation of some articulations of Irish English [t̪] and [d̪] corresponding to the alveolar articulation of received pronunciation [t] and [d]. See **ARTICULATION, CONSONANT, PLACE OF ARTICULATION**.

DEONTIC MODALITY

See **MODALITY**.

DEPENDENCY

In a **construction**, the relationship between the **head** and the items that **modify** it. These depend on the head (and imply it): e.g. in the English **noun phrase** *the big house*, *the* and *big* depend on *house*, and *the big* by themselves imply that there is a noun that they modify.

DEPENDENCY GRAMMAR

Any grammar that takes **dependency** relations as primary and represents **syntactic structure** by means of trees or strings of words showing dependencies rather than **constituent structure**. See CONSTRUCTION, VERB DEPENDENCY GRAMMAR.

DEPENDENCY PHONOLOGY

A **non-linear phonology** that centres around the structure of the **syllable**. This typically has a **vowel** as **head** since this is the **sonority peak** of the syllable, is perceptually most salient, and is the focus for **tone** or **stress**. Syllable onsets and coda are seen as dependents on the head. The dependencies are usually represented in a tree structure. Dependency phonology also concerns itself with **feature geometry**. See DEPENDENCY GRAMMAR, FEATURE GEOMETRY.

DEPENDENT

Any unit that is dependent on another. In a **noun phrase** any **determiner** or **adjective** is a dependent of the **noun**. Subordinate **clauses** are dependents: **relative clauses** are dependent on nouns, **complement clauses** are dependent on verbs, nouns or adjectives; **adverbial clauses** are dependent on other clauses.

DEPENDENT CLAUSE

A clause that is dependent on a head, typically a noun (**relative clause, noun complement clause**) or a verb (**complement clause**). See DEPENDENCY, DEPENDENT.

DEPENDENT-MARKING

Marking dependencies on the dependent items in a **construction**. E.g. in the Russian **prepositional phrase** *v Moskvu* 'to Moscow', the fact that *Moskvu* is dependent on *v* 'to' is marked by the **accusative** case suffix *-u*. See CASE, HEAD-MARKING.

DEPONENT VERB

Especially in **Latin**, a verb that is **passive** in form but **active** in meaning, such as *utor* 'I use' (vs *rego* 'I rule', which is active in both form and meaning). The term is sometimes used for any verb whose **morphology** does not match its meaning.

DEPTH HYPOTHESIS

The hypothesis that **left-branching** structures are more difficult to process than **right-branching** ones.

DERIVATION

1. A sequence of steps by which one structure is 'created' or derived from another. E.g. in **transformational grammar** the sentence *What will Fiona choose* has in its derivation the strings *Fiona will choose what, what Fiona will choose, What will Fiona choose?*. In written English *drummer* might have the derivation *drum+ er, drummer*. 2. The process by which affixes are added to roots and stems to build

up new **lexical words**. Thus, the prefix *re-* is added to the root *write* to create the stem *rewrite* realizing the lexical item *rewrite*. To this stem can be added the suffix *-able*, to create the stem *rewriteable* realizing the lexical word *rewriteable*. See DERIVATIONAL MORPHOLOGY, INFLECTION.

DERIVATIONAL MORPHOLOGY

The processes by which new **lexical words** are created from **stems** and **roots**. The branch of **morphology** that is concerned with these processes. E.g. the addition of the **suffix** *-hood* to the stem *child* yields *childhood*. The addition of *-ion* to *educate* yields *education*. *-hood* is class-maintaining, in that it does not change the class of the stem to which it is added. *Child* is a noun and so is *childhood*. *-ion* is class-changing in that it changes the class of the stem to which it is added. *Educate* is a verb, *education* is a noun. **Prefixes** also play a role in derivational morphology; for instance, the addition of *re-* to the stem *write* yields *rewrite*. An alternative term for these processes is word formation. See INFLECTION, MORPH.

DERIVATIONAL NEGATION

Negation signalled by the presence of a negative affix; e.g. *un* in *unworthy*, *in* in *incomplete*, *non* in *non-alcoholic*. See CONSTITUENT NEGATION, CLAUSAL NEGATION.

DERIVATIVE

A form produced by a derivational process. See DERIVATION.

DERIVE

See DERIVATION.

DERIVED STRUCTURE

In early **transformational grammar**, a structure produced as the result of a **derivation**. Passive sentences were derived structures, being derived from the structure of active sentences: e.g. *Susan pushed him aside* → *He was pushed aside by Susan*. See VOICE.

DESCRIPTIVE ADEQUACY

See ADEQUACY.

DESCRIPTIVE GRAMMAR

1. A systematic, complete and objective account of the facts of a language, based on the usage of native speakers, at a given point in time and without giving rules for how it is assumed the language ought to be used. This approach contrasts with **prescriptive grammar**. 2. A grammar that uses well-defined concepts to analyse and describe a set of data without setting the analysis within a formal model such as some type of generative grammar. See ADEQUACY.

DESCRIPTIVE LINGUISTICS
That branch of linguistics focusing on a synchronic, as opposed to a historic description of a language. Often opposed to **prescriptive** and **theoretical linguistics**. See DESCRIPTIVE GRAMMAR.

DESCRIPTIVE MEANING
Also called cognitive meaning, ideational meaning and propositional meaning. The component of meaning that helps listeners to identify the **referent** of a noun phrase and determines whether a **proposition** expressed by a **sentence** is true or false. Non-descriptive meaning has to do with speaker's attitude, formal vs colloquial style, technical vs non-technical usage, neutral words vs words that carry associations with particular places, events and so on. *Lake* and *loch* have the same descriptive meaning, but *loch* evokes Scottish landscape; *shin* is an everyday term, *tibia* is a medical term. Such associations are referred to, depending on the analyst, as 'connotations', 'evoked meaning' or 'associative meaning'. See DENOTATION, REFERENCE, SYNONYMY.

DE-SEMANTICIZATION
Part of the process of **grammaticalization** in which a **lexical word** loses its lexical meaning. See GRAMMATICALIZATION.

DESIDERATIVE
A **mood**, signalled by special **affixes** or syntactic **constructions**, expressing desires or wants; e.g. *Would it were summer.* See OPTATIVE.

DESIGN FEATURES
A set of properties of language held to be distinctive of human language and not shared by other **animal communication** systems. See ARBITRARINESS, DISPLACEMENT, DOUBLE ARTICULATION, PRODUCTIVITY.

DET
Especially in generative grammar. See **Determiner**.

DETERMINATIVE
CGEL distinguishes 'determinative' and 'determiner'. 'Determinative' is the label for the class of words including *this, that,* etc. usually known as determiners and 'determiner' denotes the function of this class. So in *that book, that* is a determinative with the function of a determiner.

DETERMINATIVE COMPOUND
See COMPOUND WORD.

DETERMINER
The class of items occurring in a **noun phrase** outside the core, which consists of **adjective – noun – prepositional phrase/relative clause**. It includes **articles** – *the/a (fierce dog)*, **demonstratives** – *this/that fierce dog*, **possessive pronouns** – *her (fierce dog)*, and **quantifiers** – *some/many/no (fierce dogs)*. The core specifies the type of entity – dogs, fierce dogs, dogs in kennels, dogs chasing cats and so on.

The determiner specifies whether the speaker is referring to a definite dog or dogs, specifying the possessor, or loosely specifying the quantity. See **REFERENCE**.

DETERMINER PHRASE

A phrase with a **determiner** as its **head**, such as *no* in [*no support*] and *few* in [*few spectators*]. In Chomskian **generative grammar** phrases such as *the lofty spire*, which used to be analysed as **noun phrases**, are now analysed as determiner phrases, In this phrase *the* is both obligatory and indicates the type of phrase; the phrase is complete, whereas a phrase such as *lofty spires* allows the addition of adjectives or determiners, as in *splendid lofty spires* or *few lofty spires*. The NP analysis continues to be used in **descriptive grammar** and in many formal models.

DETERMINISM

See **LINGUISTIC DETERMINISM, SAPIR–WHORF HYPOTHESIS**.

DEVELOPMENTAL LINGUISTICS

See **DEVELOPMENTAL PSYCHOLINGUISTICS**.

DEVELOPMENTAL PSYCHOLINGUISTICS

The study of psychological changes over the human life span. This may concentrate on changes affecting infants and children, adolescence, ageing, etc. When it is focused on language issues (acquisition, loss, etc.), it is often known as developmental linguistics.

DEVERBAL

Formed from a **verb**. E.g. the deverbal **noun** *drainage* derives from the verb *drain*, the deverbal noun *throw* (a rug) derives from the verb *throw*. See **DERIVATIONAL MORPHOLOGY**.

DEVIANCE

1. See **UNGRAMMATICALITY**. 2. The property of language that deliberately flouts the grammatical and collocational conventions of a language for stylistic effect. See **COLLOCATION, UNGRAMMATICALITY**.

DEVOICING

A process whereby a **segment** that is normally voiced loses its **voicing** either partially or totally in some particular environment; for example [l̥] in the consonant **cluster** [pl̥] in *please*.

DHIVEHI

Indo-Iranian, Indo-European. Approx. 3.2M speakers, Maldive Islands (official language).

DIACHRONIC LINGUISTICS

The study of language through time, cf. **comparative linguistics**. The opposite is **synchronic linguistics**.

DIACHRONIC TYPOLOGY
The study of the types of historical change attested in the languages of the world.

DIACRITIC
A subscript or superscript added to a symbol to indicate a different sound value. For example, the sound change in some German plurals is orthographically represented by the umlaut superscript [¨] over a **vowel**, e.g. *Mann* (man sg) [man]; *Männer* (man pl) [mɛnnə]. See DIAERESIS, UMLAUT. For the diacritics used in IPA, see Figure 'IPA diacritics' at INTERNATIONAL PHONETIC ALPHABET.

DIADOCHOKINESIS
The ability to perform rapidly alternating muscular movement. Used as an assessment tool by speech pathologists.

DIAERESIS
The symbol [¨] placed over the second of two **vowels** to indicate that the two vowels are to be pronounced independently and not as a **diphthong** or long vowel, etc. E.g. *coöperate* [kəʊˈɔpəreɪt] vs *coop* [kuːp].

DIALECT
A form of a language differentiated from the **standard language** by particular features of **grammar**, vocabulary and **accent** and associated with a particular region, for instance Norfolk dialect, or social background, for instance English RP.

DIALECT ATLAS
An atlas showing the geographical distribution of **dialect** forms. This often shows isoglosses of particular linguistic features as points where recordings have been made. See ISOGLOSS.

DIALECT CONTACT
Contact between speakers of different but mutually intelligible **dialects**.
In such cases **accommodation** and perhaps **dialect mixture** is likely to occur.

DIALECT CONTINUUM
Geographically neighbouring **dialects** that differ from each other minimally and are mutually intelligible. Across a territory neighbouring dialects form a **chain** such that adjacent dialects are mutually intelligible but the dialects at either end of the chain and geographically distant from each other may not be. Thus, in the British Isles, a native of Cornwall may not be intelligible to a native of Glasgow when each is speaking their local dialect.

DIALECT FORMATION
The formation of new **dialects**. See DIALECT MIXTURE, DIALECT CONTACT.

DIALECT GEOGRAPHY
The study of the **dialects** of a particular geographical area, often associated with a **dialect atlas**, such as *The Linguistic Survey of England*, *The Linguistic Survey of Scotland*.

DIALECT MIXTURE
A consequence of **dialect contact**. A dialect mixture may give rise to new dialects.

DIALECTOLOGY
1. The study of **dialects**. Originally the study of rural dialects and particularly their **phonology**, **morphology** and **lexicon**, and also of their distribution. See **DIALECT GEOGRAPHY**. More recently, the study of urban dialects, including their syntax. Urban dialectology also interests itself in the social distribution of dialects. See **SOCIOLECT**.

DIALOGUE
Speech between two or more people. See **MONOLOGUE**.

DIAPHONE
An abstract phonological unit that represents the different **realizations** of a **phoneme** that occur in two or more **dialects**: thus a single diaphone might represent the pronunciation of *put* as [pʌt] and [pʊt] in different **accents**.

DIASYSTEM
A phonological system that fuses two or more dialect systems in order to show similarities and differences between the two dialects.

DICTION
The choice of vocabulary to create different types of literary text.

DICTIONARY
See **LEXICON**.

DICTIONARY MEANING
Dictionary entries contain information about the senses of **lexical words**. They are contrasted with entries in encyclopaedias, which provide information that relates to the world and to specific cultures. But, since dictionaries also give information about the **denotation** of lexical words, there is no clear boundary between dictionary meaning and encyclopaedic meaning. See **SENSE**.

DIEGESIS
The recounting of facts or events by a narrator.

DIFFUSE
In J&H distinctive feature theory, an acoustic distinctive feature involving a spread of energy throughout the spectrum associated with high vowels and front consonants. Opposite **compact**. See **DISTINCTIVE FEATURES**.

DIFFUSION
The spread of linguistic forms (pronunciations, words, grammatical properties, etc.) from one geographical or social variety to another via **dialect contact** and **accommodation**.

DIGLOSSIA

The existence of two separate varieties of a language within a **speech community**, each associated with a different communicative function, level of **formality** and so on. For example, in Greece, until recently, there were two varieties, Katharevousa, the 'high', formal variety of Greek, and Dhimotiki, the 'low' or informal variety. Diglossic situations exist in Arabic-speaking communities between the **colloquial** and the formal.

DIGRAPH

Two symbols representing a single speech sound. E.g. the consonantal digraphs th and ng representing the sounds [θ] and [ŋ].

DIMENSION

In the analysis of genres, a dimension is a set of properties. There are no definite boundaries between one genre or text-type and another. Rather, there are different sets (six or seven) of features to do with **derivational morphology, tense and aspect**, **modal verbs, syntax** and vocabulary. Text-types have to be rated for each dimension. E.g. one dimension involves the occurrence of simple past, third-person pronouns, free participial clauses, and verbs such as *admit* and *declare*. Fiction scores highly for this dimension, i.e. has many instances of the features. Broadcasts, professional letters, academic prose and official documents score very low. See **FREE PARTICIPLE, PRONOUN**.

DIMENSIONS OF LEXICAL MEANING

Two **lexical words** may be close in basic meaning but differ in a number of properties which have been called 'dimensions'. Some have to do with **descriptive meaning**: *big* and *colossal* both denote above-average size but differ in the dimension of intensity – *not just big but colossal*. Others have to do with non-descriptive meaning: in *Taranaki is stunningly/very beautiful in winter*, *stunningly* differs from *very* on the dimension of expressive meaning.

DIMINUTIVE

A word indicating small size – *duckling, flatlet* – and/or affection – Russian *ruka* 'hand', but *ruchka* 'handie' when talking to a small child.

DINKA

Nilotic. Approx. 1.4M speakers, South Sudan.

DIONYSIUS THRAX (C. 170–C. 90 BCE)

A Greek philologist who worked in Alexandria and wrote a grammar handbook, *Tekhne Grammatike*, which was the source for the Western tradition of grammatical analysis.

DIPHTHONG

If in the **articulation** of a **vowel** there is a perceptible **glide** in **vowel** quality such that the starting point of the glide is perceptually distinct from the finishing point, we have a diphthong, as in the British English Pronunciation of *day* [deı] or *cow* [kɑʊ]. Diphthongs are usually treated as single **phonemes**.

DIRECT CASE

The **case** of the **subject** of the **verb** in a **clause** (in grammars of **Latin**, e.g.) or the subject and **object** (in grammars of **Slavic** languages, e.g.). See **OBLIQUE 1**.

DIRECT OBJECT

Depending on the language, the **noun** typically denoting the **patient** and typically next to the **verb** but not connected to it by a **preposition**. In the grammars of languages with **case** affixes the direct object is said to be in the **accusative** case. The direct object in active clauses corresponds to the grammatical subject in passive clauses: *The tiger caught the deer, The deer was caught by the tiger*. See **GRAMMATICAL FUNCTION, TRANSITIVITY**.

DIRECT QUESTION

A question reported directly, i.e. using the speaker's actual words: e.g. *'Where have you been', he asked me*, as opposed to the **indirect question** *He asked me where I had been*. See **INTERROGATIVE, INTERROGATIVE CLAUSE, INDIRECT SPEECH**.

DIRECT SPEECH

The direct quotation of something said or thought: e.g. *'I'll be back in ten minutes', he said* and *'What a prat!', she thought*. An archaic term is 'oratio recta' (Latin 'speech straight, direct speech'). See **INDIRECT SPEECH**.

DIRECT SPEECH ACT

See **SPEECH ACT**.

DIRECTIONAL

Denoting movement. In English, *from London, towards the river, into the tunnel* and *out of the woods* are directional phrases. See **CASE, LOCALISM**.

DIRECTIONAL OPPOSITES

Pairs of **lexical words** that denote opposing directions or the opposite end-points on some axis. Examples are UP and DOWN and TOP and BOTTOM. See **OPPOSITENESS**.

DIRECTIONAL PHRASE

A phrase expressing direction of movement, such as *out of the fire, into the frying pan, (ran) up and down the hill*.

DIRECTIVES

In Searle's classification, **speech acts**, such as orders, advice and requests, by which the speaker or writer tries to get someone to do something. E.g. *Could you make some coffee please?, Why not ask him if he is serious?*. See **ASSERTIVE, COMMISSIVE, DECLARATIVE, EXPRESSIVE**.

DISCONTINUITY

The splitting up of parts of a constituent that go together. For example, the **phrasal verb** *eat up* is discontinuous in *He ate his dinner up*.

DISCONTINUOUS CONSTRUCTION

A constituent of a sentence that is split into two chunks separated from each other. E.g. the separation of a relative clause from the rest of the noun phrase – *A house that meets your requirements is for sale* vs *A house is for sale that meets your requirements*, or of a verb and particle – *The banker gave up his yacht* vs *The banker gave his yacht up*. See **CONSTITUENT STRUCTURE**.

DISCOURS

See **HISTOIRE**.

DISCOURSE

1. Any coherent sequence of **sentences** with a structure, typically marked by various cohesive devices. A discourse can be in writing or speech. 2. A style of language; e.g. legal discourse, political discourse, literary discourse. See **COHESION, COHERENCE, DISCOURSE ANALYSIS, GENRE, DIMENSION, HISTOIRE**.

DISCOURSE ANALYSIS

The analysis of discourse from any perspective: the connections between **sentences, information structure**, ideology and choice of grammar and vocabulary, etc. See **CRITICAL DISCOURSE ANALYSIS, CRITICAL LANGUAGE AWARENESS, TEXT LINGUISTICS**.

DISCOURSE COMPETENCE

The ability to understand and produce chunks of coherent and cohesive discourse. See **COHERENCE, COHESION, DISCOURSE**.

DISCOURSE DEIXIS

Deixis that has to do with pointing linguistically at texts or portions of texts. *This* points to a text that is near in the sense of about to be heard or read: *This is The News at Ten*. *That* points to a text that is distant in that it has been heard or read: *That was an interesting phrase*. Other examples of discourse deixis are *the former, the latter, the following*. See **ANAPHORA, CATAPHORA, OBVIATIVE, SOCIAL DEIXIS**.

DISCOURSE GRAMMAR

A grammar which takes as primary the functioning of language in communication and not **syntactic structures**.

DISCOURSE MARKER

See **DISCOURSE PARTICLE**.

DISCOURSE PARTICLE

Optional but frequent items, not an integral part of the syntax of **clauses**, that are used by speakers and writers for various purposes, all connected with social interaction. They indicate attitude to some **proposition** – *surely* in *Surely you're not inviting her?*; connections between chunks of discourse (**cohesion**) – *so* in *You're not coming? So you've found something more interesting to do?*; interpretation of a piece of text – *in other words* in *You suddenly have a report to write. In other words, you can't be bothered to come and see us*; agreement – *indeed* in *You've a reason for their decision. Indeed, I think you're quite right*; a mismatch with the previous speaker's expectations – *Can we go round to Kenneth's? Well, only for half an hour*; reluctance to agree – *Are you going to invite him? Oh, I don't think so.* See **ADVERBIAL**.

DISCOURSE REPRESENTATION THEORY

An application of **logic** and **model-theoretic semantics** to the analysis of discourse, in particular the handling of anaphora across clause and sentence boundaries. See **ANAPHORA, CATAPHORA**.

DISCOVERY PROCEDURES

Informally, a set of procedures introduced by structural linguists as tests to establish **constituent structure**. They include **commutation**, the exchange of one element for another in a particular **context** to establish whether there is a significant contrast (e.g. /pɪn/, /bɪn/; see **PHONEME**); **substitution**, a test to determine whether one string can be substituted for another longer or shorter string suggests that they are members of the same class (e.g. *the man next door, he*); omission is a test to determine if a string can be omitted without affecting grammaticality (e.g. adverbials are optional: *he kissed her (on the nose)*). Formally, a set of procedures which, when applied mechanically to a corpus of data, say by a computer program, will produce a grammar. See **CONTRASTIVE DISTRIBUTION, DISTRIBUTION**.

DISCRETE

Having an identity independent of other items of the same type. Thus the word /kat/ consists of the three discrete **phonemes** /k/, /a/ and /t/.

DISJUNCT

See **ADVERBIAL**.

DISJUNCTION

A type of **coordination** that presents alternatives: *Tea or coffee?* Some examples of disjunction can only be understood as presenting events as disjoined, either one or the other but not both: *Are you staying or leaving?* This is exclusive disjunction: one alternative excludes the other. Others can be understood as allowing the possibility of both or all alternatives: *Either James or Gordon, or both, will help Edward*. This is inclusive disjunction. In **logic**, disjunction is interpreted as 'at least one of two alternatives and possibly both'. The disjunctive operator V is interpreted as inclusive disjunction: p V q is read as 'Either p is true or q is true or both p and q are true'.

DISJUNCTIVE

Applied to a **coordinator** such as *or* that marks a **disjunction**.

DISJUNCTIVE ORDERING

Especially in **transformational grammar** of the 1960s in which rules applied in a particular order, the ordering of two rules, such that one of them, but not both, would apply to a given constituent. See **CONSTITUENT STRUCTURE**.

DISPERSION

The amount of **variation** in a set of data. For example, in a set of ten speakers represented in a sample of conversation, six may produce 400 lexical items, three may produce 300 and one may produce 350. The total number of lexical items produced is 3,050, the mean number of lexical items produced is 305 and the range is from 300 to 400. In another set of ten speakers, three produce 200 lexical items, two produce 400, one produces 500, two produce 300 and two produce 275. The total is again 3,050 and the mean is 305. The range is from 200 to 500 and the variation among the speakers is greater. This variation in totals produced by individual speakers and the range constitute the dispersion of the set. See **STANDARD DEVIATION**.

DISPLACEMENT

The property of human language whereby speech can refer to times, situations, individuals, etc. not in the immediate environment. Often taken to be one of the defining properties of human language. See **DESIGN FEATURES**.

DISSIMILATION

A process whereby a **segment** changes to become less similar to a contiguous segment. In some English dialects, in a sequence of two nasals the second is dissimilated, thus *chimney* becomes *chimley*. The process is particularly common in historical change. See **ASSIMILATION**.

DISSONANCE

A combination of sounds that produce a harsh effect. See **ASSONANCE**.

DISTANT ASSIMILATION

See **ASSIMILATION**.

DISTINCTIVE FEATURES

Much of contemporary phonological theory assumes that speech sounds are not indivisible units, like the classical **phoneme**, but can best be characterized by a set of smaller abstract properties called 'distinctive features'. Every **segment** can be characterized by some combination of these features. The features are usually held to be universal.

In modern phonological theory features are most usually defined as binary oppositions, ie [+/− feature]. This was not always so – see **opposition** and **flat/plain/sharp**. The features are designed to capture any phonological

contrast between segments: thus [i] as in *beat* is a **close, front, unrounded** vowel and which might be characterized in feature terms as [+vocalic], [+high], [−back], [−round] and [u] as in *boot* is a **close, back, round** vowel, as [+vocalic], [+high], +back], [+round]. The two vowels contrast in the features [+/−back], [+/−round]. As these examples show features are usually presented in terms of a **feature matrix**.

Features can be defined in **acoustic** or in articulatory terms. See **ARTICULATION**. Acoustic definitions are in terms of the distribution of acoustic energy as revealed in the analysis of sound spectrograms and other instrumental investigations. This system was introduced by Jakobsen and Halle in the 1950s, and is introduced in **J&H Distinctive Feature Theory**. Among the features identified are **compact: diffuse; strident: mellow; checked: unchecked; grave: acute; flat: plain; sharp: plain**. Articulatory distinctive features were proposed by Chomsky and Halle in *Sound Pattern of English* (1968) and are introduced in **SPE Distinctive Feature Theory** The features are all binary and can be grouped into several classes in terms of 'natural' groupings: **major class features:** (vowels, consonants, etc: **consonantal, sonorant, syllabic**); **source features, phonation types: voice, strident**, subglottal pressure); **cavity features** (the place of articulation and the configuration of the vocal tract: **coronal, anterior, high, low, back, round**); **manner features** (the manner of articulation) **nasal, continuant, strident, lateral, delayed release, implosion, ejective, tense, velaric** activity. See **ACOUSTIC DISTINCTIVE FEATURE, ARTICULATORY DISTINCTIVE FEATURE, DISTINCTIVE FEATURES: MAJOR CLASS FEATURES, DISTINCTIVE FEATURES: PLACE FEATURES, DISTINCTIVE FEATURES: SOURCE FEATURES, SOUND SPECTROGRAPH.**

DISTINCTIVE FEATURES, ACOUSTIC

Acoustic definitions of distinctive features are in terms of the distribution of acoustic energy as revealed in the analysis of sound spectrograms and other instrumental investigations, etc. This system is associated with the work of Jakobsen and Halle in the 1950s, as presented in *Fundamentals of Language*. It is thus sometimes referred to as **J&H Distinctive Feature Theory**. Although the features can be regarded as binary oppositions (that is [+/− feature]), they are usually presented with independent names: **vocalic/non-vocalic; consonantal/ non-consonantal; compact/diffuse; tense/lax; voiced/voiceless; nasal/ oral; discontinuous/continuous; strident/mellow; checked/ unchecked; grave/ acute; flat/plain; sharp/plain**. See individual entries for fuller specification. Today this system is largely superseded by articulatory distinctive features. See **ARTICULATION**.

DISTINCTIVE FEATURES, ARTICULATORY

Proposed by Chomsky and Halle in *Sound Pattern of English* (1968). The features are all binary, that is [+/−feature]. They can be grouped into several 'natural' classes: **major class features**: (vowels, consonants, etc:); **source features** (phonation types); **cavity features** (the place of articulation and the configuration of the vocal tract); manner features (the manner of articulation). See DISTINCTIVE FEATURES, FEATURE GEOMETRY, SPE DISTINCTIVE FEATURE THEORY.

DISTINCTIVE FEATURES: MANNER FEATURES

In SPE Distinctive Feature Theory, features that characterize the **manner of articulation**: continuant, nasal, strident, lateral, delayed release, implosion, ejective, tense, and see FEATURE GEOMETRY.

DISTINCTIVE FEATURES: PLACE FEATURES

In SPE Distinctive Feature Theory, features that specify the **place of articulation** and the configuration of the **vocal tract**. Also known as **cavity features**. See FEATURE GEOMETRY.

DISTINCTIVE FEATURES: MAJOR CLASS FEATURES

In SPE Distinctive Feature Theory, a set of features that distinguish major segment types such as **vocalic, consonantal, sonorant** and **syllabic**. See FEATURE GEOMETRY.

DISTINCTIVE FEATURES: SOURCE FEATURES

In SPE Distinctive Feature Theory, features that characterize the state of the larynx, hence phonation types: **voice, spread glottis, constricted glottis, strident**, and see FEATURE GEOMETRY.

DISTRIBUTED MORPHOLOGY

An approach in which morphological phenomena are not handled in a single special component of a **formal grammar** but are distributed over **syntax**, the **lexicon** and **phonology**. See MORPHOLOGY.

DISTRIBUTION

The set of contexts in which a constituent or class of constituents can appear. E.g. the distribution of the class of **nouns** in English is, partly, [V__] in **clauses**, that is, following a verb as in *read novels* and [Det__] in **noun phrases**, that is, following a determiner as in *a surprise*. Part of the distribution of *whisky* can be can stated in terms of specific lexical items: [*Scotch*__], following Scotch or Irish as in *Scotch whisky, Irish whisky*; [__*barrel*], preceding *barrel* as in *whisky barrel*; [*a dram of*__], following the string *a dram of* as in *a dram of whisky*; *distil*__], following the verb *distil* as in *They distil whisky* See FRAME, PHRASE, WORD CLASS.

DISTRIBUTIVE

1. Of **quantifiers**, *each* is distributive: an action is assigned (or distributed) to each individual in a set – *Each girl bought a present*. *All* may or may not be distributive. *All the girls bought a present* may have the interpretation that the girls collectively bought a single present or that each girl individually bought a present. Russian, for example, has two **constructions**: *devushki kupili podarok* 'girls bought present' (collectively, so only one present) vs *devushki kupili po podarku* 'girls bought PREPOSITION present' (individually, so as many presents as there are girls). 2. An **Aktionsart** or lexical aspect pertaining to situations where an

action or process affects several entities: e.g. Russian *Mal'chik zabolel* '(the) boy fell-ill' vs *Vse mal'chiki pereboleli* 'All (the) boys fell-ill'.

DISYLLABLE
A word consisting of two **syllables**. The English iambic foot is disyllabic.

DITRANSITIVE VERB
In the grammar of English, a **verb** that takes two **objects**: e.g. *She taught them maths.* *Them* is the **direct object** and *maths* is the **second object**, as shown by the **passive** *They were taught maths by her.*

DO
See **DIRECT OBJECT**.

DOGON
Niger-Congo. Approx. 540K speakers, Mali.

DOMAIN
1. The range of some rule or pattern. For instance, the **clause** is the domain of **case** – verbs assign case to **nouns** in the same clause. 2. Especially in **Cognitive Grammar**, different domains of the real world in which verbs and case markers such as **prepositions** have parallel uses: e.g. *I got a letter from Beirut* [Beirut is the Source of the letter] and *She died from hypothermia* [hypothermia is the Source of her death}. 3. In computing, a name which identifies a website or group of websites. 4. The social context (including, for instance, participants, location and topic) that influences choice of language, dialect and style. 5. In **Conceptual Metaphor Theory**, a relatively stable packet of information, a 'knowledge structure', about some area of human experience that is required for the interpretation of a given **lexical word**. A distinction is drawn between basic domains deriving from the physical world as experienced and conceived by humans and abstract domains that are more distant from the physical world, such as psychological states, human relationships and intellectual concerns such as number, truth and falsity, scientific theories. See **CONCEPTUAL BLENDING, MENTAL SPACE**.

DOMAIN MATRIX
In **cognitive linguistics**, the set of domains required for the analysis of some concept. For instance, 'building' requires domains such as size, shape, materials, purpose and climate. See **BASE, DOMAIN**.

DOMAIN NAME
In computing a name which identifies a website or group of websites.

DOMARI
Indo-Iranian, Indo-European. Spoken by nomads (Roma) throughout the Middle East. Endangered.

DOMINANCE
In a **tree diagram**, the relation between a node X and any node Y on a branch originating from X. In $_{VP}$[reported $_{NP}$[*the news* $_S$[*that the bank had collapsed*]]] the

node VP dominates the NP, the S and all the nodes inside the S. The dominance relations are indicated by the broken lines in the figure below.

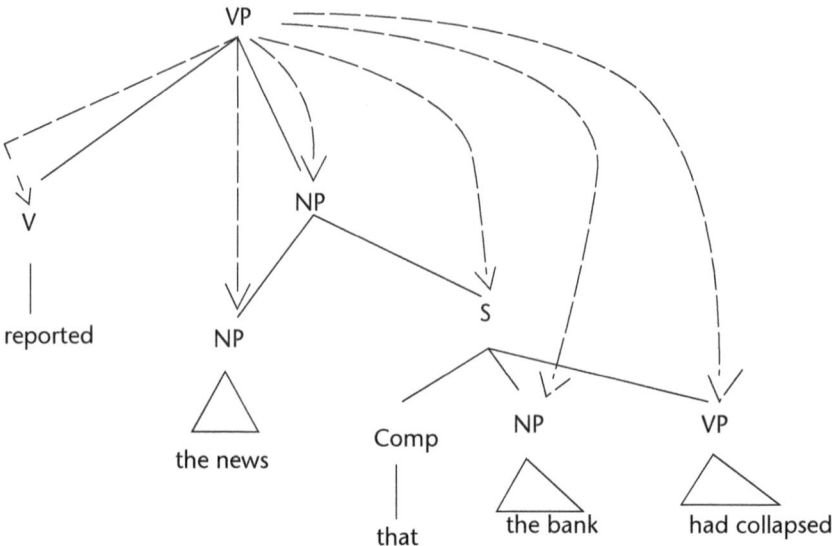

DOMINANT LANGUAGE
See **LINGUISTIC IMPERIALISM**.

DONKEY SENTENCE
Sentences used to illustrate the **lazy pronoun** phenomenon: e.g. *Every farmer who owns a donkey beats it. It* does not refer to a specific individual donkey but to the members of an unlimited set. Lazy pronouns are also known as sloppy pronouns.

DORSAL
1. A sound made with the back of the **tongue** in contact with the **velum**.
2. In **SPE Distinctive Feature Theory, segments** that are articulated with the body of the tongue raised; for example [k] [g].

DOUBLE ARTICULATION
1. In phonetics. See **ARTICULATION, CO-ARTICULATION**. 2. One of the **design features** of human language. The property of having two levels of structure: words participate in sentence structure, and also have a phonological structure. In principle the two levels of structure are independent. Also called **duality of structure**.

DOUBLE-BAR
See **X-BAR SYNTAX**.

DOWNGRADING
A process whereby a larger syntactic unit is used where a smaller one would be expected. E.g. in the **noun phrase** *the rumour that she had died* the **clause** *that she*

had died is downgraded to merely a constituent of the noun phrase; cf. *the rumour of her death*, containing the phrase *of her death*. The **imperative** clause *Publish and be damned!* is downgraded to a **modifier** of a noun in the noun phrase *His publish-and-be-damned reaction surprised me*.

DOWNDRIFT

A common **intonation** pattern in **tone languages**. The **pitch** of a high **tone** following a low tone is lower than a preceding high. Thus in a HLH sequence the second H will be lower in pitch than the first. The domain of downdrift is a **tone group**. In **Akan** for example a sequence of high tones with no intervening low will be at the same pitch, but where two highs are separated by a low the second high is lower in pitch than the first (see Figure 'downdrift & downstep').

Downdrift	H H	H L H	H H L H H L H

Downstep	H!H	L H !HL	L H !H H L	L H !H !H L

DOWNSTEP

In some **tone languages**, the second of two successive high tones is lowered slightly in **pitch** with no intervening low tone. The pitch of the downstepped high tone is lower than a high tone, but not as low as a low tone. Typically symbolized as H!H. Thus in a HH sequence the two highs will be of the same pitch; in a H!H the second high will be lower in pitch than the first, but not as low as a low pitch, and in a HLH sequence the two high tones are separated by a low tone. Downstep is usually grammatically conditioned, though it may also be lexical. It is possible to attest sequences H!H!H!H!H, where each successive high tone is lower in pitch than the preceding high. Languages with downstep are sometimes referred to as terraced level languages. Downstep may or may not be accompanied by downdrift. (See Figure 'downdrift & downstep'.)

DOWNTONER

See **INTENSIFIER**.

DP

See **DETERMINER PHRASE**.

DRAG CHAIN

See **CHAIN SHIFT**.

DRAVIDIAN

With approximately twenty-five languages, the Dravidian family is the fifth largest language family in the world. It includes **Tamil, Telugu, Kannada** and **Malayalam**, each with more than 30M speakers.

DRIFT

A set of gradual linguistic changes that appear to occur in an identifiable direction.

D-STRUCTURE

In **Government and Binding Theory** model, a level of representation developed from and replacing the earlier concept of **deep structure**. This level results after the insertion of **lexical words** but before the application of syntactic rules such as 'Move alpha'. Rather than the structure of passive sentences being derived from the structure of active sentences as in **transformational grammar** of the mid 1960s, each structure is derived from its own D-structure. A passive sentence such as *The goal was scored by the striker* has a D-structure in which a constituent containing inflections for **tense and aspect**, the Inflection Phrase or IP, contains a verb phrase, VP, dominating a constituent phrase [scored[the goal [by the striker]]]. *The goal* is the **direct object** of *scored* and is raised into subject position as part of the formation of the sentence's **S-structure**. The latter is a representation close to but not necessarily identical with the surface syntax. There is no conversion of an NP to a PP as there was in transformational grammar; the PP *by the striker* is present in D-structure. The relationship between *scored* and *the goal* is captured by having *the goal* as the direct object of *scored* in D-structure. See **LOGICAL FORM, SURFACE STRUCTURE**.

DUAL

Forms expressing the concept 'two of (something)'. E.g. Maori *raua* 'they two', *ratou* 'they (three or more)'; classical Greek (but rare) *krites* 'a judge', *krita* '(two) judges', *kritai* '(three or more) judges'. See **TRIAL**.

DUALISM

The theory that there is a direct relationship between language and the external world, as opposed to a relationship between language and mental representations, with the latter being mapped onto the external world.

DUALITY OF STRUCTURE

See **DOUBLE ARTICULATION**.

DUMMY SUBJECT

In *Whether she resigns or not is crucial*, the subject is *Whether she resigns or not*. The sentence can be reformulated as *It is crucial whether she resigns or not*. The property of being crucial still belongs to *whether she resigns or not* but the subject of *is crucial* is *It*. It is a dummy subject anticipating the *whether* **clause** (although some analysts see it as a referential pronoun referring to, and anticipating, the *whether* clause). Dummy *it* also occurs in clauses describing weather, time and distance: *It's snowing, It's midnight, It's five miles to Matakana*. Dummy *it* is also called 'pleonastic *it*'. (Greek *pleon* 'more' – the pronoun is more than is required.) The term 'ambient *it*' has been used, reflecting the idea that *it* in weather clauses refers to the ambient environment. See EXPLETIVE *IT*, EXTRAPOSITION, IMPERSONAL CLAUSE.

DUMMY SYMBOL

In the Standard Model of **transformational grammar**, a symbol, Δ, marking a place in a phrase structure tree where another tree can be inserted.

DURATION

See LENGTH.

DURATION ADVERB/ADVERBIAL

A label traditionally applied to **noun phrases** and **prepositional phrases** denoting the period of time for which a given state or event lasts, e.g. *She slept for ten hours*, *They walked along the coast all day*. The label is standardly used in work on **aspect** and **Aktionsart**, in which such phrases play an important role. Duration adverbs distinguish a **state** (*She slept for hours*) or an **activity** (*We chopped logs for hours*) from an **accomplishment** (**We walked to the shops for hours*) or an **achievement** (**They reached the summit for hours*). See TENSE AND ASPECT.

DURATIVE

Expressing **duration**.

DUTCH

Germanic, Indo-European. Approx. 13.5M speakers Netherlands, 6.3M Belgium, 200K Surinam. The official language of the Netherlands, one of the official languages of Belgium and the language of administration of former Dutch possessions in South America.

DVANDVA

See COMPOUND WORD.

DYNAMIC

1. Of **verbs**, denoting an **action** or process as opposed to a **state**. See AKTIONSART.
2. Of **modality**, not deontic or epistemic but relating to abilities and characteristics.

DYNAMIC CONSTRUAL

The theory that the denotations of lexical items only provide clues to the meanings and that the full interpretations of **lexical words** emerge in **context**, subject to constraints arising from a particular culture and from the immediate context of utterance. E.g. the meaning assigned to *Ball* in *The ball hit him on the arm* depends on whether the game is football, cricket, tennis, etc. See CONSTRUE, DENOTATION, DOMAIN, EMERGENT MEANING.

DYNAMIC SYNTAX

A model of grammar based on left-to-right parsing, assumed to be the process by which listeners and readers construct semantic representations for chunks of syntactic structure. See PARSE.

DYNAMIC PASSIVE

See VOICE.

DYNAMIC TONE
See **CONTOUR TONE**.

DYSARTHRIA
A speech disorder caused by lack of control over the muscles that move the vocal apparatus.

DYSFLUENCY
In **clinical linguistics**, disorders affecting fluency.

DYSGRAPHIA
The loss of the ability to write, which may be a result of trauma; also the delayed acquisition of writing skills. See **DYSLEXIA**.

DYSKINESIA
In **clinical linguistics**, a movement disorder involving loss of voluntary movements and presence of involuntary movement. See **HUNTINGTON'S DISEASE**.

DYSLALIA
In **clinical linguistics**, speech defects due to abnormalities in the articulatory organs or impaired hearing.

DYSLEXIA
In **clinical linguistics**, the loss of the ability to read, which may be acquired, through accident, etc., or be developmental. Dyslexia may be the result of an impairment in the visual system or difficulties with processing language.

DYSNOMIA
In **clinical linguistics**, loss of the ability to name things. See **ANOMIA**.

DYSPHASIA
In **clinical linguistics**, delayed or deviant speech acquisition.

DYSPHEMISM
See **EUPHEMISM**.

DYSPHONIA
In **clinical linguistics**, impairment of the vocal folds leading to an in ability to produce **voice**.

DYSPRAXIA
In **clinical linguistics**, an impairment of the ability to make physical movements thus causing speech difficulties and writing problems. See **APRAXIA**.

DYSPROSODY
In **clinical linguistics**, loss or impairment of the ability to produce intonation.

DYSRHYTHMIA
In **clinical linguistics**, loss or impairment of the ability to produce rhythm.

DYSTONIA
A neurological disorder causing repetitive movement and abnormal posture.

E

EAP
See ENGLISH FOR ACADEMIC PURPOSES.

EAR
The organ that detects sound. The outer part of the ear collects sound vibrations which are transmitted via the eardrum to the **middle ear** and thence to the inner ear, which includes the organ of hearing, the **cochlea**.

EAR TRAINING
The technique for teaching students of **phonetics** to recognize and identify speech sounds by listening to them.

EBLAITE
Semitic, Afroasiatic. Spoken in Mesapotamia in the third millennium BCE. It survives in some 3,000 clay tablets in cuneiform writing.

EBONICS
See AAVE.

ECHO-QUESTION
Especially in spoken language, an **interrogative construction** echoing a preceding **statement** by another speaker: *They're voting for Smoot. – They're voting for who?* (or simply *For who?*). See **INTERROGATIVE CLAUSE**.

ECHOIC
See ONOMATOPOEIA.

ECHOLALIA
In **clinical linguistics**, the usually involuntary repetition of words phrases and clauses just spoken by others.

ECM
See EXCEPTIONAL CASE MARKING.

ECONOMIC MOTIVATION
The explanation proposed for the general property of natural languages whereby, for ease of processing, two or more meanings are expressed by one form. This is a characteristic of **fusional** morphology in **Indo-European** languages, for instance **Russian**, where the case suffix *-om* in *molotom* 'with a hammer' signals masculine **gender**, singular **number** and instrumental **case**.

The property is found in frequently used **constructions**, in which words may be coalesced, as in *dja find him?* (= *Did you find him?*) or ellipted, as in *Find him?* (= *Did you find him?*). **Iconic motivation** may counteract the effects of economic motivation. See **ECONOMY, FUSION**.

ECONOMY

1. Especially in formal models, the principle that it is desirable to use as few rules and symbols, and resort to as few exceptions, as possible. 2. The expression of meanings using as few words and phrases as possible.

ECP

See **EMPTY CATEGORY PRINCIPLE**.

ED-FORM

In English, a **passive participle**, a **past participle** or a **simple past** form. These typically have the **suffix** *-ed*.

E-LANGUAGE

A Chomskyan term for language as 'externalized' by speakers, i.e. seen as a set of audible or legible **utterances**. See **I-LANGUAGE, PERFORMANCE**.

EFFECTED OBJECT

Direct object noun phrase denoting an entity that is created by the **action** denoted by a **verb**: e.g. *We baked scones, The mole dug tunnels across the lawn, She painted his portrait.* See **AFFECTED OBJECT**.

EFIK

Benue-Congo, Niger-Congo. Approx. 750K speakers, south-east Nigeria.

EGOCENTRISM

Especially in Piaget's work on child language, the characteristic of very young children which leads them to behave and talk as though all points of view were identical with theirs.

EGRESSIVE

Applied to the **airstream** moving out of the lungs. See **AIRSTREAM MECHANISM**.

EGYPTIAN

Afroasiatic. The language of ancient Egypt, first attested in hieroglyphic inscriptions before 3000 BCE. The hieroglyphic writing system gradually developed into a hieratic and then into a demotic form of script, which was the forerunner of **Coptic**, the language of mediaeval, Christian Egypt. Coptic is written in a modified form of the Greek script and has approx. 8.8M speakers.

EJECTIVE

A **consonant** produced on a glottalic **egressive airstream mechanism**. Such a consonant is typically a **stop** but can also be an **affricate** or a **fricative**. They are represented in IPA with a following apostrophe: p', t', s', c', k', etc. In British

English they are sometimes found in emphatic positions, e.g. the [k'] in ['k'ʌm'hiə] _Come_ here and word final, as in _ba__c__k_. See **GLOTTALIC AIRSTREAM**.

ELABORATED CODE

Part of a theory of language and its relation to social structure. Elaborated code is said to be used in public situations and hence to be less dependent on extra-linguistic clues, shared assumptions and so on. Language that is formal rather than intimate and characterized by formal vocabulary and complex syntactic structures such as **embedding** which are sometimes incorrectly associated with **standard language**. Elaborated code lies at one end of a **cline** which at its other end has **restricted code**. Restricted code was originally said to be characteristic of disadvantaged working-class children, but its properties are typical of spontaneous spoken English (or any other language) produced in context, irrespective of the socio-economic class of the speakers. See **EMBEDDING**.

ELABORATION

See **RHETORICAL STRUCTURE**.

ELAMITE

Language isolate. It was spoken in Iran until the end of the Persian Empire in the fourth century BCE. It exists in royal Achaemenid monumental inscriptions and in several thousand documents from the administrative centres of the Persian Empire.

ELATIVE

A **case** marking signalling movement out-of: e.g. **Finnish** _talo_ 'house', _talosta_ 'house-ELAT, out of the house'. See **ABLATIVE, FINNISH**.

ELECTROAEROMETER

See **AEROMETRY**.

ELECTROKYMOGRAPH

See **KYMOGRAPH**.

ELECTROLARYNGOGRAPH

See **LARYNGOGRAPH**.

ELECTROMYOGRAPHY

See **MYOGRAPHY**.

ELECTROPALATOGRAPH

See **PALATOGRAPHY**.

ELEMENT

1. A basic or indivisible unit of analysis: e.g. **words** (syntax – **morphemes** in some theories), phonemes, individual features or **articulatory gestures** (phonology), etc. 2. A term or role in a **construction**: e.g. in **clause** constructions, **subject, object, complement, adverbial**; in syllable structure, **onset, nucleus, coda**. See **GRAMMATICAL FUNCTION, SYLLABLE**.

ELF

See **ENGLISH AS A LINGUA FRANCA**.

ELICIT

To obtain information about the grammar or uses of a language or variety of a language, typically indirectly, using elicitation techniques. See **ELICITATION TECHNIQUES**.

ELICITATION TECHNIQUES

Methods for drawing information from informants without researchers asking them directly about the grammar, vocabulary or uses of a language. For instance, informants may be asked to fill in gaps in sentences, to complete sentences or to choose between alternative completions. They may do tasks online, for instance, pressing a button as soon as they match an interpretation to a given sentence.

ELISION

The omission or suppression of a sound or **syllable** in pronunciation, as in *do not → don't; I will → I'll*.

ELLIPSIS

The omission of **words, phrases** or **clauses** that are recoverable from the **context**. Sometimes they can be recovered directly from the text, as in *Have you seen the book that was on the table? – Sorry, I haven't [seen...table]*, where the chunk *seen the book that was on the table* is said to be ellipted. Sometimes they have to be recovered indirectly from text plus other context (*Have you done your homework? – I am [doing my homework]*, where *doing* and *my* do not occur in the first utterance.)

ELSEWHERE CONDITION

In **generative grammar**, the principle that specific **rules** apply first, then the general rules. For example, the rules handling the irregular **past tense** forms in English apply first and the general rule handling the *-ed* **suffix** applies 'elsewhere'.

EMBEDDING

The inclusion of a sentence or **clause** inside a larger **sentence** or **clause** or inside a **phrase**. E.g. in *I like the picture you painted*, the **relative clause** *you painted* is included in the main clause *I like the picture you painted* (and also in the **noun phrase** *the picture you painted*, which is the object in the main clause). In *the very idea that we would abandon them*, the clause *that we would abandon them* is embedded in the phrase *the very idea*.

EMBLEM

A non-verbal gesture that has a verbal equivalent in a specific language and culture. For instance, holding one's arm straight out in front with the hand positioned so that the palm is facing another person is equivalent to *Stop!*

EMERGENT MEANING

The meanings constructed by listeners and readers as they process texts, in particular, the meanings that arise as a result of **conceptual blending**. See **CONSTRUAL, METAPHOR**.

EMG

See **ELECTROMYOGRAPHY**.

EMIC

An emic analysis focuses on the relationship between the units in a system; by contrast an etic analysis focuses on details of the units concerned. For example, a **phonemic** analysis of the sounds of Tamil would focus on the fact that [t], [d] and [ð] are in **complementary distribution**. A **phonetic** analysis focuses on the physical properties of the sounds: e.g. that [t] is a voiceless, dental **stop**. 'Emic' and 'etic' are now applied outside linguistics. See **DISTRIBUTION**.

EMOTICON

A set of keyboard symbols representing the expression on a face, used in informal writing such as e-mail to represent the feelings of the sender of the message. For example, :-) and :-(represent pleased and displeased expressions. See **ICON**.

EMOTIVE FUNCTION

In semiotics, the emotional effect that a speaker or writer wishes to produce by communicating something to an addressee.

EMOTIVE MEANING

See **AFFECTIVE MEANING**.

EMPHATIC

Any **construction** signalling emphasis, by means of **stress** – I <u>didn't</u> invite him, special **pronoun** – French *moi, je suis crevé* [I don't know about you but] 'me, I am done', or **word order** – <u>down</u> came the rain, <u>out</u> came the sun or, an authentic example, *He thought we would give up but <u>give up</u> we didn't*. Since emphasis is typically used for contrast, the more general term contrastive is often used.

EMPIRICAL PRINCIPLE

Hjelmslev's term for a principle whereby analyses of a language system should be consistent (free of internal contradictions), cover as much of the relevant data as possible and be as simple as possible. Consistency outweighs coverage of the data and neither of these should be sacrificed for simplicity.

EMPTY CATEGORY

In the **Principles and Parameters** model, an element such as **PRO**, **pro** and **trace** that has a position in a syntactic structure but has no phonological **realization**.

EMPTY CATEGORY PRINCIPLE
Principle requiring a phonetically null element to be syntactically licensed either by a **verb** or by an **antecedent**. See **LICENSING, PROPER GOVERNMENT**.

EMPTY MORPH
A **morph** that is not the **realization** of a **morpheme**. E.g. **Latin** *laborabam* 'I-was-working' divides into *labor* 'work', *ba* 'ipfv', *m* '1sg'. The remainder, *-a-*, has no meaning and serves to connect the **stem** *labor* to the grammatical **suffixes**.

EMPTY NODE
See **DUMMY SYMBOL**.

EMPTY SET
See **NULL SET**.

en-FORM
A label sometimes applied to the **past participle** forms of the English verb, although only some **irregular** verbs have the *-en* **suffix**.

ENCLITIC
See **CLITIC**.

ENCODER
An **algorithm** or tool that converts information from one format to another. In language generation the component that encodes grammatical, phonological or semantic information.

ENCODING
The signalling of meaning in the **grammar** or vocabulary of a language. The forms used in a given language to encode meaning are arbitrary: *dog*, Russian *sobaka* and Turkish *köpek* all denote the same set of entities. Languages do not encode exactly the same contrasts of meaning. French *apparition* corresponds to the English *appearance* (as in 'make an appearance') and not *apparition*, and the contrast between *was writing a letter* and *wrote/have written a letter* is not the same as the contrast between Russian *pisal* (IMPFV) and *napisal* (PFV) *pis'mo*. Finally, a given language may encode in a single lexical item a meaning that can only be encoded in a phrase in another language. Where English has the one lexical item *hand*, Turkish has two. *El* denotes the whole hand, *avuç* denotes the palm and fingers and corresponds to the English phrase *hollow of the hand*. *Avuç dolusu* 'hollow-of-the-hand full-its' is the equivalent of *handful*. See **ARBITRARY SIGN, SOUND SYMBOLISM, TENSE AND ASPECT**.

ENCYCLOPAEDIC MEANING
See **DICTIONARY MEANING**.

END FOCUS
The placement at the end of a **clause** of whatever **phrase** carries new information. The **focus** does not contrast one piece of information with

another but merely fills in a gap in the hearer's knowledge. In English the **focal accent** falls on the last major lexical item. E.g. *When did you write the report? – (I wrote it) last month*, where *last month* carries new information and the focal accent falls on *month*. See GIVEN AND NEW, INFORMATION STRUCTURE.

END WEIGHT

The principle that a long and complex (heavy) constituent is optionally relegated to the end of a **sentence**. E.g. *The news surprised us that she was proposing radical changes* vs *The news that she was proposing radical changes surprised us*. The principle is optional but widely followed in informal and/or unplanned spoken language.

ENDING

A traditional but informal term for any **suffix** or combination of suffixes at the end of a word, especially in grammars of **inflecting languages**.

ENDOCENTRIC CONSTRUCTION

1. Originally defined as a **construction** with a **head** whose **distribution** is the same as that of the construction as a whole: e.g. *outside the house* occurs in the same general frames as *outside*, as in *We met outside the concert hall*, *We met outside*. (Greek *endo* 'within', Latin *centrum* 'centre'.) **2.** In contemporary generative syntax an endocentric construction is the projection of a head and thus all constructions are endocentric. See EXOCENTRIC CONSTRUCTION, FRAME, X-BAR SYNTAX.

ENDOPHORA

A cover term for **cataphora** and **anaphora**, the relationship between **deictics** in a text and the items in the text that they point to. (Greek *endo* 'inside'.) See ANAPHOR, EXOPHORA.

ENHANCEMENT

See RHETORICAL STRUCTURE.

ENGLISH

Germanic, Indo-European. Approx. 364M speakers: 60M UK, 20M Australia, 24M Canada, 4M New Zealand, 251M USA, 3.5M South Africa. Smaller numbers of speakers in other countries. There is an extensive literature in 'Old English', from the seventh century to the Norman conquest in 1066. 'Middle English', heavily influenced by French, gradually developed into the standard language, acquiring the general shape it has today during the 'early modern' period (1500–1700). From the seventeenth century English spread, first to North America and then to Australia, New Zealand, Southern Africa, India and other countries in the former British Empire.

ENGLISH AS A LINGUA FRANCA (ELF)
English used as a common means of communication by speakers of different first languages, as in the European Union. By definition ELF is nobody's native language. See ENGLISH AS AN INTERNATIONAL LANGUAGE, NATIVE LANGUAGE.

ENGLISH AS AN INTERNATIONAL LANGUAGE
See ENGLISH AS A LINGUA FRANCA.

ENGLISH FOR ACADEMIC PURPOSES (EAP)
A restricted form of English supposed to be suitable for the use of students and teachers in higher education. See ENGLISH FOR SPECIAL PURPOSES.

ENGLISH FOR SPECIAL PURPOSES (ESP)
Delimited English intended to provide the language needed for a particular area of study, thus 'Business English', 'English for Medicine', etc. See ENGLISH FOR ACADEMIC PURPOSES.

ENRICHMENT
See EXPLICATURE.

ENTAILMENT
The relationship between two **propositions** p and q such that whenever p is true, q is also true. E.g. p could be *Someone has broken the vase* and q could be *The vase is broken*. See DEDUCTION, IMPLICATURE.

ENTRENCHMENT
In **cognitive linguistics**, the process whereby linguistic units that occur frequently become established (or *entrenched*) as a cognitive pattern or routine. *Slept* and *ate* are irregular **past tense** forms but are entrenched because they occur very frequently. *Hove*, as in *The ship hove to*, is the past tense of *heave* but occurs so rarely that it is not entrenched and is coming to be used as a **present tense** or **bare infinitive**. See ESTABLISHMENT.

ENTRY CONDITION
In **Systemic Functional Grammar**, the condition that must be met for a system to operate. For example, the entry condition for the system **declarative** vs **interrogative** vs **imperative** is that a given clause be a main **clause**.

ENVIRONMENT
A context in which some **constituent** can occur. See DISTRIBUTION, FRAME.

EPENTHESIS
The insertion into a word of an additional **vowel** or **syllable**. Epenthetic vowels often break up a consonant or vowel sequence, as *filum* for *film*. In English past-tense formations there is an epenthetic /ɪ/ when a verb root ends in an alveolar– *bat: batted*. Epenthesis at the beginning of word is known as prothesis – cf. Hindi loans from English with initial *sp-*, *sk*, etc. as in *iskuul*. Also known as anapytxis and excrescence, and by the Sanskrit term *svarabhakti*.

EPENTHETIC
The adjective from epenthesis. See **EPENTHESIS**.

EPG
See **ELECTROPALATOGRAPH**.

EPICENE
A **noun** or **pronoun** used to refer to individuals of either sex: e.g. **English** *teacher*, **Turkish** third-person pronoun *on* 'he'/'she' – and 'it'. (Greek *epi* 'upon', *koinos* 'common'.)

EPIDEMIOLOGY
The evidence-based study of factors that affect the health or illness of a population. It forms the basis of interventions made for the public health.

EPIGLOTTIS
The cartilage at the root of the **tongue** which is depressed during swallowing to protect the glottis. See Figure 'Articulators' at **ARTICULATION**.

EPISTEMIC MODALITY
See **MODALITY**.

EPITHET
1. An older term for **adjective**. 2. A descriptive word or phrase added to someone's name: e.g. *Charles the Bold*, *Suleiman the Magnificent*.

EQUATIONAL
See **EQUATIVE**.

EQUATIVE
1. A **copula** construction identifying one entity with another: e.g. *The consultant is Peter's wife*. Equative sentences can be reversed: *Peter's wife is the consultant*.
2. In some languages, a **case** marking indicating a **predicative** noun: e.g. **Russian** *vrach* 'doctor', *Petr byl vrachom* 'Peter was doctor-INSTR, 'Peter was a doctor'.

EQUI
See **EQUI NP DELETION**.

EQUI NP DELETION
A **construction** involving **control**. The label reflects early transformational **derivations** of, e.g., *Angus expects to be promoted* from *Angus expects (Angus be promoted)* with two equivalent NPs, the second instance of *Angus* being deleted. The derivation has been abandoned, but the label has been kept for the construction. See **TRANSFORMATIONAL GRAMMAR**.

EQUIPOLLENT ANTONYMS
See **ANTONYMY**.

EQUIPOLLENT OPPOSITIONS

An **opposition** between two **segments** which is neither privative nor **gradual** but involves several contrasts. Thus the contrast between /p/ and /x/ involves both **place of articulation** and **manner of articulation**.

EQUIVALENCE

1. See **BICONDITIONAL**. 2. In **generative grammar**, a relationship of **adequacy** among alternative grammars with respect to the strings of symbols they generate and the structures they assign to the sequences. See **STRONG GENERATIVE CAPACITY, WEAK GENERATIVE CAPACITY**.

ERGATIVE

1. Applied to a language or **construction** which possesses **ergativity**. 2. Designating the **case marking** of the **subject** of a **transitive verb** in a language with ergativity, such as **Basque** and most Australian languages. 3. With respect to verbs such as *sink, melt, boil*, etc., applied to the role of, e.g. *water* in *The water boiled*, with **patient** as subject, and *We boiled the water*, with patient as **direct object**. (This usage condemned by some linguists.) See **CASE, GRAMMATICAL FUNCTION**.

ERGATIVE VERB

See **ERGATIVE**.

ERGATIVITY

The property ascribed to grammatical systems in which the **subject** of an **intransitive verb** and the **direct object** of a **transitive verb** are similar in grammar, while the subject of a transitive verb is different. The latter may have a special ergative **case marking**, as opposed to absolutive on the former two, and/or behave differently with respect to **coordination** and **control**. Some ergative languages have an **antipassive** construction that allows patients to be left unspecified, much as the passive in English allows agents to remain unspecified. Languages can have ergative morphology without having ergative syntax. See **CASE, VOICE**.

ESKIMO-ALEUT

A family of languages spoken from Greenland to Siberia. There are two main branches, Eskimo, with subfamilies Yupik and Inuit, and Aleut.

ESOPHAGEAL

See **OESOPHAGUS**.

ESP

See **ENGLISH FOR SPECIAL PURPOSES**.

ESPERANTO

An artificial language created in 1887 and originally intended for use as an international language. It has adherents in over a hundred countries and speakers are estimated at more than 200K.

ESSENTIAL CONDITION
See **FELICITY CONDITIONS**.

ESSENTIALISM
In medieval philosophy, the idea that **concepts** represent individuals essentially assigned to natural kinds and not sorted into natural kinds by the operation of human intellect on concepts or by linguistic convention. See **NATURAL KIND TERMS**.

ESSIVE
In some languages with **case** inflections, a case marking signalling a temporary state. E.g. Finnish *poika* 'boy' – *poikana* 'boy-ESS, as a boy (I did not know him)'. See **INFLECTION**.

EST
See **EXTENDED STANDARD THEORY**.

ESTABLISHMENT
The process by which a **lexical word** becomes familiar to all or many of the linguistic community in which it is used. See **ENTRENCHMENT**.

ESTONIAN
Finno-Ugric, Uralic. 900K speakers, Estonia (official language).

ESTUARY ENGLISH
A form of English spoken predominantly in the south-east of England along the Thames estuary. It has been described as 'Standard English spoken with the accent of the south-east of England', that is with features of working-class London speech.

ETHIC DATIVE
Noun or **pronoun** in the dative **case** used to refer to someone affected by an action or with an interest in the outcome of an action. E.g. Russian *Ona nastupila Petru na nogu* 'she stepped Peter-DAT on foot-ACC, She stepped on Peter's foot', *Ty Petru ne opozdaj* 'you Peter-DAT not be-late, Don't be late for/to Peter', i.e. 'Don't do that to Peter'. See **DATIVE**.

ETHICAL DATIVE
See **ETHIC DATIVE**.

ETHIOPIAN LANGUAGES
There are approximately eighty languages in the Ethiopian linguistic area. They mainly belong to three **Afroasiatic** families – **Semitic**, **Cushitic** and **Omotic**. They share a number of phonological, grammatical and lexical features.

ETHNOGRAPHY OF SPEAKING
In **linguistic anthropology**, the rules and conventions governing interaction in a **speech community**, such as the use of formal language in greeting and

leave-taking and who is permitted to speak to whom, how and on what occasions. See **PRAGMALINGUISTIC NORMS, SOCIOPRAGMATIC NORMS, SPEAKING.**

ETHNOLINGUISTICS
The study of language in its social and cultural contexts. See **ETHNOMETHODOLOGY, ETHNOGRAPHY OF SPEAKING.**

ETHNOMETHODOLOGY
An approach to the analysis of social groups and relationships which requires analysts to work with categories valid for the members of whatever social group they are studying and based on observed patterns of behaviour in interactions. The approach was the basis for **conversation analysis**.

ETIC
See **EMIC**.

ETIOLOGY
In **clinical linguistics**, the science of causes of diseases and disorders.

ETRUSCAN
Language Isolate. The ancient language of Tuscany, apparently unrelated to any other language.

ETYMOLOGICAL FALLACY
The common but erroneous belief that the meaning of words can be investigated by tracing their etymology. *Bead* in the sense of a small round object with a hole through it enabling it to be put onto a thread can be traced back to *bead* in the sense of a prayer, but the earlier sense is irrelevant to contemporary usage and understanding.

ETYMOLOGY
The study of the history of **words** and their meanings, especially the way they have developed, or are assumed to have developed, from an earlier form of 'the same' word in the same language (e.g. English *mother* derives from Old English *modor*) or in some **cognate** language (e.g. German *Mutter*) or an ancestor language (both English and German are related to an Indo-European root which Latin *mater* is also related to). See **COMPARATIVE LINGUISTICS.**

EUPHEMISM
The use of a polite, indirect expression instead of a direct, offensive one: the converse is dysphemism. E.g. the neutral *die*, the euphemism *pass away* and the dysphemism *snuff it*. (Greek *eu* 'well', *dus* 'un-, mis-, as in *mischance, phemi* 'I speak'.)

EVALUATION
See **NARRATIVE**.

EVALUATION PROCEDURE

In the theory of **generative grammar**, a mechanical procedure proposed by Chomsky in the 1950s for determining which of two grammars, of the same format and generating the same language, is the better. Such a procedure employs various evaluation measures.

EVENKI

Tungusic. Approx. 30K speakers, Siberia, North China, Mongolia.

EVENT TIME

In Reichenbach's theory of **tense**, the time at which an event occurs as opposed to the **speech time**, **reference time** or perspectives adopted by the speaker. See **TENSE AND ASPECT**.

EVENT TYPES

See **AKTIONSART**.

EVENTIVE

1. Designating an event, a **dynamic** situation, as opposed to a **state**: e.g. *The building collapsed* is eventive, *The building lay in ruins* denotes a state. 2. Applied to noun phrases denoting events: e.g. in *The invasion took the country by surprise*, *The invasion* is an eventive subject. See **AKTIONSART**.

EVIDENTIAL

A construction with modal marking signalling the evidence on which a statement is based. E.g. Turkish *Ali şeker al-dı* 'Ali sugar buy-PST, Ali bought sugar' (speaker knows this on his or her own authority), *Ali şeker al-mış-tı* 'Ali sugar buy-NONWITNESSED-PST, Ali, so I've heard/so I'm told/apparently bought sugar'. See **HEDGE, HEDGING, MODALITY**.

EVOKED MEANING

See **DESCRIPTIVE MEANING**.

EVOLUTIVE

An **Aktionsart** recognized by some analysts for Russian, as exemplified by *krichat'* 'shout' vs *raskrichat'sja* 'to work oneself up to shouting'; not just the beginning of the action but the development or evolution of the action from zero to full intensity. See **AKTIONSART**.

EWE

Kwa languages, Niger-Congo. Approx. 5M speakers, south-east Ghana, Togo.

EXCEPTIONAL CASE MARKING

Exceptional **case** marking is said to apply in the derivation of sentences such as *They believe him to be honest*. The structure assigned to such examples is [*They believe* ₛ[*him to be honest*]], with *him* as the **subject** of the embedded sentence *him to be honest*. As subject, the pronoun should receive **nominative** case and be realized as *he*, but, exceptionally, it is assigned **accusative** case and realized as *him*. See **RAISING, SUBJECT-TO-OBJECT RAISING**.

EXCHANGE
In the analysis of conversation, the smallest interaction between two or more interlocutors consisting of a move followed by a response. The move could be a **statement**, a **question**, a **command** and the response could be a reply to a question, a comment on a statement, a verbal response to a command and so on. Moves combine to form transactions. See **ADJACENCY PAIRS, BACKCHANNEL, CHECKING, INTERPERSONAL MEANING, TURN**.

EXCLAMATION
See **EXCLAMATIVE**.

EXCLAMATION MARK
1. Used in writing to mark a **word, phrase** or **clause** spoken with emphasis or shouted. **2.** Used in writing to mark the content of some sentence, clause or phrase as important or surprising. E.g. *They told him to leave – and he left without saying a word!*. *They got fewer votes than the others but are now in government!!* **2.** Used to mark an example that is grammatical in one sense but not in another. E.g. *The beans got spilled (all over the floor)* is grammatical in its literal meaning but not in the metaphorical meaning of telling everything: ! *The interrogation began and the beans got spilled* (though the example might be used for humorous effect).

EXCLAMATIVE
A set of constructions used in exclamations. They range from fixed phrases such as *Good grief!* and *No way!*, through wh forms, noun phrases such as *What an idiot!* and **adjective** phrases such as *How unfortunate!*, to **yes/no questions** such as *Isn't that just amazing!* and the special **clause** construction contrasting with **declarative, interrogative** and **imperative** clauses; e.g. *What a fright you gave me!*, *How thoughtful you are!*. As a **speech act**, an exclamation contrasts with a **statement, question** or **command**. See **CLAUSE, CONSTRUCTION**.

EXCLAMATORY CLAUSE
See **EXCLAMATIVE**.

EXCLUSIVE DISJUNCTION
See **DISJUNCTION**.

EXCLUSIVE WE
Designating the **speaker** and at least one other person, but not the **addressee**. Maori *maua* 'We = He/she and I', *matou* 'We = They and I, but not you'. See **INCLUSIVE**.

EXCRESCENT
See **EPENTHETIC**.

EXEMPLAR THEORY
See **PROTOTYPE THEORY**.

EXHORTATIVE
A **construction** expressing a modal meaning of exhortation or encouragement. E.g. English *Let's visit Sarah*, *Do borrow my car*; Russian *Daj knigu* 'give-IMP-PFV, Give me the book' vs *Daj-ka knigu* 'give-IMP-PFV-EXHORT book, Do give me the book'. See **MODALITY**.

EXISTENTIAL
A **construction** used to assert the (non-) existence of some entity or entities. In English the classic construction begins with *there*: *There's a policeman at the door*, *There are black swans in Australia*, *There are no snakes in Ireland*. The construction is also called 'existential-presentational', since it used to present entities to the listener, or to introduce them, as in *There was an inspector visiting the restaurant last Friday*. *There* is also known as the introductory *there*.

EXISTENTIAL-PRESENTATIONAL
See **EXISTENTIAL**.

EXISTENTIAL QUANTIFIER
An **operator** in **logic** used in **propositions** asserting the existence of something. E.g. *I saw a tiger* is expressed in predicate logic as $\exists x\ \&\ tiger\ (x)\ \&\ see\ (I, x)$ 'There is an x and x is a tiger and I saw x'.

EXOCENTRIC COMPOUND
See **COMPOUND WORD**.

EXOCENTRIC CONSTRUCTION
1. Originally defined as a **construction** in which the whole structure has a different **distribution** from that of any of its **constituents**: e.g. *in Lapland* has a different distribution from either *in* or *Lapland*. In contemporary theory all constructions are treated as having a **head** and as endocentric. 2. In earlier generative syntax, a construction without a head, such as S (sentence).
3. **Compound words** such as *scarecrow* and *pickpocket* which do not denote a type of crow or scaring, or a type of picking or pocket. The compound denotes a different type of entity from either of its constituent words. (Greek *exo* 'outside', Latin *centrum* 'centre'.) See **ENDOCENTRIC CONSTRUCTION**.

EXONYM
The name of a place in one language that differs from the name in the language of the country in which the place is situated. E.g. German *Mailand* Italian *Milano*. Exonyms are found in national states where two or more languages are spoken: in Belgium, French *Courtrai*, Flemish *Kortrijk*. (Greek *exo* 'outside', *onoma* 'name'.)

EXOPHORA

The use of **deictic** expressions to point to items outside a **text**: e.g. *They've arrived*, referring to guests, or *This is no use*, referring to a book, a tool, a recipe and so on. (Greek *exo* 'outside'.) See **ANAPHORA, CATAPHORA, DEIXIS, ENDOPHORA**.

EXPANDING CIRCLE

The diffusion of English as an international language in territories where English is mainly used as a foreign language, rather than as a first or second language. See **ENGLISH AS A LINGUA FRANCA, LINGUA FRANCA**.

EXPANSION

A criterion for determining whether a sequence of words forms a single **constituent** of a particular class: e.g. in *Dogs can be frightening*, *dogs* can be replaced by, or expanded into, the sequences *barking dogs, dogs with sharp teeth, dogs which are large and bad-tempered* and so on. In *They are hungry*, *they* expands into *the children, the boys who play in my garden* and so on. *Dogs, they, dogs with sharp teeth*, etc. are all classed as **noun phrases**. See **CONSTITUENT STRUCTURE**.

EXPANSION RULE

See **REWRITE RULE**.

EXPERIENCER

A participant **role** pertaining to psychological and certain physical states. In a number of languages the role is signalled by the **dative** case. E.g. Russian *Petru grustno* 'Peter-DAT sad, Peter is sad' vs *Petr umnyj* 'Peter-NOM clever, Peter is clever'.

EXPERIMENTAL PHONETICS

See **INSTRUMENTAL PHONETICS**.

EXPLANATORY ADEQUACY

See **ADEQUACY**.

EXPLETIVE *IT*

1. The *it* that acts as a **dummy subject** in examples such as *It is nine o'clock*, *It is very exciting to see the results*, *It is muddy in that field*. It fills out the syntax to the correct shape. (Latin *pleo* 'fill'.) 2. A swear word that, from a logical point of view, adds nothing to the meaning of a sentence but simply fills it out. See **IMPERSONAL CLAUSE**.

EXPLICATURE

In **relevance theory**, a set of processes whereby what is said explicitly in **utterances** is elaborated by hearers in order to arrive at a complete, interpretable **proposition**. Explicature supplies information to resolve **ambiguity** (*grub* in *I'm eating my grub* probably just denotes ordinary food if uttered in a restaurant in Britain but might denote a creature if uttered in some jungle) and to interpret definite referring expressions that presuppose familiarity with a culture or knowledge of a situation. (In *At Christmas my parents are buying the tree*, the speaker uses the definite referring expression *the tree* on the assumption that the hearer understands the reference by virtue of knowing the culture.) Enrichment is the component of explicature in which incomplete propositions are made complete. Instances of **ellipsis** are filled out: e.g. the reply *I will* or indeed *uhuh* to the question *Could you give me a hand with the cases?* is filled out to *I will give you a hand with the cases*. It supplies standards for assessing extent: the interpretations of *near* in *New Zealand is near Australia* and *Our house is near the supermarket* are very different, a thousand miles in one case, possibly just half-a-mile in the other. Explicature also deals with indirect speech acts: *There's black ice* is a statement, but it is also a warning, though not signalled as such, not even by a phrase such as *Be careful*. The role of explicature in relevance theory is similar to the role of the **maxims of conversation** and the various principles in neo-Gricean pragmatics. See **BRIDGING**.

EXPLICIT

Applied to analyses, especially in **formal grammar**, which leave nothing to be inferred or guessed by the reader. See **FORMALIZATION**.

EXPONENT

The **realization** of a linguistic unit. E.g. /s/, /z/ and /ɪz/ are exponents of **Plural**. In **phonology**, the exponents of **stress** may be the **length** of a **vowel**, a change in vowel quality or change in **pitch**. (Latin *exponere* 'set out, display'.) See **MORPH**.

EXPRESSION RULES

In **functional grammar**, rules that map complexes of semantic, syntactic and functional information into sound or writing.

EXPRESSION STRUCTURE

See **F-STRUCTURE**.

EXPRESSIVE

In Searle's classification, a speech act, such as praising, blaming or congratulating, by which speakers and writers convey their attitude towards some situation. E.g. *Excellent result!*, *That was stupid!*. See **ASSERTIVE, COMMISSIVE, DECLARATIVE, DIRECTIVE, SPEECH ACT**.

EXPRESSIVE MEANING

A dimension of non-descriptive meaning relating to speakers expressing an emotional state or attitude: *Wow!* Expressing astonishment, as Burns' poem 'Tam o' Shanter' (1790): *And, wow! He saw an unco sicht!* (Wow! He saw an extraordinary sight.); *Stop whingeing*, expressing contempt, as opposed to *Stop complaining*, which is neutral; *He's damn well spent our money*, expressing anger and surprise. See **DESCRIPTIVE MEANING**.

EXTENDED EXPONENCE

The **realization** of a single morpheme by two or more parts of a word. E.g. in *swollen* the morpheme past participle is realized by the *-o-* in *swoll-* and the suffix *-en*. See **MORPH**.

EXTENDED STANDARD THEORY

The model of **transformational grammar** current in the mid 1970s. It was distinguished from the preceding **standard theory** by three main properties: semantic interpretation was determined by **surface structure** and not **deep structure**; transformations were restricted in their operations, and general restrictions on movement and **coreference** were formulated, replacing restrictions on individual transformations. See **COREFERENTIAL, TRANSFORMATION**.

EXTENSION

1. See **RHETORICAL STRUCTURE**. 2. The individual members of some set. An extensional definition of, e.g. the denotation of the lexical item *kiwi* is simply a listing one by one of all the members of the set of kiwis. See **DENOTATION, INTENSION, SENSE**.

EXTENSIONAL MEANING

See **EXTENSION**.

EXTERNAL ADEQUACY

The extent to which a **grammar** corresponds to the data.

EXTERNAL POSSESSOR

In a clause such as *Peter's head hurts* the noun phrase *Peter's* denotes the possessor of the head and is inside the bigger noun phrase *Peter's head*. In the Russian *Petru bolit golova* 'Peter-DAT hurt head, Peter's head hurts', the pronoun *Petru* denotes the possessor of the head but does not combine with *golova* 'head' to form a larger noun phrase. *Petru* is an external possessor. See **CASE, DATIVE, ETHIC DATIVE**.

EXTERNAL SANDHI

See **SANDHI**.

EXTERNALIZED LANGUAGE

See **E-LANGUAGE**.

EXTRA-LINGUISTIC

Applied to phenomena related to language use but external to language and any particular language system, e.g. the extra-linguistic world as opposed to speakers' mental representations of the world.

EXTRAPOSE

See **EXTRAPOSITION**.

EXTRAPOSITION

Term introduced by **Jespersen** for the movement of a **phrase** or **clause** to the end of a sentence although it is logically the subject and belongs at the beginning of the sentence. In *It was interesting to see how the project has developed* the **infinitive** *to see how the project has developed* is logically the subject of *was interesting*. Alternative phrasing makes this clear: *To see how the project has developed was interesting*. The latter **construction** is hardly ever used in spoken English. Similar pairs of structures are *It was reported on the news that the road was completely closed* (with extraposed clause) and *That the road was completely closed was reported on the news*; *It was strange finding the house empty* (with extraposed **gerund**) and *Finding the house empty was strange*. The concept has been extended to constructions in which a **relative clause** has been moved to the end of the sentence. In *A guy that my sister hated came to the party*, the relative clause can be extraposed to give *A guy came to the party that my sister hated*. See **DUMMY SUBJECT, POSTPOSING**.

EXTRINSIC ORDERING

See **RULE ORDERING**.

F

F⁰
> See **FUNDAMENTAL FREQUENCY**.

F¹
> Formant 1. See **FORMANT**.

F-STRUCTURE
In **Lexical-Functional Grammar**, c-structure handles the basic **constituent structure** of a **sentence** or **clause** while f-structure handles information about **grammatical functions** such as subject, direct object, etc. but also information about **grammatical categories** such as **number**, tense and **case**. This information is represented as pairs of attributes and values, where an attribute is a symbol such as S, TENSE, NUM, PRED (predicate) and the values can be symbols such as PL (plural), semantic forms such as 'lion', or whole f-structures. The f-structure relates **argument structure** – events and participants such as agent, patient, instrument and so on – with constituent structure, also called expression structure. See **AGREEMENT, GOVERNMENT, ROLE, TENSE AND ASPECT, UNIFICATION**.

FABULA
See **HISTOIRE**.

FACE
In politeness theory, the self-image projected by a speaker in an interaction such as a conversational **exchange**. Positive face represents a speaker's desire that their self-image be approved of, and negative face represents a speaker's desire not to be imposed on. See **POLITENESS PRINCIPLE**.

FACETS
Different senses of **lexical words** which are not distinct enough to count as completely separate readings and therefore as straightforward **polysemy** but which are discrete enough to be more than just contextual **modulation**. A much-used example is *book*, which has a [text] facet and a [tome] facet. In *I love this book*, it is possible that *this book* refers to the text (the plot, the characters, the writing) but at the same time to the physical copy of the book (its binding, the quality of the paper, the type, the illustrations). See **ANTAGONISM, HOMONYMY, MONOSEMY, SENSE**.

FACTITIVE

A **verb** denoting an **action** or **process** that causes an entity to change its state. E.g. *kill* is 'make dead' and *blacken* is 'make black', whereas the action of reading does not make books change their state. See **AFFECTED OBJECT, EFFECTED OBJECT**.

FACTIVE VERB

Know and *realize* are factive verbs. They take a **complement clause**, and speakers who use factive verbs presuppose that the complement clause is true. It does not matter whether the main **clause** is **declarative** or **interrogative**, **positive** or **negative**. *She knows that Bill is leaving, She doesn't know that Bill is leaving* and *Does she know that Bill is leaving* are all appropriate only if the speaker assumes that *Bill is leaving* is true. An alternative view is that, e.g., *She doesn't know that Bill is leaving* entails *Bill is leaving*. See **ENTAILMENT, NON-FACTIVE VERB, PRESUPPOSITION**.

FACTOR ANALYSIS

A statistical method for analysing **variation** among observable **variables** in terms of more general but hidden variables called factors. Suppose certain texts have wh **relative clauses** in both subject and object **noun phrases**, and a high incidence of **nominalizations**. This combination of properties constitutes a factor. When certain other properties are taken into account, this factor turns out to be associated with highly explicit, context-independent reference such as is found in official documents and academic prose. The factor is not visible without detailed automatic statistical analysis of texts.

FALLING

1. A **tone** or **intonation** pattern where the **pitch** moves from relatively high to relatively low. In English the unmarked intonation pattern associated with statements is falling. 2. Of a **diphthong**, where the second element of the diphthong is less prominent that the first, compare [iə] in *here* which is falling, with [eɪ] in *say* which is **rising**.

FAMILY TREE

The graphic representation of the relationship of languages within a family. The root of the tree is the ancestor language (e.g. **Latin**) and the branches represent **daughter languages** or families (e.g. **Italian, Spanish**, or **French**). See **LANGUAGE CLASSIFICATION**.

FALSE VOCAL CORDS

See **VOCAL CORDS**.

FANAGALO

A **pidgin** language developed in the mines of Southern Africa some two hundred years ago and still used. It contains elements of **Afrikaans, Xhosa** and **English**.

FAROESE
Germanic, Indo-European. 45K speakers, Faroe Islands.

FEATURE
1. In **generative grammar**, an element in the representation of properties used to classify **lexical words**: e.g. [animate], [count], [abstract], etc. 2. In various models of generative grammar, representation of the properties used to classify syntactic categories: e.g. [+N] for **Noun**, [+/− sg] for **singular** or **plural**, [+/− past] for **past tense** or **present tense**. See COUNT NOUN, MASS NOUN.

FEATURE CO-OCCURRENCE RESTRICTION
In **generalized phrase structure grammar**, a restriction on possible combinations of **features** for any one item. E.g. any item that has the feature SUBCAT, i.e. that is subcategorized, also has the feature BAR 0, i.e. is a lexical item. See STRICT SUBCATEGORIZATION.

FEATURE GEOMETRY
A development of **distinctive feature** theory where features are grouped together under superordinate properties called '**gestures**'. Thus the **laryngeal** gesture gathers together features associated with the activity of the **larynx**. Articulatory gestures cover **cavity features** (the place of articulation and the configuration of the vocal tract) and **manner features** (the manner of articulation). See DISTINCTIVE FEATURES, ARTICULATORY. See SOURCE FEATURES.

FEATURE INSTANTIATION
In **Generalized Phrase Structure Grammar**, the central mechanism of the model that allows features to be freely assigned to categories in local trees provided they do not infringe any general condition specified by the grammar. See TREE DIAGRAM.

FEATURE MATRIX
A display of features in rows and columns used to characterize **lexical words** or **phonemes**. See FEATURE.

FEATURE SPECIFICATION
In **Generalized Phrase Structure Grammar**, the specification of categories by means of pairs of features and feature values. For example, a **finite verb** phrase has the feature 'V' and the value '+', the feature 'N' and the value '−', the feature VFORM (the form of the verb) and the value 'FIN' (finite) and so on.

FEEDBACK
Responses which enable **speakers** to judge how successfully they are communicating with an **addressee**. The responses may be verbal, such as *right, ok, what?*, or non-verbal. The latter may be vocal, such as sighs or groans, or non-vocal, such as eye-movements, facial expressions, hand gestures,

head movements. See **BACKCHANNEL, COMPLETE FEEDBACK, EXCHANGE, SEQUENCE, TURN.**

FEEDING

In a rule system with ordered rules, the ordering of the rules may be such that the output of a particular rule produces the necessary conditions for the application of a subsequent rule. The first rule feeds the second. Opposite **bleeding**. See **GENERATIVE PHONOLOGY, RULE ORDERING.**

FELICITY CONDITIONS

Austin's theory of **speech acts** recognized that for a **performative** to be successful, certain conditions, Felicity conditions, have to be met. A person sitting in judgement in a court must have been properly appointed by the legal authorities; a person carrying out a marriage ceremony must have the authority to do so; the procedure for carrying out some act must be properly and completely followed. Even everyday acts such as giving orders only succeed if the person giving the orders is entitled by their position or rank to do so.

Searle recognizes preparatory conditions, sincerity conditions and essential conditions. Preparatory conditions must hold if a speech act is to be successfully performed, as with the above-mentioned conditions for passing judgement and conducting marriages. Speakers making statements ideally have evidence that their statements are true and that their hearers do not know the content of the statement. Sincerity conditions must hold if an act is to be performed sincerely. Speakers asking questions must genuinely desire to have the answers. If preparatory conditions are not met, an act misfires, does not take place. If sincerity conditions are not met, an act is performed but is abused. Essential conditions have to do with speakers' intending their utterance to be recognized as a particular type of speech act. Thus, an utterance such as *Come and have a meal with us* might be intended as a genuine invitation, or it might just be a polite form of words. See **NEO-GRICEAN PRAGMATICS.**

FEMININE

Especially in many **Indo-European** languages, a grammatical **gender**, or **noun** class, whose central members denote female humans, although most of the nouns in the class denote inanimate and/or abstract entities. E.g. in French, *femme* 'woman' and *fille* 'girl' are feminine but so are *vérité* 'truth' and *viande* 'meat'. See **COMMON GENDER, COMMON NOUN, COUNT NOUN, MASS NOUN.**

FEMINIST LINGUISTICS

Studies of women's language and language and sexism.

FICTIVE MOTION

In the theory of **force dynamics**, the use of forms and **constructions** basically denoting movement through space to refer to situations that, in the external world, do not involve movement. E.g. *The path went across the field and into the* *wood, The mountain shoots up precipitously to a height of 8,000 feet.* **Cognitive linguistics** uses the term **subjective motion**. See **CONSTRUAL, CONSTRUE**.

FIELD
See **FIELD OF DISCOURSE**.

FIELD OF DISCOURSE
An area of linguistic activity, such as science, journalism, advertising, etc. See **FORMALITY**.

FIELD THEORY
A theory of how the vocabulary in a given language is structured. Lexical items are seen as organized into groups relating to particular fields of the external world. The members of a lexical field are held together by their denotation but also, crucially, by the **sense relations** that hold among them. See **HYPONYMY, OPPOSITENESS, SENSE, SYNONYMY**.

FIELDWORK
Work done in 'the field'; the practical side of linguistic research, as distinguished from laboratory work and the application and development of theory.

FIGURATIVE
A use of language in which a basic, concrete, literal **meaning** is extended to another **domain**, which may be abstract. E.g. *Frosty* is applied to (part of) a day or some area affected by frost: *a frosty morning, a frosty landscape. Thaw* is applied to snow melting: *The snow thawed slowly over several days. Frosty* and *thaw* can be extended to a look – *She gave him a very frosty look* – or to relationships – *Relations with our neighbours have been frosty but are now thawing.* The last two examples illustrate figurative language. See **FIGURE OF SPEECH, HYPERBOLE, LITOTES, METAPHOR, SIMILE, SYNECDOCHE**.

FIGURE
In a given **situation** or scene, there is usually one entity, the figure, that stands out against the rest of the scene, the ground. In **Cognitive Grammar** these concepts are applied in the analysis of examples such as *A kangaroo was crushed by the roadtrain*, which presents the kangaroo as figure, and *The roadtrain crushed a kangaroo*, which presents the roadtrain as figure. Certain types of scene, such as locational ones, have a typical figure-ground organization. In a location scene containing an **animate** entity, the latter is typically the figure and is denoted by the subject **noun phrase**: *The chairman sat in a vast leather armchair* is far more usual than *A vast leather armchair contained/supported the chairman.* See **COGNITIVE GRAMMAR, GRAMMATICAL FUNCTION**.

FIGURE OF SPEECH
Any of the constructions employed in the use of figurative language. See **FIGURATIVE, METAPHOR, SIMILE, SYNECDOCHE**.

FIJIAN

Malayo Polynesian, **Austronesian**. Approx. 541K speakers, Fiji and neighbouring communities in the South-west Pacific between the Solomon Islands and Samoa.

FILLED PAUSE

A pause which speakers fill in order to signal that they are going to resume addressing their audience. Typical fillers in English are *ah, eh* and *erm*.

FILLER

In **slot** and filler representations, items that can fill a particular slot in a given **construction**. E.g. **noun phrases** contain a **determiner** slot which can be filled by an **article**, *the* or *a*, a **demonstrative** such as *this* or *that*, or a **quantifier** such as *some* or *any*.

FILTER

In **generative grammar**, a condition that applies to the output of a grammar, or component of a grammar, to check for structures that do not conform. For example, a grammar might generate as output a structure for *What$_i$ did you hear that t$_i$ collapsed?* This structure is filtered out by a condition stipulating that the **complementizer** *that* cannot be immediately followed by the **trace** of a **wh form** that has been moved.

FINAL

Occurring in the last position in a particular **construction**: e.g. a **consonant** in the last position of a **syllable** is syllable-final; a **particle** occurring in the last position in a **clause** is clause-final and so on.

FINAL CLAUSE

See ADVERBIAL CLAUSE OF PURPOSE.

FINGER SPELLING

A type of **signing** where each letter of a word is represented by a configuration of the fingers.

FINITE CLASS

See CLOSED CLASS.

FINITE CLAUSE

A clause containing a **finite verb**.

FINITE-STATE GRAMMAR

A generative device based on the idea of **sentences** as **strings** of **words**. The device starts off in an initial state and passes to another state, then to yet another state and so on. Depending on which state the device moves to, it writes a word. In generating the string *The dog barked*, the device moves to a state along a connection that allows it to write *the*, then along a connection that allows it to write *dog*, and finally along a connection that allows it to write *barked*.

The device was formulated by Chomsky in the 1950s as part of his demonstration that some generative devices were inadequate for the handling of human language. See **ADEQUACY, GENERATIVE GRAMMAR, TRANSFORMATIONAL GRAMMAR**.

FINITE VERB

Traditionally **verbs** marked for tense, **person** and **number** are regarded as finite; these markings are numerous and easily recognized in languages such as Russian, Italian and written French, but rare in English. The term 'finite verb' contrasts with '**non-finite verb**' and '**infinitive**'. It derives from the Latin *finitus*, the past **passive participle** of *finire* 'to limit', from the same root as *finis* 'a boundary, limit'. The underlying **metaphor** is that, for example, the Latin infinitive form *currere* 'to run' denotes running without any limitations, whereas finite forms such as *currebam* run-PST-1sg 'I was running' tie the event down to a (general) time and to a certain participant or to certain participants. See **TENSE AND ASPECT**.

FINNISH

Finno-Ugric, Uralic. 5.2M speakers, Finland. Small numbers of speakers in Russia and Sweden. Very closely related to Estonian.

FINNO-UGRIC

Language family including, in Europe, **Finnish**, **Saami** (Lapp), **Hungarian**, and, in north and central Russia, Komi, Mari (Cheremis), Mordva (Mordvin), Mansi (Vogul).

FIRST LANGUAGE

1. The language a speaker acquires first as a **native language**. 2. A speaker's preferred language. See **SECOND LANGUAGE**.

FIRST PERSON

See **PERSON**.

'FIS' PHENOMENON

The refusal by children to accept an adult's imitation of a childish pronunciation. For example, children may say *fis* instead of *fish* but get upset when addressed by adults who imitate their pronunciation by also saying *fis*. The phenomenon is interpreted as showing that children's perception of sounds is ahead of their ability to produce them.

FIXATION

In reading, a period of rest between rapid eye-movements as the reader scans a text. See **SACCADES**.

FIXED EXPRESSION

A general term, along with 'set expression', for combinations of words that cannot be changed in any way, or that can only be changed in minor detail, that function like individual **lexemes**: e.g. *in a nutshell* (= briefly), *once and for all*.

Some expressions allow relatively large variation, as in *as I/we/you was/were saying/mentioning, as far as I/we/they can see/make out*; others allow less variation, such as *the more the merrier*. 'Frozen expression' is equivalent to 'fixed expression' but is sometimes restricted to combinations containing words that do not occur anywhere else: e.g. *spick and span*. Many fixed expressions, both phrases and clauses, are idioms, that is, fixed expressions whose meaning cannot be guessed from their individual words: e.g. *It takes two to tango* (= People need to cooperate), *She put her foot in it* (= She offended someone greatly). Many fixed expressions are distinguished by their function in specific contexts, such as personal social exchanges (*Good morning!*, *Guten Appetit!*, *Slainte mhath* (= Scots Gaelic), 'good health'), public transactions (*Single to Glasgow, please*; *Do you have a table for four?*); ritual activities such as religious services or proceedings in courts of law; expressions used by oral poets and storytellers. Expressions with specific functions in specific contexts are known as formulas. Unlike idioms, their meanings can typically be inferred from the individual lexical items and the context of use. Every language and culture has many proverbs and aphorisms; they too are fixed expressions: e.g. *a rolling stone (gathers no moss)*, *The early bird catches the worm*, etc. A term for the study of all types of fixed expressions is 'phraseology'.

FIXED WORD ORDER
See **WORD ORDER**.

FLAP
A term in the description of the **manner of articulation** of oral **consonant** sounds. The **active articulator**, typically the **tip** of the **tongue**, briefly strikes against a **passive articulator**, typically the **alveolar** ridge, forming a single brief oral closure. A one tap **trill** is sometimes referred to as a tapped *r*. The **retroflex** consonants of some Indian languages are flaps. See **ARTICULATION**.

FLAT
In **J&H Distinctive Feature Theory**, an acoustic distinctive feature representing a downward shift of the upper frequencies of the spectrum, associated with lip-rounding, **retroflex** and pharyngealization. It is in opposition to both sharp and plain, so **flat, plain, sharp** is in effect a ternary opposition.

FLOATING TONE
A **tone** that is not associated with a particular tone bearing unit in an underlying representation, but which may have an effect on an adjacent tone bearing unit.

FLORES LANGUAGES
Austronesian. Southern Indonesia.

FLOUT A MAXIM
To deliberately disregard one of the **maxims of conversation**.

FOCAL ACCENT
See **NUCLEUS**.

FOCAL AREA
In **dialect geography**, an area whose dialect has influenced surrounding areas as a source of innovation, usually a centre of relatively high economic or cultural activity.

FOCAL REGION
In **prototype** theory, the set of entities that are good central members of some set; e.g. in the UK *oak*, *beech*, *birch* and *ash* are in the focal area of trees, whereas *totara*, *kauri* and *rata* are peripheral. (In New Zealand, *totara*, etc. are focal.) See **PROTOTYPE THEORY**.

FOCALIZATION
The perspective from which a narrative is told; e.g. from the perspective of the author of a novel or one of the characters in the novel. See **AUTHORIAL VOICE**, **VOICE**.

FOCUS
Focus has to do with giving prominence to **constituents** and the information they carry. Such prominence serves different purposes – the introduction of new entities or new **propositions**, the contrast of one entity with another, 'exhaustive listing' (one particular entity and no other). This may be achieved by means of **pitch**, as in English *We're going to SOUTHWOLD (not SOUTHEND)*, by syntactic **constructions**, such as an English **cleft construction**: *It's Southwold we're going to, Where we're going is Southwold*, by word order – *You should avoid Southend* vs *Southend you should avoid*, or by particle – *It's really Southwold we're going to*. Constituents are said to be given prominence, made prominent, highlighted, made salient or given salience. See **END FOCUS, GIVEN AND NEW, THEME, FOCUS PARTICLE**.

FOCUS PARTICLE
A set of words such as *only* and *even* which highlight different **constituents**. Cf. *Even Freya liked this book* (highlighting *Freya*) and *Freya liked even this book* (highlighting *this book*). See **DISCOURSE PARTICLE, FOCUS**.

FOLK LINGUISTICS
The knowledge, beliefs, theories, etc. that members of a speech community hold about their own language, language in general, etc.

FOOT
1. In **phonology**, a rhythmical unit consisting of one or more **syllables**, typically a stressed syllable and the unstressed syllables following it up to but not including the next stressed syllable: e.g. in the line |MEAdows| TRIM with| DAISies| PIEd, foot divisions are marked with | and stressed syllables are capitalized. Compare also the foot divisions in a|GENda| and |ALgebra|. In a

stress timed language feet tend to be isochronous. **2.** In poetics, the basic unit of rhythm consisting of one or more syllables, one of which is stressed. Traditional feet include the **iamb** (unstress, stress) as in |to BE| or NOT| to BE|, the trochee (stress unstress) as in |MEAdows| TRIM with| DAISies| PIEd|, the **dactyl** (stress unstress unstress) as in the As|SYRian came |DOWN like a| WOLF on the| FOLD| and the spondee (stress stress). Note that the traditional metrical foot and the contemporary phonological foot do not always correspond. See **ISOCHRONY**.

FOOTING
See **STANCE**.

FORCE DYNAMICS
A model of causation based on the concepts of entities exercising forces and other entities resisting the forces. *Keep the dog in the kitchen* is interpreted as someone exercising a force on the dog to prevent it from going out of the kitchen. *Let the dog out* is interpreted in terms of removing a force that was acting on the dog so that the dog's energy takes it out. See **COGNITIVE GRAMMAR, COGNITIVE LINGUISTICS, CONSTRUAL**.

FOREGROUNDING
In **discourse analysis**, making certain parts of a text prominent. For example, the main events in a **narrative** (which move the narrative on) are foregrounded by being presented in a main **clause** with a **finite verb**, typically in the **Simple Past** (in English). Events which do not move the narrative on are backgrounded by being presented in either a main or **subordinate clause**, often by a **non-finite verb**. See **BACKGROUNDING**.

FOREIGN PLURAL
In English, words borrowed from Latin which have their Latin **plural**: e.g. *gladiolus* and *gladioli*, *focus* and *foci*. Some words, such as *referendum* and *stadium*, have Latin and English plurals: *referenda* and *referendums*, *stadia* and *stadiums*. *Data*, a plural in Latin, has the **singular** *datum* in the usage of academics, but for most speakers is a singular, **mass noun**. *Bacteria* is a Latin plural but is beginning to be used as a singular, by speakers who are not doctors or scientists. See **COUNT NOUN, MASS NOUN**.

FOREIGNER TALK
The deliberate simplification of their language often used by native speakers when addressing non-native speakers. It is sometimes said to represent a native speaker's notion of how a foreigner speaks their language. Foreigner talk stereotypes are common in most societies.

FORENSIC LINGUISTICS
The use of linguistic techniques in the investigation of crime, e.g. voice recognition, dialect recognition.

FORM

The written or spoken shape assumed by a unit as opposed to its content or meaning, the **lexeme** it realizes or its function. E.g. *mouse* and *mice* are forms of the lexeme MOUSE. See **MORPH**.

FORM CLASS

A set of **morphs, words, phrases** or **clauses** whose members have the same **distribution**. E.g. in English *the* and *a* make up the form class of **articles**, *-ed* and *-s* and make up the form class of tense **suffixes**, *sand, water*, etc. belong to the form class of mass nouns. See **DISTRIBUTION, NOTIONAL, PART OF SPEECH**.

FORM OF ADDRESS

Features of style used in addressing someone. They often express personal relationships (*auntie, grandpa*) or the degree of intimacy or difference in status between interlocutors. At a more formal level, they are legal or official titles, often associated with institutions such as the monarchy, the judiciary or legislative bodies. See **INTERLOCUTOR, T/V FORMS**.

FORM WORD

See **GRAMMATICAL WORD**.

FORMAL

1. Relating to **form** and **form class**, rather than meaning or function. A formal account of a **word class** focuses on **distribution**. 2. Relating to **formal grammar**.

FORMAL GRAMMAR

1. In its original and strongest sense, an explicit, mathematically based set of rules that specify the strings of symbols in a given language, which may be artificial or natural. In natural languages the symbols represent words, phrases and so on. In its weaker sense, a formal grammar is any account of a natural language which is explicit, leaving as little as possible to the reader's intuition, and uses some clearly defined notation. 2. A grammar that takes **form, form class** and **distribution** as central. See **NOTIONAL GRAMMAR**.

FORMAL LANGUAGE

See **PROGRAMMING LANGUAGE**.

FORMAL ROLE

One of the **qualia roles**, related to the perspective of an entity as having a particular form and belonging to a particular kind. For example, the view of a house as belonging to the set of dwellings that includes cottages and villas but excludes castles and caravans. See **AGENTIVE ROLE, CONSTITUTIVE ROLE, TELIC ROLE**.

FORMAL LOGIC

The study of systems for assigning exact representations to the **propositions** expressed by sentences of any natural language and determining the **entailments** of any given set of propositions. One such system is the propositional **calculus**, another more complex one is the predicate calculus. See DEDUCTION, IMPLICATURE, PRESUPPOSITION.

FORMAL SEMANTICS

Originally a means of assigning precise interpretations to expressions in the formal languages of logic and mathematics. In the 1960s the techniques of formal semantics were extended to the analysis of natural language, primarily through the work of Richard Montague. See CALCULUS, CATEGORIAL GRAMMAR, COMPOSITIONALITY.

FORMALISM

Any notation or rules for representing items, their properties and relations, such as number (mathematics), propositions (logic) and syntactic or phonological structures (linguistics).

FORMALIST LINGUISTICS

An approach to the analysis of language focusing on **form** rather than **function**. An opposition between formal and functional linguistics is sometimes invoked but most language analysis employs both form and function.

FORMALITY

The formality of a text is determined, sometimes in a very subtle fashion, by particular combinations of **topic, medium, channel, setting** and **tenor**. A conversation that is being recorded is more formal than one that is not; a dialogue between father and son is more formal than one between son and a friend of the same age; a dialogue in familiar domestic surroundings is less formal than one in a lawyer's office. See DIMENSION, REGISTER.

FORMALIZATION

Any analysis that is **formal 2**.

FORMANT

A concentration of **acoustic** energy in a particular **frequency** band. Formants are displayed graphically on a **sound spectrograph** showing up as thick dark bars. **Vowels** are associated with several formants, and every vowel has a different distribution of energy between the formants. The positions of the three lowest formants (F1, F2 and F3) distinguish vowels apart. **Sonorant** consonants also produce formants. When a vowel precedes or follows a **consonant**, the **transitions** as the formants pass from a vowel to a consonant distinguish between different **stop** consonants.

FORMATION RULE

In **logic** and **formal semantics**, rules specifying possible sequences of symbols.

FORMATIVE

1. A general term for the result of any morphological **process**. This may be an **affix**, such as the *-ion* and *-s*, realizing the **morpheme** 'Plural', in *transmissions*, an empty **morph** such as *-s* in the German **compound word** *Liebesbrief* 'love+s

+letter', a change in vowel as in *sang* vs *sing*, or a change in vowel length or in tone. 2. In mid-1960s generative grammar, a **morpheme** or minimal unit of syntax.

FORMOSAN LANGUAGES
Austronesian. Taiwan. The fourteen extant indigenous languages of Taiwan are mostly endangered. They are considered the ancestors of the Austronesian languages.

FORMULA
See **FIXED EXPRESSION**.

FORTIS
A **consonant** articulated with special muscular effort or particularly strong exhalation of breath. See **LENIS, TENSE**.

FORTITION
The process whereby a segment is perceived to be articulated with 'more force', thus 'strengthened', e.g. a fricative becoming a stop. See **LENITION**.

FOSSILIZATION
The process by which a **phrase** or **clause** becomes **fossilized**.

FOSSILIZED
A fossilized **phrase** or **clause** is one that has become a **fixed expression**, often preserving a word or grammatical feature that has been lost from the language. E.g. *if I were you*, preserving the subjunctive *were*, *to shy away from doing something*, preserving the verb *shy*, which is a fossil except perhaps in the domain of equestrianism.

FOUCAULT, Michel (1926–1984)
A French philosopher and sociologist. He elaborated the ideas that particular social groups have particular **discourse** practice and that language has a key role in maintaining ideologies and social power.

FOURTH PERSON
See **OBVIATIVE**.

FOWLER, Henry Watson (1858–1933)
An English schoolteacher and journalist who wrote the *Dictionary of Modern English Usage* (1926), now in its third edition (1996).

FRAME
1. In the analysis of **distribution**, the representation of a context or **environment** in which an item can occur. E.g. *happy* occurs in the frames [*the __ baby*] or [*__er*]; *delicious* occurs in the frames [*the __ pear*] or [*more __*]. 2. In **generative grammar**, the representation of the syntactic context in which a lexical item occurs or which, in the later models, a lexical item licenses: e.g. VANISH has the frame [__Ø] – *The rabbit vanished*. PUT has the frame

[___ NP PP] – *(Fiona) put her purse on the counter-top*. See **DISTRIBUTION, FRAME, PHRASE, SUBCATEGORIZATION, WORD CLASS**. **3.** In generative grammar, the representation of the roles obligatory or optional for a given **predicate**: e.g. TAKE [agent, patient, goal], *Keith took the letter to the Post Office*. **4.** In AI, part of a mental representation of the external world in a given culture, a schema of some area of experience containing the main types of actors and the relations between them: e.g. shopping in a British supermarket vs shopping in a Middle Eastern souk. Frames are constantly updated and are used in reasoning. **5.** Any cultural or other setting that involves different language practices; e.g. the use of colloquial language in domestic settings vs the use of formal language in school classrooms. Sense (5) can be seen as dependent on (4). See **CASE GRAMMAR, FRAME SEMANTICS, LICENSING, ROLE**.

FRAME ANALYSIS

A research method used to analyse how people understand situations, activities, etc. It seeks to understand how issues of public interest or controversy are presented in the communication media. See **FRAME, FRAME SEMANTICS**.

FRAME SEMANTICS

An analysis of word meaning which focuses on **lexical words** in relation to particular frames of reference. Thus in the frame relating to the collection and delivery of mail, *letter* denotes envelopes containing written messages on paper and is in a lexical field with *parcel, packet, envelope*. In the frame relating to typography, *letter* denotes a particular set of marks on paper representing sounds. In the frame 'tennis', *server* is the player serving the ball; in the frame 'computing', *server* is the piece of equipment that distributes mail and other documents to individual PCs. See **CONTEXT, DOMAIN, LEXICAL FIELD**.

FRANGLAIS

A portmanteau word from French (français) and English (anglais) indicating the use of French words in English (*Bien je jamais* for 'well I never') and vice-versa (*le weekend* for '*la fin de semaine*'). English speakers generally regard this as humorous; some French speakers regard this as an unwelcome and unacceptable import into French.

FREE

1. Applied to a **morph** or morpheme that can occur on its own as a **word**. E.g. *educational* in *educational advantages* but also the stem *education*, since it occurs as an independent word in *He has no education*. **2.** Initially in the **Government and Binding Theory** but now generally, any **noun** or **pronoun** whose **reference** is not bound to an **antecedent**. E.g. in *Lionel fancies himself*, *Lionel* controls the reference of *himself* but is itself free. In *We are leaving now*, *we* has no antecedent but refers to the speaker and others.

FREE DATIVE

See **ETHIC DATIVE**.

FREE INDIRECT SPEECH

A type of narration which avoids direct and indirect speech but instead presents a character's words or thoughts as part of the narrative. E.g. *'Will you want to be in on this part of the inquiry, sir?' – 'Certainly' – Oh dear. 'Oh good!'* (Lindsey Davis, *Three Hands in the Fountain*.) The phrase *oh dear* is an example of free indirect speech.

FREE MODIFIER

See **ADJUNCT**.

FREE PARTICIPLE

A **participle** or participial phrase that modifies a complete **clause**. E.g. in *Opening the window, I shouted for help*, the free participle *opening the window* modifies the clause *I shouted for help*. It is a type of non-finite clause. See **GERUND, NON-FINITE VERB**.

FREE RELATIVE CLAUSE

A **clause** that is like a **relative clause** in having a wh word at the beginning: *what you said* in *What you said is unacceptable* and *I heard what you said*. The label 'headless relative clause' reflects the view that the clause does not have a noun as **antecedent**. This view also lies behind the label 'free relative clause', along with the fact that the clause behaves like a **noun phrase**; e.g. *what you said* is the subject of *is unacceptable* and the **direct object** of *heard* in *I heard what you said*. Its behaviour as a noun phrase is captured in the alternative label 'nominal relative clause'. One analysis of the **construction** sees the single wh word as both **head** and **relative pronoun**, a fusion of *that which* – hence the label 'fused relative clause'. An alternative analysis takes the wh word as the head modified by the rest of the sequence. The latter is regarded as a **contact clause** with a missing or ellipted **personal pronoun**: e.g. *What [you said it] is unacceptable* is realized as *What$_i$ [you said __$_i$] is unacceptable*.

FREE VARIATION

Variation in which either of two (or more) sounds or **forms** can be used without any contrast or change in meaning. In **phonology** it designates the substitutability of one **segment** for another in the same **environment**, thus /i/ or /ɛ/ in the first syllable of *economics* or /ei/ or /a/ in the second syllable of *tomato*. For many speakers, in the pronunciation of many words ending in a final voiceless stop, as *bit*, the final stop may be either released, [bɪt^h], or unreleased [bɪt], and if unreleased may be glottalized [bɪtʔ]. In syntax, the comparative of some comparative adjectives can involve either *more* or the suffix *-er* – *sillier; more silly*. E.g. *Neither* can be pronounced with [i:] or [aɪ], the **comparative** of *polite* can be *politer* or *more polite* and the **past tense** of *plead* can be *pled* or *pleaded*. *Politer* and *more polite*, for example, are said to be free variants. Although such variation seems free, the choice of sound or form may be affected by stylistic or sociolinguistic factors. This is in contrast with complementary distribution, in which the choice of one or other form is controlled by linguistic factors and is obligatory: e.g. the use of *a* before nouns beginning with a consonant and *an* before nouns beginning with a vowel. See **COMPLEMENTARY DISTRIBUTION, DISTRIBUTION, ENVIRONMENT, FRAME**.

FREE WORD ORDER

See **WORD ORDER**.

FREGE, Gottlob (1848–1925)

A German mathematician, logician and philosopher who developed the theory of **reference**, including the distinction between reference and **sense**, and laid the foundations of **compositionality**.

FRENCH

Romance language, **Indo-European**. 64M speakers France, 4.1M Belgium, 1.6M Switzerland, 7.2M Canada. Official language of French Overseas Territories and several former French colonies.

FREQUENCY

The frequency of a given entity is the number of occurrences of the entity in a particular context.

FREQUENCY ADVERB

An **adverb, adverb phrase** or **adverbial clause** stating how often an event happens. E.g. *often, twice a year, whenever we are in Paris*. A phrase such as *every Sunday* is a noun phrase but in work on aspect such phrases are also called frequency adverbs. See **DURATION ADVERB**.

FREQUENCY ADVERBIAL

See **FREQUENCY ADVERB**.

FREQUENTATIVE

See **ITERATIVE**.

FRICATIVE

A term in the description of the **manner of articulation** of oral **consonant** sounds, as in [f] *fin*. The sound made when two **articulators** come into **close approximation** resulting in a turbulent airflow thus producing audible **friction**. See **ARTICULATION**.

FRICTION

The sound produced when air passes a constriction in the **vocal tract** caused by **articulators** approaching each other thus creating a turbulent **airstream**. Audible friction is characteristic of **fricative** consonants; by contrast **vowels** are frictionless. Friction can occur at all **places of articulation** – there are **bilabial** fricatives, **dental** fricatives, etc. See **AIRSTREAM MECHANISM**.

FRICTIONLESS CONTINUANT

A term in the description of the **manner of articulation** of oral **consonant** sounds, as in [w] in *win*, [j] in *year*, [l] in *leaf*. The **articulators** approach each other and there is a non-turbulent **airstream** without **closure** or friction. Such sounds are sometimes called **approximants**. See **FRICTION**.

FRISIAN

Germanic, Indo-European. Approx. 700K speakers Netherlands, 21K Germany.

FRONT

1. A term used in the description of the **manner of articulation** of sounds. It can refer either to sounds articulated in the front of the mouth as opposed to the back, such as the **vowels** [i] or [e], or to sounds articulated with the front of the tongue, such as **consonants** [t], [d], [s] or [z]. In distinctive feature analyses, sounds articulated in the front of the mouth are **anterior** and those articulated with the front of the tongue are **coronal**. 2. That part of the tongue that lies below the hard palate; see Figure 'Articulators' at **ARTICULATION**. 3. In SPE **Distinctive Feature Theory**, segments, especially vowel segments, that are articulated with the tongue pushed towards the front of the mouth. **Tense**, with muscular tension in the tongue, **lax**, with the tongue relatively relaxed. for example [i], [e] Opposite **back**.

	front (rounded)		back (unrounded)	
close	9	[y]	16	[ɯ]
half-close	10	[ø]	15	[ɤ]
half-open	11	[a]	14	[ʌ]
open	12	[œ]	13	[ɑ]

	front (unrounded)		back (rounded)	
close	1	[i]	8	[u]
half-close	2	[e]	7	[o]
half-open	3	[ɛ]	6	[ɔ]
open	4	[a]	5	[ɒ]

FRONTING

1. In **phonetics**, the process whereby a segment moves closer to the front of the mouth, for example the /k/ in *key* is fronted in comparison with the /k/ in *car*. See **PLACE OF ARTICULATION**. 2. In grammar and discourse, the process whereby a **constituent** is moved to the front of a larger constituent. See **PREPOSING, WH-MOVEMENT**.

FROZEN EXPRESSION

See **FIXED EXPRESSION**.

FULFULDE
Niger-Congo. App 6.5K speakers, Cameroon, Chad, parts of Nigeria and Sudan.

FULL VERB
See **LEXICAL VERB**.

FUNCTION
The role played by a **morph**, **word**, **phrase** or **clause** in a particular **context**, as opposed to the shape of the **constituent** or the order in which they are arranged. **Noun phrases** function as (grammatical) **subject** or **object** and as **complement** or **adjunct**. In sequences such as *What happened to Angus? – He crashed his car*, *He crashed his car* functions as a response to the question *What happened?*, *he* functions as **theme** or **topic** of the second clause and *crashed his car* as rheme or comment. The function of clauses is to convey statements, questions, commands, exclamations, etc. A clause can also function as a **complement clause**, a **relative clause** or an **adverbial clause** depending on what it modifies. The function of some clauses is to highlight a particular constituent, possibly for contrast. See **CLEFT CONSTRUCTION, GRAMMATICAL FUNCTION, INFORMATION STRUCTURE, PREDICATE FOCUS, SENTENCE FOCUS, THEMATIC FRONTING**.

FUNCTION WORD
See **GRAMMATICAL WORD**.

FUNCTIONAL GRAMMAR
1. Any account of the **syntax** and **morphology** of a language that takes the concept of **function**, including **speech act**, as primary, and focuses on how the language is used in interactions of all sorts. **Word** structure, **phrase** structure and **clause** structure are treated as secondary. 2. The name of a model of syntax, **text** and **information structure** developed in the Netherlands. Information structure, **argument structure** and relations between **head** and **modifier** are defined and constructed by explicit sets of rules. A separate set of expression rules realize these structures as **constituent structure** involving **voice**, **prepositions** or **postpositions** or **case** suffixes, **word order** and **intonation**. See **FUNCTION, GRAMMATICAL FUNCTION**.

FUNCTIONAL SENTENCE PERSPECTIVE
An approach to the analysis of sentence structure arising out of work by the Prague School in the 1920s and 1930s and applied and refined by contemporary linguists. It emphasizes **information structure** and communicative dynamism. Parts of a sentence communicating given information constitute the **theme** and convey the least to the addressee. The parts communicating new information constitute the rheme and convey the most. The approach has been influential in Europe. See **FOCUS, GIVEN AND NEW, THEMATIC FRONTING**.

FUNCTIONAL SHIFT
See **CONVERSION**.

FUNCTIONAL STRUCTURE
See F-STRUCTURE.

FUNCTIONALIST
See FORMALIST LINGUISTICS.

FUNCTOR
See GRAMMATICAL WORD.

FUNDAMENTAL FREQUENCY
In speech, the fundamental frequency of a **vowel** is the frequency with which the **vocal cords** vibrate.

FUSED RELATIVE CLAUSE
See FREE RELATIVE CLAUSE.

FUSION
1. The phenomenon of a **word** form that realizes two or more **morphemes** but cannot be neatly separated into individual morphs. E.g. *swam* realizes *swim* and **past tense** but consists of one indivisible **morph**. In some varieties of southern English *flyer* is realized as /fla:/, in which the long /a:/ realizes both part of *fly* and the suffix *-er*. 2. In some analyses of English, the concept has been extended to the wh word in **free relative clauses** and to examples such as *The few who turned up* and *The rich don't always pay their taxes*, in which *few* and *rich* are treated as a fusion of *few/rich* with *ones/people*. See REALIZATION.

FUSIONAL LANGUAGE
Languages in which many or all word forms display **fusion**.

FUTHARK
The Runic alphabet.

FUTURE TENSE
A genuine future tense verb form refers to future time and nothing else. So-called 'future tenses' typically involve other meanings, such as intention, obligation and movement. The English **construction** *will/shall* + Verb is based on *will*, which originally denoted intention, and *shall*, which denoted obligation. Intention and reference to future time are intertwined, especially with animate subjects: *I'll meet you at the airport* signals the speaker's intention as well as future time. *I'm going to meet you at the airport* is based on the verb *go*. The intention component is weakest with inanimate subjects, as in *The suit will be ready next week*. Speakers of English can also refer to future events by means of the **Present tense**: *I'm meeting you at the airport*. The choice depends on their presentation of the event: they can treat it as fixed and as already in their (personal) present time – *'m meeting* – or as dependent on their intention – *'ll go* or *'m going to*. In some languages future events are referred to by means of verb forms which are irrealis, that is, which present events as not real or observable, because

they have not taken place and are not taking place. Such irrealis forms have to do with **mood**, not with **tense**. See TENSE AND ASPECT.

FUZZY

A fuzzy set is one whose members cannot be rigorously determined and delimited from the members of other sets. Fuzzy logic works with a scale of truth rather than an absolute distinction between true and false. Fuzzy boundaries are not clear-cut. See PROTOTYPE.

FUZZY BOUNDARIES

See FUZZY.

FUZZY GRAMMAR

A grammar that distinguishes grammatical and ungrammatical sentences but also recognizes sentences that are not clearly one or the other. See GRADIENCE.

FUZZY LOGIC

See FUZZY.

FUZZY SET

See FUZZY.

G

GABELENTZ, Hans Georg Conon von der (1840–1893)
A German linguist and orientalist. He followed Humboldt's ideas on inner and outer form and not the Neogrammarians, and focused on synchronic rather than diachronic analysis. He developed and elaborated the distinction between language use and language system, which was central to **Saussure's** theory and much current linguistics.

GALICIAN
Romance, Indo-European. 3M speakers, north-west Spain, northern Portugal.

GAMILARAAY
Pama-Nyungan, Australian languages. Once spoken over a large area of New South Wales. Now nearly extinct but is the subject of a language revival initiative.

GAP
1. A gap in the vocabulary of a language. In English, *parent* is a **superordinate** for *father* and *mother*, and *grandparent* for *grandfather* and *grandmother*, but there is no corresponding superordinate for *uncle* and *aunt*. 2. An empty slot where we would expect to find a **constituent**, usually a **noun phrase**. E.g. in *the book she borrowed* we expect a **direct object** after *borrowed*, since in main **clauses** the **verb** requires one: *She borrowed a book* but not **She borrowed*. Gaps can be created by **ellipsis**, such as the ellipsis of the **subject** of the second clause in *Philippa ran downstairs and [she] leapt into her sports car*. See **ELLIPSIS, CONJUNCTION, RELATIVE CLAUSE**.

GAPPING
Gapping is a type of **ellipsis** applying in a specific linguistic context. Where two or more **clauses** are conjoined the first clause is complete, but in the other clause or clauses a repeated verb, along with any repeated **direct object**, is ellipted. E.g. *John likes claret and Juliet [likes] shiraz, Fiona is sitting her driving test next week and Susan [is sitting her driving test] the week after*. See **CONJUNCTION, ELLIPSIS**.

GB
See **GOVERNMENT AND BINDING THEORY**.

GE'EZ
Semitic, Afroasiatic. The earliest records date back to the third century, and it was used in Ethiopia as a formal language until the nineteenth century. Now used only as the official liturgical language of the Ethiopian Orthodox Church.

GEMINATED
Doubled, usually of **consonants**. English does not have phonologically distinctive geminated consonants, though it may have phonetically geminated consonants especially at a **morpheme** or **word boundary**, e.g. *meanness, hard disk*. Geminated consonants are distinctive in Italian and Spanish, as in Spanish *pero* 'but' vs *perro* 'dog'.

GEMINATION
The doubling of a **consonant** as a morphological operation. E.g. the formation of causative verbs in Arabic – *kataba* 'he wrote' vs *kattaba* 'he caused to write'. See **GEMINATED**.

GENDER
Connected with *genre*, this term originally meant 'type' or 'class' but in European linguistics usage was narrowed to that of natural gender, 'male' vs 'female', plus 'neuter' (neither male nor female). **Nouns** in many **Indo-European** languages are divided into **classes** which have a basis in natural gender. The division is reflected in grammatical properties such as **agreement**, as in the Italian noun phrases *quest-o ragazz-o* 'this boy', *quest-a ragazz-a* 'this girl', *quest-i ragazz-i* 'these boys', *quest-e ragazz-e* 'these girls'. Note also the **copula** constructions: *Il ragazz-o è piccol-o* 'The boy is small', *La ragazz-a è piccol-a* 'The girl is small'; *Il ragazz-o è arrivat-o* 'The boy is/has arrived', *La ragazz-a è arrivat-a* 'The girl is/has arrived'. On the basis of their meaning, *ragazzo* and *ragazza* are said to be masculine (gender) and feminine (gender) and the gender can be called natural gender. However, many nouns in Italian which do not denote male or female beings but which have the above grammatical properties are also said to be masculine or feminine, and this can be called grammatical gender. E.g. *telefono* 'telephone' is masculine (*questo telefono*) and *tavola* 'table' is feminine (*questa tavola*). 'Gender' has been extended to accounts of languages with different and/or more complex classes of nouns. See **GOVERNMENT, PERSON**.

GENDERLECT
A variety of language, or **lect**, typically associated with one gender.

GENERAL LINGUISTICS
Linguistic theory in general, as opposed to **applied linguistics, sociolinguistics** or **theoretical linguistics**.

GENERAL ONTOLOGY FOR LINGUISTIC DESCRIPTION (GOLD)
A formalized account of the basic categories and relations used in the scientific description of languages. Originally proposed as a way of resolving differences in mark-up schemes for linguistic data, especially from endangered languages.

GENERAL PHONETICS

The study of speech sounds independent of their use in a language. See **PHONETICS**.

GENERALIZATION

A statement or analysis applicable to a large number of examples.

GENERALIZED CONVERSATIONAL IMPLICATURE

See **IMPLICATURE**.

GENERALIZED PHRASE STRUCTURE GRAMMAR

A generative grammar with no **transformations** but just one level of syntactic structure generated by **context-free** phrase structure rules. It was developed in the early 1980s. Within any one **construction**, say **active declarative**, the mother node, say **VP**, carries a (large) number of features which are passed on to the **head** of the construction and from the head to its modifiers. These features ensure, *inter alia*, **agreement** in number and person between the **subject** and the **finite verb** in a **clause**, the correct type of **complement** – finite or non-finite (*reported that snow was falling* vs *was keen to play in the snow*, *that* or *wh* – *regretted that she had resigned* vs *inquired where the manager was*). Relations between constructions are handled by **metarules** specifying that, for example, if a grammar has rules generating active declarative structures, then it also has rules generating passive declarative structures, active **interrogative** structures and so on. The model had the merits of being explicit and restricting the power of the grammar. A variant of the model, **Head-Driven Phrase Structure Grammar**, appeared in the late 1980s and has now replaced it. See **PHRASE STRUCTURE RULE**.

GENERALIZED TRANSFORMATION

In early **transformational grammar**, a **transformation** that combined two phrase structure trees, e.g. deriving a **complex sentence** with a **relative clause** by inserting the tree for *the boy threw the ball* into the tree for *the boy broke the window* to generate the tree for *The boy who threw the ball broke the window*. Generalized transformations were abandoned by Chomsky in *Aspects of the Theory of Syntax* (1965) but have reappeared in the most recent models in the **Minimalist Program**. See **TREE DIAGRAM**.

GENERATIVE GRAMMAR

1. Any **grammar** consisting of a set of formal and completely explicit rules intended to generate all and only the sentences of a given language. 2. In the 1960s, the model developed by Chomsky and his followers but now extended to any model meeting the criteria in (1). Examples of generative grammars are **Generalized Phrase Structure Grammar, Head-driven Phrase Structure Grammar, Lexical Functional Grammar, Lexicase, transformational grammar**. See **PHRASE STRUCTURE RULE**.

GENERATIVE LINGUISTICS
See **GENERATIVE GRAMMAR**.

GENERATIVE PHONOLOGY
Generative phonology developed as the phonological component of a **generative grammar** (see Chomsky and Halle, *The Sound Pattern of English*, 1968). Naturally it adopted the assumptions of generative grammar in that it reflected the linguistic **competence** of the native speaker. The classical **phoneme**, and hence a level of **phonemic** representation, was rejected as inconsistent and replaced by an abstract level of **representation** expressed as a string of **distinctive feature** matrices. **Phonetic** representations are derived by a set of ordered phonological **rules** and in particular rules capturing phonological **alternations**, like, as a simple example, the [s –z] alternation in English plurals (*cats: dogs*), etc. This led on to an analysis of the **vowel** and **consonant** alternations in the **Great Vowel Shift** and the reflexes of these alternations in modern English – *divine: divinity; profane: profanity*, etc. The **underlying structure** for such alternations were abstract, often exceedingly so, and the rules required to derive a phonetic representation increasingly complex: this was partly responsible for the downfall of this particular model. Underlying representations in the generative phonology models of the 70s were strings of distinctive feature matrices together with **boundary** symbols indicating **word, phrase** and **sentence** boundaries. Later models included **suprasgmental phonology** properties such as tone and stress markers, and the introduction of these suprasegmentals led to attempts to accommodate the phonology of tone languages and to a proliferation of new models. See **AUTOSEGMENTAL PHONOLOGY, FEATURE GEOMETRY, LEXICAL PHONOLOGY, OPTIMALITY THEORY**.

GENERATIVE RULE
An explicit **rule** specifying a general structure or sequence that generates a large number of phrases or sentences. E.g. VP → V NP NP generates *sold Harry the car, sent Susan a card, gave Jane a piano*, and so on. (In mathematics, a function such as $x + 2x$ is said to generate a set of numbers, depending on the value of x: 3, if x=1; 6 if x=2; 9 if x=3 and so on.)

GENERATIVE SEMANTICS
A generative grammar in which the **base** component specified semantic structures that were converted to surface syntactic structures without any intermediate level of **deep structure**. The theory was developed from the mid 1960s to the mid 1970s. Chunks of semantic structure were converted to lexical items, which were units only in **surface structure**, an idea that has reappeared in the work of some proponents of the **Minimalist Program**. The basic and complex semantic structures allowed the analysis of **entailment, presupposition** and **quantifier** constructions. The theory gave rise in the 1970s to intensive work on the concept of **speech act** and was a precursor of **Cognitive Grammar**.

GENERATIVE SYNTAX

A grammar that handles syntactic structures by means of explicit rules, especially the **phrase structure grammar** and **transformational grammar** developed by Chomsky and others in the 1950s and 1960s. See GENERATIVE GRAMMAR.

GENERIC

Referring to an entire **class** of individuals rather than to specific members of a class. The **sentence** *Kilts are worn by caber-throwers* is used to make a generic statement, or to express a generic **proposition**, about kilts in general. Generic statements may also concern a permanent property of individuals, a distinction being drawn between stages of individuals and individuals. *Sue can't cook* may refer to a stage in Sue's life (*because she has broken both arms*) or to the entire existence of the individual named Sue (*because she is too lazy*). Generic statements may require special **noun phrase** structures – compare English *Wine is good* (no article) with French *le vin est bon* 'the wine is good' (definite article *le*). Some languages have special verb forms for generic statements such as the **aorist** in **Turkish**: *Bu kahve sev-iyor-um* 'this coffee like-PROG-1sg, I like/am enjoying this coffee' vs *Kahve sev-er-im* 'coffee like-AOR-1sg, I like coffee (in general)'.

GENERIC SPACE

See CONCEPTUAL BLENDING.

GENERIC REFERENCE

See REFERENCE.

GENETIC CLASSIFICATION

See LANGUAGE CLASSIFICATION.

GENITIVE

A **case** marking on a **noun** or noun phrase **dependent** on another noun. The dependent noun typically denotes a possessor (in the broadest sense): e.g. **Russian** *syn Ivana* 'son Ivan-GEN, 'Ivan's son', **Turkish** *Mehmet-in ev-i* 'Mehmet-GEN house-POSS-3sg, of-Mehmet his-house, Mehmet's house'. Genitive case marking can be assigned by a verb, such as Russian *bojat'sja* 'to fear', German *gedenken* 'remember', and by a **preposition**, such as Russian *do* 'as far as' and *iz* 'out of'.

GENRE

Traditionally applied to bodies of literature such as plays (comedies, tragedies), historical novels, sonnets, epic poetry, ballads. Now applied to any types of **text**, such as academic monographs, newspaper editorials, business reports, sports reports (with different sub-genres for football, rugby, cricket and so on). See DIMENSION.

GEOGRAPHICAL LINGUISTICS

The study of the geographical distribution of languages and their areal and typological properties, together with the political status and prestige of languages and language varieties. See **AREAL LINGUISTICS, DIALECT GEOGRAPHY, TYPOLOGY**.

GEORGIAN

Kartvelian, **Caucasian**. Approx. 4M speakers, Georgia (official language) and neighbouring countries. The oldest inscription dates from circa 430 CE and the oldest manuscript from 864 CE.

GERMAN

Germanic, **Indo-European**. Approx. 75M speakers Germany, 7.5M Austria, 150K Belgium, Approx. 13M in other countries. Ranks tenth among the languages of the world and has the most first-language speakers in the European Union.

GERMANIC

Indo-European. There are three major subgroupings of Germanic languages: West Germanic (including **Afrikaans, English, German, Dutch** and **Frisian**); North Germanic (including **Icelandic, Norwegian, Swedish** and **Danish**) and East Germanic (**Gothic** and other now extinct Central European languages).

GERUND

Originally applied to noun-like forms of the **verb** in Latin. E.g. *leg-imus* 'read-PRS+1pl 'we are reading', *ars leg-en-di* 'the-art read-GER-GEN, the art of reading'. *Legendi*, like ordinary Latin nouns, takes **case**, here the **genitive** case. In English grammar, the term applies to noun-like forms in *-ing*, derived from verbs, which can be the **subject** or **object** of a verb: e.g. *Paragliding* scares me vs *I love paragliding*. Gerunds are verb-like in that they can have a **direct object** as their **complement** and can be modified by an **adverb** of place, time, etc. but the phrase containing them functions as **subject** – *Sitting exams in May amuses me* – or as object, *I hate sitting exams in May*. A **construction** known as the full gerund has a **possessive** subject noun: *Everybody criticized the new manager's resigning so soon*. The term is used differently in the grammars of different languages. In grammars of Spanish 'gerundio' is applied to forms that are not noun-like and do not function as subject or object: e.g. in *Juan está estudiando* 'Juan is studying' *estudiando* is labelled a gerund. (Possibly from Latin *gero* 'I act/carry', the label *verbum gerendi* 'verb of acting/carrying' capturing the active meaning of gerunds as opposed to **gerundives**.) See **NON-FINITE VERB**.

GERUNDIVE

In Latin grammar, **adjective**-like forms probably derived from **gerunds**. A gerundive functions as a **predicative** adjective expressing necessity and has a passive meaning in contrast with a **gerund**. E.g. *Del-end-a est Carthago* 'destroy-GER-FEM-sg is Carthage, Carthage must be destroyed'.

GESTALT

A single mental image enabling humans to construe partial or disconnected perceptions as a single object. A basic concept in **cognitive linguistics** because of the hypothesis that language relates to mental representations and not directly to the external world. Individuation and **force dynamics** are central parts of the process by which humans constitute experience and give it a gestalt.
See **BOUNDEDNESS, CONSTRUAL**.

GESTURE

1. Movement of the hands, head, face, etc. used in communication. 2. In phonology, a development of the theory of **distinctive features**, where features are grouped together under superordinate properties called 'gestures'. Thus the **laryngeal** gesture gathers together features associated with the activity of the larynx. See **DISTINCTIVE FEATURES: SOURCE FEATURES**.

GET PASSIVE

See **VOICE**.

GIKUYU

Bantu, Niger-Congo. Spoken by approx. 5.5M people in Kenya.

GILLIÉRON, Jules (1854–1926)

A Swiss-born linguist and dialectologist who founded scientific dialectology in France, taking a structural approach to the analysis of **dialects**.

GIVEN AND NEW

Given information is what speakers and writers assume their listeners and readers can pick up, either because it has already been mentioned, or is unique or salient in the context of utterance or is in their world-knowledge. New information is what speakers and writers assume their listeners cannot pick up, possibly because it is being mentioned for the first time. In many languages, such as English, there is a tendency for given information to come first in clauses and for new information to come at the end of clauses. Given information may be conveyed by a **pronoun** or a definite **noun phrase** and typically does not carry the focal **accent**. The **theme** of a clause typically carries given information. New information often carries the focal accent. Languages may have special constructions for introducing new entities into a text, such as the English **existential**-presentational construction: *There's a suggestion we need to discuss*.
See **DEFINITE DESCRIPTION, FOCUS, REFERENCE**.

GLIDE

In **phonetics**, the auditory effect as **articulators** move from one segment to another. There is sometimes an audible glide, e.g. [j] between *tea* and *and* in *tea and sympathy*. See **OFF-GLIDE, ON-GLIDE, INTRUSIVE R**.

GLIDING VOWEL

See **DIPHTHONG**.

GLOBAL DERIVATION CONSTRAINT
See GLOBAL RULES.

GLOBAL RULE
A **rule** or **constraint** that can look back over earlier stages in a **derivation**. Global rules were a feature of **Generative Semantics** and have reappeared in early work on the **Minimalist Program** in the guise of global economy principles such as **Last Resort**.

GLOSS
A rough translation of a **word**, **phrase** or **clause** from one language into another, in order to explain the meaning of the unit and to show its structure. For example, from the entry for genitive: **Turkish** *Mehmet-in ev-i* 'Mehmet-GEN house-POSS-3sg, of-Mehmet his-house, Mehmet's house'.

GLOSSARY
An alphabetically sorted word list, e.g. a list of technical or special words, or the words in a particular text, explaining their meanings.

GLOSSECTOMY
In **clinical linguistics**, the removal of the tongue or part of the tongue.

GLOSSEMATICS
The theory of linguistic structure developed by the Danish linguist Hjelmslev and his colleagues in the Copenhagen School in the 1930s and 1940s.

GLOTTAL
A term in the description of the **place of articulation**. In consonants the **glottis** can be closed or constricted. In English the complete **closure** of the glottis produces a **glottal stop**, symbolized in IPA transcriptions as [ʔ]. In English the audible release of the stop can be heard before a strongly articulated vowel as in [ʔam ai] *AM I*. In many, especially urban, accents of English it occurs intervocalically as in *butter* [bʌʔʌ] and word finally, as in *but* [bʌʔ] where received pronunciation would have a voiceless plosive. If the glottis is constricted, there can be audible friction, as in the English glottal fricative [h] *hat*. In vowels **breathy voice** and **creaky voice** are the most audible properties. See **PLACE OF ARTICULATION**.

GLOTTAL CONSTRICTION
See GLOTTAL.

GLOTTAL STOP
See GLOTTAL.

GLOTTALIC AIRSTREAM
This is produced by drawing the **glottis** sharply downwards for a glottalic ingressive **airstream**. A **consonant** produced on a glottalic **ingressive** airstream is an **implosive**. The glottalic egressive airstream is created by closing the glottis

and drawing it sharply upwards. A consonant produced on a glottalic egressive airstream is an **ejective**.

GLOTTALIZATION

A glottal **constriction** articulated simultaneously with another **segment**. In English voiceless **plosives** are often reinforced by glottalization, thus in many, especially urban, accents of English glottalization occurs intervocalically as in *butter* [bʌʔə] and word finally as in *but* [bʌtʔ] where received pronunciation would have a simple voiceless plosive.

GLOTTIS

The aperture between the **vocal cords**.

GLOTTOCHRONOLOGY

A technique for determining the time divergence between languages, dialects, etc. by comparing the numbers of shared **cognate** forms for basic concepts, e.g. body parts, kinship terms, pronouns, etc. – the hypothesis is that the lexicon for basic concepts is most resistant to change and least likely to include borrowed words and that there is a constant rate of loss of vocabulary for basic concepts. So, by comparing the number of cognate forms, the number of years involved in the separation of two languages can be calculated. The technique is no longer thought to be reliable. See **SWADESH LIST**.

GOAL

1. A **role** expressing the place towards which an entity moves, as in *We drove to Berlin*. The role is extended to **recipients**, as in *Alice gave the key to Ethel* and metaphorically to abstract events, as in *This fact indicated to Jan that her theory was correct*. 2. In some analyses, especially in grammars of Philippine languages, the term 'goal' is used instead of **patient** or **direct object**. See **GRAMMATICAL FUNCTION**.

GOD'S TRUTH VERSUS HOCUS-POCUS

A phrase coined by Fred Householder of Indiana University with reference to analysts who believed their analyses revealed categories actually existing in a given language, as opposed to analysts who thought the categories were simply constructs in their analysis.

GOLD

See **GENERAL ONTOLOGY FOR LINGUISTIC DESCRIPTION**.

GONDI

Dravidian. Approx. 2M speakers, central India.

GOODNESS OF EXEMPLAR RATING

In prototype theory, the extent to which a possible member of a category does or does not meet the relevant properties. For example, in the UK, *kiwi* has a low rating as a member of the category of birds, whereas *robin* has a high rating. See **PROTOTYPE**.

GOTHIC
East **Germanic**. Now extinct.

GOVERN
See GOVERNMENT.

GOVERNING CATEGORY
The smallest structures, **NP** and **S** or **IP** (Inflectional Phrase, roughly = Sentence), within which an NP can be **bound** to an **antecedent**. E.g. in *The reporter claimed* ₛ[*that the policeman blamed himself*], *himself* has *the policeman* as its antecedent (is bound by *the policeman*), which is within the same clause. It cannot have *the reporter* as its antecedent, as this NP is outside the sentence.

GOVERNMENT
1. The relation between the **head** of a phrase and its **complements**, a type of **syntactic linkage**. The head governs the **complements** in a phrase, determining how many complements can combine with it and what sort. E.g. *vanish* allows no complements in the verb phrase – *The rabbit vanished* vs **The rabbit vanished Alice*; *destroy* requires one complement – *The fire destroyed the church*, **The fire destroyed*; *put* requires two complements, an NP and a PP – *She put the vase on the sideboard*, **She put the vase*, **She put on the sideboard*, **She put*. In languages with **case** marking, **verbs** and **prepositions** govern their complements and may assign **case** to them (but do not themselves change their form). E.g. Russian *videl devushku* 'saw-PST girl-ACC, saw the girl', *pomog devushke*, help-PST girl-DAT, helped the girl'; *za domom* 'behind house-INSTR, behind the house', *iz doma* 'out-of house-GEN, out of the house'. 2. In the **Government and Binding Theory** model, government is a relation between one constituent and another that **m-commands** it. Constituents are assigned cases by other constituents that govern them. See AGREEMENT, C-COMMAND, M-COMMAND, X-BAR SYNTAX.

GOVERNMENT AND BINDING THEORY
See PRINCIPLES AND PARAMETERS.

GOVERNMENT THEORY
The theory in the **Principles and Parameters** model that controls the occurrence of a **trace** and its government by an **antecedent**. See GOVERNMENT.

GOVERNOR
Any **constituent** that **governs** another, such as the lexical **head** in **dependency** relations or the antecedents to which **anaphors** are bound in **Government and Binding Theory**. See CONSTRUCTION, TRACE.

GPSG
See GENERALIZED PHRASE STRUCTURE GRAMMAR.

GRADABILITY
The property of being gradable. See **OPPOSITENESS**.

GRADABLE
Applied to properties that vary in quantity or intensity and to the adjectives that denote them. For instance, being wooden is a property that does not vary. Questions such as *How wooden is that house?* and statements such as *That house is very wooden* would be very unusual and difficult to interpret. In contrast, size does vary, and it is quite normal to ask questions such as *How big is their house?* or make statements such as *Their house is very big*. See **ABSOLUTE ADJECTIVE, ANTONYMY, GRADABLE ADJECTIVE**.

GRADABLE ADJECTIVE
Certain **adjectives** denote properties, such as height, that can be graded. For example, a given person may have a greater grade or degree of height than another or have the greatest grade of height in a particular group of people: *Susan is taller than Jane, Susan is the tallest in her class. Taller* is the **comparative** form of *tall*, or in the comparative grade; *tallest* is the superlative form, or in the **superlative** grade. The basic form *tall* is said to be positive or in the positive grade.

GRADIENCE
1. The property of classes whose members are graded into central, less central and peripheral members. E.g. *thin* is accounted a central **adjective** because it has many properties of adjectives – *thinner, the thin man, The man is thin, the very thin man. Utter* is accounted a peripheral member, having only one property – *in utter darkness* (but not **utterest, *The darkness is utter, *the very utter darkness*). This type of gradience has been called subsective (Latin *sub* 'under', *seco* 'I cut', to cut up a class into members). 2. The property of **lexical words** possessing characteristics of two different **word classes**. A given lexical word may possess more characteristics of one class than the other in particular contexts; in a given context lexical words may differ in the number of characteristics they possess. Thus, in *a working hypothesis, working* has more adjectival than verbal characteristics: it typically cannot be negated by *not*, as in *a not working hypothesis*, and it does not combine with aspect, as shown by **a having worked hypothesis*. It occurs in an **environment** that is typical of adjectives, but it does not combine with *very*, nor with *more* and *most. Encouraging* in *this encouraging news* is like *working* in having more adjectival than verbal characteristics in this environment but has more adjectival characteristics than *working*: *very encouraging news, more encouraging news*. This type of gradience has been called intersective (Latin *inter* 'between', *seco* 'I cut').

GRADUAL
See **DISTINCTIVE FEATURES**.

GRADUAL OPPOSITION

A graded opposition in which segments show different grades of some feature. Thus, the English front unrounded vowels /ɪ/, /ɛ/ and /a/ differ in their height. See **PRAGUE SCHOOL, OPPOSITION**.

GRAMMAR

1. In its narrow sense, the structure of sentences (**syntax**) and the structure of words (**morphology**) in a language. 2. In its broad sense, the morphology and syntax plus the **phonology**, the **semantics** and even the **pragmatics** of a language. 3. A description of the **grammar** of a language. 4. The sense introduced by Chomsky, the set of rules known by (internalized by) the members of a speech community and now called **I-language**. See **I-LANGUAGE, INTERNALIZATION**

GRAMMATICAL

1. Relating to **grammar** in any of its senses. 2. Conforming to the rules of a particular language: e.g. *some shiny cars* is a grammatical **noun phrase** of English, *cars some shiny* is not. See **GRAMMATICALITY, GRADIENCE, NON-DISCRETE**.

GRAMMATICAL AMBIGUITY

See **AMBIGUITY**.

GRAMMATICAL ASPECT

See **VIEWPOINT ASPECT**.

GRAMMATICAL CASE

A **case** whose only function is to mark some **construction**. E.g. the Turkish **accusative** case, which simply marks a **direct object** noun with a specific referent. Opposed to **semantic case**. See **REFERENCE**.

GRAMMATICAL CATEGORIES

Word classes and the **grammatical meanings** typically associated with each class. Grammatical meanings are generally expressed not by **lexical words** but by **grammatical words, affixes, particles** and even patterns of **tones**. In many languages some meanings are associated with nouns, e.g. **case, number, gender**; other meanings are associated with verbs, e.g. **tense and aspect, mood, person and number**. Despite the association with single words, grammatical categories like **case** play a role in connecting the constituents in a **phrase**, and tense, aspect and mood affect an entire **clause**. In *Cedric wrote the program, wrote* carries past tense and simple aspect, but it is the event denoted by the entire clause that is presented as taking place in past time and as completed. See **GRAMMATICALIZATION**.

GRAMMATICAL COMPETENCE

An idealization of speakers' knowledge of the **grammar** of their language. The content of this idealized knowledge does not include tongue slips, memory limitations and distractions. See **COMMUNICATIVE COMPETENCE**.

GRAMMATICAL CONDITIONING

See **CONDITIONING**.

GRAMMATICAL FUNCTION

'Function' is a very general term denoting functions such as **complement**, **adjunct**, **determiner**, **adverbial** and others. The term 'grammatical function' or 'grammatical relation' is typically applied to relations in a **clause** between noun phrases and the main verb. A **noun phrase** can function as grammatical **subject**, direct object, second or indirect object or **oblique** object of a verb.

In active main clauses in English, a number of properties converge on one noun phrase, the grammatical subject. For example, the finite verb agrees with it in **person** and **number**, it controls the understood subject of a **non-finite verb** and is ellipted (undergoes **ellipsis**) when clauses are conjoined – *Susan went out to the cinema and [] forgot to lock the front door*. Grammatical subjects of **transitive verbs** typically denote agents. Direct object nouns in English basic clauses immediately follow the main verb and correspond to the grammatical subjects of **passive** clauses. They typically denote patients. Oblique objects are connected to verbs by prepositions: *gave the book to Bill, bought a present for Juliet, talked about her family*, etc.

There is controversy over the appropriate grammatical functions for non-subject noun phrases with a ditransitive verb, i.e. a verb followed by two noun phrases, as in *gave Bill the book* and *spared Fiona the details*. The underlined nouns are not principal direct objects, since *Bill* and *Fiona* correspond to the grammatical subjects in the passive: *Bill was given the book, Fiona was spared the details*. On the other hand, *Bill* and *Fiona* can be seen as denoting recipients and not patients. If this criterion is considered primary, *Bill* and *Fiona* can be given the traditional label 'indirect object', a term that was also applied to noun phrases preceded by the preposition *to*, denoting recipients and connected to verbs of giving, telling, as in *gave the book to Bill*. *To* being a preposition, *Bill* in *gave the book to Bill* is now called an oblique object.

LFG analyses of the above ditransitive examples treat *Bill* and *Fiona* as objects and *the book* and *the details* as second objects, thereby avoiding the unclearly defined traditional concept of indirect object. The LFG analysis gives primacy to the grammatical criterion: *Bill* and *Fiona* become the subjects of the corresponding passive clauses. A further distinction comes from typology, arising from the grammatical patterns found in languages such as Yokuts (a native American language of California). The distinction is between primary object and secondary object. The primary objects occur with transitive verbs and denote patients, rather like direct object in English. Secondary objects occur with ditransitive verbs and denote recipients. Both primary and secondary objects can be thought of as equivalent to direct objects in English but secondary object is different from second object. This is shown by the Yokuts clause *'ama' nan wan+xo k'exa+ni nim* 'He me give+durative money+oo my, He gives me my money'. *Nan* is the secondary object and in the accusative case. *k'exa+ni* is in an oblique case. A literal English translation might be *He gives me with my money*. See **AGREEMENT, CASE, CONTROL, FINITE VERB.**

GRAMMATICAL GENDER
See GENDER.

GRAMMATICAL HIERARCHY
A scale on which items can be arranged depending on how susceptible they are to some grammatical process or construction. For example, there is a well-known animacy hierarchy on which first- and second-person **pronouns** outrank third-person pronouns, which in turn outrank human nouns, which outrank animate nouns, which outrank inanimate nouns. There is a general tendency across languages for verbs to have **agreement** markings for first and second **person** but not for third person. In many languages first- and second-person pronouns are treated as natural agents and third-person pronouns as natural patients. First- and second-person patients are given special markings, as are third-person agents. In a variation on that pattern, in many languages if the subject noun is lower on the hierarchy than the direct object noun, a special verb form is required. Hierarchies are a convenient way of representing implicational universals. See ACCESSIBILITY HIERARCHY, IMPLICATIONAL UNIVERSAL.

GRAMMATICAL MEANING
Whatever meaning is contributed to the interpretation of a clause or sentence by morphology or syntax (**grammatical words**, **affixes**, patterns of **tone**) as opposed to the **denotation** of each **lexical word**. Examples are the 'event in progress' interpretation of *be* + *-ing* in English – *wrote* vs *was writing*, the 'polite request' interpretation of isolated *if* clauses – *If you could just roll up your sleeve*, the concessive interpretation of *although* – *Although it's much better, it still won't do*, and the interpretation of **interrogative** constructions as signalling that the speaker is asking a question. See CONSTRUCTION, GRAMMATICAL CATEGORY.

GRAMMATICAL RELATION
See GRAMMATICAL FUNCTION.

GRAMMATICAL SUBJECT
See GRAMMATICAL FUNCTION.

GRAMMATICAL WORD
1. In contrast with a **lexical word**, a grammatical word does not denote an entity – a thing, a being, an event, an abstract idea and so on – but carries information about the grammar of clauses: e.g. definiteness – *the* vs *a*, finiteness – *to* vs the (English) **tense** suffixes *-ed* and *-s*. The **preposition** *of* is generally considered a grammatical word but other prepositions denote locations and are lexical, e.g. *below* vs *above*, *inside* vs *outside*. The more general term 'grammatical morpheme' includes **affixes** such as the **gerund** *-ing* in English and **case** suffixes in Russian. Alternative terms for grammatical word are empty

word, form word, functor. See **DEFINITE ARTICLE**, **FINITE VERB**, **MORPH**, **MORPHOSYNTACTIC WORD**.

GRAMMATICALITY

1. The property possessed by a **phrase**, **clause** or **sentence** that conforms to the rules of a particular language. 2. The property possessed by phrases, clauses and sentences that are judged acceptable by the speakers of a particular language. Constituents may be judged more or less acceptable; degrees of grammaticality are recognized. See **GRADIENCE**, **ACCEPTABILITY**.

GRAMMATICALIZATION

The process by which a **word**, **phrase** or **clause** loses its original, referential meaning, which changes into a **grammatical meaning**. For instance, in **Greek** and **Bulgarian** the original verb 'want, wish (to do something)' has become the marker of future tense. The Early English *while* was a **lexical word**, as in the fixed phrases *wait a while*, *in a little while*, but developed into a subordinating conjunction, as in *While I was waiting, I read the notices*. 2. The process by which a distinction in meaning is reflected in an obligatory part of the grammar. For example, the distinction between an event witnessed by the speaker and one not witnessed is signalled in Turkish by the obligatory presence or absence of the **evidential** suffix *miş*. The distinction can be signalled in English by adverbs such as *apparently*, but their use is optional and the distinction is not grammaticalized in English. See **DE-GRAMMATICALIZATION**, **LAYERING**, **REANALYSIS**.

GRAMMATICIZATION

See **GRAMMATICALIZATION**.

GRAPH

A symbol representing a phoneme or letter of the alphabet.

GRAPHEME

The smallest unit in a writing system compare **phoneme**. See also **ALLOGRAPH**.

GRAPHEMICS

The study of graphemes.

GRAPHETICS

The study of **graphic substance**.

GRAPHIC SUBSTANCE

The written or printed form of a language, as opposed to **phonic substance**, the range of sounds used in a language. See **MEDIUM**.

GRAPHOLOGY

The study of the written forms of language.

GRASSMAN, Hermann Günther (1809–1877)

A German mathematician and linguist who published original work on algebraic curves and vectors before becoming a **Sanskrit** scholar. He is famous for Grassman's law, explaining, for example, the alternation of *th* and *t* in Greek *thriks* (hair, nominative case) and *trikhos* (hair, genitive case) and a parallel change in **Sanskrit**.

GRAVE

In **J&H Distinctive Feature Theory**, an acoustic **distinctive feature** involving a concentration of energy in the lower frequencies of the spectrum, associated with back vowels and consonants with a peripheral articulation, e.g. labial, velar, uvular. Opposite **acute**. See DISTINCTIVE FEATURES, ACOUSTIC.

GRAVE

See DISTINCTIVE FEATURES.

GREAT VOWEL SHIFT

a chain of sound changes in late Middle English in which **low** and mid long **vowels** were raised,

/æ:/ > /ɛ:/   /ɔ:/ > /o:/
/ɛ:/ > /e:/   /o:/ > /u:/
/e:/ > /i:/

and long high vowels became **diphthongs**

/i:/ > /ai/
/u:/ > /au/

For example Old English /bek/ > Modern English /bik/ (beak); Old English /mis/ > Modern English /mais/; Old English /mus/ > Modern English /maus/ (mouse).

Many of the mismatches in English orthography between spelling and pronunciation are the result, as can be seen in the examples.

GREEK

Greek, **Indo-European**. 10.7M speakers, Greece. Greek has a continuous development from the fourteenth century BCE to the present. The earliest form of Ancient Greek, Mycenaean, was spoken on Crete and various parts of the mainland and written in a syllabary known as Linear B. Homeric Greek is the language of the *Iliad* and *Odyssey*. Hellenistic Greek (300 BCE–300 CE) is the language of the New Testament and of the authors of early grammatical and philosophical works and was the form of Greek spread by Alexander the Great's conquests. Byzantine Greek (300–1650 CE) was the language of Constantinople. Modern Greek is spoken worldwide by some 12M people (Greece 10.7M).

A particular feature of Modern Greek until very recently was the institutionalized **diglossia**, distinguishing between 'high' (official and formal) and 'low' (colloquial and informal) forms of the language.

GREENBERG, Joseph (1915–2001)
An American linguist who founded **typology** and a particular approach to the study of **language universals**. He carried out original work in the genetic **classification** of languages, demonstrating in particular that all African languages fell into four families.

GRICE, Herbert Paul (1913–1988)
An English philosopher who taught at Oxford and Berkeley. He is famous for his work on the logic of conversation and especially for his **maxims of conversation**.

GRICEAN MAXIMS
See MAXIMS OF CONVERSATION.

GRIMM, Jacob Ludwig Carl (1785–1863)
A German linguist who wrote a seminal historical grammar of **German** and is renowned for the lexicographical research he carried out with his brother Wilhelm which resulted in their German dictionary, *Deutsches Wörterbuch*. The first volume was published in 1854, the sixteenth and last in 1950.

GRIMM'S LAW
A series of interrelated **sound correspondences** associated with the name of Jacob Grimm, famous for his collection of fairy tales. The voiced aspirated **stops** of proto Indo-European lost their **aspiration** in proto Germanic to become simple voiced stops; then by a **drag chain** the voiced **stops** became **voiceless**, and the voiceless stops **fricatives**:

voiced aspirated stops /b^h, d^h, g^h/ > voiced stops /b,d,g /
voiced stops /b,d,g/ > voiceless stops /p,t,k/
voiceless stops /p,t,k/ > fricatives: /f,θ,h/

Words in Germanic languages show these changes whereas words in other Indo-European languages do not: e.g. French *pied, dent, coeur*; English *foot, tooth, heart*. See VERNER'S LAW, VOICE.

GROOVE FRICATIVE
A fricative articulated with the central line of the **tongue** slightly grooved, [s]. This produces a higher frequency than the **slit fricative** like [θ].

GROUND
See FIGURE.

GROUP
1. A group whose members identify with each other in terms of a common heritage (including ancestry, language, religion). The British census invites people to identify themselves as 'white', 'Asian', 'black' and so on. 2. In **Systemic Functional Grammar**, any constituent that ranks between a **word** and a **clause**. E.g. *many confusing terms* is a nominal group, *has been writing* is a verbal group.

GROUP GENITIVE

The English **construction** in which the **possessive** suffix 's is added to an entire **noun phrase** and not to an individual **noun**: e.g. *the guy I met yesterday's house, my father and mother's views on TV.*

GUARANI

Tupian. Spoken in Paraguay, where it is the official language along with Spanish, and in parts of Argentina, Bolivia and Brazil.

GUJARATI

Indo-Iranian, Indo-European. Approx. 52M speakers, Indian states of Gujarat, Maharashtra, Rajasthan. Emigrant speakers in South Asia and Africa.

GULLAH

Creole. An English-based Creole with strong influences from several West African languages, spoken by African Americans in South Carolina and Georgia.

GUR LANGUAGES

Volta-Congo, **Niger-Congo**. The 85 or so Gur languages are spoken in a belt which stretches from the northern Ivory Coast, through northern Ghana and into north-west Nigeria. They are also called Voltaic languages.

GUUGU YIMIDHIRR

Pama-Nyungan, Australian languages. Spoken in Queensland. Severely endangered.

H

HABITUAL
An **aspect** signalling that an event happens as a habit or regular pattern. In English the aspect is realized by *used to*, as in *We used to go there every Easter*, or by **simple present** tense verbs; e.g. *We go there every Easter* vs *We are going there this Easter*. Often habitual aspect is signalled by **adverbs** such as *every Easter* in the above example or *each day* in *We sell thirty copies each day at the moment*.
See AORIST, TENSE AND ASPECT, SIMPLE PAST.

HALF-CLOSE
A term in the description of the **place of articulation** of **cardinal vowels**, which recognizes four **tongue** heights – **close**; half-close; **half-open** and **open**. [e] and [o] are respectively front half-close and back half-close vowels.

HALF-OPEN
A term in the description of the **place of articulation** of **cardinal vowels**, which recognizes four **tongue** heights – **close**; **half-close**; half-open and **open**. [ɛ] and [ɔ] are respectively front **half-close** and back **half-close** vowels.

HAPAX LEGOMENON
A word attested only once in a text or set of texts. Originally applied to texts of *The Iliad* and *The Odyssey*. (Greek *hapax* 'once', *legomenon* 'spoken'.)

HAPLOLOGY
The omission of sounds or **syllables** in a sequence of similar **articulations**, e.g. *probly* for *probably*, *libry* for *library*.

HAPTICS
In **semiotics**, the study of touch as a means of communication.

HARD CONSONANT
A **consonant** pronounced without **palatalization**. In Russian there is a contrast between soft (palatalized) and hard consonants.

HARD CONTACT
In **clinical linguistics**, a tense **articulation** producing strong contact between the **tongue** and some **passive articulators**. A characteristic of **stuttering**.

HARD PALATE
See **PALATE**.

HARMONIC
In **acoustics**, a **frequency** which is a multiple of the **fundamental frequency** of a vibrating body. The lowest harmonic is the first harmonic, the next lowest, the second harmonic and so on. The configuration of the vibrating body will dampen some harmonics and enhance others. In speech this gives rise to vowel **formants**.

HARMONY
In **typology**, a relationship between two properties A and B such that property A only occurs with property B (A is said to be harmonic with B) or property B only occurs with property A (B is said to be harmonic with A). For instance, across languages the order **Adjective** followed by **Noun**, as in *hot water*, is harmonic with the order **Demonstrative** Noun, as in *this house*. The order Demonstrative Noun is not harmonic with Adjective Noun because it also occurs with Noun Adjective as in French *ce chat* 'that cat' and *le chat noir* 'the cat black, the black cat'. See **VOWEL HARMONY, CONSONANT HARMONY**.

HARRIS, James (1709–1780)
An English lawyer who wrote a large philosophical grammar, *Hermes: or, a philosophical inquiry concerning language and universal grammar* (1751). He argued that a theory of language required a theory of mind and logical inquiry.

HARRIS, Zellig Sabbettai (1909–1992)
A major American linguist. He developed his own transformational analysis of syntactic structures and **discourse**. His 1946 paper 'From **morpheme** to utterance' anticipates key components of **X-Bar syntax**.

HARSH VOICE
See **VENTRICULAR VOICE**.

HART, John (1501–1574)
A member of the Heralds' College, he wrote three books on English spelling and pronunciation which show him to have been an outstanding phonetician.

HAUSA
Chadic, Afroasiatic. Approx. 18.5M speakers northern Nigeria, 8.5M Southern Niger.

HAWAIIAN
Malayo-Polynesian, Austronesian. Fewer than 1M speakers and severely endangered.

HEAD

In a **phrase** or **clause**, the **word** that is obligatory and controls the other words, its **dependents**. A growing number of analysts consider the **head** of a **clause** to be a **verb**. In, e.g., *The police blamed Ken for the accident*, *blame* requires a **subject**, *the police* and a **direct object**, *Ken*. It allows a **prepositional phrase**, but requires the **preposition** *for*. Prepositions are the heads of prepositional phrases; *with* requires a **noun phrase** – *with friends*, but excludes any following preposition – **with beside his friends*. *In* requires a noun phrase but allows another following preposition, e.g. *behind* in the phrase *in behind the bookcase*.

With respect to **meaning** heads convey central pieces of information and their dependents contribute extra information. *Blame* denotes the set of events of blaming. *Blamed Ken* narrows that to the set of events of blaming people named Ken. *Blamed Ken for the accident* narrows the set further, and *the police blamed Ken for the accident* narrows the set to events of blaming carried out by police, directed at people named Ken and related to an accident.

Some analysts propose to distinguish syntactic heads from semantic heads. In *The editor might publish the story tomorrow*, *might* can be treated as the syntactic head of the clause, but *publish* is the semantic head which controls, in particular, the **roles** assigned to the NPs. In phrases such as *the soldiers*, the syntactic head is *the* but *soldiers* is the semantic head, controlling the type of **adjectives** that can occur and involved in **agreement** and **government** links with the verb in a clause. See **ADJUNCT, COMPLEMENT, DEPENDENCY GRAMMAR, DETERMINER PHRASE, SUBCATEGORIZATION**.

HEAD-DRIVEN PHRASE STRUCTURE GRAMMAR (HPSG)

A development of **Generalized Phrase Structure Grammar** created in the late 1980s. Like GPSG it has no **transformations** and a single level of representation of syntactic **structure**; unlike GPSG, it has no phrase structure rules; instead, the syntactic structure is projected ('thrown out') by whatever **lexical word** is the **head** of a **phrase**, and words and phrases are combined by **unification**. The head of a **clause** is a **verb**. For example, in one of its meanings *take* requires a **prepositional phrase** with *against*, *took against bankers* (= 'conceived a dislike for bankers') and *against*, the head of the prepositional phrase, requires a **noun** and so on. *Take* unifies with *against the bankers* to produce the phrase *took against the bankers*, and this phrase, which must have the properties of its head, unifies with a noun and its dependents to produce a clause, such as *The politicians took against the bankers*. Lexical words consist of complex sets of **attributes** (**features**) and **values** for the attributes. Various **constraints** check that combined or unified sets of attributes are well formed. Because HPSG is amenable to computer applications, it has been widely adopted in cognitive science. See **PHRASE STRUCTURE GRAMMAR, PHRASE STRUCTURE RULE, PROJECTION, UNIFICATION**.

HEAD FEATURE

In any head-driven model of grammar, such as **Head-Driven Phrase Structure Grammar** or **Generalized Phrase Structure Grammar**, features assigned to the **head** of a **construction**. These features control the number and type of other constituents in the construction. E.g. in Russian **adjectives** modifying nouns with the **features** [masculine], [singular] and [dative case] acquire those features; verbs with the feature [__NP **direct object, accusative**] require a direct object noun in the accusative case. See ADJUNCT, AGREEMENT, COMPLEMENT, GOVERNMENT.

HEAD FEATURE CONVENTION

In **Generalized Phrase Structure Grammar**, the **constraint** that ensures that a **construction** has the **features** inherent in its **head**. See HEAD FEATURES.

HEAD FEATURE PRINCIPLE

In Head-Driven Phrase Structure Grammar, the equivalent of the **Head Feature Convention**.

HEAD-FIRST LANGUAGE

See HEAD PARAMETER.

HEAD-LAST LANGUAGE

See HEAD PARAMETER.

HEAD-MARKING

In a **construction** one constituent is the **head** and the others are **dependents/modifiers**. Which constituents are which is signalled by their order (see HEAD PARAMETER) but also marked by **affixes**. In some constructions in some languages the **dependent** is marked; e.g. in **Russian** *boitsja tsarja* 'fears the-tsar', the dependent **object** noun *tsarja* has the **genitive** case affix *-ja*. Russian is said to be a dependent-marking language. In other languages the head of a construction is marked; e.g. in the **Luganda clause** *omukazi enkoko aligigoba* 'the-woman the-chicken will-chase', the initial *a* on the **verb** signals that *omukazi* is **subject** and *-gi-* signals that *enkoko* is **direct object**. Luganda is said to be a head-marking language. In some constructions in some languages both head and dependent are marked; e.g. in the **Turkish** *Mehmetin evi* 'Mehmet-GEN house-POSS3, Mehmet's house', *Mehmet* is the dependent noun, marked by the genitive **case** suffix *-in*. *ev-* is the head noun, marked by the third-person possessive suffix *-i*. It appears to be constructions rather than whole languages that are head- or dependent-marking, though there are languages, such as Russian and Dyirbal, in which all constructions have dependent-marking and languages, such as Lakota, in which all constructions have head-marking. See CONSTITUENT STRUCTURE, DEPENDENCY, DEPENDENT, HEAD, MODIFIER.

HEAD MOVEMENT

In **Principles and Parameters**, the **Minimalist Program**, movement of the **head** of a phrase to another head position.

HEAD PARAMETER

A proposed **parameter** of **Universal Grammar** that determines the order of **head** and **dependent** for a given language. For English the parameter would be set 'head first', i.e the order is **head** followed by **modifiers**: Preposition + NP as in *on the beach*, Verb + NP as in *invented many machines* and Det + N as in *the cheese, a mouse, our cat* (on the assumption that **determiners** are the heads of **noun phrases**). For **Japanese** the setting would be 'head last'. See **ADJUNCT, COMPLEMENT, LINGUISTIC UNIVERSALS**.

HEADLESS RELATIVE CLAUSE

See **FREE RELATIVE CLAUSE**.

HEARER

See **ADDRESSEE**.

HEARING ACUITY

The ability of listeners to distinguish different sounds.

HEARSAY

Information, etc. learned at second or third hand and not necessarily true.

HEAVY NOUN PHRASE

A long or complex **noun phrase**. Typically heavy noun phrases are moved to the end of a **construction** because it is too long or complex. E.g. *I sent the parcel to Catriona*, with the simple noun phrase *the parcel*, but *I sent to Catriona the parcel of new detective novels that she had agreed to review*, wth the long and complex underlined noun phrase. See **END WEIGHT, EXTRAPOSITION**.

HEAVY SYLLABLE

A **syllable** that contains a **diphthong** or long **vowel** or a final **consonant**. See **LIGHT SYLLABLE**.

HEBREW

Semitic, Afroasiatic. 5M speakers , Israel. Biblical Hebrew is the language of the Jewish Bible. Superseded by **Aramaic** in second century CE, becoming a literary and liturgical language. Revived in the twentieth century as Israeli Hebrew, an amalgam of revived Biblical Hebrew and **Yiddish**.

HEDGE

A **discourse particle**, a **word**, **phrase** or **clause**, that speakers and writers use to avoid committing themselves to some proposition: e.g. *as far as I can see, this will work; you wouldn't find any problems, probably*. See **EVIDENTIAL, HEDGING**.

HEDGING

The process of using a **hedge**. The **metaphor** appears to derive from using a hedge as protection against wind and rain. Cf. *to hedge one's bets*. See **HEDGE**.

HERDER, Johann Gottfried (1744–1803)
A German philosopher and Lutheran divine, he emphasized the interconnections between thought and language, argued that language had a human origin and was not God-given, and proposed that the properties of a given language reflected the national characteristics of its speakers.

HERTZ
The unit for measuring **frequency** of a **sound wave**, 1Hz = one **cycle** per second.

HESITATION
A delay in the production of an **utterance**, caused, for example, by problems in planning the **syntax** to use or in finding the appropriate **lexical word**. Pauses caused by hesitation in speech are usually filled by hesitation forms such as *ehm* or *er* in British English. Hesitations occur in writing and, in handwritten documents, are betrayed by scored-out words and phrases or by insertions marked by a **caret**.

HESTERNAL PAST
See **REMOTE PAST**.

HETEROCLISIS
A mixture of different **inflectional** classes within one and the same **paradigm**. E.g. Russian *ton* 'a shade of colour' has **masculine** inflections in the **singular** but **neuter** inflections in the **plural**. See **GENDER**, **INFLECTION**.

HETEROCLITE
Any **lexical word**, typically a noun or verb, that is characterized by **heteroclisis**. See **HETEROCLISIS**.

HETERORGANIC
Having different places of articulation. Most **consonant clusters** are heterorganic: /sk/ (alveolar /s/ and velar /k/). Most striking are co-articulated **labiovelar** consonants [kp] and [gb] found in some West African languages. Opposite **HOMORGANIC**. See **CO-ARTICULATION**.

HEURISTIC
A process of problem-solving by using past experience as a practical way of solving problems.

HEXAMETER
A line of verse consisting of six feet. See **FOOT**.

HIERARCHICAL STRUCTURE
See **CONSTITUENT STRUCTURE**.

HFC
See **HEAD FEATURE CONVENTION**.

HIATUS

In verse, a break in the middle of a line, as in *to be | or not to be*. In **phonology**, a break where adjacent **vowels** belong in different **syllables**, e.g. *coloperate*.

HIERARCHY

A system in which items, etc. are classified into different levels, in terms of importance, size or some other property. In society, people may be organized into different hierarchical levels depending on their social importance. In linguistics, sentence **structure** is held to be hierarchical: a sentence consists of **words**, grouped into **phrases**, which are then grouped into **clauses**, etc. See **ACCESSIBILITY HIERARCHY, GRAMMATICAL HIERARCHY**.

HIGH

In **SPE Distinctive Feature Theory**, **segments**, especially **vowel** segments, that are articulated with the **tongue** close to the **palate**, for example [i], [u], opposite **low**.

HIGH VOWEL

See **CLOSE, LOW, MID**.

HILIGAYNON

Malayo-Polynesian. Approx. 7M speakers, the Philippines.

HINDI

Indo-Iranian, Indo-European. Approx. 450M speakers, India (official language with English). Many speakers in Africa and South-East Asia. It is written in the Devanagari script. Very closely related to **Urdu**, which is written in an Arabic script and is the national language of Pakistan. Hindustani is a Hindi-based contact language developed for communication between the rulers and the common people. It is a widespread colloquial language.

HISTOIRE

In **narrative** theory a distinction is drawn between histoire and **discours**, and **fabula** and **sjuzhet**. The first pair are used by French theorists, the latter by Russian. English language theorists use **story** and **discourse**. 'Histoire', 'fabula' and 'story' denote the basic skeleton of events and characters in a narrative. 'Discours', 'sjuzhet' and 'discourse' denote the realization of the basic skeleton in some **medium**, whether language, film, dance or song, including the different techniques by which, for example, different authors present stories in writing, or by which different film producers present stories in cinematic form. 'Realization' denotes both the product, i.e. a particular version in a particular medium, and the process of creating the product.

HISTORIC CONJUNCTIVE

Old-fashioned term. See **OPTATIVE**.

HISTORIC PRESENT

The use of the **present tense** in descriptions of events in past time. In using the present tense speakers present the events as thought they were taking place in present time and thereby make them more vivid. E.g. *I was crossing the road – suddenly this car roars round the corner.* In English the historic present is typical of the telling of jokes and stories in colloquial speech but is also used in history programmes on radio and television. In other languages it also belongs to formal genres, as in French the present tense is regularly used in written accounts of historical events. See **TENSE AND ASPECT**.

HITTITE

Anatolian, **Indo-European**. Spoken in the second millennium BCE in Anatolia. It is written in Mesopotamian cuneiform script.

HJELMSLEV, Louis Trolle (1899–1965)

A Danish linguist who developed a theory of language called **glossematics**. The theory was set against a broad **semiotic** background and was to be incorporated in a rigorously formalized model.

HMONG-MIEN LANGUAGES

Approx. 4M speakers, China, North Vietnam, Laos, Thailand. Also known as Miao-Yao.

HOCKETT, Charles Francis (1916–2000)

A leading American linguist of the mid twentieth century, he followed Bloomfield's strict structuralism, producing excellent work in **phonology** and **morphology**, inventing the classic distinction between three models of morphology, **Item and Arrangement, Item and Process** and **Word and Paradigm**.

HODIERNAL PAST

See **REMOTE PAST**.

HOKAN LANGUAGES

A language family spoken in North-West America.

HOKKIEN

See **CHINESE**.

HOLD

When the vocal organs maintain an **articulation** position, as in a **geminated** consonant or in the **closure** of a consonant.

HOLISTIC

Applied to a theory of word meaning that focuses on the **sense** relations holding between a given **lexical word** and other lexical words and does not analyse its meaning into a set of **components** in isolation from the meanings of other lexical words. See **COMPONENTIAL ANALYSIS, LEXICAL DECOMPOSITION**.

HOLOGRAPH
A piece of handwriting.

HOLONYM
See **MERONYMY**.

HOLOPHRASE
An **utterance** consisting of a single **word** which is interpreted as conveying a more complex **meaning** corresponding to a **sentence**. Holophrases are typical of the language of very young children, as in *car*, interpreted according to the context as 'Give me my toy car' or 'We're going in the car' and so on. Holophrases are used by adults, as in the stereotypical *Scalpel!* ('Pass the scalpel, immediately'), or *Down!* ('Lie flat' or 'Take cover behind the wall', etc.).

HOMOGRAPHS
Word forms with identical spelling but different pronunciations such as *lead*, /liːd/ (base form of verb *lead*) and /lɛd/ (metal). See **WORD**.

HOMONYM
See **HOMONYMY**.

HOMONYMY
Where a single word form has two meanings for which analysts cannot provide a plausible relationship, the word form is analysed as realizing two **lexical words**. The relationship between the two lexical words is **homonymy** and the items are called homonyms. An example is *file*, a tool for smoothing rough edges and *file*, a container for loose leaves of paper. Judgements of homonymy differ because they depend on awareness of etymologies and the vitality of **metaphors**. Thus at an earlier stage in the history of English, *ear* as in *ear of corn* and *ear* denoting the ears of humans were separate lexical words realized by separate word forms. The word forms became identical, and it is possible that *ear* was regarded as a homonym. It is very natural to imagine ears of corn as named thus by analogy with human ears and *ear* is now considered a instance of **polysemy**, that is, one word form realizing one lexical item which has a basic meaning and a related metaphorical meaning. Perhaps fewer speakers of English are aware of the **metaphor** by which pieces of paper in books were called *leaves*, by analogy with leaves on trees. See **ETYMOLOGY**.

HOMOPHONES
Word forms with different spellings but the same pronunciation, such as *plane* and *plain*.

HOMORGANIC
Having the same place of **articulation**. This is common with **affixes** ending with a **nasal** consonant, as in *embrace; indecent; impotent;* and in consonant **clusters** beginning with a nasal within a **morpheme**, as in *pump, tent, pink*.

HONORIFIC

A special form of a **verb** or **pronoun** or term of address used to indicate respect and politeness. Honorifics may apply to the **addressee**, as in the use, in French, of the **second-person** singular *tu* which signals intimacy and friendship between **speaker** and addressee, while the use of *vous*, second-person plural, signals formality and lack of intimacy. Honorifics may apply to bystanders or third persons. In English a speaker might refer to a third person as *he* or *she* (very informal), as *John* or *Sandy* (not so informal) or as *Professor and Mrs X* (formal and respectful). See **MAXIMS OF POLITENESS**.

HOPI

Uto-Aztecan. Arizona.

HORTATIVE

See **EXHORTATIVE**.

HPSG

See **HEAD-DRIVEN PHRASE STRUCTURE GRAMMAR**.

HUMBOLDT, Wilhelm von (1767–1835)

A German linguist and Prussian diplomat and statesman, he held that each language realizes in its own particular way a set of universal concepts and that language is not a rigid unchanging structure but an activity reflecting the intentions and creativity of speakers. See **LANGUAGE UNIVERSAL, LINGUISTIC UNIVERSALS**.

HUNGARIAN

Finno-Ugric, Uralic. 11M speakers Hungary, 3M Romania, approx. 658K Slovakia.

HUNTINGTON'S CHOREA

See **HUNTINGTON'S DISEASE**.

HUNTINGTON'S DISEASE

A neurological disease that causes abrupt movements of the limbs and sudden involuntary changes in the pitch and loudness of the voice.

HURRIAN

Mesopotamia. *c.* 3000 BCE. It was written in the cuneiform script.

HYBRID

A **compound word** whose component parts come from different languages. E.g. *television*, in which *tele-* is from Greek and *vision* is from Latin. A Greek-English hybrid is *tele-working*.

HYPERADAPTATION

The adaptation by speakers of one variety to another by using linguistic features of the other variety, usually perceived as more prestigious. See **HYPERCORRECTION**.

HYPERBOLE

Exaggeration: *There must have been hundreds of people at the party* (when in fact there were eighty). See **LITOTES**.

HYPERCORRECTION

1. A pronunciation or grammatical **construction** often arising from a mistaken analogy with standard usage and produced out of the wish to be 'correct', but usually resulting in incorrect or stilted forms, as in *whom do you want?* 2. Extravagant style-shifting, surpassing an overtly prestigious **norm**. Examples are /sɑmən/ for /samən/ (*salmon*), perhaps modelled on the pronunciation of *psalm*, and *with you and I* for *with you and me*.

HYPERLEXIA

In **clinical linguistics**, a syndrome characterized by difficulties in using language but by a high level of skill at reading words.

HYPERNASALITY

A flow of air through the nasal cavity affecting all **segments** in a speaker's **utterances**, e.g. because the speaker's **velum** is paralysed or split, making **velic closure** impossible.

HYPERONYM

See **HYPONYMY**.

HYPOCORISTIC

A form typical of child language, e.g. *tootsie* 'toe', *tummy* 'stomach' or a **diminutive**, especially of names: e.g. *Lottie* 'Charlotte', *Sandy* for *Alexander*. (Greek *kore* 'boy/girl', *hupo* 'below', *hupokorizesthai* 'to use childish language'.)

HYPONASALITY

Reduced airflow through the **nasal** cavity, say because of a head cold.

HYPONYM

See **HYPONYMY**.

HYPONYMY

A central relation between **lexical words** in the vocabulary of a given language. Two lexical words are said to be in a relation of hyponymy, if the set of things denoted by one includes the set of things denoted by the other. E.g. hyponymy holds between *tree* and *beech* as the set of trees includes the set of beeches. *Tree* is the **hyperonym** or superordinate of *beech* (and of *oak, ash, rowan*, etc.) and *beech* is a hyponym of *tree*. The figure below shows the hyponymy relations among some lexical items relating to animals. *Mammal* is the superordinate of *dog, cat, tiger*, etc. *Tiger, lion, leopard, cheetah* and *(domestic) cat*, etc. are hyponyms of *cat* (and are co-hyponyms). *Dog* and *cat* are hyponyms of *mammal* and co-hyponyms. See **DENOTATION, MERONYMY, OPPOSITENESS, SENSE RELATION, SYNONYMY**.

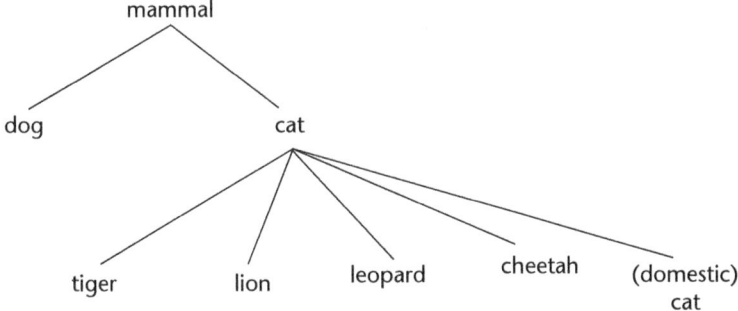

HYPOTAXIS

Subordination, especially of **clauses** and **sentences**. In the more general sense all subordinate clauses are hypotactic; in the stricter sense only subordinate clauses embedded in other constituents are hypotactic. E.g. in the stricter sense, relative clauses as in *the definition <u>which you accept</u>* and **complement** clauses as in *realized <u>that the game was up</u>* are instances of **hypotaxis**. *Which you accept* is embedded in the **noun phrase** *the definition which you accept* and *that...up* is embedded in the **verb phrase** *realized that ...up*. If **adverbial clauses** are analysed as not embedded, they are not hypotactic. E.g. in *After I saw the appeal, I made a donation*, the adverbial clause of time *After I saw the appeal* is not hypotactic but paratactic. In parataxis, clauses are not embedded one in the other but are adjacent to each other: e.g. *She arrived, I left* and *She arrived and I left*. (Greek *taxis* 'arrangement, rank'; *hupo* 'underneath', *para* 'beside'.)

HYPOTHETICAL PAST

See REMOTE PAST.

HYPOTHETICO-DEDUCTIVE METHOD

A research method used in science. A general proposition about some set of data is developed and used as a hypothesis. The **propositions** that can be deduced from the general proposition are then tested experimentally. If the propositions turn out to be false, the hypothesis is rejected. (In the real world of scientific research, the procedures are more convoluted and hypotheses are often re-formed and defended rather than abandoned immediately.) See ABDUCTION, DEDUCTION, INDUCTION.

I

IA
See ITEM AND ARRANGEMENT.

IAMB
See FOOT.

IAMBIC REVERSAL
In some **words** in English, **stress** is shifted to a preceding **syllable** to avoid having two adjacent stresses. Thus, in isolation *thir'teen, Prin'cess*, but in context *'thirteen 'men, 'Princess Di'ana*. Also known as the **'THIRTEEN MEN RULE'** or **RHYTHM RULE**.

IBN JANAH (c. 990–1050)
Born in Cordoba, died in Saragossa, Ibn Janah was a physician. He wrote, in Arabic, the first complete account of Hebrew grammar and vocabulary.

IBN JINNI (died 1200)
Born in Musil in northern Iraq, he belonged to the Baghdad school of linguistics. His major works dealt with vocabulary and **morphology**. He was the leading linguist of his time in the Arab world.

IC
See IMMEDIATE CONSTITUENT, CONSTITUENT STRUCTURE.

ICELANDIC
Germanic, Indo-European. 307K speakers, Iceland.

ICON
A non-arbitrary symbol, for example a symbol on a computer screen representing a file or program.

ICONIC MOTIVATION
The explanation proposed for a property of many **grammatical** patterns across languages, whereby the syntactic and morphological structures reflect the semantic and **pragmatic** information conveyed by a given **clause**. For instance, the written English example *the box in which we found the documents* contains the **relative clause** *in which we found the documents*. The clause is immediately next to *box*, about which it supplies extra information. The **preposition** *in* is immediately next to the relative **pronoun** *which* and the phrase *in which* signals clearly that the relative clause is connected with *box*

and that the documents were in the interior of the box. In spoken English we find **constructions** such as *the box we found the documents in*, in which *in* is right at the end of the relative clause and the link between the relative clause and *box* is signalled only by the position of the clause. A **word** or **phrase** that a speaker wishes to highlight can be put right at the beginning of a clause, as in *That country I've never visited*. Alternatively, a special construction can be used, as in *It's that country I've never visited*, and yet more highlighting can be provided by **adverbs**, as in *It's precisely that country I've never visited*. The highlighting is effected by putting the **constituent** in an unusual position, at the front of the clause, or by using a special construction, and degrees of highlighting are achieved by using just a special construction or the construction plus a highlighting **adverb**. Iconic motivation and **economic motivation** may counteract each other. See **ARBITRARY SIGN, CLEFT CONSTRUCTION, ICONICITY, ICONIC SIGN, ONOMATOPOEIA, SOUND SYMBOLISM**.

ICONIC SIGN

A **sign** whose form has some connection with its meaning. For example, the sound of the English word *splosh* resembles the noise made by a heavy object falling into deep water. See **ARBITRARY SIGN, ICONIC MOTIVATION, ICONICITY, ONOMATOPOEIA**.

ICONICITY

The property of natural language whereby semantic and pragmatic properties are paralleled in **grammar** and in sound. For example, in grammar derivational affixes, involved in the creation of new **lexical words**, are typically closer to the **root** or **stem** than **inflectional** affixes, and **direct object** nouns, denoting a central **participant** in events, are typically closer to the **verb** in a **clause** than **oblique** object nouns, denoting peripheral participants. In sound, languages have onomatopoeic words such as English *miaow*, a verb imitating the noise produced by cats, and **phonaesthemes** such as *fl-* associated with rapid repeated movements in *flicker, flit* and *flap*. See **ARBITRARY SIGN, ICONIC SIGN, ONOMATOPOEIA, SOUND SYMBOLISM**.

ICTUS

1. First position in a **foot**. 2. The rhythmical or metrical beat in a line of verse, typically falling on a stressed syllable. See **RHYTHM**.

ID

See **IMMEDIATE DOMINANCE**.

IDEALIZATION

In constructing a **grammar**, data is usually idealized to some extent, by disregarding such phenomena as hesitations, repetitions and pauses.

IDEALIZED COGNITIVE MODEL

In **cognitive linguistics**, a relatively stable mental representation of some area of culture or some aspect of the world. Not unlike **frames**, but can handle a wider range of **concepts**. A stock example is love as a container – *He was in love, He fell in love, He fell out of love*. An alternative label is **image schema**. See FRAME SEMANTICS, SCRIPT.

IDEATIONAL MEANING

A term in Halliday's **Systemic Functional Grammar**. A later term is 'representation', which captures the idea that **clauses** encode speakers' representations of the external world. See CONSTRUE, DESCRIPTIVE MEANING, INTERPERSONAL MEANING, TEXTUAL MEANING.

IDENTIFYING RELATIVE CLAUSE

See RESTRICTIVE, RELATIVE CLAUSE.

IDEOGRAM

A graphic symbol representing a **concept**. Early writing systems often contain ideograms, e.g. some Egyptian hieroglyphs or early Chinese characters. In contemporary text messaging **emoticons** like the 'smiling face', :-) and 'sad face', :-(are ideograms.

IDEOPHONE

A **word** with onomatopoeic characteristics, **sound symbolism**, **reduplication**, etc. often used adverbially, as in *The tap was leaking, plip plop*. Ideophones are found in many Bantu languages.

IDIOLECT

A distinctive way of speaking associated with a single individual.

IDIOM

See FIXED EXPRESSION.

IDIOM PRINCIPLE

The principle that the basic unit of analysis of language is not the **word** but combinations of **words** such as **phrases**, whether **fixed expressions** or semi-fixed expressions and **clauses**. The principle arose out of work on digital corpora which revealed how frequently combinations of **lexical words** recurred. See COLLIGATION, COLLOCATION.

IDIOMATIZATION

1. The formation of **idioms**, that is, expressions whose **meaning** cannot be (easily) worked out from the meanings of their component **words**. *To be hard-boiled* was originally applied to eggs, which can be boiled until they are hard. Applied to persons, the phrase means hardened by experience and not susceptible to appeals or arguments based on emotion rather than reason. See FIXED EXPRESSION. 2. In **derivational morphology**, the process by which complex **words** acquire a non-compositional meaning. E.g. *transmission* originally denoted the act of transmitting; with this sense the meaning is composed of the meaning of the **stem** *transmiss-* and the meaning of the **suffix** *–ion*. *Transmission* has

acquired the additional meaning of that part of a car that transmits power from the engine to the wheels. With this **sense** its meaning is non-compositional. See **COMPOSITIONALITY**.

IDENTIFYING RELATIVE CLAUSE
See **RESTRICTIVE RELATIVE CLAUSE, RELATIVE CLAUSE**.

IF CLAUSE
See **CONDITIONAL CLAUSE**.

IGBO
Benue-Congo, Niger-Congo. Approx. 26.9M speakers, southern Nigeria.

I-LANGUAGE
Chomsky's term for language internalized in the minds of speakers as a set of **rules** and principles. See **GRAMMATICAL COMPETENCE, COMMUNICATIVE COMPETENCE**.

ILL-FORMED
Not conforming to the **rules** and **constraints** of a **formal grammar**.

ILLATIVE
A **case** marking signalling movement into the interior of something. Finnish: *talo* 'house' *talon* 'into the house'. See **CASE**.

ILLOCUTIONARY ACT
In **speech act** theory, the act a speaker (or writer) intends to perform by producing an **utterance**: e.g. making a **statement**, asking a **question**, making a request, giving a **command**. A given utterance is said to have an **illocutionary force**, though this concept is not easy to apply. The utterance *Could you let me have the car back by three o'clock?* has **interrogative** force and is used to perform the illocutionary act of asking a **question**. It is also used to perform an act of requesting and has the force of a request, but there is some unclarity as to whether the request is a secondary illocutionary act or a **perlocutionary act**. See **LOCUTIONARY ACT, PERLOCUTIONARY ACT**.

ILLOCUTIONARY FORCE
See **ILLOCUTIONARY ACT**.

ILOCANO
Austronesian. Approx. 9M speakers. The Philippines.

IMAGE METAPHOR
In **cognitive linguistics**, **metaphors** based on physical resemblance. E.g. *Their new defender is the large ferocious gorilla charging at the opposing forwards*.

IMAGE SCHEMA
See **IDEALIZED COGNITIVE MODEL**.

IMAGINED COMMUNITY

A **group** in which each member knows, and communicates face to face with, few other members but considers him- or herself to belong to the group. Such communities are held together by communication in written language. Examples of such a group are the set of university lecturers in the UK, the set of general practitioners in the UK, the set of supporters of Manchester United. The set of people who control formal written English is an imagined community, but its members share many linguistic norms to do with what is acceptable in formal written texts. See **SPEECH COMMUNITY**.

IMITATION

In **language acquisition**, copying the **utterances** and **paralinguistic** behaviour of other speakers.

IMITATIVE

See **ONOMATOPOEIA**.

IMMEDIATE CONSTITUENT

See **CONSTITUENT STRUCTURE**.

IMMEDIATE DOMINANCE

In a **phrase structure tree**, the relation between a **node** X and a node Y where Y is on a **branch** originating from X and there are no intervening nodes. X is said to immediately dominate Y. In the figure below, A immediately dominates B and C, and C immediately dominates D and E. A dominates D and E, but it does not immediately dominate them.

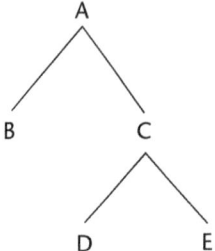

IMPERATIVE

1. A **construction** typically used for issuing **orders** or instructions. The English imperative construction typically has no **subject** and uses the bare verb **stem**, as in *Take this file to the secretary.* When a subject noun occurs, it is usually *you*, as in *You just stay there*, but can be *someone*, as in *Someone open the door.* 2. The **verb** forms that occur in imperative constructions, just the bare verb in English, but in, e.g., Russian a singular form – *daj* 'give', and a plural form – *dajte*.

IMPERFECT

Notably, but not solely, a set of **verb** forms in the **Romance** languages that contrast with the **perfect** and **past historic** forms. They are used to present individual **states** or **habitual** states (e.g. French *il dormait* 'He was-sleeping' or 'He used to sleep' vs *Il a dormi chez nous* 'He has slept at us, He has slept at our house (before)' or simply 'He slept at our house (last night)') or to present **actions** and **processes** as on-going (e.g. French *il lisait ces journaux* 'He was-reading these newspapers' or 'He used to read these newspapers' vs *il a lu ces journaux* 'He has read these newspapers', 'He read these newspapers'. Not to be confused with **Imperfective**. See TENSE AND ASPECT, SIMPLE PAST.

IMPERFECTIVE

In languages with a perfective-imperfective system of grammatical **aspect**, **perfective** verb forms present an **action** or **process** as completed, whereas imperfective forms do not specify whether an action or process was completed but are used to present them as on-going or as **habitual**. E.g. Russian *Tat'jana pisala pis'ma* 'Tatiana was-writing/used to write letters'. The Russian imperfective can also be used to state that some **action** or **process** took place, without drawing attention to its completion. E.g. *Tat'jana pisala pis'mo* 'Tatjana (once upon a time) wrote a letter'. See TENSE AND ASPECT.

IMPERSONAL CLAUSE

Impersonal clauses describe **situations** presented as not involving an **agent**. Typical are clauses describing weather (occasionally called **ambient clauses**) as in *It is blowing a gale*. *It* does not refer to any person or thing; the clause refers to the ambient weather conditions. An English **clause** requires a **subject**, which is supplied by *it*. It is variously known as **dummy subject** *it* (it has no **referent**), prop *it* (it props up the syntax) and **expletive** it (it fills out the syntax – Latin *pleo* 'fill'). Other examples are *It is nine o'clock*, *It is very exciting to see the results*, *It is muddy in that field*.

IMPLICATE

In Grice's theory of inferencing in conversation, speakers carry out acts of implicating or implication. The acts of implication point listeners towards inferences, to which Grice gave the technical term **implicature**. See ENTAILMENT, PRESUPPOSITION.

IMPLICATION

See ENTAILMENT.

IMPLICATIONAL UNIVERSAL

A type of universal in which the existence of one grammatical pattern in a given language implies or entails the existence of another one. Thus, if a language has **overt** verb **suffixes** marking **agreement** with third-person **pronouns**, it will have overt **verb** suffixes marking agreement with first- and second-person pronouns, but not vice versa. If in a given language **oblique** object nouns can be modified by **relative clauses**, then **direct object** and **subject** nouns can also be relativized, but not vice versa. See **ACCESSIBILITY HIERARCHY, GRAMMATICAL HIERARCHY**.

IMPLICATURE

Implicatures are inferences that enable **interlocutors** to go beyond what speakers say to what speakers actually mean. The inferences are not part of the **truth conditions** of **propositions** conveyed by **utterances** nor are they logical **entailments**. They are based on assumptions about speakers following the **maxims of conversation**. If the question *Is Jane a good cook?* elicits the response *Her mother's a good cook*, the questioner will probably infer, not that the interlocutor is maliciously changing the topic, but that he or she is saying indirectly that Jane is not a good cook. Such an inference is a **conversational implicature**. Some analysts distinguish generalized conversational implicatures and particularized conversational implicatures. The former require no context, the latter need a particular context. The utterance *Katarina is looking very happy today* only implies *Katarina has passed her exam* in the context of the question *Do you think Katarina has passed her exam?* Conventional implicatures are attached by convention to particular words. *Jane could cook that* and *Even Jane could cook that* have the same **descriptive meaning** and truth conditions, but from the word *even* listeners infer that the dish must be very simple and that Jane's culinary skills are rated very low by the speaker. This information belongs to the **non-descriptive meaning** of the sentence. See **NEO-GRICEAN PRAGMATICS, POLITENESS PRINCIPLE, PROPOSITION**.

IMPLOSION

In **SPE Distinctive Feature Theory**, the velaric suction producing an **ingressive airstream** mechanism, typical of an **implosive**.

IMPLOSIVE

A term in the description of the **manner of articulation** of **consonant** sounds relating to the nature of the **airstream mechanism**. For glottalic ingressive consonants, an **articulation** is formed in the mouth, the **glottis** is closed and the oral and glottalic closures are released simultaneously. Air is drawn into the mouth (**ingressive**) by the downward movement of the glottis, and this causes the effect of voicing. Implosive stops are not found in English; bilabial, [ɓ], and alveolar, [ɗ], implosives are found in many West African languages. See **AIRSTREAM**.

IMPRECATIVE

A minor type of **construction** containing a swear word (imprecation). E.g. *Blast it! Where's my key?*, *Damn the lot of them!*, *Well, bugger me if it isn't a tax demand!*

INALIENABLE

See **ALIENABLE POSSESSION**.

INANIMATE
Of **nouns**, not denoting an **animate** being.

INCEPTIVE
See **INCHOATIVE**.

INCHOATIVE
An **Aktionsart** denoting movement into a state or the beginning of an action or process. E.g. Russian *sedoj* 'grey' – *sedet'* 'become grey'; *pet'* 'sing' – *zapet'* 'begin to sing'.

INCLUSION
Relationship between sets. If the members of a set A are also all members of a set B, which also contains other members, set B is said to include set A.

INCLUSIVE
Of a **verb** or **pronoun**, designating the speaker and the **addressee**, as opposed to exclusive verbs and pronouns, which designate the speaker and someone other than the addressee. E.g. Maori *taua* 'We = You and I', *tatou* 'We = You, and I and at least one more person'. English *we* is used inclusively and exclusively. Some uses are only exclusive, such as the royal *we* in Queen Victoria's possibly apocryphal *We are not amused* and Margaret Thatcher's *We are a grandmother*. See **EXCLUSIVE WE**.

INCLUSIVE DISJUNCTION
See **DISJUNCTION**.

INCLUSIVENESS
In the **Minimalist Program**, a restriction preventing properties being added to or removed from **lexical words** during the syntactic part of a **derivation**.

INCOMPATIBILITY
A general sense relation holding between two **lexical words** that cannot be applied simultaneously to one and the same entity. E.g. a rugby jersey cannot be both all black and all white; a particular animal cannot be both a small elephant and a large elephant, though a small elephant is a large animal. See **OPPOSITENESS, SYNONYMY**.

INCONGRUITY
The phenomenon of a **phrase** or **clause** that cannot be given a sensible interpretation except in terms of extreme **figurative** language, as in Chomsky's *Colorless green ideas sleep furiously*.

INCORPORATION
A **process** by which **object** nouns are made part of, or incorporated into, **verbs**. The process typically applies to nouns with non-specific or **generic reference**. E.g. Dulay (Eastern **Cushitic**) – *Wosho an-tayad'a* 'field verb FOC-1sg guard, I-guard a – (particular) – field' vs *An-wosho^tayad'a* 'verb FOC-1sg-field guard-IPFV-1sg,

I guard fields/I am a field-guard'. The first example consists of a separate **noun phrase** *wosho* followed by the verb *an-tayad'a*; the speaker refers to one specific field. The second example consists of a single verb; part of the verb is the **noun** *wosho*, which is said to be incorporated into the verb. The speaker does not refer to any specific field but states his occupation. In English incorporation occurs in compound nouns such as *deer stalking*: *I am stalking a (particular) deer* vs *I go deer-stalking*. See REFERENCE, TRANSITIVITY.

INDECLINABLE

In a language in which a **noun** typically takes a **suffix** indicating **case**, **number**, etc., nouns which do not take **suffixes** are called indeclinable. E.g. **Russian** *kakadu* 'cockatoo' and *pal'to* 'overcoat' do not take any suffixes. A typical noun such as *student* 'student' does: e.g. *student-a* 'student-GEN', *student-u* 'student-DAT'.

INDEFINITE ARTICLE

See INDEFINITE NOUN PHRASE.

INDEFINITE NOUN PHRASE

In English, a **noun phrase** with the indefinite **article** *a/an*. The article signals that the speaker is referring to someone or something not previously mentioned or not known to the **addressee**. Indefinite noun phrases may consist of just an indefinite **pronoun**, such as *someone, something, anyone, anything*, or they may have *some* or *any* as **determiner**: *Would you like some apples?*, *Are there any copies of this book?* Languages with no articles may signal the same information by **word order** or by not using **plural** or **case** affixes: e.g. Turkish *Resmi ver* 'picture-ACC give-IMP, Give me the picture', *Resim ver* 'Give me pictures/a picture'. See REFERENCE.

INDEFINITE PRONOUN

See INDEFINITE NOUN PHRASE.

INDEFINITE REFERENCE

See REFERENCE.

INDEFINITE REFERRING EXPRESSION

See REFERENCE.

INDEFINITE RELATIVE

See RELATIVE CLAUSE.

INDEPENDENT CLAUSE

See CLAUSE.

INDEPENDENT PRONOUN

A **pronoun** that is not **anaphoric** to another **noun phrase** but refers directly to someone or something: *You are fired!*, *It is just what we need* (e.g. some kind of tool), *That is amazing* (e.g. some picture, act or piece of news).

INDETERMINACY

1. Applied to cases where a clear border cannot be established between one **category** and another or where different criteria lead to different divisions between categories. See **GRADIENCE**. 2. See **VAGUENESS**.

INDEX

1. Any **feature** of a **speaker** or writer that indicates their age, gender, socio-economic status, level of education, and emotional or psychological state. For example, inability to remember lexical items may indicate the effects of a stroke; the use of complex syntactic constructions or literary vocabulary may indicate advanced education. 2. In philosophy, any deictic pointing to time or place. See **DEIXIS**. 3. A device for coding the relationship between **anaphors** or **pronouns** and their **antecedents**. E.g. in *Bill$_i$ has removed himself$_i$ from the list of candidates*, the subscript *i* on *Bill$_i$* and on *himself$_i$* signals that *Bill* is the antecedent of *himself*.

INDEXICAL

In philosophy, **deictic**. See **DEIXIS**.

INDEXICALITY

See **DEIXIS**.

INDICATIVE

Where languages have a contrast between **indicative** and **subjunctive**, **imperative** or **optative**, indicative applies to verb forms in a main **clause** and expressing statements about **states**, **actions** and events treated as fact. The actions, etc. can be indicated or pointed at because they are fact. E.g. French *Jean revient* 'John is-coming-back-IND' vs *Que Jean revienne* 'that John come-back-SUB, Let John come back'. See **MOOD**.

INDIRECT OBJECT

See **GRAMMATICAL FUNCTION**.

INDIRECT QUESTION

1. A **question** reported in **indirect speech**. The **direct question** *Where are you going?* changes to, e.g., *He/she asked* followed by *where I was going*. The indirect question has the **word order** of a declarative clause, not *where was I going* but *where I was going*, with **subject** *I* followed by the **auxiliary** verb *was*. *You* is not used because the speaker is not reproducing the exact words of the questioner. A slightly old-fashioned term is *oratio obliqua* (Latin: *oratio* 'speech', *obliqua* 'indirect'). 2. In the sense of an indirect **speech act**; the speaker does not encode a request for information directly in the form of a question, *When will they arrive?*, but utters a **statement**: *I wonder when they will arrive*. See **DIRECT SPEECH**.

INDIRECT REFLEXIVE

See **LOGOPHORICITY**.

INDIRECT SPEECH

The report of some **utterance** or thought, not using the speaker's actual words and from the **viewpoint** of the reporter. E.g. *I'll phone you on Tuesday* is reported as *He/she said* and then *he/she* (since the reporter is referring to a person other than the **addressee**), *would* (since the reporter is describing a past event) *phone me* (since the original statement was made to the reporter, who refers to him- or herself as *me*: *He/she said he/she would phone me on Tuesday*. Note the phenomenon of **backshifting** in English, whereby **tenses** are shifted back; **Present tense** becomes **Past tense**, Past tense becomes **Past Perfect**. E.g. *I saw him last week* is reported as *He/She said that she had seen him the previous week*. Note too the change of first-person **pronouns** to third-person and other changes such as that of *last* to *the previous*. An older term is *oratio obliqua* (**Latin** 'oblique speech').

INDIRECT SPEECH ACT

See **SPEECH ACT**.

INDIVIDUAL LEVEL

See **GENERIC**.

INDIVIDUATION

In **cognitive linguistics**, see **BOUNDEDNESS**.

INDO-ARYAN

See Indo-Iranian.

INDO-EUROPEAN

Most of the languages of Europe and north India belong to the Indo-European family. There are a number of branches that contain a single language (**Albanian**, Armenian, Hellenic; two branches that are now extinct (**Anatolian** and **Tocharian**) and many thriving branches including **Baltic**, **Celtic**, **Germanic**, Indo Iranian, **Romance** and **Slavic**.

INDO-IRANIAN

Major branch of **Indo-European** with two substantial sub-branches, **Indo Aryan** and **Iranian**. The oldest recorded texts, the Vedic hymns, written in an early form of **Sanskrit**, date back to 1500 BCE. Modern Indo-Aryan languages are spoken in northern and central India and fall into four geographical groups: North-western (**Sindhi**, **Punjabi**, Lahnda, **Kashmiri** and other Dardic languages) South-western (**Gujarati**, **Marathi**, **Sinhala**); Midland (**Hindi**, **Urdu**) and Eastern (Assamese, **Bengali**). Hindi with over 337M speakers and Bengali with 70M speakers are the largest languages and several other languages have tens of millions of speakers.

INDONESIAN

Malayo-Polynesian, Austronesian. Approx. 23.5M, Indonesia. Very closely related to (Bahasa) **Malay**.

INDUCTION

A process of reasoning that moves from the observation of particular entities to a general **proposition** about the class of entities. Observers of swans in, say, Britain or France, might conclude after seeing two thousand white swans that all swans are white. A visit to the Antipodes will reveal that their inductive reasoning is incorrect, as there are black swans in Australia. Inductive reasoning can yield general propositions which are true; the difficulty is knowing when they are true. See **ABDUCTION, DEDUCTION**.

INDUCTIVE REASONING

See **INDUCTION**.

INESSIVE

A **case** marking signalling location in the interior of something. Finnish *talo* 'house' *on talossa* 'is in-the-house'. (Latin *in* 'in', *esse* 'to be'.)

INFINITIVE

A **verb** form denoting an **action**, **process** or **state** not limited to particular participants or a particular time. Infinitives in **English** are signalled by *to* preceding a verb, as in *To travel is better than to arrive*. Infinitives in **Turkish** are signalled by a special suffix: *git-ti-k* 'We went' vs *git-mek* 'to go'. See **FINITE VERB, NON-FINITE VERB, ROLE**.

INFINITIVE CLAUSE

A **non-finite clause** with an **infinitive** as its **head**.

INFIX

An **affix** inserted inside another form. The classical Greek verb *lambano* 'I take' has the root *lab-*, as in *elabon* 'I took', *lep-somai* 'I shall take'. The *m* in the *lamb* of *lambano* is an infix. See **INTERFIX**.

INFL

Introduced in Chomsky's **GB** model as a **node** in a **tree** carrying verbal **inflections** and information about **tense**, **person**, **gender** and **number**. In the P&P model the node was split into AGR, carrying **agreement** features to do with person, number and gender, and tense. In a further change, to reflect the fact that some languages have agreement between the **object** NP and the **verb**, AGR was split into AGR $_S$, carrying information about **subject** agreement, and AGR $_O$, carrying information about object agreement. INFL, which can have the features [+finite] and [−finite], captures the relationship between finite and non-finite **clauses** and enables clauses to be handled as endocentric, with INFL, later I, as their **head**. See **FINITE VERB**.

INFLECTION

Variation in the form of a **lexical word** reflecting different **morphosyntactic categories**. (Inflection contrasts with **derivation**, which has to do with the building-up of lexical words.) The variation is typically, but not only, by means of a **suffix**. E.g. in Russian *molotom* 'with a hammer' *-om* realizes instrumental **case**, singular **number** and masculine **gender**. In *molotov* the suffix *-ov* realizes genitive case, masculine gender and plural number. In Latin *regat* 'May he rule' *-at* realizes third person, singular number, active voice, subjunctive mood, present tense. *Regit* realizes the same morphosyntactic properties except for the change of **subjunctive** to **indicative**. See AGGLUTINATIVE, DERIVATIONAL MORPHOLOGY, MORPH.

INFLECTIONAL AFFIX

An **affix** that signals **morphosyntactic categories** such as **number** and **case** and syntactic linkages such as **agreement** and **government**. See INFLECTIONAL MORPHOLOGY.

INFLECTIONAL CLASS

A class of **words** or **morphemes** (**stems**, **roots**) which take the same inflectional **suffixes**. Verbs are gathered into classes, each class being a **conjugation**, and **nouns** and **adjectives** are gathered into classes, each class being a **declension**.

INFLECTING LANGUAGE

A language in which **words** are constructed from **stems** and typically one **inflectional affix**.

INFLECTIONAL MORPHOLOGY

The branch of **morphology** dealing with variation in the form of **words** that signals **morphosyntactic categories** such as **number**, **person** and **case** and the syntactic linkages of **agreement** and **government**. The variation typically, but not always, involves an **inflectional affix**.

INFORMANT

A person who willingly takes part in a research project as a language consultant.

INFORMATION EXTRACTION

A computational operation that searches a **database** to extract information. See TEXT MINING.

INFORMATION PACKAGING

See INFORMATION STRUCTURE.

INFORMATION RETRIEVAL

A computational operation that searches a **database** in response to a query. Depending on the program used, the query could be expressed in natural language or as a set of key words. See NATURAL LANGUAGE PROCESSING.

INFORMATION STRUCTURE

The structure of a **clause** or **sentence** as part of a larger **text** and viewed as a means by which speakers or writers present or package information to be transmitted to hearers and readers. Information can be presented as given or new; it can be contrasted or emphasized, stated overtly or left to inference, and so on. Information structure is handled in terms of **accessibility**, **focus**, **given** and **new**, **reference tracking**, **referential distance**, **theme** and **rheme**, **topic** and **comment**. See, ANAPHORA, ARGUMENT FOCUS, CATAPHORA, END FOCUS, FUNCTIONAL SENTENCE PERSPECTIVE, HIERARCHY, PREDICATE FOCUS, SENTENCE FOCUS, THEMATIC FRONTING, THETIC SENTENCE, TOPICALIZATION.

INFORMATION THEORY

A mathematical theory, based on probability, of the quantity of information conveyed by a given message.

INFORMATIVITY

The extent to which the information in a **text** is new.

INGRESSIVE AIRSTREAM

The main initiator of an **airstream** is the lungs, a **pulmonic airstream**. Air can be drawn into the lungs on an **ingressive** airstream, or expelled on an **egressive** airstream. Other airstreams are the **glottalic airstream** and the **velaric airstream**. The ingressive glottalic airstream is produced by closing the **glottis** and drawing it sharply downwards – **consonants** produced on a glottalic ingressive air stream are **implosive**. Consonants produced on an ingressive velaric airstream are **clicks**.

-ING CLAUSE

In English, a non-finite **clause** containing an -*ing* form. It may be a **gerund** (*I love reading detective novels*) or a **participial clause**, which may be a **reduced adverbial clause** (*Sitting at the window I saw the accident (Because/while I was sitting at the window)*) or a **reduced relative clause** (*The person waiting to see you) seems agitated (who is waiting to see you)*).

-ING FORM

In grammars of English, applied to verb forms with the suffix -*ing*: *playing*, *swimming*. Such forms may be **gerunds** or **participles**.

INGRESSIVE

See INCHOATIVE.

INHERENT FEATURE

Especially in **generative grammar**, a **feature** possessed by a **noun** in the lexicon/dictionary in contrast with features assigned by a syntactic **construction**. E.g. in Latin *mensa* 'table' is inherently **feminine**, count, common but receives **case** features such as **nominative** and **accusative** in particular **constructions**. See CONSTRUCTION, CASE, GENDER, SUBCATEGORIZATION.

INHERENT INFLECTION

An **inflection** inherent in a **lexical word** and not assigned by a syntactic **construction**. E.g. **tense** is inherent in verbs but **indicative** or **subjunctive** mood are assigned by constructions, subjunctive mood being assigned by particular types of subordinate **clause**. See **MOOD, TENSE AND ASPECT**.

INHERENT VARIABILITY
The property whereby the grammar of any language is subject to variation.

INHERITANCE
The transfer of properties from one **constituent** to another. A **verb** in a **passive** construction inherits the **feature** [passive]. The noun *blame* inherits from the verb *blame* the property of taking the **preposition** *for*: *They blamed Gordon for the mess*, *The blame for the mess fell on Gordon*.

INHERITED FEATURE SPECIFICATION
In **Generalized Phrase Structure Grammar**, the process by which **constituents** lower in a **tree** inherit **features** from constituents higher in the tree and immediately dominating them. See **INHERITANCE**.

INITIAL
Occurring at the beginning of a construction, e.g. a **word**, **phrase** or **clause**.

INITIAL SYMBOL
See **REWRITE RULE**.

INITIALISM
An **abbreviation** formed from the initial components of two or more **words**, e.g. *radar* from 'radio detection and ranging'; *NATO* from North Atlantic Treaty Organization. See **ACRONYM**.

INITIATOR
The organ that initiates an **airstream**, usually the lungs, which initiate the **pulmonic airstream**, but also the **glottis**, initiating the **glottalic airstream**, or the **velum**, initiating the **velaric airstream**. See **AIRSTREAM MECHANISM**.

INNATENESS HYPOTHESIS
The hypothesis that humans are born with a knowledge of the principles and constraints applying to the **grammars** of every natural language and that this knowledge enables children to acquire their native language rapidly and without instruction from adults.

INNER CIRCLE
In work on English as an international language or **English as a Lingua Franca**, those countries where English is the **native language** and the primary language of education and so on; that is, countries such as the United Kingdom, the United States, Canada, etc. See **EXPANDING CIRCLE, OUTER CIRCLE**.

INNER EAR
See **EAR**.

INPUT SPACES
See **CONCEPTUAL BLENDING**.

INSERTION
In the Standard Model of **transformational grammar**, any **transformation** that inserts new **constituents** into an existing **structure**; e.g. *do*-insertion, which inserts *do* to carry **tense** in an **interrogative clause**, e.g. *They know* and *Do they know?* See **CONSTITUENT STRUCTURE**.

INSERTION SEQUENCE
Especially in conversation, a **move** that breaks the **coherence** of the discourse or represents a different activity but is typically not felt by the interlocutors to be an interruption. Thus, in the sequence of utterances *Got any large envelopes? – We do. Depressing weather isn't it? – Yes – That's £1 for the packet* the buying–selling **exchange** has inserted into it an **utterance** that is a weather comment and an instance of **phatic communion**.

INSTANTANEOUS RELEASE
See **ABRUPT RELEASE, DISTINCTIVE FEATURES**.

INSTANTIATION
1. The representation of an abstract item by a concrete example. E.g. *mouse* and *mice* are both **instantiations** of the **lexical word** MOUSE. 2. In **Generalized Phrase Structure Grammar**, the assignment of a constant **value** to a **variable** feature. E.g. in a **clause** such as *The mice are eating the cheese*, both MOUSE and BE have the feature NUMBER and for both items NUMBER must be Plural to yield *mice* and *are*, agreeing in **number**. In grammars of English, NUMBER is said to be instantiated as Singular or Plural, as appropriate.

INSTRUCTIVE
A **case** expressing manner or means. E.g. Finnish *palja* 'bare', *pää* 'head', *paljain päin* 'bare-headed'.

INSTRUMENT
A participant **role** relating to things used as instruments or tools: *e.g., glue* in *We mended the box with glue*.

INSTRUMENTAL
A **case** expressing manner or means. E.g. Russian *molot* 'hammer', *molotom* 'with a hammer', *les* 'forest', *lesom* 'through the forest'. See **INSTRUMENT**.

INSTRUMENTAL FUNCTION
In early work on child language acquisition in **Systemic Functional Grammar**, the use of language as a means of meeting the needs of the speaker, for example obtaining food and drink.

INSTRUMENTAL PHONETICS

The study of speech sounds by the use of instruments that record and analyse data.

INTEGRATION

In syntax, the degree to which one **clause**, typically subordinate, is linked with another clause. E.g. a speaker might say *I have a filing cabinet. The drawers don't shut.* The two main clauses are quite independent of each other in their grammar and are said to be unintegrated. *I have a filing cabinet. Its drawers don't shut* has at least a **discourse** link, since *its* picks up the referent of *filing cabinet*. In *I have a filing cabinet whose drawers don't shut* the two clauses are more closely integrated, the **relative clause** having the **relative pronoun** *whose* as subject. An **infinitive** possesses an even higher degree of integration, as shown by *We want to win*, in which the **non-finite clause** *to win* has no **tense** or **aspect** and no subject NP. Unintegrated clauses are typical of spontaneous spoken language and highly integrated clauses are typical of edited written language.

INTELLIGIBILITY

A property of **utterances** such that their phonetic **segments, intonation** and **rhythm** are clear enough for listeners to begin the process of interpretation. See COMPREHENSIBILITY, INTERPRETABILITY.

INTENSIFIER

In CGEL, an alternative term for **degree adverb**. **Amplifiers** include words such as *absolutely, utterly*: *absolutely idiotic, utterly amazing*. **Downtoners** include words with a negative meaning, such as *hardly*: *hardly credible*.

INTENSIFYING ADJECTIVE

An **adjective** used to intensify or emphasize the meaning of a noun: *utter madness, complete fool, absolute genius*.

INTENSION

The set of properties that an entity must have in order to belong to one set of entities rather than another; e.g. in order to be referred to as a *kiwi* and not as a *kea*. An intensional definition of the **denotation** of *kiwi* is the set of properties of prototypical kiwis: having brown feathers and a very long beak, being flightless and nocturnal, living in burrows, laying eggs and so on. See EXTENSION, PROTOTYPE, REFERENCE, SENSE.

INTENSIONAL MEANING

See INTENSION.

INTENSIONAL WORLD

In **truth-conditional semantics**, a set of **propositions** providing an **intension** for some state of affairs. See TRUTH CONDITIONS.

INTENTIONALITY

The property of **utterances** such that **speakers** have particular intentions in producing them and are aware that their listeners also have intentions. A complete interpretation of a given utterance must include an understanding of the speaker's intentions. See **SPEECH ACT**.

INTENSITY

The strength of a sound signal measured in **decibels**. See **LOUDNESS**.

INTENSIVE

Applied to a **construction** where there is a referential link between two **constituents**. E.g. in *John is the man with alpacas*, *John* and *the man with alpacas* refer to the same person. In *Juliet is busy*, *Juliet* and *busy* pick out the same busy person. In *The drink made Mike ill*, *Mike* and *ill* pick out the same ill person. See **CONSTITUENT STRUCTURE, REFERENCE**.

INTERACTIONAL SOCIOLINGUISTICS

The study of the language of face-to-face interaction, that is, the production and reception of social meanings in talk.

INTERCHANGEABILITY

The principle that hearers are also speakers.

INTERDENTAL

A term in the description of the **place of articulation** of **consonant** sounds. The **tip** of the **tongue** comes between the teeth as in some pronunciations of the **voiceless** interdental **fricative** [θ], *thigh*; or the **voiced** dental fricative [ð] *thy*. See **ARTICULATION**.

INTERFACE

In the **Minimalist Program**, any level on which syntactic **structures** interact ('interface') either with the **Conceptual-Intentional structure** (CI) or the **Articulatory-Perceptual structure** (AP). Syntax does not interact directly with the AP but via a set of operations called **Spellout** that map syntactic structures onto a representation called **Phonetic Form** (PF). It interacts with the CI via a representation known as **Logical Form**. Spellout and Logical Form are interface levels.

INTERFERENCE

The transfer of features from speakers' first languages into their second languages, as when native speakers of Russian do not use definite and indefinite articles in English.

INTERFIX

An empty **morph** used to link two parts of a **compound word** or to link a **stem** to a **suffix**. German *Arbeit* 'work', *Anfall* 'load', *Arbeit+s+anfall* 'workload', Latin *labor* 'work', *-bam* 'PST, IPFV, 1sg', *labor+a+bam* 'I was working'. See **INFIX**.

INTERJECTION
Typically a **word** that expresses an emotion and is not connected grammatically to the other words in a **sentence**. (But some interjections are a **phrase** or **clause**.) E.g. *ouch, wow, hell's bells, stone the crows*.

INTERLINGUA
1. An international auxiliary language with a simple grammar and a vocabulary derived from a wide range of languages, mostly Indo-European, and designed to be comprehensible to a wide variety of people. See **ESPERANTO**.
2. A language-independent interface used in **machine translation**.

INTERLOCUTOR
Any person taking part in a **dialogue**, playing in turn the **roles** of **speaker** and **hearer**.

INTERMEDIATE PROJECTION
See **X-BAR SYNTAX**.

INTERNAL ADEQUACY
The **adequacy** of a grammar measured by its internal organization, its simplicity and elegance.

INTERNAL COHESION
A key property of a **word**. The order of a **stem** and its **affixes**, or stem and stem in the case of a **compound word**, cannot be changed nor can the **constituents** of a word be separated. E.g. in *fearlessly*, *fear*, *less* and *ly* must be in that order; in the Turkish *evleri* 'her/his houses', *ev* 'house', *ler* 'pl' and *i* 'POSS' must be in that order and cannot be separated by any other **morph**.

INTERNAL RECONSTRUCTION
A technique for reconstructing earlier stages of a language by comparing variant forms within that language on the assumption that alternate forms descend from a single ancestor and the alternation was introduced by regular processes of **sound change**. For example, given the English forms /lɔŋ/ (*long*) and /lɔŋɡə/ (*longer*), parallel to *strong* and *stronger*, we postulate that the original stem is /lɔŋɡ/ and in *long* the /ɡ/ has been lost following a nasal. By contrast, the **comparative method** compares variant forms between languages on the assumption that they descend from a common ancestor.

INTERNALIZATION
In Chomsky's theory of **language acquisition**, the process by which children create internal representations of linguistic structure in their minds without instruction and following universal principles. See **I-LANGUAGE**.

INTERNALIZED-LANGUAGE
See **I-LANGUAGE**.

INTERNAL MODIFICATION
See MODIFICATION.

INTERNAL SANDHI
See SANDHI.

INTERNAL STABILITY
See INTERNAL COHESION.

INTERNATIONAL PHONETIC ALPHABET (IPA)

A system of phonetic **transcription** first devised by the International Phonetic Association in 1888 and frequently modified since then, the most recent revision being published in 2005. The aim is to provide a transcription system for all known languages. **Consonants** are classified in terms of **place of articulation**, **manner of articulation** and **voice**. **Vowels** are classified in terms of the **cardinal vowel** system. As far as possible, symbols are based on the roman alphabet, though a number of specially designed characters are also used. **Diacritics** are generally used sparingly.

THE INTERNATIONAL PHONETIC ALPHABET (revised to 2005)

CONSONANTS (PULMONIC)   2005 IPA

	Bilabial	Labio dental	Dental	Alveolar	Postalveolar	Retroflex	Palatal	Velar	Uvular	Pharyngeal	Glottal
Place	p b		t d			ʈ ɖ	c ɟ	k ɡ	q ɢ		ʔ
Nasal	m	ɱ		n		ɳ	ɲ	ŋ	ɴ		
Trill	ʙ			r					ʀ		
Tap or Flap		ⱱ		ɾ		ɽ					
Fricative	ɸ β	f v	θ ð	s z	ʃ ʒ	ʂ ʐ	ç ʝ	x ɣ	χ ʁ	ħ ʕ	h ɦ
Lateral fricative				ɬ ɮ							
Approximant		ʋ		ɹ		ɻ	j	ɰ			
Lateral approximant				l		ɭ	ʎ	ʟ			

Where symbols appear in pairs the one to the right represents a voiced consonant.

CONSONANTS (NON-PULMONIC)

Clicks		Voiced implosives		Ejectives	
ʘ	Bilabial	ɓ	Bilabial	ʼ	Examples
ǀ	Dental	ɗ	Dental alveolar	pʼ	Bilabial
ǃ	(Post)alveolar	ʄ	Palatal	tʼ	Dental alveolar
ǂ	Palatoalveolar	ɠ	Velar	kʼ	Velar
ǁ	Alveolar lateral	ʛ	Uvular	sʼ	Alveolar fricative

INTERNATIONAL PHONETIC ALPHABET (IPA)

VOWELS

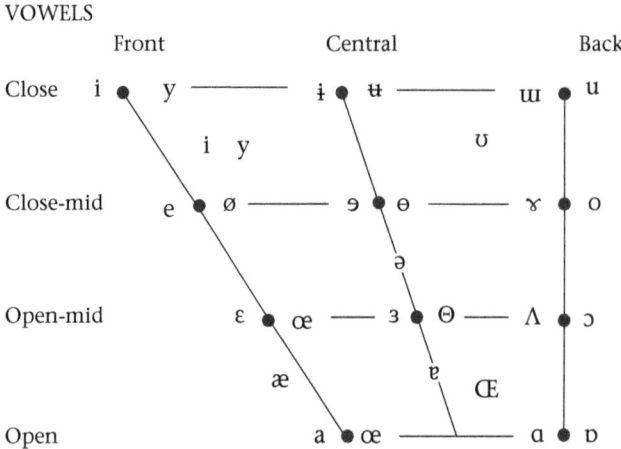

Where symbols appear in pairs the one to the right represents a rounded vowel.

DIACRITICS Diacrities may be placed above a symbol with a descender. e.g. ŋ̊

̥	Voiceless	n̥ d̥	̈	Breathy voiced	b̈ ä	̪	Dental	t̪ d̪
̬	Voiced	s̬ t̬	̰	Creaky voiced	b̰ ḭ	̺	Apical	t̺ d̺
ʰ	Aspirated	tʰ dʰ	̼	Linguolabial	t̼ d̼	̻	Laminal	t̻ d̻
̹	More rounded	ɔ̹	ʷ	Labialized	tʷ dʷ	̃	Nasalized	ẽ
̜	Less rounded	ɔ̜	ʲ	Palatalized	tʲ dʲ	ⁿ	Nasal release	dⁿ
̟	Advanced	u̟	ˠ	Velarized	tˠ dˠ	ˡ	Lateral release	dˡ
̠	Retraced	e̠	ˤ	Pharyngealized	tˤ dˤ	̚	No audible release	d̚
̈	Centralized	ë	̴	Velarized or pharyngealized ɫ				
̽	Mid-centralized	ė	̝	Raised	e̝	(ɹ̝ = voiced alveolar fricative)		
̩	Syllabic	n̩	̞	Lowered	e̞	(β̞ = voiced bilabial approximant)		
̯	Non-syllabic	e̯	̘	Advanced Tongue Root	e̘			
˞	Rhoticity	ɚ a˞	̙	Retracted Tongue Root	e̙			

SUPRASEGMENTALS

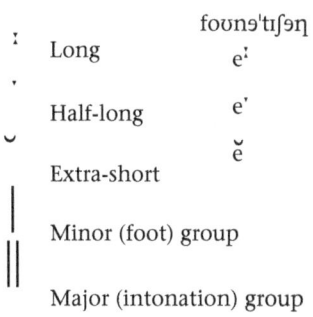

ˈ Primary stress

ˌ Secondary stress

ː Long   foʊnəˈtɪʃən
                eː

ˑ Half-long   eˑ

˘ Extra-short ĕ

| Minor (foot) group

‖ Major (intonation) group

. Syllable break   win.tə

‿ Linking (absence of a break)

INTERPERSONAL MEANING
In Halliday's **Systemic Functional Grammar**, interpersonal meaning has to do with the use of language to make **statements** to others, to ask questions and to issue **commands**. A later term is **exchange**, and the **clause** is regarded as the essential linguistic instrument by means of which speakers and listeners exchange information and what Halliday calls 'goods and services'. The former are, e.g., statements and **questions**, the latter are, e.g., commands and offers. See **IDEATIONAL MEANING, TEXTUAL MEANING**.

INTERPRETABILITY
The property of **utterances** such that listeners can go beyond the literal meaning of **phrases**, **clauses** and **sentences** to understand the meanings that speakers and writers intend to convey. See **COMPREHENSIBILITY, EXPLICATURE, INTELLIGIBILITY, INTENTIONALITY**.

INTERPRETABLE FEATURE
See **CHECKING**.

INTERPRETATION
1. An act of interpreting a spoken or written **text** or the understanding of the text produced by such an act. 2. In any formal **model**, the application of a set of rules in one **component** of the model to representations generated in another

component. For example, in various Chomskyan models of **generative grammar**, the representations of **syntactic structure** become the input to rules that generate semantic structures or rules that generate phonological structures.

INTERPRETIVE SEMANTICS

In the early 1970s, the principle, and models of **transformational grammar** incorporating that principle, that representations of the meaning of sentences were derived from representations of syntax, especially surface **syntax**. The principle and the models were opposed to **Generative Semantics**. See **GENERATIVE SEMANTICS**.

INTERROGATIVE

Applied to **constructions** (**words, phrases, clauses**) used for asking **questions**: *Where?, Which road?, Are you leaving?* are all interrogative.

INTERROGATIVE ADJECTIVE

An **adjective** that marks interrogative **constructions**, such as *which* in *Which team won?* or *what* in *What films will be on at Christmas?* In many analyses of English, *Which* and *What* in these examples are treated as **determiners**.

INTERROGATIVE ADVERB

An **adverb** that is the focus of a wh-**interrogative clause**/sentence and in English is typically at the beginning of the **clause**: *Why did you refuse? How did you escape?, Where did you go?*

INTERROGATIVE CLAUSE

A **clause** whose primary use is in the asking of **questions**. Two main clause types are recognized, yes/no or polar interrogatives and wh interrogatives. Yes/no interrogatives are occasionally called closed interrogatives, being used to ask questions about a situation in general which can be answered by *yes* or *no* – *Did she leave?, Are they buying a flat?* Wh interrogatives are used by speakers who presuppose a particular situation but ask about particular **participants** and circumstances. Thus, in asking *What is Kirsty buying?* the speaker presupposes that Kirsty is buying something and asks what the something is. See **DIRECT QUESTION, INDIRECT QUESTION, OPEN INTERROGATIVE**.

INTERROGATIVE PRONOUN

Pronoun that is the focus of a wh-**interrogative clause/sentence** and in English is typically at the beginning of the **clause**: *Who did you meet?, What did you buy?*

INTERROGATIVE SENTENCE

See **INTERROGATIVE CLAUSE**.

INTERSECTIVE GRADIENCE

See **GRADIENCE**.

INTERSENTENTIAL CODE SWITCHING
See **CODE SWITCHING**.

INTERTEXTUALITY
The property of **texts** whereby a given text is linked, or can be linked by a user, to many other texts. One text (or its creator) may allude to another one, may quote from another one, parody another one and so on. Intertextuality is illustrated in the entry for **free indirect speech**. The title of Lindsey Davis' novel *Three Hands in the Fountain* echoes the song and the film entitled *Three Coins in the Fountain*.

INTERVOCALIC
Occurring between two **vowels**.

INTONATION
Variation in **pitch** over a stretch of **utterance**. Intonation **contours** may also be accompanied by variation in **loudness** and **tempo** and by **pauses** of various lengths. Intonation can be used for a variety of purposes, such as signalling grammatical boundaries (**phrase**, **clause**, etc), **sentence** types (**statement**, **question**, etc.) and speakers's attitude (for instance, surprise, irony).

INTONATION CONTOUR
The **intonation** pattern over a stretch of **utterance**.

INTRANSITIVE CONSTRUCTION
A construction in which a **verb** combines with only one **noun**, e.g. *The tree fell, The paint dried quickly, The surface scratches easily.*

INTRANSITIVE PREDICATE
In **logic**, a **predicate** that is not transitive. See **TRANSITIVE PREDICATE**.

INTRANSITIVE VERB
A verb that combines with a single noun that is not a direct object, as in *The dog barked, My watch stopped.* See **TRANSITIVITY**.

INTRASENTENTIAL CODE SWITCHING
See **CODE SWITCHING**.

INTRINSIC ORDERING
See **RULE ORDERING**.

INTRODUCTORY *IT*
See **DUMMY SUBJECT, EXTRAPOSITION**.

INTRODUCTORY *THERE*
See **EXISTENTIAL**.

INTRUSION
In pronunciation, the introduction of additional sounds in particular environments, e.g. the **intrusive r** found in some pronunciations where there

is no 'r' in the spelling and no 'r' is generally pronounced, as in *law and order* [*law[r]and order*], Where there is an 'r' in the spelling and it is pronounced, this is known as a **linking r**, as in *rear end* [*rea[r]end*]. See **LIAISON**.

INTRUSIVE R
See **INTRUSION**.

INTUITION
The ability to know something by direct or immediate insight, rather than by a consideration of facts. In linguistics, the ability of a **native speaker** to make judgements about the **acceptability** of sentences, etc. on the basis of unconscious knowledge.

INUPIAQ
An **Eskimo-Aleut** language spoken in Alaska.

INVARIABLE WORD
A **word** which does not change its form. Especially relevant to languages such as Russian in which most nouns take **case** suffixes but some invariable ones do not: e.g. *moloko* nominative case 'milk', *moloka* genitive case vs *pal'to* 'coat', nominative, genitive and the other four cases.

INVARIANCE
The principle that a particular **phone** should always be assigned to a particular **phoneme**. This ensures that the phonetic **realization** of a particular phoneme will not overlap with that of another phoneme. Transcription conventions insist on **biuniqueness**.

INVERSION
Any operation changing the order of items in a string from $x + y$ to $y + x$. See **SUBJECT-AUX INVERSION**.

INVERTED PSEUDO-CLEFT SENTENCE
See **REVERSE WH CLEFT, CLEFT CONSTRUCTION**.

IO
See **INDIRECT OBJECT, GRAMMATICAL FUNCTION**.

IP
1. In the GB and P&P models, a phrase with an **auxiliary** or a tense **inflection** as its **head**. ('I' stands for 'Inflection'.) E.g. the structure underlying *Freya ate a biscuit* would contain a verb phrase [*Freya eat a biscuit*] and this would be part of an IP headed by **tense**: [*Past* [*Freya eat a biscuit*]]. IP replaced the older 'S' for 'Sentence' (and 'clause'). 2. See **ITEM AND PROCESS**.

IPA
See **INTERNATIONAL PHONETIC ALPHABET**.

IRANIAN

A major branch of **Indo-Iranian**, itself a branch of **Indo-European**. The oldest texts are in **Avestan**, the language of the Zoroastrian scriptures, and Old **Persian**. The modern languages are spoken in an arc from eastern Turkey to Afghanistan and include Bactrian, **Baluchi**, Chorasmian, Khotanese, **Kurdish**, **Pashto**, **Persian** and **Sogdian**.

IRISH GAELIC

Celtic, **Indo-European**. 355K speakers, Ireland.

IROQUOIAN

Spoken in the south-east and north-east states of the USA and in Canada. Cherokee 15K speakers, Oklahoma and North Carolina; **Oneida** approx. 250, Canada.

IRREALIS

See **MOOD**.

IRREFLEXIVE

See **REFLEXIVE PREDICATE**.

IRREGULAR

Applied to any **word** that does not follow the normal pattern for its class. E.g. *dog* and *dogs* but *mouse* and *mice*, *big* and *bigger* but *bad* and *worse*, *remind* and *reminded* but *swim* and *swam*.

ISLAND

Any unit in a **sentence** whose boundaries act as **barriers** to particular **relations** or **processes**. E.g. wh questions cannot extract NPs from a **relative clause**: in *Rene deleted the e-mail [which contained the list]*, *the list* cannot be extracted and questioned. **Which list did Rene delete the e-mail [which contained]* is gobbledygook. See **COMPLEX NOUN PHRASE CONSTRAINT**, **COORDINATE STRUCTURE CONSTRAINT**.

ISLAND CONDITION

Any **constraint** defining an **island**.

ISOCHRONY

The rhythmic speech pattern whereby particular units occur at (roughly) regular intervals. In **stress-timed** languages like English, stressed **syllables** occur at regular intervals. In **syllable-timed** languages like French, each syllable tends to take the same time. See **RHYTHM**.

ISOGLOSS

In **geographical linguistics**, a line on a map indicating the boundary of an area showing some linguistic characteristic, e.g. of pronunciation or vocabulary.

ISOLATED
See DISTINCTIVE FEATURES.

ISOLATING LANGUAGE
A language in which each **word** form consists of a single **morph**, with no **stem** or **affix**. See AGGLUTINATIVE, FUSION, INFLECTIONAL CLASS.

ISOSYLLABISM
See SYLLABLE-TIMED.

IT CLEFT
See CLEFT CONSTRUCTION.

ITALIAN
Romance, Indo-European. 55M speakers, Italy.

ITALIC
Indo-European. Italic includes the now extinct Oscan, the language of Pompeii, and **Latin**, the language of ancient Rome and the ancestor of the **Romance** languages.

ITEM AND ARRANGEMENT
A type of analysis in which a **word** is taken to consist of a sequence of **morphs** or **morphemes**. The analysis states which morphemes a given word consists of and the **order** in which they are arranged. E.g. *taught* might be analysed into the morphemes '*taugh*' and '*-t*'. The model has no abstract underlying forms and no **processes** converting these into surface forms. The Latin *nominative* form *reks* 'king' would be analysed as consisting of the **root** *rek-* and the **suffix** *-s*, the **accusative** form *regem* as consisting of the root *reg-* and the suffix *-em*. *Rek-* and *reg-* would be treated as alternative roots equal in status. See ITEM AND PROCESS, WORD AND PARADIGM, ZERO MORPH.

ITEM AND PROCESS
A type of analysis in which a surface **word** form is derived from an underlying **root** by a series of **processes**. E.g. Latin *reks* 'king-NOM' is derived from the root *reg*. *Reg-* is realized as *reg-* when preceding a vowel, as in the genitive singular *regis* and the nominative plural *reges*. *Reks-* is derived by two processes: one adds the **nominative** case **suffix** *-s* and a second devoices /g/ to /k/ before the **voiceless consonant** /s/. See ITEM AND ARRANGEMENT, WORD AND PARADIGM.

ITERATIVE
An **Aktionsart** or syntactic construction signalling repetition of an event. Compare the English *I wrote a letter*, describing a single event, with *I used to write letters on Sunday evening*, describing repeated or iterated events. Another iterative construction is based on *keep*, as in *I keep telephoning*. A given event may be repeated over a short time, as in *I kept telephoning all that day*, or over a longer time, as in *she kept writing to her friend for years*. Some languages have special iterative

verb forms, such as Czech *psal* 'wrote (once)' vs *psával* 'used to write'. See **TENSE AND ASPECT**.

ITERATIVE RULES

Any **rule** that applies over and over but does not invoke itself as recursive rules do. E.g. in **transformational grammar** many transformations, such as **passive** and **raising**, were iterative, applying wherever the appropriate structure was met.

I-TO-C MOVEMENT

In **GB** and **P&P**, the **movement** of an **auxiliary** from the I node (**Inflection**) to the C node (**Complementizer**). The movement maps **declarative** clauses such as *She has read this book* and *Lucie can speak Czech* into the corresponding **interrogative clauses**, *Has she read this book* and *Can Lucie speak Czech?* In the classic Standard Model of **transformational grammar** the movement was called **Subject-Aux Inversion**, a label that is still in use and reflects the **inversion** in the order of subject noun phrase and auxiliary verb, i.e. they change places.

J

J&H DISTINCTIVE FEATURE THEORY
The system of **acoustic** distinctive features associated with the work of **Jakobson** in the 1950s in *Fundamentals of Language*. His work grew out of work in the **Prague School**. See **DISTINCTIVE FEATURES, ACOUSTIC**.

JAKOBSON, Roman (1896–1982)
A leading European structuralist, he was born and educated in Moscow and emigrated to the USA in 1941. He worked on literature and aesthetics but is known in linguistics for his work on **phonology** and his analysis of **Russian** case. He developed a set of universal acoustic features which were central to the earliest model of generative phonology. See **J&H DISTINCTIVE FEATURE THEORY**.

JAPANESE
Language Isolate. 127M speakers, Japan. Attested in writing from the eighth century CE. Modern written texts use a mixture of four scripts. Chinese characters, known as kanji, represent lexical morphemes. Two syllabaries, consisting of simplified Chinese characters known as kana, are used for grammatical morphemes such as suffixes, particles and conjunctions. The hiragana are in general use but katakana are mainly used for transcribing foreign words and in imperial proclamations. Missionaries introduced the Roman alphabet in the sixteenth century CE.

JAVANESE
Austronesian. 97M speakers, Indonesia.

JERRAIAS
Romance, Indo-European. Norman French dialect spoken on the island of Jersey.

JESPERSEN, Otto (1860–1943)
A Danish linguist, Jespersen was an outstanding scholar of **English** and an excellent phonetician. His seven-volume grammar of English syntax is still consulted and referred to by scholars.

JIWARLI
Pama-Nyungan, **Australian languages**. Western Australia. The last speaker died in 1985.

JOHNSON, Dr Samuel (1709–1784)

An English scholar who prepared the first comprehensive and scientific dictionary of English, in which the definitions of **lexical words** were supported by quotations from literature. The dictionary was the authority on language use until the first volume of the *Oxford English Dictionary* appeared in 1887.

JONES, Daniel (1881–1967)

The leading British phonetician of the first half of the twentieth century. He invented the system of **cardinal vowels**, introduced the term '**phoneme**' into English and the phoneme principle into British linguistics (in 1917) and carried out fundamental and still influential work on the **phonetics** of **Received Pronunciation**.

JONES, Sir William (1746–1794)

An English lawyer who founded the Asiatic Society in Calcutta and in a lecture to it in 1786 presented his theory that **Sanskrit** was genetically related to Latin and Greek and possibly also to the Celtic, Germanic and Iranian languages. This lecture marks the beginning of scientific **comparative linguistics**.

JUNCTION

Jespersen's term for a **construction** with a **head** and constituents **dependent** on the head but containing no **predication**. E.g. the noun phrase *absolutely stunning performance*, where the head is *performance* and *absolutely stunning* is dependent on it and modifies it. See **PREDICATE**.

JUNCTURE

1. The **phonetic** features linking successive speech **segments** where there is a grammatical **boundary**. For example, the two phrases *plum pie* and *plump eye* may be identical as a series of **phonemes** in a phonemic **transcription**, /plʌmpaɪ/, but there are word boundaries between *plum* and *pie* and between *plump* and *eye*. In *plum pie*, /plʌm+paɪ/, the juncture, symbolized here as [+], between the /m/ and the /p/ is marked phonetically by the slight lengthening of the /m/, the **aspiration** on /p/ may be audible and there may even be a slight **pause** between *plum* and *pie*. By contrast in *plump eye*, /plʌmp+aɪ/ there is no comparable juncture between the /m/ and the /p/, both being in the same **word**, the /m/ is unlikely to be lengthened, the /p/ may be less audibly aspirated and, if there is a slight pause, it will be between *plump* and *eye*. See **BOUNDARY**. 2. Role and Reference Grammar recognizes three different types of linkage between units, the linkage being called '**nexus**'. Juncture has to do with the different levels on which nexus applies and the different units connected by a nexus. RRG recognizes three levels of grammar and three sorts of unit, **nucleus**, **core** and **clause**. An English example of nuclear juncture is *hammer flat* in *The blacksmith hammered flat the iron bar*. An example of core juncture is *I asked Sabrina to set the table*, the two cores being *I asked Sabrina* and *Sabrina set the table*. Examples of clausal juncture are *James fell and Freya picked him up* and *When James fell, Freya picked him up*. See **CONJUNCTION, SUBORDINATION**.

JUSSIVE

Any **verb** form, or **phrase** or **clause** construction, used for **commands**. *Give me the key* and *Let them wait* are both jussive. The term is now less frequently used than its equivalent, **imperative**.

JUXTAPOSITION

The placing of two **constituents** side by side, especially where their relationship is not signalled by an **affix** or a **complementizer**. In spoken English *What they do, they leave them to dry* the clauses *What they do* and *they leave them to dry* are juxtaposed; the listener assumes they are related. In written English the clauses are typically integrated: the second one, *leave them to dry*, has no subject and the clauses are connected by *is*: *What they do is leave them to dry*. Frequently occurring examples of juxtaposition, however, are contact **relative clauses** and contact **complement clauses**, which are typical of both spoken and written English. E.g. in *the letter I am writing* the relative clause *I am writing* is juxtaposed with the noun it modifies, *letter*. In *We said it wouldn't work*, the complement clause *it wouldn't work* is juxtaposed with the verb it modifies, *said*.

K

KANNADA
Dravidian. Approx. 35M speakers, Southern India (state of Karnataka and neighbouring states). The earliest written records date back to *c.* 450 CE.

KANURI
Nilo-Saharan. Approx. 4M speakers, Nigeria, Cameroon, Chad and Niger.

KAPAMPANGAN
Austronesian. Approx. 2M speakers. The Philippines.

KASHMIRI
Indo-Iranian, Indo-European. Approx. 4M speakers, Kashmir and surrounding states.

KATZ-POSTAL HYPOTHESIS
In early **transformational grammar**, the principle that **transformations** do not change meaning, e.g. by introducing negation.

KAYARDILD
Pama-Nyungan, **Australian languages**. An Australian aboriginal language spoken in Queensland. It is severely endangered.

KAYTETJ
Pama-Nyungan, **Australian languages**. App. 200K speakers, Northern Territory of Australia.

KAZAKH
Turkic, **Altaic**. 8.2M speakers, Kazakhstan.

KERES
Language isolate. Approx. 8K speakers, Pueblo people, New Mexico.

KERNEL SENTENCES
In early versions of **transformational grammar**, the set of elementary sentences from which all the sentences of a given language were built by means of **transformations** and combiners such as *wh*, *that*, *because* and *and*. The set of elementary sentences and combiners made up the kernel of the grammar. The kernel sentences were built round a small set of kernel **constructions**, which were the site of the major relationships of co-occurrence. For example, the sentence *I told her that she could take the book lying on the desk* was derived

from the kernel sentences *I told her something*, *She could take the book*, *The book is lying on the desk*. The concept was adopted in Chomsky's early transformational grammar. See CO-OCCURRENCE RESTRICTION, DEEP STRUCTURE.

KEY

The **pitch** range of an **utterance**. Excited speech might be uttered in a high key and depressive speech in a low key.

KEYWORD

A **word** occurring in a text or **corpus** more frequently than might be expected if it occurred by chance. Keywords are determined by comparing the frequency of a given word in some text under analysis with its frequency in a large corpus. For instance, 'fairness' is a keyword in certain political speeches, 'security' in others.

KHASI

Mon-Khmer, **Austroasiatic**. North-east India, Bangladesh.

KHMER

Mon-Khmer, **Austroasiatic**. Approx. 11M speakers, Cambodia, Thailand, Vietnam.

KHOISAN LANGUAGES

More than 500K speakers, South Africa, Namibia, Botswana. Well known for their **click** consonants.

KINETIC TONE

See CONTOUR TONE.

KINSHIP TERMS

The set of **words** in a particular language for members of a family and their relationships to each other, such as *grandmother*, *nephew* and so on. Who counts as a family member differs from culture to culture, and the set of terms is smaller or larger depending on the culture.

KINYARWANDA

Bantu, **Niger-Congo**. Approx. 20M speakers, Ruanda (national language).

KIRGHIZ

Turkic, **Altaic**. 3.5M speakers, Kirgizstan.

KOINE

Originally the popular form of written or spoken **Greek** that emerged in the Hellenistic, post-classical, period. Now used more generally as the variety of a language that arises through **dialect mixture** and may become more widely used.

KORDOFANIAN LANGUAGES

Niger-Congo. Approx. 200K speakers, Sudan.

KOREAN

Language isolate, though perhaps **Altaic**. 48.5M speakers South Korea, 22.6M North Korea, 2M China, 700K Japan, 600K USA. In grammatical structure most similar to Japanese. Originally written in Chinese characters but came to be written in an alphabet invented by the Korean Emperor over the period 1443–1446. Chinese characters have not fallen into complete disuse and are even making a comeback because of the position of Chinese as a **lingua franca** in the Far East.

KRIO

English-based **Creole**. *c.* 500K in Sierra Leone.

KRU LANGUAGES

Niger-Congo. Approx. 2M speakers, Ivory Coast, Southern Liberia. Related to **Gur** and **Kwa languages**.

KURDISH

Indo-Iranian, Indo-European. 13.8M speakers, Eastern Turkey, approx. 4.6 Northern Iran, 4.3M–5.8M Northern Iraq.

KURUKH

Dravidian. Approx. 2M speakers, Northern India, Bangladesh and Nepal.

KWA LANGUAGES

Volta-Congo, **Niger-Congo**. Spoken in Ivory Coast, Ghana, Togo and southern Nigeria.

KWAKWALA

Current name for **KWAKIUTL**.

KWAKIUTL

Wakashan. Spoken on Pacific coast of British Columbia and the adjacent coast of the USA. Much cited in work by **Boas** and **Sapir**.

KWIC

An acronym standing for Key Word in Context. **Concordance** software typically presents the result of a search with the key word under investigation in the middle of the computer screen or print-out. A given number of words preceding and following the key word are placed on either side of it. This is a concordance line. All the instances of the key word thus form a column. The preceding and following words enable the analyst to explore the meaning of the key word and its **discourse** function.

KYMOGRAPH

In **instrumental phonetics**, a device for measuring and recording changes in air pressure.

L

L2
See **SECOND LANGUAGE**.

LABELLED BRACKETING
In **syntax** and **morphology**, a way of representing the structure of a **word**, **phrase** or **clause**. **Brackets** enclose the **constituents** that group together into larger units, and subscript labels indicate the type of constituent and larger unit. E.g. the words in the phrase *a very short story* are labelled thus: $_{Det}$[a], $_{Adv}$[very], $_A$[short], $_N$[story]. Further bracketing shows that $_{Adv}$[very] and $_A$[short] combine as an Adjective Phrase AP – $_{AP}$[$_{Adv}$[very] $_A$[short]], that the AP combines with $_N$[story] – $_{N'}$[$_{AP}$[$_{Adv}$[very] $_A$[short] $_N$[story]] and that $_{Det}$[a] combines with N' to form an NP – $_{NP}$[$_{Det}$[a] $_{N'}$[$_{AP}$[$_{Adv}$[very] $_A$[short]] $_N$[story]]]. See **NOUN PHRASE**, **TREE DIAGRAM**.

LABIAL
1. A term in the description of the **place of articulation** of **consonant** sounds. A sound produced with the lip or lips as articulator. See **BILABIAL**, **LABIALIZATION**, **LABIODENTAL**. 2. In **SPE Distinctive Feature Theory**, segments articulated with the lips. May be produced with or without **lip rounding**, for example [b], [m]. See **ROUNDED**.

LABIALIZATION
A **secondary articulation** involving **lip-rounding**. Transcribed as a superscript [w] – [^{w}]. See **LABIAL**, **ROUNDED**.

LABIODENTAL
A term in the description of the **place of articulation** of **consonant** sounds. The lower lip comes against the upper teeth as in the voiceless labiodental **fricative** [f] *fin*, or the voiced **labiodental** fricative [v] *vine*.

LABIOVELAR
A term in the description of the **place of articulation** of **consonant** sounds. A sound produced with simultaneous **labial** and **velar** articulations, e.g. the velar [w] articulated with **lip-rounding**, or the **labiovelar** consonants [kp] and [gb] found in some West African languages.

LABOV, William (b 1927)
Professor of Linguistics at the University of Pennsylvania. The founder of modern **sociolinguistics**, pioneered the study of **variation** in terms of systematic

correlations between language and age, social class, sex, ethnicity, etc. His first major study of the urban **dialects** of New York City set the paradigm for later work. His interest spread into issues in educational and historical linguistics.

LAD

An acronym from 'Language Acquisition Device', the name of a hypothetical mental **language acquisition** device proposed by Chomsky which enables children to construct the **grammar** of their native language quickly and without instruction from adults.

LADEFOGED, Peter (1925–2006)

The most prominent phonetician of the latter part of the twentieth century. Trained in Edinburgh, he became Professor of Phonetics at the University of California, Los Angeles, where he established the UCLA Phonetics Laboratory. As well as having an interest in **acoustic** phonetics, he collected phonetic data from a wide range of the world's languages and helped the development of descriptive phonetic theory.

LAK

Caucasian. 119K speakers (112K in Russia).

LAKOTA

Siouan. 6K speakers, USA and Canada.

LAMINA

That part of the **tongue** that lies opposite the **alveolar** ridge between the **tip** and the **centre**, also known as the **blade**. See Figure 'Articulators' at **ARTICULATION**.

LAMINAL

A **consonant** articulated with the **blade** of the **tongue**, e.g. for most English speakers, [t] and [n].

LANDING SITE

In **Government and Binding Theory**, a position into which constituents can be moved. See **PRINCIPLES AND PARAMETERS**.

LANDMARK

In **Cognitive Grammar**, the point of **reference** in a relational expression. In any such expression one **participant**, the **trajector**, is given prominence. The other participant is the landmark. In expressions of location such as *X is behind Y*, X is the trajector whose location is specified with reference to the landmark, Y. *X is behind Y* entails *Y is in front of X*, but Cognitive Grammar treats them as different in meaning, since in the latter example Y is the trajectory and X the landmark. The contrast applies to expressions of movement; in *The train moved across the bridge*, *train* is the trajector and *bridge* the landmark. The contrast also applies in non-spatial expressions; in *The guerrillas attacked the train*, *guerrillas* is the trajector, given prominence as **subject**, and *train* is the landmark, the **goal** that the attack was aimed at. See **COGNITIVE LINGUISTICS**.

LANGAGE
See **LANGUE**.

LANGUAGE ACQUISITION
The process(es) by which children gain knowledge of their **first language** and by which speakers in general gain knowledge of one or more additional languages.

LANGUAGE ACQUISITION DEVICE
See **LAD**.

LANGUAGE ATTITUDES
The attitudes people have towards **accents**, **dialects** and languages other than their own.

LANGUAGE CLASSIFICATION
Languages can be classified in a variety of ways, most commonly genetically or typologically. A **genetic classification** is the most common – languages are classified into language families on the basis of presumed descent from a common ancestor. The Romance languages (French, Italian, etc.) are descended from Latin, and Latin, together with Oscan and other languages formerly spoken in the Italian peninsula, is a branch of **Indo-European**, which includes Balto-Slavic, Indo-Iranian, etc. Genetic classification rests on the **comparative method**. A typological classification groups languages together in terms of common structural characteristics. A typological classification may be on the basis of shared morphological properties – classifying languages into agglutinating, inflecting, isolating and polysynthetic types – or syntactic properties – classifying languages according to the most frequent order of **Subject**, **Verb** and **Object** in simple sentences – languages which are verb first (Verb, Subject, Object), like most **Celtic** languages, or verb last (Subject, Object, Verb) like most Indo-Iranian languages. Languages may also be classified into a **Sprachbund**, that is, a group of spatially contiguous languages that have developed common features. A well-known example in Europe is the Balkan Sprachbund, including Romanian, Bulgarian, Albanian and Greek. Although not genetically closely related, these languages show grammatical convergence. See **AGGLUTINATING LANGUAGE, INFLECTING LANGUAGE, INFLECTION, ISOLATING LANGUAGE, LANGUAGE FAMILY, LEXICOSTATISTICS, LINGUISTIC AREA, MORPHOLOGY, TYPOLOGY**.

LANGUAGE CODE
A term reflecting the idea that **morphology**, **syntax** and vocabulary constitute a code with which speakers express meanings. While this conception of language is limited, it is important to distinguish between a language code and the language users (the **speakers** and writers) who use the code and to recognize that the users of the code unconsciously bring about changes in it. See **CONSTRUE, DYNAMIC CONSTRUAL, EMERGENT MEANING**

LANGUAGE CONFLICT

In multilingual communities groups speaking different languages can disagree fiercely about language issues such as which language is to be used in education, the law courts or in government. An example is the conflict in recent years in Belgium between the Flemish- and French-speaking populations.

LANGUAGE CONTACT

A situation in which the speakers of different languages are in close contact in their everyday lives. The different communities of speakers may borrow vocabulary, **phonetic** features and grammatical **constructions** from each other's language, but if one community is dominant, their language will survive and the language of the non-dominant community may become extinct. See LANGUAGE DEATH.

LANGUAGE DEATH

The process by which a language becomes extinct. This commonly involves a **language contact** situation leading to **multilingualism** and to a **language shift** to the dominant language. Over time, as the non-dominant language is used in fewer and fewer contexts, its grammatical **constructions** become less complex and its range of **registers** contracts. It becomes endangered and eventually vanishes when the last speakers abandon it or die.

LANGUAGE EDUCATION POLICY

In a given political unit, political decisions about which language or languages are to be taught in schools and are to be the medium of instruction. Such policies may involve teaching knowledge about language.

LANGUAGE FAMILY

A group of languages that have developed from a common ancestor. Language families are often represented by a **tree diagram**, the root of the tree being the ancestor language (e.g. **Latin**) and the branches representing daughter languages or families (e.g. **Italian, Spanish** or **French**). The term 'language family' is not reserved for any particular branch of the tree. Some families are very large – **Austronesian** is the largest family with approximately 1,200 languages; others have only a single member, often referred to as a **language isolate**. **Basque** and **Ainu**, spoken in Japan, are usually considered to be language isolates. The term 'phylum' is sometimes applied to a group of languages thought, but not demonstrated, to be related, for example the Nostratic hypothesis proposes a macro-family including **Indo-European, Semitic** and other language families. **Mixed languages, Creole** and pidgin languages clearly do not fit into this scheme.

LANGUAGE GENERATION

The generation of **natural language** text by computational means. It usually involves a process for generating the overall structure of the **text**, a macroplanner and a microplanner that deals with textual detail. In **machine translation** an **interlingua** may be involved.

LANGUAGE-INDEPENDENT PREFERRED ORDER OF CONSTITUENTS
The principle whereby the simplest **constituents** in a **clause** or **sentence** occur first and complex constituents occur later. Abbreviated as **LIPOC**.

LANGUAGE ISOLATE
A language, such as **Basque**, that is the sole member of a **language family** and not related to any language in another language family.

LANGUAGE LOYALTY
The positive attitude of speakers towards a language that leads to **language maintenance**.

LANGUAGE MAINTENANCE
The retention of a language or **dialect** by an individual or community in spite of pressure to shift to a more dominant and prestigious variety. See **LANGUAGE SHIFT**.

LANGUAGE PATHOLOGY
In **clinical linguistics**, the science of language disorders, such as difficulty in producing sounds, in finding correct **lexical words**, in creating and understanding connected **text**, or in following the conventions of conversation in a given culture.

LANGUAGE PLANNING
Official policy towards the selection of a language, variety, **dialect**, etc. that is to be favoured for use by a particular community for official purposes, in education, the courts, etc. (status planning). This involves choices about standardization in spelling and orthography, in grammar and style, and in vocabulary, including spelling conventions, and a policy towards loanwords and other vocabulary choices (corpus planning). It will also involve educational decisions as to what languages will be taught within the curriculum, how teachers are to be trained, what pedagogical materials are to used, etc. (acquisition planning).

LANGUAGE RIGHTS
The human and civil rights individuals possess with respect to the language they can use in areas of public communication such as language education, the print media, radio and television, and communication in judicial and administrative affairs.

LANGUAGE SAMPLE
See **SAMPLING**.

LANGUAGE SHIFT
A change in the language used by an individual or community, often caused by immigration, social mobility or the perceived prestige of other varieties or languages. See **LANGUAGE MAINTENANCE**.

LANGUAGE SOCIALIZATION
In a given culture, the process of children learning what language is appropriate in which situations and who speaks when in a given type of interaction. See **PRAGMALINGUISTIC NORMS, SOCIOPRAGMATIC NORMS**.

LANGUAGE TYPES
See **TYPOLOGY**.

LANGUAGE UNIVERSAL
A property found in all, or almost all, languages or a statement that applies to all, or almost all, languages. For example, all languages distinguish **vowels** and **consonants**, and all languages have **aspect**; however, many languages do not have **tense**.

LANGUAGE USER
See **LANGUAGE CODE**.

LANGUE
The terms 'langue' and '**parole**'derive from **Saussure**. Langue is the language of a linguistic community (cf. **competence, I-language** (= internal)), which underlies an individual's performance or **parole** (cf. **performance**, E-language (= external)). In Saussure, langue is also distinguished from **langage**, the human language faculty, language in a general sense.

LAO
Also called Eastern Thai. 3.4M speakers, mostly in Laos.

LARYNGEAL
1. A speech sound produced in the **larynx**. 2. In historical linguistics, a **consonant** type hypothesized for **Indo-European** which affected the quality of adjacent **vowels**. These consonants are only found in **Hittite**.

LARYNGECTOMY
The surgical excision of the **larynx** or part of the larynx, e.g. because of a cancerous growth.

LARYNGOGRAPH
An instrument for measuring the vibration of the vocal cords, and hence the fundamental frequency of the glottis during speech.

LARYNX
That part of the windpipe that contains the 'voice box', the **vocal cords** or folds The space between the vocal folds is called the **glottis**. It is importantly

involved in the production of several types of sound effects, notably **voicing**, **whisper**, **pitch** and several glottalic sounds, notably the **glottal stop**.

LAST RESORT

In the **Minimalist Program**, a principle whereby syntactic processes apply only if some property of the grammar would not otherwise be met.

LATERAL

1. A **place of articulation** for **consonants**. The oral closure is partial and air escapes round the sides of the tongue. 2. In **SPE Distinctive Feature Theory** this relates to the shape and position of the **tongue**; in lateral segments the centre of the tongue comes in contact with the **palate**, thus forcing a lateral flow along the lowered side(s) of the tongue.

LATERAL RELEASE

When a **lateral** stop is released by dropping one or both sides of the **tongue** while retaining the **closure** at the centre of the tongue. It occurs in English in pronunciations of *middle*.

LATIN

Italic, Indo-European. Ancestor of the **Romance** languages. No longer spoken as a native language but functions as the official written language in the Vatican.

LATVIAN

Baltic, Indo-European. 1.3M speakers, Latvia.

LAX

1. A sound produced with relatively little muscular tension. Compare the lax [ɪ] and [ʊ].with the **tense** [i] and [u]. See **TENSE**. 2. In **J&H Distinctive Feature Theory**, a feature characterizing a segment with low energy, limited duration and little spread across the spectrum. Opposite **tense**. See **DISTINCTIVE FEATURES, ACOUSTIC**.

LAYERING

1. The inclusion of smaller constituents inside larger constituents, leading to layers of **constituent structure**. For instance, as shown in the Figure 'Layering', in the structure of *the book on the table in the study*, the highest layer contains the whole **phrase**, the next layer down contains *the table in the study* and the next again layer down contains *the study*. In the structure of *the book I found*, the highest layer contains the whole phrase and the next layer down contains the **relative clause** *I found*. See the figure below. 2. In **grammaticalization**, the creation of layers of structure in a given language as **lexical words** give rise to form words or **affixes** with grammatical meanings but continue in the language with their original meaning. Thus, *keep* is still a lexical word in English but has given rise to **aspect** markers in *keep running* and *keep on working*. The perfect *has written the letter*, in which *has* is an **auxiliary** and *written* is a **past participle**, derives from a **resultative** construction *has the letter written*, in which *has* denotes possession

and *written* denotes a result. The resultative construction survives and has developed into *has got the letter written*. The survival of lexical words and constructions is known as persistence.

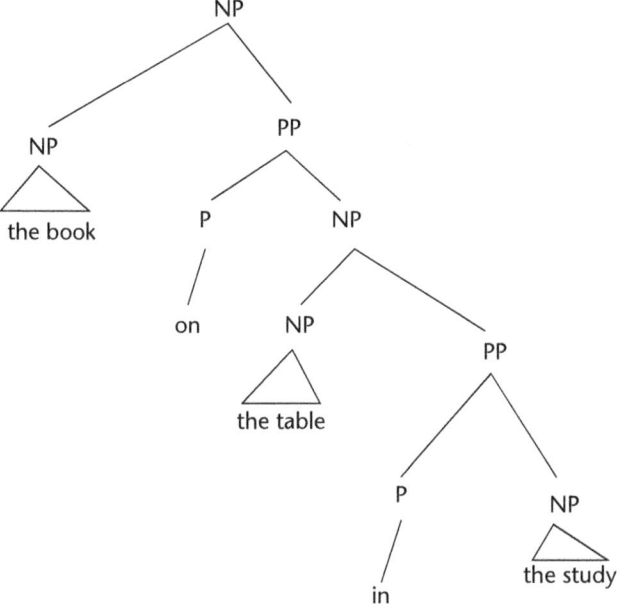

LAZY PRONOUN

A **pronoun** whose **referent** is not explicit in a situation but must be inferred by the **addressee**. E.g. in *Fiona posted her application today and Janet will post it tomorrow*, *it* is a lazy pronoun if it is not intended to pick up the referent of *her application* but to refer to Janet's application. The phenomenon is also known as 'sloppy identity'.

LCCM

See **LEXICAL CONCEPT AND COGNITIVE MODEL**.

LCS

See **LEXICAL CONCEPTUAL STRUCTURE**.

LEARNABILITY

1. The property of human languages whereby any normal child, within a given age-range, can learn any language. 2. The property of formal languages whereby an automatic procedure can construct grammars for them on the basis of **sentences** presented to it. Such a language is learnable and different degrees of learnability are recognized depending on what complexity of **embedding** is required. The mathematical theory of learnability is learnability theory or learning theory.

LEARNABILITY THEORY

See **LEARNABILITY 2**.

LEARNABLE

See **LEARNABILITY 2**.

LEARNER CORPUS

A **corpus** of written and/or spoken language produced by learners of a given language. Such a corpus can be compared with a corpus of speech and writing from native speakers, enabling persistent errors and difficulties to be identified.

LEARNING THEORY

See **LEARNABILITY 2**.

LECT

As in **dialect, sociolect**.

LEFT BRANCHING

Any **constituent structure** containing two or more **heads** whose dependents precede them. E.g. in *really seriously deteriorating situations*, *situations* is preceded by *really seriously deteriorating*, *deteriorating* is preceded by *really seriously* and *seriously* is preceded by *really*. A **tree diagram** of the **constituent structure** of this **phrase** has a series of branches to the left, as shown in the figure below. Languages with basic OV word order are typically left-branching, languages with basic VO order are typically right-branching. German is an example of a language that has both types of branching. See **DEPENDENT, RIGHT BRANCHING**.

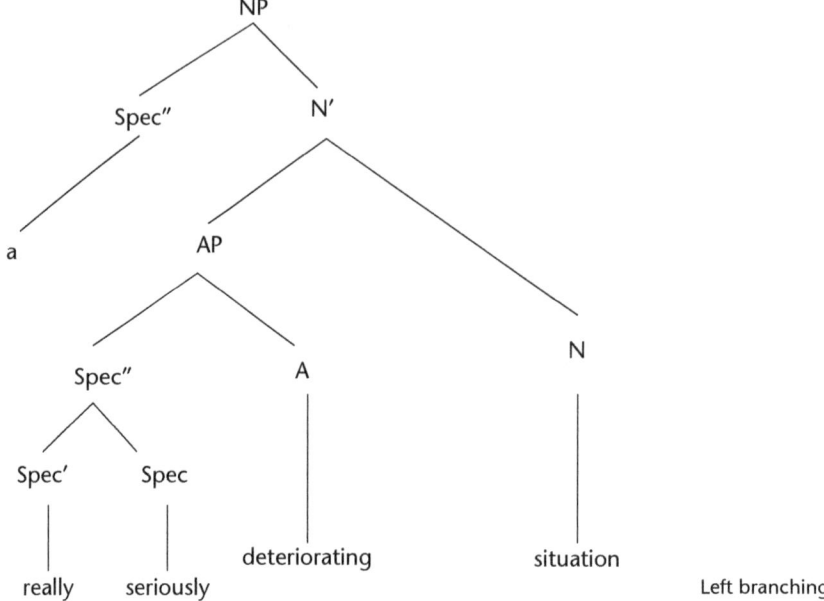

Left branching

LEFT DISLOCATION

A **construction** consisting of a **noun phrase** followed by a complete **clause** containing a pronoun **anaphoric** with the noun phrase. The construction firmly establishes a referent, as in (from a spoken narrative) *when I was [young]… I used to do these things with friends…The girl I worked beside, she used a Bible. The girl I worked beside* is said to be left-dislocated. The construction may be used for contrast, as in (from a newspaper interview) *'My youngest daughter gets embarrassed when she sees me on television,' says Stewart. 'My eldest, she doesn't mind so much because it gives her extra street-cred at school.'* See **RIGHT DISLOCATION**.

LEFT-EDGE ELLIPSIS

In English, the deletion of **constituents** at the front of the second and subsequent **clauses** in coordinations of clauses. E.g. the coordination of *The dog chased the rabbit* and *The dog failed to catch the rabbit* gives *The dog chased the rabbit but failed to catch it*. See **COORDINATION, ELLIPSIS**.

LEGAL

In **Generalized Phrase Structure Grammar**, any constituent or combination of constituents that meets the restrictions on which **features** can occur together in some piece of structure.

LEIBNIZ, Gottfried W. (1646–1716)

German philosopher and mathematician, particularly associated with the invention of calculus. His linguistic interests included the invention of an artificial universal language.

LEMMA

See **LEMMATIZATION**.

LEMMATIZATION

The reduction of the word **tokens** in a **corpus** to their **lexemes**. Thus the set of word forms or tokens *swim, swam, swum, swims* and *swimming* constitute the lemma for the lexeme SWIM. 'Lemma' is mainly used as an alternative to 'lexeme' or 'headword', the form that heads an entry in a dictionary. See **TYPE-TOKEN RATIO**.

LENGTH

In **phonetics**, the actual **duration** of a sound, **utterance**, etc. In phonetic **transcriptions**, length is frequently represented by a colon, [V:]. In **phonology**, the relative duration of a sound, etc. in contrast to some other sound. Both long and short **vowels** and long and short **consonants** may be distinguished. In many **Indo-European** languages, vowel length is represented in the orthography by a macron (e.g. Latin *mensā*). In some languages long vowels are represented by doubling the corresponding short vowel, e.g. in **Akan** – *Oba* 'he comes' but *Obaa* 'he went'. In many languages vowel length is accompanied by a difference in vowel **quality**, as, for instance, English *beat* ([biːt], long) and *bit* ([bɪt], short). Transcriptions that focus on the difference in vowel length represent the distinction by using the same vowel symbol but add a colon to represent length: *beat* [biːt] versus *bit* [bit]. Transcriptions that focus on the difference in vowel quality tend to use different vowel symbols, as above. English does not have phonologically distinctive doubled consonants, though it may have phonetically doubled consonants especially at morpheme or word boundaries; e.g. *meanness, hard disk*. Long consonants are phonologically distinctive in Spanish: *pero 'but'* vs *perro 'dog'*. See **GEMINATION**.

LENIS

A **consonant** articulated with relatively weak muscular effort or weak exhalation of breath. In English the voiced **stop** consonants, [b], [d], [g], are often referred to as lenis. See **ASPIRATION, FORTIS**.

LENITION

The process whereby a sound is perceived to be articulated with 'less force', thus 'weakened', such as a stop becoming a fricative, as in the case of **consonant mutation** in Celtic languages. See **FORTITION**.

LENTO

In phonetics, slowly.

LESKIEN, August (1840–1916)

Professor of Philology at Leipzig. A prominent **Neogrammarian** particularly associated with work on the regularity of **sound change**.

LEVEL

1. The notion of level belongs to a conception of different aspects of linguistic structure being analysed on different levels. The lowest level deals with **phonology**, the organization of the sounds of a given language into **phonemes, syllables** and so on. The next level up deals with **syntax**, the organization of **words** into **phrases**, phrases into **clauses** and clauses into **sentences**. The top level deals with **semantics**. The levels are typically considered independently of each other; the organization of sounds into syllables and words is irrelevant to the organization of words into phrases, etc.

The use of levels as part of linguistic analysis or the representation of linguistic structure is particularly associated with, though not confined to, the **structuralist** approach in linguistics practised by linguists who came after Bloomfield. Some scholars claimed that the structures on the lowest level, phonology, had to be analysed before the structures on the next level up, syntax, and so on. See **Bloomfield**. 2. In **prototype** theory three levels of **category** are recognized. Basic-level categories are denoted by **lexical words** used for everyday neutral reference; e.g. *dog, rose*. Superordinate categories are referred to with lexical words with a very general denotation; e.g. *animal, bush*. Subordinate categories are the most specialized and are denoted by lexical words such as *spaniel* and *rambler*.

LEVEL OF ADEQUACY
See ADEQUACY.

LEVEL OF REPRESENTATION
See LEVEL.

LEVEL ORDERING
In **lexical phonology**, the principle whereby **affixes** and phonological processes are divided into groups, each group belonging to a different level. E.g. affixes such as *-y* might be on level 1, and affixes such as *-ness* on level 2. Level 1 affixes are attached to **stems** before level 2 affixes, and processes applying to level 1 affixes take place before processes applying to level 2 affixes. This organization ensures, for example, that words such as *healthiness* are derived but non-existent words such as **healthnessy* are excluded.

LEVEL STRESS
When each component part of a word has the same **stress** level – compare *'black'board* (a board which is black) and *'blackboard* (the black or dark green surface that classroom teachers used to write on). See PRIMARY STRESS, SECONDARY STRESS.

LEVEL TONE
In **phonetics**, a **tone** with the same **pitch** throughout, neither **rising** or **falling**. See CONTOUR TONE.

LEXEME
See LEXICAL WORD.

LEXICAL AMBIGUITY
See AMBIGUITY.

LEXICAL ASPECT
See AKTIONSART.

LEXICAL BUNDLE
In **corpus** linguistics, a term for sets of three or more words that regularly occur together, such as *I don't think*, *the problem with this is* and so on. See FIXED EXPRESSION.

LEXICAL CATEGORY
See CATEGORY.

LEXICAL COMPONENT
In **lexical phonology**, the component containing the rules that apply inside **words**.

LEXICAL CONCEPT AND COGNITIVE MODEL
In **cognitive linguistics**, an approach to **semantics** in which the content of lexical items is analysed in terms of lexical **concepts**. These give access to

encyclopaedic knowledge and are sharply distinguished from **meaning**, which is held to be a property of language use in particular situations. In its broad outline, the Lexical and Cognitive Model is reminiscent of Wittgenstein's slogan about looking for the use of a **word** or **phrase** and of the theory developed by J. R. Firth and his colleagues.

LEXICAL CONCEPTUAL STRUCTURE

In some models of grammar, the basic semantic level. Its content resembles the content of **predicate-argument** structures found in a number of current models, such as **Lexical-Functional Grammar**. E.g. the lexical conceptual structure for *enter* contains the information that an entity moves along a path to the interior of something.

LEXICAL CONDITIONING

See **CONDITIONING**.

LEXICAL DECOMPOSITION

The theory that the meanings of the **lexical words** in a given language can be analysed as combinations of a small number of **concepts** that form structures just as words combine to form syntactic **constructions**. This type of analysis was a central component of **Generative Semantics** and was later adopted as part of lexical entries. A famous example is the analysis of DIE as *BECOME [NOT ALIVE]* and of KILL as *CAUSE [BECOME [NOT ALIVE]]*. Some analysts use 'lexical decomposition' as a synonym of 'componential analysis'. See **COMPONENTIAL ANALYSIS, NATURAL SEMANTICS**.

LEXICAL DIFFUSION

The, usually gradual, spread of **sound change** from word to word throughout the lexicon.

LEXICAL ENTRY

An entry for a **lexical word** in a dictionary (or lexicon, if a component of a formal model). Such entries contain information about the **denotation** of lexical words and about their subcategorization. The latter information ensures that a given lexical item is inserted into an appropriate piece of syntactic structure. In the **Minimalist Program** the notion of insertion no longer applies. Instead, entries for lexical items contain instructions about which piece of syntactic structure given lexical items project or add to a tree. See **STRICT SUBCATEGORIZATION, SUBCATEGORIZATION FRAME**.

LEXICAL FIELD

A set of **lexical words** denoting entities in a particular conceptual area, say colour, kinship, fruit and vegetables, and so on. The lexical words in such a set are connected by **sense relations**. The terms 'semantic field' and 'associative field' are also used. It is useful to distinguish between lexical fields, part of the organization of the vocabulary in a given language, and conceptual fields, which apply generally across languages. See **CONCEPT, DENOTATION, DOMAIN, FIELD THEORY.**

LEXICAL FORM
See **LEXICAL WORD**.

LEXICAL-FUNCTIONAL GRAMMAR
A generative model of **syntax** developed in the late 1970s–early 1980s. It has only one level of syntactic structure and excludes the **movement** of **constituents**. The model involves three kinds of **structure**: lexical, **functional** and **constituent**. Lexical entries for **verbs** provide information about a **predicate** and its **arguments**, the latter in terms of **roles** such as **agent, theme** and **goal**. Lexical entries also provide information about which **grammatical functions** each argument is mapped onto. The relation between, say, **active** and **passive** is handled by lexical entries providing two mappings: thus, the entry for HIT specifies that the agent is **Subject** and the theme **Object**, for the active, or that theme is Subject and the agent **oblique**, for the passive. The lexical entry captures the fact that two syntactic **constructions** have the same semantics. Functional structure includes **complement** and **adjunct** as well as grammatical functions. Functional structure is universal, but constituent structure varies across languages. See **CONSTITUENT STRUCTURE, HEAD, UNIFICATION.**

LEXICAL GAP
In the study of **sense relations**, a place in the system where a **lexical word** might have existed but does not. For example, in the lexical field for utensils and dishes there is no superordinate term for all the dishes used in baking or indeed for all the dishes used in cooking in general. Department stores, which need such terms, have invented *bakeware* and *cookware*. It is useful to have a superordinate term for sons and daughters – *offspring*, and for brothers and sisters – *siblings*, but no superordinate term has been devised for nieces and nephews.

LEXICAL HIERARCHY
Areas of vocabulary in any natural language are organized into hierarchies. There are lexical words with larger **extensions**, such as *animal*, and ones with smaller extensions, such as *cat*, whose extension includes *tigers, lions, leopards*, etc. Hierarchies are represented by tree diagrams; for a given lexical field, the lexical item with the biggest extension is at the top and the extensions are smaller the lower in the tree they are. See **HYPONYMY, MERONYMIC HIERARCHY, TAXONOMIC HIERARCHY, TREE DIAGRAM.**

LEXICAL INSERTION RULES
In early models of **transformational grammar**, rules that inserted **lexical words** into syntactic structure, combining with the correct number and type of other lexical items.

LEXICAL ITEM
See LEXEME, LEXICAL WORD.

LEXICAL MEANING
The meaning or **denotation** of **lexical words**, usually taken to be sets of entities in the broadest sense – concrete individuals, **mass** stuff, abstract entities, types of **situation** (states, activities and so on). It is opposed to **grammatical meaning**. See EMERGENT MEANING, GRAMMATICAL MEANING.

LEXICAL MORPHOLOGY
1. A theory in which all aspects of derivational and inflectional morphology are handled in the **lexicon**. 2. See DERIVATIONAL MORPHOLOGY.

LEXICAL PHONOLOGY
A theory about the organisation of **phonology, morphology** and the **lexicon** developed in the 1960s. It claims that many morphological and phonological processes are carried out in the lexicon

LEXICAL RELATION
See SENSE RELATION.

LEXICAL SEMANTICS
The analysis of the meaning of lexical items. See DENOTATION, SENSE RELATIONS.

LEXICAL SET
See LEXICAL FIELD.

LEXICAL SPECIFIC CONSTRUCTIONS
See FIXED EXPRESSION.

LEXICAL STRUCTURE
The organization of the vocabulary of a language. See LEXICAL FIELD, LEXICAL HIERARCHY, LEXICON, SENSE RELATION.

LEXICAL SYNTAX
Originally a tendency in **generative grammar** to include in the lexicon much information about syntax. This tendency is now an orthodoxy in all formal models of syntax, including those in the **Minimalist Program**. See LEXICAL ENTRY, LEXICASE.

LEXICAL STRESS
See WORD STRESS.

LEXICAL TONE
The **tone** pattern inherent in a lexical **word**.

LEXICAL VERB

A **verb**, also called a full verb or main verb, which is not an **auxiliary** verb carrying grammatical meaning, to do with **tense, aspect** and **mood**, but which denotes a **state, action** or **process**. In English, *know, sit, write* and *build* are lexical verbs, while *may, will, must*, etc. are auxiliary verbs.

LEXICAL WORD

A word considered as a lexical item or **lexeme** denoting things, beings, events, abstract ideas and so on. Lexical words are sometimes represented in capitals and the surface word forms in lower case. E.g. the lexical word SWIM has the surface forms *swim, swims, swam, swum, swimming*.

LEXICALIST HYPOTHESIS

In earlier **transformational grammar**, the idea that **derivational morphology** should be handled in the **lexicon** and not by **transformations**.

LEXICALIZATION

The process by which, in a given language, **lexical words** are provided for a difference of meaning. Different languages lexicalize different distinctions of meaning. For example, Russian lexicalizes light blue and dark blue as the independent lexemes *goluboj* and *sinij*; English lexicalizes the more general category of blue as *blue*. A phrase such as *ran out* denotes an event composed of a movement, the type of movement and a path – from inside some location to the outside. English lexicalizes the movement and the type of movement as *ran* and the path as an intransitive preposition, *out*. French lexicalizes the movement and the path as *sortit* and the type of movement as a separate non-finite clause, *en courant* 'in running, running'.

LEXICASE

A formal model of syntax developed from the early 1970s onwards. The model has only one level of structure and 'the grammar is the lexicon'. The basic units of the syntax are **words**; information about **agreement, tense and aspect**, roles and so on is handled by features on words. The syntactic structures are based on dependency relations, **constituent structure** being secondary. The model anticipates **Lexical-Functional Grammar** in some respects, **Head-driven Phrase Structure Grammar** in others and **Word Grammar**. See **DEPENDENCY, FEATURE**.

LEXICON

1. The set of **lexemes** in a language. 2. A dictionary, especially of classical Greek. 3. The vocabulary of a language, as part of its description. Vocabulary is stored in dictionaries. See **DICTIONARY MEANING**. 4. In formal models of language, the component which handles the meanings of **lexical words**. 5. In theories of language processing and acquisition, the component, called the **mental lexicon**, which models the storage, retrieval and interpretation of lexical words by speakers and listeners. The information in the mental lexicon of a given speaker

of a given language does not necessarily match the information resulting from the analysis of the language by linguists.

LEXICOSTATISTICS

A comparison between languages, dialects, etc., based on the statistical analysis of shared vocabulary. Used in **glottochronology** as a technique for determining the time divergence between languages by comparing the numbers of shared **cognate** forms. See **SWADESH LIST**.

LEXIS

The vocabulary of a language and its study. See **LEXICON**.

LEZGIAN

Caucasian. Approx. 450K, southern Dagestan and northern Azerbaijan.

LF

See **LOGICAL FORM**.

LFG

See **LEXICAL-FUNCTIONAL GRAMMAR**.

LIAISON

In **phonology**, a transition feature between **words**, especially where a word-final **consonant** is silent except in a particular context, usually preceding a vowel. In French, the final 's' in the definite article *les* is only pronounced when the following word begins with a vowel – *les Anglais* [lez...] but *les Francais* [le..]. In English the **linking r** of non-**rhotic** varieties, e.g. *rear end*. See **INTRUSION**.

LICENSING

In **GB** and later Chomskyan models, the process by which **lexical items** require or allow a particular category, **constituent structure** or **case**. Thus, *blame* licenses an NP and PP – *blame someone for something*, Turkish *bakmak* 'look at' licenses an NP and a noun in the **dative** case, e.g. *adam* 'man', *adama bak-ti-m* 'man-DAT look-PST=1sg, I looked at the man'. The traditional term is still in use; verbs are still said to take an NP and PP, take the dative case and so on. See **ADJUNCT, AGREEMENT, COMPLEMENT, GOVERNMENT, HEAD**.

LIGHT VERB

Verbs such as *give, take, have, get* in **phrases** such as *give someone a surprise, take a look at something, have a read of something, get a fright* where they are weak or light in meaning. Many such phrases can be replaced by single verbs: *surprise someone, look at something, read something*.

LIGHT SYLLABLE

A syllable that contains a short **vowel** as the **nucleus** and no **coda**. See **HEAVY SYLLABLE**.

LINEAR CORRESPONDENCE AXIOM
In the **Minimalist Program**, in **linearization (2)**, the principle that if a **constituent** A **c-commands** a constituent B in a **tree** structure, A precedes B in the corresponding linear sequence of constituents.

LINEAR GRAMMAR
In **computational linguistics**, a grammar capable of generating only linear strings, and hence unable to accommodate **hierarchical structure**. It is capable of generating finite state languages. See FINITE-STATE GRAMMAR.

LINEAR PRECEDENCE RULE
In **Generalized Phrase Structure Grammar**, rules that specify permitted orders of **constituents**. See LINEARIZATION.

LINEARITY
An essential property of **words**, **phrases**, **clauses** and **sentences**, namely that, whether in writing or speech, the units out of which they are built occur in a line, one after the other.

LINEARIZATION
1. Especially in models that make **dependency** relations primary, the process of putting a **head** and its **dependents** into some permitted linear order. E.g. the English noun phrase *a complex idea* and its French equivalent *une idée complexe* have the noun, *idea* or *idée*, as head and the **article** and **adjective** as dependents. The linearization rules for English put the adjective before the noun, those for French put it after the noun. 2. In the **Minimalist Program**, the conversion of a **tree** structure to a linear string of symbols as required by the sensorimotor systems.

LINGUA FRANCA
1. The **Romance**-based **pidgin** formerly spoken around the Mediterranean.
2. Now applied to any language used between speakers with no native language in common, such as **Swahili** in East Africa and **English** and **French** in West Africa. See ENGLISH AS A LINGUA FRANCA.

LINGUAL
A sound made with the **tongue**.

LINGUAL TRILL
The trilled [r] made with the **tip** of the **tongue** against the **alveolar** ridge. Contrasts with the **uvular** trill.

LINGUIST
In linguistics, one who professes or studies the subject. In a general sense, one who commands several languages.

LINGUISTIC ANTHROPOLOGY

The study of language from the particularly anthropological perspective that language is an integral part of culture and, therefore, that a good anthropologist needs to understand and/or speak the language of the culture under study. This particularly includes cultural problems in the use of language.

LINGUISTIC AREA

A geographical area occupied by speakers of languages, possibly from different language families, with shared linguistic characteristics that arise through language contact. See **AREAL LINGUISTICS, LANGUAGE CONTACT, SPRACHBUND**.

LINGUISTIC CRITICISM

The analysis of literary texts via linguistic theory and methods.

LINGUISTIC DETERMINISM

See **SAPIR–WHORF HYPOTHESIS**.

LINGUISTIC ENVIRONMENT

See **CONTEXT 1**.

LINGUISTIC FORM

See **FORM, FORMAL GRAMMAR, FUNCTION, FUNCTIONAL GRAMMAR**.

LINGUISTIC IMPERIALISM

The relationship between dominated and dominating cultures, and hence languages. The concept is often used to explain the widespread use of English but it is equally applicable to such languages as Latin, classical Greek, French, Spanish and Mandarin Chinese.

LINGUISTIC INSECURITY

The negative attitude by a group within a larger community towards their own language or variety.

LINGUISTIC LANDSCAPE

The linguistic objects that are found in public space – signage, both public and private, advertising, etc. These (e.g. road names) are markers of power in mixed communities.

LINGUISTIC LEVELLING

The standardization process whereby variant pronunciations, grammatical forms and lexical items are reduced to a smaller number. This typically involves disregarding forms that are unusual or are used by minorities.

LINGUISTIC MINORITY

A minority group within a community whose language is different from that of the majority. Examples are speakers of Hungarian in Slovakia or speakers of Urdu in the UK.

LINGUISTIC PHILOSOPHY
See ORDINARY LANGUAGE PHILOSOPHY.

LINGUISTIC PHONETICS
The study of the speech sounds of a particular language. See PHONETICS.

LINGUISTIC RELATIVISM
See SAPIR–WHORF HYPOTHESIS.

LINGUISTIC SCIENCE
See LINGUISTICS.

LINGUISTIC SIGN
See SIGN.

LINGUISTIC UNIVERSALS
1. See LANGUAGE UNIVERSALS. 2. The universal properties of human language on which **universal grammar** (UG) is based. UG is a set of invariant general principles that determine the form of grammar and the sorts of categories it operates with. It constrains the type of grammar that children acquire. The hypothesis is that all humans acquire the same **core grammar** but that grammars differ superficially depending on which language a particular child is exposed to.

LINGUISTIC VARIABLE
A linguistic unit that varies from **accent** to accent or **dialect** to dialect and is characteristic of that accent, etc. Widely used in the investigation of variation. Variables may be lexical (e.g. *bonnet/hood* or *pavement/sidewalk* in US and British English), grammatical (e.g. present **tense** forms with and without final -s – *he go / he goes* in various English dialects), or phonological/**phonetic** (e.g. the pronunciation of *-ing* forms with final [n] or final [ŋ]: *having/havin; doing/doin* or the realization of alveolar consonants as glottal stops (e.g. *butter:* [bʌtə]/ [bʌʔə]).

LINGUISTICIAN
See LINGUIST.

LINGUISTICS
The study of language according to scientific principles. Frequently found in compounds referring to branches of linguistic study, such as **sociolinguistics, psycholinguistics, applied linguistics,** etc.

LINKING ELEMENT
See INTERFIX.

LINKING R
See LIAISON.

LINKING RULES

In models that have predicate-argument structures in the **lexicon**, the rules that link these structures with **functional** structures involving **subject**, **object**, etc. or with **constituent structure** in terms of NP, PP, VP, etc.

LINKING VERB

See **COPULA**.

LIPOC

See **LANGUAGE-INDEPENDENT PREFERRED ORDER OF CONSTITUENTS**.

LIP-ROUNDING

See **ROUND**.

LIQUIDS

Non-nasal **sonorants**, including **laterals**, such as [l], and **rhotics**, such as [r].

LITERACY

The ability to read and write, typically involving the control of complex grammar and vocabulary.

LITERAL MEANING

The meaning of a **phrase** or **clause** composed of the meanings of its component **lexical words**, with no **metaphor** or other figurative language. The term is also applied to what is said overtly as opposed to what is implied or what is added by the listener's or reader's construal or inferences. It may be that literal meaning is a small part of the interpretation of a given utterance by a given listener or reader. See **CONSTRUE**, **FIGURATIVE**, **IMPLICATURE**.

LITERARY PRAGMATICS

The application of pragmatics to the analysis of literary texts and to the interaction between authors and readers.

LITERARY SEMANTICS

The study of meaning in literary texts.

LITHUANIAN

Baltic, Indo-European. 2.9M speakers, Lithuania.

LITOTES

Understatement, often involving **negation**: e.g. *You're not wrong* (= *you have a very good point*), *Not the least of these poets is Herrick*. See **HYPERBOLE**.

LITTLE PRO

See **PRO**.

LOAN TRANSLATION

See **CALQUE**.

LOANWORD
A word borrowed from one language into another. For example French has borrowed such English words as *'le weekend'*. See **FRANGLAIS**.

LOC
See **LOCATIVE**.

LOCAL TRANSFORMATION
A **transformation** applying to the structure dominated by a single **node**.

LOCAL TREE
In **Generalized Phrase Structure Grammar**, a tree with a root node and one layer of **daughter** nodes. See **TREE DIAGRAM**.

LOCALISM
The theory that all relations are based on the concepts of location or movement in space. The metaphor on which the concept of **transitivity** is based is localist: an action originates in an **agent** and moves from an agent to a **goal** or **patient**. See **CONCEPTUAL METAPHOR THEORY, CONSTRUAL, FICTIVE MOTION**.

LOCALIST HYPOTHESIS
See **LOCALISM**.

LOCATIVE
1. A case marking signalling location. E.g. Finnish *talo* 'house' *talossa* 'in-the-house', Russian *Moskva* 'Moscow, **nominative** case' – *v Moskve* 'in Moscow, locative' vs *v Moskvu* 'to Moscow', **accusative** signalling direction. See **CASE**. 2. A **copula** construction expressing the location of some entity.

LOCKE, John (1632–1704)
English philosopher. His contribution to linguistics is in his theory of ideas, particularly the notion that there are no innate ideas, and his views on the relationship between language and thought.

LOCUTIONARY ACT
In **speech act** theory, the act of producing an **utterance**. Originally applied to speech but the concept can be extended to the production of written texts. See **ILLOCUTIONARY ACT, PERLOCUTIONARY ACT**.

LOCUTOR
See **SPEAKER, ADDRESSEE**.

LOG LIKELIHOOD
A statistical test for comparing the **frequency** of a given word in one **corpus** with the frequency of the same word in another corpus and determining whether any difference in frequency is statistically significant.

LOGIC

The study of argument, in particular relationships between propositions, formal ways of representing the content of a **proposition**, and the development of formal calculuses for automatically making correct **deductions** from a given set of **premises**. See ABDUCTION, CALCULUS, DISCOURSE REPRESENTATION THEORY, ENTAILMENT, FORMAL LOGIC, INDUCTION.

LOGICAL CONNECTIVE

See CONNECTIVE.

LOGICAL CONSTANT

See LOGICAL CONNECTIVE.

LOGICAL FORM

In **GB**, **P&P** and **MP**, underlying representations of syntactic structure, **D-structures**, are mapped onto representations of surface syntax, **S-structures**. S-structures are mapped into representations of Logical Form, or LF, an intermediate step between syntactic structures and the predicate-argument semantic structures deployed in logic and formal semantics. In current terminology, LF constitutes an interface with the **Conceptual-Intentional** (CI) system, as the semantic component is now known. The interface requires the syntactic structure to show the **scope** of a **quantifier** such as *some*, *any*, *all*, and the **antecedent** of a pronoun, and exploits semantic features on lexical words. E.g. the sentence *Jacob likes a boy* has a logical structure that can be glossed as 'There is an x such that x is a boy and Jacob likes x'. Its S-structure has the constituents in the order [Jacob likes a boy]. LF has a structure [a boy$_j$ [Jacob$_i$ [t$_i$ likes t$_j$], which can then be mapped onto a complete logical structure. See ANAPHORA, BOUND.

LOGICAL RELATIONS

1. The different types of relation (between arguments) denoted by **predicates** and the different entailments licensed by the relations. See PREDICATOR, REFLEXIVE PREDICATE, SYMMETRIC PREDICATE, TRANSITIVE PREDICATE.
2. The different relations between propositions. See CONTRADICTORY, CONTRARY, ENTAILMENT, PRESUPPOSITION 1.

LOGICAL SEMANTICS

The use of **logic** (propositional calculus, predicate calculus) to analyse meaning.

LOGICAL SUBJECT

In earlier traditional grammar, the **noun phrase** in a clause denoting an **agent**. Since in **active** clauses an agent is typically denoted by a **grammatical subject** noun phrase, the logical subject of an active clause is typically also a grammatical subject. In turn any grammatical subject of an active clause is a logical subject, which means that the concept encompasses roles such as experiencer, in *James saw the giant peach*, and recipient, in *Katarina received a prize*. In passive clauses the grammatical subject is the patient, and the agent is denoted by an oblique noun phrase. In *The tree was felled by James*, *the tree* is the grammatical subject denoting a patient (something happens to the tree) and *James* in the prepositional phrase *by James* denotes the agent. *Tree* is not a logical subject. The concept is equivalent to **macrorole**. See ACTOR, GRAMMATICAL FUNCTION, PSYCHOLOGICAL SUBJECT, ROLE, VOICE.

LOGOCENTRISM

In deconstruction, the priority given to the spoken word. See DECONSTRUCTION, POST-STRUCTURALISM.

LOGOPHORIC

See LOGOPHORICITY.

LOGOPHORICITY

Especially in African languages such as Efik, the use of devices such as a logophoric **pronoun** or logophoric verb **affix** in **indirect speech** to refer to the person whose words are reported. E.g. Donno So *Oumar Anta inyemen waa be gi* 'Oumar Anta LOG-ACC see AUX said, Oumar said that Anta had seen him (Oumar)'.

LOGORRHEA

In **clinical linguistics**, the inability to stop talking. Speakers suffering from this disorder usually produce incoherent speech.

LONG COMPONENTS

In some developments of **phoneme** theory, it was recognized that some phonological features might be realized on two or more successive segments: vowel harmony is an example. The notion is similar to that of **prosody** in prosodic phonology. See PROSODIC PHONOLOGY.

LONG-DISTANCE REFLEXIVE PRONOUN

The **antecedents** of **reflexive pronouns** are typically in the same clause, as in *Michael gave himself a reward* and *The players criticized themselves*. Occasionally the antecedent of a reflexive pronoun is in another clause. In *Lucie didn't think [that it would be so difficult for herself to abandon the flat in Paris]*, *herself* is inside the **complement clause** *that ... Paris* and the antecedent, *Lucie*, is outside the complement clause and in the main clause. Such a relationship between the reflexive pronoun and the antecedent is known as a long-distance dependency, and the reflexive pronoun in such a relationship is called a long-distance reflexive pronoun. See ANAPHORA.

LONG PASSIVE

See VOICE.

LONG VOWEL

See LENGTH.

LONGITUDINAL
Applied to research that investigates, for example, the linguistic, social or intellectual development of children over a number of years.

LOOK-AND-SAY
A method of teaching reading in which learners are taught to recognize whole words rather than sounding out individual segments. See **PHONICS**.

LOUDNESS
See **AMPLITUDE**.

LOUISIANA CREOLE
French-based creole. Approx. 70K speakers, Louisiana.

LOW
1. Of **vowels**, equivalent to **open**. For instance, [a] is an open (i.e. low) front neutral vowel. See **CARDINAL VOWELS, PLACE OF ARTICULATION**. 2. In **SPE Distinctive Feature Theory**, segments, especially vowel segments, that are articulated with the tongue as low in the mouth as possible for example [æ], [ɑ]. See **HIGH**.

LOWTH, Robert (1710–1787)
His *Short Introduction to English Grammar* (1762) was famous during his lifetime.

LP RULE
See **LINEAR PRECEDENCE RULE**.

LUGANDA
Bantu, Niger-Congo. South-east Uganda.

LUO
Nilo-Saharan. 3M speakers Kenya, 280K Tanzania.

LUXEMBOURGISH
Germanic, **Indo-European**. 490K speakers, Luxembourg. With **French** and **German**, one of the official languages of Luxembourg.

LYONS, Sir John (b 1932)
Professor of Linguistics at Edinburgh, then Sussex. Originally a classical scholar, *Structural Semantics,* his study of the **semantics** of Plato's vocabulary, was the first work on semantics to be based on the principles of **generative grammar**. He was an influential exponent of **structural linguistics**.

M

MAASAI
   Nilo-Saharan. 883K speakers Kenya, 453K Tanzania.

MACEDONIAN
   Slavic, Indo-European. 1.5M speakers, Macedonia (much smaller numbers in Albania, Bulgaria and Greece).

MACHINE TRANSLATION (MT)
   The use of computational techniques to translate text from one natural language to another.

MACROLINGUISTICS
   The study of all aspects of linguistics, as opposed to **microlinguistics**, usually held to be restricted to formal aspects of language, especially **morphology**, **syntax** and **phonology**.

MACROROLE
   In **Role and Reference Grammar**, very general **roles**, to which grammatical rules apply. E.g. the macrorole of actor covers **agents**, as in *Gertrude chopped the onions*, **experiencers**, as in *Ken knows all the answers*, and **recipients**, as in *Kirsty received a phone call*. The macrorole of **undergoer** covers **patients**, as in *Alec chopped down the tree*, **themes**, as in *The ball rolled under the car*, and perceived entities, as in *Susan heard a noise*. See **ACTOR**, **LOGICAL SUBJECT**.

MAD MAGAZINE SENTENCE
   In early **transformational grammar**, a label given to echo questions supposedly typical of *Mad Magazine*: e.g. *The plane is out of control / Plane out of control?*

MADANG
   Austronesian. Approx. 2K speakers, Sarawak.

MADURESE
   Austronesian. Approx. 13.5M speakers, Java and Bali.

MAIN CLAUSE
   See **CLAUSE**

MAIN VERB
   See **LEXICAL VERB**.

MAJOR CLASS FEATURES
See DISTINCTIVE FEATURES: MAJOR CLASS FEATURES.

MAJOR PATTERN
A pattern of **construction** that is very common: e.g. NP VP *Maggots work medical miracles*; There BE NP PP *There's a crocodile on that mudbank*; and so on. Patterns of construction that are rare are called minor: e.g. *Would that* + clause *Would that she had sold the property earlier!*

MAJOR WORD CLASS
See WORD CLASS.

MALAGASY
Austronesian. Approx. 10.5M speakers, Madagascar.

MALAY
Austronesian. 13M speakers, Malaysia (also spoken in Brunei and Singapore). Very closely related to (Bahasa) **Indonesian**.

MALAYALAM
Dravidian. 37M speakers, Southern India.

MALAYO-POLYNESIAN
Austronesian, or the largest family within Austronesian. Includes **Fijian**, **Hawaiian**, **Maori**, **Niuean**, **Samoan**, **Tamambo**, **Tongan**.

MALINOWSKI, Bronislaw (1884–1942)
Polish anthropologist whose work on the interaction between language and culture among the Trobriand islanders was influential in sociolinguistics. He coined the phrases '**phatic communion**' and '**context of situation**'.

MALTESE
Semitic, **Afroasiatic**. 405K speakers, Malta. Strong **Italian** influence on vocabulary and grammar.

MALUKAN
Malayo-Polynesian, **Austronesian**. In the islands between East Timor and West Papua.

MAMBILA
Niger-Congo. Approx. 99K, Nigeria.

MANAMBU
Sepik-Ramu language. Papua New Guinea.

MAND
In **speech act** theory, a cover term for commands, requests, suggestions, etc.

MANDARIN
A group of dialects of Chinese spoken in the north and southwest of China. The Beijing dialect forms the basis of Standard Chinese, also referred to as Putonghua.

MANDE
Language family within **Niger-Congo**. West Africa. Includes Bambara and Mandinka.

MANNER ADVERB
See ADVERB.

MANNER FEATURES
See SPE DISTINCTIVE FEATURE THEORY.

MANNER OF ARTICULATION
In classifying speech sounds, the manner of articulation identifies the type of obstruction that occurs in its production. See CONSONANT, CLOSE APPROXIMATION, OPEN APPROXIMATION, STOP, FRICATIVE, AFFRICATE, NASAL, CLOSE, OPEN, MONOPHTHONG.

MANNER OF DISCOURSE
See FORMALITY.

MAORI
Polynesian, Austronesian. New Zealand. According to 2006 Census, 23.7% (approx. 90K) of Maori people could discuss everyday things in Maori.

MAPPING
A mathematical term for the relationship between a set A of items and a set B, when a **function** connects each member of A with a member of B. The function maps A into B or onto B. There is a mapping between A and B. E.g. in **transformational grammar** the passive **transformation** mapped the structure of **active** clauses onto the structure of passive **clauses**.

MAPUDUNGAN
Araucanian. Approx. 300K speakers. Chile.

MARATHI
Indo-Iranian, Indo-European. Approx. 68M, India (state of Maharashtra, official language).

MARGIN
The **syllable** is composed of a syllabic nucleus, typically a vowel, optionally preceded by an onset, usually a consonant and optionally followed by a coda, also typically a consonant. The segment(s) that form the margins of a syllable are the onset and coda.

MARGINAL MODAL
See **SEMI-AUXILIARY**.

MARKED
1. Having some change of form signalling **case, tense, aspect, number**, etc. *Children* is marked for number, having the suffix *-ren*, child is unmarked, having no suffix. 2. In an analysis, being treated as the positive value of a feature; e.g. /n/ is marked, being [+ nasal], while /d/ is unmarked, being [−nasal]. 3. In **Prague School** analyses, definitely having a property as opposed to possibly having a property. Thus Jakobson treats the Russian **accusative** case as marked for movement, since it always denotes movement, concrete or metaphorical. The **nominative** case is unmarked for movement, since it may or may not denote movement. 4. Unusual, unexpected or complex in some way, and therefore infrequent. Thus the Russian **high** back **vowel** with spread lips in *syn* 'son' is marked; a high back vowel with **lip- rounding** is unmarked. In English simple active declarative **sentences** are unmarked in comparison with, say, **imperative** sentences; regular morphology in, e.g., the formation of plural or past tense forms, is unmarked by comparison with irregular morphological forms; some infrequent consonants, like **ejectives** are marked. *Dog* has the unmarked meaning 'canine vs other types of animal' but it has the less usual, marked meaning 'male canine', as opposed to bitch 'female canine'. It is generally held that marked forms are less common cross-linguistically; have lower text frequency in a language, appear later in language acquisition; and in cases of **merger** are less stable than their unmarked counterparts. The notion first achieved prominence in **Prague School** phonology and plays a prominent part in distinctive feature phonology. In Chomskyan **generative grammar** a given language is seen as having a core of regularly occurring constructions which are quite usual for, and expected by, native speakers. The language also has a periphery of marked constructions which are unusual and unexpected. The Chomskyan theory of language acquisition holds that the core, which is subject to general constraints, is acquired early by children. In contrast, constructions in the periphery may be acquired late on.

MARKEDNESS
See **MARKED**.

MARKER
1. Any **morph** or phonological feature, e.g. **tone**, which realizes an abstract unit. E.g. an **affix** or a **preposition** are case markers; *-ed* is a **tense** marker, *the* is a marker of definiteness. See **CASE, DEFINITE ARTICLE**. 2. A morph that carries no meaning, lexical or non-lexical, but whose function is to signal the presence of a particular **construction**. E.g. *that* marks a **complement** clause or **relative clause**, *-ing* marks non-finite **gerund** clauses. 3. A feature used in the analysis of systematic relations between lexical items: e.g. the marker [male] marks *man, boy, ram, uncle* vs *woman, girl, ewe, aunt*; the marker [adult] marks *boy, girl, lamb* vs *man,*

woman, ram/ewe. **4.** In sociolinguistics a linguistic **variable** that identifies a particular social group. **5.** A feature whose presence or absence is significant, such as voice in stops. See **LINGUISTIC VARIABLE, MARKED**.

MARKUP LANGUAGE

A language for storing texts in digital form, keeping the basic or plain text separate from information about the formatting of the text in the original documents, e.g. whether a piece of text was in bold or italics, which were in headlines (in newspaper texts). XML, standing for Extensible Markup Language, is the current standard.

MASCULINE

Especially in **Indo-European** languages, a **gender**, or class, of **nouns**, whose central members denote males, although most masculine nouns denote inanimate or abstract entities. See **COMMON GENDER, COMMON NOUN, COUNT NOUN, MASS NOUN**.

MASS NOUN

A **noun** denoting an entity that is perceived as an uncountable mass of stuff as opposed to individuals that can be counted. English mass nouns combine with *much* but not *many*, *less* but not *fewer*: e.g. *much water, less sugar*. See **COUNT NOUN**.

MATCHED GUISE TECHNIQUE

A means of measuring language attitude. The original experiments involved a bilingual speaker recording texts in two languages which were then judged by other bilingual speakers on various scales, such as friendliness, reliability and having leadership qualities. The purpose of the technique is to remove personality traits from judgments of attitude.

MATCHING CONDITION

In **GOVERNMENT AND BINDING THEORY**, the constraint that a **pronoun** and its **antecedent** must have matching features of **number, gender**, etc. See **AGREEMENT**.

MATHEMATICAL LINGUISTICS

The study of the formal properties of grammatical theories, formalized in logical or mathematical terms. See **COMPUTATIONAL LINGUISTICS, PARSING**.

MATHESIUS, Vilém (1882–1945)

Czech linguist. Founder of the Prague Linguistic Circle and a prominent European structural linguist.

MATRIX

1. A clause or sentence in which other clauses/sentences are embedded. See **CLAUSE, EMBEDDING, MAIN CLAUSE**. **2.** A display of features in rows and columns. See **FEATURE MATRIX**.

MAXIM

A typically brief and pithy statement of some principle, often in the form of an instruction expressed by an **imperative** construction: e.g. *Do as you would be done by*. See APHORISM, IMPERATIVE, MAXIMS OF CONVERSATION, MAXIMS OF POLITENESS, PROVERB.

MAXIM OF MANNER

See MAXIMS OF CONVERSATION.

MAXIM OF MODESTY

See POLITENESS PRINCIPLE.

MAXIM OF PRAISE

See POLITENESS PRINCIPLE.

MAXIM OF QUALITY

See MAXIMS OF CONVERSATION.

MAXIM OF QUANTITY

See MAXIMS OF CONVERSATION.

MAXIM OF RELATION

See MAXIMS OF CONVERSATION.

MAXIM OF SYMPATHY

See POLITENESS PRINCIPLE.

MAXIMAL PROJECTION

The highest level of structure in a given phrase structure tree. See X-BAR SYNTAX.

MAXIMS OF CONVERSATION

In order to explain conversational **implicature**, **Grice** proposed that interlocutors follow a **Cooperative Principle**, consisting of four maxims of conversation. Hearers assume that speakers are following the maxims, and that when speakers do not follow a maxim (or flout a maxim), they do so intentionally to convey some piece of information indirectly. The **Maxim of Quality** enjoins speakers to say only what they believe to be true and not to say anything for which they do not have adequate evidence. The **Maxim of Quantity** enjoins speakers to avoid providing either more or less information than hearers need in a given situation. The **Maxim of Relation** enjoins speakers to be relevant, to stick to the point, and the **Maxim of Manner** enjoins speakers to put things plainly, without ambiguity, in an orderly fashion and as briefly as possible. Grice's ideas have been developed by proponents of **Neo-Gricean pragmatics**. See POLITENESS PRINCIPLE.

MAXIMS OF POLITENESS

See POLITENESS PRINCIPLE.

M-COMMAND

A **constituent** A m-commands a constituent B if the first maximal **projection** dominating A also dominates B, and if neither A nor B dominates the other. In the Figure 'M-command (a)', A m-commands B. In the Figure 'M-command (b)', A also m-commands D. M-command, a restricted form of **c-command**, is central to the definition of **government** in the **GB** model. See DOMINANCE.

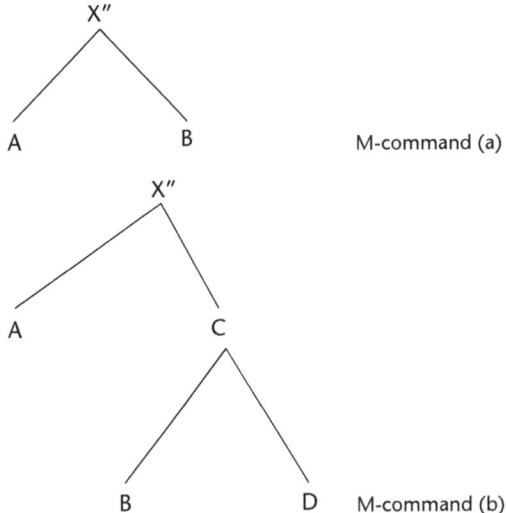

MDP

See MINIMAL DISTANCE PRINCIPLE.

MEAN LENGTH OF UTTERANCE (MLU)

A measure of children's linguistic development based on the number of morphemes in their utterances.

MEANING

Whatever information is encoded in a **sentence** and conveyed by an **utterance**. A fundamental distinction is drawn between the meaning of sentences and the meaning of utterances, since the latter require listeners and readers to take account of **context**, to enrich the meaning by their understanding of intentions and **implicatures** and by intensive use of inference. Other distinctions are between the meaning of **lexical words** and the meaning of **clauses** and sentences, and between what is said overtly and what is implied and to be added to the meaning by the exercise of inference. See DEIXIS, ENTAILMENT, EXPLICATURE, GRAMMATICAL MEANING, INTENTIONALITY, LEXICAL MEANING, LITERAL MEANING, MAXIMS OF CONVERSATION, PROPOSITION, SENTENCE MEANING, SPEECH ACT.

MEANING POSTULATE

An alternative to **lexical decomposition** as a method for stating relationships between lexical items. Meaning postulates state **entailments** between propositions containing related lexical items; e.g. for **hyponymy**, *X is an apple* entails *X is a fruit*; for **synonymy**, *X ran fast* entails *X ran quickly*..

MEANING-CHANGING TRANSFORMATION

In early **transformational grammar**, a **transformation** that changed the meaning of the structure it applied to; e.g. the transformation that converted a **declarative** clause, say *She can swim*, into an **interrogative clause**, *Can she swim?*

MEANING-PRESERVING TRANSFORMATION

In early **transformational grammar**, a **transformation** that did not change the meaning of the structure it applied to; e.g. the transformation that converted *We took down the pictures* to *We took the pictures down*.

MEDIAL

An element occurring in the middle of a unit. Thus, /a/ occurs medially in /mad/. See **FINAL, INITIAL**.

MEDIUM

The physical vehicle for the transmission of language. The spoken medium, **phonic substance**, is the vehicle for speech, and **phonetics** and **phonology** are the study of the spoken medium. The written medium, **graphic substance**, is the written or printed form of language and **graphetics** and **graphology** are the study of the written medium. Other language mediums are possible. Sign language is transmitted through the visual medium and Braille uses touch. See **HAPTICS**.

MEILLET, Antoine (1866–1936)

French Indo-Europeanist and general linguist. He was an early pupil of Saussure and other French structuralists. He coined the term **grammaticalization**.

MEIOSIS

See **LITOTES**.

MEL'CHUK, Igor Aleksandrovic (b 1932)

Russian computational linguist. He has made significant contributions to computational lexicography and machine translation.

MELLOW

In **J&H Distinctive Feature Theory** an **acoustic** distinctive feature, the opposite of **strident**. Characterizing **consonant** sounds other than those that are strident. See **DISTINCTIVE FEATURES, ACOUSTIC**.

MENTAL LEXICON

In theories of language processing by humans, the **lexicon** or **dictionary** that speakers are assumed to have stored in their minds.

MENTAL REPRESENTATION

A representation of some **situation** in the 'real' world, constructed in the mind and based on **prototypes**. An important idea in theories such as **cognitive linguistics** and in other contemporary research is that language relates directly to mental representations and via them to the world outside language. See **CONCEPT, CONSTRUE**.

MENTAL SPACE

In **cognitive linguistics**, a region of conceptual space containing specific information, and also applied to the 'packet' of information itself. In contrast with domains of knowledge, the packets of information are temporary, being constructed as part of the process of interpreting **texts** (spoken or written). For instance, in interpreting *If she accepted, he would refuse*, one mental space is created to handle the conditional construction and its counterfactual meaning, which is in a different mental space from the one occupied by the speaker speaking. See **BLENDING, CONCEPTUAL METAPHOR THEORY, DOMAIN**.

MENTALISM

The belief that mental processes such as beliefs, thoughts and intentions can be appealed to in scientific discussions and investigated objectively.

MERGE

See **MINIMALIST PROGRAM**.

MERGER

In historical linguistics or **sociolinguistics**, a loss, or partial loss, of contrast between two or more phonemes.

MERONYMIC HIERARCHY

A hierarchy in which the relationship between lexical items is one of **meronymy**. See **LEXICAL HIERARCHY, TREE DIAGRAM**.

MERONYMY

A relation holding between two **lexical words** when one denotes a part of the denotatum of the other. E.g. *leg* and *foot*, *axe* and *blade*. *Foot* and *blade* are meronyms, *leg* and *axe* are the respective **holonyms**. (Greek *meros* 'part', *holos* 'whole'.) See **HYPONYMY, SENSE RELATIONS**.

MESOLECT

In a **dialect continuum**, the variety (or **lect**) that is intermediate between the **acrolect** and the **basilect**.

METADISCOURSE

Shifts in the level of discourse by means of which speakers and writers move from immediate involvement in conversation, argument, presentation, narration and so on to comments on the form and content of their own utterances and those of other interlocutors. These shifts are signalled by various metalinguistic devices. Speakers and writers signal what their intentions are in producing a piece of text: *I wish to argue that…, The following facts explain this decision* and so on. They can anticipate the listeners' or readers' reactions: *Surprising though it may seem, It will be obvious that…, It is perhaps unnecessary to say that…* They can signal connections between sections of text: *however, nonetheless* and so on. See **METALINGUISTIC HEDGES, METALINGUISTIC NEGATION**.

METALANGUAGE

The language used to talk about or describe language in general or a particular language. What is described is the **object language**. A metalanguage may be quite distinct from the object language it describes, e.g. a **formal** or **logical** language used to describe a language. More commonly a natural language is used as a metalanguage – e.g. in a grammar of French written in English, French is the object language and English the metalanguage. In a grammar of English written in English, English is both the object language and the metalanguage.

METALINGUISTIC HEDGES

A **hedge** that functions as a comment on the sentence containing it, an **utterance** of a sentence or the **proposition** expressed by a sentence. An example is *technically*, in a sentence such as *Technically tomatoes are fruit*. The speaker is saying that while the proposition expressed by that sentence is true, the implication is that, certainly in Britain, tomatoes are not treated like fruit in the structure of meals.

METALINGUISTIC NEGATION

Negation that is metaphorically outside or above the clause in which it occurs and signals that the speaker is rejecting a previous statement. Thus, speaker A may say *Philippa has read some of these books* and speaker B may respond *She hasn't read some of them – she's read every last one of them*. Normally a negative phrase such as *hasn't read* requires *any*, but speaker B can combine it with *some* because he or she is not saying that Philippa has read none of the books but that speaker A was wrong. Similarly, speaker A may say *We're going to Firenze to see the art and architecture* and speaker B may respond *We're not going to Firenze – we're going to Florence*. 'Firenze' may be the town that appears in railway timetables, but 'Florence' is the name required when one is talking (in English) about art and architecture.

METALINGUISTIC THEORY

Any theory concerned with the nature of linguistic analyses and theories.

METAPHOR

Metaphor is the **comparison** of two categories, with the comparison not being overtly signalled. **Simile** is a metaphor in which the comparison is signalled, as in *as good as gold, as poor as a church mouse, Pleasures are like poppies spread*. Metaphors relate a **source** domain to a target domain. *The firm is on the* *rocks* takes a source domain, the business world, and maps it onto a target domain, voyaging on the ocean. The firm is compared to a ship that has been blown off course and driven onto rocks. See **CONCEPTUAL BLENDING, CONCEPTUAL METAPHOR THEORY, CONSTRUE**.

METAPRAGMATICS

1. Debate as to what **pragmatics** is, the type of phenomena pragmaticists should investigate and the demarcation of pragmatics from other disciplines, such as **semantics**, concerned with language and **language use**. 2. The theory of pragmatic patterns and practices, such as the conditions governing when **statements**, promises, instructions and so on can be issued, and the conditions allowing speakers to use their language effectively or preventing them from doing so; the conditions governing the application of pragmatic principles. See **IMPLICATURE, MAXIMS OF CONVERSATION, MAXIMS OF POLITENESS, SPEECH ACT**.

METARULE

A general **rule** expressing a property of a number of more specific rules taken individually. In **GENERALIZED PHRASE STRUCTURE GRAMMAR**, a rule defining some rules in a **grammar** on the basis of others; e.g. the metarule stating that if a grammar has a set of rules generating active **declarative** clauses it also has a set of rules, with equivalent restrictions on combinations of **lexical words**, generating **passive** declarative clauses. See **VOICE**.

METONYMY

In traditional **rhetoric**, a **figure of speech** whereby entities are referred to by means of expressions denoting something closely associated with them. In *The flute is late again*, *the flute* refers to the person who plays the flute; in *Purple Dress was the cynosure of all eyes*, *Purple Dress* refers to the woman wearing the dress. In **cognitive linguistics** metonymy is considered a central component of conceptual organization.

METRICAL GRID

See **METRICAL PHONOLOGY**.

METRICAL PHONOLOGY

A **phonological** theory that developed out of the stress rules of **Sound Patterns of English**. It focuses on prosodic phenomena, especially **stress** and the distribution of strong and weak **syllables** within the **foot**. Its principle notations are the **metrical tree**, analysing a linguistic form into a hierarchical constituent structure of strong and weak syllables, and the **metrical grid**, which depicts the stress levels of individual syllables. See Figures 'Metrical tree' and 'Metrical grid'. See **CONSTITUENT STRUCTURE, PROSODIC PHONOLOGY**.

,inde'pendence   raised stress mark – major stress
                     lowered stress mark – secondary stress
                     no stress mark – unstress

Metrical tree

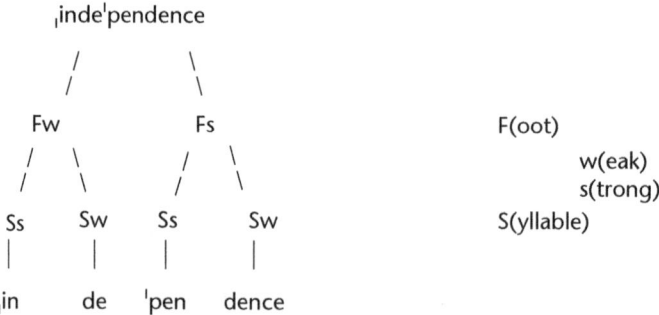

Metrical grid

[The higher the column of Xs, the more prominent the syllable]

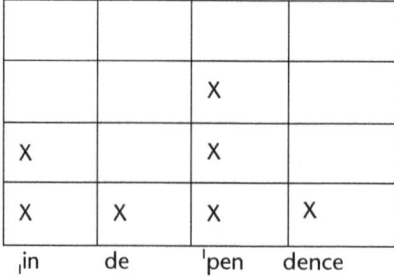

METRICAL TREE
See **METRICAL PHONOLOGY**.

MICROLINGUISTICS
See **MACROLINGUISTICS**.

MID VOWEL
A term in the three-way classification of **vowels** with respect to the position of the **tongue** within the **vowel space: high**, or **close** (the highest point of the **tongue** as close as possible to the roof of the mouth), **low** or **open** (the highest point of the tongue as far as possible from the roof of the mouth), mid (the highest point of the tongue in a mid position between high and low). In English /e/, as in *bed*, [bed].

MID-CLOSE
See **HALF-CLOSE**.

MIDDLE EAR
The part of the **ear** behind the ear drum containing the bones that transfer sound vibrations.

MIDDLE VOICE
See **VOICE**.

MID-OPEN
See **HALF-OPEN**.

MIMESIS
The communication of events by showing rather than telling. Storytellers who act out events in their stories, use **direct speech** and imitate the voices of different characters, make pointing gestures, put on costumes and so on are employing mimesis by means of these mimetic props.

MINIMAL DISTANCE PRINCIPLE
The principle that in a **sentence** such as *Philippa asked Katarina to help with the cooking* the understood **subject** of *to help* is determined (or controlled) by the nearest potential **antecedent**, here *Katarina*. See **CONTROL, UNDERSTOOD SUBJECT**.

MINIMAL FREE FORM
A free form which cannot be analysed into smaller forms that are themselves all free. E.g. *Think!, educate* – neither *educ-* nor *-ate* can stand by themselves. See **FREE**.

MINIMAL PAIR
A pair of **words** that have different meanings and differ in a single segment, such as the English words *pick* and *sick*. See **PHONEME**.

MINIMALIST PROGRAM
A programme of developments of **Principles and Parameters**, begun in the early 1990s and intended to replace the complex procedures and constraints of **Government and Binding Theory** with simple, general principles of **syntactic structure**. In one system, syntactic structures, still at the centre of the model, interface with (are mapped into) two other systems, one to do with meaning (**Conceptual-Intentional**/CI system) and the other to do with sound (**Articulatory-Perceptual**/AP system). The syntactic structure or syntactic object that interfaces with CI is **Logical Form**, whereas what interfaces with AP is a different syntactic object, created by a set of operations called **Spellout**.

The generation of syntactic structures/objects is called a **derivation**, as in early **transformational grammar**. But, unlike early transformational grammar, derivations begin by selecting items from a collection of lexical items called a numeration. The lexical items project (erect and label) small pieces of syntactic structure, all with the same arrangement and all incorporating the later developments in **X-Bar syntax**. There are no phrase structure rules. A central binary operation called **Merge** combines small pieces of syntactic structure, two at a time, until all the pieces projected by whatever lexical items have been selected are part of a larger syntactic structure (of a **clause**). Merge crucially involves checking: the selectional features belonging to one lexical item are checked against the features belonging to another to ensure that correct combinations are generated. Some features are passed from lexical items to the **heads** of syntactic structures.

A second operation, **Adjoin**, adds **adjuncts**, such as *quickly* or *yesterday*, which do not involve any selectional features. A third operation, **Move**, moves **constituents** once complete pieces of syntactic structure have been generated. The operation does this by creating copies of constituents and deleting the original one. See **CHECKING, COMPLEMENT, HEAD, INTERFACE**.

MINIMALITY CONDITION
See **MINIMAL DISTANCE PRINCIPLE**.

MINORITY LANGUAGE
A language, typically of low status, spoken by a minority of people in a given country. Examples are Australian languages in Australia, Hungarian in Slovakia, Tamil in Sri Lanka, Lapp/Saami in Finland.

MISCOMMUNICATION
An attempt to communicate that is unsuccessful, because of different perspectives, different languages or different varieties of a language, or different cultures.

MISCUE
The misinterpretation of a word by someone learning to read.

MISMATCH
In **first language** acquisition, a lack of correspondence between the word-meaning links in the vocabulary of the adult speakers of a given language and those in the vocabulary of children acquiring that language.

MIXED LANGUAGE
A mixed language arises through the fusion of two distinct languages in a bilingual situation. The classic example is Mitchif, where **nouns** and **adjectives** follow French patterns and **verbs** follow Cree patterns. To be distinguished from **pidgin** and **creole** languages.

MIXE-ZOQUEAN
Meso-American family. Mexico. Includes Mixe and Zoque.

MLU
See **MEAN LENGTH OF UTTERANCE**

MODAL AUXILIARY
See **MODAL VERB**.

MODAL VERB
Verbs expressing **modality**. Across languages, such verbs require a **main verb**, which they are seen as helping, and for that reason are also given the label modal **auxiliary**. English modal verbs, such as *can, could, may, might, must, will,* have particular syntactic properties: e.g. they combine directly with *n't* and *not* (*can't swim*) and take part in **subject-aux inversion** in **interrogative** sentences (*Can she swim?*). See **NICE PROPERTIES**.

MODALITY
Modality can be defined in either linguistic or **logical** terms. The two approaches are not the same, although they are closely related.

In linguistic terms it is helpful to start with a distinction between the **grammatical categories** of **mood** and **modality**. Mood is a grammatical category. Across languages it is typically realized by **affixes** on verbs marking **indicative** and **subjunctive** or **realis** and **irrealis**, and by **clause** types, **declarative**, **interrogative**, **imperative**. Modality has to do with the speaker's attitude. Speaker's attitude is expressed by the different clause types, by modal verbs, by the choice of indicative and subjunctive mood (not relevant in English but very relevant in languages such as French) and by **discourse particles**.

A fundamental distinction in modality has to do with whether speakers present situations as actual/factual, that is, as having happened or as happening, or as merely possible. The terms 'realis' and 'irrealis' are often applied to these modalities, and also to the verb forms expressing the modalities in particular languages. There are languages that lack specific **future tense** forms of the verb, employing instead general irrealis forms presenting a situation as merely possible.

Analyses of modal verbs employ a widely accepted distinction between epistemic and deontic modality. Epistemic modality (also sometimes called evaluative modality) is concerned with the speaker's assessment of the truth of a **proposition**. Modalized clauses with *can/may* (possibility) and *must* (necessity) can be seen as indicating the speaker's growing strength of conviction that a proposition is true; clauses with *will* often express a prediction that a proposition will become true. In *That may be the postman*, the proposition is presented as only possible or likely. Speakers who utter *That must be the postman* signal a strong presumption that what they say is true, while recognizing that it is open to challenge. *That will be the postman* expresses a prediction. In uttering the declarative clause *That is the postman* speakers signal their assumption that what they say is true; in uttering the interrogative clause *Is that the postman?* speakers ask the hearer about the truth of the proposition.

Deontic modality is concerned with the granting of permission and the imposing of obligation. Modalized clauses with *can/may* (permission) and *must* (obligation) can be seen as indicating speakers' growing strength of a sense of obligation, either for themselves or their hearers. Sentences with *will* express the speaker's insistence. In *you can go* the speaker is granting permission or enabling a possible event. In *you must go* the speaker is laying an obligation on an addressee or expressing the necessity of an event. In *you will go* the speaker is insisting. With the **imperative** clause *Go now*, speakers make a strong requirement or issue an order.

A further type of modality is **dynamic** root modality. This concerns the speaker's observations about inherent abilities (*He can sing treble*), and their own and other people's willingness (*I can sing, if you like*) and characteristics (*He can be very silly*).

Modality is pervasive in language and it can be realized, as above, by modal auxiliary verbs, but it can also be realized by a variety of other lexical means. Thus, for epistemic modality: *She must be on holiday* (modal auxiliary); *She's probably on holiday* (adverb); *Its possible she's on holiday* (adjective); *There's a possibility she's on holiday* (noun); *It seems she's on holiday* (verb of appearances); *I'm told she's on holiday* (evidential verb). For deontic modality: *You may not smoke* (modal auxiliary); *It is impermissible to smoke* (Adjective); *I insist that you do not smoke, You are required not to smoke, It is not permitted to smoke* (main verbs).

In logical terms modality is concerned with truth defined through the **operators** of (logical) necessity and (logical) possibility. A proposition is necessarily true (it is necessary that P) if it must be so and possibly true (it is possible that P) if it may be so. Necessity and possibility are mutually defining through negation: negating one modal with a non-negated proposition implies the assertion of the complementary modal with a negated proposition

[not Modal$_A$ (P)]   implies   [Modal$_B$ (not P)]
it is not necessary (that P)   implies   *it is possible (that not P)*
it is not possible (that P)   implies   *it is necessary (that not P)*

MODE OF DISCOURSE

In **Systemic Functional Grammar**, the medium in which a text is realized, e.g. in sound (speech) or marks on a surface (writing).

MODE

Especially in systemic grammar. See **MEDIUM**.

MODEL

A way of representing linguistic **concepts**, usually somewhat simplified or idealized, used as a tool for exploring the nature of the system concerned, for predicting its behaviour and so on. In linguistics usually the formal representation of a theory is modelled. Thus a syntactic model is a simple description of a grammatical system used to describe the relations between grammatical units.

MODEL-THEORETIC SEMANTICS

A theory of meaning which treats **propositions** as true or false in a particular model of the world. The theory is able to take account of **indexicality** – information about times and places, speakers and addressees that makes propositions true or false. E.g. *I will be here tomorrow* is true or false depending on who the speaker is, where the speaker is located, and the day on which the speaker produces the utterance. See DEIXIS, INDEX, POSSIBLE WORLD SEMANTICS, TRUTH CONDITION, UTTERANCE.

MODIFICATION

Any **construction** involving a **modifier**.

MODIFIER

1. An optional **constituent**, not required by a **head**, such as *great* in *great ideas* and *skilfully* in *She skilfully repaired the mechanism*. See PREMODIFIER, POSTMODIFIER. 2. Any word, phrase or clause modifying the head of a given construction. In this interpretation, a modifier is either a **complement** or an **adjunct**. See ADJECTIVE, DEPENDENCY, HEAD.

MODIFY

The relationship between some **dependent** and its **head**. **Adjectives** modify **nouns**; **adverbs**, nouns and preposition phrases modify **verbs**; adverbs modify **prepositions**.

MODULATION

1. Changes in the meaning of lexical items effected by **context**. The meaning can be enriched: in *My colleague is on maternity leave*, *colleague* acquires the extra meaning 'female'. The meaning can be impoverished: in *She drives a sort of motor-bike*, *motor-bike* does not refer to a typical machine. 2. A term used to refer to suprasegmental modulations to an utterance, such as stress and intonation, that can be manipulated for **paralinguistic** effect. See INTONATION, STRESS.

MODULE

A cognitive **domain** which functions independently of other domains. The degree to which the brain is organized into modules and functions modularly is controversial, but a constant theme in Chomskyan **generative grammar** is that there is an innate language module in the mind/brain.

MODUS PONENS

See DEDUCTION.

MODUS TOLLENS

See DEDUCTION.

MOHAWK

Iroquoian. Quebec and Ontario.

MOMENTANEOUS
See SEMELFACTIVE.

MOMENTARY
See ACHIEVEMENT, PUNCTUAL.

MONGOLIAN
Language family, the Mongolian Republic.

MONISM
A theory of meaning which takes form and content to be inseparable; a change in form brings about a change in meaning: e.g. *Pay up!* and *Please pay for the goods you have put in your basket, Depress the lever* and *Push the lever down* differ in non-descriptive meaning. See DESCRIPTIVE MEANING

MON-KHMER LANGUAGES
South-East Asia. Include Vietnamese, Khmer (Cambodian) and Mon (Burma and Thailand).

MONOGENESIS
The hypothesis that all languages, or all of a group of languages, have a single source. In **creole** linguistics the monogenesis claim is that all **pidgins** and creoles derive from a common ancestor and are differentiated by **lexicalization**, that is, by the languages from which their vocabulary is drawn. For instance, there are creoles and pidgins based on English, French and Portuguese. The contrary **polygenesis** claim is that pidgins develop independently of each other.

MONOLINGUALISM
The use of a single language by an individual or community, in contrast with bilingualism and multilingualism. See BILINGUALISM, MULTILINGUALISM.

MONOLOGUE
The production of speech by one person with no **turn-taking**. Typical monologues are stories, sermons, summings-up in court, speeches on radio and television. See DIALOGUE.

MONOMORPHEMIC
Consisting of a single **morph**: e.g. *chair*, but not *armchair*.

MONOPHTHONG
A **vowel** whose quality remains stable during its articulation. See DIPHTHONG, GLIDE.

MONOSEMIC
Applied to the organization of the **lexicon**, the view that where a **lexical word** has two meanings, and one of the meanings can be derived in a motivated fashion from the other, only the basic meaning should be included in the lexical entry. The polysemic approach includes all the meanings in the lexical entry. Thus the polysemic approach would include in the lexical entry for

drink both the basic meaning 'swallow a liquid' and the specialized meaning 'swallow an alcoholic liquid'. See **POLYSEMY**.

MONOSEMY

The phenomenon of a **lexical word** having only one meaning or sense. See **POLYSEMY**.

MONOSTRATAL

Having a single level of representation, as in **Lexical-Functional Grammar**, **Role and Reference Grammar, Generalized Phrase Structure Grammar** and **Head-driven Phrase Structure Grammar**, as opposed to early **transformational grammar**.

MONOSYLLABIC

Having a single **syllable**.

MONOVALENT

Applied especially to **verbs** that take only one **argument**: E.g. *vanish* – *The rabbit vanished* but not **He vanished the rabbit*. See **VALENCY**.

MONTAGUE, Richard (1931–1971)

American logician and philosopher whose work on semantics was one of the starting points of **formal semantics**. He worked on the idea that a natural language like English could be formally described using the techniques of formal logic.

MONTAGUE GRAMMAR

A type of **categorial grammar** developed by Richard **Montague** in the late 1960s. The treatment of **syntax** is typical of categorial grammar but Montague introduced an approach to compositional semantics in which each rule of syntax is associated with a corresponding rule of semantics.

MOOD

A **grammatical category**, usually realized by **affixes** on **verbs** but also by different types of **clause**. It relates to speakers' judgements of situations as real or factual vs unreal/irrealis or non-factual. Between factual and non-factual, situations can be judged certain, probable, possible, doubtful. They can be presented as unknown. The term 'mood' was originally applied to different sets of verb forms, such as the French **indicative** and **subjunctive**. French *a* 'has' is indicative and is used in statements of fact and in yes/no questions: *Jean a sa licence* 'John has his degree'. *Ait* 'has' is subjunctive and is used primarily in **complement** clauses dependent on verbs such as *vouloir* 'wish' and *croire* 'believe'. *Je crois que Jean a sa licence* 'I believe that John has his degree' signals the speaker's belief that the situation is factual. *Je ne crois pas que Jean ait sa licence* 'I don't believe that John has his degree' presents the situation as non-factual or irrealis. This is signalled by the negative verb *ne crois pas* but also by the subjunctive form of the verb *ait*. '**Declarative**', '**interrogative**' and '**imperative**' are labels for different types of clause but they also realize mood. Speakers choose a type of clause depending on their judgement of a **situation**, whether they want to make a **statement**, ask a **question** or issue a **command**. Across languages different verb forms occur in declarative and imperative clauses, and some languages have special verb forms for use in interrogative clauses. The term 'analytic mood' is sometimes applied to structures in which mood is expressed by independent words such as English *can*, *must*, etc. as opposed to structures in which mood is expressed by inflections, as in *were* in *If she were here*, or by bound morphs, as in Turkish *Para ver-ebil-dim* 'Money give-able-I was, I was able to give money (and did so)' vs *para ver-dim* 'money I-gave, I gave money'. See **MODALITY, MORPH**.

MORA

In **phonology** a unit that determines **syllable** weight. Typically a syllabic **nucleus** containing a short **vowel** is monomoraic, i.e. contains a single mora, and a nucleus with a long vowel or **diphthong** is bimoraic. The syllable onset does not have moraic value, but the syllable **coda** may have a moraic value in some languages. The sound system of Japanese is usually said to be based on moras rather than syllables. See also **METRICAL PHONOLOGY, SYLLABLE**.

MORPH

Morphs are the smallest chunks into which spoken or written **words** can be divided (on the basis of contrast between words). E.g. *misdirected* splits into *mis-*, *direct-* and *-ed*, *renewables* splits into *renew*, *-able* and *-s*; *renew* splits into *re-* and *new-*. *-s* and *-ed* are inflectional morphs. They carry **grammatical meaning** and play a role in **agreement** and **government**. *Renewables* combines with *are* in *Renewables are desirable*, *renewable* combines with *is* in *This renewable is not viable*. *Mis-*, *re-* and *-able* are derivational morphs. They contribute to the creation of new **lexical words**, such as *misdirect* from *direct*, *renew* from *new* and *renewable* from *renew*.

A distinction can be drawn between morphs and morphemes. Morphs typically realize abstract units of meaning called morphemes. The meanings are grammatical and lexical. *-ed* realizes [Past Tense] and *-s*, in *renewables*, realizes [Plural Number]. Morphemes such as *renew* and *direct* carry lexical meaning and are known as **lexemes**. There is a notational convention whereby morphs are written in lower case italics and morphemes are written in small capitals but the distinction is not universally observed and many analysts use only the term 'morpheme'. A small number of morphs are empty, such as the *s* in the German compound noun *Liebesbrief*, whose role is to connect *Liebe* 'love' and *Brief* 'letter'.

Morphs are **bound** or **free**. Bound morphs do not occur on their own but only as part of words, e.g. *mis-* in *misdirect*, *-ness* in *kindness*, *-es* in *fishes*. Free morphs can occur on their own as words, e.g. *quickly* in *They quickly extinguished the fire*. The stem *quick* is also free, since it can occur as a word, e.g. *The quick fox evaded the hounds*.

A morpheme may be realized by more than one morph. In spoken English, [Plural] is realized by /s/, /z/ or/z/. The choice of morph is said to be phonologically conditioned, since it depends on the final segment in the **stem** to which the plural suffix is added. /s/ is added to stems ending in a voiceless consonant: e.g. *cats* /kats/, *cups* /cʌps/; /z/ is added to stems ending in a voiced consonant or a vowel: e.g. *logs* /lɔgz/, *pillows* /piləʊz/. /s/, /z/ and /z/ are allomorphs or morpheme alternants; that is, they are alternative realizations of the one morpheme 'Plural'.

For other sets of **allomorphs** the choice is lexically conditioned, being controlled by the choice of lexeme but not by the sounds. In Latin, nominative case and singular number are realized by the inflection *-a* if the lexeme is a feminine noun such as *femina* 'woman', but by *-us* if the lexeme is a masculine noun such as *dominus* 'master'. See **AFFIX, AGGLUTINATIVE, CONDITIONING, CUMULATION, FORMATIVE, FUSION, INFLECTION, PROCESS, ROOT, ROOT-AND-PATTERN.**

MORPHEME ALTERNANT
See **MORPH**.

MORPHEME STRUCTURE CONDITION
In the **Sound Pattern of English**, a condition capturing some regular pattern in the structure of morphs; e.g. that no native English morph begins with a sequence of more than three consonants, as in *spring*.

MORPHEME
See **MORPH**.

MORPHEMICS
An approach to **morphology** that considers the **morpheme** to be the basic unit of analysis. See **MORPH, WORD AND PARADIGM**.

MORPHOLOGICAL OPERATION
Any operation that changes the shape of a stem, such as the addition of **affixes**, **gemination, reduplication** and **ablaut**.

MORPHOLOGICAL TYPOLOGY
The study of the patterns of derivational and inflectional morphology in the world's languages. See **AGGLUTINATION, FUSION, INFLECTION, MORPH.**

MORPHOLOGIZATION
A type of **grammaticalization** in which a **word** becomes a **morph** inside a word.

MORPHOLOGY
The study of the structure of **words** and of the **grammatical categories** realized by **morphs**: e.g. *trickster* consists of the **stem** *trick* and the **suffix** *-ster* indicating an agent, Turkish *evlerini* consists of the stem *ev-*, the suffix *-ler* expressing **plural**, the suffix *-i* expressing third-**person possessive**, the final suffix *-i* realizing **accusative** case, and *n*, an empty morph or **interfix** between the two morphs *i*. See **AFFIX, AGGLUTINATIVE, CONDITIONING, DERIVATIONAL**

MORPHOLOGY, FUSION, GRAMMATICAL CATEGORY, INFLECTION, PROCESS, ROOT, ROOT-AND-PATTERN.

MORPHOPHONEME

In some approaches, especially American structuralism, a unit realized as two **phonemes**. Such units were employed to deal with the problem of segments that sometimes realize different phonemes and sometimes are not in contrast. E.g. in *loaf* and *loaves*, /f/ and /v/ do not contrast, although they do in /*fine*/ and /*vine*/; *loaf* and *loaves* are not different **lexical words**. /loaf/ could be analysed as /loaF/, the capital *F* representing a morphophoneme which can be realized as /f/ in the context of [singular] and /v/ in the context of [plural].

MORPHOPHONEMIC ALTERNATION

The occurrence of two or more different **phonemes** in the same **morpheme** under different morphological conditions. E.g. the alternation between /k/ and /g/ in Latin *reks* 'king-NOM' and *regem* 'king-ACC', or between /f/ and /v/ in *hoof* and *hooves*, or between /k/ and /s/ in *electric* and *electricity*. See **BASE, CONDITIONING, MORPHOPHONEME**.

MORPHOPHONEMICS

Especially in the USA, the analysis of morphophonemic **alternations**.

MORPHOPHONOLOGY

Especially in Europe. See **MORPHOPHONEMICS**.

MORPHOSYNTACTIC CATEGORIES

Categories such as **number, case, person**, tense, **mood** that are realized by **affixes**, especially by **inflectional** affixes. Such categories are central in the interaction of **morphology** and **syntax**, in **agreement** and **government** and in the signalling of important distinctions of meaning such as **singular** vs **plural, present tense** vs **past tense** and so on. E.g. The Turkish word *ed-iyor-d-um* 'I was doing' realizes the grammatical (or morphosyntactic) categories of aspect, tense, person and **number**. It has the morphosyntactic category of **imperfective** aspect – *iyor*, past tense – *d* and first-person singular – *um*. See **GRAMMATICAL CATEGORY, INFLECTION, MOOD, MORPH, TENSE AND ASPECT**.

MORPHOSYNTACTIC WORD

A representation of a **word** as a **stem** plus the relevant **grammatical categories** or **morphosyntactic categories**. Thus, *children* is CHILD + plural, *left* is LEAVE + past tense, *was leaving* is LEAVE + past tense, progressive, singular, Latin *pugnabit* 'he/she will fight' is PUGN + future tense, singular, third person, indicative mood.

MORPHOSYNTAX

The analysis of **morphosyntactic categories**, which takes in both morphology and syntax.

MORPHOTACTICS

The study of the order of **morphemes** in **words**. For instance, in Turkish verbs the order of morphemes is **stem aspect tense person/number**, as in *ed-iyor-d-um* 'I was doing'. Also the study of the relations between morphemes in **clauses** and **sentences**, e.g. *have* and *-ed* in *have phoned*. See **AGREEMENT, GOVERNMENT, MORPH, MORPHOSYNTACTIC CATEGORIES**.

MOTHER TONGUE

The first language acquired by a speaker in childhood.

MOTHERESE

The type of simplified language used by parents or caregivers when talking to very young children in their care.

MOTIVATED

Applied to a sign which is considered non-arbitrary, to an extension of meaning that is based on conceptual parallels, such as the extension of *head* from the human head to head of a department, and to a change in grammar based on **meaning**, such as the extension of *go to* from movement in space to movement towards future events. See **ARBITRARY SIGN, ICONIC SIGN**.

MOTIVATION

Whatever need or desire leads a speaker to learn a language additional to their first language.

MOTOR THEORY OF SPEECH PERCEPTION

The theory that humans perceive speech sounds by mentally making the articulatory movements required to produce them. See **ARTICULATION**.

MOTU

Austronesian. Papua New Guinea. Basis of a pidgin, Hiri Motu or Police Motu.

MOVE

1. In the **Minimalist Program**, an operation that copies part of a **tree** and **merges** it with another part of the tree, leaving a copy behind. See **MOVE ALPHA, MOVEMENT**. 2. See **EXCHANGE**.

MOVE α

See **MOVE ALPHA**.

MOVE ALPHA

In **Government and Binding Theory** and **Principles and Parameters**, a general rule applying to **trees** showing **constituent structure** and stating that any **constituent** can be moved to any position. Many structures resulting from the application of the rule are incorrect but are filtered out by various **constraints**. The single rule replaced a number of separate movement rules, each of which moves a specific type of constituent, an NP or wh phrase or auxiliary and so on. See **SUBJACENCY CONDITION**.

MOVEMENT

In **generative grammar**, a process by which constituents are moved from one position to another. E.g. in *John is going to give this book to Sandy, is* can be moved to the front to give an **interrogative** sentence, *Is John going to give this book to Sandy?*, and *to Sandy* can be moved to the front to give *To Sandy John is going to give this book*. Early **transformational grammar** had a separate **rule** for each type of constituent moved, but in later models there was one general movement rule, made possible by the use of constraints to check the output of the rules. Movement is also called 'permutation' and constituents are said to be permuted. See MOVE, MOVE ALPHA.

MOVEMENT RULE

See MOVEMENT.

MP

See MINIMALIST PROGRAM.

M-PRINCIPLE

See NEO-GRICEAN PRAGMATICS.

MT

See MACHINE TRANSLATION.

MULTIDIMENSIONAL ANALYSIS

A complex type of statistical analysis applied to various dimensions of a set of data and the measurements for each dimension. For example, the number of wh **relative clauses** used by one speaker in casual conversation over a six-month period constitutes a one-dimensional dataset. The number of wh relative clauses used by several speakers in casual conversation over six months constitutes a two-dimensional dataset. The number of wh and th relative clauses used by several speakers in casual conversation over six months constitutes a three-dimensional dataset. Multidimensional analysis has been applied most intensely in the analysis of different types of **text**.

MULTIDIMENSIONAL SCALING

A method of analysing sets of **lexical words** by having speakers estimate, via experimental tests, the extent to which a given member of the set is like or unlike the other members.

MULTILATERAL OPPOSITION

An **opposition** between three or more segments that contrast in a particular dimension. Thus /p/, /t/ and /k/ are all **voiceless** stops that contrast in their **place of articulation**. See PRAGUE SCHOOL.

MULTILINGUAL

The use of two or more languages by an individual or community, in contrast with **bilingualism** and **monolingualism**.

MULTILINGUALISM
The use of multiple languages by an individual speaker or by a community. Multilingualism is more common than **monolingualism**. See also **BILINGUALISM**.

MULTIMODALITY
The use of several different communicative channels, as, for example, in addition to the audio-lingual modality, gestural modalities like signing and lip-reading.

MULTIVALUED FEATURE
A **feature** which involves more than just a binary split between the presence or absence of a property. E.g. **vowels** are high, mid-high, mid-low and low.

MULTI-WORD EXPRESSION
An alternative term for **lexical bundle**.

MUNDARI
Language family also known as Munda. Approx. 2M speakers, India, Bangladesh and Nepal.

MURMUR
A term used in the classification of **voice quality** as an alternative to **breathy voice**. More than the usual amount of air passes through the **glottis**, producing a husky sound quality. In English, some speakers have breathy voice as a permanent feature of their speech, but it is normally restricted to expressive effects, as the 'sexy' voice associated with some female screen idols. **Vowels** produced in this way are often referred to as 'murmured' vowels. They are not usually phonologically distinctive but are found in **Gujarati**, where they appear to have developed from a final /h/ and two open vowels, /ɛ/ and /ɔ/.

MURRAY, Sir James (1837–1915)
The editor of the *Oxford English Dictionary* from 1879–1915, he pioneered the system still in use today for the collection and analysis of data based on **synchronic linguistics** and diachronic principles.

MURRAY, Lindley (1745–1826)
A prolific writer of English school textbooks, best known for his *English Grammar* (1795) which, with its successors, was very influential in both Britain and America.

MUSKOGEAN
Language family, south-east USA. Includes Muskogee and Choctaw.

MUTATION
A morphological **process** signalling syntactic links between, in particular, nouns and other words in a **phrase** or **clause** by means of changes in a **consonant** in the noun stem. E.g. in Scottish Gaelic possessive constructions, *an cu* 'the dog' vs *mo chu* 'my dog' (the *c* becomes zero), prepositional phrases, *Màiri*

'Mary' – *do Mhàiri* 'to Mary' (the *m* becomes *v*), and other constructions; in Finnish, certain case forms, such as *tupa* 'hut' vs *tuvassa* 'in the hut'.

MUTATIVE

An **aspect** construction signalling a change of **state** or property; e.g. *She fell ill*, Russian *zabolela* 'fell ill' (from *bolet'* 'to be ill' and *za-* signalling movement into a new state). See TENSE AND ASPECT.

MUTISM

In **clinical linguistics**, a disorder characterized by the inability to produce speech, although people affected by it may be able to understand and produce written language.

MUTUAL ASSIMILATION

See ASSIMILATION.

MUTUAL INFORMATION

The information shared by two items. Where two items share information, knowing one of the items reduces how much information has to be discovered about the other one.

MYOGRAPHY

An instrumental technique for measuring airflow through the mouth and nose.

MYRINGOTOMY

In **clinical linguistics**, draining fluid from the middle ear by making an incision in the eardrum.

NA-DENE
Language family proposed by Sapir to include Athapaskan, Eyak, Tlingit and Haida.

NAGA
Sino-Tibetan Language family. Approx. 1M speakers, India.

NAHUATL
Uto-Aztecan. Approx. 1.3M speakers, Central Mexico. The language of the Aztecs.

NAME
See **PROPER NOUN**.

NARRATIVE
A story about events. They are presented as happening in a particular order. They are linked by all involving one and the same character or characters and by the fact of one event leading to another and producing effects. Narratives have plots, consisting of the evolution of events and the interactions of characters with plans and intentions. Plots have resolutions: the hero or heroine meets with success in some domain, the criminals get their comeuppance and so on.

NARROW
A transcription that tries to be as exhaustive as possible. Opposite **broad**.

NARROWING
The process by which, over time, the meaning of a lexical item is restricted. E.g. the meaning of *deer* has been narrowed from 'animal' to a particular kind of animal.

N-ARY FEATURE
See **MULTIVALUED FEATURE**.

NASAL
1. A term in the description of the **manner of articulation** of speech sounds. Sounds made when the velum is lowered so that air escapes through the nose. The term applies to both **consonants** and **vowels**. With consonants there is complete oral **closure** at some point of articulation; thus English **bilabial** [m] *ham*, **alveolar** [n] *ban*, and **velar** [ŋ] *bang*. Other languages illustrate other possibilities, thus Spanish **palatal** [ɲ] *señor*. In English, nasal consonants are usually voiced, though positionally they can be devoiced as in English

following *s* [smo]. In nasal **vowels** air escapes simultaneously through the mouth and nose. English has no distinctively nasal vowels, though they may be **nasalized** in some contexts, as in [mãn]. In French, oral and nasal vowels contrast. 2. In **J&H Distinctive Feature Theory**, a feature characterizing a **segment** exhibiting **formants**, interpreted as representing nasality 3. In **SPE Distinctive Feature Theory** nasal segments are produced by lowering the **velum** so that air can pass through the nasal tract; non nasal segments are produced with a raised velum which blocks the passage of air.

NASAL HARMONY

Nasality spreads over several **segments**, most commonly within the **word**. Characteristic of some languages in West Africa. See **HARMONY**, **VOWEL HARMONY**.

NASAL PLOSION

The release of a **plosive** consonant **homorganic** with a preceding **consonant** through the nose rather than the mouth, as in the **syllabic** nasal in *sudden* [sʌdn]]; also known as nasal release.

NASALIZED

The property of an otherwise oral sound that has acquired a nasal quality from contiguous sounds. Thus English **vowels**, which are normally non-nasal, sometimes, when preceding or following a nasal **consonant**, can be nasalized as in *man* [mãn].

NASOPHARYNX

That part of the **pharynx** adjacent to the nasal cavity.

NATIVE LANGUAGE

The **first language** acquired by a child, typically from its mother.

NATIVE SPEAKER

A person who speaks a particular language as a native language. See **FIRST LANGUAGE**.

NATIVE SPEAKER INTUITION

The intuitive grasp that native speakers of a language have of its grammatical structures, vocabulary and the interpretations of sentences.

NATURAL GENDER

See **GENDER**.

NATURAL KIND TERMS

In philosophy, many predicates apply to kinds of substances or individual entities that are considered to occur naturally in the world. Examples are *gold*, *water*, *coal*, *hyena*, and *snowdrop*. Reference to natural kinds is typically carried out, in English, by means of bare plural NPs for individual entities or by bare singular

NPs for substances: e.g. *Snowdrops flower in winter*, *Hyenas have powerful jaws*, *Water is essential for life*. See **ARGUMENT, PREDICATE, PREDICATOR, PROPOSITION**.

NATURAL LANGUAGE

1. A human language like French, English or Zulu spoken by a community, as distinguished from a **formal language** or a **computer language**. 2. **Natural language processing**, NLP, is used in **computational linguistics** to denote systems that interact between computers and humans: natural language generation converts information from computer data bases into a readable representation of human language; **natural language understanding** converts human language into formal representations that can then be manipulated by computer programs. NLP implies that computers must to able to **model** natural language in sense (1). See **ARTIFICIAL INTELLIGENCE**.

NATURAL LANGUAGE INTERFACE

The means whereby a human, or a computer, can interact with another computer, or human, using ordinary natural language, e.g. in question posing and answering.

NATURAL LANGUAGE PROCESSING

Computer processing of natural language.

NATURAL LANGUAGE UNDERSTANDING

Computational analysis of natural language input that aims to produce a semantic analysis and hence human-like understanding.

NATURAL MORPHOLOGY

A theory of **morphology**, developed in Germany and Austria and based on the idea that morphological patterns obey 'laws' of naturalness. For example, speakers prefer **words** to have a transparent structure. The addition of **affixes** to **stems**, as in *cow* vs *cows*, produces an obvious structure, but the vowel change from *mouse* to *mice* does not. Within a given language, some affixes are more transparent than others. In English *-ness* and *-ing* are very transparent; they have only one form and can be added to a very large number of stems without changing the shape of the stem. In contrast, *-ity* is added to a small number of stems, changes their shape (e.g. from *electric* to *electricity*) and its meaning is more difficult to specify. See **MORPH**.

NATURAL PHONOLOGY

A phonological theory developed in the 1970s that sought to distinguish between 'natural' processes, such as the voicing of **intervocalic** stops, which are thought to be universal and innate, and 'learned rules', such as the devoicing of final **stops** in German, which are thought to be language specific.

NATURAL SEMANTIC METALANGUAGE

See **NATURAL SEMANTICS**.

NATURAL SEMANTICS

A theory of semantics based on the idea that it is possible to arrive at a set of semantically minimal or primitive expressions which cannot be further broken down and can be used to analyse all the meanings of **lexical words**, and **grammatical categories**, in a given language. These semantic primitives constitute a natural semantic **metalanguage** and form a set of lexical universals, in the sense that every primitive has an exact translation in every human language. Although the primitives are labelled 'lexical', they include bound **morphs** and **fixed expressions** as well as words. Examples of the primitives are *I, you, someone, think, know, want, feel, good, bad, big, small, place, here, far, above, near, because, if, maybe, not*. The method of analysis using the primitives is called 'reductive paraphrase analysis'. Natural Semantics was developed and elaborated by Anna Wierzbicka.

NATURAL SIGN

See **ICONIC SIGN**.

NATURALISM

In medieval philosophy, a theory that there is an intrinsic connection between the form of a word and its meaning. See **ARBITRARY SIGN, ICONIC SIGN, ONOMATOPOEIA, NOMINALISM**.

NAVAJO

Athapaskan. Approx. 148K speakers, south-west USA.

NEAR-SYNONYMY

The relationship between **lexical words** that are not synonyms but whose meanings differ in very minor respects, such as intensity, e.g. *pull* vs *heave*, or duration, e.g. *calm* (short-term state) vs *placid* (long-term state). See **SYNONYMY**.

NECESSARY CONDITION

A condition such that if it does not exist, then some situation does not exist. For puddles to be frozen, it is necessary that the temperature falls below zero on the Celsius scale. No below-zero temperature, no frozen puddles.

NEGATION

1. In **speech act** theory, the process of denying something that has been asserted. 2. In logic, the negative connector *not* that applies to **propositions**: e.g. *Sue passed* → *not [Sue passed]* = 'It is not the case that Sue passed'. 3. The presence of a **negative** in a construction. See **CONNECTOR, LOGIC, NEGATIVE**.

NEGATIVE

1. A **clause** or **sentence** used to assert that something is not the case; e.g. *The Prime Minister has not resigned.* 2. A **phrase** or **word** denoting the absence or opposite of some property; e.g. *unhappy*. See **CLAUSAL NEGATION, CONSTITUENT NEGATION, DERIVATIONAL NEGATION**.

NEGATIVE FACE
See **FACE**.

NEGATIVE FRONTING
In English grammar, a **construction** in which a negative word or phrase is at the front of a **clause**, followed by an auxiliary verb, the subject NP and the rest of the clause. E.g. *Never have I seen such a mess*, *Nowhere will you find such delicate engraving*. See **SUBJECT-AUX INVERSION**.

NEGATIVE POLARITY ITEM
An item whose use is controlled by the contrast between **negative** and **positive** (the negative and positive poles or extremes on a scale). E.g. *some* typically occurs in positive **clauses** – *We saw some snakes, She bought some bread*. *Any* normally occurs in negative clauses – *We didn't see any snakes, She didn't buy any bread*. Some negative clauses have no overt negative but require *any* and exclude *some*; e.g. *I seldom see any snakes*. See **NEGATION**.

NEGATIVE TRANSFER
See **INTERFERENCE**.

NEGOTIATION OF MEANING
The process by which **interlocutors** agree the interpretation of their **utterances** in a given **context**. See **COMMON GROUND, CONSTRUE, CONTEXT**.

NEG-RAISING
See **TRANSFERRED NEGATION**.

NENETS
Samoyedic, Uralic. Approx. 26.5K speakers, in an area stretching from the White Sea in European Russia to the Taymyr Peninsula in Siberia.

NEOCLASSICAL COMPOUND
A compound noun in which both **combining forms** are borrowed from **Latin** or **Greek** and typically do not occur on their own as **words** of English. E.g. *anthropo-logy, leuko-cyte*. See **COMPOUND WORD, ROOT COMPOUND, STEM, SYNTHETIC COMPOUND**.

NEOGRAMMARIAN
The generation of younger German philologists in the late nineteenth century who opposed many of the older generation's ideas on sound change in **comparative linguistics**. They were particularly associated with the principle that all sound change is regular.

NEOGRAMMARIAN HYPOTHESIS
The view, adopted by the **Neogrammarians**, that sound change is regular – cf. their slogan 'sound laws suffer no exceptions'. See **COMPARATIVE METHOD**.

NEO-GRICEAN PRAGMATICS

The refinement and extension of Grice's theory of maxims of conversation. One version of the theory rests on two principles. The Q-Principle (Q stands for Quantity) enjoins speakers to make their contributions sufficient and to say as much as they can (in the light of the R-Principle). The R-Principle (R stands for Relation) enjoins speakers to make their contributions necessary and to say no more than they have to. The Q-Principle brings together Grice's Maxims of Quantity and Manner and the R-Principle unites the Maxims of Quantity, Relation and Manner.

A second version of the theory distinguishes between maxims, or principles, governing the speaker's actual utterances and maxims governing the information conveyed by utterances. The latter are divided into maxims for speakers and maxims for hearers. According to the Q-principle (Quantity) speakers should not say less than is required, and hearers should assume that propositions left unsaid are false. The I-principle (Informativeness) enjoins speakers to say only as much as is required to get their message across and encourages hearers to give utterances as rich an interpretation as is normally justified by world-knowledge and culture-specific knowledge. This enrichment is controlled by a series of sub-principles, such as the one that requires the question *Have you got the time?* to be answered, not with *yes*, but with *It's 1.30*, or whatever the time is. The M-principle (Manner) enjoins speakers not to use convoluted or unusual syntax and vocabulary unless they want to indicate that a situation is abnormal in some way. Hearers are to interpret unusual or convoluted language as indicating an abnormal situation or speakers' presenting a situation in some abnormal fashion. Thus, *It's not improbable that large bonuses will be paid* indicates that the speaker is not declaring that bonuses absolutely will be paid. See **IMPLICATURE, MAXIMS OF CONVERSATION, POLITENESS PRINCIPLE**.

NEOLOGISM

A word newly introduced into a language, e.g. by being borrowed or invented. Examples of words that are neologisms in 2012 are *biofuel, energy efficient, renewables*. In a year or two they will no longer be neologisms. In the 1940s *airlift, baby-sit, bikini* and *gremlin* were neologisms but are now just ordinary words of English.

NEPALI

Indo-Iranian, Indo-European. Approx. 17M speakers, Nepal, India and Bhutan.

NESTING

The **embedding** of a **constituent** inside another constituent. The figure below shows the structure of *That the fact that she resigned shocked everybody was obvious*. The sentence *that she resigned* is nested inside the noun phrase *the fact* and inside the sentence *That the fact [...] shocked everybody*. A special type of nesting is self-embedding or **centre-embedding**.

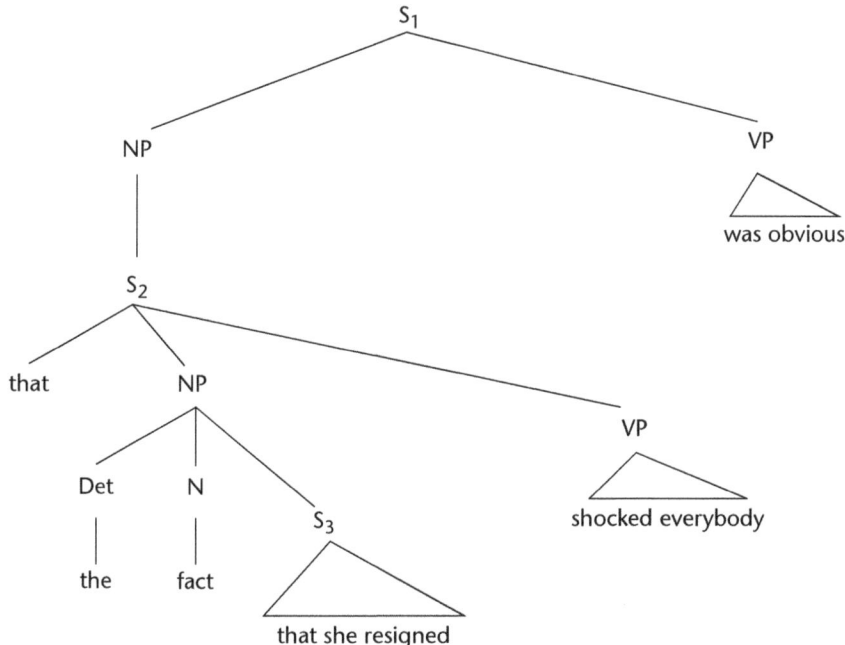

NETWORK

A number of computers and other electronic equipment that are connected together so that information, etc. can be shared.

NEUROGENIC

In **clinical linguistics**, applied to disorders of a neurological nature.

NEUROLINGUISTICS

The science of the relationship between the brain and nervous system and the knowledge and use of language.

NEUTER

Especially in **Indo-European** languages, a **gender** or class of **nouns** whose members typically denote entities perceived as **inanimate**: e.g. Russian *derevo* 'tree', German *das Wasser* 'water'. Exceptions in German are *das Weib* 'woman' and *das Mädchen* 'girl'. See AGREEMENT, FEMININE, MASCULINE.

NEUTRAL

Occupying a position between two or more specified categories. In **phonetics**, referring to a lip position that is neither **rounded** nor **spread**; or **vowels** produced in the middle of the **vowel space**, i.e. neither front nor back, high nor low; typically [ə].

NEUTRALIZATION

When in a particular context there is no **opposition** between two **segments** that elsewhere are in opposition, they are neutralized. In **phonology**, the absence in a particular **environment** of a contrast that occurs elsewhere. Thus, in English, the distinction between voiced and voiceless **stops** is neutralized in word-initial position after /s/ – so /spɪn/ and /skɪn/ but not */sbɪn/ or */sgɪn/. See **ARCHIPHONEME, DISTRIBUTION**.

NEXUS

1. In **Role and Reference Grammar**, the type of syntactic linkage between two units, including the linkage between **clauses**. Three types are recognized: **coordination, subordination, cosubordination**. 2. Jespersen's term for a construction involving predication (in contrast with **junction**); e.g. *The volcano erupted*, (*We heard*) *the volcano erupt*. See **CONJUNCTION, JUNCTURE, PREDICATE**.

N-GRAM

A sub-sequence of n items from a sequence of items. The items can be **phonemes**, letters, **syllables**, **words** or pairs of words.

NGUNI

Subgroup of **Bantu** languages. South Africa, Lesotho and Swaziland. Includes Xhosa and **Zulu**.

NICE PROPERTIES

In English grammar, the properties that distinguish **modal verbs**: they combine directly with the **negative** – *can't help* vs *doesn't help*; they occur on their own in **interrogatives** – *Can she help?* vs *Did she help?*; they combine with *so* to function as what is called 'code' in cases of **ellipsis** – *She can help and so can I* vs **She writes novels and so write I*; they carry emphasis – *She CAN help* vs *She DOES help*. The initial letters of 'negative', 'interrogative', 'code' and 'emphasis' make up the word 'nice'. See **AUXILIARY, SEMI-AUXILIARY**.

NIDA, Eugene (1914–2011)

American structural linguist well known for his *A Synopsis of English Syntax*, a full-scale grammar of English according to Bloomfieldian principles of constituent structure analysis, and his widely used textbook *Morphology, a Descriptive Analysis of Words*. He was a committed Christian and his work as the director of the Summer Institute of Linguistics was influential in translation theory in general and Bible translation in particular.

NIGER-CONGO

A large family of languages encompassing the languages of West Africa and the languages spoken south of the Sahara, including the **Bantu** family (1,500 languages, 250M speakers) but excluding the **Khoisan languages** group.

NILO-SAHARAN

A controversial grouping of the **Nilotic** languages with the other languages spoken between the upper Nile and the Congo.

NILOTIC LANGUAGES
Language family in East Africa including **Luo** and **Maasai**, both spoken in Kenya and Tanzania.

NIUEAN
Malayo-Polynesian. Approx. 11K speakers, Niue and New Zealand.

NIVKH (GILYAK)
Language isolate. Approx. 1K speakers, on the lower Amur river and Sakhalin.

NODE
Any point connected by lines in a **tree diagram** or other graph.

NOISE
In **acoustic phonetics**, randomly generated sound. It usually interferes with a signal.

NOMENCLATURE
The system of terminology used in naming objects.

NOMINAL
1. Relating to a **noun**. (From Latin *nomen* 'name, noun'.) E.g. *liquid* is a nominal **stem**. The addition of *-ize* creates the **denominal** verb *liquidize*. 2. Any **constituent** that functions like a **noun phrase**. E.g. in *That he refused shocked everyone*, the clause *that he refused* is the **subject** of *shocked everyone*; in *I know why he refused*, the clause *why he refused* is the **object** of *know*. Such subject and object clauses are called nominal clauses or noun clauses. Just as common, however, is **complement clause**. The terms 'nominal phrase' and 'nominal group' are alternatives to **noun phrase**. 3. In some phrase structure models, the N' component of a noun phrase. See **X-BAR SYNTAX**.

NOMINAL GROUP
See **NOUN PHRASE**.

NOMINAL RELATIVE CLAUSE
See **FREE RELATIVE CLAUSE**.

NOMINAL SENTENCE
A **sentence** with no **verb**. Most frequent in spoken language – *Everything in order*, *Nobody at home*, *Nothing simpler!*, but also found in literature – *Fog everywhere. Fog up the river. Fog down the river* (Dickens, *Bleak House*). Also called a verbless sentence. See **NOMINAL**.

NOMINALISM
In medieval philosophy, the doctrine that universal terms such as *dog* did not correspond to anything in reality except the individual objects that could be referred to by means of the term. The opposing doctrine was **realism**. It held that universal terms corresponded to some universal entity over and above all the

individual entities – in this case *dogness* as opposed to *(my/the/a) dog*. See **ARBITRARY SIGN, ICONIC SIGN, ONOMATOPOEIA, NATURALISM**.

NOMINALIZATION

1. Any process by which a **noun** is derived from a word belonging to another **word class**: e.g. *transmission* from *transmit*, *laziness* from *lazy*. *Transmission*, *laziness*, etc. are said to be nominalizations. 2. The process by which **clauses** or **verb phrases** are converted into **constituents** functioning like **noun phrases**: e.g. *The dog ran away* → *The dog's running away* annoyed him or *The dog running away* annoyed him. The result of the process, *The dog's/dog running away*, is a nominalization. See **NOMINAL**.

NOMINATIVE

A **case** whose main use is to mark the **subject** of a **clause**: e.g. Russian, *Anna otkryla fortochku* 'Anna-NOM open small-window-ACC, Anna opened the window'. The nominative reflects the idea that the case marks a given noun being used to name some entity. In languages with case inflections, the nominative case form is the one used in citations and as the heading for dictionary entries. See **GRAMMATICAL FUNCTION, SUBJECTIVE**.

NOMINATIVE-ACCUSATIVE LANGUAGES

Languages with a nominative and accusative case system, though it would be more accurate to talk about nominative-accusative **constructions**. See **CASE**.

NON-CONSONANTAL

In **J&H Distinctive Feature Theory**, an **acoustic** distinctive feature involving high energy and a lack of an obstruction in the vocal tract, associated with vowels. See **CONSONANTAL, DISTINCTIVE FEATURES**.

NON-ANTERIOR

See **ANTERIOR**.

NON-ASSERTIVE

A speech act that is not **assertive**. See **ASSERTIVE**.

NONCE WORD

1. See **HAPAX LEGOMENON**. 2. A word invented on some particular occasion, and afterwards used little or not at all.

NON-CONCATENATIVE MORPHOLOGY

Any morphological system in which **syntactic linkage** and **grammatical categories** are signalled, not by the addition of **affixes** to **stems** but by changes in the stems themselves. E.g. *Swim* vs *swam* v *swum*, Scottish Gaelic *an la fada* 'the day long, the long day' v *an oidhche fhada* 'the night long, the long night', where the agreement is signalled by changes in the initial segment of the adjective, *f* v *fh* (zero). See **AGREEMENT, CONCATENATION, CONCATENATIVE MORPHOLOGY, GOVERNMENT**.

NON-CONFIGURATIONAL LANGUAGES
See CONFIGURATIONAL LANGUAGES.

NON-CONSTITUENT COORDINATION
See GAPPING.

NON-CONTINUANT
See CONTINUANT.

NON-COUNT NOUN
See MASS NOUN.

NON-DEFINING RELATIVE
See RELATIVE CLAUSE.

NON-DESCRIPTIVE MEANING
See DESCRIPTIVE MEANING.

NON-DISCRETE
Applied to sets of items consisting of two subsets not separated by a distinct boundary but by zones containing intermediate categories. For a given member of such a set, it may not be clear which subset it belongs to. Such sets are called non-discrete categories. E.g. experimental evidence shows that sentences are not just grammatical or ungrammatical but that some sentences are more, or less, grammatical than others. Verbs are not just transitive or intransitive but on a scale of transitivity. A thing that is not big is not necessarily small; it may be of average size. A non-discrete grammar is one that includes non-discrete categories. See FUZZY GRAMMAR, GRADIENCE, OPPOSITENESS, TRANSITIVITY.

NON-DISCRETE GRAMMAR
See NON-DISCRETE.

NON-DURATIVE
Applied to **verbs** and **adverbs** that do not express duration. E.g. *She reached the summit* (*in two days* but not *for two days*), *They found the dog* (*after two hours* but not *for two hours*.) See ACHIEVEMENT, AKTIONSART, SEMELFACTIVE.

NON-FACTIVE VERB
Like **factive verbs**, non-factive verbs take a **complement clause**, but speakers who use non-factive verbs do not presuppose that the complement clause is true: e.g. *I supposed that Gordon was leaving*. Non-factive verbs do not normally take direct object **gerunds** – **I supposed Gordon's leaving* vs *I regretted Gordon's leaving* – but do take the **accusative and infinitive** construction, as in *I supposed Gordon to be leaving*. See ENTAILMENT, PRESUPPOSITION.

NON-FINITE CLAUSE
See CLAUSE, NON-FINITE VERB.

NON-FINITE VERB

A verb form that has no markings for **tense**, **number** or **person**. English has various non-finite verb forms: *(to)* **infinitives**, marked by a preceding *to* – *We all like to make fun of this theory*; gerunds, marked by a suffix *-ing* (*I love swimming*); **participles**, also marked by a suffix *-ing* – *Reading his latest novel, I fell asleep*; and the bare verb stem – *Can you help me move this desk?*. *Move* is called a bare or zero infinitive. Other languages have a range of parallel non-finite forms. In some recent work, being non-finite is regarded as a property of **clauses**, not of verbs. See **FINITE VERB, GERUND, GERUNDIVE, SUPINE**.

NON-LINEAR PHONOLOGY

A phonological representation which consists of more than just a linear sequence of **segments**. **Prosodic phonology** in addition to a linear string of **phonematic units** proposes a set of prosodies. **Autosegmental phonology** proposes a set of parallel **tiers** each representing some aspect of an utterance and with a variety of connections between the various tiers. See **DEPENDENCY PHONOLOGY, METRICAL PHONOLOGY, PROSODY**.

NON-NATIVE SPEAKER

A person who speaks a particular language not as a native language. See **NATIVE LANGUAGE, SECOND LANGUAGE**.

NON-PAST TENSE

In certain languages, a new label for the traditional **present tense**, which refers not just to present time but also to future time. E.g. English *April is leaving right now* and *April is leaving next month*. **Past tense** remains, as protypical past tense verbs refer to past time: e.g. *April was leaving her office when I saw her (this morning/last week/last month)*. See **FUTURE TENSE, TENSE AND ASPECT**.

NON-PRO-DROP LANGUAGE

See **PRO-DROP LANGUAGE**.

NON-RESTRICTIVE

See **RESTRICTIVE**.

NON-RESTRICTIVE RELATIVE CLAUSE

See **RELATIVE CLAUSE**.

NON-RHOTIC

See **RHOTIC**.

NON-ROUNDED

See **ROUNDED**.

NON-SEGMENTAL

See **SUPRASEGMENTAL**.

NONSENSE WORD

An invented word which follows the conventions of word structure but is meaningless, as in nonsense verse like 'Jabberwocky' by Lewis Carroll. Often used in **ear training** for phonetics students.

NON-SPECIFIC REFERENCE

See REFERENCE.

NON-STANDARD

The opposite of standard. See STANDARD LANGUAGE.

NON-STRIDENT

See DISTINCTIVE FEATURES.

NONTENSE

See LAX.

NON-TERMINAL SYMBOL

In early **generative grammar**, a symbol that can be rewritten by a **phrase structure rule**. See TERMINAL STRING, TERMINAL SYMBOL, TRANSFORMATIONAL GRAMMAR.

NON-VERBAL COMMUNICATION

Any communication not involving words; e.g. hand gestures, facial expressions, body posture, and noises such as sighs, raspberries, tutting noises and so on. See PARALINGUISTIC.

NON-VOCALIC

1. In **J&H Distinctive Feature Theory** an acoustic **distinctive feature** associated with no well-defined formant structure. Opposite **vocalic**. See DISTINCTIVE FEATURES, ACOUSTIC. 2. See VOCALIC.

NOOTKA

Wakashan. Approx. 200 speakers, British Columbia.

NORM

Behaviour that is typical or expected. See NORMATIVE RULE.

NORMALIZATION

This is a way of ensuring that a **database** has as general a structure as possible so that all sorts of enquiries can be addressed to the database and sensible answers obtained. In corpus linguistic work, normalization typically involves adjusting the analysis of frequencies so that two items can be sensibly compared. If word X occurs 25 times in a corpus of 1,000 words and word Y occurs 500 times in a corpus of 50,000 words, there is no point in saying that Y is more frequent than X. If we look instead at the number of occurrences in a thousand words, X turns out to be more frequent than Y.

NORMATIVE RULE

A **rule** setting out a norm, i.e. what users of a language should say or write according to some ideology rather than a rule describing what users actually say or write. An example is the rule that *different* is followed by *from* and not *to*. See **PRESCRIPTIVE GRAMMAR**.

NORTH GERMANIC

Germanic subgroup containing the Scandinavian languages **Norwegian**, **Swedish** and **Danish**, together with Faroese and **Icelandic**.

NORWEGIAN

Germanic, **Indo-European**. 4.3M speakers, Norway. Two main varieties, Bokmal and Nynorsk.

NOTATION

The system of signs or symbols used to represent information, as, for example, in science or music. In linguistics **phonetic transcription** is a notation for the **transcription** of speech. **Logical Form** is sometimes used to represent semantic structures.

NOTIONAL

Based on meaning, independently of the grammar of any language. Thus, time is a notional category divided into past, present and future time but **tense** is one of the **grammatical categories**, and English, e.g., can be analysed as having **past tense** and **non-past tense**. A given language may or may not have a **future tense**. For instance, English poses problems of analysis: *I will phone tomorrow* has a component of intention and *They shall pay the fine* has a component of obligation. That is, the sentences do not just refer to future time. In many other languages future time is referred to entirely by means of **mood**. Time can also be referred to by means of **adverbs** such as *today, next week, yesterday*. Word classes were traditionally given notional definitions – a **noun** was said to denote a person, place or thing – but are nowadays defined on the basis of **form** and **distribution** as well as meaning. See **FORM CLASS, MODALITY, TENSE AND ASPECT**.

NOTIONAL AGREEMENT

Agreement determined by meaning. E.g. *Committee* denotes a set of people and can take a **plural** verb although it is a **singular** noun: *The committee are coming to a decision*.

NOTIONAL GRAMMAR

A grammar of a language based on meaning, as in the traditional definitions of **word classes**. See **NOTIONAL, PROTOTYPE**.

NOUN

For a given language, a member of the **word class** whose protypical or central members denote concrete entities such as *tree* and *chair*. Less central members denote abstract entities such as *truth* or *idea* but are classed as nouns because they behave the same way in the grammar. E.g. English nouns can be preceded by *the, this* etc. or by an **adjective**. They take the plural **affixes** *-s* or *-es* (although plural mass nouns such as *wines* have the meaning 'kinds of wine') and the **possessive** affix. Nouns in Russian can be preceded by *etot* 'this', take affixes signalling plural, but also take **case** affixes. Nouns in English, Russian and other languages are the **heads** of noun phrases, by means of which speakers refer to concrete and abstract entities. See **DENOTATION, DISTRIBUTION**.

NOUN CLASS

Nouns are members of many classes, such as count nouns and abstract nouns, but the term 'noun class' is typically applied to distinctions that are reflected in systems of **agreement** and **government**, such as masculine nouns, feminine nouns and neuter nouns. See **CLASSIFIER, GENDER**.

NOUN CLAUSE

See **COMPLEMENT CLAUSE, NOMINAL**.

NOUN COMPLEMENT CLAUSE

A type of **complement clause** that complements **nouns**. In English, such **clauses** cannot be introduced by *which, who*, etc.: *We accepted the proposal that the land be sold* vs **We accepted the proposal which the land be sold*. See **COMPLEMENT**.

NOUN INCORPORATION

See **INCORPORATION**.

NOUN PHRASE

A **phrase** with a **noun** as its **head**, e.g. *the car, a book, this idea, the coffee in my cup, a cousin that he had never met, the suggestion that the project be abandoned*. Noun phrases function as subjects and objects and are used to refer to concrete and abstract entities. See **DETERMINER, GRAMMATICAL FUNCTION**.

NP

See **NOUN PHRASE**.

NP-MOVEMENT

In **Government and Binding Theory** and **Principles and Parameters**, a general rule that moves **noun phrases**. It applies in the derivation of **passives**: the direct object NP in an active sentence is moved into subject position in the corresponding passive sentence. For example, *Sue* in *John phoned Sue* is moved into subject position in *Sue was phoned by John*. NP-Movement also applies in **raising** structures – *the bank* in *It seems the bank has mislaid some money* is moved out of the clause *the bank has mislaid some money* to become the subject of *seems*, as in *The bank seems to have mislaid some money*. See **TRANSFORMATIONAL GRAMMAR**.

NP-TRACE

In **Government and Binding Theory**, a trace left behind by **noun phrases** that move. E.g. NP-Movement applies to *[John phoned $_{NP}$[Sue $_i$]]* to yield *[$_{NP}$ [Sue$_i$] was phoned NP [t$_i$] by John]*. The subscript *i* on *Sue* and *t* indicates that the trace is linked to *Sue*. NP traces are different from co-referential indices, as in *[John$_i$ congratulated himself$_i$ on his escape]*. No movement is involved in the co-indexing of *John* and *himself*. See **BINDING, BINDING THEORY, CO-INDEX, NP-MOVEMENT**.

NUCLEAR ARGUMENT

An **argument** that is in the **nucleus** of a **clause**, i.e. that is required by the **verb**.

NUCLEAR STRESS

See **SENTENCE STRESS**.

NUCLEAR SYLLABLE

See **NUCLEUS**.

NUCLEAR TONE

The most prominent pitch in an **intonation** unit.

NUCLEUS

1. In a **clause**, the **verb** plus any obligatory **arguments**: e.g. *Jane* + *found* + *the memory stick* in the clause <u>*Jane found the memory stick*</u> *in the car yesterday*. 2. In **ROLE AND REFERENCE GRAMMAR**, the verb alone forms the nucleus. The verb plus obligatory arguments form the core of a clause, and optional arguments form the periphery. 3. Every syllable requires a nucleus, usually a **vowel**. The minimal syllable consists of just a vowel.

NULL

Having no realization. E.g. the noun phrase *dogs* in *They like dogs* has no **article**, in *They like the dogs* it does. The structure of *dogs* can be thought of as having an article which is realized as Ø. *Dogs* is said to have a null article. See **MORPH**.

NULL CHARACTER

A character with the value zero included in a string for formatting, etc.

NULL HEAD

See **X-BAR SYNTAX**.

NULL SET

A set containing no members; e.g. the set of humans who have visited Mercury.

NULL-SUBJECT PARAMETER

See **PRO-DROP LANGUAGE**.

NUMBER

One of the **grammatical categories**, typically signalled by **inflections** and distinguishing reference to one entity from reference to more than one; e.g. *car* and *cars* and, with no affix, *foot* and *feet*. Some languages have special dual forms for referring to, e.g., hands and feet. See **DUAL, PLURAL, SINGULAR**.

NUMERAL

Any **word** or **phrase** denoting a number, such as *five, seventy-three, one thousand two hundred and six*. In some languages numerals combining with nouns require a **classifier**, as in Chinese *yi ben shu* 'one CL book, one book'. Combinations of numerals and nouns may follow unusual patterns of **agreement** and **government**. For instance, in Russian *dva* 'two', *tri* 'three' and *chetyre* 'four' take a noun in the genitive singular, while the numerals from *pjat'* 'five' to *dvadcat'* 'twenty' take a noun in the genitive plural: *tri mal'chika* 'three boy-GEN-sg, three boys', *pjat' mal'chikov* 'five boy-GEN-pl, five boys'.

NUMERAL CLASSIFIER

See **CLASSIFIER**.

NYANJA

Bantu, Niger-Congo. Approx. 7M speakers Malawi, 497K Mozambique and 1.6M Zambia.

O

OBJECT
See **GRAMMATICAL FUNCTION**.

OBJECT COMPLEMENT
See **COMPLEMENT**.

OBJECT LANGUAGE
The language that is the object of a given analysis.

OBJECT RAISING
An analysis in which, e.g., the **direct object** of *reach* in sentences such as *It is tough to reach the summit* is raised out of the **infinitive**, *to reach the summit*, to become the **subject** of the main **clause**, *The summit is tough to reach*. Also known as tough-movement. See **RAISING**.

OBJECTIVE
A **case** marking for **objects**, particularly in languages such as English which have only a subject-object contrast: e.g. *I avoided him* and *He avoided me*. See **GRAMMATICAL FUNCTION**.

OBJECTIVE GENITIVE
A noun in the genitive **case** or, in English, preceded by *of*, dependent on a noun denoting an action or process. The **genitive** noun denotes the patient undergoing the action or process. E.g. *the destruction of the town*, *the town's destruction*, Russian *sborka urozhaja* 'gathering harvest-GEN, the gathering of the harvest'. See **SUBJECTIVE GENITIVE**.

OBLIGATORY TRANSFORMATION
In early **transformational grammar**, a given **transformation** that had to apply wherever it could.

OBLIQUE
1. Any **case** affix other than **nominative** or **accusative** (for instance, in grammars of **Russian**). 2. Any **noun phrase** modifying a verb other than **subject** and **direct object**. E.g. *We bought lunch in an expensive restaurant in Edinburgh on Friday with Juliet's credit card* contains four obliques: *in an expensive restaurant*, *in Edinburgh*, *on Friday* and *with Juliet's credit card*. 3. Any noun phrase modifier of a verb connected to the verb by a **preposition**, such as *for the*

children in *He sent presents for the children* and *to Morocco* in *We went to Morocco*. See **GRAMMATICAL FUNCTION**.

OBSERVATIONAL ADEQUACY
See **ADEQUACY**.

OBSERVER'S PARADOX
The phenomenon of an event being influenced by the presence of an observer, even a non-participant one. This poses a particular challenge to fieldworkers since the task of gathering data may be influenced by the mere presence of the fieldworker.

OBSOLETE
Some word that is no longer in use because it has been supplanted by something newer.

OBSTRUENT
A term used in the classification of speech sounds that refers to sounds involving a **constriction** in the mouth that impedes the airflow, as in **stops**, **fricatives** and **affricates**.

OBVIATIVE
Especially in Native American languages such as **Algonquian**, a system of marking and contrasting different third-person **pronouns** as proximate or obviative. Proximate pronouns refer to participants who are more **topical** or salient in a given context and treated as closer; the **referents** of obviative pronouns are treated as distant. (Latin, *obviare* 'to prevent, obviate', i.e. to 'obviate' a participant.) Compare the French *Jean rencontra Pierre*, 'Jean met Pierre'. *Il dit...* 'He said ...'(= *Jean*, topical) vs *Celui-ci dit* 'This-one said ...' (= Pierre, not so topical). The participant treated as proximate may be the agent or patient that is more expected in a given context. See **DEIXIS**.

OCCITAN
Romance, Indo-European. Was spoken in southern France. Endangered.

OCCLUSION
The duration of the **closure** involved in the articulation of a **plosive** consonant.

OESOPHAGEAL
Sounds or phonation type initiated at or below the **oesophagus**. Oesophageal voice is a technique of voice production taught to those who have had the **larynx** removed surgically. It is in effect a belch.

OESOPHAGUS
The tube connecting the **pharynx** to the stomach. See Figure 'Articulators' at **ARTICULATION**.

OFF-GLIDE
A **glide** that is the transition occurring at the end of a **falling** diphthong, e.g. [ɪ] in the **diphthong** [ɔɪ] as in *boy*.

OFFICIAL LANGUAGE
A language that has legal status in a nation's courts, parliament, administration and so on, such as Gaelic in Ireland.

OLD CHURCH SLAVONIC
Slavic, Indo-European.
Earliest Slavic literary language (ninth century CE). Related to **Bulgarian** and **Macedonian**.

OMAHA-PONCA
Siouan. East Nebraska, Oklahoma. Endangered.

OMOTIC
Language family. Ethiopia.

ONEIDA
Iroquoian. Approx. 250K speakers Canada, 50 in the USA.

ONE-PLACE PREDICATE
See **PREDICATE**.

ONE-PLACE VERB
A verb that allows only one **argument**, such as *vanish* in *The White Rabbit vanished*. See **PREDICATE**.

ON-GLIDE
A **glide** that is the transition occurring at the beginning of a **rising** diphthong, e.g. [ə] in the **diphthong** [əʊ] as in *sew*.

ONOMATOPOEIA
The phenomenon of words, said to be onomatopoeic, which imitate or echo the sound produced by some process or creature. The imitations are not completely natural but vary across languages and conform to the phonology of the language they belong to. Thus, dogs produce *woof woof* in English but *wau wau* in German and *haf haf* in Czech. Leaves *rustle* or *susurrate* in English but *shurshat* in Russian. (Greek *onoma* 'a name', *poein* 'to make'.) See **ARBITRARY SIGN, ICONIC SIGN**.

ONSET
See **SYLLABLE**.

ONTOGENESIS
The development, during childhood, of the ability to process (linguistic) signs.

ONTOGENY
The course of language development in an individual speaker.

ONTOLOGICAL TYPES

Basic types of entities that are generally recognized in the human cognition. E.g. *thing, quantity, quality (property), place, time.* See **ONTOLOGY**.

ONTOLOGY

1. In computational linguistics a framework for organizing information about the set of concepts and the relations between them which characterize some domain. Ontologies are the structural frameworks for organizing information and are used in artificial intelligence, the Semantic Web, systems engineering, software engineering, biomedical informatics, library science, enterprise bookmarking, and information architecture as a form of knowledge representation about the world or some part of it. The creation of domain ontologies is also fundamental to the definition and use of an enterprise architecture framework. 2. A branch of philosophy dealing with existence and the types of entities that can be recognized as existing. **Conceptual semantics** recognizes a set of ontological types including *thing, quality, place, time, state, process, event.*

OPAQUE REFERENCE

See **REFERENCE**.

OPEN APPROXIMATION

A term in the description of the **manner of articulation** of **consonants** such as [w] *win,* [j] *year,* [l] *leaf.* They are sometimes called **frictionless continuants**. The **articulators** are approached to each other and there is a non-turbulent airflow without closure or friction.

OPEN CHOICE PRINCIPLE

The theory that any text is the result of a large number of complex choices. Wherever a **word**, **phrase** or **clause** is completed, the speaker or writer has to decide how to continue the text. In its early form the theory allowed only **grammaticality** as a constraint on the choice, but analysts have suggested that **context** is a major constraint too.

OPEN CLASS

See **CLOSED CLASS**.

OPEN INTERROGATIVE

A recently introduced term equivalent to 'wh interrogative' or 'wh question'. It contrasts with 'closed interrogative', a recently introduced term equivalent to 'yes–no interrogative'. The terms capture the fact that questions such as *What are you reading at the moment?* have an open-ended set of answers, whereas *Did Rene play in the orchestra?* allows two answers, *yes* or *no*. See **INTERROGATIVE CLAUSE**.

OPEN TRANSITION

See **TRANSITION**.

OPEN

A term in the classification of **vowels** referring to the position of the tongue in the **vowel space**. (See the vowel chart in the figure at **CARDINAL VOWELS**.) In an open vowel the highest point of the tongue is furthest from the roof of the mouth, the **palate**. Opposite **CLOSE**.

OPERAND

1. In **logic**, whatever an **operator** is applied to, such as a **proposition**. **2.** In morphology a **stem** that undergoes an operation of vowel change, as in *swim → swam*, or of the addition of a **suffix**, e.g. *climb → climbed*.

OPERATOR

1. In logic, symbols representing operations applying to basic propositions. E.g. basic propositions are non-negative and making them negative is conceived as an operation whereby **negation** is added. P might stand for the proposition 'Ken is at home' and ¬ P (¬ is the negation operator) for 'Ken is not at home'. Other operators are **tense**, **modality** (possibility, necessity) and **quantifiers** (*some, all*). **2.** In CGEL, the verb that moves over the subject noun in the formation of interrogative clauses. This is typically the first auxiliary in sequences such as *has written, has been writing, must have been writing*, where *has* and *must* carry tense and modality. The definition also applies to the main verb *have* (*They have a car* vs *Have they a car?*) and *be* (*He is an expert* vs *Is he an expert?*). **3.** A wh word such as *who* or a negative word such as *no* which signal that an operation has applied to a basic **declarative** clause. The operation is either that of making the clause **interrogative** or that of making it **negative**. See **CONNECTIVE**.

OPPOSITENESS

A very basic **sense** relation connecting pairs of **lexical words** whose meanings are connected by being opposed to each other within some domain. (An alternative view is that the relation holds between pairs of meanings and not between lexical words.) A number of different types of oppositeness are recognized. See **ANTIPODAL OPPOSITES, ANTONYMY, COMPLEMENTARIES, CONVERSES, DIRECTIONAL OPPOSITES, HYPONYMY, MERONYMY, OPPOSITION, REVERSIVES, SYNONYMY**.

OPPOSITION

The **paradigmatic** contrast between items in a particular environment. Thus /p/ and /t/ are in opposition in the environment /_in/ – *pin: tin*. A number of different oppositions are commonly identified: **bilateral, equipollent opposition, gradual opposition, multilateral opposition, privative opposition**. The notion of opposition is most commonly associated with phonological theories particularly in the characterization of the 'geometry' of phonological systems, especially in **Prague School** phonology and in systems of **distinctive features**. But it can apply equally to grammatical features, e.g tense [+/− past], number [+/- singular] or lexical items, e.g *man:woman; cock:hen*.

OPTATIVE

1. A **construction** expressing wishes, a category of **mood**: *May you live in interesting times, Would that he had stayed away, So be it.* 2. Especially in classical **Greek**, the set of verb forms that occur in **optative** constructions: *elthei* 'he/she/it is coming vs *eithe elthoi* 'Particle come-OPT, I wish he would come'. The optative forms also occur in various types of subordinate **clause**, such as conditional clauses presenting events as possible in the future but very unlikely. (Latin *optatum* 'a wish', *optare* 'to wish, desire'.) See **INDICATIVE, MODALITY, SUBJUNCTIVE**.

OPTIMALITY THEORY

A model of any area of a given language, especially **phonology** and **morphology**, in which structures are subject to a number of **constraints**. Each constraint is held to be universal but the constraints are ordered differently for different languages. For instance the constraint that word-initial **voiceless** stops are aspirated is highly ranked in English but not in Russian. The constraint that only voiceless stops occur at the end of words is highly ranked in the Slavic languages but not in English. Constraints can be violated, provided the violation is minimal. For any language the constraints are ordered so as to ensure the optimal **realization** of a **clause, phoneme, word**, and so on.

OPTIONAL TRANSFORMATION

In early **transformational grammar**, a **transformation** that did not have to apply to a given structure even when it could. E.g. the transformations yielding passive and **interrogative** structures were optional; examples of obligatory transformations were those involved in person and number **agreement** and in the positioning of **affixes** on **verbs**.

ORACY

Abilities in speaking and listening. See **LITERACY**.

ORAL

1. A label for the area of the mouth in which sounds are produced, the oral cavity, as opposed to other cavities, especially the nasal cavity but also the **pharynx**. 2. A label for sounds produced in the oral cavity and hence used in opposition to **nasal**.

ORAL TRADITION

The maintenance of a culture in spoken form, e.g. folktales and traditional songs.

ORALITY

1. The property of being oral, usually in opposition to nasality.

ORATIO OBLIQUA

See **INDIRECT SPEECH**.

ORATIO RECTA

See **DIRECT SPEECH**.

ORDER

The sequencing of linguistic units, as, for example, the order of elements in the **noun phrase** {determiner adjective noun}.

ORDERING

See **RULE ORDERING**.

ORDINAL NUMERAL

Forms of **numerals**, typically adjectives, having to do with the order in which entities are placed in a series. E.g. the *first* bus, The *Seventh* Seal, the *fiftieth* Pope. See **CARDINAL NUMERAL**.

ORDINARY LANGUAGE PHILOSOPHY

An approach to philosophy which, rather than developing formal logical analyses, concentrates on the use of language by ordinary speakers in everyday situations. The approach derives from Wittgenstein's later work but is associated with Oxford of the 1950s, particularly with Ryle and Austin. See **SPEECH ACT**.

ORIENTATION

In narrative studies, information that enables readers to locate the plot in time, space, etc.

OROMO

Cushitic. Three closely-related varieties. Approx. 16K Ethiopia, 152K Kenya, 41.6K Somalia.

ORO-NASAL GESTURE

See **ARTICULATORY GESTURE**.

ORTHOGRAPHIC WORD

In a given language, a **word** defined by criteria derived from orthography, such as permissible letter sequences and whether preceded or followed by a space. Thus *white water* consists of two orthographic words, *whitewater* in *whitewater rafting* consists of one.

ORTHOGRAPHY

The spelling system of a language.

OSCILLOGRAPH

An electronic instrument used to record the **acoustic** characteristics of a **speech wave**. An oscillogram is the record obtained.

OSSETIC

Indo-Iranian, Indo-European. Approx. 650K speakers, North Ossetia-Alania and South Ossetia.

OTHER-REPAIR

See **REPAIR**.

OTHER-INITIATED
See REPAIR.

OTO-MANGUEAN
Language family, Mexico. Includes subgroups of Mixtec, Otomi, Trique and Zapotec.

OUTER CIRCLE
In work on English as an international language or English as a **lingua franca**, those countries where English is not the native tongue but where it plays an important role in the nation's institutions, for instance as an **official language**. This circle includes the anglophone Commonwealth. See INNER CIRCLE.

OUTPUT CONDITION
See FILTER.

OUTPUT CONSTRAINT
See FILTER.

OUTPUT
In **generative grammar**, the structure(s) generated by a rule or set of rules.

OVEREXTENSION
In child language acquisition, extending the meaning of a lexical item beyond its normal **referents**, such as the use of *ball* to refer to oranges, doorknobs, cakes of soap. The phenomenon is common in the speech of children between one year and two and a half years.

OVERGENERALIZATION
In child language acquisition, the application of a grammatical pattern to lexical items that follow a different pattern, such as the use of the regular **past tense** suffix *-ed* to produce forms such as *taked*, *writed* and *maked*. Common in the speech of children.

OVERGENERATION
The generation by a set of rules of incorrect as well as correct sentences. The incorrect outputs have to be blocked by **constraints** on possible structures.

OVERLAPPING
In **phonology**, the property of a **phone** that can be assigned as an **allophone** to more than one **phoneme**. The classical example is the devoicing of German word final stops: *Rat (advice)*, genitive [ra:təs] and *Rad (wheel)* genitive [ra:dəs]) are both [ra:t] in word-final position. See BIUNIQUE.

OVERLAPPING ANTONYMS
See ANTONYMY.

OVERLEXICALIZATION

The phenomenon of a language having a large number of terms for the same **referent**. The concept is of doubtful value; there is no reliable standard, and any such set of terms almost certainly differ in non-descriptive meaning. See **DESCRIPTIVE MEANING**.

OVERT

Applied to a linguistic process that is observable, such as **number** marking in English, which is usually overt (*stag; stag-s*) except in a few cases like *deer: deer*, where it is **covert**.

OVERTONE

See **HARMONIC**.

OXYMORON

A phrase in which **contradictory** words are deliberately combined for stylistic effect; e.g. *friendly fire*. (Greek *oxus* 'sharp', *moros* 'foolish'.)

P&P
See **PRINCIPLES AND PARAMETERS**.

PAHLAVI
Middle **Persian (Farsi)** (seventh–eighth centuries CE).

PALATAL
A term in the description of the **place of articulation** of **consonant** sounds. The front of the tongue comes against the hard **palate**. In IPA transcriptions some palatals have a special symbol, [ç], [ʂ] [ɭ], and where there is no special symbol a leftward facing curly tail, as in the examples, represents palatalization. There are few palatal sounds in English **received pronunciation**, except as positional variants. The voiceless palatal **fricative** [ç] is heard in German *ich;* the palatal **nasal** [ɲ] is found in Spanish, e.g. *señor*.

PALATALIZATION
A term in the description of the **secondary articulation** of a **place of articulation**. The front of the tongue moves towards the **palate**. In English the most audibly palatalized sounds are the palatal **off-glides** found in some accents of English in words such as [tjun] *tune;* [sjut] *suit*.

PALATE
The area between the **alveolar** ridge and the **velum**; the roof of the mouth. Usually divided into two areas, the **hard palate**, the immobile bony area immediately behind the **alveolar** ridge, and the **soft palate**, the mobile fleshy area culminating in the velum. The velum can be raised and lowered. When it is lowered, the **airstream** escapes through the nose producing **nasal** sounds; when it is raised the airstream can only escape through the mouth producing **oral** sounds. Sounds articulated against the hard palate are **palatal** and those articulated against the soft palate are **velar**. See Figure 'Articulators' at **ARTICULATION**.

PALATO-ALVEOLAR
See **ALVEO-PALATAL**.

PALATOGRAM
A record of contact made between the **tongue** and the **palate** in **palatography**.

PALATOGRAPHY
The instrumental study of **articulations** made by the **tongue** against the **palate**.

PALENQUERO
Spanish-based creole in Colombia.

PALI
Early **Indo-Aryan**; language of many Buddhist texts.

PAMA-NYUNGAN
Proposed language family including most **Australian languages**. Non-Pama-Nyungan languages were or are spoken in Western Australia and the Northern Territory.

PANINI (fl fifth century BCE)
Indian grammarian. His grammar of **Sanskrit**, known as Ashtadhyayi ('the eight chapters') describes the **morphology** of the language spoken as his **mother tongue**. It is the earliest, and one of the finest, works of descriptive and generative linguistics. He developed algorithms for the generation of well-formed words, and his approach foreshadows in many respects the notions of **phoneme**, **morpheme** and **root**.

PANOAN LANGUAGES
Language family, South American.

PAPIAMENTU
Spanish- and **Portuguese**-based creole, Dutch Antilles and Aruba.

PAPUAN
The indigenous language family of Papua New Guinea.

PARABLE
A story told to illustrate some doctrine or moral principle, especially the stories set out in the Bible as told by Christ. Parables relate to everyday events but have a deeper interpretation. See **ALLEGORICAL**.

PARADIGM
The set of forms of a given **noun**, **verb** or **adjective**, taken as a model for a particular class of noun, etc. and set out systematically according to **case**, **number**, **person**, tense, **mood**. (Greek *paradeigma* 'a model'.) An example is the set of forms of the Russian noun *sputnik* 'fellow traveller'.

	Singular	Plural
Nominative	SPUTNIK	SPUTNIKI
Accusative	SPUTNIKA	SPUTNIKOV
Genitive	SPUTNIKA	SPUTNIKOV
Dative	SPUTNIKU	SPUTNIKAM
Instrumental	SPUTNIKOM	SPUTNIKAMI
Locative	SPUTNIKE	SPUTNIKAX

See **GRAMMATICAL CATEGORY, PARADIGMATIC, SYNTAGM, SYNTAGMATIC, TENSE AND ASPECT.**

PARADIGMATIC

1. Applied to the relation between the **affixes** in a **paradigm**. 2. Extended to the relation between any **constituents** that can replace each other at a given slot in a structure: e.g. *Cat* and *dog* in *The __ chased a rat* or *terrible* and *marvellous* in *Her performance was __*. See **SYNTAGM, SYNTAGMATIC.**

PARALANGUAGE

Non-segmental vocal features that accompany speech and have a communicative effect, e.g. tone of voice, **tempo**, **loudness**, **nasality**, **breathy voice**, hesitation, etc. Often extended to non-vocal features such as facial expression, eye movements, etc.

PARALINGUISTIC

Applied to components of communication by means of language that are not part of the language system, i.e. have nothing to do with morphology, syntax or phonology. Such components include **voice quality**, loudness, speed of delivery, hand gestures, body posture and facial expressions. They convey the speaker's attitudes and emotions but, perhaps more importantly, they help to get communication started and ensure that it proceeds smoothly and according to the intentions of the participants. A collective term for the paralinguistic components is paralanguage. See **BACKCHANNEL, CONVERSATION ANALYSIS, PARALANGUAGE.**

PARALLEL ARCHITECTURE

See **SIMPLER SYNTAX.**

PARALLEL CORPORA

A corpus of parallel texts.

PARALLEL TEXT

A text along with its translation. Most helpfully a text segment and its translation are in **alignment**.

PARAMETER

1. Any way in which languages can vary one from another. Short for 'parameter of variation', as opposed to the universal properties that languages have in common. E.g. languages vary with respect to whether the **heads** of **phrases** are followed or preceded by their **modifiers**. E.g. in **Turkish noun phrases** demonstratives and adjectives precede the head noun, while in **Swahili** noun phrases they follow the head noun. 2. In Chomsky's theory of first language acquisition, parameters control the choice of alternative structures. Parameters are said to be binary, either switched on or left off, and to be set in accordance with children's experience of a given language. Thus, assuming that the default order is modifiers preceding the head in a construction, the parameter requiring the order 'head followed by modifiers' is switched on in Swahili but left off in Turkish.

PARAMETRIC PHONETICS
The view of speech not as a sequence of **segments** but as a set of variable articulatory **parameters** like voicing, nasality, lip-rounding, tongue height, etc. Each variable changes over an utterance. See **NASAL, ROUNDED, VOICE**.

PARASITIC GAP
Especially in **Government and Binding** and **Principles and Parameters**, an empty place in a structure occupied by a **null constituent** whose interpretation depends on another null constituent. E.g., In *Burn the documents after reading [e]*, the null element *[e]* has the same **referent** as *the documents*. In *Which documents did you burn [e $_1$] after reading [e $_2$]?* the null element *[e $_2$]* has the same referent as the null element *[e $_1$]*; the null element *[e $_1$]* has the same referent as *the documents*. *[e $_1$]* relates directly to, and is licensed by, the full noun phrase *the documents*, but *[e $_2$]* is licensed by, and is said to be parasitic on, another null element or a gap. See **LICENSING**.

PARASITIC VOWEL
An additional **vowel** inserted into a word, thus producing an additional **syllable**, e.g. *filum* /filəm/. See **ANAPTYXIS**.

PARASYNTHESIS
See **CIRCUMFIX**.

PARATACTIC
See **HYPOTAXIS, PARATAXIS**.

PARATAXIS
The placing of clauses side by side. See **HYPOTAXIS**.

PARATONE
An **intonation** pattern that can be regarded as the equivalent of a paragraph. It may be a single large unit or sequence of smaller units.

PARENTHESIS
A **word**, **phrase** or **clause** inserted into a clause or sentence but not fitting into the syntax of the latter by way of, e.g., **agreement** or **government**. For instance, *My ambition – <u>didn't I tell you this before?</u> – is to see the Jim-Jim Falls, Our company – <u>we only found out this morning</u> – is being taken over.* Such interrupting chunks are said to be **parenthetical**, or parentheticals, or in parenthesis.

PARENTHETICAL
1. Having the characteristics of a **parenthesis**. 2. A clause such as *I think, she said, he whispered* used in the relaying of direct speech: e.g. *'Should we,'* <u>he whispered</u>, *'get out of here now?'*

PAROLE
A term introduced by **Saussure** for the use of language by an individual, as opposed to **langue**, the language of a community.

PARONOMASIA
Word play. (Greek *para* 'beside', *onoma* 'a name'.)

PARONYMS
Words that are similar in form, either accidentally or because one derives historically from the other. E.g. French *avoine* and Spanish *avena* are similar in form because they both derive from the Latin *avena* 'oats'. *Flaunt* and *flout* are similar in form but are not related historically and, until recently, did not have the same meaning. By a process of paronymic attraction *flaunt* is used by a growing number of speakers instead of *flout*.

PAROXYTONE
A word with the principal **stress** falling on the penultimate **syllable**, e.g. *nasality*.

PARSE
1. In traditional teaching, to assign the **words** in a **sentence** to their **word class**. Working out a syntactic structure for a sentence – different phrases, **subject**, **direct object**, etc. – was known as analysis. 2. In modern usage, especially in **computational linguistics**, the assignment of syntactic structure to sentences especially by computer programs. Such programs focus on resolving grammatical ambiguity and working out the correct groupings of constituents. The labelling of **constituents** as nouns, verbs and so on is done by part-of-speech taggers. See **AMBIGUITY, CONSTRUCTION**.

PARSER
Any computer program capable of working out the syntactic structure of **sentences**.

PARSING
See **PARSE**.

PART OF SPEECH
See **WORD CLASS**.

PARTIAL OVERLAP
The situation where two **phonemes** are realized by identical **allophones** in different **environments**. Thus in some accents of English the final consonants in *write* /raɪt/ and *ride* /raɪd/ are realized phonetically as, respectively, [t] and [d], but when the agent affix *er*, /ə/ is attached *write-r, ride-r* both are realized by the **alveolar** flap [D] – [raɪDə].

PARTICIPANT
See **ROLE**.

PARTICIPANT OBSERVATION
1. In data collection, the process in which the fieldworker becomes a member of the group under investigation. 2. A technique designed to circumvent the problem of the **observer's paradox**.

PARTICIPANT ROLE
See ROLE.

PARTICIPIAL ADJECTIVE
Adjectives with the form of **participles**: *encouraging remarks, the ploughed fields*. See GRADIENCE.

PARTICIPIAL CLAUSE
A non-finite **clause** containing a **participle** and, like **adverbial clauses**, modifying a whole clause; e.g. *arriving late* in *Arriving late, she went straight to the meeting*. (= *Because she arrived late...*). See NON-FINITE VERB.

PARTICIPLE
A **word class** first established for **Greek** and **Latin** but found in other (modern) languages. The classic participles (e.g. in classical Greek, Latin, Russian) are forms derived from **verbs**. They are marked for **tense and aspect**, which are central to verbs, and also for case, which is central to nouns and adjectives. (The term 'participle' is from the Latin *participalis* 'sharing', which reflected the view that these forms share properties of verbs and adjectives.) Examples from Latin are: *dona ferunt* 'gifts carry-3pl-PRS, they are bearing gifts, *Graeci dona ferentes* 'Greeks gifts carry-PRT-PRS-NOM-pl, Greeks bearing gifts, in which *ferentes* agrees in nominative case and plural number with *Graeci*, and *fidunt Graecis dona ferentibus* 'they-trust Greek-DAT-pl gift carry-PRT-PRS-DAT-pl, They trust Greeks bearing gifts', in which *ferentibus* agrees in dative case and plural number with *Graecis*. For participles in English, see FREE PARTICIPLE, PAST PARTICIPLE, PRESENT PARTICIPLE.

PARTICLE
1. Traditionally, any uninflected word or word that does not change its **form**, such as English *up, besides, because, but*. 2. In modern grammars of English, a class of words, mostly identical with **prepositions**, that combine with **verbs**. Like prepositions, these particles have concrete (spatial) meanings and **figurative** meanings: e.g. *picked up the rubbish, picked up the allusion*. 3. Equivalent to **discourse marker**. See PHRASAL VERB.

PARTICULARIZED CONVERSATIONAL IMPLICATURE
See IMPLICATURE.

PARTITIVE
Applied to **constructions** denoting part of some entity or some of a set of entities. The **French** construction is based on the **preposition** *de* 'of' – *du pain* 'of bread, some bread'. **Finnish** has a partitive **case** affix – *kahvi* 'coffee', *kupissa on kahvia* 'cup-in is coffee-PRTV, There's some coffee in the cup'.

PASHTO
Indo-Iranian, Indo-European. 9.9M speakers Afghanistan, 13.9M Pakistan.

PASSIVE
See **VOICE**.

PASSIVE ARTICULATOR
The description of the **place of articulation** of a **consonant** involves a description of the place of contact or **constriction** between a moveable articulator, the **active articulator**, usually the tongue, and an immobile articulator, the passive articulator, usually the roof of the mouth.

PASSIVE PARTICIPLE
A participle which is **passive**, as in French *maisons rénovées* 'houses renovated, renovated houses', in which the participle *rénovées* is derived from the verb *rénover* but is adjective-like in agreeing with *maisons* in feminine **gender** and plural **number**. See PARTICIPIAL ADJECTIVE, PARTICIPLE, PAST PARTICIPLE.

PAST HISTORIC
Especially in **Romance**, a set of verb forms used to refer to single completed events in past time. The forms are a mixture of tense (past time) and aspect (completed event). In French and Italian the Past Historic is used in the written language but not in speech. In Spanish the Past Historic is used in both speech and writing. See PERFECT, PERFECTIVE, PRETERITE, SIMPLE PAST.

PAST PARTICIPLE
In some Indo-European languages, past participles are identical in form with passive participles but combine with *have* (or its equivalent) to form the perfect tense, e.g. *renovated* as in *They have renovated those houses*. The forms are called passive participles when they combine with *be* (or its equivalent) to form a passive, e.g. *renovated* in *Those houses have been renovated*. In other Indo-European languages, the two participles are distinct. Czech has past (active) participles in *-l*, as in *Petr je pozval sestru* 'Peter is having-invited sister, Peter has invited his sister', and passive participles in *-n* and *-t*, as in *Sestra je pozvaná* 'Sister is having-been-invited, His sister has been invited'. See PARTICIPLE, PASSIVE PARTICIPLE.

PAST PERFECT
See **PERFECT**.

PAST TENSE
A tense that refers to a point or period of time preceding the speech time. *They lost the battle* refers to an event that took place before the time at which the speaker speaks or the writer writes. The exact time is not specified but could have been by means of **adverbs** such as *recently, last week, in the remote past, in 480 BCE*, etc. See PERFECT, PERFECTIVE, PRETERITE, SIMPLE PAST.

PASTICHE
A text (but also a piece of music or a painting) consisting either of bits of other writers' texts or of imitations of other writers' texts. A pastiche may be created for humorous effect.

PATH

1. In a **tree diagram**, any route from one **node** to another. 2. In analyses of movement events, the route followed by an entity moving from a **source** to a **goal**. Path is signalled by various **prepositions** in English – *along the street, by/via Sheffield, through the forest* – and by **case** affixes in other languages: Finnish *meri* 'sea', *meritse* 'by sea'; Russian *bereg* 'bank (of river, etc.) *beregom* 'along the bank', *les* 'forest', *lesom* 'through the forest'. See **AFFIX**.

PATHETIC FALLACY

The attribution of human feelings to inanimate entities.

PATIENT

See **ROLE**.

PATTERN CONGRUITY

Where there are competing possible phonological analyses, regularities or symmetries in patterning may be invoked to choose between them. In English we find word-initial sequences voiceless alveolar **fricative** + unaspirated **stop** – [spɪ..], as in *spit*, but not sequences voiceless alveolar fricative + aspirated stop *[spʰɪ..]. In English, voiced stops are normally unaspirated, as in [bɪn] *bin*, and voiceless stops normally have **aspiration**, as in [pʰɪn] *pin*. Now, the stop in [spɪ..] is unaspirated, so why should it not be analysed phonologically as a voiced stop, [b]? However, normally **clusters** of obstruents are either all voiced or all voiceless – i.e. /st/ as /past/, *past*, or /zd/ as in /bʌzd/, *buzzed* – but not */sd/. Pattern congruity would therefore favour the analysis /sp/, /st/ and /sk/ over the analysis */sb/ */sd/ and */sg/. Similarly the phonetic sequence [kʷ] might be analysed as a labialized /kʷ/ or as the sequence /kw/. If consonant clusters are dispreferred in the language under analysis and there are other labialized stops, as for example in Akan, then pattern congruity would favour the analysis /kʷ/. If on the other hand consonant clusters are common, as in English, pattern congruity would favour the analysis /kw/.

PATTERN GRAMMAR

A way of describing grammar that focuses on the relationship between lexical words, phrases and meanings. It arose out of, and is well suited to, the presentation of results obtained from the computer analysis of text corpora.

PAUCAL

A **number** category. Some languages have paucal noun forms denoting 'a few'. (**Latin** *paucus* 'little, few'.)

PAUL, Hermann (1846–1921)

Professor of Comparative Philology at Freiburg, then Munich. His five-volume *Deutsche Grammatik* (1916–1920) and *Deutsches Wörterbuch* (1921) were influential. His *Principien der Sprachgeschichte* formalized the methodology of the 'young grammarians'. He was concerned about the social nature of linguistics and his work on the relationship between linguistic norms and individuals usage contributed to the development of Saussure's *Cours de linguistique générale* (1916).

PAUSE

An interruption, usually brief, in an **utterance**. A **silent pause**, often transcribed as [+], the number of [+]s indicating the length of the pause, has no vocalization, as in *that's more ++ than I can afford*. A **filled pause** has some vocalization such as *er, um*, etc.

PEER GROUP

People of the same age, social class, occupation, gender and so on who enjoy similar status.

PEJORATION

A change that makes the meaning of a word negative and less attractive. E.g. *boor* originally meant just a farmer, like the related Dutch word *boer*. (Compare the use of *peasant* to designate someone lacking civility and sensitivity.)

PENTAMETER

A line of verse consisting of five feet.

PERCOLATION

In formal models of syntax and morphology, a process by which **features** are assigned to **words** and move or percolate upwards to the **phrase** or **clause** nodes, or are assigned to **affixes** and move upwards to the **node** dominating the entire word. E.g. the suffix *-ness* is [+noun]; when the **suffix** is added to an adjective **stem**, say *kind* [+adjective], [+noun] moves up to the word node and the whole word *kindness* is [+noun]. See **UNIFICATION**.

PERFECT

The present perfect, as in *Sue has sold her house*, is treated by some analysts as a tense and by others as an aspect. (It must not be confused with **perfective**, which is an aspect.) The classic example is the English Present Perfect, which is used to present a result as relevant at the moment of speech. The **present tense** form *has* points to the moment of speech and the **past participle** *sold* expresses the result of the event of selling, as in *The house is sold*. Since *sold* expresses a result, the action that caused the result must have taken place in past time. There is a tendency for perfects to become **simple past** tenses, as has happened in French and Italian. French *Sue a vendu sa maison* 'Sue have-3sg sell-part her house' can be translated as 'Sue has sold her house (and is very happy)' or 'Sue sold her house (many years ago)'. The present perfect has various interpretations: result – *Sue has sold her house*; experiential – *Has Sue (ever) sold a house?*; immediate past or 'hot-news' – *Sue has (just) sold her house*; persistent situation – *Sue has been selling her house since last year*.

The English Past Perfect, as in *Sue had sold her house (before we met her)*, is used to place an event in past time earlier than another event in past time – the event of selling the house is earlier than the event of meeting her. *Had* is a **past tense** form. In some languages past perfects have become remote pasts. See **PRETERITE, RESULTATIVE, TENSE AND ASPECT**.

PERFECTIVE

A verb **aspect** used for presenting an event as completed, typically a single event. (It must not be confused with **perfect**, which some analysts regard as an aspect and others as a tense.) Many languages with perfective vs **imperfective** aspect locate completed events in past time and on-going events in past or present time. In many languages perfective aspect combines only with **past tense**, and many other languages have no tense forms but the above contrast between perfective and imperfective aspect gives them a contrast between past and non-past time. E.g. **Chinese** *ta chi fan* 'He/she eat rice, he/she is eating (rice)' vs *ta chi le fan* 'he/she eat-PFV rice, he/she ate (rice)'. In the **Slavic** languages, which have a very untypical system of perfective and imperfective aspect, both aspects combine with past and **present tense**. The combination of perfective aspect and present tense is interpreted as relating to future time.

PERFORMANCE

In early **generative grammar**, the actual use of language in concrete situations as opposed to **competence**. Now replaced by the concept of performance systems. **Phonetic form** is conceived as a bridge from **I-language** to the articulatory-perceptual performance system and **Logical Form** as a bridge to the conceptual-intentional system. Performance errors are hesitations, slips of the tongue, uncompleted syntactic constructions, wrong choice of lexical items and so on that happen, not because of imperfect competence, but because of the pressures in processing and producing language in real time. See **MINIMALIST PROGRAM**.

PERFORMATIVE

See **SPEECH ACT**.

PERIODIC

In acoustics, a regularly repeated waveform.

PERIPHERY (OF A CLAUSE)

See **CLAUSE, CORE GRAMMAR**.

PERLOCUTIONARY ACT

The act, intentional or unintentional, that is performed by producing a spoken or written utterance. The speaker who exclaims *The dog has eaten the sausages* may cause someone else to shout at the dog, to berate the first person for leaving the sausages in a silly place or to go off to buy more sausages, or all three. Utterances are said to have a perlocutionary effect. See **LOCUTIONARY ACT, ILLOCUTIONARY ACT, SPEECH ACT**.

PERLOCUTIONARY EFFECT

See **PERLOCUTIONARY ACT**.

PERMUTATION

See **MOVEMENT**.

PERSEVERATIVE ASSIMILATION
See ASSIMILATION.

PERSIAN (FARSI)
Indo-Iranian, Indo-European. 33.9M speakers, Iran.

PERSIAN, OLD
Oldest attested ancestor of **Persian** (Farsi). Inscriptions from *c.* sixth century BCE.

PERSISTENCE
See LAYERING.

PERSON
A **grammatical category** typically realized by independent pronouns and by **affixes** attached to **verbs**. Traditionally the speaker, at the centre of an event of speaking, is 'first person'. Almost as central is the hearer or **addressee**, labelled 'second person'. Other persons or things are not central to an event of speaking; they may be spoken about but do not speak and are labelled 'third person'. See DEIXIS, OBVIATIVE.

PERSON DEIXIS
See DEIXIS.

PERSONAL PRONOUN
A **pronoun** pointing to first **person**, etc.

PERSONIFICATION
A peripheral type of **metaphor** in which inanimate entities, concrete and abstract, are treated as though they were human: e.g. *My computer is misbehaving; Let the rivers clap their hands, Let the hills be joyful together.*

PERSPECTIVE
See CONSTRUE.

PF
See PHONETIC FORM.

PHARYNGEAL
A term in the description of the **place of articulation** of **consonant** sounds. The root of the tongue moves toward the pharynx. Pharyngeal consonants occur in Arabic, E.g. in Arabic [ʕ]. See PHARYNX.

PHARYNGEALIZATION
A **secondary articulation** in which the root of the tongue is retracted into the pharynx. Transcribed in IPA as a superscript [ˤ].

PHARYNX
The space at the back of the mouth opposite the root of the **tongue**, at the juncture of the oral and nasal cavities, and above the larynx. See Figure 'Articulators' at ARTICULATION.

PHASE

In the **Minimalist Program**, roughly equivalent to the cycle of the standard transformational model. The essential idea is that syntactic **derivations** proceed in small steps. In the derivation of *Who does Harriet think Matt saw Imogen meeting?* the initial structure is *Harriet thinks Matt saw Imogen meeting who*. *Who* does not move to the front of the sentence in one jump but in small jumps: first to the front of the clause *Imogen meeting*, then to the front of *Matt saw Imogen meeting*, then to the front of the sentence. See **CYCLIC PRINCIPLE**.

PHATIC COMMUNION

The use of language not primarily to exchange information but to establish and then maintain good social relations, both between strangers and between friends. E.g. at bus stops in the UK, *Morning!*, *At least it's not raining*, *This bus is always late*, etc.

PHATIC FUNCTION

The orientation of language towards social relations between interlocutors.

PHOENICIAN

Semitic, Afroasiatic. Spoken in what is now Lebanon (Tyre, Sidon, Byblos) and Carthage (in what is now Tunisia). Inscriptions from eleventh century BCE in the first known alphabet.

PHONAESTHEME

See **SOUND SYMBOLISM**.

PHONAESTHESIA

See **SOUND SYMBOLISM**.

PHONAESTHETICS

The study of the aesthetic properties of sound, particularly in connection with **onomatopoeia** and sound symbolism, the correspondence of sound and meaning. See **ARBITRARY SIGN, ICONIC SIGN**.

PHONATION

The various kinds of production of vocal sound by the vibration of the **vocal folds**, especially **voicing**. See **PHONATION TYPES**.

PHONATION TYPES

Different types of glottal activity that yield distinguishable voice types.
See **BREATHY VOICE, CREAK, WHISPER**.

PHONATORY SETTING

The tendency for an individual to maintain a particular **phonation type** throughout an utterance. E.g. the **breathy voice** of some actresses.
See **ARTICULATORY SETTING, PHONATION**.

PHONE

A single phonetic **segment**. See **ALLOPHONE, PHONEME**.

PHONEMATIC UNITS

1. Discrete segmental units, consonants and vowels, that occur in linear sequence. 2. One of two basic units in **prosodic phonology**, the other being **prosody**. In prosodic phonology a phonematic unit is a discrete segmental unit, such as a **consonant** or **vowel**, that occurs in a fixed place in a structure. It may be symbolized as C, V, etc. Phonematic units are usually underspecified and receive a full phonetic realization only after the application of relevant prosodies. Thus to account for the alternation in the plural **affix** in English between /-s/, as in *cats* and /z/ as in *dogs*, the affix might be specified as /Z/, i.e. an alveolar fricative, unspecified for voice. A prosody of voice will spread the voice value of the final segment of the noun onto the plural affix, yielding either /ts/ or /gz/. See **UNDERSPECIFICATION**.

PHONEME

In many phonological theories the phoneme is the smallest contrastive unit in the sound system of a particular language or dialect. It is the minimal unit that distinguishes between meanings of words. The phonemes of a language can be found by constructing minimal pairs, that is pairs of words with different meanings that differ in a single segment. For example, the English word *pin* can be represented by the phoneme sequence /pɪn/ where /p/ contrasts with /b/ in *bin* and with /t/ in *tin*; /ɪ/ contrasts with /a/ in *pan* and /ʌ/ in *pun* and so on. Each of these words has a distinct meaning. In **autonomous phoneme** (or classical phoneme) theory, phonemes are abstract units realized by **allophones**, which are the corresponding concrete units. The allophones of a phoneme are united by their **phonetic similarity** and **complementary distribution**: thus [pʰ], an aspirated voiceless bilabial stop and [p], an unaspirated voiceless bilabial stop are allophones of /p/ by virtue of their phonetic similarity, and the two phones are in complementary distribution in that the unaspirated [p] occurs in the environment following [s] and the aspirated [pʰ] occurs elsewhere: so [spɪn] / spɪn/] and not *[spʰɪn] and [pʰɪn] /pɪn/, but not *[pɪn]. In classical phoneme theory a phoneme cannot be analysed into smaller contrastive units (see **DISTINCTIVE FEATURES**). Different languages, or different dialects of the same language, will have different phoneme systems: the systems may differ in the number of phonemes recognized or in different allophonic realizations of individual phonemes or both. There is some variation in phoneme theories. Some are strict and others less strict on issues such as whether a particular phone should always be assigned to a particular phoneme, as per the principle of **invariance**; whether there must be a strict one-to-one correspondence between a phonemic and a phonetic representation, as per the principle of biuniqueness; whether a **phone** must be assigned to only one phoneme or can be assigned to more than one, with **overlapping**.

PHONEMIC TRANSCRIPTION

A transcription of speech in terms of the **phonemes** established for that particular speech variety. It omits predictable phonetic detail See **BROAD, NARROW, PHONETIC TRANSCRIPTION**.

PHONEMICS

1. the method of analysis of the sound system of a language which involves identifying the **phonemes** of a language. 2. The term used by American structuralists for **phonology**, indicating the central position of the phoneme in their analyses.

PHONETIC ALPHABET

The set of symbols used in the transcription of speech sounds. See **BROAD, IPA, NARROW, PHONEMIC TRANSCRIPTION,**

PHONETIC FORM

The phonetic representation of a word or longer sequence. Contrasts with phonological form or **underlying form**.

PHONETIC MOTIVATION

A property of a phonological rule that appears to be motivated by phonetic considerations: for example the nasalization of a vowel in the environment of a nasal consonant. See **NASAL, NASALIZED**.

PHONETIC SETTING

See **ARTICULATORY SETTING**.

PHONETIC SIMILARITY

In phoneme theory, the requirement that the **allophones** of a **phoneme** should be phonetically similar. Thus in English [p^h], an aspirated voiced bilabial stop, and [p], an unaspirated voiced bilabial stop, are in **complementary distribution** and are considered to be allophones of /p/ by virtue of their phonetic similarity. By contrast, [h] and [ŋ] are in complementary distribution – [h] cannot appear word finally and [ŋ] cannot appear word initially – they are not considered to be allophones of the same phoneme because they are not phonetically similar.

PHONETIC SPELLING

An orthography where each letter represents a single phone.

PHONETIC TRANSCRIPTION

A transcription of the phonetic details of speech. It will usually include details that are predictable by general rules for a particular accent. See **BROAD, IPA, NARROW, PHONEMIC TRANSCRIPTION**.

PHONETIC UNIVERSAL

A phonetic property that is manifested in all languages.

PHONETICS

The scientific study of speech sounds. Often divided into **articulatory phonetics** (the study of the way speech sounds are produced by the organs of speech), **acoustic phonetics** (the study of the acoustic properties of sounds produced in speech) and instrumental phonetics (the study of speech sounds by the use of instruments that record and analyse data). General phonetics is the study of speech sounds independent of their use in a language; linguistic phonetics is the study of the speech sounds of a particular language.

PHONIC MEDIUM

The sound system as the **medium** of communication. Speech uses the phonic medium as opposed to writing which uses the graphic **medium**. See CHANNEL, PHONIC SUBSTANCE, SUBSTANCE.

PHONIC SUBSTANCE

The range of speech sounds that can be used in language.

PHONICS

A method of teaching children to read and write by recognizing sound–symbol correspondences and sounding out the individual letters in words. See LOOK-AND-SAY.

PHONOLOGICAL COMPONENT

In **generative grammar** that part of the theory concerned with **phonology** and **phonetics**. See SYNTACTIC COMPONENT.

PHONOLOGICAL CONDITIONING

The selection of an **allomorph** dependent on its phonetic or phonological environment; e.g. the English plural morpheme is realized by /z/ following a voiced segment, /bɪd-z/, and by /s/ following a voiceless segment, /bɪt-s/. See CONDITIONING, REALIZATION.

PHONOLOGICAL PROCESS

In child language acquisition the term used to describe the simplifications used by young children in their speech production. These may include the reduction of consonant clusters, the substitution of sounds and assimilations.

PHONOLOGICAL RULE

A formal way of expressing the relationship, or **mapping**, between an underlying phonological representation, in terms of **phonemes** or the like, and its **phonetic** realization, as a **phone**. Phonological rules are also found in historical linguistics to capture sound changes. See RULE.

PHONOLOGICAL SCALING

See NATURAL PHONOLOGY.

PHONOLOGICAL SPACE

A way of conceptualizing the range of possibilities for distinguishing phonological systems. For example, **vowel space** conceptualizes the space in the oral cavity used for the production of vowels, characterized in terms of tongue height and frontness and often represented in simplified form by a vowel quadrilateral. (See Figure at **CARDINAL VOWELS**.) A fuller representation could include lip-rounding, **phonation types**, etc. A consonant chart could represent the various parameters for categorising **consonants**. See **CARDINAL VOWELS, PHONATION, ROUNDED**.

PHONOLOGICAL UNIVERSAL

A phonological property common to all languages.

PHONOLOGICAL WORD

A word established by phonological rather than syntactic or semantic criteria. Typically the domain of some phonological process, **vowel harmony**, or cliticization, such as the cliticization of the negative in *can't (I can't tell you)*. See **CLITIC, GRAMMATICAL WORD, WORD**.

PHONOLOGY

The branch of linguistics concerned with the sound systems of particular languages or of language in general. Contrasting with **phonetics**. In most phonological theories before the 1960s, the **phoneme** is the central analytic concept. Somewhat different versions of phoneme theory are found in **Glossematics** and the **Prague School. Prosodic phonology**, developed by the London School in the 1950s, offered a strikingly different perspective. **Generative phonology**, developed in the 1960s, saw phonemes dissolved into bundles of **distinctive features**, and introduced the notion of an abstract **underlying form** formulated in terms of **systematic phonemes** and relating to surface phonetic forms by a complex system of phonological **rules**. Generative phonology soon proved to be too unconstrained and was followed by a range of theories designed to constrain some aspect of the theory. See **AUTOSEGMENTAL PHONOLOGY, DEPENDENCY PHONOLOGY, LEXICAL PHONOLOGY, METRICAL PHONOLOGY, NATURAL PHONOLOGY, NON-LINEAR PHONOLOGY, OPTIMALITY THEORY**.

PHONOTACTICS

Constraints on sequences of segments. In English a word-initial /s/ may be followed by a **voiceless** but not a voiced stop: /sp/, /st/ or /sk but not */sb/, */sd/ or */sg/.

PHRASAL PROJECTION

See **X-BAR SYNTAX**.

PHRASAL VERB

In English, a **verb** plus a **particle**. The combination functions as a single semantic unit, whose meaning is not always predictable from the meanings of the verb and the particle. The particle may be immediately after the verb, as in *She put down her laptop,* or immediately following the direct object, as in *She* *put her laptop down*. The meaning of *put down* is predictable in the preceding example but not in *The vet put down the dog* and *The vet put the dog down*, where *put down* is equivalent to *kill*. See **PREPOSITIONAL VERB**.

PHRASE

1. In linguistics, typically a sequence of two or more words but also just one word in a slot or **frame** where two or more words could occur: the empty slot in the frame [___ *are heavy*] could contain *books, these books, many books on linguistics* and so on. In both senses of the term, a phrase has a head, *books* in *many books on linguistics*, *rich* in *exceedingly rich in fauna and flora*, *outside* in *outside the kitchen window*. Sequences of words that count as phrases can be replaced by a single word – *they* for *these books*, *there* for *outside the kitchen window*. (This is the substitution test.) They also occur together in the same order in different frames: e.g. *these heavy books* in *Jennifer moved these heavy books*, *These heavy books were moved by Jennifer*, *These heavy books Jennifer moved (not Freya)*. (This is the transposition test, so called because the sequences of words were at one time thought of as being transposed, moved over other constituents.) 2. In **Government and Binding**, **Principles and Parameters** and the **Minimalist Program**, clauses are treated as Inflection Phrases. This analysis arose from the extension of **X-Bar syntax** from noun phrases, adjective phrases, prepositional phrases and verb phrases to functional categories such as tense and aspect.

PHRASE MARKER

Originally, the structure assigned to a sequence of **constituents** by a **phrase structure grammar**. Now used as equivalent to **phrase structure tree** or **tree diagram**.

PHRASE STRUCTURE GRAMMAR

Any grammar consisting of **phrase structure rules** alone, with no **transformations**. See **GENERALIZED PHRASE STRUCTURE GRAMMAR**, **HEAD-DRIVEN PHRASE STRUCTURE GRAMMAR**.

PHRASE STRUCTURE RULE

A rule stating that a **phrase** (or **clause**) consists of one or more **constituents**, which may be **words**, phrases or **clauses**. The rule NP → Det N generates the structure of *the flood, this flood, these floods* and so on. The rule NP → Det N S generates the structure for phrases such as *the fact that we are leaving*, where Det is *the* and N S is *fact that we are leaving*. The rules rewrite symbols representing different types of constituent. Each rule rewrites one symbol and cannot change the order of symbols. Rules can be **context-free** or **context-sensitive**. In a development in the early 1970s, phrase structure rules were interpreted not as generating structures but as well-formedness conditions on randomly generated trees. A tree containing an NP node dominating the sequence of nodes Det N S is admissible, but if the sequence is S Det N or if a PP node dominates Det N S, the tree is not admissible. In this conception, phrase structure rules were relabelled 'node admissibility conditions'.

PHRASE STRUCTURE TREE

A **tree diagram** showing the **constituent structure** of a word, phrase, clause or sentence. See **PHRASE STRUCTURE RULE**.

PHRASEOLOGY

The study of phrases, focusing on **collocations** and **fixed expressions**.

PIAGET, Jean (1896–1980)

Swiss psychologist, renowned for his work on the cognitive development of the child. He did not believe that knowledge was innate, but rather that it was constructed by children during their early years through physical interaction with the environment. His view was that the child progressed through a series of stages of cognitive development that could be studied empirically. He was not primarily interested in a child's linguistic development, but his position was very influential in studies of child language acquisition.

PICTISH

Apparently a non-Indo-European language. Spoken in eastern Scotland until c. eighth century CE.

PIDGIN

A trade language that has developed through contact between speakers who do not share a common language and that serves as a **lingua franca**. Each pidgin derives from a source language, from which it usually takes the bulk of its vocabulary, by **pidginization**. As contact languages pidgins have no native speakers, though they may in time be used as native languages, when they are known as **creoles**. Many, but by no means all, pidgins have developed from English or Portuguese. See **CREOLE** and the list of some pidgin and creole languages below.

	Source language	Where spoken
Berbice Dutch Creole	Dutch	Guyana
Bislama	English	Vanuatu
Cape Verdean Creole	Portuguese	Cape Verde
Fanagolo	Xhosa, Zulu etc.	Southern Africa
Gullah	English	South Carolina
Hawaiian Creole	English	Hawaii
Krio	English	Sierra Leone
Louisiana Creole	French	Lousiana, USA
Mobilian Jargon (extinct)	Choctaw	South-eastern US
Palenquero	Spanish	Colombia
Papamiento	Portuguese, Spanish	Curacao
Russenorsk (extinct)	Russian	Norwegian Arctic
Sango	French	Central African Republic
Sranan	English	Surinam
Tok Pisin	English	New Guinea
Tsotsi Taal	Afrikaans	South Africa

PIDGINIZATION

The language mixing, reduction, and simplification that eventually leads to a **pidgin**. The same processes are often found in imperfect adult second language learning.

PIED PIPING

The movement of **wh forms** which take their **modifiers** with them. E.g. in **transformational grammar**, **relative clauses** such as *the book [in which I read this]* or *the book [in the footnotes of which I found this]* derive from the clauses: *the book [I read this in which]* and *the book [I found this in the footnotes of which]*. *Which* moves to the front of the clause taking with it *in* and *in the footnotes of*. ('Pied piping' is a **back-formation** from 'pied piper'. Just as the rats followed the Pied Piper of Hamelin, so the constituents follow the wh word.) See **MOVEMENT, NP-MOVEMENT, TRANSFORMATION**.

PIG LATIN

A schoolchildren's antilanguage that disguises words by, for example, inserting a syllable after the initial consonant **cluster**: *l-ike th-is* > *legike thegis*. Alternatively, the initial consonant cluster is moved to the end of the word and a vowel is added: *l-ike th-is* > *ikeley isthey*. A version is found in French, where it is known as *verslan* (from *l'envers* 'the other way round'), and in a number of other languages.

PIKE, Kenneth (1912–2000)

Professor of Linguistics at the University of Michigan who on retirement moved to the Summer Institute centre in Dallas. His first interest was in phonetics and phonology, then in language and culture, then in the 1950s in grammatical analysis when he developed the theory of **tagmemics**. He was a prolific author not only on linguistics but also scripture translation.

PINYIN

See **CHINESE**.

PITCH

The auditory correlate of acoustic frequency. In perceptual terms sounds are measured on a scale from high to low; in acoustic terms this is measured as frequency. Pitch is studied by the phonologist in terms either of **intonation** or of **tone**.

PITJANTJATJARA

Pama-Nyungan, Australian languages. 2.5K speakers, Australia.

PIVOT

An NP that is associated with the verbs in successive **clauses**. Thus, in English the subject noun, typically denoting an agent, is the pivot in coordinated clauses; in *Kirsty phoned and cancelled the appointment*, *Kirsty* is the overt subject of *phoned* and the understood subject of *cancelled*. Subject nouns are also the pivots in reduced **relative clauses** such as *The dog chasing that black cat is our Labrador*. The understood subject of *chasing* is *the dog*, which is the overt subject of *is our Labrador*. In **ergative** languages pivot NPs typically denote patients and are in the **absolutive** case. A more recent name than 'pivot' is 'privileged syntactic argument'. See GRAMMATICAL FUNCTION.

PLACE ADVERBIAL

A word or phrase functioning as an **adverbial** and denoting a location: e.g. *in Wagga Wagga, under the sofa, upstairs*. See ADVERB.

PLACE FEATURES

See SPE DISTINCTIVE FEATURE THEORY.

PLACE OF ARTICULATION

Identifies the place of contact or of constriction between a moveable or **active articulator**, usually the tongue, and an immobile or passive articulator, usually the roof of the mouth. Thus, from the lips: **bilabial** (the two lips); **labiodental** (the lower lip against the teeth); **dental** (the tip of the tongue against the teeth); **alveolar** (the blade of the tongue against the teeth ridge); **retroflex** (the tip of the tongue curled back against the front part of the hard palate); **alveo-palatal** (the front of the tongue against the back of the teeth ridge); **palatal** (the front of the tongue against the hard palate); **velar** (the back of the tongue against the soft palate or velum); **uvular** (the back of the tongue against the uvula); **pharyngeal** (in the pharynx); **glottal** (in the larynx by the closure or constriction of the glottis).

PLACE PHRASE

A phrase expressing location in a place, such as *(sitting) in a large armchair, (lying) on top of the cupboard, (hiding) under the bed*. See LOCATIVE.

PLAIN

In **J&H Distinctive Feature Theory**, an acoustic distinctive feature. Unusually, it is effectively a term in a ternary **opposition**: flat, plain, sharp. Most of the unmarked consonants of English and other languages are plain.

PLEONASM

Pleonasm occurs when a **sentence** contains words and phrases that are redundant, in that they convey information already conveyed or entailed by another word or phrase. E.g. in *The intruder murdered the couple illegally*, *illegally* is redundant because murder is intrinsically illegal. The sentence is said to be pleonastic or an example of pleonasm.

PLEONASTIC PRONOUN

See DUMMY SUBJECT.

PLESIONYMY

The relationship between two lexical items that are close in meaning but not enough to count as cognitively synonymous. FOG, HAAR and ROKE are cognitively synonymous; they all apply to the fogs that affect the north-east coast of Britain when an easterly wind blows in off the North Sea. (FOG also applies more generally.) These lexical items differ with respect to variety of English: FOG is standard English, HAAR is Scottish English and ROKE is Northumbrian. None of these items is cognitively synonymous with HAZE, as demonstrated by the following example: *This isn't a haar/sea-fog/roke; it's just a haze*. Nonetheless, HAZE and FOG, and HAZE and HAAR apply in the same domain of meaning. See **SYNONYMY**.

PLOSIVE

A term in the description of the **manner of articulation** of pulmonic **egressive** stop **consonants**. English has a range of plosives both voiced and unvoiced at different **places of articulation**: from **bilabial**, [p], [b]; through **alveolar** [t] [d] to **velar** [k], [g]. In other languages there is an even wider range of places of articulation from bilabial to **pharyngeal**. See **PULMONIC AIRSTREAM**.

PLUPERFECT

See **PERFECT**.

PLURAL

A category of **number** relating to two or more entities – three or more in languages with a **dual**. Plural is marked on **nouns** – *dog–dogs*, and on verbs – **Russian** *poet* 'he/she is singing' vs *pojut* 'they are singing'. In some languages plural is marked on **determiner** and noun (**French** *le chat* 'the cat' vs *les chats* 'the cats'), in some languages it is marked only on the determiner (**Maori**), and in other languages, such as **Chinese**, it is marked in **pronouns** but not in full nouns. See **MORPH, SINGULAR**.

PLURALIA TANTUM

Nouns that only have a **plural** form. E.g. English *trousers*, *scales* (for weighing; compare the French singular noun *une balance* (sg). 'a set-of-scales'); Russian *sanki* (pl) 'sledge'. (*Pluralia tantum* is Latin and translates as 'plural only'. *Pluralia* is a neuter plural form; the singular, *plurale*, is very rarely used in descriptions of English grammar.)

POINT OF REFERENCE

See **INDEX**.

POINT OF VIEW

See **FOCALIZATION**.

POLARITY

The opposition between the **negative** pole (*no, she's not resigning*) and the **positive** pole (*yes, she is resigning*). The opposition applies to **clauses**, as in the preceding examples, but also to pairs of **lexical words**. Polarity may be signalled by a negative affix on one of the terms, e.g. *worthy–unworthy, abashed–unabashed, honest–dishonest, moral–amoral*. *Worthy* is at the positive pole, *unworthy* is at

the negative pole. Adjectives with negative affixes are privative.
See **NEGATIVE POLARITY ITEM**.

POLISH
Slavic, Indo-European. 38.4M speakers, Poland.

POLITENESS PRINCIPLE
A principle proposed by Leech to supplement the **maxims of conversation**. It consists of various maxims whose purpose is to avoid hearers losing face and to make hearers feel good. The Maxim of Praise enjoins speakers not to be (too) critical of hearers and to give praise when possible. E.g. the question *Did you like the paper I sent you?* should not be answered with *No* or *It was pretty poor* but along the lines of *I really enjoyed reading it. One or two things occurred to me. Can I send you some comments?* The Maxim of Sympathy enjoins speakers to be sympathetic to hearers as required by the situation and to avoid being unsympathetic. The Maxim of Modesty enjoins speakers not to trumpet their achievements and good qualities. Thus, a response to *You've made a real contribution to the field* might be *Well, I was lucky in having X and Y as colleagues.* The maxims of conversation are socially neutral and the maxims of politeness can be seen as specifying reasons for flouting them. The comment *What a wonderful meal!* may elicit the response *Oh, it was nothing, just a little recipe from X's cookery book.* The response would probably flout the Maxim of Quality.
See **IMPLICATURE**.

POLYGENESIS
See **MONOGENESIS**.

POLYLECTAL GRAMMAR
A grammar that attempts to accommodate several dialects of a language.

POLYNESIAN
Subgroup of **Austronesian**. Spoken in the Polynesian triangle whose points are New Zealand, Hawaii and Easter Island. Includes Samoan, Tongan, Fijian and **Maori**.

POLYSEMOUS
See **POLYSEMY**.

POLYSEMY
When a word has two or more **senses** that are related, it is said to show polysemy or to be polysemous. Thus, *head* is polysemous, having various senses in *He hit his head on the ceiling, the head of the valley, the head of the screw, the head of our Department.* See **ANTAGONISM, FACETS, HOMONYMY, MONOSEMY**.

POLYSYLLABIC
Having more than one **syllable**.

POLYSYSTEMIC

In **phonology**, particularly **prosodic phonology**, the label for analyses in which different phonological systems are recognized for different parts of a given language. For example, in a C_1VC_2 structure, the set of contrasts at C_1 may be different from those at C_2; the phonological system of the **verb** might be different from that of the **noun**, or there might be different phonological systems for different parts of the lexicon, e.g. 'native' words vs 'loan' words. Such analyses contrast with those that propose a single homogeneous phonological system for a language. See **PROSODIC PHONOLOGY**.

POMOAN LANGUAGES

Native American, some extinct. Coast Range north of San Francisco.

PORTMANTEAU MORPH

A single **morph** realizing two morphemes that elsewhere are realized by two morphs one after the other. E.g. French *aux Pyrénéés* 'to-the Pyrenees', where *aux = à* 'to' plus *les* ('the' plus **plural**), English *mice = mouse* plus **plural**; compare *dogs = dog + s*, where *dog* realizes the lexeme and *-s* realizes plural. (French *portmanteau* 'large travelling bag for carrying coats and suits'. Lewis Carroll invented the term 'portmanteau word' for words like *slithy*, a blend of *slimy* and *lithe*.) See **LEXICAL WORD, MORPHOLOGY, REALIZATION**.

PORTUGUESE

Romance, Indo-European. 10M speakers Portugal, 195M Brazil. Widely used as a second language in Angola and Mozambique.

POS TAGGER

A computer program that assigns each word in a digitally stored text to its part of speech. See **WORD CLASS**.

POSITION

In dialogue, the assumption by speakers that they are entitled or obliged to carry out certain acts, linguistic or otherwise, during a given interaction and the assignment of such entitlements and obligations to speakers by their listeners. Positions are temporary and continually under negotiation during interactions, whereas **stances** are typically of longer duration.

POSITIVE

1. Not negative. Equivalent to **affirmative**: *The book is dull* is a positive **sentence** or **clause**, *the book is not dull* is **negative**. 2. Not marked for **comparative** or **superlative**; *fast* is positive, *faster* is comparative, *fastest* is superlative. See **COMPARISON, GRADABLE ADJECTIVE, NEGATIVE POLARITY ITEM, POLARITY**.

POSSESSIVE

Applied to any **construction** denoting possession. The construction may involve a **case** affix on the **noun** denoting the possessor – Russian *Ivan* 'Ivan', *kniga Ivana* 'book Ivan-GEN, Ivan's book'; a case **affix** as in **Russian** and an affix on the noun denoting the thing possessed – **Turkish** *ev* 'house' *Mehmet, Mehmetin evisi* 'Mehmet-gen house-POSS3sg, Mehmet's house'; a **preposition** – **French** *le livre de Thérèse* 'the book of Theresa, 'Theresa's book'; or by a determiner (possessive adjective in older grammars) as in – *my house, your money, her book*. These structures focus on the thing possessed but other structures focus on the possessor, such as *the man with a Porsche* or *the dog with two tails*. Some Australian languages have a special proprietive case suffix: 'man-genitive book' is equivalent to 'the man's book' but 'man book-PROP is equivalent to 'the man with a book'.

POSSESSIVE ADJECTIVE

An older term often now replaced by **determiner**. See **POSSESSIVE**.

POSSESSIVE PRONOUN

A subset of **determiners** denoting possession in the broadest sense: *my, your, his, her, its, our, their,* as in *my house, their books, his accident*. A distinction is drawn between the determiner possessive pronouns and independent possessive pronouns such as *mine, yours,* etc in *The idea was mine/yours/hers/his/theirs*. See **POSSESSIVE**.

POSSIBLE WORLD SEMANTICS

A possible world is any possible state-of-affairs. Possible world semantics is a theory of formal semantics in which **propositions**, as expressed by **utterances**, are judged true or false with reference to possible worlds, not just to one world. E.g. *Everyone reads the poetry of Burns* is not true in the world in which this entry is being written but could be true in some other possible world. The concept of possible worlds is important in modal logic, which encompasses, not just propositions that are true or false, but propositions that are possibly true and propositions that are necessarily true. Being possibly true is interpreted as being true in some possible world; being necessarily true is interpreted as being true in all possible worlds. See **MODALITY, MODEL-THEORETIC SEMANTICS**.

POST CREOLE CONTINUUM

A dialect continuum that is the result of contact between a creole, the **basilect**, and its source language, the **acrolect**, when the creole has partially decreolized. See **DECREOLIZATION**.

POST-ALVEOLAR

See **ALVEOLAR**.

POSTCYCLIC RULES

In phonological theories, especially **lexical phonology**, that call on the **cycle**, rules that apply after all the cyclic rules have applied. In general **cyclic rules** are primarily concerned with **morphology** within the **word**, and postcyclic rules with processes within the **phrase**. See **CYCLIC PRINCIPLE**.

POSTDETERMINER

A **determiner** preceded by other determiners such as the definite **article** *the*, the **demonstratives** *this*, *that*, etc. and **possessive** adjectives such as *their*. E.g. *three* in *the three friends*, *other* in *these other books*, *many* in *their many relatives*.

POSTLEXICAL RULES

Rules that apply in a **derivation** after the insertion of lexical items. See **LEXICAL PHONOLOGY**.

POSTMODERNISM

An intellectual movement that thrived from the early 1960s to the 1990s and affected literature, art and architecture. Postmodernist writers flaunted their skill in wordplay, indulged in pastiche, produced collages of different text types and questioned accepted ideas about narrative and the distinction between fiction and reality.

POSTMODIFIER

Any **modifier** that follows its **head**. In grammars of English, any **constituent** that modifies and follows a **noun**: e.g. *inside* in *the people inside*, the postmodifying PP *of Hume* in *the influence of Hume*, the **relative clause** *that she wrote* in *the novel that she wrote*. See **PREMODIFIER**.

POSTMODIFYING GENITIVE

See **POSTMODIFIER**.

POSTPOSING

Moving to the end of a **clause** a heavy **constituent** other than the **subject**. E.g. in the previous sentence, *a heavy constituent other than the subject* is the **direct object** of *moving* but was shifted to the end of the clause for stylistic reasons. A heavy constituent may be moved out of a **noun phrase**, as in *A book about the causes of the credit crunch has just been published* → *A book has just been published about the causes of the credit crunch*. See **DUMMY SUBJECT, END WEIGHT, EXTRAPOSITION, HEAVY NOUN PHRASE**.

POSTPOSITION

A **constituent** that links **nouns** to **verbs**, **adjectives** and other nouns but follows the noun. Postpositions have the same function as **prepositions** in English and **case** suffixes in languages such as **Finnish**. E.g. Turkish *bu adam gibi* 'this man like, like this man'. See **ADPOSITION, ELATIVE**. (Latin *post* 'after', *positus* 'placed'.)

POST-STRUCTURALISM

An approach to the analysis of **texts** and literary criticism which incorporates deconstruction but goes further in emphasizing the precarious relationship between **words** and **referents** and the impossibility of a direct, simple relationship between language and a world outside language. See **COGNITIVE LINGUISTICS, CONSTRUAL, DECONSTRUCTION, REFERENCE**.

POTENTIAL PAUSE

A point in a **word** at which a speaker might pause. Potential pauses are often invoked as a diagnostic for identifying word boundaries. Thus in *gentlemen prefer blondes* there are potential pauses at word boundaries (gentlemen # prefer # blondes) but not in the middle of words (*gentle#men pre#fer blondes). See **BOUNDARY**.

POVERTY OF STIMULUS

Especially in Chomsky's theory of **first language** acquisition, the idea that children hear **utterances** realizing a limited range of **constructions** and vocabulary and full of hesitations, repetitions, unfinished **clauses** and so on. From this kind of language, it is impossible for children to infer the grammatical rules of the adult version of their native language. See **COMPETENCE, E-LANGUAGE, I-LANGUAGE, PERFORMANCE**.

PP

See **PREPOSITIONAL PHRASE**.

P-RULE

In **natural phonology**, a **PHONOLOGICAL RULE**.

PRACTICAL CRITICISM

Detailed analysis of **texts** based on intuitive reactions to them.

PRAGMALINGUISTIC NORMS

In a given society, the norms governing which linguistic structures are appropriate in a given **sociopragmatic** context. E.g. in many societies the question *What did your car cost?* is not appropriate when speaking to a stranger. *She* and *he* is not a polite way of referring to someone who is present; *your friend, Mr Crichton*, or *Robert* are examples of the expected usage. See **SOCIOPRAGMATIC NORMS**.

PRAGMATICS

In current usage, pragmatics is held to deal with the use of language in **context**. It covers the acts performed by speakers and writers when they use language, the inferences by which hearers and readers construct a rich interpretation that goes beyond what is actually said or written, the things that speakers and writers presuppose (take for granted), the conventions governing what is appropriate in particular situations. Many analysts draw a strict division between pragmatics and **semantics**. However, the analysis of real language requires both, and key concepts in pragmatics, such as **implicature, maxims of conversation, presupposition** and **speech acts** originated and were developed in philosophy and semantics. See **CONTEXT, EXPLICATURE, PRAGMALINGUISTIC NORMS, RELEVANCE THEORY, SOCIOPRAGMATIC NORMS**.

PRAGUE SCHOOL

Work associated with the Prague Linguistic Circle in the 1920s and 1930s especially **Trubetskoy** and **Jakobson**. Particularly influential in the development of **phoneme** theory, their typology of **oppositions** and theorizing relating to the **archiphoneme**, **neutralization** and **markedness** is still of interest. Prague School ideas also played an important role in the development of the theory of **distinctive features** and **generative phonology**.

PREDETERMINER

Especially in grammars of English, a **determiner** that precedes other determiners: e.g. *all, both, half* in *all the members, both these theories, half my fortune*. See **POSTDETERMINER**.

PREDICATE

1. In syntax and semantics, a predicate is a **constituent**, typically a verb, that takes a set of **arguments** within a **clause**: *vanish* takes one argument – *The rabbit vanished*, *scrape* takes two arguments – *He scraped the car*, and *put* takes three arguments – *I put the car in the garage*. *Vanish* is a one-place predicate, *scrape* is a two-place predicate and *put* is a three-place predicate. 2. In traditional **logic**, predicate was applied to an act performed by speakers. Speakers were held to refer to some entity, to put down some entity to be talked about, and then to say something about it, to assign a property to it or predicate a property of it. 3. In syntax and semantics, the part of a **clause** conveying what a speaker predicates of, or asserts about, an entity by means of a predicate (2): e.g. *The dog runs quickly*, *The dog chased the cat into the house*. A distinction is drawn between such primary predications, conveyed by **finite verbs**, and secondary predications, conveyed by other types of constituent and occurring in the same clause as a primary predication. Thus, in *He returned very happy*, *returned* conveys the primary predication, *very happy* conveys the secondary predication. 4. In modern logic, a component of predicate-**argument** structures in which a predicate denoting some property or relation is applied to an argument denoting an entity. To predicates in this sense correspond, **adjectives**, **adpositions**, **adverbs**, **nouns** and **verbs**. In *The dog is black*, *dog* corresponds to a predicate denoting the property 'being a dog' which is applied to an entity. *Black* corresponds to another property applied to that entity. In *The dog runs quickly*, *quickly* corresponds to a predicate denoting a property of running – the running is quick. See **PREDICATOR, PROPOSITION, RHEME, THEME**.

PREDICATE CALCULUS

See **CALCULUS, QUANTIFIER**.

PREDICATE FOCUS

A **proposition** consists of a **predicate** and **arguments**. When a proposition is expressed by means of a clause in an utterance the focus may be on the predicate. E.g. in *What happened to Fiona? – She got malaria*, the **focus** in the reply falls on *got malaria* and *malaria* carries the focal accent. See **ARGUMENT FOCUS, END FOCUS, SENTENCE FOCUS**.

PREDICATE LOGIC
See **PREDICATE CALCULUS**.

PREDICATE NOMINAL
A **noun phrase** that is part of a **predicate** in sense (3): e.g, *Susan is my boss*, *She is my daughter*, *That was a joke*.

PREDICATE-ARGUMENT STRUCTURE
In the analysis of clause structure, that part of the representation that shows the predicate, in the sense of **predicate** (1) and its **arguments**, in particular the number of arguments and the **role**, such as agent and patient, assigned to each one. See **PREDICATOR, SUBCATEGORIZATION**.

PREDICATION
See **PREDICATE** in sense (2).

PREDICATION THEORY
The theory of **predicates** in sense (4).

PREDICATIVE
A **constituent** that is part of a **predicate** (3).

PREDICATIVE ADJECTIVE
See **ADJECTIVE**.

PREDICATIVE EXPRESSION
Any expression conveying a **predicate** in sense (2).

PREDICATOR
1. A **constituent**, typically a **verb** or **adjective**, that is central to a **predicate** in sense (3). 2. Such a constituent seen as determining the number and type of constituents in a clause. See **DEPENDENCY, HEAD, SUBCATEGORIZATION, VERB DEPENDENCY GRAMMAR**.

PREFERENCE ORGANIZATION
In **conversation analysis**, the organization of possible responses to a **move** in an **adjacency pair** according to which is most preferred or likely and which is least preferred or likely. See **EXCHANGE**.

PREFIX
See **AFFIX**.

PREMISE
A **proposition** that is taken for granted at the initial stage of an argument. In the sequence *It is raining, There is a slate missing from the roof, The rain will come through where there is no slate* therefore *The ceiling will be wet by the time we*

get home, the sentences preceding *therefore* express the premises, and the sentence following expresses the conclusion.

PREMISS
See PREMISE.

PREMODIFIER
Any **modifier** that precedes its **head**. In grammars of English, a modifier that precedes a noun in a **noun phrase**: E.g. *Indian summer*, *wooden expression*. See POSTMODIFIER.

PREP
See PREPOSITION.

PREPARATORY CONDITION
See FELICITY CONDITIONS.

PREPOSING
The fronting of a **constituent**, i.e. moving it to the front of a **clause** or **sentence** for emphasis or contrast. E.g. *I absolutely hate broccoli* → *Broccoli I absolutely hate*, *I'll finish plastering and start painting tomorrow* → *Tomorrow I'll finish plastering and start painting*, *He isn't generous* → *Generous he isn't*. See THEMATIC FRONTING, TOPICALIZATION.

PREPOSITION
A **constituent** that protypically links a **verb, adjective** or **noun** to another **noun phrase**, which it precedes: e.g. *works in the bank, small in stature, books about caving*; Latin *ex Africa semper aliquid novi* 'out-of Africa always something of-new, There is always something new from Africa'. The *bank, stature* and *caving* are **complements** of the prepositions. Some analyses distinguish intransitive prepositions as in *He tripped over* and transitive prepositions as in *He tripped over the carpet*. (Latin *prae* 'in front of', *positus* 'placed'.) Prepositions also link verbs and adjectives, as in *What counts as expensive?*, *That passes for amusing in these parts*. Some analysts treat items such as *after* in *after we arrived* and *before* in *before he resigned* as prepositions taking a clause as a complement; an example from non-standard English is *without she helps* = *unless she helps*. See ADPOSITION, CONJUNCTION, POSTPOSITION, PREPOSITIONAL ADVERB.

PREPOSITIONAL ADVERB
Especially in grammars of English, **prepositions** that are not followed by a **noun phrase**: e.g. *She came across and spoke to us* vs *She came across the room and spoke to us*, *You're lagging behind* vs *You're lagging behind the others*, *The office is upstairs*.

PREPOSITIONAL COMPLEMENT
Whatever **constituent** follows and modifies a **preposition**: e.g. *to Moscow, after leaving the office, in behind the boxes*. See COMPLEMENT, HEAD.

PREPOSITIONAL GROUP
See PREPOSITIONAL PHRASE.

PREPOSITIONAL PHRASE
A **phrase** with a **preposition** as its **head**.

PREPOSITIONAL PRONOUN
In **Arabic**, **Hebrew** and the **Celtic** languages, **prepositions** that are marked for **person**. E.g. Scottish Gaelic *agam* 'at me', *agad* 'at you', *aice* 'at him', etc.

PREPOSITIONAL VERB
A unit consisting of a **verb** with a **prepositional phrase** as its **complement**: *look + after the children, decide + on a new carpet*. The choice of preposition is controlled by particular verbs: *decide on* but not **decide over*. The meaning of the combination may not be obvious from the meanings of the verb and the preposition separately. Prepositional verbs are not the same as **phrasal verbs**. In the latter the particle can be put after the direct object, as in *I looked up their number* and *I looked their number up*. The preposition in prepositional verbs cannot follow the direct object: *I can't cope with many problems* but not **I can't cope many problems with*. See PARTICLE.

PRESCRIPTIVE
See ADEQUACY, PRESCRIPTIVE GRAMMAR.

PRESCRIPTIVE GRAMMAR
A grammar of a language that does not describe the actual usage of speakers and writers but sets out or prescribes what the author thinks is the correct way of saying or writing something. E.g. a grammar might classify *It was them that caused the trouble* as incorrect, prescribing instead *It was they who caused the trouble* and ignoring the fact that most speakers of English use the former and never the latter.

PRESENT PARTICIPLE
A **participle** that supposedly has present tense; e.g. *jogging* in *Jacob is jogging in the park*. The participle actually takes its interpretation from context: *is jogging* is present, *was jogging* is past, but the contrast lies in *is* vs *was*. In *Today the girl sitting at the back is smiling at you* and *Yesterday the girl sitting at the back was smiling at you*, *sitting* is interpreted as present or past depending on whether it combines with *Today* and *is smiling* or *Yesterday* and *was smiling*. See FREE PARTICIPLE, PAST PARTICIPLE, PASSIVE PARTICIPLE.

PRESENT PERFECT
See PERFECT.

PRESENT TENSE
The subcategory of tense relating to present time. It is used when speakers present an event or state as occurring in a stretch of time that includes the moment of speech: e.g. *The laptop is working (as I speak, it was working just before*

I began to speak and may or may not continue after I stop speaking). Speakers choose whether to present situations as occurring in present time. Speakers who say *We are leaving/leave on Tuesday* present the event as arranged and in present time as they perceive it. Speakers who use the present tense when telling stories present the events as though they were in present time: *I go up the stairs and I see this bloke lying there...* This use of the present tense is called the **Historic Present**, but it is not a different tense, merely a special use of the present tense for narrative effect. See **NON-PAST TENSE, PAST TENSE, SIMPLE PRESENT, TENSE AND ASPECT**.

PRE-SEQUENCE

In **conversation analysis**, a turn that functions as a preliminary to some **exchange**. E.g. the utterance *Do you know anything about computers?* preceding a request *Could you have a look at my laptop?*, or *Excuse me* preceding a request for directions. See **PHATIC COMMUNION**.

PRESSURE STOP

A stop consonant made on an **egressive glottalic airstream**, an **ejective**. Contrasts with suction stop or **implosive**.

PRESTIGE

The high status enjoyed by a language or dialect within a speech community. In general the language of a higher social class, typically the **standard language**, is considered more prestigious than that of a lower social class. However, within a local community non-standard language may acquire **covert prestige** as an indicator of community membership and of desirable qualities such as friendliness.

PRESUPPOSITION

1. In philosophy, a relation between **propositions** such that a given proposition can be true or false, i.e. can have a truth value, only if some presupposed proposition is true. E.g. the proposition *John's brothers work abroad* can only be assessed as true or false if John has brothers; it presupposes the proposition *John has brothers*. Presupposition holds even if the given proposition is negated: *John's brothers don't work abroad* still presupposes *John has brothers*.
2. In pragmatics, a proposition that speakers and writers take for granted when making assertions. In asking *Who smashed the window?* the speaker presupposes that someone smashed the window. If the addressee replies *What do you mean? The window isn't smashed*, the speaker realizes that their presupposition is incorrect. See **FACTIVE 3**. The act of taking some proposition for granted.

PRETERITE

A slightly old-fashioned term, equivalent to **Simple Past**. (Latin *praeter* 'past' (as 'going past') and *itum* roughly = 'having gone'.)

PREVOCALIC

The position before a **vowel** in a **syllable**.

PRIMARY CARDINAL VOWEL
See **CARDINAL VOWELS**.

PRIMARY OBJECT
See **GRAMMATICAL FUNCTION**.

PRIMARY STRESS
The strongest **stress** that is put on a syllable in a word or a phrase when it is spoken. See **SECONDARY STRESS, LEVEL STRESS**.

PRIMARY VERBS
In **CGEL**, *be*, *do* and *have*, the three most common verbs in English. They can all function either as main verbs or **auxiliary** verbs. See **LEXICAL VERB**.

PRIME NOTATION
See **BAR NOTATION, X-BAR SYNTAX**.

PRINCIPAL EXPONENT
Where a morpheme is realized by two or more **morphs** in a single **word**, the morph that is regarded as the most salient and as the one that is focused on the morpheme. For instance, in Latin *laboravit* 'he worked' **perfective** is realized or signalled by *-v* and by *-it*. Since *-it* also realizes third **person** and singular **number**, *-v* is considered the principal exponent of perfective in Latin.

PRINCIPAL PARTS
For a given **verb** in a given language, the **form** or forms from which all the other forms can be predicted. These forms are listed in dictionaries, reference grammars and grammars for learners who are native speakers of another language. (But native speakers need to consult such lists too. *Le Petit Larousse Illustré* (2000), a dictionary-encyclopaedia for native speakers of French, lists, for each of ninety-five verbs, twenty-four forms from which all the other forms can be constructed by readers who know the patterns.) E.g. the irregular Latin verb *ferre* 'to carry' has the first-person singular present tense form *fero* 'I carry'. From this can be predicted the **future tense** and **imperfect** forms. The **perfect** is *tuli* 'I carried/have carried' and from it can be predicted the future perfect and **pluperfect**. The **supine** is *latum*, which, like the infinitive *ferre*, cannot be predicted. The principal parts of *fero* are *fero – ferre – tuli – latum*. See **TENSE AND ASPECT**.

PRINCIPLES AND PARAMETERS
The model of grammar developed by Chomsky and his colleagues from the early 1980s. It was first known as **Government and Binding Theory** (GB) because of the central role played by **government** in controlling the occurrence of **traces** and by the theory of **binding** between traces and **pronouns** and their **antecedents**. The name of the model was changed because government was not the only important concept in it and there were several other principles besides binding, which was anyway not unique to this model. In the

deepest level of representation, **D-structure**, syntactic structure was projected by individual lexical items according to **X-Bar syntax** principles. D-structure was converted into S-**structure** by two general **transformations** that substituted or adjoined any constituent for any other. The output of the transformations was controlled by various principles or theories: **bounding theory**, which constrained the movement of constituents by means of barriers; **case theory**, which constrained the occurrence of overt NPs and their relationship with empty NPs such as PRO; **government theory**, which determined the distribution of **traces**; the theory of **argument structure** and the assignment of **roles** to NPs; and **binding theory**, handling **anaphora** and free **reference**. S-structure was mapped onto Phonetic Form (PF) and Logical Form (LF), where, respectively, phonological and semantic properties were represented. See **ADJOIN, BOUND, COMPLEMENT CLAUSE, REFLEXIVE PRONOUN**.

PRISCIAN (fifth–sixth century BCE)

Lived and taught in Constantinople. His *Institutiones grammaticae* on the **morphosyntax** of Latin had a major influence on linguistic thought throughout the middle ages.

PRIVATIVE ADJECTIVE

See **POLARITY**.

PRIVATIVE OPPOSITION

An opposition between two segments one of which is **marked** for some feature and the other unmarked. Thus in the contrast between the labial **stops** /p/ and /b/, /b/ is marked by the presence of voice, i.e. [+voice], in contrast with /p/ which is unmarked, i.e. [−voice]. See **PRAGUE SCHOOL**.

PRIVILEGED SYNTACTIC ARGUMENT

See **PIVOT**.

PRO

In **Government and Binding** and **Principles and Parameters**, a null NP. Its **referent** may be arbitrary, as in *[PRO] to give in would be stupid*, where the subject PRO is interpreted as 'one' – *For one to give in would be stupid*. Typically the referent of PRO is controlled by another NP, as in *Gordon wanted [PRO] to win the election*, where PRO is **anaphoric** to *Gordon*. PRO is called 'big pro'. See **ANAPHORA, UNDERSTOOD SUBJECT**.

Pro

In **Government and Binding** and **Principles and Parameters**, the underlying pronoun subject of **finite verbs** with no overt **subject**. E.g. in Italian *Partiamo per Roma* 'we-are-leaving for Rome' the verb *partiamo* does not have a subject NP, although the suffix *-amo* points to the speaker and at least one other person. In Principles and Parameters, the structure of this **clause** has an NP containing *pro*, which is realized as zero. *Pro* is called 'little pro'. See **PRO-DROP LANGUAGE**.

PROCESS

1. In analyses of languages, an operation by which one **form** is derived from another. E.g. *The window was broken by the ball* can be thought of as derived by a syntactic process from *The ball broke the window*; *education* as derived from *educate* by a derivational process; the position of the stress in *edu'cation* by a phonological process. 2. In **Aktionsart** theory, a dynamic situation in which change takes place, energy is expended but there is no **agent**: e.g. *The snow thawed, The blossom opened*. Processes contrast with actions, which are also dynamic but have agents, as in *The gardener planted many fruit trees*, and with states, which do not involve change or the expenditure of energy: *Juliet knows the answer, Margaret understands advanced calculus*.

PROCLITIC

See **CLITIC**.

PRO-DROP LANGUAGE

A language in which **verbs** do not need an overt **subject** noun phrase. E.g. Italian *hanno telefonato* 'they-have phoned', Russian *xochesh' chaju?* 'you-want some-tea?.Would you like tea?'. Such languages are said to obey the null-subject parameter. See **GRAMMATICAL FUNCTION, pro**.

PRODUCTIVE

A productive rule or pattern allows new **words** or combinations of words to be freely created. The addition of *-ness* to **adjectives** is productive in English, as is the addition of *-able* to verbs: *do-able, persuadable*. The yes/no **interrogative** pattern is productive: *Have you seen my wallet?* Semi-productive rules and patterns apply to a number of **stems** but not to all apparently eligible ones: e.g. the addition of *-ant* to verbs yields *defendant, assailant* and so on but not **adaptant* or **creatant*. The middle pattern is extending its range but applies unpredictably: *The surface scratches easily* but *?The surface does not deface*. Unproductive rules and patterns are not used for the creation of new forms. The suffix *-id* as in *frigid* and *tepid* exists only in a limited number of words, which have to be listed. The term 'semi-productive' should be replaced by 'partially productive', since productivity is a continuum, not a three-way distinction. See **DERIVATIONAL MORPHOLOGY, VOICE**.

PRODUCTIVITY

1. One of the proposed **design features** that characterize a human language. A native speaker can produce and understand an infinite number of **sentences**. 2. The degree to which native speakers use a particular grammatical process to produce novel (new, non-established) structures. In **derivational morphology**, productive **affixes** are those frequently used for new forms (e.g. *-able* in *drinkable, readable*, etc.) in contrast to non-productive affixes (e.g. *-th* in *length, breadth*, etc.). 3. The property of being **productive**.

PROFILE AND BASE

See BASE AND PROFILE.

PRO-FORM

By analogy with **pronoun** (= pro+noun), any form thought to 'stand for' another **word**, **phrase** or **clause**. A pronoun stands for – picks up the **referent** of – a **noun phrase** of any length and complexity: thus in *Have you seen it?*, *it* picks up the reference of some noun phrase in an earlier part of the conversation: e.g. *my wallet* or *the black pigskin wallet into which I put the bundle of euro notes*. *So* functions as a pro-adjective – *Rory is worried and so is Angus*; as a pro-VP, understood as the main verb and its **modifiers** (excluding the subject) – *I'm leaving for Paris on Wednesday and so is Margaret*, where *so* = *leaving for Paris on Wednesday*; and as a pro-clause – *I believe there is a strike on Monday, at least Jane said so*, where *so* = *there is a strike on Monday*. See ANAPHOR, ANTECEDENT, BOUND.

PROGRAMMING LANGUAGE

A formal language in which instructions are given to a computer.

PROGRESSIVE

A **viewpoint aspect** which is used to present an event as in progress. The speaker who says *Sabrina is playing the piano* presents the event as on-going at the time of speaking but says nothing about when it began or how long it will continue. The classic and most-analysed progressive construction is the English one, but progressive constructions are found throughout **Bantu** and in some languages of Europe: e.g. Spanish *Ana esta trabajando en la sala* 'Ana is working in the sitting-room'. Some grammars of English use the term 'continuous'. See TENSE AND ASPECT.

PROGRESSIVE ASSIMILATION

When two words come together and the pronunciation of the first segment of the second word is influenced by the pronunciation of the final segment of the first word. E.g. *did you* [dɪd ju] becomes [dɪdʒu]. See ASSIMILATION.

PROJECTION

See X-BAR SYNTAX.

PROJECTION PRINCIPLE

See X-BAR SYNTAX.

PROLEPSIS

1. In rhetoric, narrating an event from a point in time before it would occur in real life: e.g. *For the rest of his life the unhappy Torquil would regret his mother dying from the disease that was about to be diagnosed.*

PROMOTION
See **DEMOTE**.

PRONOMINAL
Belonging to the set of **pronouns**. (Latin *pro* 'in place of', *nomina* 'names, nouns'.)

PRONOMINALIZATION
A syntactic process whereby under certain conditions full **noun phrases** are replaced by **pronouns**. Thus, in early **transformational grammar** the sentence *Janie was deluding herself* was derived from *Janie was deluding Janie* by substituting *herself* for the second instance of *Janie*. See **PRO-FORM**.

PRONOUN
A class of words which were traditionally thought of as standing for nouns (hence pro + noun) or **noun phrases**. Personal pronouns (*I, you, he, she, it, we, they*) and demonstrative pronouns (*this, that*) convey a minimum of meaning: e.g. *I* refers to the speaker, *this* is used for something relatively close to the speaker. Personal pronouns or demonstrative pronouns may function as **anaphors** or **independent pronouns**. Other types are **reflexive pronoun**, **interrogative pronoun** and **relative pronoun**. Pronouns are typically the only **constituents** in noun phrases, as in *He forgot about the party*. Occasionally they have modifiers, as in *Silly old him forgot about the party*. See **ANAPHORA, ANTECEDENT, DEIXIS**.

PRO-NP
See **PRO-FORM**.

PROPER GOVERNMENT
In Government and Binding, part of the **empty category principle**. In examples such as *Who$_i$ do you think [they'll elect t$_i$]?* the trace t_i is bound to *who$_i$*. t_i is an empty category. Traces must be properly governed. A properly governs B if A governs B and A either assigns a theta role to B or is co-indexed with B. See **C-COMMAND, GOVERNMENT, PRINCIPLES AND PARAMETERS, THETA MARKING, THETA ROLE, THETA THEORY, TRACE**.

PROPER NOUN
See **COMMON NOUN**.

PROPOSITION
A proposition is the content of an assertion about some situation. E.g. *The British Prime Minister attended the climate-change conference in Copenhagen in December 2009* is an assertion conveying a proposition about a particular event, at a particular time and in particular location. The event is one of visiting; the agent is the British Prime Minister (whoever met that description) and the object visited is the climate-change conference. Propositions are built on **propositional content**, which is information about a type of event and types of **participants**; thus, VISIT (**agent, patient**) is a representation of the propositional content of the

above proposition. Propositional content does not relate to specific situations involving specific participants, times and places.

A proposition is asserted by means of a **declarative** clause (**sentence**), as in the above example. It is not asserted by means of an **interrogative clause** or an **imperative** clause. Speakers use declarative clauses to assert a proposition – *The Prime Minister attended …* – or to deny a proposition – *The Prime Minister did not attend ….* They use interrogative clauses to ask whether a proposition is true or false – *Did the British Prime Minister attend the climate-change conference in Copenhagen in December 2009?* – or to request information about components of the proposition: *Who attended?, What did he attend?, When did he attend?* and so on. And they use imperative clauses to order a particular situation to be brought about (a particular proposition to be made true or false): *Attend the conference* (addressed to the Prime Minister), *Don't attend the conference*.

Propositions are thought of as consisting of a **predicate** and one or more **arguments**. Thus, in *The baby is sleeping*, the predicate is represented as SLEEP and its argument as BABY. The predicate expresses a property of the argument. In *The dog chased the postman*, the predicate CHASE expresses a property of the arguments, DOG and POSTMAN, that they are in a relationship of chasing.

A distinction is traditionally drawn between analytic and synthetic propositions. Analytic propositions must be true, because of the meaning of their component parts (This is sometimes put in terms of the meanings of the lexical items in the clause expressing a given proposition.) For instance, *This tree has leaves* is analytic given the nature of trees and the meaning of the lexical item *tree*. *The tree is growing at the front door* is said to be synthetic. It can be true or false and is so because of the way the world is – and the world could be different: the tree might be growing at the bottom of the garden. See **CALCULUS, PREDICATE-ARGUMENT STRUCTURE, PREDICATOR, PROPOSITIONAL CALCULUS, PREDICATE CALCULUS, RHEME, SUBJECT, THEME**.

PROPOSITIONAL CALCULUS
See **CALCULUS**.

PROPOSITIONAL CONTENT
See **PROPOSITION**.

PROPOSITIONAL MEANING.
See **DESCRIPTIVE MEANING**.

PROSODIC FEATURE
Any **suprasegmental** feature, such as **intonation, loudness, length**.

PROSODIC LEVEL
See **METRICAL PHONOLOGY**.

PROSODIC PHONOLOGY
A phonological theory developed by J. R. Firth and his followers in London in the 1950s. Its basic units are **phonematic units**, positions in a linear structure,

and prosodies which have a domain over several phonematic units. Phonematic units follow and precede one another in **syntagmatic** structures, and for prosodic analysts, at each place in structure the paradigmatic system of oppositions is different: thus in the structure [sC] the **system** of oppositions at C is between voiceless stops, /p,t,k/, nasals /m,n/ and the lateral /l/, whereas in the structure [pC] the opposition is limited to /r,l/. In this form of **polysystemic** analysis, it is impossible to identify any of the phonological units occurring in a particular position with units occurring in another position in another structure. See **PROSODY**.

PROSODIC WORD

See **METRICAL PHONOLOGY**.

PROSODY

1. The study of meter, rhythm, etc. in poetry. 2. The **suprasegmental** features of **stress, pitch, tempo, loudness** and **rhythm**. 3. One of the two basic concepts in the theory of **prosodic phonology** accounting for those features that occur over more than a single segment, like intonation, but also for **nasality** and **vowel harmony** when these occur over more than a single segment. See **LONG COMPONENT, PHONEMATIC UNIT**.

PROTASIS

See **CONDITIONAL CLAUSE**.

PROTO INDO-EUROPEAN

The hypothesized ancestor language of the **Indo-European** languages.

PROTO LANGUAGE

In historical linguistics the reconstructed, or hypothetical, ancestor of a family of known languages.

PROTOTYPE

The central members of a set of entities are prototypes, good exemplars of the set. A given lexical item has a range of **referents**, some of which are prototypes and some of which are peripheral. Prototype referents of *bird* are, e.g., robins, sparrows and thrushes, all of which have feathers, fly, build nests off the ground and so on. Emus are not prototypical referents, at least in the northern hemisphere, since they do not fly and do not build nests off the ground. In grammar, *big* is a prototypical **adjective**: it has the comparative *bigger* and the superlative *biggest* and can be attributive, as in *the big house*, and predicative, as in *The house is big*. *Awake* is a peripheral adjective: it does not take *-er* or *-est*, nor *more__* or *most__*, and it does not occur in the construction *the__N*. See **GRADIENCE, WORD CLASS**.

PROTOTYPE THEORY

The theory that conceptual categories are separated from each other by fuzzy boundaries but that each category contains good, central members that meet all or most of the criteria for membership and peripheral members that do not. There are entities that do not fit clearly into any category. For speakers of English in the UK, robins and sparrows are deemed to be prototypical instances of the category BIRD: when asked to list five birds, say, they include robin and sparrow and when shown a picture and asked to say whether it does or does not show a bird, they respond very quickly to robins and sparrows but less quickly to penguins and ostriches. See **CLASSICAL THEORY OF CONCEPTS, LEVEL**.

PROVERB

A memorable saying expressing a perceived truth or moral lesson: e.g. *He who laughs last laughs best, People who live in glass houses shouldn't throw stones*. 'Proverb' is applied particularly to traditional sayings; new **aphorisms** are coined, but not new proverbs. See **MAXIM**.

PRO-VERB

See **PRO-FORM**.

PSEUDO-CLEFT SENTENCE

See **CLEFT CONSTRUCTION**.

PSG

See **PHRASE STRUCTURE GRAMMAR**.

PSYCHOLINGUISTICS

The study of the psychological and neurobiological processes involved in the acquisition, comprehension and production of language.

PSYCHOLOGICAL SUBJECT

In earlier traditional grammar, a noun phrase that is at the front of a **clause** but is not the grammatical subject, that is, does not agree with the finite verb in **person** and **number**, and is not the **logical subject**, that is, does not denote an agent. In contemporary theory such noun phrases are called **themes** or **topics** and are moved into theme or topic position by **topicalization**. E.g. in *Haggis I enjoy, tripe I can leave, Haggis* is the psychological subject/theme/topic of the clause *Haggis I enjoy*, and *tripe* is the psychological subject, etc. of the clause *tripe I can leave*. Grammatical subjects typically occupy first position in a clause. Being in first position but not being a grammatical subject makes the psychological subject prominent, possibly for sake of contrast, as in the above example. See **GRAMMATICAL FUNCTION, THEMATIC FRONTING, THEMATIZATION, TOPIC AND COMMENT**.

PULMONIC AIRSTREAM

Speech sounds are produced by modifying a stream of air. The main initiator of the **airstream** is the lungs (pulmonic airstream). Most speech sounds are formed with the airstream moving out of the lungs, a pulmonic egressive airstream. See **AIRSTREAM MECHANISM**.

PUN

A play on words for humorous effect.

PUNCTUAL

An **Aktionsart** relating to events that are conceived as taking place instantaneously, with no duration. Typical examples are *We finally reached the top*, *He died at 6.30*. Punctual meanings are often expressed in English by means of the **light verb** *give*, as in *gave Frank a kick/punch, gave the rope a tug*, and so on. Punctual **verbs** or **clauses** do not occur naturally with the **progressive** and do not take duration phrases such as *for hours, for five minutes*. In Russian many punctual verbs have the affix *-nu*: thus, *stuchat'* 'knock repeatedly' vs *stuknut'* 'give a knock'. See TENSE AND ASPECT.

PUNCTUATION MARK

A mark that is inserted in a written text to indicate a **boundary** of some kind. Commas mark boundaries between **words**, **phrases** or **clauses**. Two clauses that are too closely connected in content to be put into separate sentences can be simultaneously separated and linked by a semi-colon. Question marks signal that a sentence conveys a question, even if the sentence does not have interrogative syntax, as in *I take it you will add relevant examples?* The dots called full stops or periods mark the end of a sentence.

PUNJABI

Indo-Iranian, Indo-European. 83.7M speakers Pakistan, 32.4M India. Three major varieties.

PURE TONE

A **sound wave** made at a single unvarying frequency, as opposed to a **complex tone**.

PURE VOWEL

A vowel whose quality remains stable during its articulation, a **monophthong** as opposed to a **diphthong**.

PUSH CHAIN

See CHAIN SHIFT.

PUTONGHUA

See CHINESE.

Q-PRINCIPLE
See **NEO-GRICEAN PRAGMATICS**.

QUALIA ROLES
Different properties of entities related to the perspective from which they are viewed. The properties were originally proposed by Aristotle but have been adapted by James Pustejovsky for use in the lexicon of a generative grammar. (Latin neuter plural of *qualis* 'what sort of?') See **AGENTIVE ROLE, CONSTITUTIVE ROLE, FORMAL ROLE, TELIC ROLE**.

QUALIFICATION
An old-fashioned term for **modification**, particularly modification of a **noun** by an **attributive adjective**, as in *a heavy parcel*. *Heavy* is a qualifier; it qualifies the meaning of *parcel*. (Late Latin *qualificare* from *qualis* 'of some kind' and *facere* 'to make'.) See **ADJECTIVE, MODIFIER**.

QUALIFIER
See **QUALIFICATION**.

QUALITATIVE TYPOLOGY
See **TYPOLOGY**.

QUALITY
See **VOICE QUALITY**.

QUANTIFIER
1. In syntax, a type of **constituent**, such as *many, most, some, all, both, few*, that expresses quantity. It is like a **determiner** in its **distribution**. Like demonstratives and articles in phrases such as *both cars* and *the cars*, quantifiers can immediately precede nouns, as in *many books* and *these books*. They also function as **predeterminers**, preceding demonstratives, articles and possessive pronouns, as in *all these people, half the money, both their children*. Some behave like postdeterminers, occurring after demonstratives, articles and possessive pronouns, as in *those few spectators, the many protesters*. Quantifiers also behave like nouns in some **constructions**: *those happy few, the both of them* (colloquial), *the many who stayed to the end*. See **FUSION 2**. 2. In predicate logic, an **operator** such as the existential quantifier $\exists x$ 'at least one x' and the universal quantifier $\forall x$ 'all x' and the quantifiers that can be handled with these operators, *some*

('at least one'), *no* ('for all x, it is not the case that such and such') and *all*.
See **DETERMINER, PREDICATE LOGIC**.

QUANTIFIER FLOATING

Especially in English **transformational grammar**, a process whereby, e.g., *The guests have all left* is derived from *All the guests have left* by the **quantifier** *all* 'floating' out of the subject noun phrase across *have*. Compare French *Tous les invités sont partis* 'All the guests have departed' and *Les invités sont tous partis* 'The guests have all departed'. See **QUANTIFIER**.

QUANTIFIER RAISING

In **Government and Binding Theory** and **Principles and Parameters**, part of the mapping of syntactic structures onto **Logical Form** (LF). In LF the interpretation of quantifiers has to be unambiguous. A sentence such as *Every voter supports some party* is ambiguous between 'Each voter supports a party (of some sort)' and 'There is one party and every voter supports it'. The ambiguity is resolved by raising one of the phrases containing a quantifier to a position outside the nucleus of the **clause**. E.g. 'For each voter there is a party that he/she supports' for the first interpretation, and 'There is a party that every voter supports' for the second. The phrase that is raised leaves, and binds, a **trace** in the **direct object** position following *supports*. See **BINDING, BINDING THEORY, BOUND, INTERFACE**.

QUANTITATIVE TYPOLOGY

See **TYPOLOGY**.

QUANTITY

A **phonetic** or **phonological** feature referring to the **length** or **duration** of segments, particularly vowels and syllables. In English vowel length is not phonologically contrastive and the same phonologically long vowel, /i/, is found in both *bee* /bi/ and *beat* /bit/. At the phonetic level, however, there is a perceived difference in the duration of the vowels where the vowel in *bee*, [bi], is perceptually longer than the vowel in *beat*, [bit]. This phonetic difference is systematically related to syllable structure: *bee* is an **open** syllable, CV, and *beat* is a **closed** syllable, CVC, closed by a voiceless stop. Vowel length is phonemic in numerous languages, e.g. Latin, Hindi, Spanish, which distinguish phonemically long and short vowels. In a very few languages, such as Mixe, three vowel lengths are distinguished. In IPA notation length is indicated by the symbol [ː], two triangles facing each other. 'half long' vowels can be indicated by the top half alone. A breve is sometimes used to indicate a short vowel. Long vowels are sometimes represented by double vowels.

QUECHUA

Quechan. Two main groups with numerous varieties. 3.5M–4.4M speakers, mainly Peru, but also Bolivia and Ecuador.

QUESTION
See **INTERROGATIVE, INTERROGATIVE CLAUSE**.

QUINE, Willard V. O. (1908–2000)
Professor of Philosophy at Harvard. He was a logical positivist philosopher and while not a linguist had a considerable influence on linguistic thinking.

QUIRK, Lord Charles Randolph (b 1920)
British grammarian and linguist. He was Professor of English Language at University College, London. He founded the Survey of English Usage in 1959. In collaboration with other British grammarians, he published *A Comprehensive Grammar of English Language* (**CGEL**), 1985, and a set of spin-off volumes which are influential in English language education both among native speakers and teachers of English as a second language.

R

RADIAL CATEGORY
A category consisting of a central, prototypical member and other members which may be more prototypical or less prototypical. The category may be a grammatical category such as dative case or subjunctive mood or the various senses of a polysemous lexical item. The non-prototypical members are not generated by rule but are created on an individual basis and have to be learned. Thus French *droit* and English *straight* share the central sense of 'rectilinear' and the closely related senses of 'honest' and 'directly', but *droit* has the extended sense of 'right hand' or 'right foot' and *straight* has acquired the extended senses of 'undiluted', as in *just straight whisky*, 'immediately' and 'classical' – *She likes straight detective novels*. Radial categories lend themselves to representation by means of a **semantic map**. See **DATIVE, POLYSEMY, PROTOTYPE, SUBJUNCTIVE**.

RADICAL
Pertaining to the root of the tongue. See **ATR**.

RAISING
In various models of **transformational grammar**, a syntactic process that 'raises' a subject **noun phrase** from a **complement clause** to be the **direct object** of the **matrix clause**. (Many matrix clauses are also main clauses.) Thus, *We considered her to be the best applicant* derives from *We considered [her to be the best applicant]*. *Her* is the subject of *to be the best applicant* but is assigned **accusative** case by **exceptional case marking**. It is raised, becoming the direct object of *considered*, and leaves a **trace**: *We considered her$_i$ [t$_i$ to be the best applicant]*. The correct semantic interpretation can be constructed from this syntactic structure, since it is clear that, although *her* is the direct object of *considered* in surface structure, in deep structure it is the subject of *to be the best applicant*. The property of being the best applicant is assigned to *her*. A second type of raising applies to examples such as *[e] seems she to be the best applicant*. *She* is raised to become the subject of *seems*: *She seems to be the best candidate*. The first type of raising is known as **subject-to-object raising**, the second as **subject-to-subject raising**. 'Raising' has become a general label for the derived constructions.
See **CLAUSE, GRAMMATICAL FUNCTION**

RANK
In **Systemic Functional Grammar**, the different levels of grammatical units. Words are on the lowest level or rank, e.g. *On + Tuesday + my + wife + and + I +*

left + *for* + *Paris*. On the next level up are phrases: *on Tuesday* + *my wife and I* + *left* + *for Paris*. On the next rank up are clauses: *On Tuesday my wife and I left for Paris* (+ *after we had tidied the house*). On the highest rank are sentences: *On Tuesday my wife and I left for Paris after we had tidied the house*. The constituent structure is relatively simple, since systemic grammar gives priority to functions. See **FUNCTION, FUNCTIONAL GRAMMAR, RANK SHIFTING**.

RANK SHIFTING

In **Systemic Functional Grammar**, the inclusion of a **clause** or **phrase** in a unit of the same or lower **rank**, as in the phrase *the book that Sally bought Andrew*, which includes the clause *that Sally bought Andrew*. In *I said that they would refuse*, the clause *that they would refuse* is included in the clause *I said___*. See **EMBEDDING, MATRIX**.

RASK, Rasmus (1787–1832)

Danish linguist. He was one of the fathers of comparative **phonology** and **morphology**. He was author of numerous grammars of **Indo-European** and other languages.

RATE

The speed with which speech is produced. Also **TEMPO**.

R-COLORED

See **RHOTICIZED**.

REALIS

See **MODALITY**.

REALISM

See **NOMINALISM**.

REALISTIC GRAMMAR

Any grammar that is claimed to mirror or represent the mental processes involved in the production and comprehension of an **utterance**. See **COGNITIVE LINGUISTICS, SENTENCE**.

REALIZATION

1. The relationship between abstract units of meaning, morphemes, and concrete units called morphs. Thus, in *played* the morph *play* realizes the lexeme PLAY and *ed* realizes the morpheme [Past Tense]. In *wrote* the single morph realizes WRITE and **Past Tense**. In the Russian word *studentov* 'of students', the morph *ov* realizes the bundle of morphemes [**masculine, plural, genitive case**]. 2. The relationship between abstract units of syntactic structure and constituents in surface structure. Thus, a subject can be realized as a noun phrase, as in *The boys walked the dog*, or as a clause, as in *Whether they will get married is quite unclear*. A noun phrase can be realized as a mass or count noun, as in *wine, women and song*, or as a pronoun, *they*. And so on. See **CASE, GENDER, NUMBER, TENSE AND ASPECT**.

REANALYSIS

1. The process whereby the analysis of a unit is changed, so that it is in a different word class, or has a different semantics or both. Frequently quoted examples include the process whereby main verbs of motion (*I am going to London by train*) acquire temporal senses (*I am going to be a lawyer when I grow up*), main verbs of necessity (*I need a bath*) take on the syntax of modal auxiliaries (*You needn't have a bath tonight*). See **GRAMMATICALIZATION**. 2. A type of historical change in which a sequence of words stays the same but the syntactic **structure** assigned to it changes. In English examples such as *It will be useful for him to discuss the matter*, the earlier structure was ...$_{AP}$ [*useful* $_{PP}$ [*for him*]], in which *for* was a **preposition** and the interpretation was 'To discuss the matter will be useful for him'. The structure was reinterpreted as $_S$ [...*useful* $_S$ [for him to discuss the matter], in which *for*, in combination with *to*, is a **complementizer**. The interpretation now is 'For him to discuss the matter will be useful'. 3. A process assumed by many linguists in order to account for passive clauses such as *The chair had been sat in by somebody very large*. The starting point is *Somebody... sat in the chair*, in which *in the chair* is a prepositional phrase. It is assumed that the structure is reanalysed as *sat-in the chair*, with *sat-in* forming a single verb. The whole clause can then be made passive. No longer the complement of a preposition, *the chair* moves to the front to become subject, *the chair had been sat-in*. See **CLAUSE, GRAMMATICAL FUNCTION, VOICE**.

REASSOCIATION

See **AUTOSEGMENTAL PHONOLOGY**.

RECEIVED PRONUNCIATION (RP)

The accent associated with standard English in England, often perceived to be the 'prestige' accent. It is the accent most used in pronunciation dictionaries and in teaching materials on programmes for English as an additional language. It is usually said to be socially defined, being the accent associated with the Court ('received at court', 'the Queen's English'), the army, the aristocracy, the public schools ('public school English'), the older universities ('Oxford English'), BBC newsreaders ('BBC English'), etc. It has no marked regional characteristics though many regional accents have been influenced by RP, perhaps especially **Estuary English**. Several varieties of RP have been described (advanced, conservative, etc.).

RECIPIENT

A **role** typically assigned to animate beings who receive something from someone, as in *Frank gave a piano to Jane*. In many languages a recipient has the same marking as a **goal**, as in Turkish *Istanbula gittim* 'to-Istanbul I-went' and *Para adama verdim* 'money to-the-man I-gave', where the dative case affix *-a* marks a goal, *Istanbula*, and a recipient, *adama*. See **CASE**.

RECIPROCAL

A **construction** indicating that an action carried out by one **agent** on a **patient** is reciprocated, i.e. also carried out by that patient on the agent. Both participants are simultaneously agent and patient, as in the situation described by *Freya and Katarina helped each other* (F helped K and K helped F). In many languages reciprocal pronouns or affixes are identical to **reflexive** ones: French *Paul s'aime* 'Paul self loves, Paul loves himself', *Paul et Claudine s'aiment* 'Paul and Claudine love each other'. See **REFLEXIVE PRONOUN**.

RECIPROCAL ASSIMILATION

An **assimilation** where adjacent sounds mutually influence each other and merger occurs. In many pronunciations of *won't you* the final /t/ of won't [wəʊnt] and the initial /j/ of *you* [ju] merge to [wəʊntʃu].

RECOVERABILITY

1. In **transformational grammar**, a desirable property of relationships that were disrupted by a **transformation** moving or deleting constituents, such as the relationship between *met* and *who* in *The girl who I was told you met at the party is my niece*. Another is the relationship between *Arthur* and *leave* in *She persuaded Arthur to leave*. Attempts to ensure recoverability led to concepts such as control and empty categories, including traces. See **CONTROL, DELETION, EMPTY CATEGORY, EQUI-NP-DELETION, TRACE**. 2. In typology, the study of the different ways in which languages signal which noun is modified by a given **relative clause**. For instance, this may be achieved by the use of relative pronouns, as in *the book which I bought for you* (*which* as opposed to *who, whom, where, when*), or by gapping, as in *the book [] I bought for you*, where there is a gap between *book* and *I bought for you*, or by resumptive pronouns, as in *the book that I went out and bought it for you*, where *it* is the resumptive pronoun. 3. A general characteristic of constructions involving **ellipsis**.

RECTION

See **GOVERNMENT**.

RECURSION

1. The repeated **embedding** of one type of **constituent** inside (typically) another type. The constituent is said to recur. In *I danced with a man who danced with a girl who danced with the Prince of Wales*, the **relative clause** *who danced with the Prince of Wales* is inside another relative clause *who danced with a girl*. In *the cupboard in the corner near the window opposite the door of the small bedroom* the PP *of the small bedroom* is inside the NP *the door...* This NP is inside the PP *opposite...* This PP in turn is inside the NP *the window...* and so on. NP and PP both recur. 2. The recurring application of a rule such as the rule NP → (Det) N (S) that produces noun phrases containing relative clauses. Such a rule is said to be recursive. (Latin *re-* 'back', *currere* 'to run' – 'to run back, return'.) See **NESTING**.

RECURSIVE RULE

See **RECURSION 2**.

RECURSIVE TRANSITION NETWORK (RTN)

A recursive transition network is a type of graph consisting of states connected by arcs (curved arrows). The arcs are labelled with symbols for lexical categories such as Noun, Adjective or Verb or with lexical items. An RTN can represent the rules of a context-free grammar. The general principle is that a computer can be programmed to, so to speak, move along the arcs from one state to another. Some the arcs can be traversed and re-traversed enabling the graph to generate or parse chunks such as *knobbly, green, crunchy apples*. This property gives rise to 'recursion'. Such graphs can be easily incorporated into computational procedures for analysing and generating syntactic structures.

REDUCED ADVERBIAL CLAUSE

An **adverbial clause** that has lost its **subject** noun and some form of *be*. Thus, *While we were searching the house, we found valuable jewellery* reduces to *While searching the house, we found valuable jewellery*; *When it is cooked, it goes orange* reduces to *When cooked, it goes orange*.

REDUCED COORDINATION

See **GAPPING**.

REDUCED RELATIVE CLAUSE

A **relative clause** in which the relative pronoun or subordinating conjunction has been omitted, along with some form of *be*. E.g. *The guy who was repairing the leak has gone* reduces to *The guy repairing the leak has gone*. (*The leak may not have gone*.) See **COMPLEMENTIZER, RELATIVIZER**.

REDUCTION

1. The conversion of finite clauses to shorter, more compressed non-finite clauses. See **REDUCED ADVERBIAL CLAUSE, REDUCED RELATIVE CLAUSE**. 2. The process by which words or phrases carrying given information are reduced to a pronoun or zero. Thus in *She thought she could paint but she can't*, paint is reduced to zero – *can't [paint]*. In *Was that helpful? I don't think so*, so = *that it was helpful*. See **ELLIPSIS, GIVEN AND NEW**.

REDUNDANCY RULES

In earlier models of **generative syntax** and **generative phonology**, rules specifying information that can be predicted, keeping underlying forms or lexical entries to a minimum. In the underlying form of *stress*, the first consonant does not need to be fully specified; in a **cluster** of three word-initial consonants in English the first consonant must be /s/. The information in a lexical entry can be reduced; if a lexical item is [human] it is also [animate] and [concrete]. Only [human] appears in the lexical entry; the other features are added by redundancy rules. See **GENERATIVE GRAMMAR, LEXICON**.

REDUPLICATION

The repetition of all or part of a form. The reduplication may be partial, as in Classical **Greek** *lu-o* 'I am freeing' – *le-lu-ka* 'I have freed', or complete, as in **Maori** *mare* 'to cough' *mare mare* 'cough many times'.

REDUPLICATIVE COMPOUND

A **compound word** formed by two words that differ only in their vowel, as in *shilly-shally* and *fiddle-faddle*. In **CGEL**, a compound whose members rhyme, as in *walkie-talkie, busy Lizzie*. See **REDUPLICATION**.

REFERENCE

Reference is the act performed by speakers when they direct their listeners' attention, or refer, to objects. They use different referring expressions depending on the situation. If they assume that their audience can follow the reference (because the object is given, i.e. has already been mentioned or is salient), they use definite referring expressions (noun phrases) such as *the CD, your key, it*: *Did you bring the CD?, Where is your key?, Where is it? The CD* and *it* have specific reference; the speaker refers to a specific object.

Definite referring expressions vary from very complex – *the key with the red tag on the highest hook* – to very simple – *it, here, Sue*. Speakers use simple expressions conveying small amounts of information when they judge that an object is salient and accessible to their audience. When objects are very salient speakers point to them linguistically using a **deictic**. They use complex expressions when they judge that an object is not very accessible and more information is required. Objects not present in a given situation may be treated as accessible if the speaker assumes that the audience has the relevant **frame** or **script**.

Speakers use indefinite referring expressions when talking about objects that are new, i.e. have not been mentioned or are not present in a given situation: *a key, keys, any keys: Have you a key?, There's a key under the mat*.

Speakers use indefinite referring expressions either with specific reference, for objects known to them and specific – *I'm looking for a book. I left it on the desk* – or with non-specific reference, for objects unknown and non-specific – *I'm looking for a book. Have you got one?*

To refer to sets of objects rather than one or more specific objects, speakers use noun phrases with generic reference. In English these are plural noun phrases with no article (*Whales are very large*) or a definite noun phrase (*The whale is very large*).

What speakers can refer to using lexical items is to some extent controlled by the **denotation** of the latter.

Reference may be opaque. The speaker who says *That's a problem for the next Dean* may have a definite person in mind (*and that's Harry Duguid*) or may not (*whoever that may be*). In the first case *the next Dean* is used de re or referentially, about the actual person; in the latter it is used de dicto or attributively, to refer to whoever turns out to match the description.

In real-life situations speakers and writers may refer incorrectly, choosing a referring expression that does not apply to the referent. They may nonetheless refer successfully in that their listeners pick out the intended referent. If A says *The manager is going to explain* and B replies *That's not the manager*, B has picked out the person A was referring to. See **ACCESSIBILITY HIERARCHY, ATTRIBUTIVE, DEFINITE REFERRING EXPRESSION, GENERIC, GIVEN AND NEW, REFERENCE TRACKING, REFERENT**.

REFERENCE GRAMMAR

A grammar containing a detailed, systematic description of a language. Such grammars are not intended to be read or used as a teaching text but to be consulted on specific points as the need arises. Examples of reference grammars are: **CGEL**, Maurice Grévisse *Le Bon Usage* (for French), Winifred Bauer *The Reed Reference Grammar of Maori*, and hundreds, if not thousands, of others.

REFERENCE TIME

Some time, which may or may not coincide with the moment of speech, that is taken as a point of reference for tense. The speaker who says *Rene is in his office (just now)* presents that situation as including the moment of speech. The reference time includes the **speech time**. *Rene left his office* locates the event of Rene leaving the office at some time in the past, prior to the moment of speech. The reference time precedes the speech time. *Rene had left his office when Juliet arrived* presents the event as occurring earlier in the past than another event, Juliet's arrival. The time of Juliet's arrival is the reference time for Rene's leaving. (The term was introduced by the logician Hans Reichenbach in 1947.)
See **EVENT TIME, TENSE AND ASPECT**.

REFERENCE TRACKING

The process of keeping track of who and what is referred to in the course of a conversation, lecture, narrative, novel and so on and the devices by which listeners and readers do it. The devices include pronouns, person suffixes on verbs, and **agreement**. Successful reference tracking is essential for the correct interpretation of text. See **ANAPHORA, CATAPHORA, GIVEN AND NEW, PRONOUN, SWITCH REFERENCE**.

REFERENT

The entity referred to by a speaker or writer. See **REFERENCE**.

REFERENTIAL DISTANCE

A measure of topicality and accessibility, consisting of the number of clauses that have elapsed between a given mention of a referent in a text and the previous mention. The more clauses, the less accessibility. See **ACCESSIBILITY HIERARCHY**.

REFERENTIAL OPACITY

See **OPAQUE REFERENCE**.

REFERRING EXPRESSION
See REFERENCE.

REFLEXIVE PREDICATE
In logic, suppose there is a predicate P and two arguments X and Y referring to the same entity. If the predicate denotes a relation holding between X and Y, it is reflexive. Thus, the predicate *as long as* is reflexive, since it is logically true that any entity is as long as itself. A predicate that is not reflexive, say *is bigger than*, is **irreflexive**. See PREDICATE, PREDICATOR, SYMMETRIC PREDICATE, TRANSITIVE PREDICATE.

REFLEXIVE
Applied to any **construction** containing a **reflexive pronoun** or indicating in some way that an agent does something to his or her self. E.g., Turkish has a bound reflexive morph *–n* or *–in*, as in *kurulamak* 'to dry (something)' vs *kurulanmak* 'to dry oneself', *giymek* 'to put on (a garment) vs *giyinmak* 'to dress oneself'. See MORPH.

REFLEXIVE PRONOUN
A **pronoun** which can only be interpreted as **coreferential** with another **noun phrase** in the same **clause**: *Mary considered herself clever* (Mary was possibly clever) vs *Mary considered her clever* (somebody other than Mary was possibly clever). Some languages have long-distance reflexive pronouns that are coreferential with noun phrases in a different clause. E.g. Chinese, *Chen Xiansheng renwei [Liu Xiansheng tai kuangwang, Ø zongshi kanbuqi ziji]*, 'Chen Mr think [Liu Mr too arrogant, (and) Ø (=Mr Liu) always look-down-on self (= Mr Chen)]'. The antecedent *Chen Xiansheng* is in the **main clause**, the reflexive pronoun *ziji* is in a coordinate clause inside a **complement clause**. See CONJUNCTION, REFERENCE.

REFLEXIVIZATION
In early **transformational grammar**, a process applying to clauses such as *Mary$_i$ blamed Mary$_i$,* replacing the second *Mary$_i$* with *herself*.

REGISTER
1. The pitch range available to a speaker dependent on anatomical factors. In singing, soprano, tenor, etc. 2. A particular combination of derivational morphology, syntactic constructions, sentence complexity and vocabulary that, in a given culture, is appropriate for particular activities in particular circumstances. Discussing a linguistic topic with a small group of students allows one register, discussing the same topic in an article for a professional journal requires quite another register. The language of *The Sun* is one register, the language of *The Times* or *The Economist* is another.

REGISTER TONE LANGUAGE
A tone language in which each tone bearing unit has an unvarying pitch. See TONE, CONTOUR TONE LANGUAGE.

REGISTER VARIATION

The analysis of the ways in which different types of text differ, e.g. in syntactic structure, choice of lexical items, choice of fixed expressions. See **CORPUS, DIMENSION, GENRE, MULTIDIMENSIONAL ANALYSIS, REGISTER**.

REGRESSIVE ASSIMILATION

When two words come together and the pronunciation of the final segment of the first word is influenced by the pronunciation of the initial segment of the second word. For example, *is* in *is she* [ɪz ʃi] becomes [ɪʒʃi]. Sometimes called anticipatory assimilation. See **ASSIMILATION**.

REGULAR

A form that fits a very general pattern in a given language. The past tense form *played* is constructed by the addition of *-ed* (in writing) to the stem *play*. This is the most general pattern in English and *played* is thus regular. The past tense form *swam* is constructed by changing the vowel in *swim*. Very few verbs follow this pattern and *swam* is irregular. See **IRREGULAR**.

REGULARITY

The property of being regular. See **REGULAR**.

RELATION

Any link between words or phrases. In *We recognized them*, *We* is linked to *recognized* as subject (*we* vs *us*) and *them* is linked to *recognized* as object (*them* vs *they*). In *the plants that have flowered early*, the relative clause *that have flowered early* is linked to the noun *plants*. (Alternatively, it is related to the noun, hence the term 'relative clause'.) See **GRAMMATICAL RELATION, GRAMMATICAL FUNCTION, PARADIGMATIC, RELATIONAL GRAMMAR, SYNTAGMATIC**.

RELATIONAL GRAMMAR

A model of syntax developed in the 1970s by David Perlmutter and Paul Postal. Whereas Chomsky took grammatical functions or relations such as subject and object to be secondary to **constituent structure**, they were the basic units of syntax in relational grammar. **Lexical-Functional Grammar** elaborated the concept and role of grammatical relations in syntax. See **FORMAL, FORMALIST LINGUISTICS, FUNCTION, FUNCTIONAL GRAMMAR, GRAMMATICAL FUNCTION**.

RELATIVE ADJECTIVE

See **ABSOLUTE ADJECTIVE**.

RELATIVE ADVERB

In some accounts of English, the label applied to *where* or *when* functioning as a **complementizer** in a **relative clause**, as in *the town where she works, the time when it rained for forty days*.

RELATIVE CLAUSE

A subordinate clause modifying the **head** noun in a **noun phrase**. English has three types of relative clause: wh relative clauses are introduced by a **relative** pronoun such as *who* or *which* – *the course which I took*; *that* relative clauses are connected to the head noun by the conjunction *that*, *the course that I took*; contact relative clauses or zero relative clauses are simply placed beside the noun they modify – *the course I took*. In non-standard English, relative clauses may be introduced by the conjunctions *as* or *what*: *the chap as I was telling you about*, *the letter what you forgot to post*. (An older term is 'adjectival clause'. This term is still used in, e.g., grammars of English as an additional language but is no longer used in formal syntax or more theoretical grammars of English.)

Spoken English (standard and non-standard) offers regular examples of **resumptive pronouns**: *she* in *they're keeping the memory of a child that they don't know where she is* (BBC Radio 4), and *it* in *He and his father ran a racing team that these three drivers were all involved in it* (BBC Radio Scotland). This construction is the standard one in some languages.

Wh relative clauses may be restrictive or non-restrictive (defining or non-defining, identifying or non-identifying). *That* relative clauses are typically restrictive. Restrictive relative clauses provide information that helps the addressee to identify the referent of the noun phrase: *The book which I bought yesterday is very helpful* (not *the book I bought last week*). Non-restrictive relative clauses merely provide incidental information: *The book, which I bought yesterday, is very helpful* (no contrast with any other book). In writing they are often, though not consistently, marked off by commas; in speech they are marked off by slight pauses and have their own **intonation**. See **CONTACT CLAUSE**.

RELATIVE PRONOUN

In the English wh **relative clause**, *who*, *whom* and *which* are relative pronouns. In *the computer which I prefer*, *which* is **anaphoric** to *the computer*. The contrast *who* vs *whom* parallels *he/him*, etc. and the contrast *who*, *whom* vs *which* parallels *he*, *she* vs *it*. See **ANAPHORA, ANTECEDENT**.

RELATIVE TENSE

More accurately, relative time reference, since the concept applies to **verb** forms whose time reference is determined by context and not with respect to the moment of speech. English participles are **non-finite** and not marked for tense but in context they refer to times. In *The book lying on the floor is a valuable antique*, the copula *is* imposes on *lying* a reference to present time; in *The book lying on the floor was a valuable antique* the copula *was* imposes a reference to past time. The English Present Perfect is often treated as a relative tense, on the grounds that the reference time of whatever situation is referred to is not specified but has to be inferred from context. Thus, *James has been in Ankara* might refer to a situation that held in the immediate past (*He just got back this morning*) or that held in the remote past (*But that was many years ago*). Relative tense contrasts with absolute tense, which is determined with respect to the moment of time, e.g. **present tense** and **past tense**. The **past perfect** is an absolute-relative tense, since it locates a situation in the past with respect to the moment of speech, but further in the past than some other situation. That is, context controls the interpretation. See **ABSOLUTE TENSE, ABSOLUTE-RELATIVE TENSE, PARTICIPLE, PRESENT PARTICIPLE, REFERENCE TIME, TENSE AND ASPECT.**

RELATIVIZER

The constituent that introduces **relative clauses**, connecting them to the noun they modify: *that* in *the car that they crashed*, *who* in *students who buy dictionaries* and zero in *the car they crashed*.

RELEASE

The phase in the articulation of a **stop** consonant when the pressure behind the stricture is released. A stop can be released in a variety of ways – by opening the oral articulators into a vowel, as in [aba], by opening the velic closure into a nasal, as it in *bottom* [bɔtm] – this is known as **nasal plosion** – or into a lateral, as in *bottle* [bɔtl] – this is known as **lateral** plosion. See **ABRUPT RELEASE, AFFRICATE, AFFRICATION, DELAYED RELEASE.**

RELEVANCE THEORY

A theory of the interpretation of utterances developed in the early 1980s by Dan Sperber and Deirdre Wilson as an alternative to Paul Grice's theory of communication and inference based on cooperation between speakers and hearers informed by his maxims of conversation. Relevance theory is based on three central ideas. One is that much, if not most, of the information traditionally thought of as being conveyed by utterances is not extracted from the code controlling the grammar of a language but is constructed inferentially by the hearers. A second idea is that hearers have to recognize speakers' communicative intentions. One major intention is to inform hearers of something and another major intention is to make hearers aware that a communication is about to take place. The third central idea is that speakers set about interpreting utterances by assessing them for relevance. Hearers assume that a given utterance is relevant to what the speaker wants to communicate and then, as Sperber and Wilson put it, 'maximize the relevance'. Relevance is a property of utterances such that, ideally, speakers produce utterances which allow listeners to extract as much information as possible with as little processing effort as possible. A central role is played by **explicature**, various processes by which hearers elaborate into complete propositions what is actually said. Another central role is played by conversational **implicature**, though they are differentiated by being strong or weak depending on how important they are for the complete interpretation of a given utterance. Conventional implicatures are reinterpreted as conveying procedural information about what sorts of inferences listeners are to draw. Thus, in *Even Matt can cook it, even* is treated as signalling to the hearer to infer that the speaker thinks Matt is a dreadful cook and that the recipe is absurdly simple.
See **BRIDGING, GIVEN AND NEW, MAXIMS OF CONVERSATION, NEO-GRICEAN PRAGMATICS.**

REMOTE PAST

1. Some languages have two pasts, a set of past tense verb forms for referring to events that took place before the **speech time** but in the same day (**hodiernal past**, from Latin *hodie* 'today'), and another set of forms for referring to events that took place before the time of speech but not in the same day (**hesternal past**, from Latin *hesternus* 'of yesterday'). 2. Speakers use past tense forms to refer to events that took place before the speech time. Such events are presented as remote in time from the present. In many languages past tense forms can be used to refer to events which are remote from the present in that they are presented as possible or hypothetical, hence the label **hypothetical past**. This function of past tense forms is associated with conditional clauses, e.g, *If Fiona phoned, I would explain the difficulty*. Fiona has not phoned but the speaker leaves the possibility open. Speakers use **past perfect** verb forms to present an event as even more remote in time, as having taking place earlier that some other event in the past. They also use the past perfect in conditional clauses to present events as very remote in that they are unlikely ever to happen: *If Fiona had phoned, I would have explained the difficulty*. See **CONDITIONAL CLAUSE, PAST TENSE, PERFECT, TENSE AND ASPECT**.

REORDERING

In theories of language change, the application of two rules in one order at an earlier stage in a given language but in the opposite order at a later stage. For instance, one analysis of English syntax considers the earlier construction *To whom did he turn for help* to be derived from *He turned for help to wh*. The wh word was first assigned case, yielding *whom*, and was then moved to the front of the sentence. The sentence *Who did he turn to for help* is judged to have appeared in English via a change in the order of the rules. The wh word is moved to the front of the sentence first, then case is assigned. Because the wh word is no longer preceded by the preposition *to*, it is not assigned accusative case and is realized as *who*. See **MORPH**.

REPAIR

In **conversation analysis**, a correction or clarification of what a speaker has just said. The speaker may perform the correction; an example of self-initiated self-repair is *Sue, I mean Sarah, can help you*. Another interlocutor may perform the repair: an example of other-initiated other-repair is A: *She's writing the letter now*. B: *Is writing! She's written it and posted it*. Another interlocutor may prompt the speaker to perform a repair: an example of an other-initiated self-repair is A: *I'll see you there at 3.15*. B: *Don't you mean 3.50?* A: *Oh, yes, see you at 3.50*.

REPERTOIRE

The set of **registers**, **genres** and standard or non-standard varieties controlled by a given speaker. See **DIMENSION, STANDARD LANGUAGE**.

REPLACIVE MORPH
A process treated as having the status of a **morph**. In English *sang* can be treated as deriving from *sing* by a process that replaces /i/ with /a/. The concept is controversial.

REPORTABILITY
As judged by narrators, the extent to which an event is worth including in a narrative.

REPORTED SPEECH
See **INDIRECT SPEECH**.

REPRESENTATION
1. Any sort of diagram or notation on paper (or computer screen) showing the structure assigned to some area of language. A **phrase structure tree** is one representation of **constituent structure**, **labelled bracketing** is another. IPA transcriptions are representations of sounds in a given language. See **INTERNATIONAL PHONETIC ALPHABET, TREE DIAGRAM**. 2. Clause as representation. See **IDEATIONAL MEANING**.

RESPIRATORY SYSTEM
The physical system that enables breathing, the lungs, etc.

RESPONSE
See **EXCHANGE**.

REST
See **REVISED EXTENDED STANDARD THEORY**.

RESTRICTED CODE
Part of a theory of language and its relation to social structure. Restricted code is said to be found among informal groups with a good deal of shared knowledge and tends to be economical in conveying meanings with few words. It is said to be characteristic of the language found among family and friends and other intimate groups. Vocabulary is informal and syntactic structures tend to be simple. Restricted code was incorrectly said to be characteristic of disadvantaged working-class children. Restricted and **elaborated code** are considered to be at opposite ends of a cline.

RESTRICTIVE
Applied to a **modifier** that helps listeners to identify what a speaker is referring to. In, e.g., *Can I have a look at the blue dress*, *blue* signals to the listener not to bring, say, the red dress. In *Can I have a look at that amazing dress*, *amazing* does not help to identify the dress and is non-restrictive. The term is usually, and most easily, applied to relative clauses. See **RELATIVE CLAUSE**.

RESTRICTIVE RELATIVE
See **RELATIVE CLAUSE**.

RESTRUCTURING
See **REANALYSIS**.

RESULT
In some analyses, a **role** assigned to noun phrases referring to entities created as the result of an **action** or **process**: e.g. *her portrait* in *Raeburn painted her portrait*. See **FACTITIVE, RESULTATIVE**.

RESULT ADVERBIAL
See **RESULT CLAUSE**.

RESULT CLAUSE
An **adverbial clause** introduced by *(so) that* or a *to* infinitive expressing a result or consequence: e.g. *I was so angry that I resigned immediately*. The adverbial clause *that…immediately* modifies *so angry*. *Gordon cut down his neighbour's enormous hedge, only to find himself in court*. An alternative name is consecutive clause.

RESULTATIVE
Any **construction** denoting the result of an **action** or **process**, as in examples with a resultative **participle**: *I've got the book finished*, *That's the book finished*, *The trees are all felled*. Another construction is *The noise made me deaf*, where the object **complement** *deaf* denotes the result of a process. *He became deaf* exemplifies the simplest resultative construction. See **PASSIVE PARTICIPLE, PERFECT**.

RESUMPTIVE PRONOUN
A **pronoun** that duplicates the work of another pronoun or full noun by referring to the same entity, as in **relative clauses** in spoken English (and many other languages): *the film which you recommended it to everybody*. *It* duplicates the reference of *which*. Another construction is **left dislocation**, as in *This film it does give a good close-up of what goes on* or French *Pierre, il les aime* 'Pierre he them likes, 'Pierre (he) likes them'.

RETRACTION
The movement of the tongue backwards towards the velum, e.g. the final [k] of *kick* [kɪk] is retracted compared with the initial [k].

RETROFLEX
A term in the description of the **place of articulation** of **consonant** sounds. The tip of the tongue is curled back against the front part of the hard palate. In IPA transcriptions a rightward-facing curly tail represents retroflection:[ʈ], [ɖ], [ɭ], etc. Some Indian languages, such as Hindi, have retroflexed [ʈ] and [ɖ] and these sound can be heard in the English of native speakers of these languages. The 'r' sounds typical of some American, many Scottish English and some South West English dialects are retroflexed: this is typical of many words

spelled with a final *r* (*bar, far*, for example). In these cases the vowel may also be retroflexed and is often said to be 'r-coloured' or '**Rhoticized**'.

REVERSATIVE
A prefix or **particle** indicating the reversal of the process denoted by the verb **stem**, as in *tie – untie, roll (up) – unroll*.

REVERSE WH CLEFT
See CLEFT CONSTRUCTION.

REVERSED POLARITY TAG
See CHECKING TAG, TAG QUESTION 1.

REVERSIVES
Pairs of verbs such that one verb 'reverses' the movement denoted by the other. Some pairs are lexical items realized by a single root, such as COME and GO, PUSH and PULL; others consist of a phrase, such as TIE UP, and a complex lexical item such as UNTIE. See OPPOSITENESS.

REVISED EXTENDED STANDARD THEORY
The model of **transformational grammar** developed in the 1970s. General constraints limited the power of transformations, the role of the lexical component was expanded (to handle, e.g., **nominalizations**) and the semantic component provided semantic interpretations for surface syntactic structures. See PRINCIPLES AND PARAMETERS, STANDARD THEORY.

REWRITE RULE
A rule which is an instruction to replace one string of symbols with another. The rule $b \rightarrow d\ e$ (rewrite *b* as *d e*) replaces, e.g., the string *a b c* with the string *a d e c*. Since in generative grammar rewrite rules typically expand one string into a longer string, they are sometimes called 'expansion rules'. Given two rules, say NP → (Det) N and S → NP VP, S is known as the initial symbol. It has to be rewritten as NP VP before the rule rewriting NP can apply. See PHRASE STRUCTURE GRAMMAR, PHRASE STRUCTURE RULE.

R-EXPRESSION
See REFERRING EXPRESSION.

RHAETO-ROMANCE
Romance, Indo-European. 76K speakers, Switzerland. Includes Romansch (south-east Switzerland, Ladin (South Tyrol) and Friulan (north-east Italy).

RHEME
See THEME.

RHETORIC
The art of the effective use of language to persuade, please, amuse, etc.
It arose from the use of language in the law courts of Ancient Greece and Rome. A central technique was the use of **figures of speech**. Many of the traditional

RHETORICAL QUESTION

A question that, in context, is not intended to be answered. E.g. *Do you expect me to climb that wall?*, uttered in a context in which it is clear that the speaker cannot climb the wall.

RHETORICAL STRUCTURE

A theory of how different types of **clause** function in texts and interrelate. Current work is based on original analyses by Halliday. He proposed that a clause can be expanded in three ways: **i.** by elaboration, as when a **non-restrictive relative clause** adds information – *We sold the car, which we didn't really like anyway*; **ii.** by extension, when one clause adds to the meaning of another, as when a clause is added to another by *and* – *We didn't like the dress, and she didn't like it either*; **iii.** by enhancment, when one clause enhances the meaning of another with information about time, place, cause, purpose, manner, etc. – *He kept the dog on the leash so that it couldn't chase the cat*. See **ADVERBIAL CLAUSE, RELATIVE CLAUSE**.

RHOTIC

The class of 'r-sounds', especially alveolar and post alveolar approximants like [r] as in *run*, [rʌn], also alveolar taps and trills and uvular approximants and fricatives. Also rhotic vowels. See **RHOTICIZED**.

RHOTICIZED

Of a vowel, articulated with a retroflex tongue position. See **RETROFLEX**.

RHYME

1. Words that have identical syllable nuclei in their stressed syllable and identical codas; *lust, crust, bust; coda coder*. 2. Also **rime**. See **SYLLABLE**.

RHYMING SLANG

In spoken or written English, particularly in Cockney dialect, a word is replaced by a rhyming word or phrase, making communication incomprehensible to those who do not understand the code (e.g. *trouble and strife* for *wife*). Sometimes the part of the phrase that rhymes with the original is omitted, making the code even more impenetrable (e.g. *whistle* for *suit* (*whistle and flute*: *suit*).

RHYTHM

The pattern produced by the regular occurrence of prominent segments – stresses in English; syllables in French, heavy syllables in Latin, etc.

RHYTHM RULE

See **IAMBIC REVERSAL**.

RIAU INDONESIAN
Austronesian. Approx. 5K speakers, East-central Sumatra.

RIGHT BRANCHING
Applied to syntactic structures in which a **modifier** follows its **head**, as in *the book on the table at the window in the study*. The **prepositional phrase** *in the study* modifies *window*, the PP *at the window in the study* modifies *table*, and the PP *on the table at the window in the study* modifies *book*. A **tree diagram** of the **constituent structure** of such a **phrase** has a series of branches to the right, as shown in the figure below. See **BRANCHING, LEFT BRANCHING**.

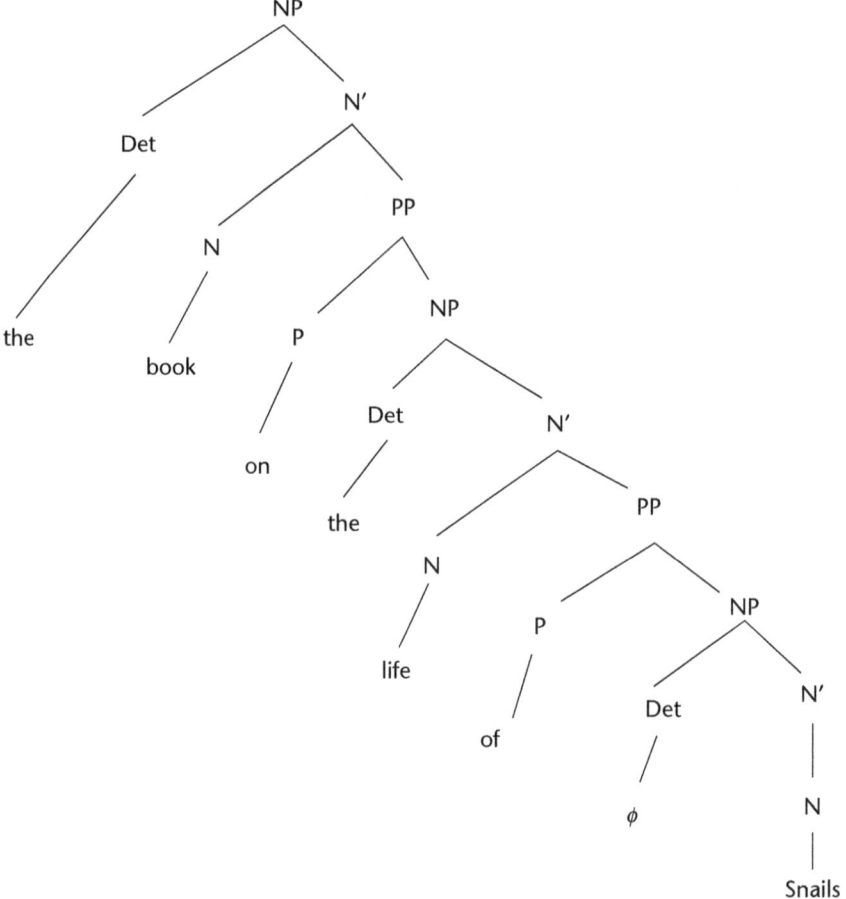

RIGHT DISLOCATION
A construction in which a complete **clause** is followed by a **noun phrase**. The clause contains a **pronoun** with the same **referent** as the noun phrase: *It's complete nonsense, his latest novel*. It allows the speaker to emphasize the important property, being complete nonsense, and to ensure that the referent, the novel, is firmly established for the **addressee**. Right dislocation contrasts with

extraposition and the movement of heavy noun phrases. See **END FOCUS, EXTRAPOSITION, HEAVY NOUN PHRASE, FOCUS, LEFT DISLOCATION.**

RIGHT NODE RAISING

In **transformational grammar**, a process deriving, e.g., *Sabrina set and Pavel cleared the table* from *Sabrina set the table and Pavel cleared the table*. The rightmost nodes, *the table* and *the table*, are raised to a higher position in the tree where they are fused to give $_S[_S[\textit{Sabrina set and Pavel cleared}]\ _{NP}[\textit{the table}]]$. The label is still used for the construction, although the process has been abandoned in formal models. See **CONJUNCTION, GAPPING.**

RIGHT-HAND HEAD RULE

The idea that the rightmost **affix** in a **word** is the **head**, determining its class. Thus, *-ous* is the head of *infelicitous* and makes the word an **adjective**. *-ity* is the head of *infelicity*, making it a **noun**, and *-ly* is the head of *infelicitously*, making it an **adverb**.

RIM

The edge(s) of the **tongue**.

RIME

See **SYLLABLE**.

RISING

A pitch movement from relatively low to relatively high. Often applied in a tone language to a rising **tone** and in an intonation language to an **intonation contour.**

RITUAL LANGUAGE

Originally the restricted language, with many fixed expressions, of religious rites and ceremonies but now extended to the conventionalized exchanges performed by interlocutors in many situations of everyday life. See **FIXED EXPRESSION, PHATIC COMMUNION.**

ROLE

Clauses denote situations, which consist of a **state** or event and participants in them. Participants play different roles. Central participants play central roles such as agent and patient and peripheral participants play peripheral roles such as location/place and time. Prototypical agents are human beings acting of their own volition, using their own energy, producing an effect on something or creating something: e.g. *Susan* in *Susan was walking the dog, Susan built a treehouse, Susan stood very still so as not to frighten the fox*. Less good examples of agents are *river* in *The river flooded the valley* and *column* in *This column supports the pediment*. Prototypical patients are animate or inanimate, do not exercise their volition or produce an effect but undergo an action or process: e.g. in the above examples *dog, fox, valley* and *pediment*.

Another major role is **experiencer**, for animate participants in situations involving mental, psychological or physical sensations: e.g. *students* in *The students knew all the answers/were ashamed/were hungry*. Other roles are **instrument** – *He painted the picture with his favourite aerosol*; location/place – *London* in *The museum is in London, The final was played in Lisbon*; goal – *Berlin* in *They flew to Berlin*; **source** – *Auckland* in *They travelled from Auckland to Wellington*.

Many languages have basic clause types which assign the same syntax to clauses with agents or experiencers and with prototypical or non-prototypical agents. Similarly, the same syntax is assigned to clauses with prototypical and non-prototypical patients. **Role and Reference Grammar**, in particular, employs the concept of **macrorole** to handle such data. One macrorole, actor, covers all the types of agent and experiencer, and the macrorole of undergoer covers all the different types of patient.

The roles of goal and source are extended to situations involving the transmission of things between people: *We received a letter from Susan* [*Susan*=source], *She sent the letter to her fiancé* [*fiancé*=goal]. Source is also extended to reason or cause, as in *He suffers from arthritis* [*arthritis*=source]. Some analysts use goal simply as an alternative to patient but others use it because they view patients as a kind of goal; that is, a sentence such as *The editor rejected the book* is analysed in terms of the action of rejecting passing from the editor (the source) to the book (the goal). This is the metaphor lying behind the traditional term *transitive* and is typical of localism, which sees location and movement in space as basic. The important point is that roles have to do with how the speakers of languages conceive and present situations in the world and a given role has to be justified on grammatical criteria. See **ACTION, AKTIONSART, ARGUMENT, CASE, CIRCUMSTANCIAL, COGNITIVE GRAMMAR, CORE OF A CLAUSE, DATIVE, FRAME 3, LOCALISM, NUCLEUS, PERIPHERY (OF A CLAUSE), PROCESS, RECIPIENT, STATIVE VERB, TRANSITIVE VERB, TRANSITIVITY**

ROLE AND REFERENCE GRAMMAR

The RRG model was developed in the early 1980s by Robert van Valin and William Foley. It is based on the analysis of a wide range of languages, including several spoken in Papua New Guinea, and gives much attention to the functioning of **clause** syntax in text, especially in the signalling of topic and focus and in reference tracking. The model offers an analysis of clauses into nucleus, core and periphery and an original account of degrees of subordination and degrees of integration between clauses. See **CORE, COSUBORDINATION, INTEGRATION, NUCLEUS**.

ROLL

See **TRILL**.

ROMANCE

Indo-European language family that developed from Latin. The major national languages are **French, Italian, Portuguese, Romanian, Spanish**. Other languages are **Catalan**, Friulian, **Galician, Occitan**, Sardinian and the **Rhaeto-Romance** subset.

ROMANI

Indo-Aryan. 6M–11M Roma speakers, mainly in Europe.

ROMANIAN

Romance, Indo-European. Approx. 19.5M speakers Romania, 2.5M Moldova.

ROOT

The central part of a word which cannot be broken up into smaller morphs. This central part carries the core meaning of a given word. *Publications* splits into *public*, *-ation* and *-s*. *Public* cannot be split up further and is the root. Roots can have alternative forms; Latin has *rek-* and *reg-*, both representing the **lexeme** REG 'king'. *Reg-* is the basic form, also found in the verb *rego* 'I rule'. /g/ becomes **voiceless** in front of the voiceless **fricative** /s/ of the **nominative** case. See **CONDITIONING, MORPH, STEM**.

ROOT COMPOUND

Compound words that are not synthetic. They consist of two roots without any affixes. E.g. *rose bush, beer can*. See **COMPOUND WORD, SYNTHETIC COMPOUND**.

ROOT TRANSFORMATION

In the **Revised Extended Standard Theory**, a **transformation** that applied only to a **main clause**, that is, in a **phrase structure tree**, to a clause dominated by the root node of the tree. See **TREE DIAGRAM**.

ROOT-AND-PATTERN

In **Semitic** languages **roots** consist of consonants. These roots combine with different patterns of vowels, which realize morphemes such as **present tense, plural** and so on. Thus, in Arabic the root *drs* occurs in the words *daras* 'he studied', *jidris* 'he will study', *madrasa* 'a school', *dars* 'a lesson'. These languages have root-and-pattern morphology. See **MORPH**.

ROOT-INFLECTING LANGUAGE

A language with **root-and-pattern** morphology. See **MORPH, ROOT**.

ROUND BRACKETS

See **BRACKET**.

ROUNDED

A term in the description of the manner of articulation of vowel sounds. The configuration of the lips is characterized in terms of the way they are stretched away from a neutral position: round as in close back vowel like [u] (*boot* [but]) or neutral as in a mid vowel like [ʌ] (*but* [bʌt]) or **spread** as typically in a close front vowel like [i] (*beat* [bit]).

RP
See **RECEIVED PRONUNCIATION**.

RRG
See **ROLE AND REFERENCE GRAMMAR**.

RULE
1. A description of the patterns followed by speakers and writers with a mature competence in a given language. It is a rule of English that **articles** precede **nouns**: *the weather, a surprise* and not **weather the* or **surprise a*.
2. A prescriptive statement made by arbiters of 'good usage' as to whether a particular construction is correct or not, such as the 'rule', completely unrelated to what native speakers say and write, that an English sentence should never end with a preposition. 3. In a **formal grammar**, the rules generating the patterns of syntax and morphology observed in the analyst's data. Thus, NP → Det N (*the weather*) but not NP → N Det (*weather the*). See **REWRITE RULE, TRANSFORMATION**.

RULE FEATURES
In generative phonology, features attached to lexical items that were exceptions to regular rules or were subject to irregular rules. In early **transformational grammar**, rules whose purpose was to block the application of particular transformations to specific lexical items.

RULE ORDERING
In some models of **generative grammar** and phonology, rules apply in a particular order. Some sets of rules order themselves, in the sense that a rule *a* cannot apply before another rule *b*. E.g. the **phrase structure rule** NP → Det N cannot apply until the rule S → NP VP has produced the symbol NP. In treatments of **extraposition** in **transformational grammar**, the rule that inserted a dummy *it* to give *It was reported that the rules had failed* could not apply until the rule of Extraposition had applied to *That the rules had failed was reported* and moved the complement clause to yield *was reported that the rules had failed*. This self-ordering is known as intrinsic ordering. For other sets of rules, analysts working in early transformational grammar had to stipulate that one rule applied before another. E.g. the Passive transformation had to apply before **Affix Hopping**. This imposed ordering is known as extrinsic ordering. See **VOICE**.

RULE SCHEMA
In formal grammar, a combination of two or more rules into a single general statement. See **BRACKET**.

RUSSENORSK

Norwegian- and **Russian-** based pidgin used by Russian and Norwegian traders throughout the nineteenth century. Extinct.

RUSSIAN

Slavic, Indo-European. 112M speakers Russia, approx. 11M Ukraine, smaller numbers in other parts of the former Soviet Union.

RYUKYUAN

Set of varieties related to Japanese. Fewer than 300K speakers, Okinawa. Highly endangered.

S

S

1. = **sentence**, especially in **generative grammar**. In **Government and Binding Theory** and **Principles and Parameters**, S was replaced by IP, for 'Inflectional Phrase'. In the **Minimalist Program**, IP in turn has been replaced by TP, for 'Tense Phrase'. 2. = **subject**. 3. The subject of an **intransitive verb**, contrasting with A and P, the subject and object of a **transitive verb**.

S´

A symbol, pronounced S-bar, standing for a subordinate clause and its **complementizer**; e.g. *(knew) that Sabrina played the piano* and *when we were in Rome*, where *that* and *when* are complementizers. In **Principles and Parameters** it was replaced by CP, for 'complementizer phrase'. See **CLAUSE, X-BAR SYNTAX**.

SAAMI
Finno-Ugric, **Uralic**. Approx. 26K speakers, Finland, Norway, Sweden and Russia. Several varieties.

SACCADES
Rapid eye movements produced as readers scan texts.

SAGITTAL SECTION
A cross-section of a body part to illustrate its structure. See Figure 'Articulators' at **ARTICULATION**.

SALISHAN
Family of endangered or extinct languages in British Columbia and north-west USA.

SAMAR-LEYTE
Austronesian. Approx. 3K speakers, Philippines.

SAMOAN
Malayo-Polynesian, Austronesian. Approx. 370K speakers, Western Samoa, American Samoa, New Zealand.

SAMOYEDIC
Uralic, include **Nenets**, Enets and Selkup.

SAMPLING

In **typology**, the selection of a number of languages which is small enough to allow analysis within the time available but large enough to yield results that are statistically significant. It is also important to ensure that the languages in any sample are spread over different language families and to avoid languages whose speakers have been in contact for a considerable time, as such languages are likely to possess some or many characteristics in common. See **LANGUAGE FAMILY**.

SANDHI

A general term, originating in the work of Sanskrit grammarians, for the phonological modifications that occur between juxtaposed forms. A distinction is sometimes made between 'internal' sandhi (sandhi rules that operate within **words**, e.g. the variant forms of the English plural, /z/ following a **voiced** segment as in /dɒgz/ and /s/ following a voiceless **segment** as in /kats/) and 'external sandhi' (sandhi rules that operate across word boundaries, as in the rules for **linking r** and **intrusive r** and **assimilation**).

SANGO

Niger-Congo. Ngbandi-based Creole, two varieties. 440K speakers, Democratic Republic of the Congo.

SANSKRIT

Indo-Iranian, Indo-European. First attested in religious chants dating from before 1000 BCE. Classical Sanskrit established as standard around 500 BCE. Still written and spoken in India as a learned language by approx. 6K.

SANTALI

Mundari, Austro-Asiatic. Approx. 6M speakers, India.

SAPIR, Edward (1884–1939)

American anthropologist; Professor of Linguistics at the University of Chicago. He worked on Native American languages in the early years of the twentieth century publishing texts and writing grammars and other descriptions. His book *Language*, 1921, remains a popular and accessible introduction to linguistics. He trained in historical and comparative linguistics and made an important contribution to the classification of American languages. His work, together with Benjamin Lee Whorf, on the mutual influence of language and culture, resulting in the **Sapir–Whorf hypothesis**, is still influential.

SAPIR–WHORF HYPOTHESIS

The view, associated with the work of Edward Sapir and Benjamin Whorf, that the way in which humans conceive the external world is subject to linguistic determinism. That is, the speakers of a given language have their conceptions of the external world determined by their native language, in particular by the semantics of its grammatical categories but also by the organization of its vocabulary. The hypothesis implies a large degree of linguistic relativism, the idea that language controls speakers' conceptions of the world and speakers of a given language have different conceptions from those held by speakers of other languages. See **GRAMMATICAL CATEGORY**.

SATELLITE

1. In **functional grammar**, a **constituent** modifying the **nucleus**, i.e. the verb and any obligatory **arguments**. In *Rene dismantled the shelves yesterday* and *Pavel sent an e-mail to find out what was happening*, the satellites are *yesterday* and *to find out what was happening*. 2. Generally, any secondary and/or **dependent** constituent in a clause such as an **adjunct**. See **MODIFIER**.

SATELLITE-FRAMED LANGUAGES

A sentence such as *We strolled down the street* describes a movement, the manner in which the movement is performed – by strolling, and the **path** followed by the people moving – down the street. English has **verbs** denoting both movement and manner, such as *stroll, swim, run, fly*. The path is denoted by a **satellite**, *down the street*. ('Satellite' is used in a broader sense than in the entry for **SATELLITE**.) Languages such as **English, German, Russian** are said to be satellite-framed languages. In contrast, languages such as **French** are said to be verb-framed. They have verbs denoting movement and path, and manner is denoted by a satellite. Thus, corresponding to *We strolled down the street* French has *Nous avons descendu la rue en flânant* 'We have descended the street in strolling'.

SATEM LANGUAGES

See **CENTUM AND SATEM LANGUAGES**.

SAUSSURE, Ferdinand de (1857–1913)

Best known for the *Cours de linguistique générale* (1916), compiled posthumously by his former students. The *Cours* is generally considered to be the foundation of structuralism, a view that extends beyond linguistics. Although he also holds a distinguished place as an historical linguist, Saussure is known for championing the **synchronic** rather than **diachronic** approach to language description. Among his many pioneering ideas is the distinction between *langage* (the general phenomenon of language), *langue* (the underlying system of a particular language) and *parole* (individual acts of speech), distinctions central to structural linguistics, and indeed to Chomsky's generative grammar (see **competence** and **performance**). He viewed a *langue* as a network of terms of interrelated axes, **syntagmatic**, items are linearly ordered, and **paradigmatic**, items form systems of oppositions.

SAXON GENITIVE

See **ADNOMINAL**.

S-BAR

See **S´**.

SC
See **STRUCTURAL CHANGE, TRANSFORMATION**.

SCAFFOLDING
A concept originally relating to the assistance that more experienced members of a culture or speakers of a language can give to less experienced members or speakers. Thus, the help that teachers give to students in the classroom, with smiles, frowns, hand-gestures, backchannelling, repetition, rephrasing and so on, is an example of scaffolding. The concept has been extended to all types of communication, since even in relaxed conversation the above-mentioned **paralinguistic** cues are crucial in establishing communication and signalling whether it is proceeding smoothly and in accordance with the participants' intentions. See **BACKCHANNEL, CONVERSATION ANALYSIS**.

SCALAR
See **SCALAR IMPLICATURE**.

SCALAR IMPLICATURE
Relating to a scale, such as the **gradable adjective** scale. The **Q-principle** applies, *inter alia*, to any **implicature** relating to scales and known as a scalar implicature, as for the scale formed by the **quantifiers** *some/any – most – all*. The **utterance** *I've replied to some of the e-mails* invites the inference *not most and not all of them*. *Poor – average/OK – good – excellent – outstanding* form a scale. If the question *Did you like the report?* elicits the reply *It's OK*, the listener is intended to infer that *It isn't good/excellent/outstanding* and *It's not poor*.
See **NEO-GRICEAN PRAGMATICS, OPPOSITENESS**.

SCALE AND CATEGORY GRAMMAR
Forerunner of **Systemic Functional Grammar**.

SCENARIO
See **SCRIPT**.

SCHEMA
See **FRAME**.

SCHWA
The **unrounded, central** vowel typically found in unstressed syllables in English as in the initial vowel in *about* [ə'baʊt] or the **vowel** in the second **syllable** of *moment* ['məʊmənt] It is represented in IPA as [ə].

SCHLEGEL, Friedrich von (1772–1829)
Indo-European scholar and comparative linguist. His book *Über die Sprache und Weisheit der Indier* was influential among his contemporaries.

SCHLEICHER, August (1821–1868)
The most distinguished Indo-Europeanist of his generation, particularly noted for his contribution to the development of the **comparative method** and in

particular the techniques of reconstruction based on laws of **sound change**. He was influenced by Darwin's *Origin of Species* in his views on the development of language.

SCHUCHARDT, Hugo (1842–1927)

Professor of Romance Philology in Graz, Austria. He worked on an enormous variety of languages including Romance, Germanic, Slavic, Celtic, Berber, Bengali and Melanesian pidgin. In his early years he turned against the **Neogrammarians'** views on rigid sound laws and also **Schleicher**'s Darwinian views on language classification. In his view language primarily relates to concepts, thoughts and meanings embedded in cultures and societies and in this respect his views are the forerunner of the discipline of Languages in Contact.

SCOPE

The extent of the influence of a form over surrounding language. Particularly used of negatives, quantifiers and adverbials and sometimes producing ambiguity, as in *you may not go* (= 'not may' [you don't have permission to go] or 'not go' [you have permission not to go].

SCOTS

Germanic. Language of literature and government from twelfth to seventeenth centuries. Many people in Scotland and Northern Ireland speak varieties descended from medieval Scots.

SCOTTISH GAELIC

Celtic, Indo-European. Approx. 59K speakers, mainly north-west Scotland, but also Nova Scotia, Canada. Endangered language.

SCRAMBLING

In languages with free **word order**, the phenomenon of the words in a **clause** being able to be arranged in (apparently) any order

SCRIPT

Scripts were originally developed to enable computers to 'understand' texts such as stories and conversations and to handle the many inferences that even a single **sentence** gives rise to. They were subsequently extended to models of language processing by humans. Scripts are structures for storing knowledge about stereotypical sequences of events and actions in given situations, the roles of the people taking part and the inanimate entities involved. For example, catching a plane involves checking in (finding the check-in desk, queuing, showing ticket and passport, putting luggage on the conveyor belt to be weighed and labelled), going to the departure lounge, the sequence of events that constitute going through security and so on.

SD

See **STRUCTURAL DESCRIPTION, TRANSFORMATION**.

SECOND LANGUAGE (L2)

A language learned after the first language, the **mother tongue**. Typically, an L2 is acquired through formal study and after puberty. Usually the speaker does not achieve the same level of fluency as in the first language. All languages acquired after the first language are second languages. A speaker may have more than one L2.

SECOND OBJECT

See GRAMMATICAL FUNCTION.

SECOND PERSON

See PERSON.

SECONDARY ARTICULATION

An articulation that accompanies a primary articulation, and with a lesser constriction than the primary articulation, such as **labialization, velarization**.

SECONDARY CARDINAL VOWEL

See CARDINAL VOWEL.

SECONDARY OBJECT

See GRAMMATICAL FUNCTION.

SECONDARY PREDICATION

See PREDICATE 3.

SEGMENT

A single speech sound, usually corresponding to a single **phone**. By convention, the **articulators** are held to be unmoving during its **articulation**.

SEGMENTAL PHONOLOGY

The analysis of speech into a string of **segments** or **phones**. Contrasting with **suprasegmental** phonology, which concerns itself with those features of speech that extend over more than one segment, particularly **intonation**.

SEGMENTAL TIER

In early versions of **autosegmental phonology**, the tier where **segments** are located. In later versions this tier is decomposed into other tiers or the segments are dissolved into **distinctive features**.

SELECTIONAL FEATURE

See SELECTIONAL RESTRICTION.

SELECTIONAL RESTRICTION

A restriction on combinations of **verb** and **noun** arising from their meanings. In early **generative grammar** such restrictions were encoded in selectional features. See FEATURE, GOVERNMENT, STRICT SUBCATEGORIZATION.

SELECTIVE LISTENING

See COCKTAIL PARTY PHENOMENON.

SELF-EMBEDDING
See **CENTRE-EMBEDDING**.

SELF-INITIATED
See **REPAIR**.

SELF-REPAIR
See **REPAIR**.

SEMANTIC ANNOTATION
Annotation relating to the meaning of **lexical words**. Typically such annotation provides information about roles such as agent, patient, **comitative** and so on, and about the senses of individual lexemes represented in a text. See **ROLE, SENSE**.

SEMANTIC CASE
A case that expresses meaning and is not merely a marker of a grammatical **construction**. See **CASE, GRAMMATICAL CASE**.

SEMANTIC COMPONENTS
See **LEXICAL DECOMPOSITION, PROTOTYPE THEORY**.

SEMANTIC MAP
A diagram displaying the meanings of **grammatical categories** or the senses of **lexical words**. The diagrams show a network of interconnected items, with a central item or pivot and other items representing extensions of the pivot. For instance, a semantic map of the **dative** case in Russian might show two sets of meanings, one set associated with **verbs** and **adjectives** that govern the dative **case** and the other with **constructions** containing the **ethic dative**. The semantic map for Russian might show the network of meanings centred on two of the first set: structures with verbs such as *vredit'* 'harm' which govern nouns in the dative case and structures such as *Petru xolodno* 'Peter-DAT cold, Peter is cold'. The maps can be used to analyse such a network for one language or to compare two languages. Thus a map of the Czech dative network would show the same meanings but might indicate that the Czech network is centred on the ethic dative constructions. The maps are a valuable tool in typology, since they can be used to compare more than two languages and to compare and contrast overlapping networks. See **RADIAL CATEGORY**.

SEMANTIC PARAPHASIA
See **VERBAL PARAPHASIA**.

SEMANTIC PROSODY
The phenomenon of apparently neutral **lexical words** acquiring positive or negative connotations through the lexical items they occur with most often. The phrase *set in* occurs frequently in the phrase *the rot set in* and has acquired a negative connotation. Other things that set in are rain, frost, infection and despair. See **COLLOCATION**.

SEMANTIC VALENCY

See **VALENCY GRAMMAR**.

SEMANTICS

The study of **meaning**. In current usage semantics is usually taken to be the study of the language code rather than the use of language in **context**, which is seen as the province of **pragmatics**. On this view semantics deals with **lexical words**, the relations between them, and how the meanings of words combine to yield the meaning of **phrases**, and the meanings of phrases combine to yield the meaning of **clauses**. In fact, much work on real language has to take account of both a particular code, say English, and its users and context. See **BRIDGING, COMPOSITIONALITY, CONSTRUAL, CONTEXT, EXPLICATURE, REFERENCE, SENSE RELATIONS**.

SEMELFACTIVE

An **Aktionsart** relating to a single **action** perceived as instantaneous, e.g. *stab, punch*, as opposed to *write*, e.g. *The boxer punched the punchbag* denotes a single action; the **progressive** *The boxer was punching the punchbag* denotes a series of actions. In contrast, *The reporter was writing his article* denotes a single action in progress. (Latin *semel* 'once', *factum*, roughly = 'done'.) See **PUNCTUAL**.

SEMI-AUXILIARY

In English grammar, combinations of *be* or *have* with a variety of words. The combinations, such as *be able to, be supposed to, be going to, have to*, express modal meanings of necessity or possibility but do not have all the NICE properties. The combinations with *be* have the NICE properties – *Is he able to help?, He isn't able to help, He's able to help and so is Jane, He IS able to help*. *Have to* patterns mainly as a main **verb**, as does *need*: *Does she have to sell the house?, She doesn't have to sell up, Does she need to sell the house? Need* is sometimes described as a marginal **modal verb**, along with *ought* and *dare*. See **MODALITY**.

SEMIOSIS

The processing of linguistic **signs**.

SEMIOTICS

The general theory of **signs**, whether linguistic or non-linguistic, such as the clothes a person wears on a particular occasion, facial expression, hand-gestures, features of buildings (such as the massive government buildings of pre-war Germany and the Soviet Union) and so on. See **ARBITRARY SIGN, EMBLEM, ICONIC SIGN, INDEX**.

SEMITIC

Language family including **Arabic, Hebrew** (Middle East, North Africa), **Amharic, Tigrinya** (Ethiopia) and **Tigrinya** (Eritrea). Semitic languages important in antiquity were **Akkadian, Aramaic, Phoenician, Syriac** and **Ugaritic**.

SENDER
The person transmitting a message, by ordinary post, by e-mail, by radio and so on.

SENSE
1. The intensional **denotation** of a lexical item. The sense of *platypus* is what enables it to be applied to platypuses but not to quolls or euros. 2. One meaning of a given **lexical word** as opposed to its other meanings; e.g. the sense of *driver* referring to the driver of a car vs its sense when referring to the driving force behind some project or policy. 3. The set of **sense relations** which a lexical item contracts with others, or which the senses of lexical items contract with each other. See EXTENSION, INTENSION, REFERENCE.

SENSE RELATIONS
The semantic relations holding between **lexical words** within the vocabulary of a given language or between the senses of different lexical words and the senses of a single lexical item. Sense relations are connected with **sense** (1) and sense (2) and play an important role in how speakers organize and store the lexical words of their language. See FACETS, HYPONYMY, MERONYMY, OPPOSITENESS, POLYSEMY, SYNONYMY.

SENTENCE
The sentence is often defined as the largest unit handled by grammar (**word order**, **morphosyntax**, obligatory and optional elements). Another analysis takes it to be a low-level unit of **discourse** consisting of one or more **clauses**. A compound sentence consists of two or more main clauses, typically conjoined by *and* or *but* – *Margaret baked scones* and *the children ate them all*. A complex sentence consists of a main clause and one or more subordinate clauses – *I love the house you live in* (*you live in* is a **relative clause**), *We left before he arrived* (*before he arrived* is an **adverbial clause of time**), *The council maintain that they own the land* (*that they own the land* is a **complement clause**).

SENTENCE ADVERB
See ADVERBIAL.

SENTENCE FOCUS
A **proposition** consists of a **predicate** and **arguments**. When a proposition is expressed by means of a **clause** in an **utterance**, the **focus** may be on the entire proposition, which is all new information. E.g. in *What happened? – Fiona stepped on a snake*, the entire sentence *Fiona stepped on a snake* and the proposition it expresses carry new information and are in focus. See ARGUMENT FOCUS, END FOCUS, GIVEN AND NEW SENTENCE FOCUS, THETIC SENTENCE.

SENTENCE FORM
The structure of **sentences** (or **clauses**). See DECLARATIVE, EXCLAMATIVE, IMPERATIVE, INTERROGATIVE CLAUSE.

SENTENCE FRAGMENT

In written **texts**, sequences of **words** and **phrases** that do not count as complete system sentences but are set down on paper with the formatting of a text sentence. E.g. *Lucie looked out of the window. Sheets of rain. Huge puddles. No taxi.* Such fragments are widely used in modern writing, serving to catch the reader's attention by highlighting some object or property. See **SENTENCE**.

SENTENCE FUNCTION

What speakers can do with different **sentence** (or main **clause**) constructions: make statements (**declarative** clause), utter exclamations (**exclamative**), issue commands (**imperative**) or ask questions (**interrogative clause**). See **FUNCTION, SENTENCE FORM, SPEECH ACT**.

SENTENCE MEANING

The meaning assigned to **sentences** in contrast with the meaning assigned to **utterances**. For instance, sentences contain information about **propositional content, role, tense and aspect, voice, mood** but only utterances in context express propositions, allow the interpretation of **deictic** items, the picking out of referents, and the performance of **speech acts**. Interpreting utterances typically requires hearers and readers to interpret the intention of the speaker or writer. See **DEIXIS, PROPOSITION**.

SENTENCE STRESS

The prominence given to a single **syllable** in a single **sentence** in an unmarked style of pronunciation. In English this is usually the final lexical item in the sentence, e.g. *Cats like 'fish*. Compare **contrastive stress**, e.g. *'Cats like fish* or *Cats 'like fish*. See **MARKED**.

SENTENTIAL NEGATION

See **CLAUSAL NEGATION**.

SEQUENCE

In **conversation analysis**, a series of turns by means of which the interlocutors organize their interaction, ensuring **coherence** and **cohesion**. See **TURN**.

SEQUENCE OF TENSES

A restriction on patterns of tenses in main clauses followed by a **subordinate clause**. The restriction applies weakly in English but past tense in main clauses tends to be followed by past tense in subordinate clauses: e.g. *Philippa says she is arriving at 6* vs *Philippa said she was arriving at 6*, *They think they have finished the job* vs *They thought they had finished the job*. See **CLAUSE, TENSE AND ASPECT**.

SERBIAN-CROATIAN-BOSNIAN LINGUISTIC COMPLEX

Slavic. Closely related varieties. Serbo-Croat was recognized as the standard language of former Yugoslavia but, with the break-up of the latter, three standard languages are in the process of elaboration, Serbian, Croatian and Bosnian.

SERIAL VERB

Serial verbs have various functions. They add an **argument** to a **verb**, thereby increasing its **valency**. **Yoruba**, for example, has the verb *fi* 'take'. This verb can occur on its own in a clause or combined with another verb in a serial verb construction, as in *Mo fi àdá gé igi nâ* '1sg take machete cut tree the, I cut the tree with a machete'. The verb serialization **construction** allows the verb *gé* 'cut' to take an additional argument, *àdá* 'machete', with the role of instrument. Typically the serial verb either has no independent tense or aspect or has a tense echoing that of the main verb. Serial verb constructions can form complex predicates without adding an argument, as in Mandarin *ta la-kai le men* 'He pull-open PFV door, He pulled open the door'. Yet other serial verb constructions encode more than one event, as in the Lango example *Án ápòyò cèggò dógólá* 'I remembered-it; I-closed door, I remembered to close the door'. See **TENSE AND ASPECT**.

SET EXPRESSION

See **FIXED EXPRESSION**.

SETTING

1. The location in which **interlocutors** interact. Politicians discussing issues in a restaurant or private house will use a register different from the register they use when taking part in a television interview in a studio or giving a public speech. 2. In narrative, the characters implicated in events, together with the locations and times of the latter. See **DOMAIN, NARRATIVE, REGISTER**.

SGML

See **STANDARD GENERALIZED MARKUP LANGUAGE**.

SHADOW PRONOUN

See **RESUMPTIVE PRONOUN**.

SHALLOW STRUCTURE

In earlier **transformational grammar**, a level of structure nearer the surface than **deep structure**.

SHANGHAIESE

See **CHINESE**.

SHARP

In **J&H Distinctive Feature Theory**, an **acoustic** distinctive feature representing an upward shift of the upper frequencies of the spectrum, associated with **palatalization**. It is in opposition to both **flat** and **plain**, so it is in effect part of a ternary opposition, flat–plain–sharp. See **DISTINCTIVE FEATURES, ACOUSTIC**.

SHONA

Bantu, Niger-Congo. Approx. 10.6M speakers, Zimbabwe.

SHORT PASSIVE
See **VOICE**.

SHORT VOWEL
A **vowel** with a relatively short duration, usually in contrast with a long vowel. Thus English [ɪ] in *bit*, in contrast with [i] in *beat*.

SHORTHAND
Various systems of speed-writing that made it possible to record speech verbatim. Also known as stenography, the practitioners being stenographers.

SIBILANT
A **groove fricative**, usually [s].

SIGN
Any kind of phenomenon (an object, a sensation, an event) correlated with some state of affairs and taken as signalling some entity or situation. Thus, smoke is taken as a sign that something is on fire, black clouds are a sign of impending rain, a damp patch on the ceiling of a room is a sign that water is coming in. Such signs are associated with the presence of whatever is signalled. The concept of sign is extended to language, and a linguistic sign is taken to be a stable association of a linguistic form (sometimes called, following Saussure, the signifier or signifiant) with a particular meaning (sometimes called the signified or signifié). A linguistic sign can be a **morph**, **word**, **phrase**, **clause** or **sentence**. Linguistic signs are not associated with the presence of what is signalled, since one key property of natural language is that it can be used to refer to entities that are distant in space and/or time. Different types of sign are recognized depending on the type of relationship between the sign and what is signalled. See **ARBITRARY SIGN, EMBLEM, ICONIC SIGN, INDEX, SEMIOTICS**.

SIGNIFIANT
See **SIGN**.

SIGNIFIÉ
See **SIGN**.

SILENT PAUSE
A pause in speech with nothing but silence (*I think … you will enjoy this*) contrasts with a **filled pause** (*I think erm you will enjoy this*).

SILENT STRESS
A **pause** in speech that occurs where a stressed **syllable** might be expected. The silent stress often maintains a rhythmic pattern, as in this analysis of the metrical pattern of a limerick (| marks the beginning of a metrical **foot**, which starts with a stressed syllable, "; ^ marks a silent syllable:

   | ^ There |"was an old |"man with a |"beard
   | ^ Who |"said it is |"just as I |"feared

| ˄ Two |″owls and a |″wren two |″larks and a |″hen
| ˄ Have |″all made their |″nests in my |″beard.

SIMILE
See **METAPHOR**.

SIMPLE ACTIVE AFFIRMATIVE DECLARATIVE
The most basic type of **sentence** (or **clause**), e.g. *The forester felled an oak.*

SIMPLE PAST
In English grammar, forms such as *wrote* in contrast with the **Progressive** *was writing*. The default interpretation is a single completed action, *Rene wrote a letter (last Friday)*; the marked interpretation is a repeated action, *Rene wrote a letter (every Friday)*. See **HABITUAL, TENSE AND ASPECT**.

SIMPLE PRESENT
In English grammar, forms such as *writes* in contrast with the **Progressive** *is writing*. The default interpretation is a repeated action, as in *Rene writes novels (for a living)* but the form with the interpretation of 'single action' is a hallmark of sports commentaries, newspaper headlines and stage directions: *Jacob passes, takes the return pass, shoots – the goalkeeper makes a diving save; Egypt rises up* (*The Economist*, 5–11 Feb. 2011), *Pavel enters stage left*. See **PRESENT TENSE, TENSE AND ASPECT**.

SIMPLE SENTENCE
A **sentence** consisting of a single main **clause** and no other clauses. Examples are *The car stopped; The tsunami was terrifying; When did they leave?; Are you going to the party?; Please leave the parcel in the porch; What a wonderful garden you have!*

SIMPLER SYNTAX
A model of syntax developed from the late 1990s. Based on constraints, the model has a syntax that employs as few principles and as little structure as possible. For example, there are no **transformations** and no **underlying subject** in the analysis of examples such as *We all like to win*. A central feature of the model is what is called 'parallel architecture'. There are independent components for **semantics**, **syntax** and **phonology**, each with its own set of rules for combining elements. The rules take the form of **constraints**. These components are connected by means of interfaces, also consisting of sets of constraints. See **EMPTY CATEGORY, GENERATIVE GRAMMAR, PRINCIPLES AND PARAMETERS, PRO, Pro, TRACE**.

SIMPLEX
A recent alternative to simple, as in 'simplex sentence'. Apparently formed by analogy with *complex*.

SIMPLICITY METRIC
A measure of simplicity applied to **grammars** as part of an **evaluation procedure**.

SINCERITY CONDITION
See FELICITY CONDITIONS.

SINDHI
Indo-Iranian, Indo-European. Approx. 18.5M speakers Pakistan, and 2.8M India.

SINGLE-BAR
See X-BAR SYNTAX.

SINGLE-BASE TRANSFORMATION
See TRANSFORMATION.

SINGLE-VALUED FEATURE
See SINGULARY FEATURE.

SINGULAR
A subcategory of **number** to do with denoting one entity. Thus, the singular form *box* denotes one box, the plural form *boxes* denotes more than one. See DUAL, PLURAL.

SINGULARY FEATURE
In some early formal models of **generative grammar**, features such as [labial] or [unvoiced] which only have a positive value, there being no features [not labial] or [not unvoiced].

SINGULARY TRANSFORMATION
See TRANSFORMATION.

SINHALA
Indo-Iranian, Indo-European. 15.8M speakers, Sri Lanka.

SINO-TIBETAN
Language family including a **Chinese** branch (Mandarin, Cantonese and Hokkien) and a Tibeto-Burman branch (**Tibetan**, **Burmese**). Far East and South-East Asia.

SIOUAN
Native American language family spoken (now and/or formerly) in the central plains from central Canada to the Mississippi delta. Includes **Lakota**, **Crow**, Hidatsa and Mandan.

SISTER
See TREE DIAGRAM.

SISTER ADJUNCTION
See ADJUNCTION.

SITUATION
See CONTEXT.

SITUATION ASPECT
See **AKTIONSART**.

SITUATION OF INTERACTION
Any situation where interlocutors can interact. See **SITUATION OF RECEPTION**.

SITUATION OF RECEPTION
Any situation where participants merely receive messages but cannot reply: e.g. listening to a formal lecture, watching a television programme. See **SITUATION OF INTERACTION**.

SITUATION SEMANTICS
A theory of **semantics** in which a **sentence** is treated as describing a situation. Situations are abstractions from actual states of affairs that speakers talk about. They consist of individual entities and the relations between them, the **role**, such as agent and **experiencer**, played by the individuals, the time and place of situations. These components of situations are primitive elements in the theory, which was developed as an alternative to **model-theoretic semantics** with its focus on truth and falsity.

SITUATIONALITY
The extent to which a **text** is relevant to the situation in which it is uttered.

SJUZHET
See **HISTOIRE**.

SKELETAL TIER
In **autosegmental phonology**, the tier which provides the anchoring for other tiers. Also called the **X tier**, or the **timing tier**.

SKOU LANGUAGES
Family of sixteen languages spoken in North New Guinea.

SLACK
See **DISTINCTIVE FEATURES, PHONATION TYPES**.

SLANG
Words and **phrases** used by speakers of standard and **non-standard** varieties, most often in very informal speech. Slang expressions are created and disappear relatively quickly, though some persist. *Booze* 'alcoholic drink' has been in use since the eighteenth century; *kick the bucket* 'die' appeared in the mid nineteenth century but is now seldom used; *dead* 'very', as in *dead brilliant* and *dead stupid*, appeared in the early 1960s but is now very infrequent.

SLASH (/)

1. An oblique line '/' that marks off the **context** in which a rule applies. Thus, k – > ts/i ___ is read 'k becomes ts following i. 2. In **Generalized Phrase Structure Grammar**, a slash was used in labels such as VP/NP to indicate a **VP** containing an empty **NP**. VP/NP is an instance of a slash category.

SLASH CATEGORY

See **SLASH**.

SLAVIC

Indo-European. Central and Eastern Europe and the Balkans. West Slavic includes **Czech, Polish, Slovak** and **Sorbian**. East Slavic includes **Russian, Belorussian** and **Ukrainian**. South Slavic includes **Slovene, Macedonian, Bulgarian** and the members of the **Serbian-Croatian-Bosnian** linguistic complex.

SLAVONIC

See **SLAVIC**.

SLIT FRICATIVE

A **fricative** produced with the tongue more or less flat, thus producing a smooth airflow. See **GROOVE FRICATIVE**.

SLOPPY IDENTITY

See **LAZY PRONOUN**.

SLOT

A position in a **construction**. See **FILLER**.

SLOT-AND-FILLER MODEL

A representation of **constructions** as consisting of slots and constituents that fill them. See **FILLER**.

SLOVAK

Slavic, Indo-European. 4.5M speakers, Slovakia.

SLOVENE

Slavic, Indo-European. 1.7M speakers Slovenia, 100K Italy, 39K Austria.

SMALL CLAUSE

A **subject complement** or **object complement** which can be thought of as expressing a **predication** and as a reduced **clause**. The clause *The pollution made him ill* contains the small clause *him ill*. The small clause is equivalent to *He was ill*. The clause *I want Bill in my office* contains the small clause *in my office* or *Bill in my office*. The small clause is equivalent to *Bill is to be in my office*. The clause *She arrived exhausted* contains the small clause *exhausted*, equivalent to *She was exhausted*. See **COMPLEMENT, REDUCED ADVERBIAL CLAUSE, REDUCED RELATIVE CLAUSE**.

SOCIAL DEIXIS

Special uses of **personal pronouns** to signal intimacy or distance in personal relationships and formality, such as the use of *tu* and *vous* in French. See **PERSON, PRAGMALINGUISTIC NORMS**.

SOCIAL NETWORK

The web of relationships (kinship, friendship, etc.) built up by an individual within a community. The concept is sometimes used to explain different linguistic behaviour by different social groups.

SOCIOLECT

A language variety determined by social rather than geographical factors, such as English **received pronunciation**. See **ACROLECT, BASILECT**.

SOCIOLINGUISTICS

The study of language in society, the way it is used and the effects it has on hearers and speakers. See **SOCIAL NETWORK, SOCIOLECT, SOCIOLINGUISTIC VARIABLE, SOCIOPRAGMATIC NORMS**.

SOCIOLINGUISTIC VARIABLE

See **LINGUISTIC VARIABLE**.

SOCIOPRAGMATIC NORMS

In a given society, the norms governing who is to perform what speech act in a particular situation. The norms relate to properties of the interlocutors: their gender and relative age, their social class and occupations, and their roles and status in the interaction. For example, a student who has borrowed a book from a lecturer and forgotten to return it is expected, in Britain at least, to apologise contritely – *I'm really sorry. I completely forgot, but it was very helpful* – and not to brush away the offence – *Oh well. I've had a lot on my mind lately.* See **PRAGMALINGUISTIC NORMS**.

SOFT CONSONANT

Some languages, like Russian, have pairs of consonants, one palatalized (the soft consonants) and the other not (the **hard consonants**). See **PALATALIZATION**.

SOFT PALATE

See **PALATE, VELUM**.

SOGDIAN

Middle **Iranian, Indo-Iranian, Indo-European**. Spoken till eighth century CE in Sogdiana, now part of Uzbekistan.

SOMALI

Cushitic, AfroAsiatic. Approx. 7.8M speakers Somalia, 3.3M Ethiopia, 420K Kenya, 291K Djibouti.

SONANT
A **voiced** sound capable of acting as a syllabic **nucleus** – **vowels**, **liquids** and **nasals**.

SONGHAY
Nilo-Saharan. Three major varieties. 740K speakers, Mali and Burkina-Faso.

SONORANT
1. A **consonant** that is **nasal** or **approximant** or one of the **liquids**, as opposed to an **obstruent**. 2. In **SPE Distinctive Feature Theory**, a **segment** that is produced without turbulence in the **vocal tract**; that is, a **vowel** or consonant that is not an **obstruent**.

SONORITY
The loudness of a sound, reflecting the openness of the articulators and the amount of energy used in its articulation. The least sonorous sounds are voiceless **plosives**, [p,t,k], then voiced plosives, [b,d,g], then voiceless **fricatives**, [f,θ,s], then voiced fricatives, [v,ð,z], then **nasals**, [m,n], then **liquids**, [l,r], then **high** vowels, [i,u]. The most sonorous sounds are **low** vowels, [ɑ,ɒ]. See **AMPLITUDE**.

SONORITY HIERARCHY
Also known as the sonority scale. A ranking of speech sounds in terms of their relative **sonority**: voiceless plosives, [p,t,k], > voiced **plosives**, [b,d,g], > voiceless fricatives, [f,θ,s], > voiced **fricatives**, [v,ð,z], > **nasals**, [m,n] and **liquids**, [l,r], > high **vowels**, [i,u]. The most sonorous sounds are low vowels, [ɑ,ɒ]. Sonority hierarchies are most useful in analysing the **onsets** and **codas** of **syllable** structure.

SONORITY PEAK
In **metrical phonology** the **nucleus** of a **syllable**, when **sonority** is greatest.

SONORITY SCALE
See **SONORITY HIERARCHY**.

SORBIAN
Slavic, Indo-European. Approx. 15K speakers, Saxony (Germany).

SOUND CHANGE
The observation that a sound in a language at one stage of its history corresponds systematically with a sound at another, later, stage. E.g. Old English /mus/ and modern English /maus/. See **GREAT VOWEL SHIFT**. Or that a sound in one language corresponds systematically with a sound in another – e.g. that certain Sanskrit sounds correspond systematically with sound in Greek and other Indo-European languages. The study of sound change is the basis of **comparative linguistics**. The systematic correspondences are formulated as sound laws – See **GRIMM'S LAW**.

SOUND CORRESPONDENCE

In historical linguistics, the set of sounds found in a set of **cognate** words that are deemed to correspond regularly. Sound correspondences among daughter languages are the basis of the reconstruction of proto-sounds from which the sound correspondence derives.

SOUND SPECTROGRAPH

A device that analyses speech input and displays it as a graph, a sound spectrogram. A spectrogram displays the **frequency** of a sound on the vertical axis, its **duration** on the horizontal axis and the darkness of the graph at any point represent its **intensity**. It is useful for the analysis of the **formant** structure of any part of an **utterance**.

SOUND SPECTRUM

See **SOUND SPECTROGRAPH**.

SOUND SYMBOLISM

A general term for different types of iconic association between **word** forms and their referents. The strongest relationship is **onomatopoeia**. A weaker one is **phonaesthesia**, in which part of a word form is associated with some meaning. E.g. in English *-ump* is associated with low-pitched noises, as in *crump, thump* and *grump,* and *gl-* is associated with light, as in *gleam, glisten, glow, glitter*. These associations are not universal but governed by the conventions applying in a given language. Sequences such as *-ump* in *bump* and *thump* and *gl-* in *glow* and *glimmer* are phonaesthemes. See **ARBITRARY SIGN, ICONIC SIGN, ONOMATOPOEIA**.

SOUND SYSTEM

See **PHONOLOGY, SYSTEM**.

SOUND WAVE

Sound is transmitted from a **source** by variations in pressure. This is usually measured in terms of its amplitude (loudness), **wavelength** and **frequency** (pitch). See **SPEECH WAVE**.

SOUNDING

Verbal duelling, typically involving insults, associated with **AAVE**.

SOURCE

1. A **role** associated with the location from which an entity moves and marked, in English, by prepositions such as *from, off, out of*. Movement-from-a-source may be concrete and literal – *We flew from London to Beirut* – or metaphorical – *The soldiers died from their injuries*. 2. The origin of a sound signal.

SOURCE FEATURE

A term in the system of feature geometry proposed in **SPE**. Distinctive features that identify **phonation types** such as **voice**.

SOURCE FEATURES
See SPE DISTINCTIVE FEATURE THEORY.

SOUTH PHILIPPINE LANGUAGES
Malayo-Polynesian, Austronesian. Three subgroups, Subanon, Danao and Manobo.

SPACE GRAMMAR
A model of language, which developed into **Cognitive Grammar**.

SPANISH
Romance, Indo-European. Approx. 333M speakers, principally in Spain 28M, Argentina 33M, Bolivia 3.5M, Chile 14M, Columbia 34M, Costa Rica 3.5M, Cuba 10M, Dominican Republic 6.9M, Ecuador 9.5M, El Salvador 6M, Guatemala 4.7M, Honduras 5.6M, Mexico 87M, Nicaragua 4.4M, Panama 2M, Peru 20M, Puerto Rico 3.5M, Uruguay 3M, USA 22.5M.

SPATIAL EXPRESSION
An expression describing location in or movement through space, such as *round the field, through the forest, in the pool*. Across languages, spatial expressions involve **prepositions**, **postpositions** and **case**. They involve lexical words denoting parts of objects such as edges and surfaces and areas of space adjacent to some part of an object, such as *beside* or *atop the building*. See ABLATIVE, ALLATIVE, ELATIVE, ILLATIVE, INESSIVE.

SPE DISTINCTIVE FEATURE THEORY
The system of articulatory distinctive features proposed by Chomsky and Halle in *Sound Pattern of English* (SPE), 1968. See DISTINCTIVE FEATURES, ARTICULATORY, FEATURE GEOMETRY.

SPE
The Sound Pattern of English (1968) by Noam Chomsky and Morris Halle. The classical account of GENERATIVE PHONOLOGY.

SPEAKER
1. The person speaking. The participants in a **dialogue** take it in turn to play the roles of speaker and hearer/**addressee**, which relate to the grammatical category of **person**, speaker being first **person** and hearer being second person. The speaker is central to **deixis**. 2. A convenient cover-term for speakers and writers which reflects the historical and acquisitional primacy of speaking and speakers over writing and writers. See GRAMMATICAL CATEGORIES.

SPEAKER RECOGNITION
In computational linguistics, the ability of a computer to recognize the identity of a speaker from an analysis of their speech

SPEAKING

A mnemonic introduced by Hymes to assist the identification of components of a linguistic interaction. S(etting) – the time and place of the interaction; P(articipants) – the speaker and audience; E(nds) – the purpose of the interaction; A(ct sequence) – the forms and order of the interaction; K(ey) – the 'tone' of the interaction; I(nstrumentality) – the form and style of the interaction; N(orms) – the characteristics of the type of interaction, e.g. friendly, formal; G(enre) – the kind of the interaction, such as anecdote or sermon.

SPECIFIC REFERENCE

See **REFERENCE**.

SPECIFIED SUBJECT CONDITION

In 1970s Chomskyan generative grammar, a constraint preventing an **anaphoric** link from crossing a subject **NP** containing a full lexical word. It prevented the generation of sentences such as *Which authors do the critics$_i$ think hates each other$_i$*. The general structure is [*Which authors*]$_i$ *do the critics$_i$ think* [e_i *hates each other*.]. The anaphor *each other* cannot have *the critics* as an **antecedent** because the anaphoric link crosses e_i, which is a specified subject by virtue of its link with *author*. See **ANAPHORA**.

SPECIFIER

See **X-BAR SYNTAX**.

SPECTROGRAPH

See **SOUND SPECTROGRAPH**.

SPEECH ACT

The classic speech acts are acts which cannot be performed unless the relevant sentences are uttered. The starting point was J. L. **Austin's** observation that many **sentences** could not be described as true or false but were an essential part of some act. He focused initially on public ceremonies such as taking an oath (as at the Inaugurations of American Presidents), marrying, passing sentence in law courts, etc. Austin called such **utterances performatives**, and opposed them to **constatives**, which were utterances conveying **propositions**. Austin came to think of constatives as also a type of performative, since stating, questioning and so on are also acts. Austin recognized three fundamental types of act. The speaker who says *Don't you think it's cold with the window open?* performs a **locutionary act** in producing the utterance, an **illocutionary act** in asking a question (or making a statement or issuing a command) and a **perlocutionary act** if the utterance has the effect of making the hearer close the window. Austin proposed that the success of performative utterances was controlled by certain **felicity conditions**.

A distinction was drawn between direct and indirect speech acts, particularly in relation to the making of requests and suggestions and the issuing of commands. It was assumed that the speech act of commanding, e.g., was directly associated with **imperative** clauses such as *Prepare an outline of your essay.* Speakers often issue commands using other **constructions**: *You should prepare an outline, Why not prepare an outline?* These are indirect and more polite ways of issuing a command. For an indirect speech act to succeed (and for direct ones too), it is necessary that the listener 'take up' the illocutionary force of the utterance; there must be illocutionary uptake.

In the late 1960s and the 1970s speech act theory was elaborated. Searle proposed various types of speech acts – **assertive** or representative, **directive**, **commissive**, **expressive** and **declarative**. He extended the felicity conditions by distinguishing preparatory conditions, sincerity conditions and essential conditions. Other researchers extended the set of speech acts, which were held to be performed (in English) by means of simple present tense verbs (performative verbs) in the first person: e.g. *I apologise, I promise to come to your wedding.* It was commented at the time that a number of performatives involve different syntax – *Four spades* (a bid in bridge), *It is forbidden to sit down on the escalator,* etc. Recent work on real dialogues has shown that many acts do not involve the use of performative verbs.

SPEECH COMMUNITY

A group of people who communicate with each other using much the same **phonetics, phonology, morphology, syntax**, vocabulary, **fixed expressions** and common **metaphors** but recognizing variation in usage. They also share **pragmalinguistic norms** and **sociopragmatic norms** and **language attitudes**. Speech communities do not come in one size. The inhabitants of a small village, the inhabitants of a city, the students at a particular school, the residents in some area of a city all count as speech communities. An important component of an individual's identity is the speech community they belong to or wish to belong to. See **IMAGINED COMMUNITY**.

SPEECH LANGUAGE PATHOLOGY (SLP)

See **CLINICAL LINGUISTICS**.

SPEECH RECOGNITION

See **NATURAL LANGUAGE PROCESSING, NATURAL LANGUAGE UNDERSTANDING**.

SPEECH SCIENCE

Speech Science explores how language develops in childhood; how it is processed, stored and produced by the brain; how it may fail to develop and how it may be impaired later in life. See **CLINICAL LINGUISTICS, SPEECH THERAPY**.

SPEECH SYNTHESIS

The generation of speech by a computer, usually based on prior acoustic analysis.

SPEECH THERAPY

The discipline dealing with the diagnosis and treatment of speech disorders. See **CLINICAL LINGUISTICS**.

SPEECH TIME
The moment of time at which a speaker is speaking, or a period of time including that moment. See **EVENT TIME, REFERENCE TIME, TENSE AND ASPECT**.

SPEECH WAVE
The **sound wave** produced by speech.

SPELLING PRONUNCIATION
The pronunciation of a word that is influenced by its spelling, such as *salmon* pronounced with an *l*, or *often* pronounced with a *t*. Children often produce spelling pronunciations of unfamiliar words they have not encountered in speech, such as [sʌbtl] for *subtle*.

SPELLOUT
See **INTERFACE**.

SPIRANT
See **FRICATIVE**.

SPLIT
A change in which what was once a single distinct unit becomes two distinct units.

SPLIT INFINITIVE
In English grammar, a **phrase** such as *to boldly go in search of adventure*, in which the *to* is split from *go* by the adverb *boldly*. The split infinitive has long been condemned in style manuals but is the normal **construction** in speech and writing, apart from the most formal written texts, and is often more elegant than unsplit infinitives.

SPLIT MORPHOLOGY
The hypothesis that **inflectional morphology** and **derivational morphology** are completely separate and handled by independent sets of rules.

SPOONERISM
A slip of the tongue affecting sequences of words in such a way that sounds, typically initial **consonants** or whole **syllables**, are transposed. E.g. *wields and foods* for *fields and woods*.

SPRACHBUND
See **AREAL LINGUISTICS, LINGUISTIC AREA**.

SPREAD GLOTTIS
In **SPE Distinctive Feature Theory**, **segments** that are accompanied by openness of the **glottis** leading to aspiration.

SPREAD
A term characterizing the configuration of the lips. Spread lips are stretched away from a neutral position, as in a **close** front **vowel** like [i] (*beat* [bit]).

Contrasted with round as in a close back **rounded** vowel like [u] (*boot* [but]) or neutral as in a **mid** vowel like [ʌ] (*but* [bʌt]).

SPREADING

1. In **phonology**, the process whereby a feature associated with one **segment**, such as nasality, high tone, etc., is realized phonetically over adjacent segments; for example, normally non-nasal vowels may become nasalized in the context of a nasal consonant. See **PROSODY**. 2. See **SPREAD, NASAL**.

S-PRUNING

In 1960s **transformational grammar**, a process by which S **nodes** whose constituents had all been deleted were removed from **constituent structure** trees. See **TREE DIAGRAM**.

SQUISH

A type of **gradience**. The term was introduced in the early 1970s. It was applied, for example, to **nouns**. A set of properties was established for nouns and it was proposed that different types of noun were more central or less central depending on how many properties they possessed. An ordinary **count noun** such as *cup* was most 'nouny', a full **gerund** such as *his leaving his money to the cattery* was less nouny and the **complement clause** *that he left his money to the cattery* was least nouny.

S-STRUCTURE

In **Principles and Parameters**, the output of the syntactic rules including **traces** and empty categories such as **pro**.

STAGE LEVEL

See **GENERIC**.

STANCE

A speaker's or writer's evaluation of and attitude towards the listener or other persons, an idea, a way of life, a type of holiday and so on. Stance may reflect an ideology and usually affects linguistic choices. Thus, the tractor driver who uses very broad Scots when talking to passers-by who are using Standard Scottish English adopts a stance reflecting his valuation of himself and his language vis-à-vis people from a different social group. See **MODALITY, POSITION, STANDARD LANGUAGE**.

STANDARD DEVIATION

A method of measuring dispersion by assessing how far, on average, the values in a set of data deviate from the mean. See **DISPERSION**.

STANDARD GENERALIZED MARKUP LANGUAGE

See **MARKUP**.

STANDARD LANGUAGE

The **dialect** normally used by educated **native speakers**. It is usually recognized by its lexical and grammatical properties, codified in **grammars** and dictionaries, rather than by **accent**. Thus standard English tends to be relatively homogeneous throughout the English-speaking world, but may be spoken with, say, a Scots, Yorkshire or Australian accent. See **NON-STANDARD**.

STANDARD THEORY

The version of **transformational grammar** presented by Chomsky in *Aspects of the Theory of Syntax* (1965). Replaced by the Extended Standard Theory and then the **Revised Extended Standard Theory**. The latter was superseded by Government and Binding Theory and **Principles and Parameters** Theory.

STATE

In **Aktionsart** theory, a situation not involving change, expenditure of energy or an agent. E.g. *I believe in miracles*, *He is ravenous*. See **ACCOMPLISHMENT, ACHIEVEMENT, ACTIVITY, DURATION ADVERB, PROCESS**.

STATE VERB

See **STATIVE VERB**.

STATEMENT

1. A **declarative** clause or **sentence** expressing a **proposition**, as in *Greece is hot in summer, This plant is poisonous*. 2. The act of making a statement, i.e. uttering a declarative clause or sentence.

STATIC TONE

See **LEVEL TONE**.

STATISTICAL LINGUISTICS

A branch of **computational linguistics** that uses statistical methodology for the analysis of linguistic data.

STATISTICAL UNIVERSAL

A universal that holds for a majority of cases and is statistically significant, but does not hold for every case without exception. See **LANGUAGE UNIVERSAL**.

STATIVE VERB

In its broadest sense, a **verb** denoting a **state**, as opposed to an **action** or **process**. E.g. *lie, know, sleep*. In its narrowest and classic sense, a verb denoting a physical or psychological state, *know, understand, be cold*. Stative verbs in English do not occur in wh clefts and do not occur easily in the **progressive** – **What she does is be cold when the heating is off, *She is knowing the city well*. (*They are being silly* describes behaviour, not a state.) Many languages have special stative constructions, as in Russian *Ivanu xolodno* 'Ivan-DAT cold, To Ivan is cold, i.e. Ivan is cold'. See **CLEFT CONSTRUCTION**.

STEM

Any chunk of a **word** to which an **affix** can be added. Stems can consist of just one **morph**, such as *like* in *likeable*, or of more than one morph, such as *computerize – compute + er + ize*, to which *-ation* can be added. Any **root** is a stem but not every stem is a root.

STEM-BASED INFLECTION

A system of **inflection** in which inflectional affixes are typically added to **stems** that are not by themselves independent **word** forms. E.g. in the Latin word *navigo* 'I am sailing' the inflectional affix *-o* is added to the stem *navig-*, which is not an independent word. The headword in dictionary entries for this lexical item is *navigo*. See **WORD-BASED INFLECTION**.

STEMMER

A computational process to find the **stem** of a word

STENOGRAPHY

See **SHORTHAND**.

STEREOTYPE

1. In semantics, a set of properties characterizing good, central members (prototypes) of a class. The properties include physical features such as size, shape, colour and behavioural features. Finches are prototypical members of the class of birds; they have the stereotypical features of having feathers, wings and beaks, being able to fly, building nests and eating seeds. Some theories of stereotypes include **connotations** in the set of stereotypical features and such features vary from culture to culture. In some cultures dogs are generally seen as desirable, in others as undesirable. Whereas a **prototype** is an actual good member of some class, a stereotype is essentially conceptual. A speaker may carry in their minds a stereotype of a crocodile without ever having seen an actual example. See **PROTOTYPE THEORY**. 2. In **sociolinguistics**, beliefs held by members of one group of speakers about members of another group. Thus, a set of speakers with one kind of **accent** may be thought of by another set as untrustworthy or unintelligent or both. The speakers in the latter group may be thought of by the speakers in the former group as arrogant. Such beliefs seldom correspond to reality but have a profound effect on how individuals in one group perceive and evaluate individuals from another group.

STEREOTYPE SEMANTICS

An approach to **semantics** in which **denotation** is handled in terms of stereotypes rather than the classical concepts of necessary and sufficient properties. See **STEREOTYPE, PROTOTYPE THEORY**.

STEREOTYPED

See **STEREOTYPE**.

STIFF

A distinctive feature proposed to account for differences in tension in the **vocal cords**. +stiff is associated with voicelessness and high **pitch**.

STOP

A term in the description of the **manner of articulation** of **consonant** sounds. With oral **stops**, the airflow through the mouth is completely blocked at some point of **articulation**, accompanied by complete **velic** closure. Pressure builds up behind the oral **stricture** and when this is released there is a small explosion. Stops can be made on any of the airstreams A stop with a pulmonic egressive airstream is called a **plosive**. English has a range of plosives, both voiced and unvoiced, at different places of articulation: from bilabial, [p], [b], through alveolar, [t] [d], to velar, [k], [g]. In other languages there is an even wider range of places of articulation, from **bilabial** to **pharyngeal**. Stops can also be made on other airstreams: a stop produced with an ingressive **glottalic airstream** is an **implosive**, sometimes called a suction stop; a stop produced with an egressive **glottalic airstream** is an **ejective**, sometimes called a **pressure stop**. A stop produced with an ingressive **velaric airstream** is a **click**. See AIRSTREAM MECHANISM.

STORY

See HISTOIRE.

STRANDING

Leaving a constituent behind, especially a **preposition**, when a constituent is moved to the front of a **sentence** or deleted: e.g. *Who did you buy your house from*, which can be thought of as derived from the structure of *You bought your house from who(m)?*.

STRATIFICATIONAL GRAMMAR

A model of grammar developed from the late 1950s on. The model is conceived as a network of relations. A central feature is a series of levels or strata with the units on each stratum realizing the units on the stratum above. See REALIZATION.

STRENGTH SCALE

In **phonology**, **segments** may be arranged on a scale with respect to some property, such as degree of **stricture**: **stop, fricative, approximant**.

STRENGTHENING

A phonological process whereby a consonantal **segment** moves up the consonantal strength hierarchy, for instance a **glide** changing to a **fricative** or **stop**, or a stop being glottalized. See LENITION.

STRESS

The perceived prominence associated with a **syllable**. Native speakers have little difficulty in identifying stressed syllables, and dictionaries characteristically mark stress on lexical items. It is not possible to identify a single phonetic feature invariably associated with stress, though it has been associated with greater **loudness**, higher **pitch** and longer **duration**. Stress is usually marked by placing the **stress mark**, ", at the beginning of the stressed syllable: "sentence "stress, em"phatic "stress: stress is associated with prosody – in English, metrical patterns are typically characterized in terms of stressed and unstressed syllables. See EMPHATIC, SENTENCE STRESS, STRESS FOOT, WORD STRESS.

STRESS ACCENT or PITCH ACCENT

A term applied to certain **tone** systems that use **pitch** variation to give prominence to a **syllable** or **mora**. The placement of the tone or its **realization** can give rise to different meanings. Pitch accent has been used in the description of the prosodic systems of Ancient **Greek** and **Japanese**.

STRESS FOOT

A prosodic unit in a **stress-timed** language. It consists of a |″ stressed |″ syllable and |″ any |″ number of |″ unstressed |″ syllables up to but not including the next stressed syllable. The stretch between vertical stress marks is a stress foot. See STRESS MARK.

STRESS MARK

The **stress** mark, ″, is usually placed at the beginning of the ″stressed ″ **syllable**. Stress marks are often replaced by a vertical mark: |stressed |syllable. The stretch between vertical stress marks is a **stress foot**.

STRESS-TIMED

A stress-timed language, such as English, is one in which stressed **syllables** are isochronous, that is they occur at regular, approximately equal, intervals of time with any number of intervening unstressed syllables. This means that unstressed syllables cannot be isochronous. Stress timing is the basis of many English verse patterns. See IAMBIC, ISOCHRONY, STRESS FOOT, SYLLABLE-TIMED.

STRICT SUBCATEGORIZATION

In **generative grammar**, the classification of **lexical words** into classes according to the **constituents** they combine with inside the relevant type of phrase. E.g. **verbs** are classified according to whether they take a **direct object** noun phrase, an **adjective phrase** and so on. See COMPLEMENT, HEAD, SUBCATEGORIZATION FRAME.

STRICTURE

Narrowing or closure of the **vocal tract** at some place of **articulation**.

STRIDENT

In **J&H Distinctive Feature Theory**, an acoustic distinctive feature characterizing sound produced with high **frequency** and intensity, e.g. [f], [v], [s] and [z]. See DISTINCTIVE FEATURES, ACOUSTIC, MELLOW.

STRING

A number of **words** set out one after the other without any regard to whether they have a structure: *some fiercely bark dogs* and *some dogs bark fiercely* are both strings.

STRIPPING
See BARE ARGUMENT ELLIPSIS.

STRONG
See METRICAL PHONOLOGY.

STRONG FORM
The full (stressed) form of a word as opposed to its unstressed form: e.g. /will/ vs /'ll/.

STRONG GENERATIVE CAPACITY
In **generative grammar**, the capacity of a formal grammar not just to generate strings of words but to assign structures to them. See ADEQUACY, STRING.

STRONG GENERATIVE POWER
See STRONG GENERATIVE CAPACITY.

STRONG VERB
In **Germanic** languages, a **verb** that forms its **past tense** by changing the **vowel** of the **stem**, e.g. German *kommen* 'come' – *kam* 'came', as opposed to adding a **past tense** suffix: e.g. *zahlen* 'count' – *zahlte* 'counted'.

STRUCTURAL AMBIGUITY
See GRAMMATICAL AMBIGUITY.

STRUCTURAL CHANGE
See TRANSFORMATION.

STRUCTURAL DESCRIPTION
See TRANSFORMATION.

STRUCTURAL LINGUISTICS
A type of analysis that focuses on constituents (**clause, morph, phrase, word**), the arrangements in which they occur and their relationships to each other. Extreme structuralist analyses avoid the concept of function and define, e.g., **subject, direct object** and so on in terms of arrangements. Thus a direct object in English is the NP immediately following the **verb** in a **VP**. See CONSTITUENT STRUCTURE, FORMALIST LINGUISTICS, FUNCTION, ITEM AND ARRANGEMENT, ITEM AND PROCESS.

STRUCTURAL MEANING
See GRAMMATICAL MEANING.

STRUCTURAL SCHEMATIZATION
In **cognitive linguistics**, the construal of entities as bounded or unbounded (as individuated countable entities or as a mass); the construal of entities with respect to their topological and geometric properties, e.g. a vase as container in 'the flowers in the vase' or as a surface in 'the fingerprints on the vase'. See BOUNDEDNESS, CONSTRUAL, COUNT NOUN, MASS NOUN.

STRUCTURALISM

An intellectual trend in the analysis of language whose various components were brought together, expounded and extended in Saussure's *Cour de linguistique générale* (1916). It was imported into anthropology by Lévi-Strauss and spread to the other social sciences and into literary theory. The key ideas in structuralism are these. Every language has a structure of its own. In a given structure or system the meaning and function of any given item, whether semantic, syntactic, lexical, morphosyntactic or phonological, can be determined only in relation to all the other items in the relevant area or system of the language. Another idea is that the historical study (diachronic) of a given language must be separated from the study (synchronic) of its contemporary structure. A third idea is that there is an essential distinction between **langue**, which is language as a social phenomenon to whose conventions all speakers are subject, and **parole**, which is the individual production of **utterances**. A fourth idea was that any given language is a system of **signs**. Especially in the USA, structuralism, influenced by behaviourist psychology and positivist philosophy, was translated into a focus on constituents (**clause, morph, phrase, word**), the arrangements in which they occur and their relationships to each other. Extreme structuralist analyses avoid the concept of function and define, e.g., **subject, direct object** and so on in terms of arrangements. Thus a direct object in English is the NP immediately following the **verb** in a **VP**. See CONSTITUENT STRUCTURE, SENTENCE.

STRUCTURALIST

To do with **structuralism** or **structural linguistics**.

STRUCTURE

1. The arrangements of elements, whether phonetic **segments, morphs, words, phrases** or **clauses**, and the relationships between them. See AGREEMENT, CONSTRUCTION, GOVERNMENT. 2. In **Systemic Functional Grammar** structure is the order and grouping of constituents in a string of constituents, in contrast with system, which relates to the substitutions that can take place at each slot in the structure. E.g. the words in *The dog inside the gate barked furiously* occur in that order and group together into the phrases *the dog inside the gate, inside the gate, the dog, the gate, barked furiously*. Substitutions can take place as follows: <u>outside</u> *the gate,* <u>near</u> *the gate, inside* <u>the house</u>, and *barked* <u>angrily</u>, <u>whined</u> and so on. See CONSTRUCTION, CONSTITUENT STRUCTURE, FILLER, PARADIGMATIC, PROSODY, SLOT-AND-FILLER MODEL, SYNTAGM, SYNTAGMATIC, SYSTEM.

STRUCTURE DEPENDENCY

The principle that a grammatical process, and any corresponding rule such as a **transformation**, applies only to valid groupings of constituents. The usual example is that of **subject-aux inversion**, as in *The hotel I was staying in* <u>is</u> *near the souk* and <u>Is</u> *the hotel I was staying in near the souk?*. The **auxiliary** that is moved is not *was*, since that is in a **relative clause** that is part of the **subject** NP *The* *hotel I was staying in*. Subject-Aux inversion moves *is*, since that is the auxiliary that actually follows the subject NP. See **CONSTITUENT STRUCTURE**.

STUTTERING
The inability to produce fluent speech. Stuttering affects initial segments in words at the beginning of **phrases** and **sentences** and leads to the repetition of initial segments or fragments of words.

STYLE
See **STYLISTICS**.

STYLISTIC RULES
In early models of **generative grammar**, rules that were to apply at a late stage in the derivation of a **sentence** and ensure that it was stylistically appropriate for its context.

STYLISTICS
The systematic study of style focusing on the choices made by speakers and writers with respect to such factors as vocabulary, **collocations**, syntactic **constructions**, **derivational morphology**, the combination of **phrases** into **clauses** and clauses into **sentences**. Different styles reflect occupation (e.g., lawyer, banker, plumber), setting, topic and personal and social relationships. See **GENRE, REGISTER, SPEAKING**.

STYLIZATION
Writing part of literary work as though it were another type of text; e.g. a letter (formal or informal) as part of a novel.

STYLOMETRY
A type of textual analysis in which statistical methods are applied to the frequency of particular vocabulary items, **collocations**, grammatical **constructions, conjunctions**, etc., to determine whether two or more texts are by the same author. See **COLLOCATION, CONSTRUCTION, CONJUNCTION**.

STYLOSTATISTICS
See **STYLOMETRY**.

SUBCATEGORIZATION
See **STRICT SUBCATEGORIZATION**.

SUBCATEGORIZATION FRAME
A notation for information about **strict subcategorization**. E.g. the information that *put* requires an **NP** and a **PP** in that order is conveyed in the frame [+ _ NP PP]. '+' is read 'can appear', ' _ 'is read 'in the context of'.

SUBJACENCY CONDITION
In **transformational grammar** up to **Principles and Parameters**, a principle controlling the movement of a **constituent**, which was blocked if it involved crossing more than one **NP** or **S** boundary. The figure below shows the

structure of the sentence *She accepted ₙₚ[the report ₛ[that what was flourishing]]* and the boundaries that *what* has to cross in order to generate the structure of the **interrogative** **What did she accept the report that was flourishing?* – The movement of *what* is blocked because it has to move across an S and an NP boundary to reach the front. See **CYCLIC NODE**.

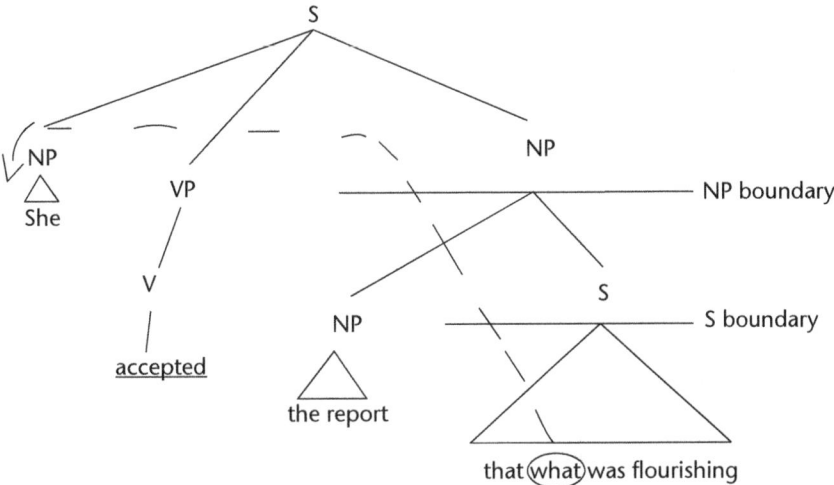

SUBJECT
See **GRAMMATICAL FUNCTION, LOGICAL SUBJECT**.

SUBJECT COMPLEMENT
In the copula **construction**, an AP, NP or PP complementing the **copula** but providing information about the **referent** of the subject NP: e.g. *The garden is enormous*, *They are real wimps*, *Andrew is in York*. In other constructions, an AP at the end of a clause, optional and not complementing the verb, which is not a copula, but providing information about the subject NP: e.g. *Sally returned downcast*. See **COMPLEMENT**.

SUBJECT-PROMINENT
In English and many other languages, one noun phrase in a **clause** has a number of properties, such as **agreement** in **person** and **number**, typically being definite and denoting agents. These **noun phrases** can be ellipted when two clauses such as *The dog barked. The dog ran away* are conjoined to give *The dog barked and [Ø] ran away*. Such languages are known as subject-prominent. In other languages, such as **Tagalog** or **Japanese**, these properties are assigned to different NPs and the concept of **subject** is not so easy to apply. In particular, Japanese and **Chinese** are said to be topic-prominent, with clauses having an initial noun phrase carrying the **topic**. A typical structure in such languages is equivalent to *The cat, I have to feed*, in which *the cat* is not an integral part of the clause *I have to feed*. The distinction between subject-prominent and topic-prominent is

not clear-cut, as some of the properties supposedly typical of topic-prominent languages are found in spoken English, spoken French, etc. See **GRAMMATICAL FUNCTION**.

SUBJECT-AUX INVERSION

In the grammar of English and other **Germanic** languages, a process by which the order subject **NP** – auxiliary – verb in a **declarative** clause is changed to auxiliary – subject NP – verb in an **interrogative clause**: e.g. *The cattle were lowing* → *Were the cattle lowing*, *The bank has sacked* who → *Who has the bank sacked*? See **GRAMMATICAL FUNCTION**.

SUBJECT-TO-OBJECT RAISING

On the assumption that *I consider her the best candidate* is derived from *I consider [her to be the best candidate] her*, the **subject** of the **complement clause** *her to be the best candidate* is thought of as being raised into the main **clause** to become the **direct object** of *consider*. See **GRAMMATICAL FUNCTION, RAISING, SUBJECT-TO-SUBJECT RAISING**.

SUBJECT-TO-SUBJECT RAISING

In transformational grammar subject-to-subject raising was a transformation that played a central role in the analysis of sentences such as *The account seems to be accurate*. The structure of this sentence was derived from an underlying structure *[e seems [the account to be accurate]]*, where *e* represents an empty category. *The account*, which is the **subject** of *to be* in the **complement clause**, is raised into the main **clause** to replace *e* as the subject of *seems*. See **EXCEPTIONAL CASE MARKING, RAISING, SUBJECT-TO-OBJECT RAISING**.

SUBJECTIVE

A **case** marking for **subjects**, particularly in languages such as English which have only a subject-**object** contrast: e.g. *I avoided him* and *He avoided me*. See **GRAMMATICAL FUNCTION, OBJECTIVE GENITIVE**.

SUBJECTIVE GENITIVE

A noun in the **genitive** case or its equivalent – e.g., 's – dependent on a noun denoting an **action** or **process**. The genitive noun denotes the agent carrying out the action. E.g. *the visitors' arrival, the bank's refusal to lend money*. See **OBJECTIVE GENITIVE, ROLE**.

SUBJECTIVE MOTION

See **FICTIVE MOTION**.

SUBJUNCT

See **ADVERBIAL**.

SUBJUNCTIVE

Where languages have a contrast between **indicative** and **subjunctive**, **imperative** or **optative**, subjunctive pertains to the verb forms that typically occur in a subordinate **clause** but are also used in a main **clause** for the expression of wishes, hopes, fears, desires, i.e. about states, actions and events treated as non-factual or **irrealis**. E.g. French *Il part* 'he leave-3sg-IND, He is leaving', *Je veux qu'il parte* 'I want that he leave-3sg-SUB', I want him to leave. (Latin *sub* 'under', *junctus* 'joined'; the metaphor is that subordinate clauses are joined under main clauses.) See **MOOD**.

SUBORDINATE CLAUSE
See **CLAUSE**.

SUBORDINATING CONJUNCTION
A conjunction connecting a clause with another clause to which it is subordinate, such as <u>whether</u> in *I asked <u>whether</u> a decision had been made* or <u>because</u> in *We came in <u>because</u> it started to rain*. See **SUBORDINATION**.

SUBORDINATION
A type of **syntactic linkage** between **clauses** in which one clause is dependent on/subordinate to the other one. Especially in **Role and Reference Grammar**, two degrees of subordination are recognized. Subordination proper (**hypotaxis**) involves one clause being embedded in another: e.g. *I know <u>that this plan is daft</u>*, the clause *that this plan is daft* is an **argument** and the direct object of *know* and is part of the main clause *I know that...* Cosubordination is a lesser degree of subordination in which one clause is dependent on another without being embedded in it. In some analyses of English, **adverbial clauses** are cosubordinate, since they are treated as not embedded in the clause they modify. Thus in <u>After you phoned</u>, *I went to the meeting*, the adverbial clause *After you phoned* is adjacent to, but not embedded in, the main clause. In contrast, in *We noticed <u>that you were at the meeting</u>* the **complement clause** *that you were at the meeting* is embedded in the VP with *noticed* as its head. See **CONJUNCTION, DEPENDENT, EMBEDDING, HYPOTAXIS**.

SUBSECTIVE GRADIENCE
See **GRADIENCE**.

SUBSTANCE
The phonic or graphic **medium** which is organized into **form** to create **meaning**. See **PHONIC SUBSTANCE, GRAPHIC SUBSTANCE**.

SUBSTANTIVE
Old-fashioned term for a **noun**. (Latin *nomen substantivum* 'noun/name self-existing', independent noun, as opposed to *nomen adjectivum* dependent noun, i.e. adjective.)

SUBSTITUTE WORD
See **PRO-FORM**.

SUBSTITUTION
See **PHRASE**.

SUBSTITUTION CLASS

The class of items that can be substituted for each other in a given **frame**. E.g. *amazingly, exceedingly, very*, etc. can replace each other in the frame $_{AP}[\_interesting]$. See **DISTRIBUTION, PHRASE, SUBCATEGORIZATION, WORD CLASS**.

SUBSTITUTION FRAME

See **FRAME**.

SUBSTRATE

In a **language contact** situation, a substrate language is an indigenous language and a superstrate language is the language of an incoming and more powerful people. Thus Irish English is said to exhibit substrate effects from the indigenous Irish Gaelic.

SUBSTRATUM

A language that has been displaced by another later language but that has influenced the incoming language, phonologically, grammatically or lexically. For example, the Gaulish substratum in French is found in river and place names.

SUBSTRING

Part of a **string**. E.g. *dogs bark* is a substring of *some dogs bark fiercely*, as are *bark fiercely* and *some dogs*.

SUBTRACTIVE BILINGUALISM

When learning a second language interferes with, or even replaces, a first language. See **BILINGUALISM**.

SUBTREE

Part of a tree. See **TREE DIAGRAM**.

SUCTION STOP

See **IMPLOSIVE**.

SUFFICIENT CONDITION

See **CLASSICAL THEORY OF CONCEPTS**.

SUFFIX

See **AFFIX**.

SUMERIAN

Sumer (S Iraq) from fourth to second millennia BCE. Written in cuneiform.

SUNDA

Austronesian. 36M speakers, Indonesia.

SUPERFIX

1. A phonological element that is simultaneous with (or superimposed upon) another element, especially **stress** or **tone**. 2. A **stem** can be modified by changes of tone or stress which have the same effect as the addition of an **affix**. An

English example is the verb *impórt*, with stress on the second **syllable**, contrasting with the noun *import*, which is stressed on the first syllable. An example from the African language Tiv is *vèndé* (low tone followed by high tone) 'refused in the recent past' vs *vèndè* (two low tones) 'refused in the past'. The term 'simulfix' is sometimes used (Latin *simul* 'at the same time'), capturing the fact that the tone or stress are pronounced at the same time as the **segment**. See **MORPH, SUPRASEGMENTAL**.

SUPERFOOT
See **METRICAL PHONOLOGY**.

SUPERLATIVE
The forms of **adjectives** and **adverbs** used for presenting entities as having some property in the highest degree or grade. The term is also applied to **constructions** containing such words. E.g. *the loudest music I have ever heard, the biggest city in the world,* French *la plus grande ville du monde* 'The biggest city of-the world'.

SUPERORDINATE
See **HYPONYM**.

SUPERSTRATE
See **SUBSTRATE**.

SUPINE
In **Latin** grammar, a **noun** formed from a **verb**. The **construction** is relatively rare, only a hundred or so verbs have been recorded in the supine and the noun only occurs in the **accusative** and **ablative** cases. The accusative forms express purpose, as in *spectatum veniunt* 'spectate-SUP-ACC they-come, They come to spectate', and the ablative case expresses the respect in which some property holds, as in *Mirabile spectatu* 'wonderful watch-SUP-ABL, wonderful to look at'.

SUPPLEMENTIVE
A **modifier** which is only loosely attached to the **clause** containing the word it modifies; e.g. *rather shy* in *Rather shy, the student hesitated to approach his tutor* and *The student, rather shy, hesitated to approach his tutor*. Participial clauses can also function as supplementives; e.g. *Sitting at the window, Freya saw the whole incident* (= *While she was sitting at the window…*) and *Freya, sitting at the window, saw the whole incident*. In the latter example, *sitting at the window* can also be analysed as a **participial clause** or a **reduced relative clause** = *who was sitting at the window*.

SUPPLETION
The use of two different **stems** for the inflected forms of what is regarded as a single lexical item. E.g. *goes* and *went*, French *bon* 'good' – *meilleur* 'better'. See **INFLECTIONAL AFFIX**.

SUPRAGLOTTAL

The area of the **vocal tract** above the **vocal cords** or **glottis**, i.e. the **pharynx** and the **oral** and **nasal** cavities. Also called **supralaryngeal**.

SUPRALARYNGEAL

See SUPRAGLOTTAL.

SUPRASEGMENTAL

A phonological element, such as **length**, **stress**, **tone** and **intonation**, that extends over more than one **segment**. See Figure 'IPA suprasegmentals' at INTERNATIONAL PHONETIC ALPHABET.

SURFACE STRUCTURE

In the **Standard Theory** and **Revised Extended Standard Theory** of **transformational grammar**, the representation of syntactic structure after all transformations have applied. It is the least abstract representation and the basis for phonetic and semantic interpretation. See D-STRUCTURE, S-STRUCTURE.

SWEET, Henry (1845–1912)

British Old English scholar, phonetician and grammarian. He was Britain's leading Old and Middle English scholar with a series of grammars, edited texts and readers. He was an original phonetician and may have been the originator of the concept of the **phoneme**. His 'broad romic' transcription was the basis for the **International Phonetic Alphabet**.

SVARABHAKTI

A term borrowed from **Sanskrit** grammatians for the process by which a **parasitic vowel** is inserted between two **consonants**, as in [fīləm] for *film*. Hence svarabhaktic vowel. See EPENTHESIS.

SWADESH LIST

A word list originally compiled by M. Swadesh designed to contain the basic vocabulary of a language and supposedly least likely to contain borrowings. Originally used for GLOTTOCHRONOLOGY.

SWAHILI

Bantu, **Niger-Congo**. 540K speakers (Tanzania, official language), 131K (Kenya). Widespread as a second language in Tanzania, Kenya and Uganda.

SWEDISH

Germanic, Indo-European. 7.8M speakers Sweden, 296K Finland.

SWITCH REFERENCE

A device for signalling whether the **subject** of a **clause** has the same **referent** as the subject of the preceding clause. E.g. Mojave (**Hokan languages**) *nya-isvar-k, iima-k* 'When-dance-3sg-Same Subject, sing-3sg, When he danced, he sang' – the same person dances and sings vs *nya-isvar-m, iima-k* 'When-dance-3sg-Different Subject, sing-3sg, When he danced, he sang (one person dances and another person sings)'. See **CONTROL, GRAMMATICAL FUNCTION, REFERENCE, UNDERSTOOD SUBJECT.**

SYLLABIC

In **SPE Distinctive Feature Theory**, segments that can function as the nucleus of a **syllable**, that is a **vowel** and a syllabic nasal such as [ŋ] in the pronunciation [beikŋ] *bacon*.

SYLLABLE

A unit for organizing speech sounds. The syllable is composed of an optional **onset**, and an obligatory **rhyme**, or **rime**. The rhyme consists of the syllabic **nucleus**, or peak, which is a **sonorant**, normally a **vowel**, optionally followed by a **coda**, typically a **consonant**. The rhyme may be preceded by an onset, typically a consonant. Thus in *man* 'm' is the onset, '*an*' is the rhyme, with '*a*' as the nucleus and '*n*' as the coda. *Man* is a monosyllable, *wo-man* is a disyllable; *wo-man-ly* is trisyllabic, etc. A syllable with no syllabic onset is an open syllable (V, VC, VCC, etc.); and a syllable with a coda is a closed syllable (CVC, CVCC, etc). The rhythmic structure, especially poetic metre, of many languages is based on syllables. The earliest writing systems are syllabic. Today, a few writing systems are syllable based, notably Japanese, which has two syllabaries, *hiragana* and *katakana*.

SYLLABLE-TIMED

A syllable-timed language, like French, is one in which syllables are isochronous; that is, the duration of every syllable is equal and they occur at regular intervals of time. This means that stressed syllables cannot be isochronous. See **STRESS-TIMED, ISOCHRONY.**

SYLLEPSIS

1. A **coordinate structure** in which one form of a main verb combines, possibly ungrammatically, with different NPs or **auxiliary** verbs: e.g. *He does his work, and I mine*, where the missing verb is *do*. 2. A coordinate structure in which a verb, combining with NPs with different roles, has different interpretations. E.g. in *She gave me some food and a piece of advice*, *gave* has a literal interpretation with *some food* and a metaphorical interpretation with *a piece of advice*. (Greek *sun* 'with', *lepsis* 'taking'.) This structure is also called zeugma. (Greek *zeugma* 'bond'.)

SYMMETRIC PREDICATE

In logic, a **predicate** holding of two entities X and Y that applies in either direction. For example, given the arguments X and Y, the predicate *is the cousin of* applies from X to Y and from Y to X. If X is the cousin of Y, it follows that Y is the cousin of X. See **REFLEXIVE PREDICATE, TRANSITIVE PREDICATE.**

SYMPTOM

An **index** conveying information about a speaker's or writer's mental, emotional or physical state. E.g. being very red in the face, shouting and thumping a table are symptomatic of a speaker's being angry.

SYNAESTHESIA
A link between sound and the other senses, such as a sound evoking a particular colour or smell for a given speaker.

SYNCHRONIC LINGUISTICS
The study of language at a particular point in time, cf. **descriptive linguistics**. The opposite is **diachronic linguistics**.

SYNCOPE
The omission in pronunciation of a medial **vowel** (e.g. [medsən] for *medicine*) or **consonant** ([laibrɪ] for *library*).

SYNCRETISM
A **morph** that realizes two or more members of a **morphosyntactic category** displays syncretism or results from a process of syncretism. E.g. the Latin **noun** *puella* 'girl' has *puellae* as its **dative singular** and *puella* as its **ablative** singular, with the one form *puellis* being both dative **plural** and ablative plural. The suffix *-is* displays syncretism. See CASE, GENITIVE.

SYNECDOCHE
A figure of speech in which an expression referring to a part of some entity is used to refer to the whole entity, as in *Forty sail appeared over the horizon*, where *sail* stands for *ships*. Synecdoche is a special case of **metonymy**.

SYNONYMY
A **sense relation** holding between two **lexical words**, or the senses of two lexical words, that typically have (almost) the same general **descriptive** (or cognitive) **meaning** but differ in some aspect of their **non-descriptive meaning**. E.g. *ear* and *lug* denote the same body part but *lug* is Scots and dialectal; *delay* and *procrastinate* both mean to put off doing something, but *delay* is a neutral term while *procrastinate* is typical of formal written English. See HYPONYMY, MERONYMY, OPPOSITENESS, PLESIONYMY.

SYNTACTIC COMPONENT
In **generative grammar**, the set of rules dealing with syntactic **structure**.

SYNTACTIC LINKAGE
The various devices for signalling that a particular **noun** combines in a particular way with a particular **verb**, **adjective** or **preposition**. See AGREEMENT, GOVERNMENT, HEAD, MODIFIER.

SYNTACTIC STRUCTURE
The arrangement of words into **phrases**, phrases into **clauses** and clauses into **sentences**. See CONSTITUENT STRUCTURE.

SYNTACTIC VALENCY
See VALENCY GRAMMAR.

SYNTAGM

Any syntactic **construction**, that is, sequences such as **words** in **phrases** and phrases in **clauses**. (Greek *sun* 'with', *tag* 'to place', an alternant of *tak* in *taksis*, as in *syntax*.) See **CONSTRUCTION, PARADIGM**.

SYNTAGMATIC

The label for relations between constituents that combine to form a **sequence**, such as the sounds in a **word**, the **morphs** in a word, the words in a **phrase** and so on. See **CONSTITUENT STRUCTURE, PARADIGMATIC**.

SYNTAX

The analysis of the arrangements of **words** in **phrases**, phrases in **clauses** and clauses in **sentences** and the grammatical relations between them. It deals with the order of constituents, **syntactic linkage**, relations between **head** and **modifier** and **dependency** relations. (Greek *sun* 'with', *taksis* 'placing'.) See **AGREEMENT, CONSTITUENT STRUCTURE, CONSTRUCTION, GOVERNMENT, SYNTAGMATIC, WORD ORDER**.

SYNTHETIC

See **ANALYTIC**.

SYNTHETIC COMPOUND

A **compound word** consisting of two words, the second one being a verb **root** plus an **affix**, the first one being a **noun**. Such compounds correspond to verb-**direct object** or verb-**oblique** object constructions; e.g. *woodcarver* is equivalent to *carves wood*; *wood* is a noun and *carver* consists of the verb root *carve* plus the affix *-er*. See **ROOT COMPOUND**.

SYNTHETIC PROPOSITION

See **PROPOSITION**.

SYRIAC

Semitic, Afroasiatic. The language of the Syrian Church from the fourth century CE. Still in use as a liturgical language.

SYSTEM

1. A set of linguistic units in a **paradigmatic** relation, that is, there is an **opposition** between the units and there is a **choice** between them. It is often useful to talk of the system of opposition at some point in a **structure**. Thus in the structure /sC/ the system of oppositions available at C is the voiceless **stops**, /p,t,k/, as in *spit*, etc. **nasals** /m,n/ as in *snip*, etc., and the **lateral** /l/ as in *slip*, etc. See **PROSODIC PHONOLOGY**. 2. By extension a system is an organized set of linguistic items, thus the **phoneme** system, the **tone** system, etc.

SYSTEM SENTENCE

System sentences are units in the language system or in the grammatical **systems** constructed by linguists. Text sentences are units used by writers in their written texts. For instance, grammars of English recognize as one system sentence *Johnny inherited the family fortune, while Timothy got nothing*. A given writer might convey the system sentence as one text sentence or as two, as in *Johnny inherited the family fortune. While Timothy got nothing*. In certain types of spoken language, such as dialogues, impromptu narratives and contributions to interviews, text sentences are difficult to identify and many analysts use clause combinations rather than system sentences. See **CLAUSE, SENTENCE**.

SYSTEMATIC GAP

The absence of a form because it violates some phonological **constraint**. For example, in English the non-occurring form *[sbin] is a systematic gap, because in word-initial **clusters** [sC] the C must be a voiceless **stop**, i.e. [sp], [st], [sk]. See **ACCIDENTAL GAP**.

SYSTEMATIC PHONEME

The abstract conception of the **phoneme** found in early **generative phonology**.

SYSTEMATIC PHONEMICS

The phonological representation in terms of systematic phonemes found in early **generative phonology**. This level of representation is the input to phonological rules.

SYSTEMATIC PHONETICS

In early **generative phonology**, the output of phonological rules.

SYSTEMIC FUNCTIONAL GRAMMAR

A model of **functional grammar** developed by M. A. K. Halliday from the late 1950s with many adherents, especially in the UK and Australia. The model has three systems, one dealing with **syntax**, one with **interpersonal meaning** (**mood** and **modality**) and one with **information structure**. Each system offers a series of choices, e.g. between **declarative** and **interrogative**, then between a **yes/no question** and a wh question, and so on. Which choices are made determines the structure of the clause or clauses. Not to be confused with Dik's Functional Grammar. See **FUNCTIONAL GRAMMAR 2, INTERROGATIVE CLAUSE**.

T/V FORMS
From the French **pronoun** forms *tu* (second-**person** singular, also used in informal and intimate styles of address and situations) and *vous* (second-person plural, also used formally or as an **honorific**). The labels are extended to the analysis of other languages. See **SOCIAL DEIXIS**.

TAG
1. See **TAG QUESTION**. 2. See **TAGGING**.

TAG QUESTION
1. In English, a **construction** (checking tag) in which a **declarative** clause conveying a statement is followed by a tag, a reduced **interrogative clause**, seeking confirmation of the statement: *Jane has accepted, hasn't she?*, *Fiona isn't leaving, is she?* If the first **clause** is positive, the second is **negative**, and vice versa. 2. A construction (copy tag) in which both clauses are positive or negative: *You're going to Glasgow, are you?*, *She won't leave, won't she?* Copy tags challenge a statement: *She won't leave, won't she? We'll see about that!* Many languages have tags of fixed form, e.g. French *n'est-ce pas?*, Russian *ne pravda li?* – but also English *You're going to Glasgow, right/yes/eh?* and Estuary English *innit?*
3. A construction in which an **imperative** clause is followed by a tag: e.g. *Send an e-mail to the organizer, will you?*

TAGALOG
Malayo-Polynesian, Austronesian. 27.5M speakers, Philippines.

TAGGING
The addition of information to the plain text of a corpus. Annotation may convey information about, e.g., **word class**, **verb** subclasses, types of **relative clause**, types of conversational **exchange** and so on. This information is separated from the basic text, e.g., by being put inside special brackets, and is generally added at the end of a word. The marks constituting the annotation are called **tags**. Most annotation is done manually, though computational taggers are becoming increasingly sophisticated.

TAGMEME
A unit of syntactic analysis employed by Bloomfield. Taxemes are formal features of syntax. A tagmeme is a taxeme plus its meaning. Thus, in English a sequence of **noun phrase** + **auxiliary** verb + **main verb** is a taxeme of **word**

order; that sequence plus meanings such as '**interrogative**', 'agent' and 'patient' is a tagmeme. See **CONSTRUCTION**.

TAGMEMICS
A model of grammar elaborating the concept of **tagmeme** and incorporating **functions** as well as **constituent structure**. See **GRAMMATICAL FUNCTION, ITEM AND ARRANGEMENT**.

TAHITIAN
Malayo-Polynesian, Austronesian. Approx. 150K speakers. **Lingua franca** throughout French Polynesia.

TAI LANGUAGES
Language group. Approx. 50M speakers, Vietnam, Laos, Thailand and China.

TAJIK
Indo-Iranian, Indo-European. Related to **Persian (Farsi)** 5.8M speakers Tajikistan, 1.4M Uzbekistan.

TAMAMBO
Malayo-Polynesian, Austronesian. Approx. 3K speakers, northern Vanuatu.

TAMBER
See **TIMBRE**.

TAMIL
Dravidian. 68.3K speakers India, 3.8M Sri Lanka, 1M Malaysia, 90K Singapore.

TANOAN
Kwa languages, Niger-Congo. Family of approx. twenty languages, Ivory Coast and Ghana.

TAP
A term in the description of the **manner of articulation** of oral **consonant** sounds. The **active articulator**, typically the tip of the **tongue**, briefly strikes against a passive articulator, typically the **alveolar** ridge, forming a single brief oral closure. The 'tapped r' [ɾ] is a one-tap **trill** often heard in Scots pronunciations of, e.g., *turn*. It is common in American pronunciations of /t/ and /d/. See **FLAP**.

TARGET ARTICULATION
In phonetic accounts of speech production, an idealized articulatory posture for a sound that may not be attained because of competing postures in the context.

TARIANO
Arawakan. Approx. 100 speakers.

TARSKI, Alfred (1902–1983)
Polish logician who became Professor of Mathematics at the University of California, Berkeley. He worked in **formal semantics** and **model** theory.

TATAR

Turkic, **Altaic**. Approx. 464K speakers Tatarstan, 600K Central Asia, Turkey.

TATPURUSHA

See **COMPOUND WORD**.

TAUTOLOGY

In **logic**, a **proposition** that can only be true: e.g. *Black cats are feline*; *If there's a full moon, there's a full moon*. In ordinary language a tautology is a statement containing unnecessary repetition: e.g. *an electric locomotive powered by electricity*. But some such statements carry special **implicatures**; e.g., **utterances** such as *If it's broken, it's broken* are used to convey the message 'There's no point in worrying about it; you have to move on and do what you can.'

TAXEME

See **TAGMEME**.

TAXONOMIC HIERARCHY

A lexical **hierarchy** that reflects (to some extent) the way the speakers of a given language conceive the external world. Lexical items may be related as superordinates and hyponyms in a **hyponymy** hierarchy. The lexical items are organized on different levels. The higher levels contain very general superordinates and the lower levels contain specialized items with narrow **extensions**. Between them is a basic level on which are found lexical items which have a rich set of properties, have extensions that are not too narrow or too broad, and which speakers access most easily: e.g. *cutlery* (superordinate), *spoon* (basic level), *dessert spoon* (specialized level). See **MERONYMIC HIERARCHY, TREE DIAGRAM**.

TAXONOMY

A classification of any collection of objects according to whatever properties of the objects are regarded as essential and important.

TCU

See **TURN CONSTRUCTIONAL UNIT**.

TELEGRAPHIC

Applied to **text**, typically speech, in which **grammatical words** are omitted: e.g. *Terrible place – dangerous work – other day – five children – mother – tall lady – eating sandwiches – forgot the arch – crash – knock – children look round – mother's head off – sandwich in her hand… shocking, shocking!* (Dickens, *The Pickwick Papers*).

TELIC

See **ATELIC**.

TELIC ROLE

One of the **qualia roles**, related to the perspective of an entity as having a particular purpose or function. E.g. the view of a house as a place to live in, protected from the wind, rain, cold and sun. See **AGENTIVE ROLE, CONSTITUTIVE ROLE, FORMAL ROLE**.

TELLABILITY

In relation to stories, the property of being worth telling, and also what makes a story worth telling: having a good plot and interesting characters, being narrated in clear syntax and with good use of vocabulary, expressed in coherent and cohesive text. See **COHERENCE, COHESION**.

TELUGU

Dravidian. 83.3M speakers, Southern India.

TEMPLATE

1. A model for producing other similar examples. 2. In syntax: an outline structure, e.g. [V NP NP] is a template for double object verbs like *give*, *John gave Mary a book*.

TEMPO

The speed of speech.

TEMPORAL CLAUSE

See **ADVERBIAL CLAUSE OF TIME**.

TENOR

Especially in **Systemic Functional Grammar**, the way in which relations of power and solidarity between **interlocutors** affect choice of grammar and vocabulary, and many aspects of **non-verbal communication**, such as eye-contact, tone of voice and so on.

TENSE

1. Muscular tension in the **vocal cords** can result in tense vowels, characterized by greater muscular tension in their **articulation** and produced with a high level of effort in contrast with **lax** vowels: compare the tense [i] and [u] with the lax [ɪ] and [ʊ]. This opposition is sometimes characterized as **fortis** as opposed to **lenis**. It is sometimes claimed, especially in discussing **vowel harmony** systems, that tense vowels are articulated with an **advanced tongue root**. 2. In **J&H Distinctive Feature Theory**, a feature characterized as exhibiting high energy. 3. In **SPE Distinctive Feature Theory**, segments whose articulation requires a high level of effort, e.g. the tense [i] and [u]. See **LAX**.

TENSE AND ASPECT

Tense has to do with speakers placing situations in past, present or future time. Lexical aspect or **situation aspect** has to do with whether a situation is a state or an event, and whether an event is presented as having or not having an end-point, or is conceived as punctual, as occupying merely a point in time. Grammatical aspect relates to presenting events as, e.g., ongoing, completed or **habitual**.

States do not change, **participants** do not expend energy or willpower. Events typically involve change and action, and have beginnings and endings. Completed events are those that have reached a natural boundary, a goal – *We walked to the park*, *We crossed the road*, the final point in a period of time – *We talked for fifteen minutes*, or the natural end of an event such as planting – *We planted two trees*.

A state is denoted by a **stative verb**, such as the classic English stative verbs *know* and *understand*. *Know* does not take the **Progressive** – *They were knowing the address* is odd – and has other grammatical properties. *Understand* very rarely takes the Progressive. **Dynamic** verbs describe events. They have different properties from those of stative verbs, e.g. taking the Progressive – *Fiona was writing down the address* – and occurring in the wh **cleft construction** –*What Fiona did was write down the address*.

Speakers place events and states in time. English and many other languages have tense, a set of contrasts which signals whether a situation was in the past – *The colour was fading*, is in the present – *The colour is fading*, or will be in the future – *The colour will fade*. In many languages the contrasts affect the shape of verbs. The **speech time**, the moment at which the speaker speaks, is central. A situation preceding this moment is in the past, one including this moment is in the present, and one following this moment is in the future. Because the future situations are less certain than past or present situations, reference to future time is often made by means of phrases to do with intention (*will* in English), obligation (*shall* in English was historically a verb denoting obligation) or movement (*be going to*). Other combinations of **modal verb** and **main verb** often locate a situation in future time; e.g. *She may appear on television (this evening/next year)*, *I must submit the application next week*.

Viewpoint aspect relates to contrasts such as *was writing* and *wrote*. Speakers adopt different viewpoints in relation to situations. If they view events as extending over time and lacking an end-point, they use, in English, the Progressive for a single on-going event – *Sue was packing her case (when the taxi arrived)* – or the **Simple Present** or the Progressive for a series of events – *Sue wrote home every week*, *At that time Sue was writing home every week*. If they view events as completed, i.e. as having reached their end-point, they use the **Simple Past** – *Sue wrote a letter*, or the **Perfect** – *Sue has written a letter*, as opposed to *Sue was writing a letter* and *Sue has been writing a letter*.

Every language has grammatical aspect, but some languages lack tense. Some information about time is signalled by aspect: an event presented as completed must have taken place in the past. And such information can also be signalled by **adverbs** of time. See AKTIONSART, EVENT TIME, PAST HISTORIC, PAST TENSE, PERFECTIVE, REFERENCE TIME, REMOTE PAST, RESULTATIVE.

TENSED CLAUSE

A **clause** containing a main verb or **auxiliary** verb that is marked for tense. E.g. in *has left*, *has* is **present tense**, in *was writing*, *was* is **past tense** and in *reads* *books*, *reads* is present tense. See **FINITE CLAUSE, LEXICAL VERB, NON-FINITE CLAUSE, TENSE AND ASPECT**.

TENSED-SENTENCE CONDITION

In **transformational grammar**, a **constraint** preventing the movement of a **constituent** into or out of a tensed **subordinate clause**. In its earliest formulation the condition applied to sentences such as *[That she bribed someone] is obvious*. In transformational grammar a transformation moved wh items to the front of a sentence. An uncomplicated statement of this transformation allowed it to move *someone* out of the clause *That she bribed someone* (which is an embedded tensed sentence) to the front of the sentence, to yield the structure *[Who [that she bribed] is obvious?]*. The Tensed-Sentence Condition prevented this movement and permitted the transformation to be stated simply. See **CLAUSE, TENSED CLAUSE**.

TERM OF ENDEARMENT

Terms of address used between adults in a very intimate relationship or between adults and their children. Generally used terms are, e.g., *love* and *honey* but many couples have their own private terms. See **DIMINUTIVE**.

TERMINAL NODE

A **node** in a **tree diagram** which is not linked to any lower nodes.

TERMINAL STRING

In **phrase structure grammar**, a string of symbols in a **derivation** to which no further **phrase structure rule** applies.

TERMINAL SYMBOL

A symbol in a **terminal string**.

TERMINATION

See **AUTOSEGMENTAL PHONOLOGY**.

TESNIÈRE, Lucien (1893–1954)

French linguist and grammarian. He was the founder of dependency (or **valency**), grammar.

TESSITURA

In **voice** dynamics, the pitch range of an individual's normal voice, as in 'a high/low pitched voice'.

TEXT

The term originally denoted any coherent sequence of written sentences with a structure, typically marked by various cohesive devices. It has been extended to cover coherent stretches of speech. See **COHERENCE, COHESION**.

TEXT DEIXIS

See **DISCOURSE DEIXIS**.

TEXT LINGUISTICS
The linguistic analysis of **clauses** and **sentences** as **constituents** of **text** and the analysis of the general discourse structure of text. See **DIMENSION, GENRE, INFORMATION STRUCTURE**.

TEXT MINING
In **computational linguistics**, the process of extracting information from **text**.

TEXT SENTENCE
See **SYSTEM SENTENCE**.

TEXT TYPE
See **GENRE, DIMENSION**.

TEXT-TO-SPEECH SYSTEM
In **computational linguistics**, a program that takes as input ordinary orthography and produces spoken output, e.g. machines for reading to the blind.

TEXTUAL FUNCTION
The component of a **functional grammar** that deals with the organization of **text** and the relation between text and the world outside text.

TEXTUAL MEANING
In Halliday's systemic grammar, textual meaning has to do with the organization of messages, the handling of **given and new** information, **focus**, etc. See **IDEATIONAL MEANING, INFORMATION STRUCTURE, INTERPERSONAL MEANING**.

TG
See **TRANSFORMATIONAL GRAMMAR**.

TH CLEFT
See **CLEFT CONSTRUCTION**.

THAI
Tai-Kadai. Approx. 57M speakers, Thailand.

THAT-CLAUSE
A **complement clause** or **relative clause** introduced by the **complementizer** *that*.

THEMATIC FRONTING
In **Systemic Functional Grammar**, the movement of a constituent into position of **theme** at the front of a **clause**. E.g. *I wrote four entries yesterday* changes to *Yesterday I wrote four entries*, *I love that book* changes to *That book I love*. See **FOCUS, GIVEN AND NEW, FUNCTIONAL SENTENCE PERSPECTIVE, PREPOSING**.

THEMATIC ROLE
Equivalent to participant **role**. Not to be confused with the much older uses of **theme** and thematic in **information structure**.

THEMATIZATION

See **THEMATIC FRONTING**.

THEME

1. In one theory of **information structure**, clauses are divided into theme and rheme. The theme is the first **phrase** in a **clause**, the starting point of the message conveyed by it. Themes typically refer to given entities, that is, entities that the speaker assumes the hearer can identify because they have already been mentioned, or are salient in the context or in the speaker and hearer's knowledge of their culture and the world. The rest of the clause is the rheme, which conveys what the speaker has to say about the theme, the properties to be assigned to the entity denoted by the theme. The information in the rheme is typically new, that is, the speaker does not expect the hearer to know what it is without being told. In *That policy seems incoherent* the theme is *that policy* and the property assigned to it is 'being incoherent'. In *On Thursday morning I have four meetings* the theme is *On Thursday morning*, and the property assigned to it is that the speaker has four meetings. See **GIVEN AND NEW**. 2. Especially in **generative grammar**, a **role** assigned to an NP denoting an entity that is located or moves somewhere. E.g. *the chimney pot* in *The chimney pot fell into the rose bed*, *The chimney pot is lying in the rose bed*.

THEME PREDICATION

The process of creating a **cleft construction**.

THEORETICAL LINGUISTICS

The branch of linguistics concerned with the development of models of linguistic knowledge, particularly in phonology, morphology, syntax and semantics. See **DESCRIPTIVE LINGUISTICS**.

THERE-INSERTION

In early **transformational grammar**, a **transformation** deriving *There's an elephant in the room* from *An elephant is in the room*.

THESAURUS

A collection of words organized by semantic fields and **sense relations**. E.g. *big, small, tiny, huge, enormous, hulking, wee*, etc. might be gathered together in the semantic field of size, with *huge* and *enormous* in the relation of **synonymy** and *big* and *small* in the relation of **oppositeness**.

THETA CRITERION

In **Government and Binding Theory**, the stipulation that each **theta role** is assigned to one and only one **argument** and that each argument is assigned one and only one theta role. The Criterion ruled out **subject-to-object raising**. If *We believed her [to be cheating]* is derived from *We believed [her to be cheating]*, *her* would receive agent role as subject of *to be cheating* and patient role as **direct object** of *believed*.

THETA GOVERNMENT

A theta-governs B if A **governs** B and assigns a **theta role** to it. See ANTECEDENT-GOVERNMENT, C-COMMAND, EMPTY CATEGORY PRINCIPLE, GOVERNMENT, PROPER GOVERNMENT, ROLE.

THETA MARKING

The process by which **theta roles** are assigned to **nouns**. See THETA CRITERION.

THETA ROLE

The usual term for **thematic role**. *Thematic* is usually represented by a theta, θ.

THETA THEORY

In **Government and Binding Theory**, the component of the grammar regulating the assignment of **theta roles**. See THETA CRITERION.

THETIC SENTENCE

A **sentence** in which all the information is new to the hearer and which presents a state of affairs as a whole. Suppose that *A car collided with a train at a level-crossing in Caithness* is the first contribution to a newspaper report or a conversation. None of the participants in the event of colliding, nor the process of colliding itself, has been mentioned and the sentence cannot be split into a topic and a comment. It can be split into a **theme** and a rheme; the theme is whatever phrase is in first position, and that is *A car*. The term **categorical sentence** is also used. It focuses on the act of presenting a state of affairs as a whole, whereas 'sentence' focuses on the chunk of text. See TOPIC, TOPIC AND COMMENT.

THETIC STATEMENT

See THETIC SENTENCE.

THIRD PERSON

See PERSON.

THIRTEEN MEN RULE

In some words in English, **stress** is shifted to a preceding syllable to avoid having two adjacent stresses. Thus, in isolation *thir'teen, Prin'cess*, but in context *'thirteen 'men*, rather than *thir'teen' men, 'Princess Di'ana*. See IAMBIC REVERSAL.

THREE-PLACE PREDICATE

See PREDICATE 4.

THREE-PLACE VERB

A **verb** that takes three **complements**: **subject** and **direct object** plus an **oblique** object, for verbs such as *place* – *She placed the flowers on the table*, or a **second object**, for verbs such as *teach* and *spare* – *She teaches us maths* and *You can spare me the details*. See PREDICATE-ARGUMENT STRUCTURE.

TIBETAN

Sino-Tibetan. Approx. 3.8M speakers, China (Tibet).

TIER

In **autosegmental phonology** one of the linear sequences of elements which in combination yield a phonological representation. See **ASSOCIATION**, **SKELETAL TIER**.

TIGRINYA

Semitic, **Afroasiatic**. Approx. 3.2M speakers Ethiopia, 1.2M Eritrea.

TIMBRE

The quality of sound produced by particular orchestral instruments, and, by extension, by individual voices. Sounds of identical pitch, loudness and length may differ in timbre (also **tamber**).

TIME ADVERBIAL

An adverb or prepositional phrase expressing information about when something happened – *recently, in December*, how often something happens – *rarely, once a week*, and how long something lasts – *for two hours, all summer*. See **ADVERB**, **ADVERBIAL**.

TIME PHRASE

A phrase denoting a location in time – *at that very second, at six o'clock, on Thursday, in June* – or duration in time – *for two hours, during the winter, all day long*.

TIMING

The timing of articulations, as in geminated consonants, and of sound sequencing. Of relevance to rhythm, intonation. See **TIMING TIER**.

TIMING TIER

See **AUTOSEGMENTAL PHONOLOGY**, **SKELETAL TIER**.

TIP

The end-point of the **tongue**. See Figure 'Articulators' at **ARTICULATION**.

TIWI

Tiwian, **Australian languages**. Approx. 1K speakers, Northern Territory.

TMESIS

The splitting of a **word** by the insertion of another word. E.g. French *lorsque* 'when' → *lors même que* 'even if', English *unlikely* → *un-bloody-likely*.

TOCHARIAN

Indo-European. Separate branch containing two languages, Tocharian A and Tocharian B. Known from documents found in Turfan and Kucha (Xinjiang). Probably extinct before 1000 CE.

TODA

Dravidian. Approx. 600 speakers, Southern India.

TOHONO O'ODHAM

Uto-Aztecan. Approx. 11.8K speakers, USA.

TO-INFINITIVE
See **NON-FINITE VERB**.

TOK PISIN
English-based creole. Approx. 121K speakers, Papua New Guinea.

TOKEN
An instance of a type. *T, t,* **t**, t are all tokens of the type (letter) 't'. *Dog*, dog, DOG are tokens of the lexical word 'dog'.

TONAL TIER
See **AUTOSEGMENTAL PHONOLOGY**.

TONALITY
In **Systemic Functional Grammar**, the division of an utterance into tone groups.

TONE
The pitch carried by a word. In some languages pitch is as essential and distinctive a part of a word as its consonants and vowels, and words which have identical sequences of consonants and vowels may be distinguished by contrasts of tone: thus, in **Akan** /pápá/ [high, high] *good;* /papá/ [low, high] *father;* /papa/ [low, low] *a fan.* Tone can distinguish both **lexical meaning**, as above, and **grammatical meaning**: thus again inAkan /ɔbáá/ [L H H] *a woman;* ɔbaá/ [L L H] *he opens.* In appropriate environments mid tones can also be found: /kasa/ [L L] *to speak* /kás!á/ [H M] *a language.* Tones do not have absolute pitches, but levels relative to the tone of other segments (see Figure at **DOWNDRIFT**). In simple tone systems tone may be indicated by **diacritics** as in the examples above /á/ for high tone, unmarked or /à/ for low tone and /!á/ for mid tone, or by letters – L(ow), H(igh) M(id), etc. In some transcription systems, e.g. **Chinese**, numbers from 1 (lowest) to 5 (highest) are used, particularly for rising (high rising: 15) and falling (51) tones. Pitch variation is also used for **intonation**. See **CONTOUR TONE, TONE GROUP**

TONE GROUP
The stretch of speech over which a tonal **contour** stretches.

TONE LANGUAGE
In tone languages the **tone** carried by a **word** is as essential and distinctive a part of the word as its **consonants** and **vowels**: words which have identical sequences of consonants and vowels may be distinguished by contrasts of tone. Grammatical meaning may also be conveyed by tone. A tone language may also have intonation. A common intonation pattern is **downdrift**. See **TONE GROUP**

TONE OF VOICE
The style adopted by a narrator.

TONE UNIT
See **TONE GROUP**.

TONEME
A minimal **tone** unit (on the model of **phoneme**).

TONETICS
The study of **tone** (on the model of **phonetics**).

TONGAN
Polynesian. Approx. 105K speakers, Tonga, New Zealand.

TONGUE
The most important vocal organ used as an **active articulator** for **consonants**. The upper surface is conventionally labelled **tip** (or point), **blade** (or dorsum, immediately below the **alveolar** ridge), **front** (immediately under the **hard palate**), **back** (immediately below the **velum**) and **root** (facing the back wall of the **pharynx**). In **apical** consonants the tip of the tongue is the active articulator; in **laminal** (or **dorsal**) consonants it is the blade of the tongue. The tongue is also involved in **secondary articulation**: in **palatalization** the front of the tongue is raised; in **velarization** the back of the tongue is raised, and in **pharyngalization** the tongue is retracted towards the back wall of the pharynx. The tongue is also important in the classification of **vowels**: in **close** vowels the highest point of the tongue is nearest the palate, in **open** vowels the tongue is low in the mouth; in **front** vowels the front of the tongue is raised, and in **back** vowels the back of the tongue is raised.

TONGUE-BODY FEATURE
See **DISTINCTIVE FEATURES**.

TONIC SYLLABLE
In **Systemic Functional Grammar**, the **syllable** which is the **nucleus**, or the most prominent in an intonation pattern.

TONICITY
In **Systemic Functional Grammar**, relating to the location of the **tonic syllable**. Compare *the CAT sat on the mat* and *the cat sat on the MAT*.

TOOKE, Horne (1736–1812)
English cleric and amateur philologist whose *The Diversions of Purley* (1786) had some influence when it was published. It used dubious etymologies to reveal the true meanings of words.

TOP-DOWN
See **BOTTOM-UP**.

TOPIC
1. See **TOPIC AND COMMENT**. This type of topic is sometimes called 'sentence topic'. 2. The topic is whatever a chunk of text is about. Sentences can have topics

in this sense but so can paragraphs, chapters and whole books. Speeches and conversations, e.g., can have topics and sub-topics. This kind of topic is sometimes called 'discourse topic'. Topics influence linguistic choices. Discussing a football match or the baby's progress at crawling require a different **register** from that for discussing some serious moral question or climate change.

TOPIC AND COMMENT

Topic was first taken to be the part of a sentence expressing what the sentence was about. The comment, the remainder of the **sentence**, expressed what was said or predicated of the topic. E.g. in *That book was very helpful* the topic is *that book* and the comment is *was very helpful*. Some analysts came to associate topic with given and comment with new, which in turn led to topic being associated, but not necessarily, with first position in a sentence or clause. In contrast, **theme** is defined as whatever phrase is first in a sentence or clause. See **FOCUS, GIVEN AND NEW, TOPICALIZATION**.

TOPIC PERSISTENCE

The extent to which a **referent** remains at the centre of attention in a text, as measured by the number of times it persists as an **argument** in the clauses following the **clause** in which it is first mentioned.

TOPIC-PROMINENT

See **SUBJECT-PROMINENT**.

TOPICALITY

The extent to which a given **referent** is topical, i.e. is talked about or is at the centre of attention in a **text**.

TOPICALIZATION

A cover term for various processes which move a **constituent** into **topic** or **theme** position at the beginning of a **clause**: e.g. *I enjoy haggis* → *Haggis I enjoy*, *Haggis is what I enjoy*. Topicalization moves constituents to the front of a clause, a position which may be unusual for them. Direct objects such as *haggis* do not usually occur first in a clause. In contrast, in the passive clause *The haggis was eaten by the dog*, the **noun phrase** *The haggis* is in normal **subject** position for **passive** clauses. The movement of *the haggis* into subject position does not count as topicalization. See **PREPOSING, THEMATIC FRONTING**.

TORRICELLI

Language family with approx. 80K speakers, Papua New Guinea.

TOTONACAN

Language family, eight languages. Approx. 276K speakers, Mexico.

TOUGH-MOVEMENT

See **OBJECT RAISING**.

TRACE

In various models of **generative grammar**, an element, *t*, occupying a position from which some **constituent** has been moved; e.g. *Who did you sack?* derives from *You did sack who?* and its structure is represented as *Who$_i$ did you sack t$_i$?* with the subscript index *i* signalling that the trace is linked to *Who*. See **MOVEMENT, NP TRACE, PRINCIPLES AND PARAMETERS**.

TRACHEA

The windpipe, the passage by which air passes from the lungs to the larynx.

TRADITIONAL GRAMMAR

A body of concepts originating in classical times for the analysis of classical Greek and Latin, and elaborated and applied, more or less inappropriately, in the analysis of many other languages up to modern times. Much-extended and refined versions are widely used and form the basis of contemporary **descriptive grammar**.

TRAJECTOR

See **LANDMARK**.

TRANS NEW GUINEA

Group of 561 languages. Approx. 3.4M speakers, Australia, East Timor, Indonesia, Papua New Guinea.

TRANSACTION

See **EXCHANGE**.

TRANSCRIPTION

The representation of spoken language in writing. Such transcriptions may be extremely detailed (**narrow** transcription) or more general (**broad** transcription). They may include just the **words**, as perceived by the transcriber on the basis of the stream of speech, but may also include pauses (short, medium or long), hesitations, intonation, non-linguistic sounds such as laughter, coughing and so on. Whether **syntactic structure** should be represented in transcriptions is a controversial question.

TRANSFERRED EPITHET

A **figure of speech** in which a property that belongs to one type of entity is assigned to another type that normally cannot possess it. The process is reflected in an **adjective** (an epithet) being transferred to an inappropriate **noun**. In *They ate a hurried meal*, *hurried* modifies *meal*, but it is the eaters who are hurrying, and being hurried along by events, not the meal.

TRANSFERRED NEGATION

A **construction** in which a **negative** that logically modifies a **complement clause** instead modifies the main **clause**. Thus, *I think that Jane is not happy with the decision* becomes *I don't think that Jane is happy with the decision*. *Not* is transferred, or raised, from the complement clause to the main clause.

In **transformational grammar** the **raising** was accomplished by a **transformation** called **Neg-raising**.

TRANSFORM

In Zellig Harris' model of **transformational grammar**, any two **constructions** that are related by a **transformation** are said to be transforms of each other. The **declarative** and yes/no **interrogative** constructions are transforms: any declarative clause is connected to a yes/no interrogative and vice versa. See **KERNEL SENTENCES**.

TRANSFORMATION

1. In Chomsky's **transformational grammar**, a **rule** that applied to **syntactic structure** as represented in a linear **labelled and bracketed string** or **tree diagram**. Transformations could move and delete **constituents** or add constituents to an existing structure, operations which **phrase structure rules** could not perform. They consisted of a structural description, or SD, which specified the structure to which a given transformation could apply, and a structural change, or SC, which specified the resulting structure. The SD of the classic **passive** transformation was (roughly) $NP_1 - Aux - V - NP_2$, which applied to the structure of active **declarative** clauses, and the SC was $NP_2 - Aux + be + en - V\ by + NP_1$. That is, the transformation related sentences such as *The dog chased the cat* and *The cat was chased by the dog*. See **TRANSFORMATIONAL CYCLE**. 2. In Zellig Harris' transformational grammar, transformations do not carry out structural changes but state relationships between **constructions** that are specified independently of each other. Some transformations are two-way (Harris' term is 'reversible'), such as the one relating declarative and yes/no **interrogative** clauses. All clauses such as *The dog chased the cat* have a corresponding clause *Did the dog chase the cat?*, and vice versa. Other transformations are one-way, such as that relating active and passive clauses. *The body was discovered by the waterfall* does not correspond to *The waterfall discovered the body*, but *The police discovered the body* does correspond to *The body was discovered by the police*. See **VOICE**.

TRANSFORMATIONAL COMPONENT

In models from *Syntactic Structures* (1957) to the **Revised Extended Standard Theory** of the 70s, the component of a **generative grammar** containing **transformations**. See **PHRASE STRUCTURE RULE, TRANSFORMATIONAL GRAMMAR**.

TRANSFORMATIONAL CYCLE

In Chomskyan **transformational grammar**, **transformations** were held to apply in cycles, beginning with the lowest S and NP in a tree and working up to the highest S. E.g. in *The council accepted the proposal that our firm should demolish the buildings* transformations applied in a cycle to the **complement clause** *that our firm should demolish the buildings*. The Passive transformation produced *the buildings should be demolished by our firm*. The transformations then applied to the highest S, the main clause. On this cycle the Passive applied again to produce

The proposal was accepted by the council that the buildings should be demolished by our firm. A major issue at one time was whether transformations should be allowed to apply in any order (intrinsic ordering) or whether they should have an order imposed on them (extrinsic ordering). See **CYCLIC PRINCIPLE, RULE ORDERING**.

TRANSFORMATIONAL GRAMMAR

Chomsky's transformational grammar is a **generative grammar** in which a set of **phrase structure rules** specifies basic syntactic structures, essentially the structures found in **active**, non-negative, **declarative** clauses. Lexical items are inserted into the **syntactic structures** from a **lexicon** and **transformations** operate on the structures to derive other **constructions: passives, negatives, interrogatives, imperatives** and the many structures of **complex sentences**. Harris' transformational grammar is a description involving transformations in the sense of transformation (2). See **MINIMALIST PROGRAM, PRINCIPLES AND PARAMETERS, REVISED EXTENDED STANDARD THEORY, STANDARD THEORY**.

TRANSFORMATIONAL RULE

See **TRANSFORMATION**.

TRANSITION

The link between adjacent sounds, particularly when there is a **liaison** such as linking r. See **INTRUSION**.

TRANSITION RELEVANCE PLACE

In **conversation analysis**, any point at which a new speaker can take over from the current speaker. The current speaker may call on someone else to take a **turn**, or a new speaker may judge that the current speaker has reached the end of their **turn constructional unit** and begin a turn. The conventions governing such transitions are not always obeyed by adult speakers and are not among the earliest language habits learned by children. See **SEQUENCE**,

TRANSITIVE CONSTRUCTION

A structure in which a **verb** is linked to a **subject** and an **object**, especially a direct object. *Jane renovated the house, Jane sent an invitation to Susan* and *Jane admired the house* are traditionally all examples of transitive constructions, but a recent alternative view is that constructions are more transitive or less transitive rather than just transitive or not transitive. For instance, a house is affected physically by being renovated but not by being admired. In many languages the difference is reflected in different **case** markings; e.g. the Turkish verb *yenilemek* 'renovate' assigns **accusative** case to its direct object while the verb *bakmak* 'look at' assigns **dative** case. Transitivity is reduced by negation – *Jane didn't invite Susan* describes a situation in which Susan is not affected by an action of Jane's – and in some languages, such as Russian, direct objects may take **genitive** case instead of accusative case in **negative** clauses. See **GRADIENCE, PREDICATE, PREDICATE-ARGUMENT STRUCTURE, TRANSITIVITY**.

TRANSITIVE PREDICATE

In logic, given a two-place transitive predicate P, if P holds between arguments X and Y and between arguments Y and Z, then P also holds between X and Z. Thus *be the same age as* is a transitive predicate. If X is the same age as Y, and Y is the same age as Z, it must be true that X is the same age as Z. See **PREDICATE, PREDICATOR, REFLEXIVE PREDICATE, SYMMETRIC PREDICATE**.

TRANSITIVE VERB

A verb that combines with two nouns, one of which is a direct object denoting a patient. See **ROLE, TRANSITIVITY**.

TRANSITIVITY

The property of **verbs** according to which they were traditionally divided into two classes. **Intransitive verbs** either exclude **direct objects** – *The cat vanished*, *The baby slept* – or have several senses, one of which excludes direct objects – *The tree fell* (intransitive) vs *The forester felled the tree* (transitive). **Transitive verbs** take direct objects. Recent work has introduced the concept of a scale of transitivity. At one end of the scale are completely intransitive verbs, which may combine with an agent or a patient **noun phrase**. At the other end are completely transitive verbs which combine with an agent noun phrase and a patient noun phrase. In between are verbs of varying degrees of transitivity which may be marked by, e.g., different **case** affixes. (Latin *trans* 'across', *itus* 'having gone'. The metaphor is of an action crossing from an agent to a patient.) See **INTRANSITIVE CONSTRUCTION, ROLE, TRANSITIVE CONSTRUCTION**.

TRANSLATION CORPUS

See **PARALLEL CORPORA**.

TRANSLATIVE

A **case** marking denoting change of state or purpose. **Finnish** *vede* 'water', *lumi muuttui vedeksi* 'snow turned water-TRANSL, The snow turned to water' (Latin *trans* 'across', *latum* 'carried').

TRANSPARENCY

1. A property of a complex form such that its structure is obvious. The structure of *illnesses* is transparent, consisting of the **stem** *illness* and the plural **suffix** *-es*. For many speakers of English, the structure of *bacteria*, the plural of *bacterium*, is not transparent. Since *bacterium* is seldom used except in technical literature, *bacteria* now occurs frequently as a **singular**. 2. A property of the relationship between the structure of a form and its meaning, such that the meaning can be deduced from the structure. The meaning of *inadequate* can be deduced from the meaning of *in* 'not' plus the meaning of *adequate*. The meaning of *inflammable* cannot be deduced according to that pattern, and the possible results of misinterpretations are so serious that the word *flammable* was invented. See **NATURAL MORPHOLOGY**.

TRANSPOSITION
See **PHRASE**.

TREE
See **TREE DIAGRAM**.

TREE DIAGRAM
A diagram consisting of lines connecting two or more points or **nodes**. Such diagrams have the form of upside-down trees. The topmost node is the root and the lines are **branches**. Two or more nodes hanging from the same node X are said to be sisters to each other and daughters of node X. In the figure below, B is a daughter of A, and D and E are daughters of C. Such diagrams can be used to represent families of languages, superordinates and **hyponyms**, **dependency** relations and **constituent structure**. For the latter purpose the root node is 'S' for 'Sentence'. Tree diagrams are a kind of graph. See **DEPENDENCY GRAMMAR**, **DEPENDENT**.

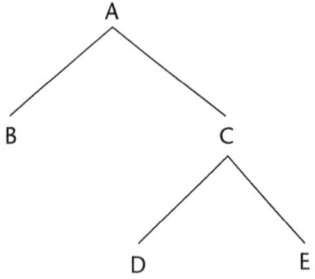

TREEBANK
A corpus consisting of parsed trees.

TREE-ONLY PHONOLOGY
See **METRICAL PHONOLOGY**.

TRIAL
A form of a noun denoting three entities. See **DUAL**.

TRIGRAM
A group or n-gram of three items. See **N-GRAM**.

TRIGRAPH
Three symbols representing a single sound, e.g. *sch* in German.

TRILL
In the articulation of an oral **consonant** if the **closure** is very brief the result is a tap, if there is a single contact, or a trill if the closure is repeated. The most familiar trills are **alveolar** [r], the 'rolled r', and **uvular** [ʀ], found in some southern varieties of French.

TRIPHTHONG
A combination of three vowels, as, for example, /aɪə/ in *fire*.

TRIVALENT
Applied to **verbs** that require or allow three **arguments**; e.g. *She*, *him*, and *his dishonesty* in *She forgave him his dishonesty*; *I*, *the book*, and *on the top shelf* in *I put the book on the top shelf*. See **COMPLEMENT, PREDICATE, PREDICATE-ARGUMENT STRUCTURE, VALENCY**.

TRUBETSKOY, Prince Nikolai (1890–1938)
Professor of Slavic Philology in Vienna. His *Grundzüge der Phonologie* (1939) is the foundation of the structuralist theory of the **phoneme** and phonological systems.

TRUNCATION
See **CLIPPING**.

TRUTH CONDITIONS
The circumstances or conditions that must exist for a given **proposition** to be true. E.g. the proposition *It's −10 outside* is true if in a given place, on a given day and at a given time the temperature outside whatever building the speaker is in is −10 degrees Celsius. What conditions must exist for the proposition *X is a bird* to be true? The classical theory of truth conditions distinguished between **necessary conditions** and sufficient conditions. For X to be a bird, it is not necessary that it fly or build nests in trees. There are flightless birds; there are birds that live in burrows, such as kiwis, which cannot fly, and puffins, which can. For X to count as a bird, it is necessary that it have feathers and a beak and lay eggs. These three conditions together are necessary and sufficient. That X lay eggs is not on its own sufficient, as snakes, turtles, crocodiles and other reptiles also lay eggs. The classical theory of truth conditions is no longer considered adequate as a theory of human categorization. See **CLASSICAL THEORY OF CONCEPTS, COGNITIVE SEMANTICS, CONSTRUAL, CONSTRUE, PROTOTYPE**.

TRUTH-CONDITIONAL SEMANTICS
Any theories of meaning that focus on the circumstances in the external world under which **propositions** are true. See **CONCEPTUAL SEMANTICS, CONSTRUE, TRUTH CONDITIONS**.

TRUTH-VALUE
In **logic** the properties of being true or false are truth-values assigned to **propositions**. Some systems of logic recognize a third value, being neither true nor false.

T-SCORE
See **T-TEST**.

TSOTSI TAAL
Afrikaans-based creole, now extinct.

TSWANA
Bantu, Niger-Congo. Approx. 4.5M speakers, Botswana and South Africa, Zimbabwe and Namibia.

T-TEST
A statistical test for determining if the variation found in a small sample of data – its **standard deviation** – can be extended to the larger set of data from which the sample comes. The result yielded by a t-test is known as the t-score.

TUCANOAN
Language family, Brazil and Colombia.

TUNE
See **NUCLEAR TONE**.

TUNGUSIC
Language family, twelve languages. Includes Even and **Evenki**. Approx. 20K speakers, Siberia, northern China. Possibly a branch of **Altaic**.

TUPIAN
Language family, Brazil and Paraguay. Includes **Guaraní**.

TURING TEST
A test of whether a computer can understand natural language and vice versa. Usually the test is whether a computer can have a conversation with a human being and the human thinks it is having a conversation with another human.

TURKIC
Language family, from Siberia, across Central Asia to the Balkans. Includes **Azerbaijani**, Kazakh, Kirghiz, **Turkish**, **Turkmen** and **Uyghur**.

TURKISH
Turkic Altaic. Approx. 55M speakers Turkey, 690K Bulgaria, 198K Cyprus, smaller numbers in Macedonia and Uzbekistan.

TURKMEN
Turkic, Altaic. 3.6M speakers Turkmenistan, 1.3M Iran, 500K Afghanistan.

TURN CONSTRUCTIONAL UNIT
Whatever structure is employed by a speaker when taking a turn in a conversation. The structure may be extremely simple, consisting of a backchannel such as *right*, *OK*, or more complex, consisting of a word, a phrase, a clause or a combination of clauses. The units play an important role in enabling participants in a conversation to recognize **transition relevance places**. See **CLAUSE, CLAUSE COMBINATION**.

TURN

In a well-regulated conversation, the participants take it in turn to play the roles of **speaker** and **hearer**. Each contribution of the speaker is a turn and the process of giving up one role and taking on the other is known as turn-taking. Turns need not consist of complete **clauses** and may just contain a **backchannel**. Not all conversations are well regulated and turns can be interrupted.

TURN-TAKING

See TURN.

TWO-PLACE PREDICATE

See PREDICATE.

TWO-PLACE VERB

See ARGUMENT, TRANSITIVE VERB.

TYPE-TOKEN RATIO

The ratio of types to tokens in a particular text. Types are abstract units, tokens are instances of that unit. Thus, the type 'cat' is realized by the following tokens *cat*, **cat**, *CAT*, **CAT**. Each letter on the page is a token of a type: *c*, **c**, *C* and C are all tokens of the type 'c'. The distinction between type and token is crucial because of the ambiguity in the word '**word**'. A computer analysis might show that a text contains 500 words. For some purposes the number of tokens is important, say in working out the relative length of contributions from different speakers. For other purposes the number of types is important, that is, the number of different lexical items.

TYPOLOGY

The analysis and comparison of the phonetic, phonological, morphological, syntactic patterns that occur in the languages of the world, the classification of languages in terms of those patterns and the deployment of those patterns in exploring the diversity of human languages. It is possible to distinguish qualitative and quantitative typology: the former focuses on the types of pattern on which language classification might be based, such as **word order**, **case** marking, **tense and aspect** and **mood** systems, and patterns of **clause combinations**; the latter focuses on the frequency of given patterns in the world's languages, on which patterns occur in which languages and on which patterns occur together.

TZ'UTUJIL

Mayan. Approx. 50K speakers, Guatemala.

TZOTZIL

Mayan. Family of six languages. Approx. 265K speakers, Mexico.

U

U AND NON-U
Terms popularized in the late 1950s by Nancy Mitford to characterize particular lexical words as socially 'acceptable', 'U', or unacceptable, 'non-U'. For instance, *napkin* and *lavatory* were considered to be 'U' and *serviette* and *toilet* to be non-U.

UC
See **ULTIMATE CONSTITUENTS**.

UGARITIC
Semitic, Afroasiatic. City of Ugarit, second millennium BCE.

UKRAINIAN
Slavic, Indo-European. Approx. 30.6K speakers Ukraine, 150K Poland.

ULTIMATE CONSTITUENTS
The smallest **constituents** in a piece of **constituent structure**, typically **morphs**.

UMLAUT
1. A phonological change in which **vowels** front in some contexts. E.g. in German *Mann* [man] (MAN singular) *Männer* [mɛnə] (plural). 2. The mark placed over a vowel to show the alternation.

UNACCEPTABLE
See **ACCEPTABILITY**.

UNACCUSATIVE
Intransitive verbs that take a patient noun phrase as subject are 'unaccusative'; intransitive verbs that take an agent noun phrase as subject are labelled 'unergative'. Compare *What happened to my ice cream? – It melted* (patient + unaccusative verb) and *What did Fiona do? – She ran away* (agent + unergative verb). In some approaches unaccusative verbs are analysed as having an underlying **direct object**; that is, the underlying structure of *The ice-cream melted* is *[] melted the ice-cream*. *Ice-cream* turns up as the subject noun phrase in the surface syntax. Unergative verbs have one and the same noun phrase as their underlying and surface subject. See **GRAMMATICAL FUNCTION, ROLE, TRANSITIVITY**.

UNARY FEATURE
See **SINGULARY FEATURE**.

UNATTACHED CLAUSE
See DANGLING PARTICIPLE.

UNBOUNDED DEPENDENCY CONSTRUCTION
A **construction** in which a **modifier** and a **head** can be separated by structures of any length and complexity. Compare, e.g., *the offer which he had accepted* and *the offer which you said Kirsty thought she heard Gordon say he had accepted*. In both examples *which* is the direct object of *accepted*, although it is separated from it by three clauses. See DEPENDENCY.

UNCHECKED
In J&H Distinctive Feature Theory, an acoustic distinctive feature characterizing segments with no **glottalization**. See CHECKED, DISTINCTIVE FEATURES, ACOUSTIC.

UNCOUNTABLE NOUN
See MASS NOUN.

UNDEREXTENSION
In child language acquisition, restricting the meaning of a **lexical item** in comparison with adult use, as when a child uses *dog* to refer to prototypical dogs but not to Chihuahuas. See PROTOTYPE.

UNDERGOER
Especially in **Role and Reference Grammar**, a macrorole covering what are seen as different microroles presented as **patients**. E.g. on one analysis, *tank* is an undergoer in *The workmen drained the tank* (*tank* is a location) and *water* is an undergoer in *The workmen drained the water from the tank* (*water* is a theme or patient). See ACTOR.

UNDERLYING FORM
See BASE.

UNDERLYING STRUCTURE
In **generative grammar**, any abstract level of representation, whether syntactic or phonological. In syntax, the structure assigned to a **sentence** such as *The first snow fell yesterday* shows explicitly that *yesterday* is a **modifier** of *The first snow fell*: [[*The first snow fell*] *yesterday*]. The structures assigned to *Visiting relatives can be a nuisance* bring out the **ambiguity**: either the relatives are a nuisance or the business of visiting one's relatives can be a nuisance. Phonological underlying structures show, for instance, that the Latin **noun** forms *reks* 'king-NOM' and *regis* 'king-GEN' have the underlying form *reg*. The *g* becomes **voiceless**, i.e. *k*, before the voiceless *s*. See DEEP STRUCTURE.

UNDERLYING SUBJECT
Especially in **generative grammar**, the **subject** in underlying structure. In the **surface structure** of a **sentence** such as *The mouse was killed by the rattlesnake* the subject is *the mouse*. On one analysis the underlying structure is *The rattlesnake killed the mouse*, in which *the rattlesnake* is the underlying subject. See DEEP STRUCTURE, TRANSFORMATIONAL GRAMMAR, UNDERLYING STRUCTURE.

UNDERSPECIFICATION

The omission from underlying representations of some information, for example particular distinctive feature values, that can be automatically supplied by some **redundancy rule**.

UNDERSTOOD SUBJECT

A **subject** which is missing but can be restored in a principled way. In an example such as *Angus wanted to live in Paris*, *Angus* is the subject of *wanted* and the understood subject of *live*. In *Angus persuaded Fiona to live in Paris*, *Fiona* is the **direct object** of *persuaded* and the understood subject of *live*. See **CONTROL, PRO**.

UNERGATIVE

See **UNACCUSATIVE**.

UNGRAMMATICALITY

The property of not obeying the rules of **morphology** or **syntax** of a particular language. E.g. **Car fast very man old a down knocked* does not obey the syntactic rules of English though an interpretation can be worked out. See **ACCEPTABILITY, GRAMMATICAL, GRAMMATICALITY**.

UNIFICATION

A process for combining matrices of attributes and values. E.g. *that* has the attribute NUMBER with the value SING (**singular**). *House* has the attribute NUMBER also with the value SING. Unification unifies the two matrices (which contain other attributes and values), yielding a matrix for the **noun phrase** *that house*, which contains NUMBER:SING. The verb *impresses* has the attribute NUMBER with the value SING. This matrix can be unified with the matrix for the noun phrase *that house* to yield a fragment of the matrix for the entire clause *that house impresses (my friends)*. The Figures 'Unification A' and 'Unification B' show the attribute-value matrices for French *cette maison* 'this house' and *ces maisons* 'these houses'. Matrices of attributes and values can be used to handle complex sentences or to combine information relating to semantics and pragmatics. Unification is central to **Lexical-Functional Grammar** and **Head-Driven Phrase Structure Grammar** and is implicit in **Construction Grammar**.

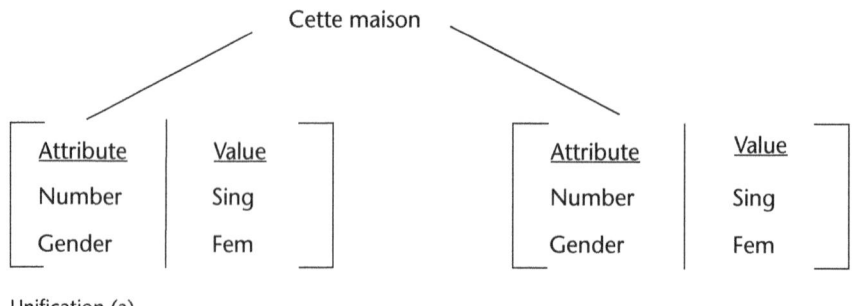

Unification (a)

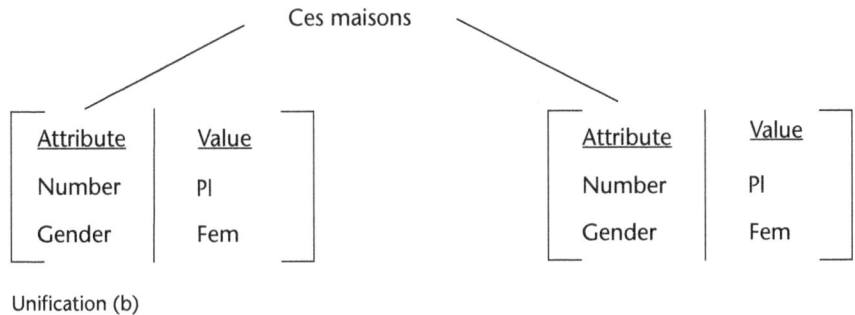

Unification (b)

UNINTERPRETABLE FEATURE
See CHECKING.

UNINTERRUPTABILITY
A property of **words** whereby a sequence of **morphs** constituting a word cannot be interrupted by some other **constituent**. Thus, in *all these fascinating exhibits*, other words can be inserted between *these* and *fascinating* or *fascinating* and *exhibits* – *all these extremely fascinating Japanese exhibits*, but not between *fascinat* and *ing* or *exhibit* and *-s*. See TMESIS.

UNIQUE MORPH
See CRANBERRY MORPH.

UNIT
Any entity that plays a role in analysis, not broken into any component parts, such as features, but as a whole. A **segment** is a phonological unit in **phonology**, say the /s/ in /sat/; **stems** and **affixes** are units in **morphology**, say the *un-*, *change-* and *-able* in *unchangeable*; words are syntactic units – say *unchangeable*. Many fixed **expressions** function as units, e.g. *kith and kin, to battle cancer, between a rock and a hard place*. The term '**constituent**' differs from 'unit': it is typically applied only to the building blocks of syntax and sequences of words that function as a unit, such as *to battle cancer*, and have **constituent structure**, the constituents being a **verb phrase** containing a **verb**, *battle*, and a **noun phrase**, *cancer*.

UNIVERSAL CONDITIONAL CLAUSE
A **clause** introduced by **words** in *-ever*: *whoever, whenever, however*, etc. E.g. *Whoever is appointed, the bank must cut staff*; *However you tackle it, you can't avoid this problem*.

UNIVERSAL GRAMMAR
See LINGUISTIC UNIVERSALS.

UNIVERSAL QUANTIFIER
See CALCULUS, QUANTIFIER.

UNMARKED
See MARKED.

UNMOTIVATED
See ARBITRARY SIGN, ICONIC SIGN.

UNPRODUCTIVE
See PRODUCTIVE.

UNROUNDED
Not ROUNDED.

UNSTRESSED
Not STRESSED.

UNTENSED CLAUSE
See CLAUSE, NON-FINITE VERB.

UPTAKE
See SPEECH ACT.

URALIC
Language family containing the **Samoyedic** group (including **Nenets**, Enets and Selkup) and the **Finno-Ugric** group, including, in Europe, **Finnish**, **Saami** (Lapp), **Hungarian**, and, in North and Central Russia, Komi, Mari (Cheremis), Mordva (Mordvin), Mansi (Vogul).

URBAN DIALECTOLOGY
The study of dialects spoken in urban areas.

URDU
Indo-Iranian, **Indo-European**. 10.7M speakers Pakistan, 48M India.

UTO-AZTECAN LANGUAGES
Family of fifty-six languages, including **Hopi**, Huichol, Luiseno, **Nahuatl**. Approx. 2M speakers, El Salvador, Mexico, USA.

UTTERANCE
1. Typically understood as a sequence of sounds produced by a speaker on a particular occasion. Utterances produced at different times by the same speaker or by different speakers may relate to one and the same abstract unit. Utterances are said to realize **sentences** or fragments of sentences and no two spoken utterances are identical. The concept of utterance can be extended to written language and understood as sequences of marks on paper or computer screen. 2. The act of producing utterances. See REALIZATION, SENTENCE MEANING, SPEECH ACT.

UTTERANCE MEANING
See **SENTENCE MEANING**.

UVULA
As shown in the Figure 'Articulators' at **ARTICULATION**, the flap of tissue hanging from the back of the velum. See **CONSONANT**.

UVULAR
A term in the description of the **place of articulation** of consonant sounds. The **back** of the tongue comes against the uvula as in the 'uvular r', [ʁ] found in some dialects of English or the uvular fricative, [χ] found in Arabic.

UYGHUR
Turkic, Altaic. 7.2M speakers China, mainly Sinkiang, 300K Kazakhstan.

UZBEK
Turkic, Altaic. 20.5M speakers Uzbekistan, 1.1M Tajikistan, 200K Turkmenistan, 2.5M Afghanistan.

V

VAGUENESS

The property of **lexical words**, **phrases** and syntactic **constructions** whose meaning cannot be stated precisely or whose application in a given context is not clearly valid. For instance, the meaning of *elderly* is not sharply delimited. When does a person cease to be middle-aged and become elderly? Or cease to be elderly and become old? What counts as a large village or a small town? A **lexical item** may be vague by virtue of having a clearly statable meaning which is very general. Thus in *We went to Dunedin*, *went* denotes movement but does not specify whether the people went on foot (if starting from some place in New Zealand), by car, by boat, by plane and so on. The meaning of the English **possessive** construction as in *my books* is likewise very general. Perhaps the speaker does own the books but it is equally possible that the speaker has borrowed the books, has written the books, has agreed to carry that pile of books to the library, to check the books for missing pages or some reference and so on. See **AMBIGUITY, GRAMMATICAL AMBIGUITY, LEXICAL AMBIGUITY**.

VALENCE

See **VALENCY**.

VALENCY

The set of **complements** that a given lexical **verb** requires or permits. *Vanish* requires only a **subject** noun phrase, *destroy* requires a subject **noun phrase** and a **direct object** noun phrase, *insert* requires a subject noun phrase and a direct object noun phrase and permits an **oblique** noun phrase – *inserted the key (in the lock)*. The set of complements for a given verb are its syntactic valents. Verbs also have semantic valents, since a given verb imposes particular roles on its complements. For instance, *built* in *The stonemasons built a new church for the town* imposes the agent **role** on *the stonemasons*, the **patient** role on *a new church* and the role of **goal** on *for the town*. It also imposes further information, such as that the church is created by the act of building and the town is the beneficiary and **recipient** of the church. 'Valency' was originally a technical term in chemistry denoting the combining power of atoms. As a given atom combines with a certain number and type of other atoms, so a given verb combines with a certain number and type of complement. See **ARGUMENT, PREDICATE, PREDICATE-ARGUMENT STRUCTURE**.

VALENCY GRAMMAR

A framework developed in East and West Germany in the late 1960s in which **verbs** were treated as **heads** of **clauses**, controlling the number and type of syntactic valents – **NP, PP, AP, subject, oblique** object, **object**, etc. – and controlling the semantic **valency**, especially the assignment of participant **roles** to the valents. A type of **verb-dependency grammar**. See COMPLEMENT, DEPENDENCY, GOVERNMENT, PREDICATE, PREDICATE-ARGUMENT STRUCTURE.

VALENT

See VALENCY.

VALUE

See FEATURE SPECIFICATION.

VARIABLE

1. See CONSTANT. 2. Any item of pronunciation, **grammar** or vocabulary that varies, often with sociolinguistic or stylistic effects. Examples are the use of *seen* as a **past tense** or **past participle** and the realization of /t/ as an **alveolar** or **glottal** stop. See SOCIOLINGUISTICS.

VARIATION

1. In **stylistics**, the use of different grammatical patterns, vocabulary, etc. in different situations for different effects. 2. In **sociolinguistics**, the variability in use of different linguistic forms depending on social situations.

VELAR

A term in the description of the **place of articulation** of **consonant** sounds. The back of the **tongue** comes against the soft **palate** or **velum** as in the voiced and **voiceless** velar **stops** [g], *gate* and [k], *Kate* and the velar nasal [ŋ] *hang*. The velar **fricative** [x] occurs in Scottish English in words like *loch*. See VOICE.

VELARIC

Concerning the activity of the **velum**, especially in its role as initiator of the **velaric airstream**.

VELARIC AIRSTREAM

The velaric airstream is created by two oral closures: one towards the front of the mouth (**bilabial, alveolar, palatal**, etc.) and the other by the back of the **tongue** against the **velum**. When the front closure is released and simultaneously the tongue moves backward against the velum, an **ingressive airstream** is produced. This is the (ingressive) velaric airstream. If the tongue moves forwards, an **egressive** velaric airstream is produced. **Consonants** produced on an ingressive velaric airstream are **clicks**. Clicks are not common as speech sounds except in some South African languages such as **Zulu** and **Xhosa**. They are commonly used in English as interjections. The egressive velaric airstream does not seem to be used for any communicative purposes.

VELARIZATION

A term in the description of the **secondary articulation** of a **place of articulation**. The back of the **tongue** moves toward the **velum**. In English the most audibly velarized **consonant** is /l/, which is often velarized in word-final position after a **back** vowel as in *fall*, [fɒɫ], in contrast with the palatalized [l̡] following a front vowel in *fill* [fɪl̡]. The contrast is sometimes referred to as a contrast between 'dark l', velarized, [ɫ] and 'light l', palatalized, [l̡]. The IPA symbol for velarization is placed over the letter concerned, as in [ɫ]. Some dialects of English, particularly in the Midlands, are characterized by velarization.

VELIC CLOSURE

Closure of the velum, thus cutting off the nasal tract.

VELO-PHARYNGEAL

The area between the **velum** and the **pharynx**.

VELUM

The soft tissue at the back of the soft palate that can be raised to allow air to escape through the nose, or lowered to allow air to escape through the mouth. It ends in the **uvula**. See Figure 'Articulators' at **ARTICULATION**.

VENITIVE

See **ANDATIVE**.

VENTRICULAR FOLDS

The false **vocal cords** which lie immediately above the **vocal cords**. They are not normally used in speech but can be set in motion to produce **ventricular voice**.

VENTRICULAR VOICE

An unusual phonation type produced by the **ventricular folds** vibrating. Also called harsh voice. Ventricular **fricatives**, **stops** and **trills** are reported in some **Caucasian** languages. It can be combined with ordinary voicing to produce double voice, the simultaneous production of two different notes. It is used in some forms of chanting by Tibetan monks.

VENTRIS, Michael (1922–1956)

An architect by training and occupation, he became obsessed by the problem of the decipherment of the Mycenaean Linear B script. He showed that the language encoded was an archaic dialect of Greek.

VERB

For a given language, a **word class** whose prototypical or central members are dynamic and denote events. In many languages a number of verbs denote **states** (e.g. *know* and *own* in English). Verbs typically denote single events which are temporary, whereas **adjectives** denote relatively long-lasting properties. In many languages verbs are marked for **person** and **number**, **tense and aspect**, and **mood**. In **clauses**, verbs combine with phrases such as NPs referring to agents and patients and PPs referring to location and direction. Verbs are used for making predications. See **AKTIONSART, PREDICATE, TENSE AND ASPECT**.

VERB DEPENDENCY GRAMMAR

A type of **dependency grammar** which takes **verbs** to be the **heads** of **clauses**, controlling how many **constituents** occur in a given clause and what type. Verb dependency models were developed particularly in East and West Germany and Eastern Europe, though the classic modern account was by Tesnière, a French linguist, and there were interesting American contributions to the formalism of the model in the late 1960s and early 1970s. See **ADJUNCT, COMPLEMENT, PREDICATE-ARGUMENT STRUCTURE, VALENCY GRAMMAR**.

VERB-FRAMED LANGUAGE

See **SATELLITE-FRAMED LANGUAGE**.

VERB PHRASE

A simple definition is a **phrase** with a **verb** as its **head**, but there are different views as to what combines with a verb in a verb phrase. On one analysis the clause *Alan is meeting Lucie in Prague* contains the VP *is meeting Lucie in Prague*, that is, the verb and all its **complements** and **adjuncts**. Another view is that VPs consist of the verb and its complement(s), i.e. *is meeting Lucie*. Yet another view is that VPs consist merely of **auxiliary** and main verbs, i.e. *is meeting*. Phrases such as *is meeting Lucie* or *might meet Lucie* are also given different analyses. For some analysts the auxiliary verb is the head of a VP containing a smaller VP: $_{VP}[might\ _{VP}[meet\ Lucie]]$. For other analysts the VP is $_{VP}[might\ meet\ Lucie]$; whether *might* or *meet* is the head of the phrase is another controversy. In **Principles and Parameters** the VP is a **constituent** containing the verb and all its complements, including the subject NP. The VP is embedded in functional constituents such as I″ or Inflectional Phrase and the subject NP is raised into I″. See **X-BAR SYNTAX**.

VERBAL DUELLING

See **SOUNDING**.

VERBAL GROUP

See **VERB PHRASE**.

VERBAL NOUN

See **GERUND**.

VERBAL PARAPHASIA

In **clinical linguistics**, a disorder in which a correct lexical item in a given context is replaced by one related in meaning, such as the use of *hammer* instead of *axe*.

VERBLESS CLAUSE

A **clause** lacking a **finite verb**, typically BE. E.g. *If at all possible, get here by midday*; *When in Rome, do as the Romans do*; *While in Paris, she met her future*

husband; <u>Although delayed in Brussels</u>, *he arrived in Lisbon in time for the meeting.*
See **SMALL CLAUSE**.

VERNACULAR

The variety that is typical of a particular **speech community**, usually applied to **non-standard** varieties.

VARRO, Marcus Terentius (116–27 BCE)

After a distinguished military and political career, he became an encyclopedic polymath. Unfortunately only six out of an original twenty-five books of his *De Lingua Latina* survive. They cover etymological issues and, most importantly, Latin inflectional morphology.

VERNER, Karl (1846–1896)

Danish scholar, provided an explanation for a set of apparent exceptions to **Grimm's Law** thus reinforcing the notion that **sound change** operates without exception. It became a cornerstone of the **Neogrammarian** approach to sound change.

VERNER'S LAW

Named after its proposer, Karl **Verner**, a sound change which tidies up an exception to **Grimm's law**.

VIEWPOINT

See **CONSTRUE**.

VIEWPOINT ASPECT

The speaker's perspective on a given situation. **Actions** and **processes** can be presented (viewed) as completed or on-going, as one-off or as repeated or **habitual**, as having results or with any results deemed irrelevant. The choice of viewpoint aspect determines the choice of grammatical aspect: in English, the choice of **Simple Past** or **Progressive**, or of **Perfect** vs **Simple Past**; in **Russian**, the choice of **Perfective** or **Imperfective**. Viewpoint aspect contrasts with situation aspect (**Aktionsart**). See **TENSE AND ASPECT, RESULTATIVE, SPEECH TIME**.

VISUAL CHANNEL

See **CHANNEL**.

VLAAMS

Germanic. Closely related to **Dutch**. Approx. 6M speakers, Belgium.

V-MOVEMENT

In Government and Binding Theory and **Principles and Parameters**, a **verb** (V) and its **arguments** are in the lowest position in a tree and I″ (Inflection) containing, e.g., tense, is higher up in the tree. To derive *Will Fred return the money* from *Fred will return the money*, *will*, which is a V in this analysis, moves to I″ and then from I″ into the **Complementizer**, at the front of the **sentence**. See **MOVEMENT, VERB PHRASE**.

VOCAL BANDS
See **VOCAL CORDS**.

VOCAL CORDS
The thin strips of muscular tissue that run form the thyroid cartilage back to the arytenoid cartilage (See the figure at **ARTICULATION**.). The space between them is the **glottis**. They are involved in the production of a variety of **phonation types**. When air flows between the vocal cords, they vibrate, producing **voice**. They can be held open in a **voiceless** segment, or partially closed to make a **stricture** producing friction, as in **whisper** or **consonants** such as [h]. Varying the mode of vibration produces **breathy voice** and **creaky voice**, and varying the rate and strength of vibration produces variations in **pitch** and volume. They can be tightly closed to produce a **glottal stop**. They are also known as vocal bands or vocal folds.

VOCAL FOLDS
See **VOCAL CORDS**.

VOCAL FRY
See **CREAKY VOICE**.

VOCAL ORGANS
The various organs used in the production of speech: the respiratory system, the **larynx** and the various organs in the **vocal tract**.

VOCAL TRACT
The tube-like cavity from the **larynx** to the lips, including the **tongue**, **velum**, **nasal** cavity and so on. Sounds are produced by various configurations of the **articulators** within this tract.

VOCALIC
1. Relating to a vowel. 2. In **SPE Distinctive Feature Theory**, one of the **major class features** identifying **segments** which are articulated with **open approximation** and voicing, that is, **vowels** and **liquids**. 3. In **J&H Distinctive Feature Theory**, one of the acoustic **distinctive features** associated with a well-defined formant structure indicating a voiced sound and air flowing without obstruction through the vocal tract. Associated with vowels and liquids. Opposite **non-vocalic**.

VOCALIZATION
1. The production of speech sounds. 2. The process whereby a phonological **consonant** segment is realized as a **vowel** or **glide**, as when in Estuary English [l] is frequently realised as [w]. *pill*, for instance, is pronounced [pɪw].

VOCATIVE

A form of a **noun** used when addressing someone. E.g. **Czech** *Jakob* 'Jacob, NOM' – *Jakobe* 'Jacob-VOC'; *Anna* 'Anne NOM' – *Anno* 'Anne-VOC'. Such vocative **affixes** are not **case** marking, as they play no part in **syntactic linkage**.

VOCOID

See **PHONETIC, VOWEL**.

VOICE

1. See **AUTHORIAL VOICE, NARRATIVE**. 2. The category of voice has to do with the different constructions, traditionally called 'active', 'passive' and 'middle', for presenting a situation from different perspectives. ('Voice' derives from the Latin *vox*, which was used for voice in its phonetic sense and for the form of a word. It was extended to active and passive constructions: Latin and Greek **verbs** changed their form, having different **suffixes** in the different constructions, e.g. *occidit* 'is killing' vs *occiditur* 'is being killed'.)

The active construction, as in *The critics savaged her latest novel*, allows speakers to present a situation, here an event of savaging, with the central participants, an **agent** and **patient**. The verb is said to be active or in the active voice. The subject of the verb typically denotes an agent, here *The critics*, and the direct object of the verb typically denotes a patient, here *her latest novel*.

In the passive the patient noun is the **theme**, as in the long passive *Her latest novel was savaged by the critics*. The verb is said to be passive or in the passive voice. Long passives have an agent noun phrase, but it is optional; most instances of the passive are agentless or short passives. Speakers typically use the passive to present a situation with the patient central and the agent unspecified, as in *Her latest novel was savaged*.

English has two major passive constructions. Passives with *be*, as in *The vase was broken*, describe **states**, **actions** or **processes**. Passives with *get*, known as dynamic passives, describe actions or processes only, as in *The vase got broken*. It has been suggested that a *get* passive such as *The fans got provoked by a rival group* is appropriate only if the fans acted deliberately, and that a sentence such as *Six students got shot accidentally* is unacceptable. This analysis is not supported by data from any British corpus. Rather, deliberate action is conveyed by **reflexive pronouns** – *He got himself arrested by throwing stones at the police car*. Examples such as *Some gifts get used a dozen or so times a year* (advertisement) cannot involve deliberate action by the patients. A rare passive construction involves *become*, as in *The cable became snapped* (BBC news bulletin).

The middle construction in English is exemplified by *This sweater washes well*, denoting a permanent property of the sweater, and *One bomb didn't guide and crashed* (Army communiqué) and *The course is jumping well* (TV presenter). The last two examples denote single events or temporary properties. English middle and passive constructions are very different: middles only have one **noun phrase** and an active verb, whereas passives can have two noun phrases and the **auxiliary** verb *be* or *get*. In middles the single noun phrase denotes a participant that is neither agent nor patient but controls the situation. The sweater washing well has nothing to with the person washing and the bomb was blamed for not guiding.

Ergative languages typically have an **antipassive** construction which allows patients to remain unspecified. Tzutujil, a Mayan language of Guatemala, has a basic active construction, as in *xuuch'ey jar iixoq jar aachi* 'hit the woman the man, the man hit the woman'. It has a short or agentless passive: *xch'ejyi jar iixoq* 'was-hit the woman, the woman was-hit'. It also has the classic antipassive, as in *xch'eyooni jar aachi* 'was-hitting the man, the man was hitting (someone)'. The patient may be clear from the context or may be unspecifiable – 'I saw the man hitting someone but couldn't make out who or what he was hitting'. See ERGATIVITY, GRAMMATICAL FUNCTION, ROLE, THEME. **3.** A **phonation type** caused by the vibration of the vocal cords. Thus, in phonetics, a classificatory label for **phones** involving vibration of the **vocal cords** as in **vowels**, voiced **stops** like [b] in *bin* or [d] in *din*. **Voicing** is the presence of voice during articulation. It is fundamental to the description and classification of both **vowels** and **consonants** both phonetically and phonologically. See J&H DISTINCTIVE FEATURE THEORY, VOICED, VOICELESS

VOICE DISORDER

A disorder that prevents the production of normal **voice quality**.

VOICE ONSET TIME

The time that elapses between the release of a **plosive** and the onset of voice in the following **segment**, usually a **vowel**. In many languages, including English, Voice Onset Time is an important indicator of whether a **consonant** is voiced or **voiceless**. Thus in the **articulation** of *peat*, [pʰit], there is a delay or lag between the release of [p] and the onset of voice in the following vowel. This is usually heard as **aspiration** on [p], represented as a superscript [ʰ]. This compares with the articulation of *beat*, [bit], where there is no such delay or lag.

VOICE QUALITY

Those features that characterize a speaker's voice production either habitually, the speaker's **articulatory setting**, or temporarily, e.g. nasality, breathiness, etc.

VOICED

1. In phonetics, a classificatory label for **phones** with vibration of the vocal cords as in the articulation of vowels or voiced stops like [b] *bin*. 2. In J&H **Distinctive Feature Theory** a phonation type involving no vibration.

VOICELESS

1. In phonetics, a classificatory label for **phones** without vibration of the vocal cords, as in the **articulation** of voiceless **stops** like [p] in *pin*. 2. In J&H **Distinctive Feature Theory**, a **phonation type** involving no vibration.

VOICEPRINT
A sound spectrogram which is used in **forensic linguistics** as an aid to the identification of an individual.

VOICING
See **VOICE**.

VOICING LAG
The delay in onset of **voice** after the release of a **plosive**.

VOLITIVE MODALITY
See **BOULOMAIC MODALITY**.

VOT
See **VOICE ONSET TIME**.

VOWEL
1. **Phonetic**. Vowels can be defined either phonetically, i.e. in terms of their properties as speech sounds, or phonologically, i.e. in terms of their value within a phonological system.

Phonetically, vowels are characteristically produced on a pulmonic egressive **airstream** with the air flowing smoothly over the upper surface of the **tongue**. They are usually **voiced**. They may in context be phonetically devoiced. The primary **articulation** of a vowel is a sound produced with open approximation, that is, with no constriction of the airstream within the vocal tract, which would produce audible friction. The primary articulation of a vowel is usually described in terms of phonetic parameters relating to the general configuration of the tongue and the lips. The position of the tongue in the **vowel space** (see Figure 'IPA vowels' at **INTERNATIONAL PHONETIC ALPHABET**) is characterized by the highest point of the tongue, **close** (nearest the palate) or **open**, and intermediate points, **half-close**, **half-open**, and which part of the tongue is raised. In English, **front** (nearest the lips), **back** (furthest from the lips) or mid. The configuration of the lips is characterized in terms of their **spreading**, the way they are stretched away from a neutral position: **spread**, as typically in a close front vowel like [i] (*beat* [bit]), **rounded**, as in a close back vowel like [u] (*boot* [but]) or neutral as in a mid vowel like [ʌ] (*but* [bʌt]). The vowel chart shows the **unmarked** lip positions: front vowels as unrounded and back vowels as rounded. For **marked** lip positions see below. This characterization yields a three-term label for vowels: in these terms [i] is a close front spread vowel, [u] is a close back rounded vowel and [a] is an open front neutral vowel.

Vowels may have a variety of **secondary articulations**. These include **length** and nasalization (acquiring a **nasal** quality). Phonetic vowels are sometimes referred to as vocoids to distinguish them from phonological vowels.

2. **Phonological**. A **segment** that forms the nucleus of a **syllable** of CV, CVC and so on. (See Figure 'IPA vowels' at **INTERNATIONAL PHONETIC ALPHABET, PHONOLOGICAL**.)

VOWEL GRADATION
See **ABLAUT**.

VOWEL HARMONY
A feature of some languages where all the vowels in a word must share some phonological property. Thus Akan verb stems may, *inter alia*, have any of the oral vowels [i, ɪ, e, ɛ, u, ʊ, o, ɔ], but the vowels in verbal prefixes fall into two sets [i, e, u, o] and [ɪ, ɛ, ʊ, ɔ]. A prefix to a word must have a vowel from the same set as the stem vowel. Thus, for example, the pronoun prefix meaning 'he, she' is [o] in odi 'she eats', but [ɔ] in ɔhwɛ 'he looks at it', because the verb stem vowels [i] and [ɛ] belong to different sets. See **ADVANCED TONGUE ROOT**.

VOWEL MUTATION
See **ABLAUT**.

VOWEL SPACE
The space in the **oral** cavity used for the production of **vowels**. This is often represented by a vowel quadrilateral (see the figure at **CARDINAL VOWELS**) which is used to represent both the cardinal vowels and the vowel system of particular languages and **dialects**.

VP
See **VERB PHRASE**.

W

WA
Mon-Khmer. Approx. 838K speakers, Burma.

WACKERNAGEL'S LAW
The generalization that **auxiliary** verbs and some **particles** and other unstressed items occupy second position in a **clause**.

WAKASHAN
Family of languages including Haida, Kwakiutl (Kwak'wala), **Nootka** (Nuuchahaulth)); 1.2K speakers, British Columbia, Washington State.

WAMBAYA
Non-**Pama-Nyungan**, **Australian languages**. Possibly twelve speakers in the Northern Territory. Highly endangered.

WANNA-CONTRACTION
The contraction of *want to* to *wanna* and of *going to* to *gonna*.

WARLPIRI
Pama-Nyungan, Australian languages. 3K, in and NW of Alice Springs.

WAVE THEORY
An alternative to the **family tree** model of linguistic change. It hypothesizes that linguistic change spreads through a **speech community** by contact, like waves in a pond. Under this view, adjacent **dialects** will be more affected than distant ones.

WAVEFORM
The shape of a sound wave, shown by plotting an oscillation against time.

WAVELENGTH
The distance a sound wave travels during a single cycle of vibration.

WEAK EQUIVALENCE
Generative grammars of different types are said to be weakly equivalent if they generate the same sets of sequences of symbols, regardless of the structures they assign to the sequences. See **ADEQUACY, STRONG GENERATIVE CAPACITY**.

WEAK FORM
1. In grammars of **Germanic** languages, verbs that form their **past tense** by the addition of a **suffix** are said to be weak, while verbs that form their

past tense by changing the stem vowel are said to be **strong verbs**. *Rain-rained* is weak, *swim-swam* is strong.

WEAK GENERATIVE CAPACITY
See ADEQUACY.

WEAK GENERATIVE POWER
See WEAK GENERATIVE CAPACITY.

WEAK VERB
See WEAK FORM.

WEAKLY ADEQUATE
See ADEQUACY.

WEBSTER, Noah (1758–1843)
American grammarian, lexicographer and spelling reformer. His *An American Dictionary of the English Language* (1848), and its subequent editions, remains authoritative.

WELL-FORMED
A **sentence** is well formed if it conforms to whatever **constraints** have been set up for judging sentences as acceptable (**grammatical**) or unacceptable (ungrammatical). Well-formed sentences possess the property of well-formedness.

WELSH
Celtic, Indo-European. Approx. 508K speakers UK, 25K Patagonia.

WERNICKE, Carl (1848–1905)
German physician, psychiatrist and neuropathologist. Following **Broca's** finding on language deficit caused by brain damage in what is now called **Broca's area**, he researched language deficits caused by damage to other areas of the brain than Broca's area. See WERNICKE'S AREA.

WERNICKE'S APHASIA
A type of aphasia, caused by injury to **Wernicke's area**, which results in speakers being unable to understand language and producing fluent but uninterpretable speech.

WERNICKE'S AREA
A part of the brain involved in the comprehension of language.

WEST PAPUAN LANGUAGES
Family of twenty-six languages. 310K speakers, Indonesia.

WFR
See WORD FORMATION RULE.

WH CLEFT
See CLEFT CONSTRUCTION.

WH FORM

Originally in analyses of English, forms beginning with *wh*, such as *who*, *which*, *whose* and also *how*. These forms occur in main **interrogative clauses** (*Who phoned?*, *Whose car is that?*, *How did you get there?*), interrogative **complements** (*I asked who was coming*, *She explained how the machine worked*), and in **relative clauses** (*the guy whose car I borrowed*, *the dog which didn't bark*). The term has become a convenient shorthand for forms that have similar functions in any other language.

WH-FRONTING

See **WH-MOVEMENT**.

WHISPER

One of the **phonation types**. In whisper the **glottis** is partially closed, so that friction is caused by the air passing through. Whispery voice involves a smaller volume of air than **breathy voice**.

WHISTLE SPEECH

A type of speech in which the speech melody, **intonation**, etc, is whistled. Found in the Canary Islands.

WHITE NOISE

A noise that is a mixture of all audible frequencies. Perceived as a featureless hiss.

WHITNEY, William Dwight (1827–1894)

American linguist and **Sanskrit** scholar.

WHIZ-DELETION

In **transformational grammar**, the rule deriving, e.g., *the book lying on the desk* from *the book which is lying on the desk*. It deletes the wh form and some form of *be*, usually *is* or *are*, *was* or *were* and yields a **reduced relative clause**.

WH-MOVEMENT

The process by which **wh forms** are moved to the front of **interrogative clauses**, **relative clauses** and **complement clauses**. The process was central to the idea that **generative grammars** should abandon individual **constructions** and focus on **rules** and **constraints** applying to many constructions. See **MOVE ALPHA, MOVEMENT, TRANSFORMATION, TRANSFORMATIONAL GRAMMAR**.

WHORF, Benjamin Lee (1897–1941)

Best known for the '**Sapir–Whorf**' hypothesis on linguistic relativity. The claim that language shapes thought by casting it in the mould of language-specific patterns.

WILLIAMS SYNDROME

A genetic disorder that delays cognitive development, though in individual children language may be more strongly developed than motor, visual or spatial skills.

WITTGENSTEIN, Ludwig (1889–1951)

Austrian philosopher. In his *Philosophical Investigations* he developed a theory of meaning based on language in use.

WOLAITTA

Omotic. Approx. 1.2M speakers, 1M in Ethiopia.

WOLOF

Niger-Congo. Approx. 3.5M speakers Senegal, 165K Gambia.

WORD

Morphs are the smallest **constituents** recognized in **morphology**, but the smallest units handled by syntax are words, which may consist of one morph or more than one. Words have a number of properties. They are the smallest forms that can be used on their own: *What did you do? – Screamed*. Smaller forms can be mentioned but not used, as in *I said 'de' not 're'*. They are uninterruptible. Constituents cannot be inserted between a **stem** and its **affixes** or into a sequence of affixes. Words are essential for the analysis of **stress**; across languages stress typically falls on some syllable in a word. There may be strict rules, as in **Spanish** and **Finnish**, or the placement may be unpredictable, as in **Russian** and **English**. Phonological phenomena such as **vowel harmony** apply within words but not from one word to the next.

Various types of words are recognized. Orthographic words are simply words on the printed page. **Lexical words** or lexemes are convenient abstract units for dictionaries, and lexemes are said to be realized by word forms. Thus, the lexeme SWIM is realized in the word forms *swim, swims, swam, swum, swimming*. Phonological words are word forms viewed as sequences of sounds following the patterns of a given language. See **MORPHOSYNTACTIC WORD**, **UNINTERRUPTIBILITY**.

WORD ACCENT

See **ACCENT**.

WORD AND PARADIGM

A general framework for **morphology** in which words are analysed in terms of contrasts within a **paradigm** and any internal structure is considered incidental. E.g. Latin *laborabant* 'they were working' contrasts with *laborabat* 'he/she was working', with *laborant* 'they are working' and so on. The question of how *laborabant* might be split into **morphs** is secondary. See **AFFIX**, **STEM**, **WORD**.

WORD-BASED HYPOTHESIS

In **generative grammar**, a hypothesis that **words** are the basic units of morphological analysis and that **derivational morphology** deals with the formation of new words from existing whole words. See **WORD AND PARADIGM**.

WORD-BASED INFLECTION

A system of **inflection** in which inflectional **affixes** are typically added to **stems** that are by themselves independent **words**. E.g. the English stems *lamp* and *grumble* take the affixes *-s* and *-ed* but are independent words, as in *Light the lamp* and *They grumble all the time*. See **STEM-BASED INFLECTION**.

WORD BLINDNESS

See **DYSLEXIA**.

WORD CLASS

Classes of **words** established primarily on the basis of grammar: where they occur in **clauses**, what words they combine with, patterns of **agreement** and **government**. The central, prototypical members of each class have distinct meanings; e.g. central **nouns** denote concrete entities, central **verbs** denote **actions**, **processes** and states, central **adjectives** denote properties. Each class has distinct uses. Nouns are used for referring to entities. Verbs, either on their own, as in *Bill snores*, or in combination with **modifiers**, as in *Bill left home unexpectedly*, are used for predicating properties of entities. In many languages the traditional major classes of noun, verb, adjective and **adverb** are easily recognized, but in many other languages only nouns and verbs are obvious. In addition to these major word classes, there are smaller word classes such as **preposition**, **postposition**, **modal verb**, **auxiliary** verb. See **AGREEMENT, DISTRIBUTION, GOVERNMENT, PREDICATE, SUBCATEGORIZATION**.

WORD FAMILY

Any group of **words**, some of which will be derived and/or inflected, based on a common **root**. E.g. *stick, stuck, sticks, sticky, stickiness* and *stickability* form a small word family based on the root *stick*. See **DERIVATIONAL MORPHOLOGY, INFLECTIONAL MORPHOLOGY**.

WORD FORMATION

See **DERIVATIONAL MORPHOLOGY**.

WORD FORMATION RULE

Any **rule** for deriving new **lexical words** from **roots**. A simple example is the rule that adds *-ness* to adjectives to produce nouns: *well – wellness*.

WORD MEANING

See **LEXICAL MEANING**.

WORD ORDER

A term applied to the order both of words within **phrases** and of phrases within **clauses**. The term 'constituent order' would be more appropriate but 'word order' is very common. Every language has basic and non-basic word orders. The non-basic word order is that of the most frequent clause type – **declarative**, **active** and **positive**. Yes/no **interrogative clauses** can be formed by changing word order, as in English, by using a particle, as in Turkish (*geldi* 'He came' vs *geldi mi* 'Did he come?'), or, in spoken language, by changing the intonation. Different languages have different basic word orders; English has SVO (Subject-Verb-Object), Turkish has SOV and Classical Arabic has VSO. Many languages that have OV order, as in Turkish, also have N-Postposition structures, such as Turkish *ev-in iç-in-de*; 'of-the-house in-its-interior, inside the house'. Many languages with VO order, such as English, have Preposition-N structures. Languages differ as to whether their word order is fixed or free. English has fixed word order; to highlight any of the phrases in *My sister has bought a Jaguar*, speakers of English use cleft constructions: *It's a Jaguar my sister has bought, It's my sister who has bought a Jaguar, What my sister has bought is a Jaguar*. Many other languages allow their speakers to simply change the word order, as though in English one could say **Has bought my sister a Jaguar, *A Jaguar my sister has bought*, etc. While it is true that in such languages the word order is free in the sense that (almost) any order is possible, the different word orders typically signal a difference in information structure. See **CONSTRUCTION, FOCUS, GIVEN AND NEW, INFORMATION STRUCTURE, PSYCHOLOGICAL SUBJECT, THEMATIC FRONTING, THEME, TOPICALIZATION.**

WORD ORDER UNIVERSALS
See **WORD ORDER**.

WORD STRESS
Stress that occurs on a **syllable** or **morph** in a word. A given **lexical word** may have stress on the same syllable in all its forms; e.g. Russian *dévushka* 'girl' has stress on its first syllable in all its **case** forms. In contrast, when the **suffix** *-a*, signalling **plural** and **nominative**, is added to a masculine **noun**, it takes the stress: e.g. Russian *gorod* 'town' – *gorodá* 'towns'.

WORLD ENGLISHES
The different varieties of English used either as a first or second language, often 'non-native' varieties such as Jamaican English and Singaporean English. The term is also used of English as an international language, as a global means of communication. See **EXPANDING CIRCLE, INNER CIRCLE, LINGUA FRANCA.**

WP
See **WORD AND PARADIGM**.

W-STAR LANGUAGES
See **NON-CONFIGURATIONAL LANGUAGES, CONFIGURATIONAL LANGUAGES.**

WUG TEST
A test to determine whether young children have control of, e.g., the noun-plural pattern in English. Children are presented with a picture of a bird-like creature and told *This is a wug* or *This is a gutch*. Another picture shows two of the creatures and children are asked to complete the sentence *Now there are two __*. This use of nonsense words can be extended to other grammatical patterns.

X

X TIER
See **SKELETAL TIER**.

X-BAR SYNTAX
A theory of **constituent structure** in which the notation represents both the structure of phrases and the relationships between **heads** and **modifiers**. Every phrase has a head, which in the initial version of the theory was a **lexical item**. The head of a **noun phrase** was the **noun**, of a **prepositional phrase** the **preposition**, and so on. Items to the left of the noun are specifiers and items to the right of the noun are **complements**. Each phrase has two levels of structure. The top level is represented by N for noun, P for preposition, etc., and two bars over them (hence the name X-Bar). The bars have been replaced by what mathematicians call primes but the term 'bar' has been retained: N″, P″, A″, V″. N″ splits into the Specifier and the core of the noun phrase, consisting of the noun and its complement. Figure 'X-Bar syntax (a)' shows the X-Bar structure for *the dog with a woolly coat*. The whole phrase is N″. *The* is the specifier and *dog with a woolly coat* is N', the core of the phrase. N' splits into N, the lexical item, and its complement, P″: *dog* + *with a woolly coat*.

In Figure 'X-Bar syntax (b)', an adjective phrase such as *exceedingly rich in wildlife* is represented by A″. This splits into the specifier *exceedingly* and A', the core of the adjective phrase, consisting of the **adjective** *rich* and its complement, *in wildlife*.

Any X″ is called the maximal projection, the highest level of structure in a given phrase. Any X' is an intermediate projection, and X, with no bars, is the minimal level.

One important development was the idea that phrases could have null heads. This fitted with the analysis of 'noun phrases' as having as their head, not nouns, but **determiners**. Phrases such as *the players*, *many doctors* and *which flights* are analysed as determiner phrases having as their heads *the*, *many* and *which*. Plural **count nouns** in English and singular **mass nouns**, as in *Books are expensive* and *Water is scarce*, do not require articles but can be analysed as having null heads: Det' splits into Ø + *books* or Ø + *water*.

A second important development was the projection principle, the idea that lexical items project phrase structure. That is, lexical items control what structure is required – actually, always the same general arrangement of specifier plus a core of head and complement. Crucially, lexical items determine how many and what kind of complements are required. The preposition *from* allows either a noun/determiner phrase as complement or another prepositional phrase: *from the station, from behind the hedge*. The verb *place* requires a noun/determiner phrase and a prepositional phrase: *placed the bag under his seat.*

An extension of the second development is bare phrase structure, unlabelled structures which could be labelled by lexical items. A further extension is the idea that phrase structure rules are not required, since the concept of projection can be elaborated to allow lexical items to specify the construction of particular arrangements of **constituents**. See **GOVERNMENT, ZERO DETERMINER**.

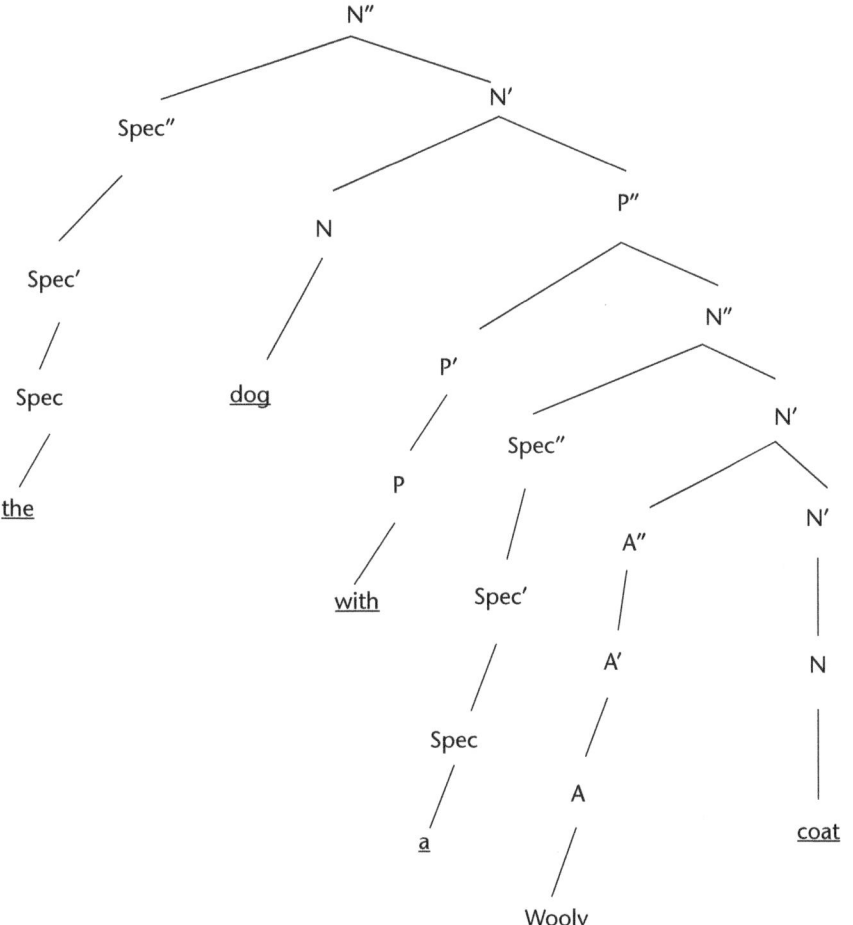

X-Bar syntax (a)

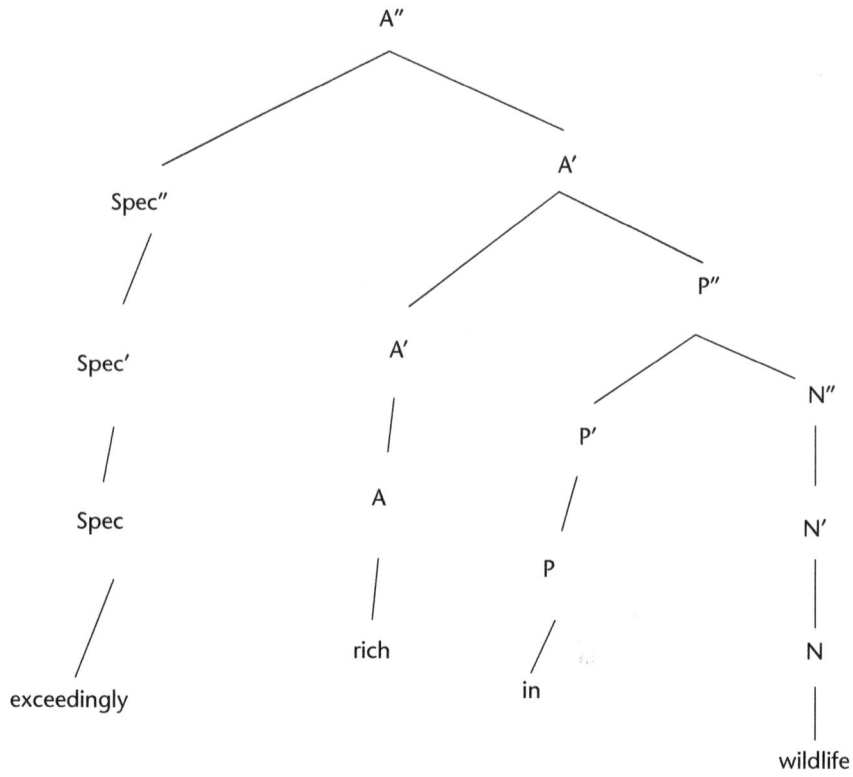

X-Bar syntax (b)

XHOSA
Bantu, Niger-Congo. Approx. 8.6M speakers, South Africa, 18K (Lesotho).

XML
See **MARKUP LANGUAGE**.

Y

YAKUT
Turkic, **Altaic**. Approx. 363K speakers, Russia (on and east of the Lena.) Also called Sakha.

YANITO
Variety of English influenced by Spanish. 3K speakers, Gibraltar.

YES/NO QUESTION
See **INTERROGATIVE CLAUSE**.

YI
Sino-Tibetan. Previously known as Luo. Approx. 6M speakers, China (Sichuan, Yunnan, Guizhou, Guangxi). Related to Burmese.

YIDDISH
Germanic. 3.1M speakers (215K in Israel).

YORUBA
Niger-Congo. Approx. 31.3M speakers Nigeria, 465K Benin.

YUKAGHIR
A family of two closely related languages, Tundra Yukaghir and Kolyma (Southern) Yukaghir. Approx. 140 speakers in north-east Siberia (Kolyma and to the north of Kolyma).

Z

ZAPOTEC
Oto-Manguean. Fifty-eight languages or dialects; 517K speakers in Mexico.

ZERO-ANAPHORA
Anaphora holding between a zero or **null NP** and an **antecedent**. In the English *Anna said she would help*, *she* is an **anaphor** and its antecedent is *Anna*. In the Russian *Anna skazala, chto pomozhet* 'Anna said that will-help', the verb in the **complement clause**, *pomozhet*, has no overt subject NP. In some analyses *pomozhet* would have an **underlying subject** NP which is realized as zero and has *Anna* as its antecedent. See MORPH, ZERO DETERMINER, ZERO MORPH.

ZERO-BAR CATEGORY
See ZERO LEVEL CATEGORY.

ZERO DERIVATION
See CONVERSION.

ZERO DETERMINER
A **determiner** that is realized as zero. This concept is particularly useful in analyses that consider determiners to be the **head** of what other analyses call **noun phrases** with nouns as their head. In *the dogs*, *the* is the head; in *these books*, *these* is the head; in *Books bore me*, *books* is analysed as a determiner phrase, – $_{DP}$ [$_{Det}$ [Ø] $_N$ [books]] The phrase does have a determiner, but it is zero. See MORPH, X-BAR SYNTAX.

ZERO ELEMENT
See ZERO MORPH.

ZERO INFINITIVE
See NON-FINITE VERB.

ZERO LEVEL CATEGORY
In **X-bar syntax**, **lexical items**, which have no bars.

ZERO MORPH
In analyses of English, *sheep* and *cows* are both treated as realizing a **lexical item**, SHEEP or COW, and the grammatical morpheme **plural**. Some analyses treat them as having the same number of surface **morphs**, namely *cow + s*, and *sheep + Ø*. Ø is a zero morph, a type of unit that was particularly useful in Item-and-Arrangement analyses. For example, it enabled both *cows* and *sheep* to

be analysed as consisting of the same number of morphs realizing the same number and type of morphemes. See **ITEM-AND-ARRANGEMENT, REALIZATION**.

ZERO RELATIVE CLAUSE

See **CONTACT CLAUSE**.

ZERO VALENT

A **verb** that has no **valents** or **arguments**. E.g. Latin *pluit* 'rain- 3sg-PRS, it is raining' excludes a **subject** NP. If *it* in clauses such as *It is raining* is treated as a **dummy subject**, English weather verbs are also zero valent. See **IMPERSONAL CLAUSE, PREDICATE-ARGUMENT STRUCTURE, VALENCY**.

ZEUGMA

See **SYLLEPSIS**.

ZULU

Bantu, **Niger-Congo**. 11.7M speakers South Africa, 248K Lesotho.